The authors

Rebecca Walker is a freelance trainer and and writer on welfare rights.

Timothy Lawrence is a solicitor specialising in immigration and asylum work at Southwark Law Centre in London.

Aideen Woods is a legal adviser at the Asylum Support Appeals Project.

Acknowledgements

The authors would like to thank everyone who has contributed to this book and all the authors of previous editions.

Thanks are particularly due this year to Henri Krishna, Fiona Ripley, Kelly Smith, Deborah Gellner and everyone at the Asylum Support Appeals Project.

We would also like to thank Alison Key for editing and managing the production of the book, Katherine Dawson for compiling the index and Kathleen Armstrong for proofreading the text.

The law covered in this book was correct on 1 July 2017. It includes regulations laid and judgments delivered up to this date.

Contents

Abbreviations   x

Part 1   Introduction
Chapter 1   How to use this book   3
1. About this *Handbook*   3
2. Checking the rules that affect you   5
3. Finding the relevant law   6
4. Immigration advice   7

Part 2   Immigration law
Chapter 2   Immigration and nationality law: overview   11
1. Immigration and nationality law   11
2. The main types of immigration status   13
3. British nationality   15
4. Immigration and nationality applications   16
5. Appeals and other remedies   18
6. Deportation   20

Chapter 3   Leave to enter or remain   21
1. Leave to enter or remain   21
2. Time-limited leave   23
3. Indefinite leave   23
4. Employment   24
5. Recourse to public funds   25
6. Sponsorship   26

Chapter 4   Asylum and human rights   31
1. Asylum seekers   31
2. Refugee leave and humanitarian protection   32
3. Stateless people   34
4. Leave for human rights and compassionate reasons   34
5. Fresh applications   38

Chapter 5   European Economic Area nationals and their families 40
1. The European Economic Area states   40
2. Rights of admission and residence   40
3. Documentation   41
4. Exclusion and removal   41

Chapter 6   Checking your immigration status   43
1. Introduction   43
2. British nationals and people with the right of abode   43
3. People with leave to enter or remain   44
4. People without leave   49
5. Asylum seekers   49
6. European Economic Area and Swiss nationals   50
7. Passport issues   50

Part 3   Benefits and immigration status
Chapter 7   People subject to immigration control   55
1. Introduction   55
2. The effect of immigration status on benefits and tax credits   56
3. Who is a 'person subject to immigration control'   57

Chapter 8   People subject to immigration control and benefits   66
1. Benefits and tax credits affected by immigration status   66
2. People subject to immigration control who can be entitled   67
3. Partners and children who are subject to immigration control   74

Chapter 9   Asylum seekers and refugees   80
1. Asylum seekers   80
2. Benefits and tax credits for people granted leave   81
3. Integration loans   84

Part 4   Benefits and residence rules
Chapter 10   Residence and presence rules: overview   91
1. Introduction   92
2. Presence   94
3. Past presence   94
4. Living in for three months   95
5. Residence   98
6. Ordinary residence   99
7. Habitual residence   103
8. The right to reside   103

Chapter 11   Habitual residence and the right to reside   106
1. The habitual residence test   106
2. 'Habitual residence in fact'   112
3. The right to reside   117

Chapter 12   Who has a right to reside   124
1. Introduction   124
2. Non-European Economic Area nationals   125
3. British, Irish and Commonwealth citizens   125

4. European Economic Area nationals   126
5. Croatian, A2 and A8 nationals   129
6. Initial right of residence   134
7. Jobseekers   135
8. Workers   142
9. Retaining worker status   149
10. Self-employed people   159
11. Retaining self-employed status   163
12. Self-sufficient people and students   165
13. Family members of European Economic Area nationals   170
14. Derivative residence rights   181
15. Permanent right to reside   190

Chapter 13   Residence and presence: rules for individual benefits   210
1. Means-tested benefits   210
2. Bereavement benefits   215
3. Child benefit and guardian's allowance   216
4. Disability and carers' benefits   218
5. Industrial injuries benefits   221
6. Contribution-based jobseeker's allowance and contributory   223
   employment and support allowance
7. Maternity allowance   225
8. Retirement pensions   225
9. Social fund funeral and winter fuel payments   226
10. Tax credits   227

Part 5   Benefits while abroad
Chapter 14   Going abroad   237
1. Introduction   237
2. How your benefits and tax credits are affected   239

Chapter 15   Going abroad: rules for individual benefits   246
1. Means-tested benefits   246
2. Bereavement benefits   256
3. Child benefit and guardian's allowance   257
4. Disability and carers' benefits   259
5. Incapacity benefit, severe disablement allowance and maternity   263
   allowance
6. Industrial injuries benefits   265
7. Contribution-based jobseeker's allowance and contributory   266
   employment and support allowance
8. Retirement pensions   267
9. Statutory payments   269
10. Tax credits   269

Part 6   **European co-ordination rules and international agreements**

Chapter 16   European Union co-ordination rules   277
1. Introduction   277
2. Who is covered   281
3. Which benefits are covered   284
4. Principles of co-ordination   288

Chapter 17   International agreements   309
1. Reciprocal agreements   309
2. Council of Europe conventions and agreements   317
3. European Union co-operation and association agreements   319

Part 7   Claims and getting paid

Chapter 18   Delays   325
1. Dealing with delays   325
2. Waiting for a decision on a claim   326
3. Delays when challenging a decision   341
4. Delays getting paid   347

Chapter 19   National insurance numbers   354
1. The national insurance number requirement   354
2. Obtaining a national insurance number   357
3. Common problems   360

Chapter 20   Providing evidence   365
1. General points about evidence   365
2. Evidence of immigration status   373
3. Evidence of residence rights   374
4. Types of evidence   376

Part 8   Support for asylum seekers

Chapter 21   Asylum support   389
1. Introduction   389
2. Support for asylum seekers   391
3. Temporary support   397
4. Support for failed asylum seekers   398
5. Support for people on temporary admission, temporary release or 407
   immigration bail
6. Support from your local authority   408

Chapter 22   Applying for asylum support   415
1. Applying for section 95 support   415
2. Making a decision on your application   416
3. Applying for section 4 support   423

Chapter 23   Payment and accommodation   427
1. Section 95 support   427
2. Section 4 support   433
3. Recovery of support   435

Chapter 24   Appeals   439
1. Introduction   439
2. The right to appeal   440
3. How to appeal   440
4. Decisions the First-tier Tribunal can make   450

Part 9   Other sources of help
Chapter 25   Other sources of help   455
1. Council tax reduction   457
2. Local welfare assistance schemes   462
3. Healthy Start food and vitamins   463
4. Education benefits   466
5. Free milk for children   468
6. Community care support from the local authority   468
7. Support under the Children Act 1989   470
8. NHS healthcare   470
9. Other financial help   472

Appendices
Appendix 1   Glossary of terms   479
Appendix 2   Information and advice   487
Appendix 3   Useful addresses   493
Appendix 4   Useful publications   505
Appendix 5   Reciprocal agreements   509
Appendix 6   Passport stamps and other endorsements   511
Appendix 7   Abbreviations used in the notes   523

Index   531

Abbreviations

AA	attendance allowance	IS	income support
ARC	application registration card	JSA	jobseeker's allowance
ASAP	Asylum Support Appeals Project	MA	maternity allowance
ASU	Asylum Screening Unit	MP	Member of Parliament
BIA	Border and Immigration Agency	NASS	National Asylum Support Service
CA	carer's allowance	NI	national insurance
CAB	Citizens Advice Bureau	OISC	Office of the Immigration Services
CJEU	Court of Justice of the European		Commissioner
	Union	PC	pension credit
CTC	child tax credit	PIP	personal independence payment
DLA	disability living allowance	REA	reduced earnings allowance
DWP	Department for Work and Pensions	SAL	standard acknowledgement letter
EC	European Community	SAP	statutory adoption pay
ECJ	European Court of Justice	SDA	severe disablement allowance
EEA	European Economic Area	SMP	statutory maternity pay
EFTA	European Free Trade Association	SPP	statutory paternity pay
EHIC	European health insurance card	SSP	statutory sick pay
ESA	employment and support	SSPP	statutory shared parental pay
	allowance	TFEU	Treaty on the Functioning of the
EU	European Union		European Union
FSU	Further Submissions Unit	UC	universal credit
HB	housing benefit	UK	United Kingdom
HMCTS	HM Courts and Tribunals Service	UKBA	UK Border Agency
HMRC	HM Revenue and Customs	UKVI	UK Visas and Immigration
IB	incapacity benefit	WTC	working tax credit
ICE	Independent Case Examiner		

Part 1

Introduction

Chapter 1

How to use this book

This chapter covers:
1. About this *Handbook* (below)
2. Checking the rules that affect you (p5)
3. Finding the relevant law (p6)
4. Immigration advice (p7)

1. About this *Handbook*

This *Handbook* is designed to be used by migrants and their advisers wanting advice on entitlement to social security benefits and tax credits. By 'migrants' we mean people, including British citizens, who have come or returned to Great Britain from abroad and people who have left Great Britain temporarily or to live abroad.

The law determining benefit entitlement for migrants is complex and frequently changing. As a result, migrants are often refused benefits and tax credits to which they are entitled, or not paid for family members when they should be.

This *Handbook* explains the different requirements that must be satisfied in order to be entitled to benefits and tax credits, so that you can understand whether or not you satisfy them and effectively challenge incorrect decisions.

This *Handbook* covers the rules that are most likely to affect migrant claimants and their families, and the practical problems that can arise. It is not a complete guide to the benefit rules and should be used together with general guides, such as CPAG's *Welfare Benefits and Tax Credits Handbook*.

European law after the UK referendum

The European law that is described in this *Handbook* has not changed as a result of the UK vote to leave the European Union (EU). European law continues to apply in the UK until the UK formally leaves the EU. The UK officially notified the European Council of its intention to leave in March 2017 and the terms of departure are being negotiated over a period of up to two years (or longer if both sides agree).[1] See CPAG's online service and *Welfare Rights Bulletin* for updates.

How this book is organised

The book is split into parts, and related chapters are grouped under these parts. For a description of the information covered in each part, see below. For the chapters included in each part, see the table of contents on pv.

Part 1 is an introduction to this *Handbook*.

Part 2 gives an overview of immigration law to help you identify your immigration status and understand the immigration terms that appear in the rest of this *Handbook*. **Note:** immigration law is complex and frequently changing. If you are unclear about your, or a member of your family's, immigration status, or the effects of claiming a benefit or tax credit, you should obtain advice from a specialist immigration adviser (see p7).

Part 3 covers the way your, and your family member's, immigration status affects your entitlement to benefits and tax credits. If you and all the people included in your claim are European Economic Area (EEA) nationals, the rules in this part do not apply to you.

Part 4 covers the residence and presence requirements for all benefits and tax credits and how you satisfy them, including details on how you satisfy the 'right to reside' requirement if you or your family member are an EEA national.

Part 5 explains the way your entitlement to benefits and tax credits is affected if you, or a family member who is included in your claim, go abroad.

Part 6 describes the way in which the EU social security co-ordination rules and international agreements on social security can assist you either to satisfy entitlement conditions in the UK or to be paid UK benefits abroad.

Part 7 covers some issues that can be particularly problematic for migrants – delays, satisfying the national insurance number requirement and providing evidence to show you meet the immigration, residence and presence rules.

Part 8 covers the rules on asylum support for people who have made an application for asylum in the UK.

Part 9 gives an overview of other possible sources of help that may be available to migrants.

Finding information

The two most efficient ways of finding information in this *Handbook* are to use the contents page or the index.

The contents shows the structure of the book and lists the parts, the chapters and the sections within each chapter.

The index contains entries in bold type, directing you to the general information on the subject or to the page(s) where the subject is covered more fully. Sub-entries under the bold headings are listed alphabetically and direct you to specific aspects of the subject.

Throughout this *Handbook* the text is referenced with the source of information, given in footnotes which are at the end of each chapter. For more information on finding the relevant law, see p6.

2. Checking the rules that affect you

As the rules are complicated, it is helpful to approach them systematically.

If you are not a European Economic Area (EEA) national (see p40), or if anyone you could include in your claim is not an EEA national, work through the following steps.

- **Step one:** be clear about your immigration status and that of anyone you could include in your claim. See Chapter 6 for help in determining on what basis you are in the UK. If you are unsure about your immigration status, get specialist immigration advice (see p7).
- **Step two:** check whether you are defined as a 'person subject to immigration control' (see Chapter 7). If you are not, your immigration status does not affect your benefit entitlement, but you must still satisfy any rules on residence and presence. **Note:** your partner's immigration status may still affect your entitlement (see Step five below).
- **Step three:** if you are defined as a 'person subject to immigration control', check whether the particular benefit or tax credit is one that excludes people subject to immigration control (see p57). If it is not, your immigration status does not affect your benefit entitlement, but you must still satisfy any rules on residence and presence.
- **Step four:** if the benefit you want to claim is one from which people subject to immigration control are generally excluded, check whether you come into an exempt group. These vary between the different benefits and tax credits (see p67). If you are in an exempt group, you must still satisfy all the other conditions of entitlement, including the residence and presence requirements.
- **Step five:** if you cannot claim the benefit you want, but you have a partner who may be able to include you in her/his claim, or if you can but have a partner or child who is subject to immigration control, check the rules on partners and children (see p74).
- **Step six:** if you or a member of your family have leave to enter or remain in the UK on condition that you do not have recourse to public funds, check whether any claim for benefits or tax credits could affect your/their immigration status (see p59).
- **Step seven:** if you are an asylum seeker or are dependent on an asylum seeker, you may be entitled to asylum support (see Chapter 21).

If you are an EEA national, or you are not an EEA national and your immigration status does not exclude you from entitlement, work through the following steps.

- **Step one:** check the residence and presence requirements for the benefit or tax credit you want to claim (see Chapter 13).
- **Step two:** if you are required to be 'habitually resident', check whether you are exempt from, or satisfy, this requirement (see Chapter 11).
- **Step three:** if you are required to have a right to reside, check how this test operates for the benefit or tax credit you want to claim (p117) and check whether you have a right to reside (see Chapter 12).
- **Step four:** if you are claiming a disability or carer's benefit, check Chapter 16 to see whether you are covered by the European Union (EU) social security co-ordination rules. If you are, check whether the UK is the 'competent state' to pay these benefits.
- **Step five:** if you do not satisfy the residence and presence rules, the EU co-ordination rules may assist you. The ways they may assist are explained for each benefit and tax credit in Chapter 13 and an overview of the way the rules operate and who they apply to is covered in Chapter 16.

If you are entitled to benefit and want to know whether you can continue to be paid when you, or someone who is included in your claim, go abroad, see Chapter 14 for an overview of the rules and Chapter 15 for the specific rules for individual benefits and tax credits. If you are going to another EEA country, the EU co-ordination rules may assist. Chapter 15 covers the ways they may assist for each benefit and tax credit, and an explanation of the way the rules operate and who they apply to is covered in Chapter 16.

---

3. **Finding the relevant law**

The complexity of the rules that specifically affect migrants means that it can be useful to refer to the relevant law not only when you are challenging a decision, but also when you make your claim. In order to ensure that the decision maker makes the correct decision on your claim, it may be helpful to provide an accompanying letter, setting out the legal requirement that you must satisfy and the way(s) in which you satisfy it. This may require you to set out more law – eg, relating to your immigration status, your right to reside, or the way the European Union co-ordination rules operate. You should also submit evidence that the law cited applies to you.

However, this does not guarantee that the correct decision will be made. If you are refused benefit when you believe you are entitled to it, you should challenge the decision. In any challenge, wherever possible, try to set out the relevant legal requirements and explain clearly how you meet them, citing the relevant law as appropriate and providing as much evidence as you can to show you meet the requirements.

This *Handbook* provides references to the law (both legislation and caselaw) and to guidance, so you can locate the source of the information given in the text.

- Find the information in the book relevant to the legal requirement you must satisfy and the text on how you satisfy it that applies to you.
- Find the endnote for that information and check the endnote text at the end of the chapter for the legal reference.
- Check Appendix 7 for an explanation of the abbreviations used in the references.
- See Appendices 2 and 4 for where to find the law and guidance online and for other useful sources of information.
- See Chapter 20 for information about providing evidence to show you satisfy legal requirements.

For a useful introduction to using legal sources, see CPAG's *Welfare Benefits and Tax Credits Handbook*.

Note: the law referred to in this *Handbook* applies in Great Britain. The equivalent law in Northern Ireland is often very similar and, in most cases, has the same effect. Many of the differences are due to the fact that the legislation and the administrative and adjudicating bodies in Northern Ireland are named differently. However, sometimes the law in Northern Ireland on a particular rule is different.

Any differences in the law in Scotland or Wales are noted.

4. Immigration advice

If you are unsure about your immigration status, or that of anyone you could include in your claim, get specialist advice from your local law centre, Citizens Advice Bureau (CAB) or other advice agency that gives immigration advice (see Appendix 2).

Anyone who gives immigration advice must be:

- a solicitor, barrister or legal executive, or supervised by such a person;
- registered by the Office of the Immigration Services Commissioner (OISC); *or*
- an adviser with an organisation that is exempt from registration. For example, CABx are exempt, but only to give basic immigration advice.

It is a criminal offence for someone not covered by one of the above groups to give immigration advice.

1

Chapter 1: How to use this book
Notes
• •

Every OISC-registered or exempt advice agency should display a certificate issued by the OISC to show it meets the OISC standards.

A list of all OISC-registered and exempt advisers and advice organisations is on the OISC website, which also includes details of how to make a complaint about an immigration adviser.

Notes
• •

1. About this *Handbook*
   1 Art 50 Treaty on European Union

Part 2

Immigration law

Chapter 2

Immigration and nationality law: overview

This chapter covers:
1. Immigration and nationality law (below)
2. The main types of immigration status (p13)
3. British nationality (p15)
4. Immigration and nationality applications (p16)
5. Appeals and other remedies (p18)
6. Deportation (p20)

1. Immigration and nationality law

The right to live, work and settle in the UK is regulated and controlled by a complex system of laws. These are amended frequently.

Sources of law

The main UK Acts of Parliament that are concerned with immigration and nationality law are:
- Immigration Act 1971;
- British Nationality Act 1981;
- Immigration Act 1988;
- Asylum and Immigration Appeals Act 1993;
- Asylum and Immigration Act 1996;
- Human Rights Act 1998;
- Immigration and Asylum Act 1999;
- Nationality, Immigration and Asylum Act 2002;
- Asylum and Immigration (Treatment of Claimants, etc.) Act 2004;
- Immigration, Asylum and Nationality Act 2006;
- UK Borders Act 2007;
- Borders, Citizenship and Immigration Act 2009;
- Immigration Act 2014;
- Immigration Act 2016.

These Acts are supplemented by;
* statutory instruments (regulations);
* the Immigration Rules;
* government policies.

You can find the original (as enacted) and revised versions of Acts of Parliament and statutory instruments at www.legislation.gov.uk, although more recent revisions may not be included.

The Immigration Rules and most government policies concerning immigration can be found on the Home Office UK Visas and Immigration website at www.gov.uk/government/organisations/uk-visas-and-immigration.

The UK has also signed various international treaties and conventions, which guarantee certain rights. These include the:
* European Convention for the Protection of Human Rights and Fundamental Freedoms 1950 (the 'European Convention on Human Rights'), incorporated, in part, into UK law by the Human Rights Act 1998;
* 1951 Convention Relating to the Status of Refugees and its 1967 Protocol, commonly referred to as 'the Refugee Convention';
* 1954 Convention Relating to the Status of Stateless Persons and the 1961 Convention on the Reduction of Statelessness;
* European Council Directive 2003/9/EC, laying down minimum standards for the reception of asylum seekers ('the Reception Directive');
* European Council Directive 2004/83/EC on minimum standards for the qualification and status of third-country nationals or stateless people as refugees or as persons who otherwise need international protection, and the content of the protection granted ('the Qualification Directive');
* European Council Directive 2004/38/EC on the right of citizens of the European Union and their family members to move and reside freely within the territory of the member states ('the Citizens' Directive');
* 2005 Council of Europe Convention on Action Against Trafficking in Human Beings.

Caselaw of the tribunals and higher courts in the UK and Europe is also important in immigration and nationality law. Much of this can be accessed free of charge on the British and Irish Legal Information Institute website at www.bailii.org.

Relevant institutions

The **Home Secretary** (Secretary of State for the Home Department) is responsible for the **Home Office.** The department within the Home Office that deals with immigration control is currently called **UK Visas and Immigration (UKVI).**

Immigration officers are generally responsible for processing people who arrive at the various UK ports of entry and for arresting, detaining and enforcing the removal of people from the UK. They have powers of search, entry, seizure and arrest of those suspected of having committed a criminal offence under immigration law, and may arrest and detain people who are liable to be detained in order to enforce their departure from the UK under immigration law.

Entry clearance officers stationed overseas are responsible for immigration control prior to entry to the UK. These are usually employed by commercial organisations responsible for the initial processing of applications. They decide whether to give **entry clearance** or **visas** to applicants under the Immigration Rules (see Chapter 3). They also decide whether to issue **family permits** (visas granted to family members of European Economic Area nationals – see Chapter 5).

Civil servants in UKVI are mainly responsible for deciding immigration and nationality applications made in the UK. Some applications made from outside the UK are also referred to civil servants in UKVI by visa officers stationed overseas.

HM Passport Office is the executive agency of the Home Office responsible for issuing UK passports and for administering the civil registration process in England and Wales – eg, births, deaths, marriages and civil partnerships.

Police officers are responsible for registering certain people who require leave to enter and remain in the UK, arresting people suspected of having committed a criminal offence under immigration law, and arresting and detaining people who are liable to be detained in order to enforce their departure from the UK under immigration law.

Judges of the **Immigration and Asylum Chambers of the First-tier Tribunal and the Upper Tribunal** are responsible for hearing and determining appeals against decisions made by entry clearance officers, immigration officers and the Secretary of State, applications for bail and most immigration-related judicial review applications.

Judges of the **Social Entitlement Chamber of the First-tier Tribunal** are responsible for determining appeals against decisions refusing asylum support.

Judges of the **Court of Appeal and UK Supreme Court** hear appeals from the Upper Tribunal, and judges of the **High Court** continue to decide applications for judicial review of certain types of decisions by the Home Secretary and her/his officers and the Upper Tribunal.

Cases may also be brought in the **Court of Justice of the European Union** if the matter concerns European Union law (which now includes asylum issues) and in the **European Court of Human Rights** if the matter concerns the European Convention on Human Rights.

2. The main types of immigration status

There are four main types of immigration status in the UK. You may be a person:
- with the right of abode. This includes British citizens (see p15);
- with leave to enter or remain (see Chapter 3);

- with a right to reside as a national of the European Economic Area (EEA) or as a family member of an EEA national (see Chapter 5);
- without status – eg, if you:
  - have entered the UK illegally;
  - previously had leave to enter or remain, but no longer have any such leave;
  - have made an asylum or human rights application when you sought to enter the UK – eg, at the airport (see Chapter 4).

If you are without status, you might be given temporary admission, temporary release or bail (see below).

Note: the term 'person subject to immigration control' is important for establishing someone's entitlement to social security benefits. It has a specific meaning that is explained on p57.

Temporary admission, temporary release and bail

If you make an application for leave to enter or remain at a port of entry or while in the UK at a time when you do not have leave (including an application for asylum or on human rights grounds), you may be given temporary admission to the UK until your application is decided. If you have been detained, you may be granted temporary release or bail. Temporary admission or temporary release may also be given if:

- you were refused leave in the UK, but you have remained; *or*
- you have remained in the UK after your limited leave to enter or remain expired;
- you entered the UK illegally and have subsequently come to the attention of the immigration authorities.

Temporary admission, temporary release and bail are best understood as alternatives to detention. This type of status may continue if you have been refused asylum or another type of application, including if you have made a new application or further submissions that you would like considered as a fresh asylum and/or human rights application (see p38).

If you were given temporary admission at a port of entry, you are considered to be 'lawfully present in the UK', unless and until that status is withdrawn from you. This can be significant if you must meet the requirement to have lawfully resided in the UK for a specified period of time to become eligible for citizenship or for indefinite leave to remain on the grounds of long residence. It can also be relevant to your eligibility to claim benefits.

Temporary admission or release usually means you have conditions imposed on you. These can include a requirement to live at a specified address, to report to an immigration officer at a specified time and place, and not to engage in paid or unpaid employment. There are criminal penalties if you do not adhere to these conditions, and failing to do so can make it more likely that you will be detained.

If you have temporary admission, temporary release or bail, you should have been issued with a notice informing you of your status and any conditions that apply.

Note: in certain circumstances, UK Visas and Immigration must provide accommodation to people with, or applying for, temporary admission, temporary release and bail (see p407).

3. British nationality

You can acquire British nationality:
- at birth, depending on the date and place of your birth, and on the nationality/citizenship and immigration and/or marital status of your parents; *or*
- on adoption; *or*
- by applying to the Home Secretary for naturalisation or registration; *or*
- as the result of legislative change.

Note: the examples given in this *Handbook* of how British citizenship may be acquired are basic. British nationality law is complex and there are many other routes that are not covered here.

There are six different forms of British nationality, only one of which (British citizenship) gives the right of abode in the UK (see below). A British national may be a:
- British citizen;
- British overseas territories citizen;
- British subject;
- British protected person;
- British national (overseas);
- British overseas citizen.

Some of the above forms of British nationality are rare and can no longer be acquired. In time, only British citizenship and British overseas territories citizenship will exist.

Multiple nationalities

Although some countries do not allow dual or multiple nationality or citizenship, UK law permits you to be a British national and a national of any number of other countries.

British nationals and the right of abode

'The right of abode' gives you the freedom to live in, and to come to and go from, the UK.

All full British citizens have the right of abode, but most people who have some other form of British nationality do not. Some Commonwealth citizens also have the right of abode, including people who are British nationals and not British citizens. However, it has not been possible to gain the right of abode since 1983 without also being a British citizen.

British nationals who do not have the right of abode generally require leave to enter or remain in the UK, but may have certain advantages over other foreign nationals in relation to applications for full British citizenship.

Acquiring British citizenship at birth

Most people, except children of diplomats and 'enemy aliens', born in the UK before 1 January 1983 automatically acquired British citizenship on that date.[1]

If you were born in the UK on or after 1 January 1983, you only acquired British citizenship if, at the time of your birth:

- your mother was a British citizen or was 'settled' in the UK – eg, she had indefinite leave to remain or permanent residence;[2] *or*
- your father was a British citizen or was 'settled' in the UK. If you were born before 1 July 2006, you could only gain citizenship from your father in this way if your parents were married, either at the time or subsequently. Since 1 July 2006, this restriction has no longer applied. If you were born before this date and did not acquire British citizenship because your parents were not married, you may now be able to register as a British citizen.

From 1 January 1983, a child born overseas acquires British citizenship if either parent is a British citizen, unless that parent is her/himself a British citizen by descent – eg, because s/he was also born overseas.[3] The same provisions as above apply to unmarried British fathers of children born abroad.

---

4. Immigration and nationality applications

Applying from outside the UK

You must obtain entry clearance before travelling to the UK to seek entry for most purposes.

Nationals of countries or territories listed in Appendix 1 of the Immigration Rules are known as **'visa nationals'**. If you are a visa national, you must obtain a visa before travelling to the UK for any purpose (unless you are a refugee – see Chapter 4).

Nationals of all other countries (**'non-visa nationals'**) may apply to an immigration officer at the port of arrival for entry for certain purposes, mainly for short-term visits. If you intend to stay for a longer period, you must usually obtain entry clearance before travelling.

Note: a European Economic Area (EEA) family permit is a visa issued to a non-EEA family member of an EEA national. However, it is not always necessary to obtain a family permit before being admitted to the UK. See p41 for more details.

An exempt vignette is issued to people, such as diplomats, who are exempt from the requirements of the Immigration Act 1971.

In most countries, you can apply for entry clearance online. In some countries, you must complete a printed application form. All applicants must attend a visa application centre in person. There is not a centre in every country in the world, so some applicants must travel to a different country to apply. Most applicants must have their fingerprints and facial image (known as 'biometric information') recorded at the visa application centre.

If you wish to apply for British nationality from outside the UK, you must usually send your application to UK Visas and Immigration (UKVI) in the UK.

Applying from within the UK

UKVI is responsible for processing applications made by people in the UK:
- for leave to remain in the UK, including for asylum;
- to extend their leave to remain or vary their leave to remain – ie, to change the type of leave or the conditions attached to it;
- for confirmation of their right to reside as an EEA national or the family member of an EEA national;
- for British nationality.

Some types of application can be made online from within the UK, but all applications must be supported by original documents.

Certain types of application must usually be made in person at a specified location. These include applications for asylum (except those made under Article 3 of the European Convention on Human Rights for health reasons) and further asylum and/or human rights submissions from someone who has previously applied for asylum unsuccessfully. Other types of application may also be made in person. A 'premium service' is available, with a shorter processing time (applications are sometimes dealt with on the same day), at an increased cost.

A fee is charged for most in-country applications. Exceptions to this include:[4]
- an application for leave to enter or remain for asylum reasons, including applications made under Article 3 of the European Convention on Human Rights for health reasons;
- an application for leave to enter or remain by a child who is being looked after by a local authority;
- an application for limited leave to enter or remain by a victim of trafficking (in limited circumstances only);
- an application for limited leave to enter or remain for certain purposes if UKVI accepts that the applicant is destitute or that other exceptional circumstances

apply. In these circumstances, you must complete an application form for a fee waiver and provide evidence.

Health surcharge

Additional fees, described as a 'health surcharge' are charged by the UK government for many applications for limited leave to enter or remain. Exceptions include applications for:[5]

- indefinite leave to enter or remain;
- entry clearance for leave to enter for six months or less;
- a child under 18 who is being looked after by a local authority;
- leave to enter or remain for asylum reasons, including applications made under Article 3 of the European Convention on Human Rights for health reasons;
- leave to remain which relates to someone being identified as a victim of human trafficking;
- leave to remain outside the Immigration Rules with access to public funds under the Home Office policy known as the 'destitution domestic violence concession' (see p35);
- entry clearance or leave to remain as the dependant of a person who benefits from certain other exemptions.

The standard surcharge fee is £150 a year per person for students and each of their dependants and £200 a year per person for everyone else.

For information on NHS healthcare, including charges and on who is exempt from them, see p470.

---

5. Appeals and other remedies

Appeals to the First-tier Tribunal

The First-tier Tribunal (Immigration and Asylum Chamber) is a judicial authority that is independent of the UK government.

You can appeal to the First-tier Tribunal against either an 'immigration decision' (see below) or a 'European Economic Area (EEA) decision' (see p19). You can also apply to the First-tier Tribunal for bail from immigration detention.

Only the following are 'immigration decisions':[6]

- a decision by the Secretary of State that you can be removed from the UK where you have made a claim that you cannot be removed because of the Refugee Convention or because you are eligible for humanitarian protection;
- a decision by the Secretary of State to refuse a human rights application you have made (including an application made from abroad);
- a decision by the Secretary of State to revoke your leave to enter or remain as a refugee or as a person eligible for humanitarian protection.

Only decisions under the Immigration (European Economic Area) Regulations 2006 that concern the following are 'EEA decisions':[7]
* your entitlement to be admitted to the UK;
* your entitlement to be issued with, have renewed or not to have revoked, a registration certificate, a residence card, a derivative residence card, a document certifying permanent residence or a permanent residence card;
* your removal from the UK; *or*
* the cancellation of your right to reside in the UK.

You can also appeal against a decision to deprive you of British citizenship.[8]

In certain circumstances, the Secretary of State has powers to prevent you from appealing until after you have left the UK or to prevent you from appealing altogether.

For example, if you wish to appeal on grounds that do not include a claim for asylum, you may be denied a right to appeal from within the UK (unless to do so would be contrary to your human rights). You may also be refused a right of appeal from within the UK if the Secretary of State (lawfully) considers your chances of succeeding in an appeal are hopeless.

You may be prevented from appealing altogether if you could have raised the grounds on which you wish to appeal when given an earlier opportunity to state your case but you chose not to do so.

In most cases, you must pay a fee when you appeal. This does not currently apply if you are appealing against a decision to remove you from the UK and you are receiving legal aid, you are a child being supported by a local authority or if you apply to the tribunal and are accepted as requiring a fee remission because you are unable to pay.

If you win your appeal, UK Visas and Immigration (UKVI) decides whether this means you must be granted leave or, in EEA law cases, whether your right to reside must be confirmed by issuing you with an appropriate document. Delays can occur while this is being considered (see p47).

Administrative review

If a decision has been made about you by UKVI that is not an 'immigration decision' or an 'EEA decision' (see above), you may be able to apply to the Home Office for an administrative review. This is not carried out by an independent body. Examples of such decisions include a decision to refuse you entry clearance or to refuse you leave to enter or remain where you have not made an asylum, humanitarian protection or human rights claim.

Judicial review

If a decision has been made about you that does not have a right to appeal, you may be able to challenge its lawfulness by applying for a judicial review to the

Upper Tribunal or to the Administrative Court, depending on the nature of the decision. This could include a decision to uphold a refusal after an administrative review.

The Administrative Court also hears applications for bail from people in immigration detention if the grounds for bail cannot be considered by the First-tier Tribunal – ie, if they relate to the lawfulness of the detention.

6. Deportation

'**Deportation**' is a procedure under which a person without the right of abode (see p15) is removed from the UK and excluded from re-entering for as long as the deportation order remains in force. Deportation is most often used when someone has been convicted of a serious criminal offence or is considered to be a persistent offender, but anyone whose presence is deemed by the Secretery of State to not be conducive to the public good is liable to be deported.

Deportation is not the same as '**administrative removal**', which is the procedure for removing someone who has entered the UK illegally or breached her/his conditions of leave – eg, by overstaying.

If you are being considered for deportation you may, whether or not you have leave to enter or remain, be detained, given temporary admission, or released or bailed with conditions. See p14 for further information.

Notes

3. British nationality
1 s11 BNA 1981
2 s1 BNA 1981
3 s2 BNA 1981

4. Immigration and nationality
   applications
4 The Immigration and Nationality (Fees)
   Regulations 2016, No.226
5 The Immigration (Health Charge) Order
   2015, No.792

5. Appeals and other remedies
6 s82 NIAA 2002, as amended by IA 2014
7 Reg 2(1) I(EEA) Regs
8 s40A BNA 1981

• • • •

Chapter 3

· ·

Leave to enter or remain

This chapter covers:
1. Leave to enter or remain (below)
2. Time-limited leave (p23)
3. Indefinite leave (p23)
4. Employment (p24)
5. Recourse to public funds (p25)
6. Sponsorship (p26)

---

1. Leave to enter or remain

You are likely to require leave to enter or remain in the UK unless you have:
- the right of abode. This includes British citizens (see p15);
- a right to reside as a national of the European Economic Area (EEA), or as a family member of an EEA national (see p40).

The Immigration Rules set out the circumstances in which leave to enter or remain can be granted for various purposes, including for study, employment and business, family connections, long residence, human rights and asylum. The Immigration Rules also stipulate the duration of the leave and any conditions attached to it, the circumstances in which leave will be refused, curtailed or revoked, and the criteria for deporting people whose presence in the UK is considered to be against the public interest – eg, if someone has committed a serious criminal offence.

Changes to the Immigration Rules must be notified to Parliament, but there does not need to be any debate before the changes take effect. The Rules are currently extremely lengthy, complicated and difficult to navigate. A consolidated version is published on the UK Visas and Immigration (UKVI) website at www.gov.uk/government/organisations/uk-visas-and-immigration. The website also contains policy guidance that explains the Immigration Rules. The explanation given in the guidance is not always followed by tribunals and courts, but the guidance must usually be followed by UKVI decision makers and you can therefore rely on it if it is beneficial in your case.

Note: leave may also be granted outside the Immigration Rules (see p38).

Conditions of your leave

Leave to enter or remain in the UK may be given subject to a limited number of conditions. If you breach the conditions attached to your leave, you may commit a criminal offence, your current leave could be curtailed or revoked, and future applications for leave could be refused. You could also be detained and removed from the UK.

The conditions that may be attached to leave granted under the Immigration Rules that is subject to a time limit are:

- a condition about residence;
- a requirement to register with the police and/or report to the Home Office;
- restrictions on your taking employment or studying (see p24);
- a requirement to maintain and accommodate yourself and any dependants without having recourse to 'public funds' (see p25).

Who is exempt from the usual conditions

Some people are exempt from some of the usual conditions attached to permission to enter and remain in the UK. The main categories of people who are exempt are seamen and women, aircrew, diplomats and members of the UK or visiting armed forces.[1]

EEA and Swiss nationals and their family members have separate rights and conditions of entry and residence in the UK (see Chapter 5).

Nationals of some other non-EEA states also have special rights to establish themselves or provide services in the UK for economic purposes under agreements of 'association'. The most notable of these is the agreement between the European Community (EC) and Turkey (see below).

Turkish nationals

Turkish nationals can establish themselves in the UK for economic purposes under an agreement of 'association' between the EC (as it was at the date of the agreement) and Turkey.

This EC-Turkey association agreement of 12 September 1963 is known as the 'Ankara Agreement'. Its purpose was to promote a move towards abolishing the restrictions on people who wished to move between Turkey and the (then) EC in order to establish themselves or provide services. This was to be achieved by certain Association Council decisions[2] and by prohibiting the introduction of new national restrictions that were less favourable than those in force on the 'relevant date'. In the case of the UK, this is 1 January 1973, the date the UK joined the EC. The Immigration Rules in effect on 1 January 1973 were less restrictive in certain respects than the current ones. Turkish nationals can therefore have any relevant applications considered under these old, less restrictive, Immigration Rules.[3]

2. Time-limited leave

Leave may be granted for a limited period of time. Depending on the requirements in the Immigration Rules, you may be able to have it extended or varied (switched) to another category.

Note: any time-limited leave is automatically extended beyond the date it is due to expire if you make a valid application to extend or vary the leave before the expiry date. Your leave is extended until UK Visas and Immigration (UKVI) makes a decision on your application and, if this is refused, until any appeal rights or rights to administrative review are exhausted (see p47).[4] Leave is not extended if you appeal or apply for administrative review against a refusal of leave to remain and you did not have leave to enter or remain at the time you applied.

UKVI can take many months or even years to process some applications (eg, those from people who have applied to extend leave given outside the Immigration Rules for human rights reasons) and appeals can take many months, sometimes years, before they are determined. This can cause problems when you need to satisfy others that your leave has been extended in this way.

Note: in certain circumstances, the Secretary of State has powers to prevent you from appealing until after you have left the UK. For example, if you have made a non-asylum human rights claim that has been refused, you can be prevented from appealing until after you have left the UK if it would not breach your human rights to appeal from overseas. The government plans to extend this power to all non-asylum human rights appeals cases, but at the time of writing, regulations to bring this into force had not been laid.

3. Indefinite leave

Indefinite leave to enter or remain in the UK is leave without a time restriction. Indefinite leave is sometimes referred to as 'settlement'.

There are no conditions (eg, on employment and claiming 'public funds' – see p25) attached to indefinite leave.[5] However, you may still be classed as a 'person subject to immigration control' for benefit purposes and therefore restricted from claiming benefits for a specific period of time if the leave was given on the basis of an undertaking by a sponsor that s/he would be responsible for your maintenance (see p61). Your sponsor may also be liable to repay any benefits claimed and may face criminal penalties (see p28). If you have been granted entry clearance or leave to enter on the basis of a maintenance undertaking, this is not stated on the document issued to you confirming this, and this may need to be checked with a decision maker. If you are in any doubt about whether the decision maker is correct, get specialist advice.

Indefinite leave can lapse if you are absent from the UK for too long (see below). It can also be revoked (see below).

If you have indefinite leave, you can leave the UK and return without your leave lapsing if:

- you wish to return to settle in the UK; *and*
- you have not been away from the UK for more than two years, unless there are special circumstances – eg, a previous long period of residence; *and*
- you did not receive any assistance from public funds towards the cost of leaving the UK. **Note:** 'public funds' in this context is the scheme that allows people to be reimbursed the costs of resettling in their country of origin. It does *not* refer to the fact that you may have claimed benefits and other public funds while in the UK (see p25).[6]

Your indefinite leave may be revoked for reasons including if:

- you become liable to deportation (see p20); *or*
- the leave was obtained by deception.

Note: if you have been granted indefinite leave to enter the UK, your visa shows an 'expiry' or 'valid until' date. This is the date by which your entry clearance must be presented to enter the UK for the first time, after which you have indefinite leave and the date becomes irrelevant.[7]

4. Employment

Certain types of leave are granted with a condition prohibiting employment. For example, visitors are usually prohibited from working in the UK. Other types of leave limit the employment you may do to a certain number of hours in a week (eg, if you are given leave as a student), or for a specific period of employment or business activity. This may be described as 'authorised' work. The details of what is authorised may be found in the relevant government policy, published on the UK Visas and Immigration (UKVI) website.

If you have been given leave for specific employment (eg, under tier two of the points-based system – see p29 – or, in the past, under a work permit) or a specific activity (such as self-employment, or as a writer, composer or artist), you can only work in the employment or undertake the activity for which you were given leave. If you wish to change employment, you must apply to UKVI for permission.

Employers must check that all new employees have the right to work in the UK and can be prosecuted for employing a migrant who cannot lawfully work. The law on the employment of migrant workers has changed several times since this requirement was introduced (in 1997) and the checks an employer must make (or should have made) depend on the date the worker was first employed by the employer. Applying such checks might raise race discrimination issues. If you think you have been treated unfavourably by an employer or potential employer, get specialist advice.

Note: since 1 December 2014, some landlords must check that you have the right to live in the UK before letting a property to you. This includes landlords who take in lodgers or sublet property.

5. Recourse to public funds

Leave to enter or remain for certain purposes is only granted if you can show that you and your dependants can, and will, be adequately maintained and accommodated without recourse to 'public funds'.

In addition, when leave is granted that is subject to a time limit, a condition prohibiting you from having recourse to public funds is usually imposed. This now includes most limited leave to enter or remain for family or private life reasons granted under Article 8 of the European Convention on Human Rights (see p34). If you have such a condition on your leave to remain, it is stated on the document issued to you confirming the leave.

If you breach this condition, you may commit a criminal offence, your current leave could be curtailed or revoked, and future applications for leave could be refused. You could also be detained and removed from the UK and/or refused citizenship on character grounds.

What are public funds

'Public funds' for the purposes of the Immigration Rules are:[8]
* attendance allowance;
* carer's allowance;
* child benefit;
* child tax credit;
* council tax benefit (now abolished);
* council tax reduction;
* disability living allowance;
* income-related employment and support allowance;
* housing benefit;
* income support;
* income-based jobseeker's allowance;
* pension credit;
* personal independence payment;
* severe disablement allowance;
* social fund payments;
* universal credit;

- working tax credit;
- housing and homelessness assistance;
- local welfare assistance.

Only the above are public funds; nothing else counts under the Immigration Rules, including other social security benefits and education. NHS services are not public funds under this definition, but they are restricted (see p470).

Note: in certain cases, you can still claim benefits defined as public funds without breaching the condition not to have recourse to public funds. This applies if you come into one of the exempt groups who can claim these benefits, despite being a 'person subject to immigration control' (see p67).[9]

6. Sponsorship

Who is a sponsor

The Immigration Rules define a sponsor as the person in relation to whom you are seeking leave to enter or remain as a spouse, fiancé/e, civil partner, proposed civil partner, unmarried partner (including same-sex partner) or dependent relative.

Your sponsor must usually demonstrate that s/he can maintain and support you in the UK without recourse to public funds. Parents must fulfil a similar role in the case of child applicants.[10] Support by third parties is permitted for some types of application,[11] but not for most 'family' applications.

Financial requirements

For most family applications, your sponsor must have a minimum specified annual income in order for you to be given leave to enter or remain as her/his family member.[12] The amount increases depending on the number of children in the family. A sponsor who is getting attendance allowance (AA), disability living allowance (DLA), personal independence payment (PIP), carer's allowance, industrial injuries disablement benefit and certain military and veteran payments does not have to have income above this threshold.

If your sponsor has more than a certain amount of savings, these can be used to make up any shortfall in her/his annual income.

Your own income, savings and prospective income, and (in most cases) any support from a third party, are all disregarded.

Adequate maintenance

For leave to be granted under other parts of the Immigration Rules, including some family cases, you must show that you can, and will, be maintained adequately without recourse to public funds. Whether or not there is adequate maintenance depends on the number of people who need maintaining and the income of the person or family unit concerned. The standard of adequacy currently required is that the income of the family as a whole must be equal to or greater than the amount an equivalent family would receive from income support (IS) if all the family members were entitled to have recourse to public funds. The use of this benchmark has been justified as necessary to prevent immigrant families or communities having a lower standard of living in the UK than the poorest British citizens.[13] However, the minimum income requirement used in most other cases is significantly higher than that.

Note: support from third parties can be counted for some types of applications not made under Appendix FM of the Immigration Rules.[14]

AA, DLA and PIP claimed by a sponsor can be included when establishing whether a family's income is the same or higher than the IS amount.[15] It is arguable that the same approach should be applied to industrial injuries disablement benefit, and severe disablement allowance and its replacement employment and support allowance. You should obtain specialist advice if this might be an issue.

Adequate accommodation

In most cases, in order to be given leave to enter or remain as a family member, a certain standard and/or type of accommodation must be available to you.

There must be adequate accommodation for you and any dependants, without your having recourse to public funds and which the family owns or occupies exclusively.

The accommodation must not be overcowded. The Housing Act 1985 contains statutory definitions of overcrowding for both privately rented and local authority accommodation. Your accommodation is considered overcrowded if two people aged 10 years or older of the opposite sex (other than husband and wife) have to sleep in the same room, or if the number of people sleeping in the accommodation exceeds that permitted in the Act, which specifies the number of people for a given number of rooms or given floor area.

The Immigration Rules often require that the accommodation must be owned or occupied 'exclusively' by the family unit concerned. A separate bedroom for the exclusive use of the applicant and sponsor is sufficient to meet this requirement, so a family may live in shared accommodation, sharing other rooms (such as a kitchen and bathroom) with other occupants.[16]

If your circumstances change

If you needed to satisfy financial, maintenance or accommodation requirements under the Immigration Rules before your leave was granted, your leave may be curtailed and/or a further application refused if you or your sponsor do not continue to meet these requirements throughout the period of leave granted.[17] **Note:** this only applies if your leave is subject to a time limit – ie, it does not apply if you have been granted indefinite leave to enter or remain (see p23). UK Visas and Immigration (UKVI) might discover that your circumstances have changed if, for example, you or your sponsor make a claim for social security benefits.

In addition, it appears that if you have been issued with a biometric residence permit (see p47), you must notify UKVI as soon as reasonably practicable if you know (or suspect) that a change in your circumstances means that you no longer qualify for leave under the Immigration Rules.[18] It is unclear whether this only applies to time-limited leave to remain or also to indefinite leave to remain.

If a change in your circumstances means you might not meet the requirements for the leave you have been granted, you should get specialist advice urgently.

See p35 if a qualifying relationship has ended because of domestic violence.

Maintenance undertakings

A sponsor may be asked to give a written undertaking to be responsible for your maintenance and accommodation, or for your care, for the period of leave granted and any further period of leave to remain that you may be granted while in the UK.[19] Undertakings are often requested for:

- dependent relatives, although not for children under 16 years coming for settlement;
- students relying on a private individual in the UK.

The benefit authorities sometimes mistakenly assume that every person referred to as a 'sponsor' will have given such an undertaking, but this is not the case. The definition of 'sponsor' is wider than this and not all sponsors are required to give a written undertaking.

If you have been granted leave to enter or remain as a result of a maintenance undertaking, you are excluded from claiming benefits.[20] If you subsequently claim benefit while in the UK, your sponsor may be required to pay back the value of the benefit claimed.[21] This restriction applies until you have been in the UK for five years since the date of the undertaking or the date of entry. If your sponsor dies, the restriction ends immediately.

A maintenance undertaking may be enforceable, even if it is not formally drafted, and vice versa.[22] In one case, a formal declaration that a sponsor was able and willing to maintain and accommodate was held not to amount to an undertaking, as it did not include a promise to support.[23]

Unlike the condition not to have recourse to public funds, a maintenance undertaking is not stated on the document issued to you when your leave to enter or remain is granted.

Sponsorship under the points-based system

For some categories in the Immigration Rules, points are awarded to someone applying for leave to enter or remain for having various attributes and levels of income and/or savings. This is different from points-based schemes in other countries, as all the categories in the Immigration Rules require applicants to have all the attributes for which points are notionally awarded and so, in reality, the UK system is a points-based system in name only.

There are five 'tiers', or categories, of purpose under which leave may be granted under this system. These are:

- tier one: entrepreneurs, investors and exceptionally talented people – eg, scientists, engineers and artists;
- tier two: skilled workers with a job offer (usually only for occupations in which UKVI recognises there is a shortage of appropriately skilled workers available in the UK and European Economic Area labour market);
- tier four: students;
- tier five: youth mobility (previously called 'working holidays') and temporary workers – eg, for short-term creative or sporting events.

Note: tier three is not currently in use.

If you are applying under any tier, you must usually be sponsored by an employer or educational institution. The sponsor must hold a certificate of sponsorship. This is a unique reference number that the sponsor issues to you to enable you to remain in the UK, as opposed to an actual certificate or document.

Sponsors must report to UKVI any significant changes in the sponsored person's circumstances, suspicions that s/he is breaching the conditions of her/his leave or significant changes in the sponsor's own circumstances – eg, if s/he stops trading or becomes insolvent.

Notes

1. Leave to enter or remain
1 s8 IA 1971
2 Association Council decisions 2/76 and 1/80
3 Art 41.1 Additional Protocol to the Ankara Agreement; *R (Veli Tum and Mehmet Dari) v Secretary of State for the Home Department,* C-16/05 [2007] ECR I-07415

2. Time-limited leave
4 The extension of leave while a right of appeal can be exercised only applies within the time limit for appealing and when an out-of-time appeal has been accepted.

3. Indefinite leave
5 s3(3)(a) IA 1971
6 paras 18-19 IR

7 See UKVI policy guidance ECB9.4, at
   www.gov.uk/government/publications/
   entry-clearance-vignettes-ecb09

5. Recourse to public funds
8 para 6 IR
9 SS(IA)CA Regs, as amended by The
   Social Security (Croatian) (Amendment)
   Regulations 2013, No.1474; para 6B IR

6. Sponsorship
10 para 297 and Appendix FM IR
11 *Mahad (previously referred to as AM)
    (Ethiopia) v Entry Clearance Officer* [2009]
    UKSC 16, 16 December 2009
12 Appendix FM IR
13 *KA (Pakistan)* [2006] UKAIT 00065;
    approved in *AM (Ethiopia) and Others
    and Another v Entry Clearance Officer*
    [2008] EWCA Civ 1082, 16 October
    2008
14 *Mahad (previously referred to as AM)
    (Ethiopia) v Entry Clearance Officer* [2009]
    UKSC 16, 16 December 2009
15 *MK (Somalia) v Entry Clearance Officer*
    [2007] EWCA Civ 1521, 28 November
    2007
16 Ch8, s1, annex F IDI. This includes
    information on the minimum size of a
    room and a table showing the
    maximum number of people allowed for
    any specific number of rooms.
17 paras 322(4)-23 IR
18 Reg 18 Immigration (Biometric
    Registration) Regulations 2008,
    No.3048
19 para 35 IR
20 s115(9)(c) IAA 1999
21 para 35 IR; ss78, 105 and 106 SSAA
    1992
22 *R (Begum)* [2003] *The Times*, 4
    December 2003
23 *Ahmed v SSWP* [2005] EWCA Civ 535

Chapter 4
• •
Asylum and human rights

This chapter covers:
1. Asylum seekers (below)
2. Refugee leave and humanitarian protection (p32)
3. Stateless people (p34)
4. Leave for human rights and compassionate reasons (p34)
5. Fresh applications (p38)

1. Asylum seekers

Applying for asylum

Someone who has applied for recognition as a refugee or as a person requiring international protection in the UK is commonly called an 'asylum seeker'.

Asylum applications to UK Visas and Immigration (UKVI) can be made on one or more of the following grounds:
- under the Refugee Convention (see p12);
- under Article 3 of the Human Rights Convention (see p12). This prescribes that no one shall be subjected to torture or to inhuman or degrading treatment or punishment;
- under the Qualification Directive (see p12).

The most common other Human Rights Convention Article raised in immigration cases is Article 8, which protects a person's right to enjoy private and family life without unnecessary or disproportionate interference (see p34).

'Temporary protection' is a separate and specific category of leave introduced by the Qualification Directive. It is intended to be given to people following a declaration by the European Union (EU) Council in recognition of a mass influx of displaced people. However, there have been no declarations since the Directive came into force.

The definition of an asylum seeker for the purpose of support and accommodation (see p391) is limited to people who have applied under the Refugee Convention and/or Article 3 of the Human Rights Convention – eg, an application based only on Article 8 does not make someone an asylum seeker for asylum support purposes.[1] However, in certain situations, UKVI can provide accommodation to people who are subject to immigration control who are not asylum seekers (see p407).

An asylum seeker may have applied for asylum at a port of entry before passing through passport control, or from inside the country, having entered the UK illegally or with leave for a different purpose under the Immigration Rules.

Note: if you delay making an in-country asylum application, your entitlement to asylum support may be affected (see p391).

If your asylum application is refused or withdrawn, and you have not successfully appealed, you may be able to make a fresh application (see p38).

Detention and removal

Many asylum seekers are given temporary admission while their asylum application is considered, but a significant number have been detained while their application is considered, in the expectation that their application will be considered quickly and they can then be quickly removed from the UK if refused. Other asylum seekers are detained waiting for removal to a third country (ie, not the UK or their country of nationality), which is deemed to be responsible for considering their application.

If you are a failed asylum seeker, you can be detained without a time limit, provided the purpose of the detention is your removal from the UK and there is some prospect of that.

Permission to work

If you are an asylum seeker who has not received a decision on your initial application for asylum after one year, and the delay was not your fault, you can apply to UKVI for permission to work.[2]

However, the work you can do is restricted to a shortlist of skilled occupations for which UKVI recognises there is a shortage of workers available in the UK. So, in practice, this is of no benefit to most asylum seekers.

2. **Refugee leave and humanitarian protection**

If you are an asylum seeker who is recognised by UK Visas and Immigration (UKVI) as a refugee or as being in need of humanitarian protection, you are granted refugee leave or humanitarian protection leave respectively.

Refugees and humanitarian protection
A 'refugee' is someone who, owing to a well-founded fear of being persecuted because of race, religion, nationality, membership of a particular social group or political opinion, is

outside the country of her/his nationality, and is unable to or, owing to such fear, is unwilling to avail her/himself of the protection of that country.

A person in need of **'humanitarian protection'** is someone who does not qualify as a refugee, but there are substantial grounds for believing that if s/he were returned to her/his country of origin, s/he would face a real risk of suffering serious harm. A person could, for example, face a risk of serious harm for reasons other than race, religion, nationality, membership of a particular social group or political opinion.

An initial five years' leave to remain is usually granted, with the option of applying for indefinite leave shortly before this leave expires.

Refugee leave and humanitarian protection leave can be reviewed and revoked, or not extended (when you apply for indefinite leave), if:

- you are a refugee, but your actions bring you within the scope of the 1951 Refugee Convention 'cessation clauses' – eg, if you travel back to your country of origin without a reasonable explanation;[3] *or*
- there is a 'significant or non-temporary' change in the conditions in your country of origin (or part of the country) that means your continuing need for protection is now placed in doubt and a formal declaration of the change is made by the responsible state authority.

Family reunion

If you have been given refugee or humanitarian protection leave, your spouse, civil partner or, in some circumstances, your unmarried partner, and dependent children under 18 who formed part of your family unit prior to your departure from your country can apply to be reunited with you in the UK. This is commonly called 'family reunion'. There are no maintenance and accommodation requirements that must be met.

Successful family reunion applicants are granted leave in line with your leave, but they may not be granted refugee or humanitarian protection as they are not necessarily recognised as refugees. The leave granted will expire at the same time as yours, and therefore may be limited leave of up to five years or indefinite leave.[4]

Exclusions

You can be excluded from refugee status or humanitarian protection status if:

- you have committed a crime against peace, a war crime, a crime against humanity or a serious non-political crime outside the UK before being admitted as a refugee; *or*
- you have been guilty of acts that are contrary to the purposes and principles of the United Nations. This could include being involved in terrorism or encouraging others to do that.

If you are excluded from refugee or humanitarian protection status for these reasons or your application is 'certified' (see below), but you cannot be removed to your home country for human rights reasons (eg, because you face a risk of torture), you may be granted restricted leave (see p37).

Your application can be 'certified' if you have committed a serious offence – eg, if you have been sentenced to 26 months (for refugee status) or 12 months (for humanitarian protection) in prison.

If you cannot be excluded, but your presence is considered to be undesirable, the Home Office may grant leave for shorter periods than five years and/or with a slower route to settlement.

3. Stateless people

A stateless person is defined by international law as someone who is 'not considered a national by any state under the operation of its law'.[5] On 6 April 2013, the UK introduced a provision in the Immigration Rules to recognise and grant leave to remain to certain stateless people.[6] Before this date, stateless people could obtain travel documents, but could not obtain leave. If you are recognised as being stateless in the UK, you can still obtain a stateless person's travel document.

4. Leave for human rights and compassionate reasons

Leave granted for Article 8 of the Human Rights Convention reasons

Article 8 of the European Convention on Human Rights guarantees enjoyment of private and family life without unnecessary or disproportionate interference. You may be able to rely on this Article if you have family in the UK and/or have lived in the UK for some time and developed ties here. If UK Visas and Immigration (UKVI) is considering removing you from the UK and this would disrupt (interfere with) these aspects of your life (eg, it would separate you from a loved one), under Article 8 you should only be removed if it is necessary and reasonable in the particular circumstances of your case. Since 9 July 2012, the Immigration Rules have set out the circumstances in which UKVI accepts it must allow you to stay in the UK for private and family life reasons if you do not satisfy the requirements of any other part of the Rules – eg, the minimum income requirement in family cases (see p26).[7] However, there are some cases that fall outside the Rules but where leave must be granted in order to comply with Article 8.

From 9 July 2012, leave is given for periods of no longer than 30 months, potentially leading to indefinite leave after 10 continuous years. This is twice the length of time in which a family member can become eligible for settlement under other parts of the Immigration Rules. UKVI policy is to grant you leave subject to a condition that you do not have recourse to public funds, unless there are exceptional circumstances that you have raised in your application for leave. It is possible to apply for this condition to be lifted if there has been a change in your circumstances, or if the circumstances were not known to UKVI at the time the leave was granted.[8] UKVI policy is that 'exceptional circumstances' only exist if you are destitute or if you are a parent on a low income and there are particularly compelling reasons relating to the welfare of your child.[9]

Note: if you are a carer or sibling of a child who is a British citizen, you may have immigration rights under Article 8 of the European Convention on Human Rights, the Immigration Rules and/or under European Economic Area (EEA) law (see Chapter 12). There are potential advantages and disadvantages of relying on one or the other of these rights for your being able to obtain permanent settlement in the UK in the longer term, and in relation to the uncertain consequences of the UK leaving the European Union. In addition, if you have rights under Article 8 or the Immigration Rules, you might be able to access public funds, but not if you rely on EEA law.

Before 9 July 2012, leave to remain given for Article 8 reasons was granted outside the Immigration Rules and was called **'discretionary leave'** (see p36).

Leave granted in cases of domestic violence and bereavement

If you are granted leave to enter or remain in the UK as a spouse, unmarried partner (including a same-sex partner) or civil partner of a British citizen, or of a person with indefinite leave to enter or remain in the UK or a member of HM Forces who has served for at least four years, you must usually complete a probationary period of limited leave in the UK with your partner before you can apply for indefinite leave to remain, in order to settle in the UK permanently with your partner. The probationary period is currently five or 10 years. However, you may be able to apply for indefinite leave to remain earlier than this if your relationship has broken down as a result of domestic violence or if you are bereaved.[10]

In addition to the above, you might have limited leave for a probationary period, which has been granted with a condition that you do not have recourse to public funds. Or you might have no leave because the probationary period has expired without your applying for further leave. In either situation, you can apply for a short period of limited leave (with no restrictions on public funds) under what is known as the 'destitution domestic violence' concession.[11]

If successful, you are granted limited leave to remain for three months with access to public funds, during which time you can apply for indefinite leave to remain under the domestic violence rule. If you do so, your 'destitution domestic violence' leave is extended until your application (and any appeal or administrative review) has been decided (see p47).

Discretionary leave

Discretionary leave is granted:
- in medical cases. The threshold for leave on this basis is high: an applicant must face a real risk of being exposed to a serious, rapid and irreversable decline in her/his health, which would result in 'intense suffering', due to the absence of appropriate treatment were s/he to be removed from the UK;[12]
- if returning you would breach the European Convention on Human Rights – eg, if the government of the country to which you would need to go if you were not granted leave in the UK would flagrantly deny your rights to a fair trial under Article 6 of the Convention or your rights to enjoy family and private life. This is different to cases where the UK government would breach your rights by removing you or refusing to grant you leave to enter or remain in the UK;
- in other exceptional circumstances specified in UKVI enforcement policies;
- if you have been identified as a victim of trafficking within the meaning of Article 4 of the Council of Europe Convention on Action Against Trafficking in Human Beings and your personal circumstances are so compelling that it is considered appropriate to grant some form of leave;
- if you are an unsuccessful asylum seeker, but it is considered appropriate to grant leave to you (the scope of this is unclear);
- under transitional arrangements, if you have been previously granted discretionary leave.

Note: from 9 July 2012, discretionary leave is no longer granted for reasons relating to Article 8 of the European Convention on Human Rights (see p34) or to unaccompanied children. Both categories are now included in the Immigration Rules.

If you have been granted discretionary leave, you can have access to public funds (see p25) and are entitled to work.

Discretionary leave is normally granted for a period of 30 months, with the possibility of a further 30-month extension period. After you have had 10 continuous years of this type of leave, you can apply for indefinite leave to remain, unless you do not satisfy the indefinite leave rules – eg, because of a criminal conviction or a recent out-of-court settlement such as a caution or for a county court debt. The previous policy was normally to grant discretionary leave for three years, with the possibility of being able to apply to extend this, and of indefinite leave to remain after six continuous years. If you were granted leave before 9 July 2012, the previous policy continues to apply to you, with the benefit of a shorter required period before you can apply for indefinite leave to remain. The exception to this is if you were granted discretionary leave before 9 July 2012 because you were excluded from refugee or humanitarian protection leave but could not be removed from the UK for human rights reasons. In this case, the restricted leave policy now applies to you (see below).

If you apply to have your discretionary leave extended, or for indefinite leave to remain after completing the required period of time, your case is 'actively reviewed'. This means your circumstances are reviewed and leave is only extended if there have been no significant changes or criminality.

Unaccompanied children

In the case of an unaccompanied child, limited leave may be granted within the Immigration Rules for up to 30 months or until the child is 17 and a half, whichever is the shorter period. At 17 and a half years, if s/he is not eligible for settlement, the child's case is actively reviewed on her/his application for further leave, and this may well be refused.

Restricted leave

If you are excluded from refugee or humanitarian protection leave (see p32) for the reasons outlined on p33, but you cannot be removed from the UK for human rights reasons (eg, because you face a risk of torture if you were to be removed), you may be granted restricted leave. The previous policy was to grant discretionary leave for short periods.

Restricted leave is usually only granted for a maximum of six months at a time, with restrictions:
- on your employment or occupation in the UK;
- on where you can reside;
- requiring you to report to an immigration officer or UKVI at regular intervals;
- prohibiting your studying at an educational institution; *and*
- prohibiting your doing voluntary work with children and/or vulnerable adults.

If you knowingly fail to comply with any restrictions imposed, you may commit a criminal offence.

Exceptional leave

Exceptional leave was replaced by humanitarian protection and discretionary leave in 2003. It was granted for similar reasons but also under blanket policies to applicants from countries experiencing civil or military upheaval.

Leave outside the Immigration Rules

It is possible to be given leave outside the Immigration Rules in special or unusual situations that would not otherwise be covered, including in Article 8 cases (see p34).

If you are given leave to enter or remain outside the Immigration Rules for compassionate reasons, UKVI policy is to grant the leave subject to a condition of no public funds, unless there are exceptional circumstances. The policy is as for leave granted for human rights reasons described on p34.

If you or a member of your family applied for asylum before July 2006, instead of refugee or humanitarian protection leave, you may have been granted indefinite leave to remain or discretionary leave under the asylum 'legacy' case resolution exercise. This was intended to deal with a backlog of unresolved cases that were identified at the time by the Home Secretary.

---

5. **Fresh applications**

If you made an asylum and/or human rights application that was unsuccessful and a decision was made to remove you from the UK, including if you appealed against such a decision and were unsuccessful, you must make further submissions to UK Visas and Immigration (UKVI) if you want to avoid being removed. The submissions must usually be made in person.

If it refuses to grant leave, UKVI should consider whether the further submissions amount to a 'fresh application' – ie, an application that is significantly different to the failed one and which has a realistic prospect of leading to leave being granted (including as the outcome of an appeal). If it decides that there is no fresh claim, you may be removed without an appeal and your only remedy is judicial review. It might take many months or years before a decision is reached and you might only be notified of the decision when you are detained for imminent removal.

If you are a failed asylum seeker, UKVI must usually provide you with accommodation if you have made further submissions that have yet to be considered and you would otherwise be destitute (see p391). The definition of a failed asylum seeker for these purposes includes someone who has made a refugee application and/or an application under Article 3 of the Human Rights Convention, which protects against torture and inhuman or degrading treatment.[13] It is likely that the definition also includes someone who has made a failed application for humanitarian protection. You may also be eligible to receive accommodation if you have been given temporary admission, temporary release or if you are seeking bail (see p407).

Notes

1. **Asylum seekers**
   1   s94(1) IAA 1999
   2   Art 11 EU Dir 2003/9; paras 360-61 IR

2. **Refugee leave and humanitarian protection**
   3   Art 1C(1)-(6) 1951 Convention Relating to the Status of Refugees
   4   Part 11, paras 352A-FJ IR and policy instructions

3. **Stateless people**
   5   1954 Convention Relating to the Status of Stateless Persons
   6   Part 14 IR

4. **Leave for human rights and compassionate reasons**
   7   See Appendix FM: exception and para 2764DE IR
   8   See www.gov.uk/government/uploads/system/uploads/attachment_data/file/286132/change-condition.pdf
   9   The policy is contained in the IDI, 'Family Life (as a Partner or Parent)' FM 1.0a, and 'Partner and ECHR Article 8 Guidance', FM 8.0, which has been amended on several occasions.
   10 paras 289A-C IR
   11 www.gov.uk/government/publications/application-for-benefits-for-visa-holder-domestic-violence
   12 *Paposhvili v Belgium* (Application No. 41738/10) [2016] ECHR 1113, 13 December 2016

5. **Fresh applications**
   13 s94(1) IAA 1999

5

Chapter 5
. . . .
European Economic Area nationals and their families

This chapter covers:
1. The European Economic Area states (below)
2. Rights of admission and residence (below)
3. Documentation (p41)
4. Exclusion and removal (p41)

1. The European Economic Area states

. . . .

The European Economic Area

The **'European Economic Area'** comprises the member states of the European Union (EU) plus the European Free Trade Association (EFTA) countries Norway, Liechtenstein and Iceland.

The current member states of the EU are: Austria, Belgium, Bulgaria, Croatia, Cyprus, Czech Republic, Denmark, Estonia, Finland, France, Germany, Greece, Hungary, Ireland, Italy, Latvia, Lithuania, Luxembourg, Malta, Netherlands, Poland, Portugal, Romania, Slovenia, Slovakia, Spain, Sweden and the UK.

Switzerland has a separate bilateral agreement with the EU.

. . . .

2. Rights of admission and residence

If you are a European Economic Area (EEA) or Swiss national, you have an absolute right to be admitted to the UK (except for public policy, public security or public health reasons – see p41), provided you produce an identity card or passport, or you can otherwise prove your status.[1]

Certain family members of EEA and Swiss nationals have similar rights to be admitted to the UK. In limited circumstances, these rights also apply to family members of British citizens, including of British citizen children.

. . . .

These rights and the rights of EEA and Swiss nationals and their family members to reside in the UK are covered in detail in Chapter 12.

British citizens are also EEA nationals, but the rights of residence described here only apply to family members of British citizens in limited circumstances (see Chapter 12).

3. Documentation

If you are a European Economic Area (EEA) or Swiss national and have a right to reside in the UK, you have the right to be issued with a registration certificate by the Home Office. If you have acquired permanent residence, you have the right to be issued with a document certifying this. These documents are in the form of a vignette (sticker) fixed on a card booklet, separate from your passport.

If you are the family member of an EEA or a Swiss national and have a right to reside in the UK, you have the right to be issued with a residence card, or a permanent residence card if you have permanent residence. Alternatively, you may have been issued with a family permit entry visa before travelling to the UK. Each of these is usually a vignette (sticker) fixed in your passport.

If you have a right of residence derived from a relationship with an EEA or Swiss national, you have the right to be issued with a derivative residence card. Again, this is usually a vignette (sticker) fixed in your passport. Biometric residence permits may replace these documents for non-EEA national family members in the future.

Note: the above documents are declaratory. It is not necessary to obtain such a document in order to have the rights recognised by it, and the period of validity does not mean you have been granted permission to to reside for that period – ie, the fact that you hold a valid residence card or registration certificate does not necessarily mean that you continue to have the rights recognised by the Home Office at the time the document was issued. However, although it is currently not known what rights EEA nationals and their family members will have after the UK leaves the European Union, it may be helpful to have a document confirming your residence rights. You should get specialist immigration advice if you are concerned about your future residence in the UK.

4. Exclusion and removal

If you are a European Economic Area (EEA) or Swiss national, the family member of an EEA or Swiss national, or a person with a right of residence derived from a relationship with an EEA or Swiss national, you can be refused admission to the UK, refused a right to reside, refused the documentation associated with such rights and removed from the UK for public policy, public security or public health reasons.[2]

A decision made on public policy, public security or public health grounds must:

- not be taken for the economic benefit of the UK;
- be 'proportionate';
- be based exclusively on the conduct of the individual concerned, which must represent a genuine, present and sufficiently serious threat, affecting one of the fundamental interests of society;
- be for reasons that relate to your case in particular, rather than being intended to deter others;
- not be justified by a person's previous criminal convictions alone; *and*
- only be made after taking into account the person's age, state of health, family and economic situation, her/his length of residence in the UK, her/his social and cultural integration in the UK, and the extent of her/his links with her/his country of origin.

If you have permanent residence (acquired after five years' continuous lawful residence), the grounds for exclusion must be 'serious'.[3] An EEA or Swiss national aged under 18 cannot be excluded or removed unless it is in her/his best interests or her/his removal is imperative on grounds of public security.[4] Similarly, an EEA or Swiss national who has resided in the UK for 10 years cannot be excluded or removed except on imperative grounds of public security.[5]

You may be prevented from re-entering the UK if you have been removed in the preceding 12 months on the grounds of not having a right to reside. The stated aim of this is to avoid someone repeatedly exiting and re-entering the UK, getting a new three-month period of residence each time.[6]

If UK Visas and Immigration thinks you are involved in a 'marriage of convenience' or other fraud, you may be refused entry, or have your right to reside taken away.[7]

Notes

2. **Rights of admission and residence**
 1 Reg 11 I(EEA) Regs

4. **Exclusion and removal**
 2 Reg 19(5) I(EEA) Regs
 3 Reg 21(3) I(EEA) Regs
 4 Reg 21(4)(b) I(EEA) Regs
 5 Reg 21(4)(a) I(EEA) Regs
 6 Reg 21B I(EEA) Regs

 7 Reg 21B I(EEA) Regs

Chapter 6

· ·

Checking your immigration status

This chapter covers:
1. Introduction (below)
2. British nationals and people with the right of abode (below)
3. People with leave to enter or remain (p44)
4. People without leave (p49)
5. Asylum seekers (p49)
6. European Economic Area and Swiss nationals (p50)
7. Passport issues (p50)

1. Introduction

This chapter explains how to check your immigration status in order to establish your entitlement to social security benefits.

You can usually identify your immigration status in the UK from your passport and any endorsements in it by the UK immigration authorities (eg, stamps, stickers or vignettes) or, increasingly, from your biometric residence permit.

Note: your status (or nationality) may have changed since your passport, endorsement or card was issued, or you may not hold any of these.

If your immigration status is uncertain, you should contact a specialist adviser. A list of advisers and organisations is included in Appendix 2.

Note: anyone who gives immigration advice must be professionally regulated. For further details, see p7.

2. British nationals and people with the right of abode

If you are a British national, you can apply to HM Passport Office for a UK **passport** (see Appendix 6, Figure 1). However, not all British nationals have been

· · · ·

issued with a passport and your British nationality does not depend on your being a passport holder.

UK passports are issued to all British nationals, not just British citizens, and it is important to distinguish between the different types of British nationality when checking your immigration status (see p15). Your passport specifies the type of British nationality you have. Holders of UK passports who have the right of abode in the UK are described as: 'British citizens or British subjects with the right of abode in the UK'.

Note: UK passports may also be issued to people whose right of abode is awaiting verification. The passport contains the endorsement: 'The holder's status under the Immigration Act 1971 has not yet been determined.'

If you have been granted British citizenship after applying to register or naturalise, you will have been issued with a certificate confirming this (see Appendix 6, Figure 2).

If you have the right of abode in the UK and are also a national of another Commonwealth country, you may have a **certificate of entitlement** endorsed in a passport issued by that country (see Appendix 6, Figure 3).

Although rare, a **certificate of patriality** issued under the Immigration Act 1971, and which was valid immediately before 1 January 1983, is regarded as a certificate of entitlement unless the holder no longer has the right of abode – eg, if you have renounced this, or if there has been independence legislation.[1]

Some people with the right of abode in the UK may hold a **confirmation of 'right of abode' document**. This was a non-statutory document issued for a brief period before the commencement of the Immigration Act 1988 to dual nationals with the right of abode who had opted to travel on non-British passports.

If you do not hold a passport or certificate confirming your British citizenship or right of abode, you may be able to prove that you have this status in some other way – eg, by producing a birth certificate showing that you were born in the UK before 1983. If your claim to British citizenship or the right of abode is complicated, you may need to prove descent from your parents and/or grandparents, and/or marriage to a person and that person's place of birth, ancestry and/or nationality status at specific times. If this applies to you, it may be helpful to get specialist advice to check your citizenship and/or right of abode.

3. People with leave to enter or remain

Entry clearance confirming leave to enter

Entry clearance is endorsed by a sticker (known as a **'vignette'**) placed in a person's passport or travel document, or by data stored digitally in an identity card and government database (see p47).

The vignette endorsement may be designated as a visa (for visa nationals, stateless people and refugees), entry clearance (for non-visa nationals and British nationals other than British citizens) or a family permit (for dependants of European Economic Area nationals).

Two types of vignette are now issued. Which is used depends on the type of entry clearance you are given. Both include a photograph of the holder (see Appendix 6, Figure 9). Older versions look similar, but without a photograph (see Appendix 6, Figure 8). Even older ones were a smaller sticker, signed and date-stamped by an official (similar to the leave to remain endorsement vignette shown in Appendix 6, Figure 8).

Accompanying dependants whose details were included in the main applicant's passport might have received their own vignettes, fixed in the main applicant's passport.

Entry clearance granting you leave to enter allows you to enter the UK at a port without having to demonstrate that you satisfy the requirements of the Immigration Rules (unless you commit an act of fraud or there is a material change in circumstances). The vignette endorsement is usually date-stamped on entry (see Appendix 6, Figure 10) and confirms that you have been granted leave to enter the UK, often for the remaining period of validity stated on the vignette.

In some circumstances, an immigration officer can vary or extend your leave on your arrival in the UK.

The date the entry clearance first becomes valid is usually the same as the date of authorisation. As the holder, you may present yourself for initial entry under the entry clearance at any time during its validity. However, entry clearance officers have the discretion to defer the date the entry clearance first becomes valid for up to three months after authorisation if, for example, you wish to delay travelling to the UK.

If you are granted entry clearance, you may travel to, and remain in, the UK for the purpose for which it was granted. You may be able to travel in and out of the UK repeatedly, provided your entry clearance remains valid. However, if entry clearance has been authorised for multiple journeys to the UK of a fixed duration (eg, under the visitor category of the Immigration Rules), the duration of each visit is limited to a maximum of six months. This limitation is stated on the vignette under the heading 'duration of stay'.

If you have been granted indefinite leave to enter the UK, your visa shows an 'expiry' or 'valid until' date. This is the date by when the entry clearance needs to be presented to enter the UK for the first time, after which you have indefinite leave and the date becomes irrelevant.[2]

If you have presented the entry clearance at a port, there should be an ink stamp showing where and on which date that occurred. The date when the entry clearance was presented is the date when the entry clearance took effect as indefinite leave.

If you are granted entry clearance with a vignette for leave to enter on certain conditions (eg, as a student on condition that you do not work except in authorised employment and do not have recourse to public funds), these should be stated on the endorsement (see Appendix 6, Figure 9). However, if you have been granted entry clearance for leave to enter on the basis of a sponsorship undertaking (see p28), the reference on the vignette may be the name of the family member whom you are joining and there may be no indication that a sponsorship undertaking has been given.

Leave to enter without entry clearance

Nationals of some countries cannot enter the UK for any purpose without first obtaining entry clearance (visa nationals). Others can apply at the port of entry for leave to enter for some of the purposes provided for under the Immigration Rules.

It is sometimes difficult to identify the purpose for which an endorsement of leave to enter has been given if someone made an application at the port of entry. If limited leave has been granted, the endorsement may be an **ink stamp**, stating the duration of the leave period for which leave is granted and the conditions (if any) attached to the leave (see Appendix 6, Figure 8). Each stamped endorsement by an immigration officer granting leave to someone without entry clearance should be accompanied by a rectangular date stamp, showing when the leave was granted.

The example shown in Appendix 6, Figure 8 is the endorsement usually made in the passport of someone given leave to enter at a port of entry as a visitor or student on a short course (of six months or less). The endorsement shows that leave has been granted on condition that the holder does not engage in any employment or have recourse to public funds.

If you are returning to the UK and already have indefinite leave to enter or remain, you may simply be given a date stamp on being readmitted.

If you leave the UK and return during a period of leave that has been given for more than six months, an immigration officer may endorse a grant of leave to enter with the same conditions, using an ink stamp stating this.[3]

Some people, usually Commonwealth citizens, who entered the UK before the Immigration Act 1971 came into force may have received an ink stamp on entry with no conditions attached. These people are referred to as 'freely landed'. They may have been treated as having been given indefinite leave to enter or remain when the 1971 Act came into force and might have retained this status by remaining resident in the UK (see p23).

Leave to remain granted in the UK

The UK **residence permit** replaced all former stamp and ink endorsements for permission to stay in the UK for longer than six months. The permit is a vignette, similar in appearance to that used to endorse entry clearance (see p44), and includes a photograph of the holder (see Appendix 6, Figure 8).

Previously, leave may have been endorsed using a smaller vignette sticker or by a rectangular stamp accompanied by a pentagonal date stamp (see Appendix 6, Figure 8).

If you were granted leave to remain on certain conditions (eg, as a student on condition that you do not work except in authorised employment and do not have recourse to public funds), these should be stated on the permit (see Appendix 6, Figure 9). However, if you were granted leave to remain on the basis of a sponsorship undertaking (see p28), this is not stated on the permit.

Biometric residence permits

Biometric residence permit cards for foreign nationals are now replacing the vignette (sticker) endorsements and other UK immigration status documents (see Appendix 6, Figure 5). You are issued with one as an alternative to having a sticker or ink stamp endorsement placed in your passport, which is not endorsed with your immigration status at all.

A biometric residence permit is a plastic card, the same size as a debit or credit card, which bears the holder's photograph, name, date of birth, nationality and immigration status. An electronic chip attached to the card holds digitised biometric details, including fingerprints, a facial image and biographical information (including name, and date and place of birth).

The card also shows details of your immigration status and entitlements in the UK, including what kind of leave you have and whether you can work. A database holds a record of the biometrics of every person to whom a card has been issued, so these can be cross-checked.

If you have the new identity card, you may need to inform UK Visas and Immigration (UKVI) of specified changes in your circumstances. If you fail to do so, you may face prosecution or other sanctions (see p27).

Leave extended for an application, appeal or administrative review

Limited leave is automatically extended beyond the date it is due to expire if you make a valid application to extend or vary your leave before this date.[4] Leave extended in this way continues until a decision is made by UKVI. If you are then refused further leave after your original leave expires, your leave is deemed to continue until any in-country appeal rights or rights to administrative review are exhausted. The same conditions attached to your original leave continue to apply during the extension (apart from the time limit).

It is not completely clear whether you are defined as a 'person subject to immigration control' and therefore excluded from most benefits during the time when you are appealing or seeking an administrative review (see p63).

UKVI can take a long time to decide applications, and appeals against refusals to vary or to extend leave can take still longer, so you may have your leave extended in this way for many months, or even years. Also, if the result of the administrative review is significantly different or additional reasons are given for upholding the decision, you may apply for a further review which, if done in time, extends your leave even further. Your passport or biometric residence permit, if you had one when you applied, may be retained during this time. For these reasons, it can be difficult to show that your leave is ongoing. UKVI may acknowledge a valid application for leave with a letter, but does not always do so. However, it offers to confirm specifically that you have ongoing leave if you request this. There is a helpline for employers, prospective employers and prospective landlords: the number for this service is available from the UKVI website.

Travel and status documents issued to non-UK nationals

Where necessary, leave to enter or leave to remain may have been endorsed on an **immigration status document** (which is simply an A4-sized piece of paper) – eg, because your passport was not available when your leave was granted. Refugee leave and humanitarian protection are never endorsed in a passport issued by the holder's government, because the use of such a passport is considered to be an indication that you are happy to be protected by the government that issued it, which would be incompatible with having asylum in the UK (see Appendix 6, Figure 4).

Refugees are entitled to a **Refugee Convention travel document** (coloured blue), which is similar in format to a passport (see Appendix 6, Figure 11).

A dependant of a refugee or person with humanitarian protection may be granted entry clearance on the basis of refugee family reunion on a standard **European Union form**, if s/he has no passport or cannot obtain one. The previous version, **a GV3 document**, had an endorsement stating: 'visa family reunion – sponsor'. The sponsor referred to is the relative with refugee status who the dependant is joining in the UK. The endorsement does not indicate that a sponsorship undertaking has been given.

People recognised as stateless under the terms of the 1954 United Nations Convention Relating to the Status of Stateless Persons are entitled to a **stateless person's document** (coloured red).

Someone granted indefinite leave but not recognised as a refugee, and someone granted exceptional leave, discretionary leave or humanitarian protection can apply for a **certificate of travel** (coloured black). However, to qualify for such a document, usually you must have applied to your national authorities (if they have a presence in the UK) for a passport or travel document and been formally and unreasonably refused one.

4. People without leave

If you have entered the UK without permission or remained in the UK after your limited leave to enter or remain has expired, you may have committed a criminal offence and could be arrested and detained for removal from the UK. This also applies if you have remained in the UK after you have been refused further leave or had your leave revoked or curtailed and any appeal rights have been exhausted. Any conditions attached to the limited leave that has expired or been revoked or curtailed ceases to apply.

If you are in the UK without leave and come to the attention of the authorities, you are likely to be served with a **notice** informing you that you are liable to be removed from the UK, and explaining why (see Appendix 6, Figure 12). You may also be detained or given temporary admission, temporary release or bail (see p14). If you have any of these types of status, you should have been issued with a notice informing you of this and of any conditions.

If further leave has been refused, a line may be drawn through the previous endorsement of leave in your passport. A decision refusing leave to enter at a port may be endorsed by a crossed-through ink date stamp.

You must be notified of any immigration decision in writing. Sending a notice to your last known address or the address of a representative (eg, a solicitor or other regulated person) might be sufficient, so you may not necessarily be aware of a decision concerning you. Get specialist advice if you are in any doubt.

5. Asylum seekers

People who have applied for refugee or humanitarian protection leave or other forms of international protection are commonly called 'asylum seekers' (see p31).

Until 2002, asylum seekers were issued with a **standard acknowledgement letter** (SAL). A SAL1 was issued to those claiming asylum at the port of entry and a SAL2 was issued to those who applied for asylum once they were already in the UK. From 2002, UK Visas and Immigration (UKVI) has issued asylum seekers with an **application registration card** (ARC) (see Appendix 6, Figure 8). The ARC may state whether you have any dependants or permission to work.

Asylum seekers who apply at a port of entry and in-country applicants who do not have leave at the time of their application are usually given temporary admission to the UK until their application is decided. If they have been detained, they might have subsequently been granted temporary release or bail. If you have any of these types of status, you should have been issued with a notice informing you of this and of any conditions (see Appendix 6, Figure 13). See p14 for further information.

If you apply for asylum when you have leave to enter or remain for another purpose, your leave might be automatically extended on the same conditions beyond the date it is due to expire until a decision is made by UKVI and, if the application is refused, any appeal rights are exhausted.

6. European Economic Area and Swiss nationals

If you are a European Economic Area (EEA) or Swiss national and have a right to reside in the UK, you have the right to be issued with a **registration certificate** by the Home Office. If you have acquired permanent residence, you have the right to be issued with a **document certifying permanent residence** (see Appendix 6, Figure 6). These documents are in the form of a vignette (sticker) fixed on a card booklet, separate from your passport.

If you are the family member of an EEA or a Swiss national and have a right to reside in the UK, you have the right to be issued with a **residence card** (see Appendix 6, Figure 7). **Note:** this only includes family members of British citizens in limited circumstances (see Chapter 12). If you are the family member of an EEA or a Swiss national and have permanent residency, you have the right to be issued with a permanent residence card. Alternatively, you may have been issued with a family permit entry visa before travelling to the UK. Each of these is usually a vignette (sticker) fixed in your passport.

If you have a right of residence derived from a relationship with an EEA or Swiss national, you have the right to be issued with a **derivative residence card** (see Appendix 6, Figure 7). Again, this is usually a vignette (sticker) fixed in your passport.

Note: the above documents are declaratory. It is not necessary to obtain such a document in order to have the rights recognised by it, and the period of validity does not mean you have been granted permission to reside for that period – ie, the fact that you hold a valid residence card or registration certificate does not necessarily mean that you continue to have the rights recognised by the Home Office at the time the document was issued. However, although it is currently not known what rights EEA nationals and their family members will have after the UK leaves the European Union, it may be helpful to have a document confirming your residence rights. You should get specialist immigration advice if you are concerned about your future residence in the UK.

7. Passport issues

Leaving the UK

Embarkation from (leaving) the UK used to be endorsed by a triangular ink stamp in the embarking person's passport (see Appendix 6, Figure 14). This practice was suspended in March 1998, but then reintroduced in 2015.

New or lost passports

If you have been granted leave to enter or remain that has been endorsed in a passport that has expired or been lost before your leave is due to expire, the expiry or loss of the passport does not affect your leave. This is most common for people granted indefinite leave – eg, if you had your leave endorsed in your passport, but this has now expired and your new passport is not endorsed.

In this situation, you can apply for confirmation of your status. This now takes the form of a biometric residence permit card (see p47).

Illegible passport stamps

Problems may arise if an endorsement on a passport is either unclear or illegible, or if you required leave and your passport was not endorsed on your last entry.

If your passport has been endorsed illegibly, you may be deemed to have been granted leave to enter for six months with a condition prohibiting employment,[5] or, if you arrived in the UK before 10 July 1998, to have been given indefinite leave to enter the UK.[6] If you required leave to enter the UK, but your passport was not endorsed on entry, you may be considered an illegal entrant.[7] You should obtain specialist advice .

Note: certain documents, such as a passport that indicates that you have indefinite leave to remain, must be current in order to demonstrate that you have a right to work in the UK. Other documents, such as a UK passport, can demonstrate a right to work if they are either current or if they have expired.[8]

Notes

2. **British nationals and people with the right of abode**
   1 s39(8) BNA 1981

3. **People with leave to enter or remain**
   2 See UKVI policy guidance ECB9.4, at www.gov.uk/government/publications/entry-clearance-vignettes-ecb09
   3 s3(3)(b) IA 1971
   4 s3C IA 1971

7. **Passport issues**
   5 Sch 2 para 6(1) IA 1971, as amended
   6 Sch 2 para 6(1) IA 1971, prior to amendment and as interpreted by the courts
   7 *Rehal v SSHD* [1989] Imm AR 576

8 The Immigration (Restrictions on Employment) (Codes of Practice and Amendment) Order 2014, No.1183 and Home Office guidance, *An Employer's Guide to Right to Work Checks* at www.gov.uk/government/publications/right-to-work-checks-employers-guide, updated 12 July 2016

Part 3

Benefits and immigration status

Chapter 7

People subject to immigration control

This chapter covers:
1. Introduction (below)
2. The effect of immigration status on benefits and tax credits (p56)
3. Who is a 'person subject to immigration control' (p57)

You should check this chapter, together with Chapter 8, if you, your partner and children are not all European Economic Area (EEA) nationals (see p40). If you, your partner and children are all EEA nationals, the rules in these two chapters do not apply to you. If you, your partner, your parent, or your child, has applied for asylum in the UK, see also Chapter 9.

1. Introduction

Entitlement to many benefits and tax credits can depend on your immigration status. The immigration status of your partner can also affect how much you are paid. It is also important to know the immigration status of any partner or child included in your claim, because if s/he has leave which is subject to the condition that s/he has no recourse to public funds, her/his right to remain in the UK could be jeopardised if you are paid an additional amount for her/him. This chapter provides an overview of how immigration status affects your benefit and tax credit entitlement and how a benefit claim can affect your partner's or child's right to remain in the UK.

If you are defined as a 'person subject to immigration control', the general rule is that you are excluded from many benefits and tax credits. However, there are limited exceptions. The relevant benefits and tax credits and the exempt groups are covered in Chapter 8, which also covers the rules on how your benefits or tax credits are affected if your partner or child is a 'person subject to immigration control'.

7

Chapter 7: People subject to immigration control
2. The effect of immigration status on benefits and tax credits

If you applied for asylum in the UK and have been granted refugee leave, humanitarian protection or discretionary leave to be in the UK, more generous benefit rules can apply (see Chapter 9).

In addition to immigration status restrictions, most benefits also have presence and residence conditions. If your immigration status does not exclude you from a benefit or tax credit, you must still satisfy these. See Part 4 for more details.

2. The effect of immigration status on benefits and tax credits

It is important to know your immigration status, and that of anyone included in your claim, before making a claim for a benefit or tax credit. This is because your immigration status can affect your entitlement to benefits and tax credits. Also, an increased amount for someone included in your claim can affect her/his right to remain in the UK if her/his leave is subject to a condition that s/he has no recourse to public funds.

There are two ways in which your immigration status affects your entitlement to benefits and tax credits.

- Your immigration status may mean that you come within the definition of a 'person subject to immigration control'. In most cases, this means that you are excluded from many benefits and tax credits (although there are exceptions).
- Your immigration status can mean that you satisfy, or are exempt from, the residence requirements for the benefit or tax credit you want to claim.

As the rules are complicated, it is helpful to approach them systematically. If you, or anyone who you could include in your claim, are not a European Economic Area national (see p40), work through the following steps.

- **Step one:** be clear about your immigration status. See Chapter 6 for help in determining on what basis you are in the UK. If you are unsure about your immigration status, or that of anyone included in your claim, get specialist advice from your local law centre, Citizens Advice Bureau or other advice agency that gives immigration advice (see Appendix 2).
- **Step two:** check whether you are defined as a 'person subject to immigration control' (see p57). If you are not, you can claim the benefits you want, provided you meet the other conditions of entitlement, including any rules on residence and presence (see Part 4). Your partner's immigration status may still affect the amount you are entitled to (see Step five).
- **Step three:** if you are a 'person subject to immigration control' check whether this excludes you from the particular benefit or tax credit you want to claim (see p66).

- **Step four:** if the benefit you want to claim is one from which 'people subject to immigration control' are generally excluded, check whether you are in one of the exempt groups. These vary between the different benefits and tax credits (see p67). Even if you are in an exempt group, you must still satisfy all the other conditions of entitlement, including the residence and presence requirements (see Part 4).
- **Step five:** if you cannot claim the benefit you want, but you have a partner who can (or if you can but have a partner or child who is subject to immigration control), check the rules on partners and children (see p74).
- **Step six:** if you, or a member of your family, have leave to enter or remain in the UK that is subject to a condition not to have recourse to public funds, check whether any claim for benefits or tax credits could affect your (or her/his) immigration status (see p59).

---

3. **Who is a 'person subject to immigration control'**

Most people, apart from British citizens, are subject to immigration control. However, for benefit and tax credit purposes, the term 'person subject to immigration control' has a specific meaning (see below). It is this meaning that is referred to when the phrase 'person subject to immigration control' is used in this *Handbook*.

In order to establish whether you are a 'person subject to immigration control', you must know:

- whether or not you require leave to enter or remain in the UK;
- if you require leave, whether or not you have it;
- if you have leave, what, if any, conditions are attached to it; *and*
- if you have leave, whether this was granted as a result of someone giving an undertaking to maintain and accommodate you.

For benefit and tax credit purposes, you are a **'person subject to immigration control'** if you are not a European Economic Area (EEA) national (see p40) and you:[1]

- require leave to enter or remain in the UK, but do not have it (see p58); *or*
- have leave to enter or remain in the UK which is subject to the condition that you do not have recourse to public funds (see p59); *or*
- have leave to enter or remain in the UK, given as a result of a maintenance undertaking (see p61); *or*
- have leave to remain in the UK solely because you are appealing against a refusal to vary your previous leave (see p63).

Note:
- An EEA national (including a British national) can never be a 'person subject to immigration control' because the definition only applies to non-EEA nationals. If you are an EEA national, you cannot be refused benefit as a person subject to immigration control, and the rules in this part of this *Handbook* do not apply to you unless you are claiming for a partner or child who is a person subject to immigration control. However, if you are an EEA national, you may still be refused benefit for other reasons, including if you do not satisfy the presence and residence conditions (see Part 4).
- If you are not an EEA national, but you have a right to reside under European Union (EU) law (eg, as a family member of an EEA worker – see p170), you do not require leave to enter or remain.[2] If this applies to you, you cannot be refused benefit on the basis of your immigration status even if, for example, you have been given leave to enter or remain on condition that you do not have recourse to public funds, or as a result of a maintenance undertaking. There are specific provisions in UK law that mean that if you have a condition attached to your leave (eg, that you do not have recourse to public funds), these do not have any effect while you have a right to reside under the EEA Regulations.[3]

You require leave to enter or remain, but do not have it

If you are not an EEA national and require leave to enter or remain in the UK but do not have it, you are 'a person subject to immigration control'.[4] If you are not an EEA national, you require leave to enter or remain in the UK unless you are:
- a person with the right of abode;
- a person with a right of residence in EU law. This applies if, for example, you are:
  - a family member of an EEA national who has a right to reside in the UK (see p170);[5]
  - a Swiss national with a right to reside. As a result of an agreement between Switzerland and the EU, Swiss nationals, in general, have the same residence rights as EEA nationals and do not require leave to enter or, if they have a right to reside, leave to remain in the UK;[6]
  - a family member of a Swiss national with a right to reside;
  - the primary carer of a British citizen who is in the UK, and it is necessary for you to have a right to reside in the UK so that s/he can continue to reside within the EU.[7] **Note:** although you do not require leave and are therefore not defined as a 'person subject to immigration control', you are still excluded from benefits that require a right to reside, because this particular right to reside does not satisfy the right to reside requirement (see p117). However, you are not excluded from other benefits that do not require a right to reside, such as personal independence payment (PIP) and carer's

allowance (CA). If the British citizen is a child, you may also be able to get support under the Children Act 1989 (or Children (Scotland) Act 1995) from your local authority (see p470). If you are a primary carer in this category, you should obtain specialist immigration advice as it may be possible for you to obtain leave to remain that would give you access to benefits.

All other non-EEA nationals require leave to enter or remain in the UK. If you are not an EEA national and not in any of the above groups, you are a person subject to immigration control if you do not have leave to enter or remain. For more information on when leave to enter or remain is granted, see Chapter 3.

Examples of when you require leave to enter or remain but do not have it include if you:

- are an asylum seeker with temporary admission (see p14);
- have overstayed your limited leave to remain – ie, you did not apply for further leave before your period of leave expired. **Note:** if you apply for further leave on the same or a different basis before your current leave expires, your leave is extended from the date it would have expired until your application is decided or withdrawn (but it may be cancelled in certain circumstances, such as if you breach a condition attached to the leave). If your leave has been extended, you are not someone who requires leave but does not have it;[8]
- have entered the UK without leave, or a right to enter under EU law, and since then have not obtained any leave to remain;
- are subject to a deportation order.

Note: there are close links between the benefit authorities and the Home Office UK Visas and Immigration (UKVI). Making a claim for benefit could alert the immigration authorities to your presence and status in the UK. If you need immigration leave but do not have it, or you are unsure of your immigration status, get specialist immigration advice before making a claim for benefits (see Appendix 2).

Your leave has a no recourse to public funds condition

You are a 'person subject to immigration control' if you have leave to enter or remain in the UK which is subject to a condition that you do not have recourse to public funds.[9]

Most people admitted to the UK with time-limited leave given for a particular purpose, such as spouses/civil partners, students or visitors, are given leave to stay on condition that they do not have recourse to public funds. Increasingly, this condition is also being added to those given time-limited leave to remain for other reasons, such as family ties, so you should always check whether your leave is subject to this condition.

People granted refugee leave, humanitarian protection (see p32) or, in most cases, discretionary leave (see p36) do *not* have a no recourse to public funds condition attached to their leave.

Indefinite leave (see p23) is never given with this condition attached.[10] However, if you have been granted indefinite leave as a result of someone else undertaking to maintain and accommodate you, you come under the definition of a 'person subject to immigration control' (see p61).

Public funds

'Public funds' are defined in the Immigration Rules as:[11]
 – attendance allowance;
 – CA;
 – child benefit;
 – child tax credit;
 – council tax benefit (now abolished);
 – council tax reduction;
 – disability living allowance;
 – income-related employment and support allowance (ESA);
 – homelessness assistance and housing provided under specific provisions;
 – housing benefit (HB);
 – income support (IS);
 – income-based jobseeker's allowance (JSA);
 – local welfare assistance (except the Discretionary Assistance Fund for Wales);
 – pension credit;
 – PIP;
 – severe disablement allowance;
 – social fund payments;
 – universal credit (UC);
 – working tax credit.

Only the benefits, tax credits and other assistance listed in the Immigration Rules are public funds. Therefore, if you get any other benefit, or other financial help, you are not in breach of any no recourse to public funds condition attached to your leave.

If you have recourse to public funds when your leave prohibits you, you have breached a condition of your leave. This may affect your right to remain in the UK. You could have your leave curtailed, be liable to be deported, have further leave refused and/or be prosecuted for committing a criminal offence.[12]

If you have leave which is subject to a no recourse to public funds condition, you are defined as a 'person subject to immigration control' and (unless you are exempt – see Chapter 8) are not entitled to the above benefits and tax credits.

However, if you come within one of the exceptions, you can claim and receive these benefits as (except for council tax reduction), you are not regarded as having recourse to public funds under the Immigration Rules.[13] If you claim council tax reduction as a result of being exempt, you still count as having recourse to public funds. This is because the council tax reduction regulations are not referred to by the part of the Immigration Rules that disregards claims made as a result of exemptions.[14]

Note: you *are* regarded as having recourse to public funds if someone else's benefit is increased because of your presence.[15] For example, if the amount of your partner's HB is greater because you are included in her/his claim, this counts as recourse to public funds. This recourse means you have breached a condition of your leave, which could jeopardise your immigration status (see p25). Get specialist immigration advice before someone makes a claim that includes extra benefit because of your presence (see Appendix 2).

Domestic violence

If you were granted leave to enter or remain in the UK as a spouse, civil partner or unmarried partner (including a same-sex partner), but that relationship has broken down because of domestic violence, you may be able to apply for leave to remain under the 'destitution domestic violence' concession (see p35). This leave lasts for three months and is not subject to any condition that you do not have recourse to public funds. During this period of leave, you are not defined as a 'person subject to immigration control' and can, therefore, claim all benefits, subject to the normal conditions of entitlement.[16] **Note:** having this type of leave means you are exempt from the habitual residence test for means-tested benefits (see p108) and the requirement to have been living in the UK for the past three months for child benefit and child tax credit (see p97).

If you apply for indefinite leave (under what is commonly known as the 'domestic violence rule'[17]) before this period of leave expires, your leave is extended while the Home Office decides your application. You continue not to be a person subject to immigration control and continue to be entitled to benefits.

If you do not apply for indefinite leave by the end of the three months, you become someone who requires leave but does not have it and, therefore, once again a person subject to immigration control. If you are claiming any of the benefits listed on p66, your entitlement ceases unless you are in one of the exempt groups listed on p67.

Your leave is given as a result of a maintenance undertaking

If you are a non-EEA national who has leave to enter or remain in the UK given as a result of a maintenance undertaking, you are a 'person subject to immigration control'.[18]

Maintenance undertaking

A **'maintenance undertaking'** means a written undertaking given by another person, under the Immigration Rules, to be responsible for your maintenance and accommodation.[19]

There are specific Home Office forms on which an undertaking can be given. However, no official form need be used, provided the undertaking is sufficiently formal and definite.[20] The document must contain a promise or agreement that the other person will maintain and accommodate you in the future. If it merely contains a statement about her/his present abilities and intentions, it does not amount to an undertaking.[21]

Your leave is considered to be 'as a result of a maintenance undertaking' if this was a factor in granting it. It does not need to have been the only, or even a major, factor.[22] However, if the maintenance undertaking was not relevant to your being granted leave, the fact that it exists does not make you a person subject to immigration control.

If it is unclear whether or not your leave was granted as a result of a maintenance undertaking, the onus is on the benefit authority to prove that it was.[23] If your leave has been granted outside the Immigration Rules, the causal connection between the leave and the undertaking cannot be inferred.[24]

If you are in doubt about whether you have leave given as a result of an undertaking, get specialist immigration advice (see Appendix 2).

Consequences for your sponsor if you claim benefits

If you have leave to enter or remain as a result of a maintenance undertaking and you claim benefits, it is possible that the person(s) who signed the undertaking to maintain and accommodate you could be asked to repay any IS, income-based JSA, income-related ESA or UC paid to you. However, in practice, this provision is rarely used because the rules for these benefits exclude people with this form of leave from entitlement for the first five years (unless the person(s) who gave the undertaking has died – see p68).

In certain circumstances, the DWP can recover any IS or UC paid to you from the person who gave the undertaking.[25] Recovery is through the family court (in Scotland, the sheriff court).

The DWP can also prosecute someone for failure to maintain if this results in IS, income-based JSA, income-related ESA or UC being paid.[26]

As the DWP can recover benefit or to take court action, if it asks you about an undertaking, you should obtain independent advice (see Appendix 2).

Sponsors

People who have been given leave to enter or remain as the result of a maintenance undertaking are often referred to as **'sponsored people'**, and those giving the undertakings as **'sponsors'**. This terminology is used by the benefit authorities, including in their guidance to decision makers. However, the term 'sponsor' is also used in connection with other types of leave and this can lead to confusion and errors in decision making. For example, the word occurs in the Immigration Rules in relation to those seeking leave to enter or remain on the basis of their relationship to their partner (see p26),[27] and people commonly describe themselves as having been 'sponsored' by their partner when they are granted such leave. The Upper Tribunal has provided a helpful discussion of this confusion.[28]

Another common area of confusion is when a family member of someone with refugee leave or humanitarian protection is given leave to enter or remain under the family reunion provisions (see p82). Although the person with refugee leave or humanitarian protection is not required to provide a maintenance undertaking, the confusion arises because the Home Office policy on family reunion and the entry visa given to the family member uses the word 'sponsor'.

It is only if you have been given leave to enter or remain *as a result* of an undertaking that you come within this definition of a person subject to immigration control. However, if you have been given time-limited leave to enter or remain because, for example, you were 'sponsored' by your spouse/civil partner, your leave is subject to a no recourse to public funds condition and you come within the second group of people subject to immigration control (see p59).

In order not to add to any existing confusion, this *Handbook* makes minimal use of the word 'sponsor'.

If you only have leave to remain because you are appealing

If you are a non-EEA national who has leave to enter or remain, but only because your leave has been extended while you appeal against a decision to vary, or refuse to vary, your leave (see p47), you may be a 'person subject to immigration control'.[29]

If you have time-limited leave (see p44), you can apply to extend your leave or apply for further leave to remain on a different basis. Provided you do this before your existing leave expires, this leave is extended from the date it would have expired until your application is decided by UKVI.[30] You therefore continue to have the same type of leave, subject to the same conditions, until your application is decided.

If your application is refused and you are entitled to appeal (or seek an administrative review) against the refusal from within the UK, you continue to have the same type of leave during the short time period in which you can do this.[31]

If you do so within the time limit, your leave is extended until the appeal or review is dealt with.[32] You continue to have the same type of leave, subject to the same conditions, while your appeal (or review) is pending.

However, during the time when your leave is extended because your appeal is pending, you *may* count as a 'person subject to immigration control'.[33]

The reason why this is not completely clear is because the relevant part of the definition of a 'person subject to immigration control' cross-refers to a provision that has now been revoked. So, you are only covered by that part of the definition if the cross reference is read as a reference to a different, subsequent provision.

There is no caselaw on this issue and it may be arguable that no one is is defined as a 'person subject to immigration control' on this basis.

In practice, if this part of the definition does apply, it only makes a difference to your benefit and tax credit entitlement if your original leave did not have a no recourse to public funds condition. Otherwise, you were already a person subject to immigration control and an extension of your leave simply means that you carry on being so.

Example

Banu is an Iranian national who was granted 30 months' discretionary leave in the UK without any public funds condition attached. She is not a person subject to immigration control and so has full access to benefits and tax credits during the period of her leave. Just before her discretionary leave expires, she applies for a further period of discretionary leave. Her application is refused. Banu has a right to appeal against this decision from within the UK, and she does so immediately. Her discretionary leave is extended while the appeal is pending. The benefit authorities may argue that she is now a person subject to immigration control as she has leave only because she is appealing.

Notes

3. **Who is a 'person subject to immigration control'**
1 s115(9) IAA 1999
2 s7 IA 1988
3 Sch 3 para 1 I(EEA) Regs
4 s115(9)(a) IAA 1999
5 s7 IA 1988; regs 11 and 14(2) I(EEA) Regs
6 *The Agreement Between the European Community and its Member States, of the one part, and the Swiss Confederation, of the other, on the Free Movement of Persons,* Luxembourg, 21 June 1999, Cmd 5639; reg 2 I(EEA) Regs defines Switzerland as an EEA state; reg 11 provides that no EEA national requires leave to enter the UK, and Part 2 of I(EEA) Regs provides rights of residence.
7 *Zambrano,* C-34/09 [2011] ECR I-01177; *Dereci and Others,* C-256/11 [2011] ECR I-11315; reg 16(1) and (5) I(EEA) Regs
8 s3C IA 1971
9 s115(9)(b) IAA 1999
10 s3(1) IA 1971
11 para 6 IR
12 s24(1)(b)(ii) IA 1971
13 para 6B IR
14 para 6B IR
15 para 6A IR
16 Confirmed in Vol 2, paras 073191-94 DMG
17 paras 289A-C IR
18 s115(9)(c) IAA 1999
19 s115(10) IAA 1999
20 *R (Begum) v Social Security Commissioner* [2003] EWHC 3380 (Admin); CIS/2474/1999; CIS/2816/2002 and CIS/47/2002

21 *Ahmed v SSWP* [2005] EWCA Civ 535;
   CIS/426/2003
22 CIS/3508/2001
23 R(PC) 1/09
24 R(PC) 1/09; *SJ v SSWP (SPC)* [2015]
   UKUT 505 (AAC), reported as [2016]
   AACR 17
25 s106 SSAA 1992
26 s105 SSAA 1992
27 para 6 IR
28 *OO v SSWP (SPC)* [2013] UKUT 335
   (AAC)
29 s115(9)(d) IAA 1999
30 s3C(2)(a) IA 1971
31 s3C(2)(b) and (d) IA 1971
32 s3C(2)(c) and (d) IA 1971
33 s115(9)(d) IAA 1999 refers to leave
   continuing while you appeal because of
   the rule in Sch 4 para 17. Sch 4 para 17
   was repealed by NIAA 2002, which also
   inserted s3C into IA 1971. The reference
   to Sch 4 para 17 in s115(9)(d),
   therefore, now arguably must be read as
   a reference to s3C IA 1971 (see s17(2) IA
   1978).

People subject to immigration control and benefits

This chapter covers:
1. Benefits and tax credits affected by immigration status (below)
2. People subject to immigration control who can be entitled (p67)
3. Partners and children who are subject to immigration control (p74)

Before using the information in this chapter, you should establish whether you, your partner or child are a 'person subject to immigration control'. This is explained in Chapter 7.

1. Benefits and tax credits affected by immigration status

The general rule is that if you are defined as a 'person subject to immigration control' (see p57), you are excluded from council tax reduction[1] (see p457) and the following benefits and tax credits:[2]

- attendance allowance;
- carer's allowance;
- child benefit;
- child tax credit;
- disability living allowance;
- contributory employment and support allowance (ESA) in youth;[3]
- income-related ESA;
- housing benefit;
- incapacity benefit in youth;[4]
- income support;
- income-based jobseeker's allowance (JSA);
- pension credit;
- personal independence payment;
- severe disablement allowance;
- social fund payments;

Chapter 8: People subject to immigration control and benefits
2. People subject to immigration control who can be entitled

8

- universal credit;
- working tax credit.

However, there are limited exceptions which mean that, despite being a person subject to immigration control, you can claim means-tested benefits (see below), non-means-tested benefits (see p69) and tax credits (see p72).

Even if cannot claim yourself, a family member may be able to claim a benefit that includes an amount for you, or you might be able to make a joint claim (see p74).

A person subject to immigration control is only excluded from the above benefits and tax credits, so you can claim any other benefit. For example, if you have paid sufficient national insurance contributions, you can claim any of the contributory benefits – eg, retirement pension, contribution-based JSA and contributory ESA. You can also claim benefits that depend on previous employment – eg, maternity allowance (MA) or industrial injuries benefits. You may also be able to get help from your local welfare assistance scheme (see p462). **Note:** there are currently provisions to make it a condition of entitlement to contribution-based JSA, contributory ESA, MA and statutory sick, maternity, adoption, paternity and shared parental pay that you be entitled to work in the UK.[5] However, at the time of writing, these provisions were not in force. See CPAG's online service and *Welfare Rights Bulletin* for updates.

2. People subject to immigration control who can be entitled

There are exceptions to the general rule that you are excluded from the benefits and tax credits on p66 if you are defined as a 'person subject to immigration control'. The exceptions vary between the different categories of benefits and tax credits, so being exempt for one category does not necessarily mean you can receive a benefit in a different category.

Note: if your leave prohibits you from having recourse to public funds (see p25), you can still claim any benefit to which you are entitled on the basis of being in an exempt group (but not council tax reduction), even though these benefits (except employment and support allowance (ESA) in youth and incapacity benefit (IB) in youth) are defined as 'public funds'. This is because the Immigration Rules do not regard you as having recourse to public funds, if you are entitled to them because you are in an exempt group (see p59).[6]

Means-tested benefits

If you are in any of the exempt groups on pp68–69, being a person subject to immigration control does not exclude you from getting:[7]

8

Chapter 8: People subject to immigration control and benefits
2. People subject to immigration control who can be entitled

- income support (IS);
- income-based jobseeker's allowance (JSA);
- income-related ESA;
- pension credit;
- housing benefit;
- universal credit (UC).

Your leave is on the basis of a maintenance undertaking and you have been resident for five years

You are not excluded from the above means-tested benefits on the basis of being a person subject to immigration control if you have:[8]

- leave to enter or remain given as a result of a maintenance undertaking (see p61); *and*
- been resident in the UK for at least five years since either the date the undertaking was given or the date when you came to the UK, whichever is later.

If you go abroad during the five years, you may still count as resident in the UK during your absence. This depends on the duration and circumstances of your absence (see p98).[9] If your absence abroad is such that you cease to be resident in the UK, you can add together periods of residence either side of the gaps in order to meet the five-year rule.[10]

Your leave is on the basis of a maintenance undertaking and your sponsor has died

You are not excluded from the above means-tested benefits on the basis of being a person subject to immigration control if:[11]

- you have leave to enter or remain given as a result of a maintenance undertaking (see p61); *and*
- the person who gave the undertaking (often referred to as your 'sponsor') has died. If the undertaking was given by more than one person, they must all have died.

Nationals of Turkey and Macedonia

You are not excluded from the above means-tested benefits on the basis of being a person subject to immigration control if you are:[12]

- a national of a country that has ratified either the European Convention on Social and Medical Assistance or the European Social Charter (1961). The only non-European Economic Area (EEA) countries to which this applies are Turkey and Macedonia; *and*
- lawfully present in the UK. You satisfy this if you currently have leave to enter or remain in the UK.

Chapter 8: People subject to immigration control and benefits
2. People subject to immigration control who can be entitled

8

Note:
- You are also not excluded from council tax reduction by your immigration status if you come into this category.[13] However, if your leave is subject to a 'no recourse to public funds' condition and you receive council tax reduction as a result of being in this category, this counts as having recourse to public funds and so breaches the condition of your leave.[14] This is because the council tax reduction regulations are not referred to by the part of the Immigration Rules that disregards claims made as a result of exemptions.[15]
- You must satisfy all the other conditions of entitlement, including the requirement to have a right to reside (see p117).[16] Therefore, if you are an asylum seeker with temporary admission in the UK, although you are 'lawfully present', you are likely to be excluded from benefit or council tax reduction, because having temporary admission does not give you a right to reside.[17]

You applied for asylum before April 2000

You are not excluded from the above means-tested benefits (except UC) on the basis of being a person subject to immigration control if:[18]
- you claimed asylum before 3 April 2000 and you have not had a decision on your asylum application (or appeal if it was against a decision made before 5 February 1996), or you were part of the benefit family of someone who applied for asylum and was receiving a means-tested benefit on 4 February 1996; *and*
- you are covered by the rules on transitional protection. See Chapter 58 of the 2011/12 edition of CPAG's *Welfare Benefits and Tax Credits Handbook* for these.

Non-means-tested benefits

If you are in any of the exempt groups below, being a person subject to immigration control does not exclude you from getting any of the following non-means-tested benefits:[19]
- attendance allowance (AA);
- carer's allowance;
- child benefit;
- disability living allowance (DLA);
- ESA in youth;
- IB for incapacity in youth;
- personal independence payment (PIP);
- severe disablement allowance.

Note: your entitlement to benefit still depends on your satisfying all the other conditions of entitlement, including those on presence and residence (see Part 4).

8

Chapter 8: People subject to immigration control and benefits
2. People subject to immigration control who can be entitled

Your leave is as a result of a maintenance undertaking

You are not excluded from the above non-means-tested benefits on the basis of being a person subject to immigration control if your leave to enter or remain was given as a result of a maintenance undertaking (see p61).[20]

You are a family member of a European Economic Area national

You are not excluded from the above non-means-tested benefits on the basis of being a person subject to immigration control if you are a 'family member' of an EEA national.[21]

'Family member' is not defined in the regulations and it is therefore arguable that it should be given its ordinary everyday meaning and include, for example, a sister or uncle, as well as a partner.

It is also arguable that no additional conditions should be placed on who counts as an 'EEA national'. So, for example, British citizens who have never left the UK should be covered, as should other EEA nationals in the UK who do not have a right to reside.

In practice, decision makers often interpret who is covered in this way quite broadly, and child benefit guidance states that you are covered if your family member is an EEA, Swiss or UK national, including if s/he is the child for whom you are claiming child benefit, or your spouse or partner.[22]

However, a much more restrictive view was taken by a commissioner in a case concerning DLA. This held that someone only comes into this exempt group if s/he is a 'family member' as narrowly defined in European law (see p171) and that EEA nationals are only covered if they are exercising certain European Union (EU) rights – eg, as a 'worker'.[23]

If you are refused benefit because the decision maker has followed this decision and used a more restrictive interpretation of who is a family member of an EEA national, you should challenge the decision on the basis that the case was wrongly decided. In support of your challenge, cite a more recent case in which a Northern Ireland commissioner considered this earlier decision in detail, but rejected its reasoning.[24] However, Northern Irish decisions are not binding on the First-tier Tribunal in Great Britain and so you would need to appeal the First-tier Tribunal decision to the Upper Tribunal, which could then follow the reasoning of the Northern Irish decision. **Note:** the Upper Tribunal has since considered both judgments and preferred the reasoning of the earlier, more restrictive, decision.[25] However, this view was not part of the actual decision and is, therefore, not legally binding.

If your leave is subject to the condition that you do not have recourse to public funds, the Home Office does not regard you as having recourse if you are entitled to a benefit because you are in an exempt group (see p59). If you are paid a non-contributory benefit because the benefit authority accepts that you are in an exempt group, but the Home Office takes the view (due to the above caselaw) that you are not, receipt of that benefit could then be regarded as having recourse to

Chapter 8: People subject to immigration control and benefits
2. People subject to immigration control who can be entitled

8

public funds and, therefore, a breach of the conditions of your leave. CPAG is not aware of any such cases, but get specialist immigration advice if this could affect you.

Note: 'family members' (as defined in European law) of EEA nationals who have residence rights in the UK (eg, as workers) are not excluded from non-means-tested benefits because they are not defined as 'people subject to immigration control'.

This is because they do not require leave to be in the UK, as they have rights under EU residence law (see p57).

Even if you were granted immigration leave that was subject to a 'no recourse to public funds' condition, this condition does not have any effect while you have a right to reside under the EEA Regulations – eg, as the family member of an EEA worker.[26]

Nationals of Algeria, Morocco, San Marino, Tunisia and Turkey

You are not excluded from the non-means-tested benefits listed above on the basis of being a person subject to immigration control if you:[27]

- are a national of Algeria, Morocco, San Marino, Tunisia or Turkey and you are either currently lawfully working (see below) in Great Britain, or you have ceased lawfully working for a reason such as pregnancy, childcare, illness or accident, or because you have reached retirement age;[28] *or*
- you are living with a member of your family (see p282) covered by the above bullet point.

Lawfully working

'Lawfully working' has been equated with being an 'insured person' under the EU co-ordination rules (see p281).[29] In broad terms, this means that you must have been insured by paying (or being credited with) national insurance (NI) contributions.[30] It is likely that you will only be accepted as lawfully working if your work does not breach any work restrictions attached to your leave or, if you are an asylum seeker, you have permission to work from UK Visas and Immigration (UKVI).

For further details on the agreements with these countries, see p319.

You are covered by a reciprocal agreement

You are not excluded from claiming AA, DLA, PIP or child benefit (but not the other non-means-tested benefits listed on p69) on the basis of being a person subject to immigration control if you are covered by a reciprocal agreement the UK has with another country.[31] In practice, due to very few countries having reciprocal agreements in relation to AA, DLA or PIP, this tends to be only relevant for child benefit. In particular, you may be able to claim child benefit if you are

8

Chapter 8: People subject to immigration control and benefits
2. People subject to immigration control who can be entitled

covered by the agreement with former Yugoslavia which applies to Bosnia-Herzegovina, Kosovo, Macedonia, Montenegro and Serbia.[32]

See p309 for more information about reciprocal agreements.

You have been in receipt of a benefit since 1996

You are not excluded from the non-means-tested benefits on p69 on the basis of being a person subject to immigration control if you have received that particular benefit continuously since 4 February 1996 (6 October 1996 for child benefit).[33]

This transitional protection only enables you to continue to receive that benefit. You cannot make a new claim. If you are receiving benefit on this basis, your transitional protection (and therefore your entitlement) ends if:

• your benefit award ends;
• you request a revision or supersession; or
• your asylum application (if any) is decided or abandoned.

If you think you may be getting benefit as a result of this transitional protection, it is important that you do not request a revision or supersession, as this will bring your entitlement to an end. However, given that you must have been getting benefit continuously since 1996 and still be a person subject to immigration control, the number of claimants affected will be extremely small.

Tax credits

If you are in any of the exempt groups below, being a person subject to immigration control does not exclude you from getting child tax credit (CTC) or working tax credit (WTC).[34] Some of the exempt groups only apply to one of the tax credits, and some apply to both.

Note: if you are a person subject to immigration control, but your partner is not (or s/he is in one of the groups below), you can make a joint claim for tax credits (see p77).

Your leave is on the basis of a maintenance undertaking and you have been resident for five years

You are not excluded from CTC or WTC on the basis of being a person subject to immigration control if you have:[35]

• leave to enter or remain given as a result of a maintenance undertaking (see p61); and
• been resident in the UK for at least five years since either the date the undertaking was given or the date when you came to the UK, whichever is later.

If you go abroad during the five years, you may still count as resident in the UK during your absence. This depends on the duration and circumstances of your absence (see p98).[36] If your absence abroad is such that you cease to be resident in

Chapter 8: People subject to immigration control and benefits
2. People subject to immigration control who can be entitled

8

the UK, you can add together periods of residence either side of the gaps in order to meet the five-year rule.[37]

Your leave is on the basis of a maintenance undertaking and your sponsor has died

You are not excluded from CTC or WTC on the basis of being a person subject to immigration control if:[38]

- you have leave to enter or remain given as a result of a maintenance undertaking (see p61); *and*
- the person who gave the undertaking (often referred to as your 'sponsor') has died. If the undertaking was given by more than one person, they must all have died.

Nationals of Turkey and Macedonia

You are not excluded from WTC on the basis of being a person subject to immigration control if you are:[39]

- a national of a country that has ratified either the European Convention on Social and Medical Assistance or the European Social Charter (1961). The only non-EEA countries to which this applies are Turkey and Macedonia; *and*
- lawfully present. You satisfy this if you currently have leave to enter or remain in the UK.

Note: you must still satisfy all the other conditions of entitlement, including working a sufficient number of hours to count as working 'full time' under the WTC rules.

If you are an asylum seeker with temporary admission in the UK (see p14), you are accepted as 'lawfully present',[40] but you are only entitled to WTC if you satisfy the other conditions of entitlement. In practice, therefore, since you must work a sufficient number of hours and temporary admission usually prohibits you from working, you cannot benefit from this provision unless you have obtained permission to work from UKVI and you work in accordance with this (see p32).

Nationals of Algeria, Morocco, San Marino, Tunisia and Turkey

You are not excluded from CTC on the basis of being a person subject to immigration control if you are a national of Algeria, Morocco, San Marino, Tunisia or Turkey and:[41]

- you are currently lawfully working in the UK (see p71); *or*
- have ceased lawfully working for a reason such as pregnancy, childcare, illness or accident, or because you have reached retirement age.[42]

For further details on the agreements with these countries, see p319.

8

Chapter 8: People subject to immigration control and benefits
3. Partners and children who are subject to immigration control

You are transferring to child tax credit from income support or income-based jobseeker's allowance

You are not excluded from CTC on the basis of being a person subject to immigration control if you:[43]

- claim CTC on or after 6 April 2004; *and*
- immediately before you claimed CTC, you were entitled to an increase in your IS or income-based JSA for a child because either:
  - you are Turkish and lawfully present (see p68); *or*
  - you applied for asylum before 3 April 2000 and are covered by the transitional protection rules (see p69).

This only applies if you are transferring to CTC from an IS or JSA claim that included amounts for a child. It does not apply if you have not been receiving IS or income-based JSA for a child.

Note: as Macedonia only ratified the European Social Charter on 31 March 2005, nationals of Macedonia cannot benefit from this provision (because they could not have established their entitlement to IS or income-based JSA for a child before 6 April 2004).

Social fund payments

You are not excluded from social fund payments on the basis of being a person subject to immigration control if you are in one of the exempt groups for either means-tested benefits (see p67) or non-means-tested benefits (see p69).[44]

You must meet the other conditions of entitlement, including (except for winter fuel payments) being in receipt of a qualifying benefit. What counts as a qualifying benefit varies for different social fund payments but is broadly the means-tested benefits and, in some circumstances, tax credits. See CPAG's *Welfare Benefits and Tax Credits Handbook* for details.

---

3. Partners and children who are subject to immigration control

Some benefits and tax credits have special rules that apply if your partner or child who lives with you is a 'person subject to immigration control'. These rules vary, so check the rules for the benefit or tax credit you want to claim.

Means-tested benefits

Income support, income-based jobseeker's allowance and income-related employment and support allowance

If your partner is a person subject to immigration control (see p57), s/he is included in your claim for income support (IS), income-based jobseeker's

Chapter 8: People subject to immigration control and benefits
3. Partners and children who are subject to immigration control

8

allowance (JSA), including if you are a joint-claim couple, or income-related employment and support allowance (ESA). However, you are only paid a personal allowance at the single person's rate, unless s/he comes into one of the exempt groups that can get the means-tested benefits on p67, in which case you are paid at the couple rate.[45]

In all cases, your partner is still treated as part of your household and part of your claim. Therefore, her/his work, income and capital can all affect your benefit entitlement. Her/his presence also means you cannot claim IS as a lone parent. Similarly, unless your partner receives a qualifying benefit or is severely sight impaired or blind, her/his presence might mean that you are not entitled to a severe disability premium.

Premiums are payable if either you or your partner satisfy the qualifying conditions and should be paid at the couple rate.

Note: if your partner's leave to enter or remain in the UK is subject to the condition that s/he does not have recourse to public funds, you should be aware that receiving the couple rate of a premium breaches this condition and could affect her/his right to remain in the UK. Obtain specialist immigration advice before making a claim that includes a higher premium because of your partner.

Pension credit

If your partner is a person subject to immigration control (irrespective of whether or not s/he is in one of the exempt groups listed on pp67–69), s/he is treated as not being part of your household.[46] This means that you are paid as a single person and your partner's income and capital do not affect your claim. If you would otherwise be entitled to the additional amount for severe disability, your partner's presence may mean that you are not entitled to it, as the DWP may count her/him as 'normally residing with' you for this purpose.[47]

Housing benefit

If your partner and/or child for whom you are responsible is a person subject to immigration control, this does not affect the amount of housing benefit (HB) you are paid. Your partner is included in your claim and your applicable amount includes the couple rate of the personal allowance and any premiums to which either of you are entitled. Similarly, your child is included in your claim and your applicable amount includes a personal allowance for her/him, together with any premiums for which s/he qualifies. **Note:** from 6 April 2017, you can only be paid HB for your third or subsequent child in limited circumstances (known as the 'two-child limit'). These include if you are covered by the transitional rules (which cease to apply if you make a new HB claim), and if you receive child tax credit (CTC) for that child. For details of the 'two-child limit' rule, including when you can get amounts for your third or subsequent child, see CPAG's *Welfare Benefits and Tax Credits Handbook*.

8

Chapter 8: People subject to immigration control and benefits
3. Partners and children who are subject to immigration control

If your partner's and/or child's leave is subject to a no recourse to public funds condition and you claim HB, this could result in additional public funds being paid as a result of her/his presence. This breaches that condition of her/his leave and could affect her/his right to remain in the UK (see p59). Obtain specialist immigration advice before making a claim (see Appendix 2).

Council tax reduction (see p457) is also defined as public funds, so if your council tax reduction is greater (eg, because you lose a single person's discount) as a result of the presence of someone whose leave is subject to a no recourse to public funds condition, that person's right to remain in the UK could be affected. Obtain specialist immigration advice before making a claim (see Appendix 2).

Universal credit

If your **partner** is a person subject to immigration control (see p57) and is not in one of the groups who can get universal credit (UC) listed on p67, you must claim UC as a single person.[48] Your award is based on the maximum amount for a single person, but your partner's income and capital are taken into account.[49] **Note:** because your partner is not a UC claimant, s/he does not need to accept a claimant commitment nor comply with any conditionality requirements.

If your partner has leave which is subject to a no recourse ot public funds condition, your claim for UC as a single person does not breach this condition as no additional UC is paid in respect of her/him.

If your **child** is a person subject to immigration control, this does not affect the amount you are paid. S/he is included in your claim and you are paid a child element (subject to the 'two-child limit' – see below) and any disabled child addition for her/him. If your child has leave which is subject to a no recourse to public funds condition, receiving UC for her/him breaches that condition and could affect her/his right to remain in the UK. Obtain specialist immigration advice before making a claim (see Appendix 2).

Note: from 6 April 2017, you can only be paid UC for your third or subsequent child in limited circumstances (known as the 'two-child limit'). These include if you have adopted the child, or s/he has been placed with you for adoption (but not if, before the adoption under UK law, you had adopted the child under the law of another country).[50] Until 1 November 2018, if you are responsible for more than two children, you cannot make a new claim for UC (unless it is linked by less than six months to a previous UC claim). Instead, you can claim CTC and other means-tested benefits (the 'two-child limit' also applies to CTC). For details of the 'two-child limit' rule, including when you can get amounts for your third or subsequent child, see CPAG's *Welfare Benefits and Tax Credits Handbook*.

Non-means-tested benefits

Non-means-tested benefits that are either contributory or based on employment are not affected by your or your partner's or child's immigration status. **Note:**

Chapter 8: People subject to immigration control and benefits
3. Partners and children who are subject to immigration control

8

there are provisions to make it a condition of entitlement to contribution-based JSA, contributory ESA, maternity allowance and statutory sick, maternity, adoption, paternity and shared parental pay that you be entitled to work in the UK.[51] However, at the time of writing, these provisions had not been brought into force. See CPAG's online service and *Welfare Rights Bulletin* for updates.

Only the claimant's immigration status affects entitlement to non-contributory, non-means-tested benefits. Therefore, for **child benefit,** if you are not a person subject to immigration control, or you are but are in one of the exempt groups (see p69), you can claim for any child for whom you are responsible, regardless of the child's immigration status. However, if your child has leave which is subject to a no recourse to public funds condition, a claim for child benefit will result in additional public funds being paid as a result of her/his presence. This could affect her/his right to remain in the UK (see p59). Obtain specialist immigration advice before making a claim.

If your child is not a person subject to immigration control, or s/he is but s/he comes into one of the exempt groups on p69, s/he can claim disability living allowance (even if you are a person subject to immigration control).

S/he must still satisfy all the other conditions of entitlement, including the residence and presence rules (see Part 4).

Tax credits

If your partner is a person subject to immigration control and you are not, or you are but are in one of the exempt groups on p72, your joint claim for tax credits is treated as if your partner were not subject to immigration control. You are therefore entitled to working tax credit (WTC) and child tax credit (CTC).[52] However, unless you or your partner are responsible for a child, or your partner is a national of Macedonia or Turkey and is lawfully present in the UK, your WTC does not include the couple element.[53]

Note: if your partner is a person subject to immigration control because s/he requires leave and does not have it and you make a joint claim for CTC, in practice an award is often made. This is despite the fact that each partner making a joint claim for CTC is required to have a right to reside (see p120). It appears that HM Revenue and Customs (HMRC) often treats the above exception as overriding this. To avoid your claim being refused, explain to HMRC that you wish to either make a joint claim (and give all the details of both you and your partner) or, if HMRC does not accept that your partner is entitled, that you wish to make a single claim. Get advice if HMRC does not accept this.

If your partner is a person subject to immigration control because s/he requires leave and does not have it and does not have a national insurance (NI) number, you can still make a joint claim as s/he is exempt from the NI number requirement (see p355).

There are no immigration status conditions for children. Any child for whom you are responsible is included in your claim and your CTC and/or WTC includes amounts for her/him, provided you meet all the conditions of entitlement, including, for example, that the child normally lives with you and, for CTC, s/he is not excluded under the 'two-child limit' (see below).

If you are not a person subject to immigration control, but your partner is because her/his leave is subject to a no recourse to public funds condition, s/he is *not* regarded as having such recourse by making a joint tax credits claim with you. This means that you and your partner can make the joint claim without it affecting her/his right to remain in the UK. If such a joint claim includes a child whose leave is subject to a no recourse to public funds condition, any tax credits awarded in respect of that child are also not regarded as having had recourse.[54]

However, if your claim for CTC or WTC is not a joint claim as described above (ie, it is a single claim or a joint claim but neither you nor your partner are a person subject to immigration control) and it includes an amount for a child whose leave is subject to a no recourse to public funds condition, this breaches that condition and could affect her/his right to remain in the UK (see p59). Obtain specialist immigration advice before making a claim (see Appendix 2).

Note: from 6 April 2017, you can only be paid CTC for your third or subsequent child in limited circumstances (known as the 'two-child limit'). These include if you have adopted the child or if s/he has been placed with you for adoption (but not if, before the adoption under UK law, you had adopted the child under the law of another country).[55] For details of the 'two-child limit' rule, including when you can get amounts for your third or subsequent child, see CPAG's *Welfare Benefits and Tax Credits Handbook*.

Notes

1. Benefits and tax credits affected by immigration status
1 Reg 13 CTRS(PR)E Regs; reg 19 CTR(SPC)S Regs; reg 19 CTR(S) Regs; reg 29 CTRSPR(W) Regs; Sch para 20 CTRS(DS)W Regs
2 s115(1) IAA 1999; reg 3(1) TC(Imm) Regs
3 Reg 11(1)(b) ESA Regs; reg 12(1)(b) ESA Regs 2013
4 Reg 16(1)(b) SS(IB) Regs
5 ss61-63 WRA 2012

2. People subject to immigration control who can be entitled
6 para 6B IR
7 Reg 2(1)-(1A) and Sch Part 1 SS(IA)CA Regs
8 Reg 2(1)-(1A) and Sch Part 1 para 3 SS(IA)CA Regs
9 CPC/1035/2005
10 R(IS) 2/02
11 Reg 2(1)-(1A) and Sch Part 1 para 2 SS(IA)CA Regs

12 Reg 2(1)-(1A) and Sch Part 1 para 4
SS(IA)CA Regs, confirmed in *OD v SSWP
(JSA)* [2015] UKUT 438 (AAC)
13 Reg 13(1A) CTRS(PR)E Regs; reg 19(2)
CTR(S) Regs; reg 19(2) CTR(SPC)S Regs;
reg 29(2) CTRSPR(W) Regs; Sch para
20(2) CTRS(DS)W Regs
14 para 6A IR
15 para 6B IR
16 *Yesiloz v London Borough of Camden*
[2009] EWCA Civ 415
17 *Szoma v SSWP* [2005] UKHL 64,
reported as R(IS) 2/06 and see *Yesiloz v
London Borough of Camden* [2009]
EWCA Civ 415
18 Reg 12 SS(IA)CA Regs; reg 12
SS(PFA)MA Regs
19 Reg 2(2), (3) and (4)(b) and Sch Part 2
SS(IA)CA Regs; reg 2(1)(a)(ib) SS(AA)
Regs; reg 9(1)(ia) SS(ICA) Regs; reg
16(d)(ii) SS(PIP) Regs; reg 2(1)(a)(ib)
SS(DLA) Regs; reg 11(1)(b) and (3) ESA
Regs; reg 12(1)(b) and (3) ESA Regs
2013; reg 16(1)(b) and (5) SS(IB) Regs
20 Reg 2 and Sch Part 2 para 4 SS(IA)CA
Regs
21 Reg 2 and Sch Part 2 para 1 SS(IA)CA
Regs
22 para 10140 CBTM
23 CDLA/708/2007
24 *JFP v DSD (DLA)* [2012] NICom 267
25 *MS v SSWP (DLA)* [2016] UKUT 42 (AAC)
26 Sch 3 para 1 I(EEA) Regs
27 Reg 2 and Sch Part II SS(IA)CA Regs
28 *Krid v Caisse Nationale d'Assurance
Vieillesse des Travailleurs Salariés
(CNAVTS)*, C-103/94 [1995] ECR I-
00719, para 26
29 *Sürül v Bundesanstalt für Arbeit*, C-262/
96 [1999] ECR I-02685
30 *Sürül v Bundesanstalt für Arbeit*, C-262/
96 [1999] ECR I-02685, in particular
paras 85-86 and 93
31 Reg 2(3) SS(IA)CA Regs
32 FANIII(Y)O
33 Reg 12(10) SS(IA)CA Regs
34 Reg 3(1) TC(Imm) Regs
35 Reg 3(1) TC(Imm) Regs, case 1
36 CPC/1035/2005
37 R(IS) 2/02
38 Reg 3(1) TC(Imm) Regs, case 2
39 Reg 3(1) TC(Imm) Regs, case 4
40 *Szoma v SSWP* [2005] UKHL 64,
reported as R(IS) 2/06 and see *Yesiloz v
London Borough of Camden* [2009]
EWCA Civ 415
41 Reg 3(1) TC(Imm) Regs, case 5

42 *Krid v Caisse Nationale d'Assurance
Vieillesse des Travailleurs Salariés
(CNAVTS)*, C-103/94 [1995] ECR I-
00719, para 26
43 Reg 3(1) TC(Imm) Regs, case 4
44 Reg 2 SS(IA)CA Regs

**3. Partners and children who are subject
to immigration control**
45 **IS** Reg 21(3) and Sch 7 para 16A IS Regs
JSA Reg 85(4) and Sch 5 para 13A JSA
Regs
ESA Reg 69 and Sch 5 para 10 ESA Regs
46 Reg 5(1)(h) SPC Regs
47 Vol 13, para 78946 DMG
48 Reg 3(3) UC Regs
49 Regs 18(2), 22(3) and 36(3) UC Regs
50 Sch 12 para 3, UC Regs; ADM Memo
10/17, paras 15 and 29
51 ss61-63 WRA 2012
52 Reg 3(2) TC(Imm) Regs
53 Reg 11(4) and (5) WTC(EMR) Regs
54 para 6B IR. The TC(Imm) Regs are made
under s42 TCA 2002.
55 Reg 11(2) CTC Regs

9

Chapter 9

Asylum seekers and refugees

This chapter covers:
1. Asylum seekers (below)
2. Benefits and tax credits for people granted leave (p81)
3. Integration loans (p84)

This chapter explains some of the specific benefit and tax credit rules that apply to asylum seekers and to people granted refugee leave, humanitarian protection or discretionary leave following an asylum application. It also covers the rules on integration loans available to people granted refugee leave or humanitarian protection and their dependants. For more information about these categories of leave, see Chapter 4.

1. Asylum seekers

You are referred to as an **'asylum seeker'** while you are waiting for a Home Office decision on your application for refugee status (see p31). If you are a non-European Economic Area (EEA) national seeking asylum in the UK, unless you have leave on some other basis or you do not require it (eg, because you are a family member of an EEA national with a right to reside in the UK as a 'worker' – see p58), you come within the definition of a 'person subject to immigration control'. This is because you are someone who requires leave, but does not have it (see p58). You are therefore excluded from the social security benefits listed on p66, unless you are in one of the exempt groups (see p67).

Remember, even if you are in one of the exempt groups, you must still satisfy all the other conditions of entitlement for the particular benefit or tax credit, including the presence and residence conditions (see Part 4).

If benefit can be paid for you, either because you are not excluded from making a claim or because your partner can include you in her/his claim, this does not affect your asylum application. You can receive any benefit defined as a 'public fund' (see p60) because asylum seekers are not subject to the no recourse to public funds condition (see p59). If you receive public funds, this does not affect the outcome of your asylum application.

If your partner is entitled to benefits and you are included in her/his benefit claim, or you make a joint tax credit claim with her/him, and you do not already have a national insurance (NI) number, you are exempt from the NI number requirement (see p355).

If you are excluded from claiming social security benefits because you are a person subject to immigration control, you may be entitled to alternative forms of state support. If you are destitute, you may be eligible for asylum support from the Home Office (see Chapter 21).

Note: asylum support for essential living needs is taken into account as income when calculating any housing benefit your partner claims. It is not taken into account for universal credit (UC) and, if it is 'income in kind', is disregarded for income support (IS), income-based jobseeker's allowance (JSA) and income-related employment and support allowance (ESA).[1]

However, any IS, income-based JSA, income-related ESA or UC your partner receives is taken into account as income when calculating your asylum support (see p416).

If you are not eligible for asylum support or benefits, ask your local authority for help. If you have children, you may be eligible for support under the Children Act 1989 or Children (Scotland) Act 1995 (see p411). You may be able to get assistance from your local authority under one or more of the community care provisions, particularly if you have additional needs as a result of your age, health or disability (see p409). You may also be entitled to help from your local welfare assistance scheme (see p462).

See Chapter 21 for details of the support available for asylum seekers.

2. Benefits and tax credits for people granted leave

If, following your asylum application, you are granted leave that is not subject to the condition that you do not have recourse to public funds, you are no longer a 'person subject to immigration control'. For example, if you are granted refugee leave, humanitarian protection or discretionary leave, you are not a person subject to immigration control during that period of leave. However, if you are granted leave that is subject to the condition that you do not have recourse to public funds, you come within the definition of a 'person subject to immigration control' (see p59) and you are excluded from the benefits and tax credits listed on p66, unless you are exempt (see p67).

Guidance summarising how to access benefits once you are granted leave as a result of your asylum application is available online and covers information such as the documents you should take to your first interview with Jobcentre Plus after you make a claim for benefit.[2]

If your leave means you are not a person subject to immigration control, you are no longer excluded from the benefits listed on p66 and can claim all benefits, provided you meet the usual conditions of entitlement. The following rules may also affect you.

• If you are granted refugee leave, humanitarian protection or discretionary leave, you are exempt from the habitual residence test (see p108).

• If you are granted refugee leave or humanitarian protection, you can be joined by certain family members under family reunion provisions (see p33). The benefit authorities sometimes make mistakes about their benefit rights (see below).

• If you, or the family member who you have joined under the family reunion provisions, have been granted refugee leave or humanitarian protection, you are exempt from the past presence test for personal independence payment, disability living allowance, attendance allowance and carer's allowance (see p219).

• If you are granted refugee leave, you may be able to claim child benefit, guardian's allowance, child tax credit and working tax credit (WTC) backdated to the date of your asylum application (see p83).

• If you are granted refugee leave, you may be entitled to income support (IS) while you study English (see p83).

• If you are granted refugee leave or humanitarian protection, you may be eligible for an integration loan (see p84).

Family reunion

If you have been granted refugee leave or humanitarian protection, certain family members may join you under the family reunion rules (see p33).

A family member who comes to the UK and is given leave under these provisions is not a person subject to immigration control for the duration of that leave and can claim all benefits, provided s/he meets the usual rules of entitlement.

However, sometimes the benefit authorities decide that your family member is a person subject to immigration control on the basis that her/his Home Office documents describe you as her/his 'sponsor' and they wrongly conclude from this that s/he has been given leave as a result of a maintenance undertaking (see p61). This is incorrect. No undertaking is required from a person with refugee leave or humanitarian protection and your family members who come to the UK under the family reunion provisions are not given leave as a result of an undertaking. DWP guidance states this clearly (although it incorrectly states the family member will have indefinite leave).[3]

If you are a family member with leave in the UK under the family reunion provisions and you are refused benefits or tax credits because the decision maker decides you are a person subject to immigration control, you should challenge the decision and refer the decision maker to the DWP guidance.

Backdated child benefit and tax credits

If you have been granted refugee leave (not humanitarian protection or discretionary leave), you can claim child benefit, guardian's allowance and tax credits and have them backdated to the date of your asylum application (or 6 April 2003 for tax credits, if this is later).[4] Generally, you are required to reclaim tax credits each year. However, under the special backdating rules for refugees, the claim is treated as having been renewed each April.[5] You are treated as having made your claim on the date you claimed asylum and each subsequent April and, therefore, even if you are not currently entitled to tax credits, you can claim for the past period. This also applies if you cannot claim tax credits now because you come under the universal credit system, but you came under the tax credits system at the time you applied for asylum. You can claim backdated tax credits as your claim is treated as having been made at the date of your asylum application. You should explain this to HM Revenue and Customs (HMRC) when you make your claim and request that, if your claim cannot be processed through the usual computer-based sytems, it be processed clerically. Get advice if HMRC refuses to accept your claim.

You must claim backdated tax credits within one month, and child benefit and guardian's allowance within three months, of receiving the Home Office letter granting you leave as a refugee.[6] If the Home Office letter is sent to a solicitor acting for you, the three- or one-month period starts from the date your solicitor receives it.[7]

The amount of tax credits paid is reduced by the amount of asylum support you received for your essential living needs over the period.[8] (An argument that the reduction should only be for the amounts of asylum support paid in respect of children was rejected by the Upper Tribunal.[9]) In many cases, the total amount of asylum support paid for essential living needs is more than the amount of tax credits and, therefore, cancels out any entitlement over the backdated period. However, if you did not receive asylum support or your tax credit entitlement exceeds the amount of asylum support paid (eg, if you worked sufficient hours to qualify for WTC), you can be entitled to an amount of backdated tax credits.

The amount of child benefit and guardian's allowance paid is not reduced by any asylum support you may have received.

Income support for refugees studying English

Refugees who are studying English are one of the categories of people who are entitled to IS.

If you have been granted refugee leave (not humanitarian protection or discretionary leave), you can claim IS for up to nine months while you are studying if you:[10]

- attend, for more than 15 hours a week, a course for the purpose of learning English so you may obtain employment; *and*

• have been in Great Britain for not more than 12 months on the date the course began.

Note: there is no equivalent rule for universal credit.

3. Integration loans

Integration loans are interest-free loans, made to assist people who have recently been granted either refugee status or humanitarian protection to integrate into UK society.

Note: you may also be entitled to help from local welfare assistance schemes (see p462). Depending on the nature of your local scheme, you may want to apply to this before applying for a repayable integration loan, but be aware that many local authorities do not give cash and some require the assistance to be repaid. You may also want to get advice on charitable and other assistance that may be available in your area before applying for a repayable integration loan.

Who is eligible

An application for an integration loan is only considered if you are eligible to apply for one and you make a valid application (see p85). Whether or not you are awarded a loan is at the discretion of the decision maker (see below).

You are eligible to apply for an integration loan if you:[11]

• have been granted, after 11 June 2007, refugee leave, humanitarian protection (see p32), or leave to enter or remain as a dependant of someone with either refugee leave or humanitarian protection;
• are aged 18 or over;
• have not previously had an integration loan; *and*
• are, in the view of the Home Secretary, capable of repaying the loan.

When deciding whether to give you a loan, the decision maker must take into account:[12]

• the length of time since your leave was granted;
• your financial position – ie, your income, assets, liabilities and outgoings;
• your likely ability to repay the loan;
• what you intend to use the loan for; *and*
• the total available budget for loans.

Although the legislation does not specify which intended uses of a loan are more likely to be accepted, the application form provides the following headings for you to set amounts against, and guidance to decision makers confirms that these examples of 'integration needs' can be accepted (if they cannot be met through assistance available from Jobcentre Plus):[13]

- help with housing, including:
  - deposits for rented accommodation;
  - rent payments;
  - house-moving expenses;
  - essential items;
- help with finding work, including:
  - travel expenses to attend interviews;
  - work clothing/equipment;
  - initial childcare costs;
  - subsistence while training;
- help with education, including:
  - the cost of a training programme;
  - requalification/professional qualification.

There is also space on the form for other needs that would assist your integration. However, the guidance states that a loan should normally be refused for:[14]

- non-essential items;
- domestic assistance and respite care;
- mobility items;
- general living expenses (including utility bills);
- council tax payments;
- medical items;
- cars, including driving lessons and a licence, unless this is essential for your employment;
- repayment of debts;
- airfares for dependants to join you in the UK.

It is helpful to read the guidance before making your application, as it covers examples of factors that can be relevant. For example, in addition to how long you have been in the UK, your financial independence can also be relevant – your application may be considered weaker if you have been working and living independently in the UK for a long time before you apply than if you were not working or living independently – eg, if you have been receiving asylum support. The guidance also states that decision makers can take your 'character' into account – eg, a loan will usually be refused if you have been convicted of an offence.

The guidance states that the minimum amount of a loan is £100 and there is no fixed maximum amount.[15]

Making a valid application

You should apply for a loan by completing the form on the UK Visas and Immigration (UKVI) website. If fully completed, this ensures your application is valid.[16]

To be valid, the application must be in writing and contain:[17]
- your full name;
- your other names you have used;
- your date of birth;
- your address;
- your telephone number (if you have one);
- your email address (if you have one);
- evidence about your leave to remain and your age;
- your national insurance number;
- details of your (and any dependants') income, assets, liabilities and outgoings;
- confirmation of whether any member of your household has applied for or received an integration loan; *and*
- the amount requested.

Decisions, payment and repayments

After you have applied for a loan, you should be sent a written decision stating:[18]
- whether the application was valid;
- if so, whether a loan will be made;
- if so, the amount, conditions and terms of repayment; *and*
- the deadline for responding to say whether you wish to take the loan.

If you are entitled to a loan, a loan agreement should be attached to the decision letter, which you can sign and return to the decision maker. Usually, you must do this within 14 days of being sent the decision. If you are unhappy with the decision, either because you were refused a loan or offered a smaller amount than you need, you can ask for a reconsideration, which is carried out by a different decision maker. Your request for a reconsideration must be received within 14 days of the date on the decision letter.[19] There is no right to an independent appeal.

If UKVI decides that you are entitled to an integration loan, it passes your details to the DWP, which then pays the loan and manages your repayments.

Integration loans are recovered through direct deductions from benefits in the same way as for other third-party debts.[20] The rate of recovery and the start date of deductions should be notified to you. See CPAG's *Welfare Benefits and Tax Credits Handbook* for further details about deductions from benefit.

If direct deductions from your benefit are not possible (eg, because you do not receive a relevant benefit), you should be notified when repayments will begin, and the method, amount and frequency of these.

If your circumstances change, you can ask the DWP to revise the terms of recovery. These should be notified to you in writing.[21]

Notes

1. Asylum seekers
1 **IS** Sch 9 para 21 IS Regs
JSA Sch 7 para 22 JSA Regs
ESA Sch 8 para 22 ESA Regs
HB Sch 5 para 23 HB Regs
UC Reg 66 UC Regs

2. Benefits and tax credits for people granted leave
2 www.gov.uk/government/publications/
refugees-guidance-about-benefits-and-
pensions/help-available-from-the-
department-for-work-and-pensions-
for-people-who-have-been-granted-
leave-to-remain-in-the-uk
3 Vol 2, para 070709 DMG
4 **CB/GA** Reg 6(2)(d) CB&GA(Admin)
Regs
TC Regs 3(4)-(9) and 4 TC(Imm) Regs
5 Reg 3(6)(b) TC(Imm) Regs
6 **CB/GA** Reg 6(2)(d) CB&GA(Admin)
Regs
TC Reg 3(5) TC(Imm) Regs
7 *Tkachuk v SSWP* [2007] EWCA Civ 515;
CIS/3797/2003
8 Reg 3(9) TC(Imm) Regs
9 CTC/3692/2008
10 Reg 4ZA(3)(b) and Sch 1B para 18 IS
Regs

3. Integration loans
11 Reg 4 ILRFO Regs
12 Reg 6 ILRFO Regs
13 *Integration Loans Policy Guidance*,
available at www.gov.uk/government/
uploads/system/uploads/
attachment_data/file/257390/
integration-loans-policyguidance.pdf,
para 9
14 *Integration Loans Policy Guidance*,
available at www.gov.uk/government/
uploads/system/uploads/
attachment_data/file/257390/
integration-loans-policyguidance.pdf,
para 9.3
15 *Integration Loans Policy Guidance*,
available at www.gov.uk/government/
uploads/system/uploads/
attachment_data/file/257390/
integration-loans-policyguidance.pdf,
para 6.2

16 www.gov.uk/refugee-integration-loan
17 Reg 5 and Sch ILRFO Regs
18 Reg 8(1) ILRFO Regs
19 *Integration Loans Policy Guidance*,
available at www.gov.uk/government/
uploads/system/uploads/
attachment_data/file/257390/
integration-loans-policyguidance.pdf,
Part 12
20 Reg 9(1) and (3) ILRFO Regs; Sch 9 para
1 SS(C&P) Regs; Sch 6 para 12
UC,PIP,JSA&ESA(C&P) Regs
21 Reg 10 ILRFO Regs

Part 4

Benefits and residence rules

Chapter 10

Residence and presence rules: overview

This chapter covers:
1. Introduction (p92)
2. Presence (p94)
3. Past presence (p94)
4. Living in for three months (p95)
5. Residence (p98)
6. Ordinary residence (p99)
7. Habitual residence (p103)
8. The right to reside (p103)

This chapter describes the different residence and presence conditions that apply when you make a claim for benefits and tax credits in the UK. The two most significant conditions are the habitual residence test and the right to reside requirement, which are covered in more detail in Chapter 11. The groups of people who have a right to reside are covered in Chapter 12. The residence and presence requirements for individual benefits and tax credits are covered in Chapter 13.

If you are not a European Economic Area (EEA) national (see p40), first check Part 3 to see whether your immigration status means you are excluded from benefits as a 'person subject to immigration control'. If you are not excluded, you must still satisfy the residence and presence conditions described in this chapter.

If you live with a partner or child who is not an EEA national, you should check whether her/his immigration status affects your benefits. If her/his immigration leave is subject to a no recourse to public funds condition, check whether any claim you make could affect her/his right to stay in the UK (see p74).

If you, or a member of your family included in your claim, go abroad (either temporarily or to stay), see Part 5 for the way this affects your benefits and tax credits.

1. Introduction

There are residence and presence conditions for the following benefits and tax credits:
- attendance allowance;
- bereavement support payment;
- carer's allowance;
- child benefit;
- child tax credit;
- disability living allowance;
- contributory employment and support allowance (ESA) in youth;
- income-related ESA;
- guardian's allowance;
- housing benefit (residence conditions only, except during an absence from your home);
- incapacity benefit (IB) for incapacity in youth;
- income support;
- income-based jobseeker's allowance (JSA);
- pension credit;
- personal independence payment;
- category D retirement pension;
- severe disablement allowance;
- social fund payments;
- universal credit;
- working tax credit.

There are presence conditions for the following benefits:
- bereavement payment;
- contributory ESA;
- IB;
- industrial injuries benefit;
- contribution-based JSA;
- maternity allowance;
- retirement pensions;
- severe disablement allowance.

Council tax reduction also has residence conditions (see p457).

There are no residence or presence requirements for statutory sick pay, statutory maternity pay, statutory adoption pay, statutory paternity pay or statutory shared parental pay paid by your employer.

The residence and presence conditions vary between the different benefits and tax credits. If you satisfy the rules for one, it does not necessarily mean you will satisfy the rules for another.

The way in which the different residence and presence conditions affect your entitlement to benefit is set out in the UK benefits and tax credits legislation. Depending on the benefit or tax credit, you may be required to satisfy tests for:

- presence;
- past presence;
- 'living in' for three months;
- residence;
- ordinary residence;
- habitual residence;
- the right to reside.

However, these can be modified by the following.

- The European Union (EU) rules on the co-ordination of social security systems. If these rules apply to you (see p281), they can help you get benefits or tax credits in the UK – eg, by exempting you from certain past presence requirements or by enabling you to count periods of residence in another European Economic Area (EEA) country to satisfy the conditions of entitlement (see p298). They can also allow you to 'export' certain benefits to other EEA states. **Note:** the EU co-ordination rules are different from the residence rights provided under EU law, which can enable you to satisfy the right to reside requirement. In general, you do not need to know whether you are covered by the co-ordination rules to know if you have a right to reside under EU law. The EU co-ordination rules are covered in Chapter 16, and the main ways they can assist with the residence and presence tests, or affect your entitlement in other ways, are highlighted for each benefit in Chapter 13.
- International agreements, including reciprocal agreements. There are reciprocal agreements between Great Britain and Northern Ireland and between the UK and some other EEA and non-EEA countries. These can help you to qualify for benefits and tax credits if you have recently moved between Great Britain and Northern Ireland, or come to the UK or gone abroad. They operate in similar ways to the EU co-ordination rules and, in general, apply only when the EU co-ordination rules cannot assist you. There are also international agreements between EU and non-EU countries, which can also have similar effects (see Chapter 17).

Note: you must also check *where* you are required to satisfy a particular residence or presence test. This varies for different benefits and tax credits, and can be Great Britain, the UK or the 'common travel area' – ie, the UK, Ireland, the Channel Islands and the Isle of Man.

2. Presence

Most benefits and tax credits have rules about presence and absence. You usually must be present in Great Britain at the time you make your claim and continue to be present. There are specific rules that allow you to be treated as present during some temporary absences (see p240) and the European Union co-ordination rules can also mean that the presence requirement does not apply if you are staying or living in another European Economic Area state (see p40). All these exceptions to the requirement to be present vary between the different benefits and tax credits and are covered in Chapters 14 and 15.

To satisfy the presence requirement, you must show that you are physically present in Great Britain. If a benefits authority wants to disqualify you from benefit because you were absent from Great Britain, it must show you were absent throughout that day.[1] This means that, on the day you leave Great Britain and the day you arrive in Great Britain, you count as present.[2]

3. Past presence

The following benefits have a past presence requirement:
- attendance allowance;
- carer's allowance;
- disability living allowance;
- employment and support allowance in youth;
- incapacity benefit in youth;
- personal independence payment;
- severe disablement allowance.

In addition to being present at the time you make your claim for the above benefits, you must also have been present in Great Britain for a period of time before you become entitled. The requirement depends on the benefit you are claiming.

If you are covered by the European Union co-ordination rules (see p281), depending on the benefit, these can assist either by exempting you from the past presence requirement or by enabling you add certain periods of residence in another European Economic Area state to your period of presence in Great Britain.

For more details of the past presence test, including exemptions, for each benefit, see Chapter 13.

4. Living in for three months

You must have been living for the past three months in:

* the common travel area (the UK, Ireland, Channel Islands and the Isle of Man) in order to satisfy the habitual residence test for income-based jobseeker's allowance (JSA) (see below); *or*
* the UK for child benefit and child tax credit (CTC) (see p97).

The phrase 'living in' is not defined in the regulations and should, therefore, be given its ordinary, everyday meaning. When deciding whether you have stopped 'living in' the UK/common travel area, the following factors are relevant:[3]

* the reasons for your absence;
* the intended, and actual, length of your absence;
* the duration and connectedness of your previous residence in the UK/common travel area;
* whether you maintained your accommodation in the UK/common travel area while you were abroad; *and*
* the nature of your accommodation abroad.

The Upper Tribunal has recently held that a man had continued 'living in' the UK despite a 15-month temporary absence while he was abroad travelling.[4]

For child benefit and CTC only, if you return to the UK after a specific temporary absence, you are exempt from this requirement (see p97). See p240 for more information about temporary absences.

If you are covered by the European Union (EU) co-ordination rules (see p281) and have moved to the UK from another European Economic Area (EEA) country, you may be able to use periods of residence there to satisfy this condition by applying the aggregation principle (see p298). This is confirmed in guidance to child benefit and CTC decision makers.[5] However, it is arguable that this guidance is overly restrictive as it suggests that this only applies if your residence would satisfy an entitlement condition to a 'family benefit' in the other country, which would only be the case in Croatia, Cyprus, Denmark and Hungary.

Income-based Jobseeker's allowance

To satisfy the habitual residence test (see p106) for income-based JSA, you must have been living in the common travel area for the past three months (in addition to having a right to reside and being habitually resident 'in fact').[6] This requirement does not apply if:

* you are exempt from the habitual residence test (see p108);
* at any time during the last three months you have worked abroad and paid class 1 or 2 national insurance (NI) contributions, or been posted abroad as a Crown servant or while a member of HM forces. **Note:** in November 2015 the

government said that this also applied to family members of HM forces, but the legislation has not been amended;[7]

- your claim began before 1 January 2014.[8]

Note: you cannot make an 'advance claim' for income-based JSA to start on a future date when you will have lived in the common travel area for three months because the rules do not allow your claim to be treated as having been made on a future date if you do not satisfy the habitual residence test.[9]

Have you moved from another European Economic Area state?

If you have moved from another EEA state, it may be possible to argue that this requirement is unlawful.

If you are are covered by the EU co-ordination rules (see p281), the Court of Justice of the European Union (CJEU) held, in the case of *Swaddling,* that you cannot be deemed not to be habitually resident in a state merely because the period of actual residence there is too short.[10] See p116 for more details.

If you are an EEA national moving from another EEA state, you may also be able to argue that you must be allowed to show another kind of link to the UK labour market, and that not to permit this is contrary to the principle of equal treatment (see p297). The starting point of this argument is that JSA is a benefit intended to facilitate access to the labour market.[11] The CJEU has held that it is legitimate for a state to pay such a benefit to someone only after s/he has established a real link with that state's labour market.[12] However, it has been held to be unlawful to require a single condition to be satisfied without allowing any other method of establishing a real link to the national labour market.[13] It is arguable that the requirement to have been living in the common travel area for three months is such an unlawful condition. This argument is supported by the Advocate General's opinion that a three-month residence requirement for EEA jobseekers to be entitled to a German benefit is unlawful.[14] However, the CJEU did not address this question in its judgment, as it had already been held that the German benefit was not a benefit designed to facilitate access to the labour market.[15]

This argument was considered by a commissioner in Northern Ireland, who held that it does not apply to the income-based JSA requirement to have been living in the common travel area for three months. The commissioner was clear that *if* the expression 'living in' was effectively reduced to a test of presence that did not address other factors, the requirement *would* be contrary to EU law. However the expression should be given 'a broad construction that was capable of admitting and assessing evidence of the connection of the claimant with the common travel area', and therefore was not contrary to EU law.[16] **Note:** it is arguable that since this case did not involve any movement between EEA states (as the claimant was returning to the UK from New Zealand), the question of the compatibility of the test with EU law did not even arise and therefore remains to be addressed in a future case.

Child benefit and child tax credit

To be treated as present in Great Britain for child benefit, and present in the UK for CTC, you must have been living in the UK for three months, ending on the first day of your entitlement.[17] This requirement does not apply if you:[18]

* are an EEA national who is a 'worker' in the UK (see p142), including if you have retained that status (see p149);
* are an EEA national who is a self-employed person in the UK (see p159), including if you have retained that status (see p163);
* are a Croatian national working in accordance with your worker authorisation document (see p129);
* are a non-EEA national who would be classed as a worker or self-employed person if you were an EEA national;
* are a family member, other than an extended family member (see p171), of someone in any of the above four groups;
* are a refugee;
* have been granted humanitarian protection;
* have been granted leave to remain in the UK under the 'destitution domestic violence' concession, pending an application for indefinite leave to remain under the 'domestic violence rule' (see p35);
* have leave granted outside the Immigration Rules with no restriction on accessing public funds;
* have leave under the displaced persons provisions;
* have been deported or otherwise legally removed from another country to the UK;[19]
* are returning to the UK after a period working abroad and, other than for last three months of your absence, you were paying UK class 1 or class 2 NI contributions;
* are returning to the UK after an absence of less than 52 weeks and either:
  - before departing the UK you were ordinarily resident for three months; *or*
  - you were covered by the rules that treat you as present during a temporary absence for eight or 12 weeks during payment of child benefit (see p257) or CTC (see p269).

Note: the child benefit regulations exclude the UK from the definition of EEA state.[20]

If you are not covered by one of the above exemptions, you must satisfy the requirement to have been living in the UK for three months. However, see p95 for ways that you may be able to include time spent outside the UK.

5. Residence

The requirement to be simply 'resident', rather than 'ordinarily resident' or 'habitually resident', is only a condition for category D retirement pension. However, it is a necessary part of being ordinarily resident (see p99) or habitually resident (see p103).

Residence is more than a physical presence in a country and you can be resident without being present – eg, if you are abroad for a short holiday. Similarly, you can be present without being resident.

To be resident in a country, you must be seen to be making your home there for the time being; it need not be your only home, nor a permanent one.[21] You can remain resident during a temporary absence, depending on the duration and circumstances of your absence.[22] Your intentions to return, your accommodation, and where your family and your personal belongings are can all be relevant. It is possible to be resident in two countries at once.[23]

Children

The only benefits that can be claimed by a child under 16 that have residence requirements are disability living allowance (DLA), housing benefit (HB) and child benefit. For DLA and HB, the claimant must be habitually resident (unless, for DLA, s/he claimed before 8 April 2013, in which case s/he must be ordinarily resident until her/his award is terminated, revised or superseded, from which point s/he must be habitually resident). For child benefit, the claimant must be ordinarily resident and have a right to reside.

Although children are covered by the same rules as for adults, in order to decide whether or not they satisfy the residence requirement,[24] in practice, a child's ordinary or habitual residence is usually decided by looking at the residence of her/his parent(s) or person(s) with parental responsibility (in Scotland, parental rights and responsibilities) for her/him. A child who lives with that person usually has the same ordinary or habitual residence as her/him, so a child who joins a parent (or person with parental responsibility) may become ordinarily and habitually resident almost immediately.[25] If there is only one person with parental responsibility, the child has the same ordinary and habitual residence as her/him.[26]

However, the Upper Tribunal held that a non-European Economic Area national child was not ordinarily resident because he had overstayed his immigration leave and was therefore not lawfully resident, despite the child living with his mother who was both lawfully and ordinarily resident (see p102).[27]

Whether or not a child has a right to reside is determined in the same way as it is for an adult. So if a child under 16 is claiming child benefit, s/he (but not the child s/he is responsible for) must have a right to reside. If a child under 16 is claiming HB, s/he must have a right to reside in order to satisfy the habitual residence test.

6. Ordinary residence

The following benefits and tax credits have a requirement to be ordinarily resident:

* bereavement support payment;
* child benefit;
* child tax credit (CTC);
* employment and support allowance in youth;
* incapacity benefit in youth;
* category D retirement pension;
* severe disablement allowance;
* social fund funeral payments and winter fuel payments;
* working tax credit (WTC);
* (if claimed before 8 April 2013 until the award is terminated, revised or superseded) attendance allowance (AA), carer's allowance (CA) and disability living allowance (DLA).

There are some limited exceptions to the requirement to be ordinarily resident and, if you are covered by the European Union (EU) co-ordination rules, these may assist you in satisfying it. The exceptions and assistance provided by the co-ordination rules vary between the different benefits and tax credits and are covered in Chapter 13.

In practice, claims are rarely refused on the basis of ordinary residence.

You cannot be ordinarily resident without being resident (see p98).

The term 'ordinary residence' is not defined in the legislation, but caselaw has confirmed:

* the words should have their natural and ordinary meaning;[28]
* you are ordinarily resident in a country if you have a home there that you have adopted for a settled purpose and where you live for the time being (whether for a short or long duration);[29]
* ordinary residence can start on arrival (see p100);
* a person in the UK for a temporary purpose can be ordinarily resident in the UK (see p100);
* in general, your residence must be voluntary for you to be ordinarily resident (see p100);
* ordinary residence can continue during absences abroad, but leaving to settle abroad usually ends ordinary residence (see p101);
* although rare, it is possible for a person to be ordinarily resident in more than one place or country;[30]
* a person who lives in the UK but has no fixed abode can be ordinarily resident;[31]
* ordinary residence is different from the concept of 'domicile'.[32]

Ordinary residence on arrival

Ordinary residence can begin immediately on arrival in Great Britain.[33] In a family law case, a man who separated from his wife in one country (where he had lived and worked for three years) and went to live at his parents' house in another was found to become immediately ordinarily resident there. The Court of Appeal found that, where there is evidence that a person intends to make a place her/his home for an indefinite period, s/he is ordinarily resident when s/he arrives there.[34] In another case, a court decided that a woman returning from Australia after some months there had never lost her ordinary residence in England. However, if she had, she would have become ordinarily resident again when the boat embarked from Australia.[35] In a case involving students, they had to show that they were ordinarily resident within a few weeks of first arriving in the UK, and it was not argued that they could not be ordinarily resident because they had only just come to Great Britain.[36]

Ordinary residence while here for a temporary purpose

To be ordinarily resident in Great Britain, you do not have to intend, or be able, to live here permanently. The purpose can be for a limited period. In the the case of *Shah,* Lord Scarman said that, 'Education, business or profession, employment, health, family, or merely love of the place spring to mind as common reasons for a choice of regular abode.'[37] If you are solely in the UK for business purposes, you can still be ordinarily resident here.[38] You may have several different reasons for a single stay – eg, to visit relatives, get medical advice, attend religious ceremonies and sort out personal affairs.[39]

The reason must be a settled one. This does not mean that the reason has to be long-standing,[40] but there must be evidence of it. Although in some cases concerning ordinary residence, the courts have looked back to see whether a person had been ordinarily resident months or years beforehand,[41] there is no minimum period of residence required before you are ordinarily resident. If, for example, you have arrived in the UK and started work, the benefit authorities should consider how long you are likely to reside in the UK. If you intend to live here for the time being, they should accept your intention as sufficient, unless it is clearly unlikely that you are going to be able to stay. The benefit authorities should not make a deep examination of your long-term intentions.[42] The type of accommodation you occupy may be relevant.[43] If you have made regular visits to the UK, this may be relevant.[44]

Involuntary residence

Ordinary residence generally requires that you have '*voluntarily* adopted' to live somewhere with a settled purpose.[45] Therefore, a person who is held in a place against her/his will is not usually ordinarily resident there. It can be arguable that if you were taken out of the UK against your will (eg, as a child or for a forced marriage), you should be ordinarily resident on your return. However, if you are in the UK because of circumstances that limit or remove your choice, this does not necessarily prevent you from being ordinarily resident here.

In practice, the question of determining ordinary residence if you lack the capacity to 'voluntarily adopt' your place of residence rarely arises when determining entitlement to benefits and tax credits. However, it is far more common when trying to determine local authority responsibility for providing support, and so the principles established in that caselaw can be relevant. Depending on the facts, if you lack capacity you can be held to be ordinarily resident where the person who makes decisions on your behalf resides, if that is where you are based, or alternatively, where your residence is sufficiently settled, omitting the criteria for it to be 'voluntarily adopted'.[46]

Deportation to the UK does not prevent you from becoming ordinarily resident here.[47] The issue is whether your residence is part of your settled purpose. If you have decided to live in the UK, it does not matter if the reason for your decision is because you were deported here. For the purposes of tax credits and child benefit, you are treated as ordinarily resident if you are in the UK as a result of deportation or having been otherwise legally removed from another country.[48]

Absence from the UK

If you are ordinarily resident, you may lose this status if you go abroad. This depends on all the facts of your situation, including:

- your stated intentions when you go abroad and whether these are followed by your subsequent actions;
- why you go abroad;
- how long you stay abroad;
- what connections you keep with the UK – eg, accommodation, furniture and other possessions, and visits back to the UK.[49]

If you decide to move abroad for the foreseeable future, you usually stop being ordinarily resident in the UK on the day you leave.[50] There can be exceptions, which depend on your circumstances, including if your plans are clearly impractical and you return to the UK very quickly.

If your absence abroad is part of your normal pattern of life, your ordinary residence may not be affected.[51] This can apply if you are out of the UK for half, or even most, of the year – eg, if you spend each summer in the UK and the winter abroad, you may still be ordinarily resident in the UK.[52]

If your absence abroad is extraordinary or temporary and you intend to return to the UK, your ordinary residence may not be affected.[53] Your subsequent actions can add weight to the relevance of your intentions – eg, if you intended to return to the UK and by the time of the decision you have, in fact, returned.[54]

However, if despite intending to return, you are away from the UK for a long time and do not keep strong connections with Great Britain, you may lose your ordinary residence. In one case, a citizen of the UK and colonies lived in the UK for over four years and then returned to Kenya for two years and five months because her business here failed and there was a business opportunity in Kenya. She intended to make enough money to support herself on her return to the UK. Her parents and parents-in-law remained in the UK. She was found to have lost her ordinary residence during her absence.[55]

In deciding whether an absence affects your ordinary residence, the decision maker must consider all your circumstances. Every absence is unique and distinct, and you should provide full details of all your circumstances including:

- why you wish to go abroad;
- how long you intend to be abroad; *and*
- what you intend to do while you are abroad.

Each of these considerations needs to be taken into account, and it is your responsibility to demonstrate that your absence is to be a temporary one.[56]

Note: in addition to affecting your ordinary residence, an absence may also affect your benefit entitlement if it means you cease to satisfy other residence or presence requirements for the benefit or tax credit you are claiming (see p239), or if it means you cease to be treated as a couple (see p242).

Legal residence

It is arguable that whether or not residence must be legal or lawful to count as ordinary residence depends on the context. However, caselaw suggests that if this entails entitlement to a state benefit, the residence must be lawful.[57] This approach was applied recently to exclude from DLA a non-European Economic Area (EEA) national child who had overstayed his immigration leave in the UK, on the basis that he was not ordinarily resident.[58]

This reasoning is problematic if you are a non-EEA national claimant defined as a 'person subject to immigration control' because you require leave and do not have it (see p58), but you are not excluded from benefits on this basis because you are in an exempt group. See p72 for the exempt groups for tax credits, p69 for child benefit and p74 for social fund payments. The requirement for residence to be lawful could also affect your entitlement to category D retirement pension (see p225). **Note:** ordinary residence ceased to be a requirement for DLA or AA, CA and personal independence payment for claims made since 8 April 2013 (see p218).

Note: if you require leave but do not have it, but are entitled to tax credits because you are making a joint claim with a partner who is not excluded by her/his immigration status, HM Revenue and Customs appears to treat the provision that allows the immigration status of one partner to be ignored in a joint claim as overriding the right to reside requirement for CTC (see p77). Arguably, it should also override the requirement to be ordinarily resident.

7. Habitual residence

The following benefits and tax credits have a habitual residence requirement:
* attendance allowance (AA);
* carer's allowance (CA);
* disability living allowance (DLA);
* income-related employment and support allowance;
* housing benefit;
* income support;
* income-based jobseeker's allowance;
* pension credit;
* personal independence payment;
* universal credit.

You must satisfy (or be exempt from) the habitual residence requirement to get the above benefits (see p108). See Chapter 11 for details of the way the test works.
Note:
* You are also excluded from council tax reduction if you do not satisfy (and are not exempt from) the habitual residence requirement (see p459).[59]
* You may be entitled to a winter fuel payment from the social fund if, instead of being ordinarily resident in Great Britain, you are habitually resident in a non-excluded other European Economic Area country or Switzerland (see p227).
* If your claim for AA, DLA or CA began before 8 April 2013, you must be ordinarily, rather than habitually, resident until your award is revised or superseded.[60]

8. The right to reside

The following benefits and tax credits have a right to reside requirement:
* child benefit;
* child tax credit (CTC);
* income-related employment and support allowance;
* housing benefit;
* income support;
* income-based jobseeker's allowance;
* pension credit;
* universal credit.

The right to reside requirement for all the above benefits, other than child benefit and CTC, is part of the habitual residence test. For all the benefits and tax credits listed above, you must satisfy the right to reside requirement, unless, for the means-tested benefits only, you are exempt from the habitual residence test (see p108).

You are also excluded from council tax reduction if you do not satisfy the right to reside requirement (see p459).[61]

See Chapter 11 for details of the way the test works for each benefit and tax credit and Chapter 12 for who has a right to reside.

Notes

2. Presence
1 R(S) 1/66
2 Vol 2, para 070642 DMG; para C1122 ADM

4. Living in for three months
3 AEKM v Department for Communities (JSA) [2016] NICom 80, paras 21, 46-48 and 61; TC v SSWP (JSA) [2017] UKUT 222 (AAC), paras 21 and 32-38
4 TC v SSWP (JSA) [2017] UKUT 222 (AAC)
5 CCM 02035; CBTM 10025
6 Reg 85A(2) JSA Regs
7 Reg 85A(2A) JSA Regs; 'Changes to jobseeker's allowance to benefit armed forces families', announced 1 November 2015 on www.gov.uk
8 Reg 3 JSA(HR)A Regs
9 Reg 13(9) SS(C&P) Regs
10 Swaddling v Chief Adjudication Officer, C-90/97 [1999] ECR I-01075
11 Collins v SSWP, C-138/02 [2004] ECR I-02703, para 63
12 Vatsouras and Koupatantze v Arbeitsgemeinschaft Nürnberg, C-23/08 [2009] ECR I-04585, para 38 and caselaw cited
13 Prete v Office National de L'Emploi, C-367/11 [2012] para 34 and caselaw cited
14 Vestische Arbeit Jobcenter Kreis Recklinghausen v García-Nieto, C-299/14, AG Opinion, 4 June 2015

15 Vestische Arbeit Jobcenter Kreis Recklinghausen v García-Nieto, C-299/14 [2016]; Jobcenter Berlin Neukölln v Alimanovic, C-67/14 [2015]
16 AEKM v Department for Communities (JSA) [2016] NICom 80, paras 50-62
17 **CB** Reg 23(5) CB Regs
CTC Reg 3(6) TC(R) Regs
18 **CB** Reg 23(6) CB Regs
CTC Reg 3(7) TC(R) Regs
19 **CB** Reg 23(3) CB Regs
CTC Reg 3(3) TC(R) Regs
20 Reg 1(3) CB Regs

5. Residence
21 R(IS) 6/96, para 19; R(P) 2/67
22 CPC/1035/2005
23 R(IS) 9/99, para 10
24 Re A (A Minor) (Abduction: Child's Objections) [1994] 2 FLR 126: on habitual residence, but also applies to ordinary residence
25 Re M (Minors) (Residence Order: Jurisdiction) [1993] 1 FLR 495
26 Re J (A Minor) (Abduction: Custody Rights) [1990] 2 AC 562, at p578
27 MS v SSWP (DLA) [2016] UKUT 42 (AAC)

6. Ordinary residence
28 Levene v Inland Revenue Commissioners [1928] AC 217; R(M) 1/85
29 R v Barnet London Borough Council ex parte Shah [1983] 2 AC 309
30 IRC v Lysaght [1928] AC 234; Britto v SSHD [1984] Imm AR 93; R(P) 1/01; CIS/1691/2004; GC v HMRC (TC) [2014] UKUT 251 (AAC)

31 *Levene v Inland Revenue Commissioners*
[1928] AC 217
32 *R v Barnet London Borough Council ex
parte Shah* [1983] 2 AC 309, Lord
Scarman at p345E-H
33 R(F) 1/62
34 *Macrae v Macrae* [1949] 2 All ER 34. The
countries were Scotland and England,
which are separate for family law
purposes. In R(IS) 6/96, para 27 the
commissioner doubted the correctness
of *Macrae* because he considered it used
a test very close to the 'real home' test
rejected in *Shah*. He does not seem to
have heard any argument about this;
Macrae was cited in *Shah* and was not
one of the cases mentioned there as
wrong: pp342-43.
35 *Lewis v Lewis* [1956] 1 All ER 375
36 *R v Barnet London Borough Council ex
parte Shah* [1982] QB 688, at p717E
37 *R v Barnet London Borough Council ex
parte Shah* [1983] 2 AC 309, Lord
Scarman at p344C-D
38 *Inland Revenue Commissioners v Lysaght*
[1928] AC 234; *AA v SSWP (IS)* [2013]
UKUT 406 (AAC)
39 *Levene v Inland Revenue Commissioners*
[1928] AC 217, HL; *GC v HMRC (TC)*
[2014] UKUT 251 (AAC)
40 *Macrae v Macrae* [1949] 2 All ER 34
41 *R v Barnet London Borough Council ex
parte Shah* [1983] 2 AC 309
42 *R v Barnet London Borough Council ex
parte Shah* [1983] 2 AC 309, Lord
Scarman at p344G
43 R(F) 1/82; R(F) 1/62; R(P) 1/62; R(P) 4/
54
44 *GC v HMRC (TC)* [2014] UKUT 251 (AAC)
45 *R v Barnet London Borough Council ex
parte Shah* [1983] 2 AC 309
46 *R Waltham Forest LBC ex parte Vale*,
unreported 11 February 1985; but see
also *R (Cornwall Council) SSH And Another*
[2015] UKSC 46
47 *Gout v Cimitian* [1922] 1 AC 105
48 **TC** Reg 3(3) TC(R) Regs
CB Reg 23(3) CB Regs
49 R(F) 1/62; R(M) 1/85; *Britto v SSHD*
[1984] Imm AR 93
50 *Hopkins v Hopkins* [1951]; *R v Hussain*
[1971] 56 Crim App R 165; *R v IAT ex
parte Ng* [1986] Imm AR 23 (QBD); *Al
Habtoor v Fotheringham* [2001] EWCA
Civ 186
51 *R v Barnet London Borough Council ex
parte Shah* [1983] 2 AC 309

52 *Levene v Inland Revenue Commissioners*
[1928] AC 217; *Inland Revenue
Commissioners v Lysaght* [1928] AC 234;
AA v SSWP (IS) [2013] UKUT 406 (AAC)
53 *R v Barnet London Borough Council ex
parte Shah* [1983] 2 AC 309, Lord
Scarman at p342D
54 *R v IAT Ex parte Siggins* [1985] Imm AR
14
55 *SSHD v Haria* [1986] Imm AR 165
56 *Chief Adjudication Officer v Ahmed and
Others*, 16 March 1994 (CA), reported
as R(S) 1/96
57 *R v Barnet London Borough Council ex
parte Shah* [1983] 2 AC 309, Lord
Scarman – comments obiter; *Mark v
Mark* [2005] UKHL 42, para 36
58 *MS v SSWP (DLA)* [2016] UKUT 42 (AAC)

7. Habitual residence
59 Reg 12 CTRS(PR)E Regs; reg 16
CTR(SPC)S Regs; reg 16 CTR(S) Regs;
reg 28 CTRSPR(W) Regs; Sch para 19
CTRS(DS)W Regs
60 Reg 1(2),(3) and (4) SS(DLA,AA&CA)(A)
Regs

8. The right to reside
61 Reg 12 CTRS(PR)E Regs; reg 16
CTR(SPC)S Regs; reg 16 CTR(S) Regs;
reg 28 CTRSPR(W) Regs; Sch para 19
CTRS(DS)W Regs

Chapter 11

· ·

Habitual residence and the right to reside

This chapter covers:
1. The habitual residence test (below)
2. 'Habitual residence in fact' (p112)
3. The right to reside (p117)

This chapter explains the way in which the habitual residence test and the right to reside requirement apply to the various benefits and tax credits. For information on who has a right to reside, see Chapter 12.

---

1. The habitual residence test

The habitual residence test applies to the following benefits:
- attendance allowance (AA);
- carer's allowance (CA);
- disability living allowance (DLA);
- income-related employment and support allowance (ESA);
- housing benefit (HB);
- income support (IS);
- income-based jobseeker's allowance (JSA);
- pension credit (PC);
- personal independence payment (PIP);
- universal credit (UC).

To be entitled to one of the above benefits, you must be habitually resident in the 'common travel area' – ie, the UK, Ireland, the Channel Islands and the Isle of Man.

To satisfy the habitual residence test for **means-tested benefits** you must:
- be 'habitually resident in fact' in the common travel area (see p112); *and*
- have a right to reside in the common travel area that is not excluded for the benefit you want to claim (see p117); *and*
- (for income-based JSA only) have been living in the common travel area for the past three months (see p95).

Some groups of people are exempt from the habitual residence test for means-tested benefits (see p108). If you are in one of these groups, you are treated as satisfying the test.

To satisfy the habitual residence test for **AA, DLA, PIP and CA**, unless you are treated as habitually resident (see p108), you must be 'habitually resident in fact' (see p112).

Note:
- If your claim for AA, DLA or CA began before 8 April 2013, the previous requirement to be ordinarily, rather than habitually, resident continues to apply until your award is revised or superseded.[1]
- You are also excluded from council tax reduction (see p457) if you do not satisfy (and are not exempt from) the habitual residence test.[2]
- You may be entitled to a winter fuel payment from the social fund if, instead of being ordinarily resident in Great Britain, you are habitually resident in a non-excluded European Economic Area (EEA) country or Switzerland (see p227).

The habitual residence test for means-tested benefits

If you are exempt (see p108), your residence should not be examined further. Provided you meet the other conditions of entitlement, you are eligible for benefit. However, in practice, the DWP or local authority does not always consider whether you are exempt. The administration of the test, either by requiring you to complete an online or paper form, or by asking you questions at an interview, tends to follow the same format regardless of whether you are in an exempt group or not. In general, the decision maker first considers your right to reside. If you satisfy this requirement and you are claiming income-based JSA, s/he then considers whether you have been living here for the past three months and then (for all means-tested benefits) whether you are 'habitually resident in fact'.

Therefore, if you are in one of the exempt groups, make this clear to the DWP or local authority, particularly if you might not otherwise be accepted as satisfying the habitual residence test – eg, because you have only recently arrived in the common travel area.

The DWP sometimes develops policies for varying the usual procedures for specific groups. For example, at the time of writing, internal guidance states that if, when you make your new claim, you can provide evidence that you have come to the UK under the 'gateway protection programme' or 'vulnerable person relocation scheme', or you have been granted leave as a refugee in the last eight weeks, you are subject to a shorter habitual residence test (because you are clearly exempt) and your claim is fast-tracked.[3]

Who is exempt from the habitual residence test

You are exempt from the habitual residence test for **means-tested benefits** if you:[4]

- are an EEA national and are a 'worker' (see p142), including if you retain this status (see p149);
- are an EEA national and are a self-employed person (see p159), including if you retain this status (see p163);
- are the family member (see p170), other than an extended family member, of someone in either of the above two bullet points;
- are an EEA national with a permanent right of residence that you acquired in less than five years (the main groups cover certain former workers or self-employed people who have retired or are permanently incapacitated, and their family members – see p197);
- are a refugee. If you are a family member of a refugee, see p109;
- have humanitarian protection;
- have discretionary leave (see p36), leave granted under the 'destitution domestic violence' concession (see p35) or temporary protection granted under the displaced persons' provisions;
- have been deported, expelled or otherwise legally removed from another country to the UK and you are not a 'person subject to immigration control' (see p57);
- (for income-related ESA only) are being transferred from an award of IS which was transitionally protected from the requirement to have a right to reside (see p120);
- (for HB only) receive IS, income-related ESA or PC;[5]
- (for HB only) receive income-based JSA and either:
  - you have a right to reside other than one that is excluded for HB (see p118); *or*
  - you have been receiving both HB and income-based JSA since 31 March 2014. Your exemption on this basis ends when either you cease to be entitled to that income-based JSA or you make a new claim for HB.[6]

If you are not in one of the above groups, you must show that you have established 'habitual residence in fact' (see p112) in the common travel area and that you have a right to reside that is not excluded for the means-tested benefit you want to claim (see p117). For income-based JSA only, you must also show that you have been living in the common travel area for the past three months (see p95).

The above exemptions do not apply to **AA, DLA, PIP and CA**. For these benefits, you must show that you have established 'habitual residence in fact' (see p112) in the common travel area, unless you are treated as being habitually resident (as well as treated as being present) because you:[7]

- are abroad in your capacity as a serving member of the forces; *or*
- are living with someone who is abroad as a serving member of the forces and s/he is your spouse, civil partner, son, stepson, daughter, stepdaughter, father, stepfather, father-in-law, mother, stepmother or mother-in-law.

Family members of refugees

If you are the family member of a refugee and have leave on the basis that you joined her/him under the family reunion provisions (see p33), your leave does not mean you are exempt from the habitual residence test. You are therefore not entitled to means-tested benefits until you have established your habitual residence, and for income-based JSA, until you have been living in the common travel area for three months.

Note: if you live with your partner and claim UC, both of you must satisfy, or be exempt from, the habitual residence test. If only your partner does so, s/he must make a single claim. Her/his award is based on the maximum amount for a single person, but your income and capital are taken into account (see p210).[8]

If you have leave as a family member of a refugee or someone with humanitarian protection, this exclusion from benefits is arguably unlawful discrimination. In relation to the past presence test for DLA, the Upper Tribunal held that the requirement was unlawful, not only for a claimant with leave as a refugee but also for a claimant with leave as a family member of a refugee and the DWP accepts that the argument also applies if you, or the family member you are joining, have humanitarian protection (see p219).[9]

Who does the habitual residence test apply to

The habitual residence test applies to the benefit claimant.

For means-tested benefits, other than income-based JSA claimed as a joint-claim couple and UC, this means that it does not matter if your partner does not satisfy, or is not exempt, from the test; you are still paid as a couple. You and your partner should therefore consider which one of you is most likely to satisfy, or be exempt from, the habitual residence test.

For couples claiming joint-claim JSA or UC, the rules are different (see below).

Joint-claim jobseeker's allowance

If you are a member of a 'joint-claim couple' for income-based JSA (see CPAG's *Welfare Benefits and Tax Credits Handbook* for what this means) and either you or your partner do not satisfy, or you are not exempt from, the habitual residence test, a special rule applies. The partner who is habitually resident can claim income-based JSA for both of you without the other partner being required to be a claimant as part of the joint claim – ie, you do not need to make a joint claim.[10] You are paid as a couple.

Couples claiming universal credit

If you live with your partner and claim UC, you are generally required to make a joint claim, and you and your partner must each satisfy the habitual residence test. However, if only one of you satisfies, or is exempt from, the habitual residence test, you cannot make a joint claim for UC. Instead the person who satisfies, or is exempt from, the habitual residence test can claim UC as a single person.[11]

If you satisfy, or are exempt from, the habitual residence test, but your partner does not, the following special rules apply to the calculation of your UC.

- The maximum amount of UC is that for a single person.[12]
- Only you have to accept a claimant commitment and comply with the conditionality requirements.[13]
- Your partner's capital is included in the amount of capital taken into account.[14]
- Your partner's income is included in the amount of income taken into account when calculating how much should be deducted from the maximum amount of UC.[15]

If you fail the habitual residence test

The way in which your failure to satisfy, or be exempt from, the habitual residence test affects your benefit is slightly different for each benefit, but the outcome is the same: if you are not habitually resident in the common travel area, you are not entitled to be paid IS, income-based JSA, income-related ESA, PC, HB, UC, AA, DLA, PIP and CA. The precise way in which this is achieved is as follows.

- For IS, income-based JSA, income-related ESA and HB, you are classed as a 'person from abroad'. This means for IS, income-based JSA and income-related ESA, you have an applicable amount of nil,[16] and for HB you are treated as not liable for rent.[17]
- For PC and UC, you are treated as not present in Great Britain.[18]
- For AA, DLA, PIP and CA, you have failed to meet the prescribed residence requirements.[19]

Have you failed the habitual residence test?

1. If you are refused benefit because you have failed the habitual residence test, consider challenging this decision. See CPAG's *Welfare Benefits and Tax Credits Handbook* for information on how to do so. You may want to contact a local advice agency for help with this.

2. While you are challenging the decision, make another claim. If this is refused, also challenge this decision and make another claim, and so on. This is because when the decision refusing your initial claim is looked at again, the decision maker (or First-tier Tribunal) cannot take account of circumstances that did not exist at the time the original

decision was made.[20] So, if the decision maker (or tribunal) considers that you were not habitually resident at the time benefit was originally refused, but you are now (eg, because you have been resident for an appreciable period of time or, for income-based JSA, you have been living here for three months), s/he cannot take this into account when looking again at the original decision. However, if by the date of the decision on your second or subsequent claim, you had, for example, completed an appreciable period of residence (or, for income-based JSA, you had been living here for three months), s/he can take this into account.

The benefit authority may say that you cannot make another claim while your appeal (or request to have the first decision looked at again) is pending. This is is not the case.[21] It may help to refer to the fact that when amending regulations were introduced, the Secretary of State said in his report that 'it needs to be emphasised that neither the fact that a person's claim for benefit has been disallowed on the grounds that the habitual residence test has not been satisfied, nor the fact that there is an outstanding appeal against that decision, prevents that individual from making a fresh claim for benefit.'[22]

3. The decision maker should consider whether you satisfy or are exempt from the habitual residence test on your date of claim and, if not, on each date from then down to the date s/he makes the decision.[23]

4. Check whether you are exempt from the habitual residence test (see p108).

5. Establish which part of the test the decision maker says you have failed (if you are exempt from the test, you do not have to show that you satisfy *any* of the parts).

6. The local authority must make its own decision on HB and not just follow a DWP decision that you are not habitually resident. Similarly, if the DWP decides you are entitled to income-based JSA on the basis of your right to reside as a jobseeker, the local authority must determine whether you have *another*, non-excluded, right to reside (see p118), which would mean you are exempt from the habitual residence test for HB (see p108 for who is exempt and p369 for the relevance of decisions on other benefit claims).[24]

7. If the decision maker considers you do not have a right to reside, check Chapter 12 for the factors relevant to demonstrating your right to reside.

8. If you have claimed income-based JSA and the decision maker considers that you have not lived in the common travel area for the past three months, see p95.

9. If the decision maker considers you not to be 'habitually resident in fact', see p112.

10. The habitual residence test applies to the claimant, so, for benefits other than UC, if you have been found not to be habitually resident, your partner may satisfy the test and may be able to include you in her/his claim. This applies even if you have claimed income-based JSA as a 'joint-claim couple' (see p109). If you are claiming UC, your partner may be able to make a claim as a single person if s/he can satisfy the habitual residence test, but will not be paid benefit for you. In all cases, you can still challenge the refusal of your claim while your partner makes a new claim.

11. Although the onus of proof is on the benefit authorities to establish that you are *not* habitually resident, produce as much evidence as possible to show that you *are*. See Chapter 20 for more information on evidence.

2. 'Habitual residence in fact'

There is no definition of 'habitual residence' in the regulations. However, there is a considerable amount of caselaw on its meaning and certain principles have emerged from this. To count as 'habitually resident in fact':
- you must be resident in the common travel area (see below);
- your residence must be voluntary (see below);
- you must have a settled intention to make the common travel area your home for the time being (see p113);
- in most cases, you must have resided in the common travel area for an 'appreciable period of time' (see p114). **Note:** this is not a fixed period and there are some exceptions.

Of the above four factors, most disputes about whether someone is 'habitually resident in fact' concern the last two bullet points.

The decision about whether or not you are habitually resident is a factual question and must be made on the 'balance of probabilities'. You should always provide as much evidence as you can about all your circumstances that are relevant to your habitual residence. Ultimately, the burden of proof lies with the benefit authority to show that you are *not* habitually resident. Therefore, in the extremely rare situation of the probabilities in favour of each answer – that you are, or are not, habitually resident in the common travel area – being exactly equal, the decision should be in your favour. However, it is preferable to examine the facts further rather than rely on this 'burden of proof'.[25] See Chapter 20 for more information about providing evidence.

Residence

You cannot be habitually resident in the common travel area unless you are resident in the common travel area. It is not enough merely to intend to reside here in the future.[26] For information on residence, see p98.

Voluntary residence

You cannot be 'habitually resident in fact' in the common travel area unless your residence is voluntary.[27] In practice, this is rarely a barrier to your being found habitually resident in fact. However, it could be relevant if you are returning to live in the common travel area after having been taken or kept away against your will (see p115). **Note:** if you have been deported, expelled or otherwise legally removed from another country to the UK and you are not a 'person subject to immigration control' (see p57), you are exempt from the habitual residence test for means-tested benefits (see p108).

Settled intention

For your residence to become habitual, you must have a settled intention to reside in the common travel area. This is not determined just by your declaring your intention, but depends on the evidence about all the factors that are relevant to it.[28]

Your settled intention to reside in the common travel area does not need to be permanent; it is enough that you intend to make the common travel area your home for the time being.

Do you have a settled intention?
The following factors are relevant when determining whether or not you have a settled intention.

1. Your reasons for coming to the common travel area. If there is one or more clear reason why you have moved here (such as a family breakdown, a desire to study here or an offer of employment), this helps to show your settled intention.

2. The steps you took to prepare for coming to the common travel area – eg, the plans you made beforehand about where you would live, enquiries about work, making arrangements for your children to attend school, contacting people you know and settling your affairs in the country you were leaving, such as closing bank accounts, disposing of property and ending a tenancy.

3. The strength of your ties to the common travel area compared with your ties to other places (this is sometimes called your 'centre of interests') – eg, whether you have family or friends living in the common travel area, whether you have registered with a doctor or joined any clubs or associations here, whether your children are in school here, whether you have begun a course of study, or whether you have spent money here (such as a deposit on a rented property). Similarly, if you have these sort of ties abroad, this may indicate a less strong settled intention.

4. The viability of your residence in the common travel area (see p114).

As with the requirement to be resident (see p98), you must be seen to be making a home here, but it need not be your only home or a permanent one.[29] Therefore, a long-standing intention to move abroad (eg, when debts are paid) does not prevent someone from being habitually resident.[30]

Events after you claim benefit or receive a decision may confirm that your intention was always to reside in the UK – eg, if you are refused benefit because the DWP does not accept that you have a settled intention to stay in the UK, the fact that you are still here by the time of the appeal hearing may help show that you always intended to reside here.[31]

There is a close connection between 'settled intention' and 'appreciable period' (see p114): the stronger your settled intention, the shorter the period you need to reside in order to count as 'habitually resident in fact'.[32]

Viability of your residence

The viability of your continued residence, although a relevant factor, is not an additional requirement. This means that the question of whether you could survive in the common travel area without claiming the benefits to which the habitual residence test applies is not a separate question that must be answered positively in order for you to count as habitually resident in fact.[33] The viability of your residence is simply one factor that can be taken into account when considering your settled intention to reside in the common travel area.[34]

This means that you can be accepted as habitually resident in fact even though you have very few or no resources.

Appreciable period

In most cases, you do not count as habitually resident in fact until you have resided in the common travel area for an 'an appreciable period of time'.[35]

However, your appreciable period is reduced or may not apply at all if you are:
* a returning resident in certain circumstances (see p115); and/or
* covered by the European Union (EU) co-ordination rules (see p116).

There is no fixed period of time that amounts to an appreciable period and it depends on your circumstances.[36] Benefit authorities must not set a standard period of time for which all claimants must be resident before they can become habitually resident, and any such policy should be challenged by judicial review. There is extensive caselaw on what constitutes an appreciable period of residence. Periods of between one and three months are frequently cited,[37] but too much weight should not be put on any one decision, nor should any general rule about a specific time period be derived from it.[38]

Your appreciable period can include visits to prepare for settled residence made before that residence is taken up.[39]

The stronger your settled intention to make your home in the common travel area for the time being, the shorter your period of actual residence need be before you can be accepted as habitually resident in fact (and vice versa).[40]

Advance claims

You can make an advance claim of carer's allowance, disability living allowance (DLA) or personal independence payment (PIP) if in the next three months (six months for attendance allowance) you will (in addition to satisfying all the other conditions of entitlement) have been resident for an appreciable period and therefore satisfy the requirement to be 'habitually resident in fact'.[41] However, in practice, this is only relevant if you are exempt from, or can satisfy, the past presence test (see p218).

You cannot make an advance claim for income-based jobseeker's allowance (JSA), income-related employment and support allowance (ESA), income support, pension credit (PC) or housing benefit for a future date when you will have been resident for an appreciable period because the rules prevent your claim from being treated as made on a future date if you do not satisfy the habitual residence test.[42]

This exclusion does not apply to universal credit (UC), but you can only make a UC claim in advance if the DWP considers you will be entitled within the next month and you are in a group accepted by the DWP (DWP guidance states this is limited to prisoners and care leavers[43]).[44]

Returning residents

If you were living in the common travel area in the past and you return here, you may count as habitually resident in fact either immediately on your return or after a much shorter period of residence than would otherwise be the case.[45]

Are you a returning resident?
If you are a returning resident, you should consider the following issues.[46]
1. Were you habitually resident when you were previously here?
2. If so, did you cease to be habitually resident when you went abroad either immediately on departure or while you were abroad?
3. If you ceased to be habitually resident while you were abroad, when did you resume habitual residence in the common travel area? This may involve deciding when you resumed residence, and then when that residence became habitual.

If you never stopped being habitually resident in fact, you continue to be habitually resident on your return. This could apply if you only went abroad for a short period – eg, for a holiday. Similarly, it can apply if your absence abroad was only ever intended to be for a temporary period. For example, in one case, a man was held not to have ceased to be habitually resident on his return from a two-year Voluntary Service Overseas placement, during which time he had given up his tenancy in the UK and put his possessions in storage.[47] It may also apply if your absence abroad was involuntary. Guidance to decision makers states that people who leave, or remain away from, the UK because of a forced marriage are not considered to have lost their habitual residence as they were abroad through no fault of their own. They are therefore considered to be habitually resident from the date of their claim.[48]

If you have ceased to count as 'habitually resident in fact' while outside the common travel area, whether or not you need to complete a further period of residence here on your return before you can resume your habitual residence depends on the following.[49]

- The circumstances in which your earlier habitual residence was lost. If you went abroad for a temporary or conditional reason and/or you stayed away longer because of circumstances beyond your control, you may be more likely to be found habitually resident immediately on your return.

- The links between you and the UK while abroad. This could include retaining property, bank accounts and membership of organisations, maintaining contact with family and friends and making visits back to the common travel area (their frequency, length and purpose are all relevant).
- The circumstances of your return to the UK. Evidence of your settled intention is relevant (see p113).

Applying the above factors in two cases that were heard jointly, a commissioner found both claimants to be habitually resident on the day of their return.[50]

Even if you are not able to resume your previous habitual residence immediately on your return, you may still be able to argue that your previous habitual residence here is a factor that reduces the period of time that counts as an appreciable period of actual residence.

If you are covered by the European Union co-ordination rules

If you are covered by the EU co-ordination rules (see p281), the period of time you must be resident before you can be found to be habitually resident in fact can be shorter than otherwise might be required, and can be outweighed by other factors that show you are habitually resident. The co-ordination rules can only assist you to be found habitually resident in fact if you are claiming a 'special non-contributory benefit' (see p287) – ie:

- income-based JSA;
- income-related ESA;
- PC;
- DLA mobility component.

Note: PIP mobility component has not yet been listed as a 'special non-contributory benefit', but the DWP treats it as such.[51]

The co-ordination rules state that you are entitled to 'special non-contributory benefits' in the member state in which you are 'resident'[52] and define 'residence' as the place where you 'habitually reside'.[53] See p289 for the factors that should be considered when deciding where you habitually reside for the purpose of the co-ordination rules.

The Court of Justice of the European Union (CJEU) has held that when assessing where someone habitually resides, her/his length of residence in the member state cannot be regarded as an intrinsic element of the concept of residence. The case concerned a British national who lived in the UK until he was 23 and then moved to France, where he worked for 14 years until he was made redundant. He returned to the UK and was refused benefit on the basis of not having completed an appreciable period of actual residence. The CJEU found that the claimant, who was covered by the EU co-ordination rules and was claiming a special non-contributory benefit, could not be deemed not to be habitually resident merely because the period of residence completed was too short.[54] Although the case concerned a returning resident, subsequent caselaw confirms that the principle applies to any claimant covered by the EU co-ordination rules.[55] So, while 'duration and continuity of presence' is one of the factors that should be considered when determining where you habitually reside, it is only one factor and can be outweighed by others. Therefore, you cannot be denied income-based JSA, income-related ESA, PC and DLA mobility component solely because you have not completed an 'appreciable period' of actual residence in the common travel area.

3. The right to reside

The right to reside requirement applies to:
* child benefit;
* child tax credit (CTC);
* income-related employment and support allowance (ESA);
* housing benefit (HB);
* income support (IS);
* income-based jobseeker's allowance (JSA);
* pension credit (PC);
* universal credit (UC).

Note: you are also excluded from council tax reduction (see p457) if you do not have a right to reside.[56]

The way the test works varies between the different benefits.

For **means-tested benefits**, the right to reside requirement forms part of the habitual residence test (see p106). Therefore, if you are exempt from the habitual residence test, you do not need to demonstrate your right to reside (see p108). If you are not exempt from the habitual residence test, in addition to being 'habitually resident in fact' (see p112), and, for income-based JSA, having lived in the common travel area for the past three months (see p95), you must satisfy the right to reside requirement.

For **child benefit** and CTC, the right to reside requirement is part of the presence test. This also requires you to be ordinarily resident (see p99) in the UK and to have lived in the UK for the past three months (see p95).

Note: if you have been claiming benefits in the UK since 30 April 2004, you may have transitional protection from the requirement and therefore not need a right to reside (see p120).

If you do not have transitional protection and if you are not exempt from the habitual residence test, you must have a right to reside that is sufficient for the benefit or tax credit you wish to claim. The regulations for each benefit or tax credit specifically exclude certain types of residence. However, you are only excluded if this is your only right to reside. If you have any other non-excluded right to reside, you satisfy the requirement for that benefit.

Means-tested benefits

To satisfy the right to reside requirement within the habitual residence test for IS, income-based JSA, income-related ESA, PC, HB, and UC, you must have a right to reside in the common travel area, other than as:[57]
* a European Economic Area (EEA) national with an initial right of residence during your first three months in the UK (see p134);
* a family member of the above;
* the 'primary carer' of a British citizen who is dependent on you and would have to leave the European Union (EU) if you left the UK (see p187). **Note:** this exclusion is arguably unlawful and although legal challenges have not yet been successful, a further challenge has been taken to the Supreme Court.[58] See CPAG's online service and *Welfare Rights Bulletin* for updates;
* (except for income-based JSA) an EEA jobseeker (see p135);
* (except for income-based JSA) a family member of an EEA jobseeker. **Note:** this exclusion does not apply if you are a former family member of a jobseeker and you have retained your right to reside (see p119).

Jobseekers

If your only right to reside is as an EEA jobseeker, you do not satisfy the right to reside test for any of the means-tested benefits *except* for income-based JSA.

If you are claiming income-based JSA and make a claim for HB, the local authority must determine whether you have a non-excluded right to reside for HB. If the DWP has recorded your residence rights as a jobseeker for the purpose of your JSA claim, this is not conclusive for the local authority (see p369).[59] If you have been receiving both HB and income-based JSA since 31 March 2014, you are exempt from the habitual residence test for HB (see p108) and can continue to receive HB, even though you would not be entitled if you were to make a new claim.

If your only right to reside is as an EEA jobseeker, you are excluded from UC. In practice, this is only relevant if:
* you live in a UC 'full service area'. If you live in area where 'gateway' conditions apply, you are excluded from UC in any case because these include the requirement to be British (see p210); *or*
* you start living with a partner who is already receiving UC. As you do not satisfy the right to reside requirement, you cannot make a joint claim and be paid as a couple. Instead, your partner claims UC as a single person. S/he is paid a maximum amount for a single person, but your income and capital are taken into account.[60]

Note: the Court of Appeal has rejected an argument that income-related ESA is a benefit designed to facilitate access to the labour market, and therefore should be available to someone whose only right to reside is as a jobseeker.[61] This decision is not being appealed.

Family members of jobseekers

If you have a right to reside as a family member (see p170) of an EEA jobseeker, this satisfies the right to reside requirement for income-based JSA. You may therefore be entitled to income-based JSA if you are either:

- an EEA national looking for work, but the DWP has decided that you do not have a right to reside as a jobseeker – eg, if you have failed to provide 'compelling' evidence that you are seeking work and have a genuine chance of being engaged (see p137); *or*
- you are a non-EEA national.

If your only right to reside is as a family member of an EEA jobseeker, this does *not* satisfy the right to reside requirement for any other means-tested benefit.

If you previously had a right to reside as a family member of an EEA jobseeker and you retain this because the EEA jobseeker has died or no longer lives in the UK or your marriage or civil partnership to her/him is terminated, your retained right to reside satisfies the right to reside requirement for *all* means-tested benefits. This was recently confirmed by the Court of Session in Scotland.[62] For further details on former family members who can retain their residence rights, see p177.

Child benefit and child tax credit

If you do not have a right to reside, you are treated as not present in the UK and therefore not entitled to child benefit or CTC.[63]

Any right of residence in the UK enables you to satisfy the requirement for child benefit and CTC *except* a right to reside as the primary carer of a British citizen who is dependent on you and who would have to leave the EU if you left the UK (see p187).[64] This exclusion is arguably unlawful and although legal challenges have not yet been successful, a further challenge has been taken to the Supreme Court.[65] See CPAG's online service and *Welfare Rights Bulletin* for updates.

Note:
- If you are not entitled to child benefit for a child living with you because you do not have a non-excluded right to reside, someone else who contributes to the cost of that child may be able to claim child benefit instead. To be entitled, that person must contribute at least the amount of child benefit that would be payable for the child.[66] See CPAG's *Welfare Benefits and Tax Credits Handbook* for further details.
- The Court of Justice of the European Union (CJEU) recently dismissed an application from the European Commission to declare the right to reside test

for child benefit and CTC unlawful, finding that it did not impose a condition that cannot be imposed under the co-ordination rules, that it was not directly discriminatory and, although it was indirectly discriminatory, this was justified (see p297).[67] The Court of Appeal in Northern Ireland, in a decision that is not being appealed further, has held that the right to reside requirement for child benefit is not unlawful, thereby overturning the decision of the Northern Ireland Chief Commissioner that the right to reside test was either directly or indirectly discriminatory.[68]

Who does the right to reside test apply to

The right to reside test only applies to the claimant.

For means-tested benefits, other than income-based JSA claimed as a joint-claim couple and UC, if your partner does not have a right to reside, you can still include her/him in your claim and you are still paid as a couple. For joint-claim JSA and UC couples, the rules are different (see p109).

If you make a joint claim for CTC, both you and your partner must have a right to reside (see p229). If your partner does not have a right to reside, you may be able to make a single claim.

The right to reside requirement does not apply to a child for whom you are claiming CTC, child benefit, HB or UC.

Transitional protection: when you do not need a right to reside

If you have been receiving benefit since before 1 May 2004, you should check whether you have transitional protection from the requirement to have a right to reside. The rules vary depending on the benefit you are claiming.

Means-tested benefits

The right to reside requirement was introduced as part of the habitual residence test for means-tested benefits on 1 May 2004. If you have been receiving a means-tested benefit continuously since 30 April 2004, you do not need a right to reside in order to continue to receive that benefit. Furthermore, you do not need a right to reside for a new claim for a different means-tested benefit (except UC), provided the periods of entitlement have been continuous since 30 April 2004. The relevant benefits are:[69]

- council tax benefit (until it was abolished from 1 April 2013);
- income-related ESA (only from 31 October 2011 – see p121);
- HB;
- IS;
- income-based JSA;
- PC.

Note: UC is not covered by this transitional protection.

The rules on transitional protection did not apply to income-related ESA when ESA was introduced, and it was only added to the list from 31 October 2011. In addition, you can make a new claim for income-related ESA without needing a right to reside if it is linked by a gap of less than 12 weeks to a previous award of income-related ESA that was part of a continuous period of entitlement to the above benefits going back to 30 April 2004.

Example
Astrid is Swedish and came to the UK in January 2004 with her baby. In March 2004 she claimed IS as a lone parent while living with friends. In 2008, she had another baby and moved into a bedsit and claimed HB. In 2012 Astrid became very ill, moved in with some friends, stopped claiming HB and claimed income-related ESA instead of IS. Today Astrid has just moved into a rented flat and makes a claim for HB.
Astrid does not need to satisfy the right to reside requirement for any of these benefit claims because she has been in receipt of one or more of the relevant benefits for every day since 30 April 2004.
If Astrid had to claim UC, rather than HB, she would not have transitional protection. She would not be entitled as she does not have a right to reside.

For transitional protection to apply, you must have been the claimant throughout the whole period of continuous entitlement, rather than a partner, child or parent of the claimant.[70]

Most people who were entitled to IS on the grounds of disability or incapacity for work have been reassessed for transfer to income-related ESA, but there are some claims that have not yet been reassessed. If you are receiving IS on this basis and it is transitionally protected (ie, you continuously received this and/or another means-tested benefit since 30 April 2004), if it is converted to income-related ESA, you are exempt from the habitual residence test at the date of transfer.[71] As these cases are rare, you may need to explain this to the decision maker if the decision maker wrongly considers you need a right to reside.

The benefit authorities rarely check, or even ask, whether you have transitional protection. So, if you have been receiving one or more of the above benefits since 30 April 2004, you should always make this clear when you make your claim, and provide evidence.

Child benefit and child tax credit

The right to reside test only applies to child benefit and CTC if you make a new claim for one of these benefits on or after 1 May 2004.[72]

If you are still receiving the same award of child benefit that began before 1 May 2004, you do not need a right to reside.

If you have been claiming CTC since before 1 May 2004, you also do not need a right to reside to continue to receive it. Although the tax credit rules treat you as making a new claim each year when you respond to your annual declaration (or when you receive a notice saying you will be treated as having made a declaration), this renewal claim does not require a right to reside.[73]

Notes

1. The habitual residence test
1 Reg 1(2), (3) and (4) SS(DLA,AA&CA)(A) Regs
2 Sch para 21 CTRS(DS)E Regs; reg 12 CTRS(PR)E Regs; reg 16 CTR(SPC)S Regs; reg 16 CTR(S) Regs; reg 28 CTRSPR(W) Regs; Sch para 19 CTRS(DS)W Regs
3 DWP email to CPAG confirming internal guidance, 6 May 2016
4 **IS** Reg 21AA(4) IS Regs
 JSA Reg 85A(4) JSA Regs
 ESA Reg 70(4) ESA Regs
 PC Reg 2(4) SPC Regs
 HB Reg 10(3B) HB Regs; reg 10(4A) HB(SPC) Regs
 UC Reg 9(4) UC Regs
5 *LB Hillingdon v MJ and Another (HB)* [2009] UKUT 151 (AAC)
6 Reg 3 HB(HR)A Regs
7 **AA** Reg 2(2)&(3A) SS(AA) Regs
 DLA Reg 2(2)&(3A) SS(DLA) Regs
 PIP Regs 19 and 20 SS(PIP) Regs
 CA Reg 9(3) SS(ICA) Regs
8 Regs 3(3), 18(2), 22(3) and 36(3) UC Regs
9 *MM and IS v SSWP (DLA)* [2016] UKUT 149 (AAC); para 071716 DMG; para C2027 ADM
10 Reg 3E(1) and (2)(d) JSA Regs
11 ss3 and 4(1)(c) and (2) WRA 2012; regs 3(3) and 9 UC Regs
12 Regs 3(3) and 36(3) UC Regs
13 ss3 and 4(1)(e) WRA 2012; reg 3(3) UC Regs
14 Regs 3(3) and 18(2) UC Regs
15 Regs 3(3) and 22(3) UC Regs

16 **IS** Regs 21 and 21AA and Sch 7 para 17 IS Regs
 JSA Regs 85 and 85A and Sch 5 para 14 JSA Regs
 ESA Regs 69 and 70 and Sch 5 para 11 ESA Regs
17 Reg 10(1) HB Regs; reg 10(1) HB(SPC) Regs
18 **PC** Reg 2 SPC Regs
 UC Reg 9 UC Regs
19 **AA** s64(1) SSCBA 1992; reg 2(1) SS(AA) Regs
 DLA s71(6) SSCBA 1992; reg 2(1) SS(DLA) Regs
 PIP s77(3) WRA 2012; reg 16 SS(PIP) Regs
 CA s70(4) SSCBA 1992; reg 9(1) SS(ICA) Regs
20 Reg 3(9) SS&CS(DA) Regs; reg(5)(2) UC,PIP,JSA&ESA(DA) Regs; s12(8)(b) SSA 1998
21 s8(2) SSA 1998
22 Statement by the Secretary of State for Work and Pensions given as part of Cm 7073, para 20, available at www.gov.uk/government/uploads/system/uploads/attachment_data/file/243307/7073.pdf
23 See for example, *GE v SSWP (ESA)* [2017] UKUT 145 (AAC), paras 52-58
24 Confirmed in *EP v SSWP (JSA)* [2016] UKUT 445 (AAC), paras 24-25

2. 'Habitual residence in fact'
25 R(IS) 6/96, para 15
26 CIS/15927/1996
27 *R v Barnet London Borough Council ex parte Shah* [1983] 2 AC 309, at p342; *Cameron v Cameron* [1996] SLT 306; R(IS) 9/99
28 *Nessa v Chief Adjudication Officer* [1999] UKHL 41

29 R(IS) 6/96, para 19
30 *M v M (Abduction: England and Scotland)* [1997] 2 FLR 263
31 R(IS) 2/00, para 30
32 CJSA/1223/2006; R(IS) 7/06; CIS/1304/97 and CJSA/5394/98, paras 29-31
33 CIS/4474/2003, paras 15-16
34 R(IS) 2/00, para 28, followed in CIS/1459/1996 and CIS/16097/1996
35 *Nessa v Chief Adjudication Officer* [1999] UKHL 41, reported in R(IS) 2/00
36 *Nessa v Chief Adjudication Officer* [1999] UKHL 41, reported in R(IS) 2/00; *Cameron v Cameron* [1996] SLT 306
37 CIS/4474/2003; R(IS) 7/06
38 CIS/1972/2003; CIS/2559/2005
39 *Nessa v Chief Adjudication Officer* [1999] UKHL 41, reported in R(IS) 2/00, para 26
40 CJSA/1223/2006; R(IS) 7/06; CIS/1304/97 and CJSA/5394/98, paras 29-31
41 **AA** s65(6) SSCBA 1992
   CA Reg 13 SS(C&P) Regs
   DLA Reg 13A(1) SS(C&P) Regs
   PIP Reg 33(1) UC,PIP,JSA&ESA(C&P) Regs
42 **IS/JSA/ESA** Reg 13(9) SS(C&P) Regs
   PC Reg 13D(4) SS(C&P) Regs
   HB Reg 83(10) HB Regs; reg 64(11) HB(SPC) Regs
43 para A2048 ADM
44 Reg 32 UC,PIP,JSA&ESA(C&P) Regs
45 *Nessa v Chief Adjudication Officer* [1999] UKHL 41, reported in R(IS)2/00
46 CIS/1304/1997 and CJSA/5394/1998, para 11
47 *KS v SSWP (SPC)* [2010] UKUT 156 (AAC)
48 HB/CTB Circular A22/2010, paras 11-12
49 CIS/1304/97 and CJSA/5394/98, paras 34-38
50 CIS/1304/97 and CJSA/5394/98, paras 40-41
51 para C2097 ADM
52 Art 70(4) EU Reg 883/04
53 Art 1(j) EU Reg 883/04
54 *Swaddling v Chief Adjudication Officer,* C-90/97 [1999] ECR I-01075
55 R(IS) 3/00

3. **The right to reside**
56 Reg 12 CTRS(PR)E Regs; reg 16 CTR(SPC)S Regs; reg 16 CTR(S) Regs; reg 28 CTRSPR(W) Regs; Sch para 19 CTRS(DS)W Regs
57 **IS** Reg 21AA(3) IS Regs
   JSA Reg 85A(3) JSA Regs
   ESA Reg 70(3) ESA Regs
   PC Reg 2(3) SPC Regs
   HB Reg 10(3A) HB Regs; reg 10(4) HB(SPC) Regs
   UC Reg 9(3) UC Regs
58 *Sanneh and Others v SSWP* [2015] EWCA Civ 49 held the exclusion was not unlawful. The appeal to the UKSC in the joined case of *HC* was heard in June 2017, judgment pending – file reference: *R (on the application of HC) v SSWP* UKSC 2015/0215
59 *EP v SSWP (JSA)* [2016] UKUT 445 (AAC), paras 24-27
60 Regs 3(3), 18(2), 22(3) and 36(3) UC Regs
61 *Alhashem v SSWP* [2016] EWCA Civ 395
62 *Slezak v SSWP* [2017] CSIH 4
63 **CB** s146 SSCBA 1992; reg 23(4) CB Regs
   TC s3(3) TCA 2002; reg 3(5) TC(R) Regs
64 **CB** Reg 23(4) CB Regs
   TC Reg 3(5) TC(R) Regs
65 *Sanneh and Others v SSWP* [2015] EWCA Civ 49 held the exclusion was not unlawful. The appeal to the UKSC in the joined case of *HC* was heard in June 2017, judgment pending – file reference: *R (on the application of HC) v SSWP* UKSC 2015/0215.
66 s143(1)(b) SSCBA 1992
67 *European Commission v UK,* C-308/14 [2016]
68 *Commissioners for HMRC v Aiga Spiridonova,* 13/115948
69 Reg 6(1) SS(HR)A Regs, preserved by reg 11(2) SS(PA)A Regs
70 CIS/1096/2007
71 Reg 70(4)(l) ESA Regs; reg 10A ESA(TP)(EA) Regs
72 **CB** Reg 23(4) CB Regs
   CTC Reg 3(5)(a) TC(R) Regs
73 Reg 3(5)(a) TC(R) Regs

Chapter 12

Who has a right to reside

This chapter covers:
1. Introduction (below)
2. Non-European Economic Area nationals (p125)
3. British, Irish and Commonwealth citizens (p125)
4. European Economic Area nationals (p126)
5. Croatian, A2 and A8 nationals (p129)
6. Initial right of residence (p134)
7. Jobseekers (p135)
8. Workers (p142)
9. Retaining worker status (p149)
10. Self-employed people (p159)
11. Retaining self-employed status (p163)
12. Self-sufficient people and students (p165)
13. Family members of European Economic Area nationals (p170)
14. Derivative residence rights (p181)
15. Permanent right to reside (p190)

This chapter explains who has a right to reside. For information on the benefits and tax credits that require a right to reside, details of how the requirement operates for each and the types of residency rights that are specifically excluded, see p117.

The right to reside requirement is only one of the residence and presence conditions that must be satisfied for each individual benefit and tax credit. For all the residence and presence rules for each benefit, see Chapter 13 .

1. Introduction

Whether or not you have a right to reside depends on the nationality, immigration status and other particular circumstances of you, your family members and certain people for whom you care. You may have a right of residence under UK law or one that comes directly from European Union law, or both. You may have more than one right of residence, or you may not have any.

Any residence right is sufficient to satisfy the right to reside requirement, unless it is specifically excluded for the benefit or tax credit you want to claim.

The residence rights of some people are more complicated than others. In general, if you are a European Economic Area (EEA) national (see p126), or a family member or primary carer of an EEA national, your residence rights are more complex. Consequently, the majority of this chapter focuses on these groups. See the checklist on p128.

Note: the phrases 'right to reside' and 'right of residence' have the same meaning and are used interchangeably in this *Handbook*.

2. Non-European Economic Area nationals

If you are a non-European Economic Area (EEA) national, you have a right to reside if:

- you have been granted leave to enter or remain under UK immigration law. You have a right to reside during your period of leave. Any form of leave gives you a right to reside – eg, indefinite leave, refugee leave, humanitarian protection, discretionary leave or limited leave granted under the Immigration Rules, such as as a spouse or visitor. However, if you have leave which is subject to a condition that you do not have recourse to public funds, or indefinite leave granted as the result of a maintenance undertaking, you are defined as a 'person subject to immigration control' (see p57) and, unless you are in an exempt group, you are excluded from benefits on this basis (see Part 3). **Note:** if you have temporary admission as an asylum seeker, this does not give you a right to reside in the UK;[1] *or*
- you are someone who does not need leave to enter or remain under UK immigration law because you have a right to reside under European law. The most common examples are if you are the family member (see p170) or primary carer (see p181) of an EEA national who has a right to reside and who confers her/his residence rights on you.

3. British, Irish and Commonwealth citizens

British citizens have an automatic right of residence in the UK. However, this right is under UK law and British citizens do not usually have residence rights in the UK under European Union law if they have not lived with a right to reside in another European Economic Area (EEA) country before returning to the UK. Therefore, unless otherwise stated, all references in this chapter to EEA nationals should be read as *not* including British citizens.

12

Chapter 12: Who has a right to reside
4. European Economic Area nationals
• •

British citizens do not automatically confer residence rights on their family members. If you are not a British citizen but you are a family member of a British citizen, or if you are a dual British/other EEA state citizen, see p174.

If you are the primary carer of a British citizen, see p187.

Commonwealth citizens with the right of abode also have a right of residence in the UK (see p15).

Irish citizens

If you are an Irish citizen you have a right to reside in Ireland, which is part of the common travel area – ie, Ireland, Channel Islands, Isle of Man and the UK. You therefore satisfy the right to reside requirement for means-tested benefits, as these require you to have a right to reside in the common travel area.

If you are the family member of an Irish citizen in the UK, your residence rights as a family member require the Irish citizen to have a relevant right to reside in the same way as family members of other EEA nationals (see p170).

---

4. European Economic Area nationals

In practice, the right to reside requirement mainly affects nationals from the European Economic Area (EEA). The residence rights of EEA nationals, their family members and carers can be complex, as both European Union (EU) law and UK law must be considered, and both are subject to a considerable amount of interpretation through caselaw.

Legal sources of European Economic Area residence rights

The right of residence of EEA nationals and their family members derives from the EU treaties, in particular the **Treaty on the Functioning of the European Union** (TFEU), or the EEA Agreement which provides similar (although not always equivalent) rights for Norway, Iceland and Liechtenstein. The most relevant provisions of the TFEU include the following.

- Discrimination on nationality grounds is prohibited wherever the provisions of the Treaty apply.[2]
- Every person holding a nationality of an EU state is an EU citizen and has certain rights that stem from this.[3]
- EU nationals have the right to move and reside freely within the territory of the EU states.

However, the right to move and reside freely within the EU is subject to the limitations and conditions set out in the TFEU and in other legislation that gives effect to it.[4] This means that those covered by the TFEU must satisfy certain conditions to have a right of residence. The most important secondary legislation that sets out residence rights and the conditions that must be satisfied is **EU Directive 2004/38**. This brings together most rights of residence under EU law into one piece of legislation and replaces many earlier directives and regulations, which previously set out EU residence rights. Directive 2004/38 has been in force since 30 April 2006 and was extended from 1 March 2009 to cover nationals of Norway, Iceland and Liechtenstein.[5] **Note:** while the EU Directive is the most important source of residence rights for EEA nationals and their family members, it is not the only one – eg, some derivative rights of residence (see p181) stem from other EU legislation.

Swiss nationals and their family members are covered by a separate agreement, which provides similar rights.[6]

Note: the EU Directive, the Swiss agreement, and the effect of both in the UK, have not changed as a result of the UK vote to leave the EU. These rules continue to apply until the UK formally leaves the EU.

The Immigration (European Economic Area) Regulations 2016, referred to in this *Handbook* as the **'EEA Regulations'**, apply to all EEA nationals (except British citizens – see p125) and Swiss nationals.[7] These give similar residence rights to those contained in the Directive. Where they conflict with, or do not completely incorporate, EU Directive 2004/38, you can rely on whichever is more favourable to you. The current EEA Regulations replace very similar regulations from 1 February 2017.[8]

Who can have European Economic Area residence rights

You may have EEA residence rights if you are:
- an EEA national (other than a British citizen, except in limited circumstances – see below) or a Swiss national; *or*
- a family member of an EEA national (other than a British citizen, except in limited circumstances – see below) or Swiss national who has a right to reside. You can have these rights whether or not you are an EEA national;
- someone who was previously in the above group; *or*
- the primary carer of certain EEA nationals (including British citizens).

In all cases, whether or not you have EEA residence rights also depends on other factors.

For a list of **EEA member states**, see p40. However, note that, unless otherwise stated, references to EEA nationals in this chapter should be read as *not* including **British citizens**.[9] This is because British citizens have different rights in the UK than other EEA nationals. If you are a British citizen, you always have a right to reside in the UK under UK law. However, most British citizens do not have residence rights in the UK under EU law.[10] This means that family members and primary carers of British citizens do not have the same rights as family members and primary carers of other EEA nationals. If you are the family member of a British citizen, see p174. If you are the primary carer of a British citizen, see p181.

In general, **Swiss nationals** have the same residence rights as EEA nationals, so, unless otherwise stated, references to EEA nationals include Swiss nationals.

Croatian, A2 and A8 nationals may have their residence rights affected by additional restrictions. For a list of these countries and explanation of the restrictions, see p129.

Checklist

As EEA residence rights can be complex and affected by many different factors, it can be helpful to work through the following checklist of the main residence rights.

- **Step one:** are you an EEA national with a right to reside as a 'qualified person'[11] – ie: in the UK as a:
  - jobseeker (see p135);
  - worker (see p142), including if you have retained this status (see p149);
  - self-employed person (see p159), including if you have retained this status (see p163);
  - self-sufficient person, including a self-sufficient student (see p165).
- **Step two:** are you a 'family member' (see p170) of someone covered in Step one? You have a right to reside even if you are not an EEA national yourself. In limited circumstances, you may have a right to reside if you were the family member of someone in Step one but s/he has now died, left the UK or your marriage or civil partnership has been terminated (see p177).
- **Step three:** do you have a permanent right of residence (see p190)? This is normally after five years of 'legal residence' in the UK which can include periods with a right to reside under Step one or two above, but in limited circumstances can be acquired before five years.
- **Step four:** do you have you have a 'derivative' right to reside through someone else's right to reside, but not as her/his family member? This covers certain children and their primary carers (see p181).

Note:
- The term 'qualified person' appears in the EEA Regulations, but is not used in the EU Directive, although the same groups of people are covered.[12]
- You can have more than one right to reside at a time – eg, you may be a self-employed person and also the family member of someone with a permanent right of residence.[13]
- If you are an EEA national or family member of an EEA national, you also have an initial right of residence for the first three months you are in the UK. However, if this is your only right to reside, it does not entitle you to means-tested benefits (see p134). It can count towards the five years of legal residence required for a permanent right of residence (see p190).
- If you are a Croatian, A2 or A8 national, a 'family member' (see p171) of a Croatian, A2 or A8 national, or if you have a derivative right to reside (see p181) as the child or primary carer of a Croatian, A2 or A8 national, see p129 for the additional restrictions that can affect your right to reside.

5. Croatian, A2 and A8 nationals

Croatia, A2 and A8 states

Croatia joined the European Union (EU) on 1 July 2013.

Restrictions are currently in force until 30 June 2018.

The A2 states are: Bulgaria and Romania.

These states joined the EU on 1 January 2007.

Restrictions applied until 31 December 2013.

The A8 states are: Czech Republic, Estonia, Hungary, Latvia, Lithuania, Poland, Slovakia and Slovenia.

These states joined the EU on 1 May 2004.

Restrictions applied until 30 April 2009 (although this date is the subject of an appeal – see below).

The treaties under which the above 'accession' states joined the EU allowed existing member states to restrict accession national's access to their labour markets, and their residence rights as workers and jobseekers. The duration of these restrictions was limited to five years from the date the states joined the EU, but could be extended for a further two years if certain conditions were met. The UK government imposed the restrictions for five years and then extended them for A8 and A2 nationals for an additional two years. However, this extension of restrictions for A8 nationals from 1 May 2009 to 30 April 2011 has been held to be unlawful.[14] This means that A8 nationals were not subject to restrictions during this two-year period. However, the DWP's appeal against this decision is due to be heard in the Court of Appeal.[15] Guidance to decision makers advises that they 'stay' (do not decide) any claims in which this two-year period is relevant, pending the outcome of the appeal, and that they invite the First-tier Tribunal to do the same.[16] See CPAG's online service and *Welfare Rights Bulletin* for updates.

Most **Croatian nationals** have restrictions on their residence rights as jobseekers, workers or people who retain worker status. These restrictions have applied since 1 July 2013 and apply until 30 June 2018, but they may be extended for a further two years.

Although the restrictions on **A2 and A8 nationals** have now ended, you need to know what the restrictions were if your current or future residence rights are affected by the residence rights you or your family member had during the relevant period of restriction – eg, when establishing permanent residence. The restrictions can also be relevant if you are the primary carer of a child in education and the child's parent is an A2 or A8 national who has worked in the UK.'

Restrictions on employment and residence rights

If you are a Croatian national, unless you are in one of the exempt groups listed on p131, you must obtain an 'accession worker authorisation document' (in most cases, an accession worker registration certificate, specifying the employer you can work for) before taking up employment, and then work in accordance with it.[17] Your residence rights are restricted until 30 June 2018 as follows.[18]

* You do not have a right to reside as a jobseeker.
* You are only defined as a 'worker' if you have an accession worker authorisation document and are working in accordance with it.
* You cannot retain your 'worker' status when you stop work in the ways other 'workers' can (see p149).

If you are an A2 national, unless you are in one of the exempt groups listed on p131, during the period of restrictions you were required to obtain an accession worker authorisation document (in most cases, an accession worker card specifying the employer you could work for) before taking up employment, and then have worked in accordance with it.[19] Your residence rights were restricted between 1 January 2007 and 31 December 2013 in the same way as Croatian nationals.[20]

If you are an A8 national, unless you are in one of the exempt groups listed on p132, during the period of restrictions you had to work for an 'authorised employer'.[21] Broadly speaking, this meant you had to register each job you took with the Worker Registration Scheme (but see p133 for the precise meaning as it can affect your residence rights). Your residence rights were restricted between 1 May 2004 and the date the restrictions ended as follows.[22]

* You did not have a right to reside as a jobseeker.
* You were only defined as a 'worker' if you were working for an 'authorised employer' (see p133).
* You could not retain your worker status when you stopped work in the ways other workers could (see p149). However, if you lost your job within the first month of employment, you could retain your status in those ways, but only until the end of the month. **Note:** questions concerning the legality of excluding A8 nationals from retaining worker status have recently been referred to the Court of Justice of the European Union.[23]

The restrictions do not affect other residence rights you may have as a European Economic Area (EEA) national – eg, as a self-employed or self-sufficient person.[24] The restrictions also do not affect the way other provisions of EU law are applied, including the co-ordination rules in Chapter 16. These apply to Croatian, A2 and A8 nationals in the same way as they do to other EEA nationals.

Croatian and A2 nationals not subject to worker authorisation

If you are a Croatian national, you are subject to worker authorisation and have additional restrictions on your residence rights, unless you are in one of the groups listed below.

If you are an A2 national, you were subject to worker authorisation until 31 December 2013 and had additional restrictions on your residence rights (see p130), unless you were in one of the groups listed below. **Note:** these restrictions for A2 nationals ended on 31 December 2013.

You are not subject to worker authorisation and your residence rights are not restricted if you:[25]

- have (or had on 30 June 2013 (Croatian) or 31 December 2006 (A2)) leave to enter or remain with no restriction on employment;
- were 'legally working' (see p133) in the UK for 12 months without breaks of more than 30 days (in total), up to and including 31 December 2006 (A2) or 30 June 2013 (Croatian);
- have 'legally worked' for 12 months (beginning before or after 31 December 2006 (A2) or 30 June 2013 (Croatian)), disregarding any breaks of less than 30 days (in total);
- are a posted worker – ie, you are working in the UK providing services on behalf of an employer who is not established in the UK;
- are a member of a diplomatic mission (or the family member of such a person) or a person otherwise entitled to diplomatic immunity;
- have dual nationality with the UK or another (non-A2/Croatian) EEA state;
- are the spouse/civil partner (or, Croatian only, unmarried or same-sex partner) of a UK national or of a person settled (ie, with indefinite leave to enter or remain – see p23[26]) in the UK;
- are the spouse/civil partner (or, Croatian only, unmarried or same-sex partner) or child under 18 of a person with leave to enter or remain in the UK that allows employment;
- have a permanent right of residence (see p190);
- are a student with a registration certificate that states that you cannot work more than 20 hours a week (unless it is part of vocational training or during vacations) and you comply with this. If the certificate confirms you can work during the four months after the course ends, the exemption continues for this period;
- are a family member of an EEA national who has a right to reside, unless the EEA national is an A2 (or, if you are Croatian, a Croatian) national subject to worker authorisation (or, A2 only, the only reason s/he is not an A2 national subject to worker authorisation is because s/he is covered by the group below);
- are a family member of an A2 (or, if you are Croatian, a Croatian) national subject to worker authorisation who has a right to reside (for an A2 national

only, as a worker, student, self-employed or self-sufficient person). If you are a Croatian national (or an A2 national relying on an A2 worker), you are a 'family member' if you are the descendant and either under 21 or dependent, the spouse/civil partner, or (Croatians only) the unmarried or same-sex partner;

- are a 'highly skilled person' – ie, you:[27]
  - met the points-based criteria in the Immigration Rules for entering the UK on this basis; *or*
  - have a qualification at degree level or higher in the UK, or Higher National Diploma in Scotland and, within 12 months of this award, you apply for a registration certificate confirming your unconditional access to the labour market.

A8 nationals who were not required to register

If you are an A8 national, during the period of restrictions (see p129) you were defined as 'requiring registration', any work you did had to be for 'an authorised employer' (see p133) and your residence rights were restricted (see p130) unless you:[28]

- had leave to enter or remain on 30 April 2004 which had no restriction on employment;
- were 'legally working' (see p133) in the UK for 12 months, without breaks of more than 30 days (in total), up to and including 30 April 2004 (see also note below);
- had 'legally worked' for 12 months (beginning before or after 30 April 2004), disregarding any breaks of less than 30 days (in total);
- were the spouse/civil partner or child under 18 of a person with leave to enter or remain in the UK that allowed employment;
- had dual nationality with the UK and another (non-A2/A8) EEA state or Switzerland;
- were a family member of another EEA or Swiss national who had a right to reside under the EEA Regulations (other than an A2/A8 national subject to registration/authorisation if her/his only right to reside was for the first three months in the UK);
- were the member of a diplomatic mission (or the family member of such a person) or a person otherwise entitled to diplomatic immunity;
- were a posted worker – ie, you were working in the UK providing services on behalf of an employer who was not established in the UK.

Note: the Upper Tribunal recently held that an A8 national who was not in one of the above exempt groups could be treated as if he were if the outcome would otherwise be disproportionate. On the particular facts of this case, it ruled that it would be disproportionate to disregard the years of work and subsequent involuntary unemployment completed by the A8 national, just because he failed to satisfy the second bullet above because he was abroad (albeit still employed in the UK) on 30 April 2004 and because he had then failed to register his employment under the Worker Registration Scheme (as he believed he did not need to). The Upper Tribunal accepted that he had therefore acquired a permanent right to reside.[29]

Legally working

The phrase 'legally working' is relevant to determine whether you have completed your 12 months of legal work in order to be exempt from restrictions (see p132 for A8 nationals and p131 for Croatian and A2 nationals), and to determine whether you are, or were, a 'worker' at any a particular time. It has a specific meaning and only refers to employment, not self-employment: periods of self-employment do not count as 'legally working' for the purpose of exempting you from restrictions.

If you are a Croatian national (or an A2 national before 1 January 2014), you are/were 'legally working' if:[30]

- you are/were working in accordance with your worker authorisation document; *or*
- you are/were working during a period when you are/were in one of the exempt groups on p131 (other than posted workers); *or*
- the work was done before 1 July 2013 (for Croatian nationals) or before 1 January 2007 (for A2 nationals), either in accordance with any leave you had under the Immigration Act 1971 or when you did not require leave. The Court of Appeal has held that this does not apply to work done with permission from the Home Office while you were an asylum seeker.[31]

If you are an A8 national, you were 'legally working' before the restrictions ended (see p129) if:[32]

- you were working for an authorised employer (see below); *or*
- you were working during a period when you were in one of the exempt groups listed above (other than if you were the spouse/civil partner or child of a person whose leave to enter or remain in the UK allowed employment); *or*
- the work was done before 1 May 2004 either in accordance with any leave you had under the Immigration Act 1971 or when you did not require leave. The Court of Appeal has held that this does not apply to work done with permission from the Home Office while you were an asylum seeker.[33]

Authorised employer

If you were an A8 national subject to restrictions, you were defined as working for an 'authorised employer' if you:[34]

– were within the first month of employment; *or*

– applied for a worker's registration certificate under the Worker Registration Scheme within the first month of work, but did not yet have a certificate or refusal; *or*

– had a valid worker's registration certificate issued under the Worker Registration Scheme for that employer; or
– had been 'legally working' for that employer since 30 April 2004; or
– began work at an agricultural camp between 1 May 2004 and 31 December 2004, and before 1 May 2004 you had been issued with leave under the Immigration Act 1971 as a seasonal worker at such a camp.

If you only applied for a registration certificate after the first month of work, you only count as working for an authorised employer from the date it was issued. It does not apply retrospectively.[35]

If you are a Croatian national subject to restrictions and your employment ends, you stop legally working, stop being a 'worker' and, unless you are exempt, you cannot retain your worker status. However, if you are still under a contract of employment, you continue to be legally working and a worker – eg, if you are on maternity leave, holiday leave, sick leave or compassionate leave (including if the leave is unpaid).[36]

The same applied to A2 nationals between 1 January 2007 and 31 December 2013 and A8 nationals between 1 May 2004 and the end of restrictions (see p129).

6. Initial right of residence

All European Economic Area (EEA) nationals have a right to enter any member state.[37] If you are an EEA national, you also have an initial right of residence in any member state for the first three months of your stay, provided you hold a valid identity card or passport.[38] You have this initial residence right whether or not you are working or seeking work, subject to your not becoming an unreasonable burden on the UK's social assistance system.[39]

You also have a right of residence if you are not an EEA national, but are a family member of an EEA national who has this initial right of residence for three months, provided you hold a valid passport.[40] For details of who counts as your family member, see p170.

Note: you can have another residence right (eg, as a family member of a worker and/or as a jobseeker) in addition to your initial right of residence – ie, you do not have to wait for the three months to end before you have another residence right.

If your *only* right of residence is on the basis of your (or your family member's) initial three-month right of residence, you are not entitled to **income support, income-based jobseeker's allowance, income-related employment and support allowance, pension credit, housing benefit and universal credit.** However, if you have another residence right during your initial three months in the UK, you can satisfy the right to reside requirement for these benefits, provided it is not a residence right that is excluded for the means-tested benefit you want to claim (see p118).

Note: the requirement for you to have been living in the common travel area for the past three months for income-based JSA is a different part of the habitual residence test (see p95) and unrelated to this initial right of residence.

If your *only* right of residence is on the basis of your (or your family member's) initial three-month right of residence, the **child benefit and child tax credit** (CTC) rules do not exclude you from entitlement. Therefore, you satisfy the right to reside requirement for child benefit and CTC, but only for the first three months of your residence in the UK, unless you have some other right of residence. However, in practice, you are unlikely to qualify for child benefit or CTC during this period because, unless you are exempt, you must have been living in the UK for the past three months (see p95).

Note: you can count a period during which this is your only right of residence as part of the continuous five-year period required for permanent residence (see p190).

7. Jobseekers

If you are a European Economic Area (EEA) national looking for work in the UK, you may have a right to reside as a 'jobseeker' (see below). You may also have a right to reside if you are a family member (see p170) of a jobseeker. However, both these residence rights only satisfy the right to reside requirement for certain benefits (see p141). Also, you may have difficulty claiming these benefits over the longer term solely on the basis of your right to reside as a jobseeker because of evidence requirements (see p137).

You should therefore always check whether you have a right of residence on some other basis.

Note:
- If you have previously been a 'worker' (see p142) and are now looking for work, in addition to having a right to reside as a jobseeker, you may also have a right to reside as someone who retains worker status (see p149). This satisfies the right to reside requirement for all benefits.
- Periods when you have a right to reside as a jobseeker count towards the five years required to acquire permanent residence (see p190). Having a right of permanent residency satisfies the right to reside requirement for all benefits.

Who has a right to reside as a jobseeker

If you are an EEA national, you have a right to reside as a jobseeker if:[41]
- you are in the UK and you can provide evidence that you are seeking employment and have a 'genuine chance of being engaged';

- you entered the UK in order to seek employment, or (under the UK EEA Regulations only) you are present in the UK seeking employment immediately after having a right to reside as a worker (except if you retained worker status while involuntarily unemployed – see p150), a student, a self-employed or self-sufficient person; *and*
- (EEA Regulations only[42]) either you have not already had a right to reside as a jobseeker for 91 days or, if you have, the evidence you provide to show that you are seeking employment and have a genuine chance of being engaged is 'compelling' (see p137).

If you *previously* had a right to reside as a jobseeker for 91 days, or you retained worker status while involuntarily unemployed (see p150) for at least six months, in order to have a right to reside as a jobseeker, under the EEA Regulations (unless you have been absent from the UK continuously for at least 12 months since having either residence right), you must:[43]

- have since had an absence from the UK. **Note:** the benefit authorities have not been enforcing this requirement, except in a very few recent cases, but this approach could become more widespread; *and*
- provide 'compelling' (see p137) evidence that you are seeking employment and have a genuine chance of being engaged from the start of your current period of residence as a jobseeker.

Note: if you are refused benefit because of a requirement that is in the EEA Regulations only, you may be able to challenge the decision on the basis that these interpret the category of jobseeker more narrowly than the Court of Justice of the European Union (CJEU).[44]

Croatian, A2 and A8 nationals

If you are a Croatian national subject to worker authorisation (see p131), you do *not* have a right to reside as a jobseeker.[45] Similarly if, during the relevant period of restrictions, you were an A2 national who was subject to worker authorisation (see p131) or an A8 national who was required to register your work (see p132), you did not have a right to reside as a jobseeker (see p130).[46]

For how long do you have a right to reside as a jobseeker

There is no time limit on how long you can have a right to reside as a jobseeker. It continues for as long as you can provide evidence that you are continuing to seek work and have a genuine chance of being engaged.[47]

However, under the EEA Regulations, in order to continue to have a right to reside as a jobseeker for longer than 91 days, you must provide 'compelling' evidence that you are continuing to seek work and have a genuine chance of being engaged. The benefit authority ends your entitlement if it decides you fail this requirement. It is known as the 'genuine prospects of work test' (see p137).

Evidence requirements

To have a right to reside as a jobseeker, you must provide evidence that you are continuing to seek work and have a genuine chance of being engaged.

See p140 for the type of employment you must be seeking and have a genuine chance of obtaining.

Under the EEA Regulations (but not European Union (EU) law), the evidence that you are looking for work, and have a genuine chance of being engaged, must be 'compelling':[48]

- to continue to have a right to reside as a jobseeker for more than 91 days;
- from the *start* of your period of residence as a jobseeker (unless you have since been absent from the UK for a period of at least 12 months – see note below) if you previously:
  – had a right to reside as a jobseeker for a total of 91 days; *or*
  – retained worker status while involuntarily unemployed (see p150) for at least six months.

Note:
- If you have had an absence from the UK for a continuous period of at least 12 months, on your return you can have 91 days with a right to reside as a jobseeker before your evidence must be 'compelling'.[49]
- The EEA Regulations require that before you can have a right to reside as a jobseeker, you must have been absent from the UK since either of the above applied.[50] However, the benefit authorities have not been enforcing this requirement, except in a very few recent cases, but this approach could become more widespread.
- The EEA Regulations also require that, in order to retain worker status while involuntarily unemployed, you must provide evidence that you are continuing to seek work and have a genuine chance of being engaged, and that after six months, this evidence must be 'compelling' (see p150).

Genuine prospects of work test

'Genuine prospects of work test'
The **'genuine prospects of work test'** is a term used by the benefit authorities, including in their guidance. It refers to the requirement in the EEA Regulations for the evidence that you are continuing to seek work and have a genuine chance of being engaged to be 'compelling' after 91 days as a jobseeker or six months as someone with worker status retained on the basis that you are involuntarily unemployed.
Although the terms and the detail of the guidance emphasise the need for evidence that you have a 'genuine chance of being engaged' over the need for evidence that you are continuing to seek work, the EEA Regulations require both.

If you are asked to provide compelling evidence to satisfy the 'genuine prospects of work test', or you are told that you have failed to do so, note the following.

- First check whether this test should be applied to you. If you have a right to reside *other than* as either a jobseeker or because you have retained worker status on the basis of involuntary unemployment, the test does not apply to you at any point.[51] You can continue to receive the benefit or tax credit you are claiming for as long as your other residency right continues. However, this is frequently overlooked. If you have another right to reside, make sure that the DWP or HM Revenue and Customs (HMRC) is aware of this and make it clear that. your other residency right means that the test should not be applied to you. **Note:** if you are claiming benefit while working part time, provided this work gives you worker (see p142) or self-employed status (see p159), the guidance to decision makers confirms you are not subject to the genuine prospects of work test.[52]

- Also check whether the test has been applied to you at the right time. If your only right to reside is as a jobseeker, the test will be applied to you after 91 days.[53] However if you *previously* had a right to reside as a jobseeker for 91 days, the test will be applied to you from the first day of this current period of residence as a jobseeker unless since then you have had an absence from the UK of a continuous period of 12 months. **Note:** although you are required to provide compelling evidence after 91 days, in practice, the decision maker only counts the period when you were entitled to income-based or contribution-based jobseeker's allowance (JSA).[54] Guidance to decision makers states that certain periods can be disregarded when calculating the 91-day period, including up to 13 weeks when you are treated as being available for work because you have experienced domestic violence, periods of temporary absence when you are treated as being in Great Britain (see p248) and periods of sickness.[55] **Note:** if you have retained worker status on the basis of being involuntarily unemployed (see p150), the test does not apply until you have retained your worker status on this basis for six months (see p152).

- The term 'compelling' is not defined in the legislation and therefore should have its ordinary, everyday meaning. When considering this meaning, the Upper Tribunal has held that your evidence should show, on the balance of probabilities, that you are seeking employment and have a genuine chance of being engaged and that to require a higher standard of proof is contrary to EU law.[56] Under EU law, although you must be able to provide evidence that you are continuing to seek work and have a genuine chance of being engaged, there is no requirement for the quality of this evidence to change after a particular period of time.[57] This was confirmed by the Upper Tribunal, which also held that in determining whether you have a genuine chance of being engaged, a period of six months or more seeking employment without success is a relevant factor to be taken into account, but only one among others.[58] For further details on the argument that the requirement to provide compelling evidence is contrary to EU law, see CPAG's website for a document written before these two Upper Tribunal decisions.[59]

- Ensure that your evidence of seeking employment and having a genuine chance of being engaged is as strong and extensive as possible. Include details of all your work search activities, any interviews or responses, your qualifications, work history (paid and unpaid, both in and out of the UK), skills and abilities that make you employable.

- Whether you have a genuine chance of being engaged requires looking forward, and so future events are also relevant.[60] Provide evidence of any qualifications and experience you expect to get in the near future. If you have appealed against a decision that you have not provided compelling evidence, the tribunal is not prevented from drawing conclusions from events that occurred after the time of the decision about circumstances at or before that time. For example, obtaining a job six weeks after the decision is evidence of your *chance* of being engaged on the date of the decision.[61]

- In rare circumstances, if you have an offer of a job that you cannot take up immediately, but which is being held open for you and is due to start in less than three months, you may have a right to reside as a 'worker' rather than as a jobseeker (see p144).[62]

- If you have been a jobseeker without obtaining work for some time, your evidence must demonstrate that you have a genuine chance of being engaged, despite the long period of unemployment.[63] If your circumstances have changed in any way to increase your current chance of being engaged, you should explain this to the decision maker.

- DWP guidance to decision makers includes lists of examples of relevant evidence.[64] This guidance was rewritten and made less restrictive following two Upper Tribunal decisions.[65] However, the guidance continues to emphasise the need for there to have been a change in your circumstances in order for your evidence to be accepted as compelling, whereas the Upper Tribunal held that a change of circumstances is not an essential criterion, but rather is one factor to take into account.[66] You should not be refused benefit just because your circumstances are not covered by the guidance. If the limited way the guidance is framed caused the decision maker to fail to ask all the relevant questions about your evidence, the First-tier Tribunal may need to ask a broader range of questions.[67] Although DWP guidance is not legally binding and can be disregarded, if it applies to your circumstances, you should still refer to it.

- If your JSA has been stopped because you have failed the 'genuine prospects of work test' and you have a partner, s/he may be able to claim JSA for you both.[68] This does not prevent you challenging the DWP's decision.

- If one benefit authority decides you have failed the test, this decision is not conclusive for another benefit or tax credit claim (see p369).

- While you are challenging a decision that you have failed the test, you should continue to keep evidence that you are seeking work and, if possible, continue to 'sign on' at the job centre. However, if you have not continued to sign on, this cannot be used as a reason not to reinstate your benefit when the decision that you ceased to be entitled to benefit is revised. The Upper Tribunal has held that requirement to sign on lapses once you are notified that you are not entitled to JSA, and you cannot later be penalised for not signing on if that decision is later held to be wrong.[69]
- For further information on the types of evidence that may be helpful, see p383.

Employment you must seek and have a genuine chance of obtaining

In order to have a right of residence as a jobseeker, you must be looking for and have a genuine chance of obtaining employment that would count as sufficient for you to be a 'worker' (see p143) if you obtained it.[70] **Note:** if you are only looking for work on a self-employed basis, because you are establishing yourself as self-employed, you may have a right of residence as a self-employed person (see p159).

In most cases, you should be accepted as seeking employment and having a genuine chance of being engaged if you are 'signing on' and satisfy the requirements to be actively seeking and available for work for JSA, or national insurance (NI) credits, or the work search and work availability requirements if you come under the universal credit (UC) system.

For an explanation of these requirements, see CPAG's *Welfare Benefits and Tax Credits Handbook*.

However, in rare circumstances, it is possible for someone to satisfy these conditions and not be accepted as having a genuine chance of being engaged.[71] If this applies to you, argue that your case is not one of the rare cases where this applies. It may help to look in detail at the requirements that you already satisfy. For example, if you have placed restrictions on your availability, but because you can still show you have reasonable prospects of securing employment, these have been accepted for the purpose of your JSA entitlement, it may be arguable that it is irrational to decide that you do not have a genuine chance of being engaged. This argument was discussed at the Upper Tribunal, but it was accepted that it did not apply in any of the cases in question, and so no decision was required.[72]

There is no change to the type of work you must be seeking and have a genuine chance of obtaining after 91 days, when you are required to provide compelling evidence of this (see p137).

If you do not claim jobseeker's allowance

You do not need to have claimed or be receiving getting JSA in order to have a right to reside as a jobseeker: you must simply be an EEA national and provide evidence that you are seeking employment and have a genuine chance of being engaged.

The most straightforward way of demonstrating that you meet these requirements is to claim contribution-based or income-based JSA on the basis of being available for and actively seeking work or, if you come under the UC system, contribution-based JSA and/or UC (if you have another right to reside – see below) on the basis that you satisfy the work search and work availability requirements, or NI credits on the basis of unemployment.

However, if you are not eligible for benefit or NI credits, or you are waiting for a decision on your claim, or you have not made a claim, you can still have a right to reside as a jobseeker if you provide evidence you are seeking employment and have a genuine chance of being engaged. This could be relevant, for example, if you want to claim child benefit or child tax credit (CTC), or you want to count the period towards the continuous five years required for permanent residence (see p190).[73]

Note: you are only entitled to UC if you have a non-excluded right to reside other than as a jobseeker (see p118). However, if you were receiving UC on the basis of having a derivative right to reside, being able to show that you also had a right to reside as a jobseeker will enable this period to count towards the continuous five years required for permanent residence (whereas the derivative residence right does not count – see p194).

Benefit entitlement

If you have a right to reside as a jobseeker, this satisfies the right to reside requirement for:

- income-based JSA;
- child benefit; and
- CTC.

Note:

- To satisfy the habitual residence test for income-based JSA, you must still be accepted as 'habitually resident in fact' (see p112) and have been living in the common travel area for the three months prior to your claim (see p95).
- You must have been living in the UK for the three months prior to your claim for child benefit and CTC, unless you are exempt from this requirement (see p97).

If you have a right to reside as a jobseeker, this does *not* satisfy the right to reside requirement for:

- housing benefit (HB) (but see p142);
- income support (IS);
- income-related employment and support allowance (ESA);
- pension credit (PC);
- UC.

You must therefore have another right to reside to get one of the benefits on p141.

Jobseekers have more limited benefit entitlement than most other groups with residence rights under EU law. EU Directive 2004/38 states that the host member state is not obliged to provide entitlement to social assistance to those with a right to reside as a jobseeker.[74] However, the UK is required to give EEA jobseekers who have established real links with the UK labour market equal access to financial benefits that are intended to facilitate access to the UK labour market as British citizens.[75] Therefore, the UK provides entitlement to income-based JSA along with child benefit and CTC. Note, however, that if you come under the UC system and your only right to reside is as a jobseeker, this only enables you to be entitled to child benefit.

Housing benefit

If you have a right to reside as a jobseeker, this does not satisfy the right to reside requirement for HB.

However, you are exempt from the habitual residence test for HB (see p108) if you are receiving income-based JSA and either:
- have a right to reside other than one that is excluded for HB (see p118); or
- have been receiving both HB and income-based JSA since 31 March 2014. Your exemption on this basis ends when either you cease to be entitled to that income-based JSA or you make a new claim for HB.[76]

Income-related employment and support allowance

If your only right to reside is as a jobseeker, the UK rules state that this is not sufficient to obtain income-related ESA.[77] Therefore, you should claim income-based JSA instead, if you can.

The Court of Appeal recently rejected an argument that this exclusion from income-related ESA of those whose only right to reside is as a jobseeker is unlawful. The argument was that, because most claimants (other than those entitled to the support component) are required to engage in work-related activity which is intended to assist them in obtaining a job, income-related ESA is a benefit intended to facilitate access to the UK labour market. The CJEU held that financial benefits intended to facilitate access to the UK labour market must be made available to EEA jobseekers who have established real links with the UK labour market on an equal basis to British citizens.[78] However, the Court of Appeal, in a decision that is not being appealed further, held that income-related ESA was not a benefit intended to facilitate access to the UK labour market.[79]

---

8. **Workers**

If you are a European Economic Area (EEA) national working in the UK, you may have a right to reside as a 'worker' (see p143). You may also have a right to reside if you are a family member (see p170) of a worker. Once you have established worker status, it is important to be clear when you cease to be a worker (see p148). In limited circumstances, you can retain your worker status after you stop being a worker (see p149).

If you have a right to reside as a worker, as someone who has retained worker status, or as the family member of a worker, your right to reside satisfies the right to reside requirement for all benefits.

Who has a right to reside as a worker

If you are an EEA national and a 'worker', you have a right to reside.[80]

The term 'worker' is not defined in European Union (EU) legislation and the EEA Regulations cross-refer to EU law.[81] It should therefore be interpreted in accordance with EU law, including the principles established through EU caselaw.

You count as a 'worker' if:

- you are in an employment relationship (see p144); *and*
- the work you do entails activities that are 'genuine and effective', rather than 'marginal and ancillary' (see p146).

The reason why you moved to the UK is irrelevant, provided you meet the above conditions.[82] For example, if your principal intention in coming to the UK was to pursue a course of study, this is not relevant when determining whether you are a worker.[83]

Your motives for seeking employment can be taken into account when determining whether you are pursuing activity as an employed person. However, once it is established that you are, your motives are irrelevant.[84]

Note: if you have been a worker, you do not necessarily lose this status just because you stop working. For more information on when you cease to be a worker see p148, and for the circumstances in which you can retain your worker status, see p149.

Croatian, A2 and A8 nationals

If you are a Croatian national subject to worker authorisation, you do not have a right to reside as a worker unless you hold an accession worker authorisation document and you are working in accordance with it (see p133).[85]

Similarly, if, during the period of restrictions (1 January 2007 to 31 December 2013), you were an A2 national who was subject to worker authorisation, you did not have a right to reside as a worker unless you held an accession worker authorisation document and worked in accordance with it (see p133).[86]

Before the restrictions ended, if you were an A8 national who was required to register your work, you did not have a right to reside as a worker unless you were working for an 'authorised employer' (see p133).[87] The Upper Tribunal has held that the restrictions on A8 nationals ended on 30 April 2009 and their extension to 30 April 2011 was unlawful (see p129). This means that if, before this judgment, you were not accepted as having worker status during these two years because you were not working for an 'authorised employer', you can retrospectively be accepted as having had worker status during this period. However, the DWP's appeal against this decision is due to be heard in the Court of Appeal[88] and guidance to decision makers advises that they 'stay' (not decide) any claims in which this two-year period is relevant, pending the outcome of the appeal, and that they invite the First-tier Tribunal to do the same.[89] See CPAG's online service and *Welfare Rights Bulletin* for updates.

Guidance to decision makers

Since March 2014, decision makers are advised to follow a two-tier process when determining whether or not someone is, or was, a worker (or self-employed).[90] Although this guidance is not legally binding, it is helpful to know its content either to offset potential problems before your claim is decided or to challenge an incorrect decision more effectively.

Firstly, the decision maker must establish whether your average gross earnings reach a 'minimum earnings threshold' equal to the level at which you start to pay national insurance contributions (called the 'primary earnings threshold'). This is £157 a week (£680 per month) in 2017/18. If your average gross earnings were at or above this amount for a continuous period of three months immediately before you claim benefit, you are automatically accepted as a worker (or self-employed).

If your earnings were below this threshold during the relevant three-month period, the decision maker should then assess your case and take into account all your circumstances to determine whether your activity was genuine and effective and not marginal and ancillary, and whether you are a worker (or self-employed).[91]

This guidance is clear that if you are not automatically accepted as a worker (or self-employed) under the first tier, the decision maker should then assess all your circumstances in relation to the criteria set out below. You should not be told that you are not a worker (or self-employed) just because you have not met the 'minimum earnings threshold' for three months.

Employment relationship

You count as being in an 'employment relationship' if you:[92]
- provide services;
- receive remuneration in return for those services (see p145);
- perform your work under the direction of another person (see p145).

The services you provide must entail activities that are 'genuine and effective' as opposed to 'marginal and ancillary' (see p146).

Although, in general, your employment must have begun for you to be a worker, you may be a worker if you have moved to the UK to take up a job offer and it is not possible for you to begin work immediately but the offer is being held open for you.[93]

What counts as remuneration

In order to be a worker, you must receive 'remuneration' in return for the services you provide.

If you do voluntary work and receive payments for expenses, you are not a worker.[94] This is because the payments you receive are not provided in return for the services you perform, but rather to compensate you for the expenses you have incurred in providing them.

You can still count as a worker if the remuneration you receive is in the form of payment in kind rather than, or in addition to, in money.[95]

Working under the direction of another person

To count as a worker, you must perform the services for, and under the direction of, someone else – ie, there must be someone who can tell you how to do the work. If you provide services in return for remuneration and you are not under the direction of another person, you count as self-employed (see p159) rather than a worker.[96]

If you are taxed as a self-employed person, this by itself does not prevent you from being in an employment relationship, although it is a relevant factor. For example, many people who work in the construction industry and pay tax as subcontractors under the Construction Industry Scheme clearly provide services in return for payment and while at work are under the direction of another person. They are therefore workers and not self-employed.

It does not matter whether the person or organisation that provides the remuneration is the same as the person or organisation to whom you provide services.[97]

'Cash in hand', agency and 'trafficked' work

You count as being in an employment relationship if you provide services in return for renumeration under the direction of another person. This is not affected by the fact that:

- you are paid 'cash in hand'. The concept of 'worker' is an economic status, rather than a legal one.[98] However, you must still provide evidence of your employment;
- you were 'trafficked' into the work. Even if you could get discretionary leave to remain in the UK as a result of the trafficking (which would mean you were exempt from the habitual residence test for means-tested benefits – see p108), this does not prevent you from establishing worker status on the basis of your work.[99] You still need to provide evidence of your employment;
- you did not declare the work to the DWP at the time.[100] This is likely to be most relevant when you are relying on past periods of employment;

- the person or organisation to whom you provide the services is different from the person or organisation that pays you for these – eg, if you are 'employed' by an employment agency.[101] However, the activities entailed in your provision of services must still be accepted as genuine and effective rather than marginal and ancillary (see below and, in particular p147, regarding the regularity of the work). There is nothing inherent in working for an agency that would exclude this and it depends on the facts of each case.[102]

Example
Nora is a Hungarian national working as a nurse 'employed' by an employment agency. The payment she receives is via the agency, but the services are provided to a private care home. The care home has a contractual relationship with the agency, rather than with Nora, and it pays the agency. Nora still counts as a worker because she is providing services and doing so in return for remuneration, even though there is a separation between the care home where she provides the services and the agency that pays her.

For your worker status to be accepted, you must provide evidence of your employment and this may be harder to do in some of the circumstances above, such as if you are paid 'cash in hand' or you were trafficked into the work. The benefit authority must take your own account of your work into account as evidence, unless it is self-contradictory or inherently improbable (see p367). If you have provided details of your employment to another government agency and these have been accepted (eg, to the police as part of an investigation of trafficking), a record of these should be accepted as relevant evidence when determining whether you have worker status.[103] See Chapter 20 for more information on evidence requirements and p381 for evidence of your work.

'Genuine and effective', not 'marginal and ancillary'

Even if you are in an employment relationship, you only have a right to reside as a worker if the services you provide entail activities that are 'genuine and effective', as opposed to those that are on such a small scale as to be regarded as 'marginal and ancillary'.[104]

When deciding this, the decision maker must must assess, as a whole, all the circumstances of your case.[105] See p144 for details of the guidance issued to decision makers. Relevant factors that must be considered include:

- the number of hours you work;
- the duration of your employment;
- the level of earnings;
- whether the work is regular or erratic;
- other employment rights;
- whether the work is not for the economic benefit of the employer or is just a small part of a larger relationship between the parties.

Number of hours worked

The number of hours you work in a given period is a relevant factor in determining whether your work is genuine and effective. There is no minimum number of hours you must work. Provided the other factors indicate that the work is genuine and effective, even work for a very small number of hours can count as genuine and effective.

In one case, the Court of Justice of the European Union held that, following an overall assessment of the employment relationship in question, the possibility could not be ruled out that someone who worked only 5.5 hours a week could be a worker.[106] However, in most circumstances, you must work for more than 5.5 hours a week for your activity to be accepted as genuine and effective. In one case, someone working as an au pair for 13 hours a week for £35 per week plus board and lodging for 5.5 weeks was held to be a worker.[107]

The duration of employment

The duration of the employment is a relevant factor to consider when deciding whether or not your work is genuine and effective. However, it is not conclusive, so if your work only lasts a short time, this fact by itself cannot exclude you from being a worker.[108]

Provided other factors indicate that the work you do is genuine and effective, even very short periods of work can still be sufficient to mean that you have the status of being a worker while doing this work. In one case, the Court of Appeal found that someone was a worker during work which was, and was always known to be, of two weeks' duration.[109] Although a short duration of employment that was fixed from the outset may not be a barrier to being a worker,[110] work that is curtailed prematurely may be more likely to be considered to be genuine and effective.[111]

Level of earnings

If the level of earnings from your employment is very low, this may be a factor that indicates that your work is not genuine and effective. However, low earnings cannot, by themselves, prevent you from being a worker. Even if the level of your earnings is so low that they do not meet your needs and you supplement them by claiming means-tested benefits, this does not prevent you from being a worker.[112]

Note: your earnings can include non-monetary payments in kind (see p145).

Irregular or erratic work

If you are in an employment relationship in which you are only occasionally called upon to work, this may indicate that the work is not genuine and effective. However, the decision maker must always look at all your circumstances. There is nothing inherent in an 'on-call' or 'zero-hour' contract that prevents you from being a worker; it depends on the work that you do.[113] Similarly, there is nothing inherent in doing temporary work for an agency that prevents you from being a worker. If the work is regular, rather than intermittent, and for a prolonged period or with a high likelihood of further work being obtained, you may be a worker.[114]

Other employment rights

Other contractual issues, such as the fact that you have a right to paid holidays or payment in the event of sickness, or that you are a member of a trade union recognised by your employer, are factors that may indicate that the employment is genuine and effective.[115]

Work not for an economic purpose or part of a wider relationship

Work may count as 'marginal' or 'ancillary' if it is done as part of some other relationship which is more significant, such as if a lodger performs a small task for her/his landlord as part of the terms of her/his tenancy.[116]

Work does not count as 'genuine and effective' if its main purpose is not for the economic benefit of the employer – eg, if the work is a means of rehabilitation to enable people with health problems to reintegrate into the labour market. Similarly, fostering children or caring for a person with disabilities have been held not to be economic activities and receipt of a fostering allowance or carer's allowance does not amount to remuneration in a commercial sense.[117]

Ceasing to be a worker

You only cease to be a worker when the employment relationship (see p144) ends. While you are still under a contract of employment, you continue to be a worker. Consequently, you are still a worker if you are a woman on maternity leave (including unpaid maternity leave), or if you are on holiday leave or sick leave (including if it is unpaid).[118]

If you have ceased to be a worker, you may retain your worker status in certain circumstances (see p149).

Benefit entitlement

You have a right to reside for as long as you continue to be a worker. See below for the circumstances in which you can retain your worker status after you have ceased to be a worker.

If you have a right to reside as a worker, or as a family member (see p170) of a worker, this satisfies the right to reside requirement for all benefits that have such a requirement (see p117). You are also exempt from the habitual residence test for means-tested benefits (see p108). You therefore do not need to be 'habitually resident in fact' nor to have lived in the common travel area for the three months prior to your claim for income-based jobseeker's allowance. You are also exempt from the requirement to have been living in the UK for the past three months for child benefit and child tax credit (see p95).

Note: to claim benefit on the basis of being a worker, or the family member of a worker, you must provide evidence of this (see p381).

9. Retaining worker status

You can retain the status of 'worker', even though you are no longer working if:[119]
- you are involuntarily unemployed and registered as a jobseeker (see p150);
- you are undertaking vocational training (see p155);
- you are temporarily unable to work because of an illness or accident (see p155);
- you are unable to work because you are in the late stages of pregnancy or have just given birth (see p156).[120]

Before arguing that you have retained your worker status, check whether you have ceased to be a worker (see p148). For example, if you are off work on unpaid sick leave but you can return to your job when you are better, you are still a worker and so do not need to argue that you have retained your worker status.

It may also be possible to argue that you can retain your worker status in other circumstances to those listed above. The Court of Justice of the European Union has held that European Union (EU) Directive 2004/38 does not provide an exhaustive list of the circumstances in which a worker who is not longer in an employment relationship can continue to have the rights of a worker.[121]

Croatian, A2 and A8 nationals

If you are a Croatian national subject to worker authorisation (see p130), you cannot retain your worker status in the ways described in this section. Similarly, if you were an A2 national subject to worker authorisation (see p130), or an A8 national who was required to register (see p130), you could not retain your worker status in the ways described in this section. However, if you were an A8 national required to register and you stopped working during the first month of employment, you could retain your worker status in the ways described in this section for the remainder of that month.[122]

The Upper Tribunal has held that the restrictions on A8 nationals ended on 30 April 2009, since their extension to 30 April 2011 was held to be unlawful (see p129). This means that if, before this judgment, you were not accepted as retaining your worker status during these two years because you were subject to restrictions, you can retrospectively be accepted as having retained your worker status during this period. However, the DWP's appeal against this decision is due to be heard in the Court of Appeal[123] and guidance issued to decision makers advises that they 'stay' (not decide) any claims in which this two-year period is relevant, pending the outcome of the appeal, and that they invite the First-tier Tribunal to do the same.[124] See CPAG's online service and *Welfare Rights Bulletin* for updates.

You are involuntarily unemployed and registered as a jobseeker

Under **EU Directive 2004/38**, you retain your status as a worker if you:[125]

- are recorded as involuntarily unemployed (see below); *and*
- have registered yourself as a jobseeker with the relevant employment office (see p151).

In addition to the above, under the **EEA Regulations** you must also:[126]
- provide evidence that you are seeking employment and have a genuine chance of being engaged. To retain your worker status while involuntarily unemployed beyond six months, this evidence must be 'compelling' (see p151); *and*
- either:
  - have entered the UK in order to seek employment; *or*
  - be present in the UK seeking employment immediately after having a right to reside as a worker (except if you retained your worker status on this basis), a student, or a self-employed or self-sufficient person.

Note: if you are refused benefit on the basis that you do not satisfy the additional requirements of the EEA Regulations, you should challenge the decision on the basis that these are not requirements under EU law.

Involuntary unemployment

You are 'involuntarily unemployed' if you are seeking and are available to take up a job. This depends on your remaining in the labour market. The circumstances in which you left your last job, including whether you left voluntarily, are relevant in determining whether you remained in the labour market. However, they are just one factor and your actions and circumstances, both at the time of leaving work and since then, should also be taken into account.[127]

Example
Karl is German. He was working at food processing factory for seven months. The shift times have changed recently, which means that when he is on late shifts he now has to catch three buses to get home from work. He finds this commute exhausting and asks his employer if he can just do the early shift when the bus connections are better. His employer says that all employees must work both early and late shifts, so Karl hands in his notice. Even while working his notice, Karl looks for other alternative work closer to home. He does not find any, but once his job ends he spends more time contacting potential employers. Karl counts as involuntarily unemployed, despite the fact that he left his previous employment voluntarily.

Registering as a jobseeker

You must register as a jobseeker with the 'relevant employment office'. In the UK, this is Jobcentre Plus.

The best way to register as a jobseeker is to claim jobseeker's allowance (JSA) and/or universal credit (UC) if you come under the UC system, and keep signing on to confirm that you are available for and actively seeking work, or that you satisfy the work search and work availability requirements. If you are not entitled to benefit, contact the job centre and claim national insurance credits on the basis of unemployment. You do not need to receive JSA or UC in order to be registered as a jobseeker.

You may also satisfy the requirement to register as a jobseeker if you claim a different benefit, such as income support (IS), and you declare to the job centre in the course of making your claim that you are looking for work – eg, by stating this on your claim form or on your habitual residence questionnaire.[128] You should provide evidence of your work search. **Note:** this way of registering as a jobseeker is only relevant to retaining your worker status and claiming benefit on the basis of having a right to reside as a worker. It does not enable you to claim benefits, such as IS, if your only right to reside is as a jobseeker.

For how long can you retain worker status

The length of time you can retain your worker status while involuntarily unemployed depends on whether or not you have already been employed in the UK for more than a year.

Under EU Directive 2004/38, if you were employed for more than a year, you can retain your worker status on this basis indefinitely, until there is an event that indicates that you have entirely withdrawn from the labour market.[129] Receipt of maternity allowance by a woman who remained registered with employment agencies has been held not to be such an event.[130]

In order to be employed for more than a year, you need not have been in one continuous job. Also, small gaps between jobs (such as around two weeks) do not necessarily mean that you were not employed for more than a year.[131]

Under the EEA Regulations, to retain your worker status while involuntarily unemployed, you must provide evidence that you are seeking employment and have a genuine chance of being engaged. If you were employed for more than a year, to continue to retain your worker status on this basis for longer than a continuous period of six months, this evidence must be 'compelling'.[132] This requirement is known as the 'genuine prospects of work test' (see p152).

If you were employed for less than a year, the EEA Regulations limit the period during which you can retain your worker status while involuntarily unemployed to a maximum of six months.[133] The EU Directive allows you to retain worker status for no less than six months.[134]

Once you have ceased to retain your worker status on this basis (eg, after six months, if you had worked for less than a year) you may be able to have a right to reside as a jobseeker (see p135). However, under the the EEA Regulations, you must:[135]

- have a period of absence from the UK. **Note:** at the time time of writing, the benefit authorities have not been enforcing this absence requirement except in a very few recent cases, but this approach could become more widespread; *and*
- (unless your absence was for at least 12 continuous months), provide 'compelling' evidence of seeking employment and having a genuine chance of being engaged from the start of your period of residence as a jobseeker (see p137).

Evidence requirements after six months

If you have been employed for more than a year, in order to continue to retain your worker status on the basis of being involuntarily unemployed for longer than a continuous period of six months under the EEA Regulations, you must provide 'compelling' evidence that you are continuing to seek work and have a genuine chance of being engaged.[136] This requirement is known as the 'genuine prospects of work test'.

There is no requirement to provide compelling evidence (nor is there any other change to the requirements) after six months of retaining your worker status on the basis of being involuntarily unemployed under EU Directive 2004/38. Consequently, it is arguable that this requirement under the EEA Regulations is contrary to EU law.

If you are asked to provide compelling evidence to show that you satisfy the 'genuine prospects of work test', or you are told that you have failed to do so, note the following.

- First check whether this test should be applied to you. If you have a right to reside other than retained worker status on the basis of involuntary unemployment (or as a jobseeker), the test does not apply to you at any point.[137] You can continue to receive the benefit or tax credit you are claiming for as long as your other right to reside continues. However, this is frequently overlooked. If you have another right to reside, make sure that the DWP or HM Revenue and Customs (HMRC) is aware of this and make it clear that your other right to reside means that the test should not be applied to you. **Note:** if you are claiming benefit while working part time, provided this work gives you worker (see p142) or self-employed status (see p159), the guidance to decision makers confirms you are not subject to the genuine prospects of work test.[138]
- Also check whether the test has been applied to you at the right time. If you have retained worker status on the basis of being involuntarily unemployed, the test does not apply until you have retained your worker status on this basis for six months. If the DWP or HMRC have applied the test after 91 days, this could be because they are assuming that your only right to reside is as a jobseeker.[139] **Note:** in practice, the decision maker only counts the period

when you were entitled to income-based JSA or contribution based JSA or UC.[140] Guidance to decision makers states that certain periods can be disregarded when calculating the 91-day period, including up to 13 weeks when you are treated as being available for work because you have experienced domestic violence, periods of temporary absence when you are treated as being in Great Britain (see p248) and periods of sickness.[141]

- The term 'compelling' is not defined in the legislation and therefore should have its ordinary, everyday meaning. At the time of writing, this meaning had been considered by the Upper Tribunal but only as it applies to the evidence requirements for jobseekers. However, several principles established by the Upper Tribunal are relevant when compelling evidence is required to retain worker status on the basis of involuntary unemployment. The Upper Tribunal held that the requirement to provide 'compelling' evidence means you are required to provide evidence that shows, on the balance of probabilities, that you are seeking employment and have a genuine chance of being engaged and that to require a higher standard of proof is contrary to EU law.[142] In a separate decision, the Upper Tribunal held that when determining whether you have a genuine chance of being engaged, a period of six months or more seeking employment without success is a relevant factor to be taken into account, but only one among others.[143] For further details on the argument that the requirement to provide compelling evidence is contrary to EU law, see CPAG's website for a document written before the above two Upper Tribunal decisions.[144]

- Ensure that your evidence of seeking employment and having a genuine chance of being engaged is as strong and extensive as possible. Include details of all your work search activities, any interviews or responses, your qualifications, work history (paid and unpaid, both in and out of the UK), skills and abilities that make you employable. Evidence of your recent employment that resulted in you having worker status for over a year will be particularly relevant evidence of your genuine chance of being engaged.

- Whether you have a genuine chance of being engaged requires looking forward, and so future events are also relevant.[145] Provide evidence of any qualifications and experience you expect to get in the near future. If you have appealed against a decision that you have not provided compelling evidence, the tribunal is not prevented from drawing conclusions from events that occurred after the time of the decision about circumstances at or before that time. For example, obtaining a job six weeks after the decision is evidence of your *chance* of being engaged on the date of the decision.[146]

- In rare circumstances, if you have an offer of a job that you cannot take up immediately, but which is being held open for you and is due to start in less than three months, you may have a right to reside as a 'worker' rather than as a jobseeker (see p144).[147]

• If you have been looking for work without obtaining any for some time, your evidence must demonstrate that you have a genuine chance of being engaged, despite the long period of unemployment.[148] If your circumstances have changed in any way to increase your current chance of being engaged, you should explain this to the decision maker.

• DWP guidance to decision makers includes lists of examples of relevant evidence.[149] This guidance was rewritten and made less restrictive following two Upper Tribunal decisions.[150] However, the guidance continues to emphasise the need for there to have been a change in your circumstances in order for your evidence to be accepted as compelling, whereas the Upper Tribunal held that a change of circumstances is not an essential criterion, but rather is one factor to take into account.[151] You should not be refused benefit just because your circumstances are not covered by the guidance. If the limited way the guidance is framed caused the decision maker to fail to ask all the relevant questions about your evidence, the First-tier Tribunal may need to ask a broader range of questions.[152] Although DWP guidance is not legally binding and can be disregarded, if it applies to your circumstances, you should still refer to it.

• If your JSA has been stopped because you have failed the test and you have a partner, s/he may be able to claim JSA for you both.[153] This does not prevent you challenging the DWP's decision.

• If you and your partner have made a joint claim for UC and the DWP decides your partner has failed the 'genuine prospects of work test' and therefore ceased to retain worker status, you will have to claim UC as a single person (but your partner's income and capital are taken into account – see p110) and your partner can still challenge the DWP's decision. However, if your partner can derive a right to reside from you as your family member (see p170), the test should not have been applied to your partner as s/he had another right to reside.

• If one benefit authority decides you have failed the test, this decision is not conclusive for another benefit or tax credit claim (see p369).

• While you are challenging a decision that you have failed the test, you should continue to keep evidence that you are seeking work and, if possible, continue to 'sign on' at the job centre. However, if you have not continued to sign on, this cannot be used as a reason not to reinstate your benefit when the decision that you ceased to be entitled to benefit is revised. The Upper Tribunal has held that requirement to 'sign on' lapses once you are notified that you are not entitled to JSA, and you cannot later be penalised for not signing on if that decision is later held to be wrong.[154]

• For further information on the types of evidence that may be helpful, see p383.

You have started vocational training

You retain your worker status if you have either:[155]
- started vocational training related to your previous employment; *or*
- started vocational training and you are 'involuntarily unemployed' (see p150). This applies if you have to retrain in order to find work that is reasonably equivalent to your former employment.[156]

In general, you should be able to argue that any training or study that can assist you in obtaining employment counts as vocational training. This can include a course leading to a qualification for a particular profession, trade or employment or a course that provides the necessary training or skills.[157] A course can be vocational for you even if it is not vocational for someone else – eg, a photography course if you want to work as a photographer.

Training related to previous employment

If you are not involuntarily unemployed, your vocational training must be related to your previous employment for you to retain your worker status. For this to apply, there must be a relationship between the purpose of the studies and your previous occupational activity.[158] The decision maker must take account of all your previous occupational activity in the UK, not just your most recent employment.[159] If you consider that the course you are pursuing is related to any of your previous employment in the UK, explain this relationship in detail to the decision maker and provide evidence.

You are temporarily unable to work because of an illness or accident

You can retain your worker status if you are temporarily unable to work as a result of an illness or accident.[160]

As a result of an illness or accident

To retain your worker status on this basis, your inability to work must be as a result of an illness or accident. The test of your inability to work is unrelated to any test in the benefits system – eg, you do not need to show you have 'limited capability for work' or that you are 'incapable of work'. Instead, the test is whether you can be fairly described as unable to do the work you were doing or, if it follows a period in which you were seeking work, the sort of work you were seeking.[161] You do not need to have claimed a benefit payable on grounds of illness or disability, such as employment and support allowance (ESA), or any benefit at all, to retain your right to reside as a worker on this basis. However, you must provide evidence of your inability to work, such as a medical certificate from your GP.

Your inability to work must be caused by an illness or accident which *you* have. You cannot retain your worker status if, for example, you are unable to work because you are looking after a child who is ill.[162]

Temporary inability to work

Your inability to work must be temporary. This simply means not permanent.[163] It is your inability to work that must be temporary not your health condition, so you can retain your worker status on the basis of a permanent illness or effect of an accident if this fluctuates and causes temporary periods when you are unable to work.[164]

You are considered temporarily unable to work if, taking into account all the available evidence, there is a realistic prospect of your being able to work again and re-enter the labour market.[165]

You are pregnant or have recently given birth

If you have established worker status and you are now not working because you are pregnant or have recently given birth, you may still count as a worker or you may be able to retain your worker status.

You do not cease to be a worker while you are still under a contract of employment (see p148). You are therefore still a worker while on maternity leave, whether or not it is paid. **Note:** this also applies to Croatian nationals from 1 July 2013, and, including during the period of restrictions, A2 and A8 nationals who have established worker status.[166]

If you have ceased to be a worker, you may retain your worker status if you have a pregnancy-related illness that prevents you from working on the basis that you are temporarily unable to work because of an illness or accident (see p155).[167] You can also retain your worker status on this basis if you have another illness, unrelated to your pregnancy, that results in your being temporarily unable to work. **Note:** pregnancy itself does not mean you are temporarily unable to work because of an illness or accident.[168]

Stopping work during the late stages of pregnancy or following childbirth

You retain your worker status if you stop work, or stop seeking work if you retained your worker status while involuntarily unemployed (see p150), because of the physical constraints of the late stages of pregnancy and the aftermath of childbirth, provided you start work again (or seeking work and thereby retain your worker status while involuntarily unemployed) within a reasonable period after the birth of your child.[169] The Upper Tribunal has held that, in most cases, a 'reasonable period' is 52 weeks, although this may differ if your circumstances are unusual.[170]

In most cases, your 'reasonable period', and therefore the period during which you retain your worker status on this basis, starts 11 weeks before your due date. However, exceptionally, it could be earlier if the physical constraints of your pregnancy require you to stop work (or to stop seeking work if you have retained worker status) sooner, and you can provide evidence of this – eg, if you have a multiple pregnancy or if you can no longer carry out particular requirements of your work.[171]

If you intend to work again within a 'reasonable period', you should always make this clear to the decision maker. You should still be accepted as retaining worker status on this basis unless you state you have absolutely no intention of returning to work under any circumstances.[172]

If the basis on which you retain your worker status changes

You can retain your worker status if you are in one of the groups on p149 and continue to do so if you move into another category.[173]

Example

Nikolas is Greek. He worked for 13 months in a hotel. The hotel was losing money and Nikolas was made redundant. He claimed income-based JSA. Five months later, Nikolas became depressed and was unable to carry on looking for work, so he claimed income-related ESA. Nikolas was entitled to ESA because he had retained his right to reside as a worker – initially, as someone who was involuntarily unemployed and who had registered as a jobseeker, and then because of his temporary inability to work as a result of his illness.

There is no limit to the number of times you can change the basis on which you retain worker status. However, if you lose worker status, you cannot regain it without undertaking further employment that is sufficient to give you worker status.

Gaps

If you cease to be a worker and do not retain your worker status, you cannot regain your worker status again. To be a worker in the future, you must acquire that status afresh. However, if there is just a gap between your having worker status and your being covered by one of the groups that can retain worker status on p149, you may not have lost the status of worker. Whether a gap prevents you from retaining worker status depends on all your circumstances, including the length of the gap.

A gap between your employment ending and your registering as a jobseeker does not necessarily mean that you lose your worker status. Its significance depends on whether the length of the gap and the reasons for it indicate that you have left the labour market.[174] If the delay is for more than a few days, all your circumstances (including the reasons for the gap and what you did during that time) should be considered to establish whether there are reasonable grounds for the delay, so that it is not considered an 'undue delay'. The longer the gap, the more compelling the reasons must be.[175]

Arguably, you should be able to retain your worker status if there is a gap between your ceasing work and your being temporarily unable to work because of illness or an accident, since there is no requirement for the illness or accident to be the reason for your ceasing work. You do not need to have been receiving any benefit while you were temporarily unable to work, so if there was a delay before you claimed benefit, this does not necessarily mean there was a gap between your being a worker and retaining your worker status on the basis of your temporary inability to work.

Example

Rita is a Portuguese national who came to the UK a year ago and began full-time work in a restaurant. After eight months she was injured in a cycling accident and so left her job. She did not claim any benefits as she lived with her partner who supported her. She has just separated from him and has made a claim for income-related ESA, as she is still unable to work because of her injuries. Rita provides the DWP with a medical certificate that confirms her inability to work since the date of her accident. She satisfies the right to reside requirement for income-related ESA as she retains her worker status because she is temporarily unable to work as a result of her accident. There is no gap between her retaining her worker status on this basis and her last day of employment.

If Rita lived in a UC 'full service area', she would satisfy the right to reside requirement for UC in exactly the same way.

You can also retain your worker status during a short gap between two different bases on which you can retain worker status. Whether the gap is relevant also depends on your circumstances, the bases you are switching between, the length of the gap and your actions during it.

Benefit entitlement

If you retain your worker status, this satisfies the right to reside requirement for all benefits that have such a requirement (see p117).

If you are a family member (see p170) of someone who retains her/his worker status, your residence rights are the same as if you were the family member of someone who is a worker, and therefore you satisfy the right to reside requirement for all the benefits that have it.

If you retain worker status (or you are a family member of someone who does), you are also exempt from the habitual residence test for means-tested benefits (see p108). You therefore do not need to be 'habitually resident in fact' nor to have been living in the common travel area for three months before your claim for income-based JSA. You are also exempt from the requirement to have been living in the UK for the past three months for child benefit and child tax credit (see p95).

10. Self-employed people

If you are a European Economic Area (EEA) national undertaking self-employed activity in the UK, you may have a right to reside as a 'self-employed person' (see below). You may also have a right to reside if you are a family member (see p170) of a self-employed person. Once you have established your status as a self-employed person, it is important to be clear when you cease to be self-employed (see p161). In limited circumstances, you can retain your status as a self-employed person even after you cease self-employed activity (see p163).

If you have a right to reside as a self-employed person, as someone who has retained status as a self-employed person, or as a family member of a self-employed person, your right to reside satisfies the right to reside requirement for all benefits.

Who has a right to reside as a self-employed person

If you are an EEA national and a 'self-employed person', you have a right to reside.[176]

The term 'self-employed person' is not defined in European Union (EU) legislation and the EEA Regulations cross-refer to EU law.[177] It should therefore be interpreted in accordance with EU law, including the principles established through EU caselaw.

You count as a self-employed person if :[178]

- you provide services;
- you receive remuneration in return for those services (see p145);
- you do not perform your work under the direction of another person (see p145); *and*
- the work you do entails activities that are 'genuine and effective', rather than 'marginal and ancillary' (see p146).

The meanings of the above conditions are the same as they are for workers. The main difference between the definition of a self-employed person and a worker is that the work a self-employed person does is not done under the direction of another person.

Whether or not you satisfy these requirements depends on all your circumstances. For example, in one case, the Upper Tribunal held that someone selling the *Big Issue* was self-employed, as the activities involved were 'genuine and effective'.[179] A subsequent case held that someone selling the *Big Issue* was not self-employed, as his activities were not genuine and effective. However, this decision was largely due to there being insufficient evidence for the whole period, and arguably the tribunal did not give adequate consideration to all the relevant circumstances.[180] Recently, the Upper Tribunal held that the First-tier Tribunal had not made an error of law in finding that someone selling the *Big Issue* was not self-employed because her activities were not genuine and effective. This was because the Upper Tribunal held that the First-tier Tribunal had considered all the relevant factors and not, for example, just looked at the person's low level of earnings.[181]

Fostering children, or caring for a person with disabilities, has been held not to be self-employment because it is not an economic activity and the fostering allowance or carer's allowance received does not amount to remuneration in a commercial sense.[182]

Since March 2014, decision makers are advised to follow a two-tier process when determining whether or not you are self-employed (or a worker).[183] Although this guidance is not legally binding, it is helpful to know its content either to offset potential problems before your claim is decided or to challenge an incorrect decision more effectively (see p144).

Croatian, A2 and A8 nationals

If you are a Croatian national, there are no additional restrictions that apply to you if you are a self-employed person. Your residence rights as a self-employed person are exactly the same as for nationals of any other EEA country.

Similarly, if you are an A2 or an A8 national, no additional restrictions applied if you were a self-employed person during the relevant period of restrictions. Your residence rights as a self-employed person were exactly the same as for nationals of any other EEA country.

For further details of the other restrictions that apply to Croatian nationals and that previously applied to A2 and A8 nationals, see p129.

What is self-employment

Whether you have become self-employed or you have ceased to be self-employed can be harder to determine than whether you have become a worker or you have ceased to be a worker. Unlike a person who is working, a person who is self-employed does not have a contract of employment that can be regarded as starting and ending on a particular date. It is possible that you may count as self-employed when you are setting yourself up to work as a self-employed person. Similarly, you may continue to count as self-employed, despite the fact that you have no work coming in for the time being.

Becoming self-employed

The EEA Regulations define you as a self-employed person if you are established in the UK in order to pursue activity as a self-employed person in accordance with Article 49 of the Treaty on the Functioning of the European Union.[184] The treaty prohibits restrictions on the freedom of establishment, including 'the right to take up and pursue activities as a self-employed person and to set up and manage undertakings'.[185]

However, you must have more than an intention to pursue self-employed activity, and you must provide evidence of the steps you have taken or the ways in which you have set yourself up as self-employed.[186] Exactly what steps you must take depends on the nature of your self-employed activity and on your particular circumstances. It helps if you have registered with HM Revenue and Customs (HMRC) as self-employed. However, if you have not registered, this does not necessarily mean you are not self-employed.[187]

Relevant steps include:

- advertising your services;
- researching opportunities to find work;
- setting up your accounts;
- registering with HMRC as self-employed for purposes of national insurance contributions and taxes;
- obtaining equipment required for the work you intend to do;
- setting up a website for your business.

The above steps are only examples of the sort of steps that can contribute to your having established yourself in order to pursue self-employed activity. You do not have to take any of these particular steps, but the more you have done, the more likely it is that you will be accepted as having a right to reside as a self-employed person.

Note: if you are told that you do not have residence rights as a self-employed person until you have been earning money on the basis of your self-employed activity for three months, this is incorrect. It is likely to be based on an incorrect interpretation of decision makers' guidance (see p144).

Ceasing to be self-employed

If you have stopped all self-employed activity and do not intend to resume that activity, it is clear that you have ceased to be a self-employed person. However, not all situations are as clear as this, and if you stop working, you do not necessarily cease to be self-employed. If you are in a temporary lull, you can continue to be self-employed. Whether you continue to be a self-employed person during a period when you have little or no work depends on your particular circumstances and the evidence you provide.[188]

Factors that are relevant in determining whether or not you have ceased self-employment include:[189]

- the amount of work you have coming in;
- steps you are taking to find new work;
- whether you are continuing to market your services;
- whether you are developing your business in new directions;
- whether you are maintaining your accounts;
- your motives and intentions.

Which factors are relevant depend on the nature of your self-employment and all your circumstances. However, the more factors that show you are still undertaking self-employed activity, the stronger your argument that you have not ceased to be a self-employed person. See below for the benefit implications of arguing that you have not ceased to be self-employed.

If you are temporarily not working because you are sick, you may be able to show that you are still self-employed, rather than needing to show that you meet the rules for retaining your self-employed status on the basis that you are temporarily unable to work due to illness or accident.

If you have ceased to be self-employed, you may be able to retain your self-employed status in certain circumstances (see p163).

Pregnancy

If you are working on a self-employed basis and you become pregnant, you can continue to count as self-employed during your maternity period when you do no self-employed work, provided you intend to resume your self-employment at the end of your maternity period.[190] The Upper Tribunal, in two linked cases, recently emphasised the need for careful fact finding to establish whether self-employment is maintained during maternity leave.[191] This includes establishing whether the self-employment was genuine and effective before the start of maternity leave and what steps are being taken to maintain that self-employment, taking into account all the circumstances, even if little, or no, actual work is done. Only one of the women in these cases was found, on her particular facts, to have maintained self-employed status during her maternity period. The question of whether the other woman could *retain* her self-employed status remains to be determined, taking into account the relevance of European caselaw on retaining worker status when stopping work because of late pregnancy (see p156)[192] and the questions referred to the Court of Justice of the European Union on retaining self-employed status after ceasing self-employment (see p163).[193]

Benefit entitlement

You have a right to reside for as long as you continue to be a self-employed person. See below for when you can retain your status as a self-employed person after you have ceased to be self-employed.

If you have a right to reside as a self-employed person, or as a family member (see p170) of a self-employed person, this satisfies the right to reside requirement for all benefits that have such a requirement (see p117). You are also exempt from the habitual residence test for means-tested benefits (see p108). You therefore do not need to be 'habitually resident in fact' nor to have lived in the common travel area for the three months prior to your claim for income-based jobseeker's allowance (JSA). You are also exempt from the requirement to have been living in the UK for the past three months for child benefit and child tax credit (see p95).

If you are not currently working, but you have not ceased to be self-employed (see p161), you may be entitled to income-based JSA based on your right to reside as a self-employed person, if you are seeking employment and satisfy the other conditions for JSA.[194] This is particularly significant if you are a Croatian national subject to restrictions and therefore with no right to reside as a jobseeker (see p130). It is also relevant if you want to claim housing benefit, as you will then have a non-excluded right to reside (as well as being in receipt of income-based JSA) and so will be exempt from the habitual residence test (see p108).

See p381 for information on providing evidence of self-employment.

11. Retaining self-employed status

You can retain the status of a self-employed person, even though you are no longer working, if you are temporarily unable to work because of an illness or accident (see p164).[195] However, before arguing that you have retained your status as a self-employed person, check whether you have ceased to be a self-employed person, as you may still count as self-employed if you are just in a temporary period with little or no work (see p160).

If you have stopped your self-employment because of pregnancy or childbirth, see p164.

The Court of Appeal has held that you do not retain your self-employed status if you are involuntarily unemployed and registered as a jobseeker. The court also took the view (although it was not the issue being appealed) that you do not retain self-employed status if you are doing vocational training.[196] However questions about whether a European Economic Area (EEA) national who ceased self-employment and registered as a jobseeker can retain self-employed status and, if not, whether exclusion from particular benefits is compatible with European Union (EU) law, have been referred to the Court of Justice of the European Union.[197] See CPAG's online service and *Welfare Rights Bulletin* for updates.

Croatian, A2 and A8 nationals

If you are a Croatian national, you can retain your status as a self-employed person in exactly the same circumstances as nationals of any other EEA country. There are no additional restrictions that apply.

Similarly, if you are an A2 or an A8 national, no additional restrictions applied if you were retaining your status as a self-employed person during the relevant periods of restrictions. The circumstances in which you could retain your status as a self-employed person were exactly the same as for nationals of any other EEA country.

For further details of the other restrictions that apply to Croatian nationals, and that previously applied to A2 and A8 nationals, see p129.

You are temporarily unable to work because of an illness or accident

If you have established self-employed status, but are currently unable to carry out your self-employed activity because of a temporary illness or accident, first check whether you are still self-employed (see p161).

If you have ceased to be self-employed, you can retain your self-employed status if you are temporarily unable to work because of an illness or accident.[198] The circumstances in which this applies are the same as those for retaining 'worker' status on this basis (see p155).

You are pregnant or have recently given birth

If you have established your status as a self-employed person and you are now not working because you are pregnant or have recently given birth, you may still count as a self-employed person or you may be able to retain your status as a self-employed person.

You can remain a self-employed person if you intend to resume your self-employment after your maternity period.[199] However, this will depend on your facts. The question of whether you can *retain* your status as a self-employed person if you have ceased to be self-employed during your maternity period is currently being considered by the Upper Tribunal (see p162).[200]

If you have ceased to be a self-employed person (see p161), you may retain this status if you have an illness, whether or not it is pregnancy related, which means that you are temporarily unable to work (see above). **Note:** pregnancy, in itself, does not mean you are temporarily unable to work because of an illness or accident.[201]

Benefit entitlement

If you retain your status as a self-employed person, this satisfies the right to reside requirement for all benefits that have such a requirement.

If you are a family member (see p171) of someone who retains her/his status as a self-employed person, your residence rights are the same as if you were the family member of someone who is a self-employed person and, therefore, you satisfy the right to reside requirement for all benefits to which this applies.

If you retain your status as a self-employed person (or you are a family member of someone who does), you are also exempt from the habitual residence test for means-tested benefits (see p108). You therefore do not need to be 'habitually resident in fact' or to have lived in the common travel area for the three months prior to your claim for income-based jobseeker's allowance. You are also exempt from the requirement to have been living in the UK for the past three months for child benefit and child tax credit (see p95).

12. Self-sufficient people and students

You have a right of residence as a self-sufficient person if you are a European Economic Area (EEA) national and you, and any family members who do not have an independent right to reside, have:[202]
- sufficient resources (see p166) not to become a burden on the social assistance system of the UK during your period of residence (see p167); *and*
- comprehensive sickness insurance cover in the UK (see p167).

You have a right to reside as a student if you are an EEA national and:[203]
- you are enrolled as a student in a government-accredited college;
- you provide an assurance that you have sufficient resources (see p166) for yourself, and any family members who do not have an independent right to reside, not to become a burden on the UK social assistance system during your intended period of residence (see p167);
- you, and any family members who do not have an independent right to reside, have comprehensive sickness insurance cover in the UK (see p167).

The requirements to have a right to reside as a student are very similar to the requirements to have a right to reside as a self-sufficient person. For this reason, those who have a right to reside as a student are referred to as 'self-sufficient students' in this section. The specific differences that apply to students are on p168.

You can also have a right to reside if you are a family member of a self-sufficient person. **Note:** the definition of 'family member' of a student is narrower than that which applies to family members of other EEA nationals (see p169).

Periods when you have a right to reside as a self-sufficient person or student, or family member of either, count as periods of having 'resided legally' for acquiring permanent residence after five years (see p190). This is the most common way in which periods of residence as a self-sufficient person or student can enable you to access benefits and tax credits, because during your period of self-sufficiency, your resources are likely to exclude you from means-tested benefits. However, this is not always the case (see p167). In addition, your resources would have to be a lot greater to exclude you from child tax credit (CTC) and would never exclude you from child benefit.

Croatian, A2 and A8 nationals

If you are a Croatian national, there are no additional restrictions that apply to you if you are a self-sufficient person or a self-sufficient student. Your residence rights as a self-sufficient person are the same as for nationals of any other EEA country.

Similarly, if you are an A2 or an A8 national, no additional restrictions applied if you were a self-sufficient person or a self-sufficient student during the relevant period of restrictions. Your residence rights as a self-sufficient person or self-sufficient student were, and are, the same as for nationals of any other EEA country.

Note: certain students are exempt from the additional restrictions that apply to Croatian nationals and that applied to A2 nationals for the seven years up to 1 January 2014. You are/were not subject to worker authorisation if you are a student with a registration certificate which states that you cannot work more than 20 hours a week (unless it is part of vocational training or during vacations) and you comply with this. If the certificate confirms that you can work during the four months after the course ends, the exemption continues for this period (see p131).

If this applies to you and you work no more than 20 hours a week, you may have a right to reside as a 'worker' (see p142). In addition, you count as 'legally working' and, after a year of legally working (see p133), you are no longer subject to worker authorisation.

If you are a Croatian national (or an A2 or an A8 national during the relevant periods of restrictions) employed in the UK but without a right to reside as a worker because your work is not in accordance with your worker authorisation document (or, if you are an A8 national, for an 'authorised employer'), you do not have a right to reside as a self-sufficient person on the basis of these earnings.[204]

For further details of other restrictions that apply to Croatian nationals and that previously applied to A2 and A8 nationals, see p129.

Sufficient resources

Your resources must be 'sufficient' to avoid you, and any family members whose right to reside depends on their being your family member, becoming a burden on the social assistance system of the UK (see p167).[205] The government cannot set a fixed amount that it regards as 'sufficient' and must take account of your personal situation.[206]

Your resources are 'sufficient' if they:[207]

- are more than the maximum level you (and your family) can have to be eligible for 'social assistance' (see below); *or*
- do not exceed that level, but the decision maker considers that you have sufficient resources, taking into account your (and those of any family member whose right to reside depends on their being your family member) personal circumstances.

The 'maximum level' is the equivalent of your means-tested benefit applicable amount, including any premiums. Your resources also include your accommodation, so if your resources are more than your applicable amount plus your rent, they should be sufficient. You may also be self-sufficient if your resources are more than your applicable amount and you are provided with free and stable accommodation by friends or family.[208]

You do not need to own the resources that make you self-sufficient. It is enough if you have access to them – eg, if you are supported by someone else.[209]

The source of the resources does not matter.[210] However, you cannot rely on your earnings from your employment in the UK to give you self-sufficient status.[211] In most circumstances, this does not matter as your employment means you have a right to reside as a 'worker', but it is relevant if, for example, you do not have worker status because you do not satisfy the additional conditions imposed on you as a Croatian, A2 or A8 national (see p129). However, you can rely on the earnings of your non-EEA national spouse/civil partner.[212]

Not a burden on the social assistance system

You count as self-sufficient if you have sufficient resources 'not to become a burden on the social assistance system of the UK during your period of residence'.

'Burden' has been held to be an 'unreasonable burden'.[213]

The 'social assistance system of the UK' includes all means-tested benefits.[214] In its guidance, the DWP does not include CTC, but lists all the means-tested benefits (although in the universal credit (UC) guidance, only UC and pension credit are listed).[215]

You must not be automatically regarded as not self-sufficient just because you make a claim for a means-tested benefit. Although a claim could indicate that you do not have sufficient resources to avoid becoming an unreasonable burden on the social assistance system of the UK, the decision maker must carry out an assessment of the specific burden that granting a benefit would make on the system as a whole. This assessment must take all your circumstances into account, including the likely duration of your claim.[216] It is done at the point you make your claim for benefit on the basis of your right to reside as a self-sufficient person – so, for example, you do not need to have had sufficient resources at the start of your period of residence. However, from the point the assessment is carried out, you must show sufficient resources for your intended period of residence, including for five years if permanent residence is sought.[217]

Comprehensive sickness insurance

To have a right of residence as a self-sufficient person, in addition to having sufficient resources (see p166), you must also have comprehensive sickness insurance cover in the UK.

This requirement is satisfied if you have private health insurance.[218] It is also satisfied if the UK can be reimbursed by another EEA state for any NHS costs you incur while in the UK.[219] This usually applies if you are covered by the European

Union co-ordination rules (see p281) and another state continues to be your 'competent state' (see p288) – eg, if you are:

- resident in the UK, but you are working or self-employed in another EEA state;
- resident in the UK, you receive a pension from another EEA state, you do not also receive a pension from the UK, and you are not working or self-employed in the UK (see p290);[220]
- living temporarily in the UK (eg, you are a student on a course in the UK) and during your 'stay' in the UK you are entitled to health treatment in another EEA state because you are insured there.[221]

In these circumstances, you can get a European health insurance card (EHIC) (or if you are working or self-employed in another EEA state, an S1 card). However, this does not, in itself, confirm that you have comprehensive sickness insurance cover in the UK. As with other residence documents (see p375), the card only confirms your rights on the date it was issued; it does not mean you retain those rights if your circumstances change and the UK becomes your competent state. For example, if your presence in the UK ceases to be a 'stay' and you become 'resident' (see p289), holding an EHIC does not mean you have comprehensive sickness insurance because the UK will no longer be able to be reimbursed for NHS costs by the state that issued the EHIC.[222]

Access to NHS treatment where the UK bears this cost has been held not to satisfy the requirement to have comprehensive sickness insurance cover in the UK.[223]

If you have sickness insurance cover but it is not 'comprehensive', you may be able to argue that it is disproportionate to insist on this requirement being met if it is the only barrier to your having a right to reside as a self-sufficient person.[224]

Arguments that it is disproportionate to insist on this requirement when you do not have any sickness insurance have, so far, failed.[225]

If you have difficulty satisfying the requirement to have comprehensive sickness insurance cover, get specialist advice, as this is an area in which caselaw is developing.

Self-sufficient students

You have a right to reside as a student if you are an EEA national and:[226]

- you are enrolled as a student in a government-accredited establishment for the principal purpose of following a course of study (including vocational training); *and*
- you provide an assurance that you have sufficient resources for yourself, and any family members (see p169) who do not have an independent right of residence, not to become a burden on the UK social assistance system during your intended period of residence (see p169); *and*
- you, and any family members who do not have an independent right of residence, have comprehensive sickness insurance (see p167).

The conditions for having a right of residence as a student are therefore very similar to those as a self-sufficient person. The only differences are as follows.

- To have the right to reside as a student, you must be enrolled on a course of study.[227]
- The requirement to have sufficient resources is met by providing an assurance, either by means of a declaration or some other equivalent means that you choose, that you have 'sufficient resources'.[228]
- The definition of family member is different (see below).

The assessment of what counts as 'sufficient resources' is the same as for a self-sufficient person (see p166). This requirement is satisfied by providing an assurance of these resources, but it is not clear what practical difference this makes. Although you may be more easily accepted as having a right to reside if you provide an assurance of your resources at the start of your studies, this does not prevent you from losing your right of residence if your circumstances change. However, such a loss is never automatic and always depends on your circumstances.[229] Also, if you are only likely to need to claim benefits on a temporary basis, depending on the length of your course, it may be easier to argue that a claim does not amount to an unreasonable burden on the social assistance system of the UK (see p167).

Family members

Family member of a student
You are the **'family member'** of a student (once s/he has been in the UK for three months) if you are:[230]
– her/his spouse or civil partner; *or*
– her/his dependent child (regardless of your age); *or*
– the dependent child (regardless of your age) of the student's spouse or civil partner.

The above definition of family member is narrower than that which generally applies (see p171), and only applies if the student does not have another right to reside that can confer a right of residence on you.

If you are the parent/grandparent of a student who has been in the UK for at least three months, or a parent/grandparent of her/his spouse or civil partner, you may be able to be treated as a family member on the basis of being an extended family member if you have the relevant documentation (see p173).[231]

This means that when assessing whether you have sufficient resources, you do not need to take account of anyone who does not come within this definition of family member after you have lived in the UK for three months – eg, your resources do not need to be sufficient for your non-dependent children under 21 or dependent parent living in the UK.

Benefit entitlement

If you have a right to reside as a self-sufficient person, a family member of a self-sufficient person, or as a student or family member of a student, this satisfies the right to reside requirement for all benefits that have such a requirement (see p117).

However, the most common way in which periods of residence as a self-sufficient person or student (or family member of a self-sufficient person or student) can assist you to access benefits and tax credits that require a right to reside is when such periods are used towards the five years of residence required for permanent residency (see p190). This is because during your period of self-sufficiency, your resources often exclude you from means-tested benefits.

Note: it cannot automatically be decided that you are not self-sufficient just because you have claimed a means-tested benefit (see p167).

13. **Family members of European Economic Area nationals**

You have a right to reside if you are a 'family member' (see p171) of a European Economic Area (EEA) national who has:[232]

- a right to reside as a 'qualified person' – ie, a:[233]
  - jobseeker (see p135);
  - worker (see p142), including if s/he has retained this status (see p149);
  - self-employed person (see p159), including if s/he has retained this status (see p163);
  - self-sufficient person, including a self-sufficient student (see p165); *or*
- a permanent right of residence (see p190); *or*
- an initial right to reside (see p134).

You have this right to reside as a family member, whether or not you are an EEA national yourself.

You have a right to reside for as long as the EEA national has one of the above residence rights and for as long as you remain her/his family member. In general, if s/he ceases to have a relevant right to reside or if you cease to be her/his family member, your right to reside ends. However, there are some limited circumstances in which you can continue to have residence rights as a former family member of an EEA national with a right to reside (see p177).

British citizens only give residence rights to their family members in limited circumstances (see p174).

The type of right to reside you have depends on the type of right to reside your family member has. For more information and the consequences of this for entitlement to benefits and tax credits with a right to reside requirement, see p180.

Croatian, A2 and A8 nationals

If you are a Croatian national and a family member of an EEA national with one of the residence rights listed above, you have a right to reside in the same way as a family member of any other EEA national. In addition, this may mean that you are not subject to worker authorisation and that you do not have additional restrictions on your residence rights (see p131).

Similarly, if you are an A2 or an A8 national and during the period of restrictions you were the family member of an EEA national with one of the residence rights listed above, you had a right to reside in the same way as a family member of an other EEA national. In addition, being such a family member could have meant you were exempt from these restrictions (see p131 for A2 nationals and p132 for A8 nationals).

For further details of the other restrictions that apply to Croatian nationals and that previously applied to A2 and A8 nationals, see p129.

Who is a family member

To have a right to reside as a family member of an EEA national who has a relevant right to reside (see p170), you must come within the definition of 'family member'.

Family member

You are a **'family member'** of the EEA national if you are her/his:[234]

– spouse or civil partner;

– child, grandchild or great-grandchild (or child, grandchild or great-grandchild of her/his spouse/civil partner) and you are under 21;

– child, grandchild or great-grandchild (or child, grandchild or great-grandchild of her/his spouse/civil partner) and you are dependent on her/him;

– parent, grandparent or great-grandparent (or parent, grandparent or great-grandparent of her/his spouse/civil partner) and you are dependent on her/him.

If you are not covered by the above definition of 'family member', you can be treated as a family member and have residence rights on that basis if:

● you are an 'extended family member' (see p173); *and*
● you have been issued with an EEA family permit, a registration certificate or a residence card (see p375). If you do not have this documentation, or it no longer remains in force, you are not treated as a family member.[235]

Note: a narrower definition applies to family members of students who have been in the UK for at least three months (see p169).

Spouses and civil partners

Spouses and civil partners are family members. If you are not married to, or in a civil partnership with, your partner, see p173.

You remain a spouse or civil partner if you have separated, including while you are in the process of getting divorced or dissolving a civil partnership. It is only once you are legally divorced (in the UK, when the *decree nisi* is given) or the civil partnership has been legally terminated that you cease to count as the spouse or civil partner of the other person.[236]

If your marriage or civil partnership has been terminated (or if your spouse/ civil partner dies or leaves the UK), in certain circumstances, you may continue to have a right to reside (see p177).

Aged under 21

You count as a family member of a person if you are her/his child (or grandchild or great-grandchild), or a child of her/his spouse/civil partner, and you are aged under 21.

You do not need to show that you are dependent on the person in order to count as her/his family member. Therefore, you do not need to live with her/him or show you are receiving support from her/him, and it is irrelevant whether you do or not.[237]

Example

Greta is a Lithuanian national aged 18. She is eight months pregnant and lives in rented accommodation. She has claimed income support (IS) and housing benefit (HB). Her father is also Lithuanian and is working full time in the UK. Greta has been estranged from her father since she got pregnant. Despite this, she is still defined as his family member, as she is his daughter and is under 21. Greta therefore has a right to reside as the family member of a worker, and this means she is exempt from the habitual residence test for IS and HB (see p108). It also means she satisfies the right to reside requirement for child benefit and child tax credit once her child is born.

If Greta lived in a universal credit (UC) 'full service area', her right to reside as the family member of a worker would mean she is exempt from the habitual residence test for UC and she would have a right to reside for child benefit.

For information on providing evidence of your age, see p380.

Dependent

To count as a family member of someone, you may need to be dependent on that person – eg, if you are her/his parent or grandparent, or child aged 21 or over.

'Dependence' is not defined in the legislation, but caselaw has established a number of principles.[238]

There are only three things you must show in order to establish that you are dependent on a person.

* You receive support from her/him.
* The support you receive is 'material'. If the person is providing you with financial help, paying your bills, buying you food or providing your meals, providing you with accommodation or is providing you with care because you are ill or disabled, this all counts as material support.
* The support contributes to the 'basic necessities of life'.

It is irrelevant if there are alternative sources of support, including potential employment, available to you, either in your country of origin or in the UK.[239]

If you only became dependent on the EEA national in the UK, this does not prevent you from being classed as a family member. It is sufficient that you are dependent at the point when your claim for benefit is decided.[240] **Note:** this does not apply if you are an extended family member on the basis of dependency, for which you must already have been dependent in the country from which you have come (see below).[241]

Receipt of benefit does not preclude you being dependent on someone else, and your dependency should be considered independently of any benefit you claim. A decision maker should not make the 'circular' decision that that you are not entitled because awarding you a benefit that depends on your residence rights as a dependent family member would mean you would to cease to be dependent. Whether you are dependent while receiving a benefit depends on whether or not your evidence shows the three things listed above.[242]

Extended family members

If you do not come within the definition of 'family member' on p171, but you have a partner or relative in the UK who is an EEA national with a relevant right to reside (see p170), you can be treated as a family member, and therefore have residence rights on that basis, if you:

* are an 'extended family member' (see below); *and*
* have been issued with an EEA family permit, a registration certificate or a residence card (see p375) and it remains in force.[243]

Extended family member
You are an **'extended family member'** of an EEA national if you are her/his:[244]
– partner and you are in a durable relationship with her/him; *or*
– relative and:
　– you have serious health problems that require her/his care; *or*
　– you previously were dependent on the EEA national, or were a member of her/his household, in a country other than the UK and you are accompanying her/him to the UK, wish to join her/him in the UK, or you have joined her/him in the UK, and you continue to be dependent on her/him or to be a member of her/his household. Your

previous connection does not need to have been the same as it is now – eg, you may have been a member of her/his household before coming to the UK and then be dependent on her/him on your arrival in the UK;[245] or

– you would satisfy the requirements (other than those relating to entry clearance) of the Immigration Rules for indefinite leave as her/his dependent relative.

The term 'dependent' is not defined in legislation and its meaning is the same as that for a family member (see p172). However, if you are relying on being dependent on (or a member of the household of) the EEA national to come within the definition of an 'extended family member', you must have previously been dependent on her/him (or a member of her/his household) in the country from which you have come.[246]

Before 1 February 2017, you were also defined as an extended family member if you were a relative of the EEA national's spouse or civil partner and:

- you had serious health problems that required her/his care; or
- you previously were dependent on her/him, or you were a member of her/his household, in a country other than the UK and you were accompanying her/him to the UK, wished to join her/him in the UK, or you had joined her/him in the UK, and you continued to be dependent on her/him or to be a member of her/his household.

If this applied, you continue to be defined as an extended family member, provided you have been continuously resident in the UK since 1 February 2017.[247]

It may be arguable that the exclusion of relatives of the EEA national's spouse/civil partner from the definition of extended family member is unlawful under European Union (EU) law. Although not explicitly covered in the EU Directive, the Court of Justice of the European Union (CJEU) has previously accepted that non-EEA national relatives of a non-EEA national man could have rights through his EEA national wife.[248]

Family members of a British citizen

British citizens do not automatically give residence rights to their family members. This is because most British citizens living in Britain do not generally have a right of residence under EU law, so they cannot confer an EU right of residence on their family members.[249]

However, there are circumstances in which a British citizen can have a right of residence under EU law. If you are that person's family member, s/he can then confer a right of residence on you.

The main ways in which s/he can do this are if:

- s/he has resided with a right to reside (eg, as a worker) in another EEA state. On her/his return to the UK, s/he has the same rights as other EEA nationals and can confer rights on you (see p175);

- s/he is self-employed and carries out some of her/his business activities in another EEA state (see p176);
- s/he is a dual British/other EEA state citizen, in limited circumstances (see p176).

In addition, you may have a right to reside in the following circumstances.

- If you are the primary carer of a British citizen who would not be able to continue live anywhere in the EEA if you were required to leave the UK, you may have a 'derivative right to reside' on this basis (see p187). **Note:** having a derivative right to reside is different from having a right to reside as a family member (see p181).
- If you are a non-EEA national joining your family member who is British, and you have been given leave by the Home Office (eg, as a spouse or civil partner), you have a right to reside during that period of leave. This is under domestic immigration law, not under EU law. See Part 2 for more information on immigration law. If your leave is subject to a condition that you do not have recourse to public funds, you are defined as a 'person subject to immigration control' (see p59) and excluded from all the benefits listed on p66, unless you are exempt (see p67).

The British citizen has resided in another state

If you are a family member (see p171) of a British citizen, you have a right to reside as her/his family member if s/he has resided in another EEA state with a right to reside as a worker, self-employed person, self-sufficient person, self-sufficient student or with permanent residency, you resided with her/him in that state and s/he has now returned to the UK.[250]

The EEA Regulations contain these rights, but interpret them more restrictively than the CJEU has done.[251] If your benefit is refused because the decision maker follows the more restrictive interpretation of the EEA Regulations, challenge the decision if the more generous interpretation by the CJEU would give you a right to reside. Get specialist advice.

The British citizen's and your residency in the other EEA state must have been 'genuine', which is more than mere physical presence.[252] The EEA Regulations list the following as being relevant when considering whether residence is 'genuine':

- whether the British citizen transferred her/his 'centre of life' to the other EEA state;
- the length of your joint residence in the other EEA state;
- the nature and quality of your joint accommodation in the other EEA state and whether it was the British citizen's principal residence;
- the degree of your and the British citizen's integration in the other EEA state;
- whether the residence in the other EEA state was your first lawful residence in the EU.

However, when considering whether residence was genuine, the CJEU has focused on whether the conditions for the relevant residence right were satisfied.[253]

In a separate case, the CJEU held that someone who had been a worker in another EEA state and then returned to her/his own state did not need to be undertaking an economic activity in her/his own state in order for her/his family member to have a right to reside.[254] However, the EEA Regulations only give you a right to reside as a family member of a British citizen if s/he *currently* has a right to reside in the UK under the regulations in the same ways as other EEA nationals, but with the following concessions.[255]

- If s/he is a self-sufficient person, the requirement to have comprehensive sickness insurance still applies, but it does not need to cover her/him.
- If s/he is a jobseeker or has retained worker status while involuntarily unemployed, the requirement to have entered the UK in order to look for work or to now be looking for work (see p135 and p150) does not apply.
- If s/he is a jobseeker, s/he is not required to have had an absence abroad since previously having a right to reside as a jobsekeer or having retained worker status while involuntarily unemployed (see p135).

If you are a non-EEA national, the EEA Regulations exclude you from having a right to reside on this basis if the purpose of your residence in the other EEA state was to circumvent the immigration laws.[256]

Note: the current EEA Regulations have been in force since 25 November 2016 and there is no protection if you had established rights under the previous version.[257]

The British citizen lives in the UK and carries out activities in another state

If you are the family member (see p171) of a British citizen who is employed or self-employed in the UK and whose business involves her/him undertaking some activities in another EEA state, you may have a right of residence, depending on your circumstances. This right is not covered in the EEA Regulations or the EU Directive, but is confirmed by the CJEU as coming directly from the Treaty on the Functioning of the European Union. One case concerned a non-EEA national who was the spouse of a British citizen who provided services to recipients in other member states from a business established in the UK.[258] A separate judgment held that a non-EEA national family member of a Dutch national residing in the Netherlands, but who regularly travelled to another member state as a worker, must have a right to reside.[259]

The British citizen also has citizenship of another state

The CJEU has held that a dual British/other EEA state citizen does not have rights under EU law if s/he has never moved between member states, but has lived all her/his life in the UK. Therefore, s/he cannot confer any rights on her/his family members.[260]

Following this judgment, the definition of 'EEA national' in the EEA Regulations was amended to exclude anyone who is also a British citizen.[261] Limited transitional protection was given to family members of dual nationals who had residence rights before 16 October 2012, when family members of someone who had both British and another EEA nationality had the same rights as family members of other EEA nationals.[262] If you had already acquired such a right before this date, it continues in limited circumstances.[263] See p1604 of the 2013/14 edition of the *Welfare Benefits and Tax Credits Handbook* for details.

If you are a family member of a dual British/other EEA state citizen who has previously resided with a permanent right of residence or a right of residence as a worker, self-employed person, self-sufficient person or self-sufficient student in another member state (other than the one of which s/he is a national), and you resided there with her/him, when you both return to the UK s/he may have residence rights and be able to confer these on you in the same way as if s/he were a British citizen (see p175).[264]

It is arguable that the amendment to the definition of EEA national went beyond the CJEU judgment, even taking into account the limited exceptions for family members, because the judgment was specific to someone who had lived all her life in the UK.

Questions on the rights of family members of dual British/other EEA citizens who have moved from another EEA state to the UK, acquired permanent residence and then acquired dual citizenship, have been referred to the CJEU. The Advocate General's opinion advised that, in such circumstances, the conditions for granting residence rights to the family member should not be stricter than those for family members of other EEA nationals.[265] See CPAG's online service and *Welfare Rights Bulletin* for updates.

Former family members who retain their right to reside

In general, if you are the family member of an EEA national who confers a right to reside on you, your right to reside ceases if s/he:

- stops being your family member (see p171); *or*
- no longer has a relevant right to reside.

However, there are some exceptions which mean that you can retain your right to reside in certain circumstances. Whether or not these apply to you depends on the type of right to reside your family member has. **Note:** several of these circumstances may mean that you have other residence rights that could be easier to prove or may apply instead (see p180).

When you may retain your right to reside

You may retain your right to reside if the EEA national who confers this right on you dies or leaves the UK, or if your marriage or civil partnership to her/him is terminated. These rights are in EU Directive 2004/38, but are not exactly reproduced in the EEA Regulations (see below). The decision maker is more likely to accept that you retain your right to reside if you satisfy the requirements of the EEA Regulations, so you should check these first. If you cannot satisfy these, check whether you satisfy the requirements of the EU Directive (see p179). Provided you satisfy the requirements, you can rely on rights under either the EEA Regulations or the EU Directive.

There are several differences in the specific wording of the provisions in the EEA Regulations and the EU Directive that could affect you. The two most significant differences are the following.

- Under the EEA Regulations, you can count periods of residence spent as a former family member who retains her/his right of residence towards the five years of residence required for permanent residence (see p190).
- Under the EU Directive, if you are an EEA national, you retain your right to reside if your relevant family member dies or leaves the UK, or if your marriage or civil partnership to her/him is terminated, without needing to satisfy any other conditions. These rights are not in the EEA Regulations.

European Economic Area Regulations

You retain your right to reside under the EEA Regulations if you are a family member of a 'qualified person' (see p128) or a person with a permanent right to reside (see p190) and:[266]

- that person dies and you are:
  - not an EEA national, but if you were, you would be a worker, or a self-employed or self-sufficient person (or you are the family member of such a non-EEA national) and you resided in the UK with a right to reside under the EEA Regulations for at least a year immediately before s/he died; *or*
  - the child or grandchild of the qualified person (or her/his spouse or civil partner) and you were in education (see p184) immediately before her/his death and you remain in education; *or*
  - a parent with custody of a child in the previous bullet point; *or*
- that person leaves the UK and you are:
  - the child or grandchild of the qualified person (or her/his spouse or civil partner) and you were in education (see p184) immediately before s/he left the UK and you remain in education; *or*
  - a parent with custody of a child in the previous bullet point; *or*
- your marriage or civil partnership to that person is terminated, and you are not an EEA national, but if you were, you would be a worker or a self-employed or self-sufficient person (or you are the family member of such a non-EEA

national), and you were residing in the UK with a right to reside under the EEA Regulations at the date of the termination and:

- the marriage/civil partnership had lasted for at least three years with you both residing in the UK for at least one of those years; *or*
- you have custody of the qualified person's child; *or*
- you have a right of access to the qualified person's child which a court has said must take place in the UK; *or*
- your continued right of residence in the UK is warranted by particularly difficult circumstances, such as your (or another family member's) being subject to domestic violence during the period of the marriage/civil partnership.

You have a right to reside on this basis for as long as the conditions apply to you,[267] until you can acquire a permanent right of residence (see p190).[268] For details on using periods with this residence right to acquire permanent residency, see p193.

European Union Directive 2004/38

The rules under the EU Directive treat you differently depending on whether you are an EEA national (see p127) or not.

You should retain your right to reside under EU Directive 2004/38 if you are a family member of an EEA national who has a right to reside as a worker, self-employed or self-sufficient person, or as a self-sufficient student and:

- the EEA national dies and you:[269]
  - are an EEA national; *or*
  - have lived in the UK as her/his family member for at least a year before her/his death and you are a non-EEA national; *or*
- the EEA national leaves the UK and you are:[270]
  - an EEA national; *or*
  - the child, grandchild or great-grandchild of the EEA national and in education; *or*
  - the parent with custody of a child in education; *or*
- your marriage or civil partnership to the EEA national is terminated and:[271]
  - you are an EEA national; *or*
  - before the termination proceedings were started, the marriage/civil partnership had lasted for at least three years with you both residing in the UK for at least one of these years. Your rights are not retained in this way if your spouse or civil partner left the UK before the termination proceedings began;[272] *or*
  - you have custody of the EEA national's child; *or*
  - you have a right of access to the EEA national's child, which a court has said must take place in the UK; *or*

- your continued right of residence in the UK is warranted by particularly difficult circumstances, such as your being subject to domestic violence during the period of the marriage/civil partnership. Your rights are not retained in this way if your spouse or civil partner left the UK before the termination proceedings began.[273]

Periods when you have retained your right to reside as a former family member are not on their own sufficient to enable you to acquire a permanent right of residence after five years, because you are also required to show that you are a worker, or a self-employed or a self-sufficient person, or you are the family member of such a person.[274]

Other residence rights

If you are covered by any of the circumstances that enable you to retain your right to reside as a family member, under either the EEA Regulations or the EU Directive, or if your circumstances are similar but you do not fit within these rules, check whether similar rights could apply to you. The main ones that might apply are the following.

- If you have had a right to reside in the UK as the family member of an EEA national who has conferred a right to reside on you for five years, you may have a permanent right to reside (see p190).
- If you were the family member of an EEA national who has died and s/he was a worker or a self-employed person, you may have a permanent right to reside (see p197).
- If you are the child of a worker and you are in education, or you are the primary carer of such a child, you may have a 'derivative right to reside' (see p181). **Note:** whereas periods during which you had a derivative right to reside do *not* count towards the five years needed to acquire permanent residence, time spent as a former family member who has retained her/his right to reside under the EEA Regulations *do* count towards the five years (see p190).

Benefit entitlement

Whether your right to reside as the family member of an EEA national satisfies the right to reside requirement depends on:
- the type of right to reside the EEA national has; *and*
- the benefit you want to claim.

Your right to reside is the equivalent of the EEA national's right to reside. This means the following.
- If you are the family member of a worker or self-employed person, you have the same residence rights as if you were a worker or a self-employed person yourself. Not only does this satisfy the right to reside requirement for all benefits that have such a requirement (see p117), but you are also exempt from

the habitual residence test for means-tested benefits (see p108). You therefore do not need to be 'habitually resident in fact' nor have lived in the common travel area for the three months before your claim for income-based jobseeker's allowance (JSA).

- If you are the family member of a self-sufficient person or self-sufficient student, you have the same residence rights as if you were a self-sufficient person or student yourself. This satisfies the right to reside requirement for all benefits that have such a requirement (see p117).

- If your only right to reside is as the family member of an EEA national who has a right to reside as a jobseeker, you have the same residence rights as if you were a jobseeker yourself. If this is your only right to reside, this does not satisfy the right to reside requirement for IS, income-related employment and support allowance (ESA), pension credit (PC), HB and UC (see p117).

- If you are the family member of an EEA national who has an initial right of residence for three months, you have an equivalent right to reside. If this is your only right to reside, this does not satisfy the right to reside requirement for IS, income-based JSA, income-related ESA, PC, HB and UC (see p117).

If you are the family member of an EEA national who has a permanent right of residence, your right to reside satisfies the right to reside requirement for all benefits that have such a requirement (see p117). However, you only have a permanent right to reside yourself (and are exempt from the habitual residence test – see p108) if you are the family member of an EEA national who acquired this permanent residency in less than five years (see p197).

If you have a right to reside as a former family member (see p177), your right to reside satisfies the right to reside requirement for all benefits that have such a requirement (see p117).

Note: to claim benefit on the basis of being a family member, you must provide evidence of this (see p377).

14. Derivative residence rights

You may be able to derive a right to reside from someone with a right to reside without being her/his family member. These rights are not listed in European Union (EU) Directive 2004/38, but are based on other provisions of EU law, as interpreted by caselaw. The EEA Regulations list these rights as 'derivative rights of residence'. However, they interpret them more narrowly in some respects and impose some additional conditions. If these mean you do not have a right to reside, you can rely on the rights confirmed by the caselaw.

Note:
- You cannot count periods when you have a derivative right to reside towards the five years of residence required for permanent residency (see p190).

- Some of the circumstances below are similar to those that enable you to retain a right to reside if you are a former family member of a European Economic Area (EEA) national who conferred a right to reside on you and who has now died or left the UK, or your marriage or civil partnership to her/him has been terminated (see p177). Check whether this may apply to you because, in some cases, you can count periods with a right to reside as a former family member towards the five years required for permanent residence.
- If you do not fit into any of the groups below, but your circumstances are similar, it may be arguable, by applying the principles of derivative residence rights, that you have a right to reside (see p188).

Who has a derivative right to reside

You have a derivative right to reside if you are not an 'exempt person' (see below) and you are:[275]
- the child of an EEA national who was a worker in the UK (see p142) while you were living in the UK, and you are currently in education (see p183);[276] *or*
- the primary carer of a child in the above bullet point and the child would be unable to continue her/his education in the UK if you left the UK for an indefinite period (see p185);[277] *or*
- the primary carer of a self-sufficient child who is an EEA national, who would be unable to remain in the UK if you left for an indefinite period (see p186);[278] *or*
- the primary carer of a British citizen residing in the UK who would be unable to reside in the UK or another EEA state if you left the UK for an indefinite period (see p187).[279] **Note:** this right to reside does not satisfy the right to reside requirement for any of the benefits that have this requirement; *or*
- aged under 18 and your primary carer is covered by either the second, third or fourth bullet points above and s/he would be prevented from residing in the UK if you left the UK for an indefinite period, and you do not have leave to enter or remain in the UK (see p188).

Who is exempt

Under the EEA Regulations, you are excluded from having a derivative right to reside if you are an 'exempt person'.[280] You are an 'exempt person' if you have a right to reside:[281]
- under any other provision of the EEA Regulations;
- as a British citizen or as a Commonwealth citizen with a right of abode;
- as a person with indefinite leave; *or*
- under provisions that exempt certain people from the requirement to have leave – eg, specified aircrew and diplomats.

If you are refused benefit on this basis, but your other right to reside (eg, as a jobseeker) does not enable you to claim benefit, you should challenge the decision on the basis that you are not excluded.

Croatian, A2 and A8 nationals

The rules about derivative residence rights apply to Croatian nationals in exactly the same way as for other EEA nationals, and they applied in exactly the same way to A2 and A8 nationals during the periods when other restrictions applied. However, if you are deriving your right to reside from being a worker's child in education, the primary carer of such a child, or a child of such a primary carer, the restrictions that apply (or applied) to workers could affect you, because they affect who can have 'worker' status.

If a Croatian national is subject to restrictions (see p130), the work s/he does only gives her/him worker status if it is done in accordance with her/his worker authorisation document. Similarly, if an A2 national subject to restrictions worked between 1 January 2007 and 31 December 2013, that work only gave her/him worker status if it was done in accordance with her/his worker authorisation document. If you are the child of a Croatian or A2 national and you are in education, or you are the primary carer of such a child, the work done by the parent must have been done in accordance with a worker authorisation document for it to enable you to have a derivative right to reside.[282]

If an A8 national was subject to restrictions (see p130), the work that s/he did between 1 May 2004 and the date the restrictions ended (see p129) only gave her/him worker status if it was done for an 'authorised employer' (see p130). Therefore, if you are the child of an A8 national and you are in education, or you are the primary carer of such a child, the work done by the parent must have been for an authorised employer for you to have a derivative right to reside. This includes a period when the parent had a valid worker's registration certificate for her/his employer, but s/he did not complete 12 months of working for an 'authorised employer'.[283] It also includes a period in which the parent was in her/his first month of employment, since the first month of any employment, even if it was never registered, counted as working for an 'authorised employer', provided s/he satisfied the requirements of being a worker, including that the work was accepted as 'genuine and effective' (see p143).[284]

For further details of other restrictions that apply to Croatian nationals and that previously applied to A2 and A8 nationals, see p129.

Worker's child in education

A child has a right to reside if:
- s/he was living in the UK at a time when one of her/his parents (or the parent's spouse or civil partner) had a right to reside in the UK as a worker (see p184); *and*
- s/he is now in education (see p184).

The purpose of this right of residence is to enable a child to take up her/his right to be educated in the member state where her/his (step-)parent is employed if s/he is also living in that state.[285] For this right to education to be effective, the child must have a right of residence.[286] The right continues for as long as s/he is a child in education.

The nationality of the child does not affect this right of residence. However, the child's parent (or step-parent) who had the right to reside as a worker must have been an EEA national when s/he was a worker.

The child's parent, or her/his parent's spouse or civil partner, must have been an EEA worker.[287] The child does not have this type of right to reside if the EEA worker is her/his grandparent,[288] a non-parent legal guardian,[289] or her/his parent's partner who is not in a formal legal relationship with the parent.[290]

Who is 'in education'

Caselaw has confirmed that the definition of 'education' excludes nursery education,[291] that a child's rights begin when s/he starts compulsory education at around the age of five (and excludes preschool)[292] or when s/he starts school in reception class, despite being under five years old.[293] The definition in the EEA Regulations excludes nursery education, but does not exclude education received before the compulsory school age if this is equivalent to the education received at or after the compulsory school age.[294]

Differences in Scotland may affect when residence rights begin. Although there is no reception class in Scotland, it may still be arguable that a child can be 'in education' when s/he is approaching age five. Furthermore, as the Scottish Curriculum for Excellence starts at the age of three, it maybe arguable that a child in Scotland can be in education well before the age of five.

Residence rights apply until at least the age of majority while the child remains in education. Residence rights can continue beyond the age of majority. The child's residence rights continue until s/he has completed her/his education. This includes all forms of education, whether vocational or general, and can include university courses. Whether or not the residence rights of the child's primary carer continue after the child reaches the age of majority depends on whether the child continues to need the presence and care of her/his primary carer in order to continue and complete her/his education.[295]

The child must have been in the UK while one of her/his parents (or step-parents) was employed as a worker in the UK, and now be in education. There are no other requirements. For example, the (step-)parent does not need to have continued to be a worker, or have remained in the UK, when the child started school or at any time since then.[296]

Who is a 'worker'

The EEA Regulations state that, for this purpose, 'worker' does not include a jobseeker or someone who retains her/his worker status (see p149).[297] It is arguable that the latter exclusion is wrong. The EU regulation that provides for the right of a child to be educated in a state does so for a child of an EEA national 'who is or has been employed' in another EEA state.[298] Caselaw consistently confirms that a child has a right to reside if s/he is now in education and was in the member state during a time when one of her/his parents was exercising rights of residence in that state as a 'worker' or a 'migrant worker'.[299] It appears from the wording of EU Directive 2004/38 that a person who retains her/his status as a worker resides in a country as a 'migrant worker', as s/he has equivalent rights to 'workers', provided s/he satisfies the conditions for retaining worker status. Also, family members of someone who has retained her/his status as a worker have equivalent rights of residence to family members of workers.

Absence of the child from the UK

A child may lose her/his right to reside as a worker's child in education if s/he leaves the UK but then returns. However, this depends on all the circumstances. The DWP's view is that if a child leaves the UK, other than for a temporary reason, s/he may lose her/his right to education (and her/his associated right to reside) when s/he returns. DWP guidance suggests that, while a substantial period of habitual residence in another EEA state means that the right to education, and hence to reside, is lost, 'an absence that can properly be regarded as temporary will not have that effect'.[300] However, it may be arguable that what matters is whether the child's studies undertaken on her/his return are a continuation of her/his earlier education. The Court of Justice of the European Union (CJEU) has held that a worker's child in education continued to have his rights, despite an absence in which the child went back to his state of origin, because he returned to continue his studies which he could not pursue in his own state.[301]

Primary carer of a worker's child in education

You have a derivative right to reside under the EEA Regulations if you:[302]
- are the 'primary carer' (see p186) of a child of a worker who is in education; *and*
- the child would be unable to continue to be educated in the UK if you were required to leave.

The basis of this right builds on the residence rights of the child, which are necessary in order to be educated in the country where her/his parent is, or was, employed.[303] It is assumed that the child needs an adult to look after her/him and, consequently, her/his primary carer must also have a right of residence.[304] Your rights as the primary carer continue until the child reaches at least the age of majority, and beyond that if s/he continues to need your presence and care in order to pursue and complete her/his education.[305]

You can have a right to reside as the primary carer of a worker's child in education if you were that worker or if the worker was someone else.

Neither you nor the child need be self-sufficient in order to have residence rights.[306]

Your nationality and the nationality of the child do not affect this right of residence.[307] However, the child's parent (or step-parent) who had the right to reside as a worker must be an EEA national.

Who is a primary carer

You are a 'primary carer' of someone if you are her/his direct relative or legal guardian, and either you:[308]

• have primary responsibility for that person's care; or
• share equally the responsibility for that person's care with one other person who is not an 'exempt person' (see p182).

If you share the responsibility for care equally with someone, you will need to explain to the decision maker that the other person is not an 'exempt person'.[309] The question of whether or not the child would be unable to continue her/his education or remain in the UK, or the British citizen would be unable to reside in the EEA, is considered on the basis of both carers leaving the UK for an indefinite period, unless the person with whom you share the care has already acquired a derivative right to reside before taking on the equally shared caring responsibilities.[310] **Note:** a challenge to this exclusion is due to be heard by the Upper Tribunal. See CPAG's online service and *Welfare Rights Bulletin* for updates.

You are not regarded as someone's primary carer solely on the basis of a financial contribution you make towards her/his care.[311]

If you do not come within the above definition of 'primary carer', you may be able to argue that you have rights based on EU caselaw (see p181) – eg, if you are the primary carer of someone who is dependent on you, but you are not her/his direct relative or legal guardian.

Primary carer of a child who is self-sufficient

You have a derivative right to reside under the EEA Regulations if:[312]

• you are the 'primary carer' (see above) of a child under 18 who is residing in the UK as a self-sufficient person (see p165); and
• the child would be unable to remain in the UK if you were required to leave.

The basis of this right of residence is to make effective the rights of the child, as it is assumed that s/he needs an adult to look after her/him and so her/his primary carer must also have a right of residence.[313]

Note: the EEA Regulations treat the primary carer as a family member of the child. Therefore, the child's resources must be sufficient for both her/him and her/his primary carer (see p166 for what counts as sufficient) and both must have comprehensive sickness insurance cover.[314]

Your nationality does not affect this right of residence. However, the child must be an EEA national to have a right to reside as a self-sufficient person.

Primary carer of a British citizen

You have a derivative right to reside under the EEA Regulations if you:[315]
- are the 'primary carer' (see p186) of a British citizen who is residing in the UK; *and*
- the British citizen would be unable to reside in the UK or another EEA state if you left the UK for an indefinite period.

This right of residence is based on the rights provided by Article 20 of the Treaty on the Functioning of the European Union (TFEU) for every person holding the nationality of an EU member state to be a citizen of the EU, and for every EU citizen to have the right to move and reside freely within the EU. If an EU citizen is dependent on another person to make her/his right effective, her/his primary carer must be given a right of residence.[316]

The British citizen, therefore, must be dependent on you, as her/his primary carer – eg, because s/he is a child or has health problems that require another person's care.

The key question is whether the British citizen would be required to leave the territory of the EU (or, under the EEA Regulations, the EEA) if you were required to leave the UK. This is a question of fact, taking all the circumstances into account.[317] However, if you are an EEA national, this will rarely be satisfied because you are able to live in another EEA state and so, other than in exceptional cases, this residence right only applies to non-EEA nationals.

Having a right to reside on the basis of being the primary carer of a British citizen does not enable you to be entitled to any benefit that requires a right to reside (see p117). Since 8 November 2012, it is listed as an excluded right of residence in each of the benefit and tax credit regulations. **Note:** this exclusion is arguably unlawful and although legal challenges have not yet been successful, future ones may be.[318] See CPAG's online service and *Welfare Rights Bulletin* for updates.

However, although this right of residence does not entitle you to benefits that require a right to reside, it can mean that you are not defined as a 'person subject to immigration control' (see p58). This means you may be able to claim attendance allowance, disability living allowance (DLA), personal independence payment and carer's allowance, provided you meet all the other presence and residence requirements (see p218). You may also be entitled to working tax credit (WTC), since you have a right to work in addition to your right to reside and the number of hours you need to work is still determined on the basis that you are responsible for a child (even though you are not entitled to child tax credit (CTC)) – see p227.

Note: if this is your only right of residence and you need to claim benefits that require a right to reside, you should obtain immigration advice, as it may be possible for you to apply for immigration leave on the basis of your right to family life (see p34). If this leave is granted without the condition that you have no recourse to public funds, you are not excluded from benefits, as you are not defined as a 'person subject to immigration control' (see p57) and you have a non-excluded right to reside (see p125).

Child of a primary carer

You have a derivative right to reside under the EEA Regulations if:[319]
* you are aged under 18 and your primary carer has a derivative right to reside as the primary carer of :
  – a worker's child in education (see p183); *or*
  – a child under 18 who is residing in the UK as a self-sufficient person (see p186); *or*
  – a British citizen who would be unable to reside in the UK or another EEA state if the primary carer left the UK (see p187); *and*
* you do not have leave to enter or remain in the UK; *and*
* your primary carer would be prevented from residing in the UK if you left the UK for an indefinite period.

The basis of this right of residence is to make effective the rights of the primary carer and the other child for whom s/he is caring. Your nationality does not affect this right of residence.

Example
Veronika is Czech. She is aged 16, has learning difficulties and is eight months pregnant. She has stopped attending school. Veronika's mother last worked in the UK in 2013. She has a right to reside as the primary carer of Patrik, Veronika's younger brother who is nine years old and in school. Veronika has a derivative right to reside because her mother has to look after her, and if Veronika left the UK, so too would her mother. Therefore, Veronika can claim income support (IS) on the basis of her pregnancy and satisfies the right to reside requirement. When Veronika's baby is born, she will be able to claim child benefit and CTC, and continue to get IS as a lone parent.
If Veronika lived in a universal credit (UC) 'full service area', she would satisfy the right to reside requirement for UC and child benefit.

Other derivative rights

It is arguable that you may have a right to reside if your circumstances do not exactly fit the criteria for the derivative rights on p182, but they are similar and the legal principles underlying derivative residence rights could be applied. For example, you may be able to argue that you have a right to reside in the following situations.

- You are the child of a self-employed person in education or the primary carer of such a child. The question of whether a primary carer has a right of residence was referred to the CJEU in two joined cases.[320] Although the CJEU stated that the provision that gives a right to education in the state where the child's parent has been a worker[321] cannot apply to the child of a self-employed person,[322] it did not consider other possible bases for such a right. It did not need to do so because the UK government conceded that, in each case, the person had a right of residence on another basis. Consequently, when the cases were referred back to the Upper Tribunal, the judge confirmed that the question of whether the primary carer of a (former) self-employed person's child in education has a right of residence remained to be determined in a future case.[323] However, when the same judge did consider the issue in two further cases, he held that the reasoning of the CJEU's judgment made it impossible to find that the primary carer of a self-employed person's child in education has a right to reside, but in the second case gave leave to appeal.[324] This appeal was recently dismissed by the Court of Appeal, which held that the CJEU's decision was conclusive and had not left open the possibility that the principle of non-discrimination might apply.[325] Permission to appeal to the Supreme Court is being sought. See CPAG's online service and *Welfare Rights Bulletin* for updates.
- You are the primary carer of a worker's child who is under school age. Such a child has a clear right to reside as the family member of a worker and, depending on the facts, it may be arguable that you need a right to reside to make the child's right effective.
- You are the primary carer of a child who has a permanent right to reside. The same principles that apply to give other primary carers residence rights arguably apply if the child has permanent residence – ie, to make effective the rights of the child.
- You are aged under 21 (but not under 18) and/or are dependent on a primary carer with a derivative right to reside and s/he would be prevented from residing in the UK if you left the UK for an indefinite period, and you do not have leave to enter or remain in the UK. The EEA Regulations only give a derivative right to reside in this situation if you are under 18.[326]

There may be other circumstances in which you need a right to reside to make effective someone else's residence rights. The strength of your argument always depends on your circumstances and those of the other relevant people, but you may be able to apply some of the principles on which derivative rights are based.

Benefit entitlement

If you have a derivative right to reside (other than on the basis of being the primary carer of a British citizen), this satisfies the right to reside requirement for any of the benefits or tax credits to which that requirement applies (see p117).

If your right to reside is as a result of your being the primary carer of a British citizen, this is specifically excluded for each of the benefits and tax credits that have a right to reside requirement. **Note:** this exclusion is arguably unlawful and although legal challenges have not yet been successful, future challenges may be.[327] See CPAG's online service and *Welfare Rights Bulletin* for updates.

Note: the period of time when you have a derivative right to reside does not count towards the five years of residence required for permanent residence (see pbelow). This means that, unless you have another right to reside, when you cease to satisfy the conditions for your derivative right to reside, your residence rights end, together with your entitlement to any benefits that require a a right to reside.

- -

Example

Rosa is an Italian national who came to the UK in 2010 with her son Roberto. She worked for five months, but left her job because Roberto began to have night-time seizures and was awarded DLA. Rosa then claimed IS as Roberto's carer for a couple of years. Her health deteriorated and so she switched to claiming income-related employment and support allowance (ESA). Roberto is just completing his A levels at school. When he leaves school, Rosa will cease to have a right to reside, as it was based on being the primary carer of a worker's child in education, and her entitlement to income-related ESA and housing benefit will end (even though she has had a derivative right to reside for over five years).

- -

Note: to claim benefit on the basis of having a derivative right to reside, you must provide evidence of this (see Chapter 20).

---

15. **Permanent right to reside**

You can acquire a permanent right of residence after periods of residing with a right to reside in the UK. In most cases, you must have resided with a right to reside for a continuous period of five years, disregarding certain gaps. However, in limited circumstances you can acquire a permanent right of residence after having resided for a shorter period of time (see p197).

Once you have a permanent right of residence, you do not need to satisfy any other conditions[328] (eg, you do not also need to be a worker) and this right of residence satisfies the right to reside requirement for all the benefits that have such a requirement.

You only lose your permanent right of residence if you are absent from the UK for more than two consecutive years (but see p200).[329]

Acquiring permanent residence after five years

You acquire a permanent right to reside if you have 'resided legally' (see below) for a continuous period of five years (see p194).[330]

You can acquire permanent residence whether you are a European Economic Area (EEA) national or non-EEA national, provided you satisfy the criteria. However, if you are a non-EEA national, there are fewer ways in which you count as having resided legally (see p193). If you are a Croatian, A2 or A8 national, additional restrictions may affect you during the years after your country of nationality joined the European Union (EU) and you can only count periods of residence in the UK before your country joined the EU in limited circumstances (see p194).

Legally resided

The EU Directive requires you to have 'resided legally', and the EEA Regulations require you to have resided 'in accordance with these regulations' (or previous regulations), for a continuous period of five years in the UK.[331] In most cases, this makes no difference, and so the phrase 'resided legally' is used in this section and any difference between the EEA Regulations and EU Directive are noted where they are significant.

You always count as residing legally during periods when you have a right to reside as a:[332]

- worker (see p142), including if you have retained this status (see p149);
- self-employed person (see p159), including if you have retained this status (see p163);
- self-sufficient person, including a self-sufficient student (see p165);
- family member (see p171) of any of the above; *or*
- (EEA Regulations only) jobseeker, or family member of a jobseeker, since 30 April 2006 (see p192).

Periods when you resided with another residence right can be more complicated.

Periods before 30 April 2006

The right of permanent residence was only introduced on 30 April 2006 when the EU Directive 2004/38 and the EEA Regulations 2006 came into force. However, you can still count periods when you had a right of residence before 30 April 2006 towards the required five years, if your residence was on the basis of one or more of those listed above (other than being the last bullet: jobseeker or a family member of a jobseeker). These periods of residence must be taken into account because each of the residence rights were listed under earlier EU[333] and UK[334] legislation.

If you completed five years' legal residence before 30 April 2006 and then had a gap of less than two years when you were either out of the UK or residing in the UK but not 'residing legally', this does not affect your acquiring permanent residency.[335] If you completed five years' legal residence and then had a gap of two or more years when you were not residing in accordance with the regulations, see p197. If you completed five years' legal residence and were then absent from the UK for more than two continuous years, you lost your right of permanent residence (see p200).

Jobseekers

You can count periods when you had a right to reside as a jobseeker (see p135) or a family member of a jobseeker from 30 April 2006 towards your five years of residing in accordance with the EEA Regulations.[336] You cannot count periods before this date, as jobseekers were not given a right to reside under earlier regulations. Therefore, if you need to rely on periods when you were seeking work before 30 April 2006, always check whether you had another residence right at that time – eg, if you retained worker status.

Guidance to decision makers confirms that if you have had a right to reside as a jobseeker, including if you have been awarded income-based jobseeker's allowance (JSA) on the basis of this right to reside for a continuous period of five years, this is sufficient for you to acquire permanent residence.[337] It further states that if your JSA is disallowed, the continuity of your legal residence is broken.[338] This is not necessarily correct, as you can have a right to reside as a jobseeker without receiving JSA (see p140).[339] The guidance also confirms that a period when your income-based JSA is not paid because of a sanction does not affect your continuity of residence as a jobseeker.[340]

You cannot count periods when your only right of residence was as a jobseeker, or as a family member of a jobseeker, towards the five years required to give you permanent residence under the EU Directive, as it does not count as 'residing legally'.[341] However, this is rarely a problem in practice since you can count such periods under the EEA Regulations.

Initial right of residence

You can count periods after 30 April 2006 when you had an initial right of residence for the first three months after your arrival in the UK (see p134), or as the family member of someone with an initial right of residence, towards your five years of residing in accordance with the EEA Regulations.[342] You cannot count such periods towards the five years required to give you permanent residency under the EU Directive.[343] There was no initial right of residence under earlier regulations or earlier EU legislation, so it is not relevant to periods before 30 April 2006.

Family members

If you are the family member (see p171) of a person who has acquired permanent residency after residing legally in the UK for five years, you have a right to reside for as long as you remain her/his family member.[344] Under the EEA Regulations, you can also use periods as a family member of a person with a permanent right of residence to count towards your five years of residing in accordance with those regulations, and so acquire a permanent right of residence yourself.[345] This is in addition to any other periods when you have a right to reside through being a family member of an EEA national with a right to reside (eg, as a worker) (see p191).

Note: if you are the family member of a person who has acquired permanent residency in less than five years, you may have permanent residency yourself (see p197).

Former family members

You can count periods since 30 April 2006 when you had a right to reside as a former family member under the EEA Regulations (see p178) towards your five years of residing in accordance with the EEA Regulations. This only applies to periods since 30 April 2006, as this right of residence was not provided under earlier regulations. If you are a non-EEA national, you must have a right to reside as a former family member at the end of your five-year period to acquire a permanent right to reside under the EEA Regulations.[346]

If you have been a former family member under the EU Directive (see p179) for five years, this is not sufficient to enable you to acquire permanent residency under that directive because you are also required to show that you are a worker, or a self-employed or self-sufficient person, or that you are the family member of such a person.[347]

Non-European Economic Area nationals

Periods when you are in the UK with leave to enter or remain do not count as periods of 'residing legally'. They do not count under the EEA Regulations as they are not periods in which you resided in accordance with those regulations and the Court of Justice of the European Union (CJEU) has held that they do not count towards the five years required to acquire permanent residency under the EU Directive.[348]

If you are a non-EEA national, you cannot have a right of residence as a worker, self-employed person, person who retains either of these statuses, a self-sufficient person or a self-sufficient student. However, you can have a right of residence as the family member of an EEA national who is in one of these groups.

In practice, therefore, the only ways for you to acquire a permanent right of residence after five years of residing legally is by either:

- residing for a five-year period as the family member of an EEA national who is legally residing; *or*
- retaining the right as a former family member on the basis of either the death of your spouse or civil partner or the termination of your marriage or civil partnership (see p179).[349]

Note: in limited circumstances, you can also acquire a right of permanent residence in less than five years if you are the family member of an EEA national who has acquired a permanent right of residence in less than five years (see p197).

Croatian, A2 and A8 nationals

If you are a Croatian, A2 or A8 national, you can acquire permanent residency after five years of residing legally in the same way as any other EEA national. However, if:

* you are relying on periods when you were subject to additional restrictions on your residence rights, these may affect whether you had a right to reside as a jobseeker or a worker, or retained worker status (see p129). **Note:**
  – The Upper Tribunal has held that the restrictions on A8 nationals ended on 30 April 2009 and their extension to 30 April 2011 was unlawful. This means that if you were not accepted as having, or retaining, worker status during these two years, retrospectively, these restrictions do not apply. If you would otherwise have had, or retained, worker status during this two-year period, it counts as residing legally. However, the DWP's appeal against this decision is due to be heard in the Court of Appeal.[350] Guidance has been issued to decision makers advising that they 'stay' (not decide) any claims in which this two-year period is relevant, pending the outcome of the appeal, and that they invite the First-tier Tribunal to do the same.[351] See CPAG's online service and *Welfare Rights Bulletin* for updates.
  – The Upper Tribunal has recently accepted, on the particular facts of the case, that it would be disproportionate to disregard the years of work by an A8 national and his subsequent involuntary unemployment, just because he had not complied with the restrictions, and accepted that as a consequence he had acquired permanent residency (see p132).[352]
* you are relying on periods when you were living in the UK before your country joined the EU, you do not count as having resided legally just on the basis that you had leave to enter or remain in the UK. However, you count as residing legally if:[353]
  – you had leave to enter or remain in the UK; *and*
  – you would have had a right of residence as a worker, self-employed person, person who retains one of those statuses, a self-sufficient person or self-sufficient student, except for the fact that you were not an EU national at the time.

Derivative right to reside

Periods when you have resided with a derivative right to reside (see p181) do not count as periods of residing legally, and so you cannot count them towards your five years for the purposes of acquiring permanent residency under either the EEA Regulations or the EU Directive.[354]

Continuity of residence

You acquire permanent residency when you have been 'residing legally' (see p191) for a continuous period of five years.[355] However, the continuity of your residence is not affected by certain absences (see below). It may also be arguable that the continuity of your residence is not affected by certain gaps during the five years when you were in the UK, but did not count as 'residing legally' (see below).

Absence from the UK

When calculating whether you have five years' continuous residence, temporary absences from the UK do not affect the continuity of your residence if:[356]
- they are not more than a total of six months a year;
- they comprise one absence of up to 12 consecutive months for important reasons, such as pregnancy and childbirth, serious illness, study or vocational training, or a posting abroad. These are just examples. If you have one absence of up to 12 months for a similar important reason, it should also not affect the continuity of your residence;[357] *or*
- they are for compulsory military service.

If you have one or more of the above temporary absences from the UK, you can count the time spent abroad as part of your five continuous years.[358] However, you are likely to need to make this argument to the benefit authority, as guidance to decision makers only refers to earlier caselaw that held that time spent abroad during a temporary absence does *not* count towards your five continuous years.[359] In support of your argument, note that the guidance is not legally binding and that the approach of the most recent caselaw (each heard by a two-judge panel rather than a single commissioner) should be followed. The Upper Tribunal recently summarised these alternative approaches, noting that the most recent caselaw has held that the absences abroad counted towards the five years.[360]

Example
Botond is a Hungarian national. In June 2012 he came to the UK and began working as a self-employed carpenter. His business was declining, so he ceased self-employment in August 2016 and returned to Hungary. Botond was then offered employment in the UK, which he returned to take up in January 2017. However, his new (British) partner became very sick and so, last month, he left work to care for her and claimed income support (IS) as her carer. Botond satisfies the right to reside right requirement for IS as he has legally resided in the UK for a continuous period of five years (including the five months he was in Hungary).

Your continuity of residence is broken if you are subject to a deportation or exclusion order, or you are removed from the UK under the EEA Regulations.[361]

Gaps while in the UK

Between periods when you are residing legally in the UK, you may have one or more temporary periods when you remain in the UK, but you are not 'residing legally'. Such periods are not covered in either the EU Directive or the EEA Regulations. However, the Upper Tribunal has recently stated that the relevant provisions of this legislation should be interpreted as requiring continuity of residence, but not necessarily continuity of having 'resided legally', provided the total period of having 'legally resided' is at least five years.[362]

You may be able to argue that the continuity of your residence is not affected by such a gap, on the grounds that if continuity is not affected by your being abroad for certain specified periods, it should also not be affected for equivalent periods when you remain in the UK but do not count as residing legally.[363] Although this argument was rejected by the Court of Appeal,[364] it is arguable that the judgment did not adequately consider all the arguments and relevant caselaw.[365] Future cases may succeed.

Guidance to decision makers states that you can have a cumulative gap of up to 30 days in any 12-month period between periods of residence on different bases – eg, a gap between having a right to reside as a self-employed person and then as a worker. However, it goes on to state that a gap between two periods of the same type of residence (eg, as a jobseeker) breaks the continuity of residence.[366] The guidance gives no legal basis for this and, as guidance, it is not legally binding.

The guidance also correctly notes that if your benefit is subject to a sanction, the continuity of your residence is not affected.[367] However, it also states that if your JSA or universal credit (UC) is disallowed, the continuity of your legal residence is broken.[368] This is not necessarily correct, as you can have a right to reside as a jobseeker, or with worker status retained while involuntarily unemployed and registered as a jobseeker, without receiving JSA or UC (see p140 and p151).[369]

If you stopped work to care for someone, you may be able to argue that you retained your worker status, as the CJEU has held that the ways in which you can retain worker status listed in the directive are not exhaustive (see p149).[370]

If the gap was while you were in prison, this interrupts the continuity of your residence and you cannot count the time spent in prison towards your five years.[371] The CJEU found that taking time spent in prison into account when calculating the five years is contrary to the EU Directive's aim of strengthening social cohesion. This aim was a key factor behind establishing the right of permanent residency and was also the reason why permanent residency depends not just on the duration, but also on the qualitative elements of residence relating to the level of integration in the member state. Receiving a prison sentence shows a person's non-compliance with the values of that state.[372]

This reasoning suggests that other gaps in your five-year period should be treated differently, particularly if they do not call into question your level of integration in the UK – eg, periods when you temporarily ceased to be a worker or self-employed because you were caring for someone.

Although a prison sentence may break your continuity of residence if you have resided in the UK for at least 10 years, it may not do so if you have already established integrating links with the UK which were not broken by the prison sentence.[373]

Gaps after five years

If you have a gap of at least two continous years after a five-year period during which you resided either:[374]

- in accordance with previous regulations – ie before the current regulations came into force on 1 February 2017 (see p191); *or*
- before the country of which you are a national joined the EU (see p194),

you cannot count those periods of residence under the EEA Regulations.

It is arguable that discounting these periods of residence which would otherwise result in permanent residence is not compatible with EU law: the EU Directive is clear that permanent residence is *only* lost if you are absent from the UK for more than two consecutive years (see p200).[375] The CJEU has held that a gap of less than two years which follows the five-year period does not affect the acquisition of permanent residence.[376] However, this does not necessarily mean that a gap of more than two years does affect it. In addition, the judgment concerned periods before the right of permanent residence exisited (ie, before 30 April 2006), whereas the exclusion in the EEA Regulations also covers periods since then. For residence before 30 April 2006, see p191.

Acquiring permanent residence in less than five years

In certain circumstances, you can acquire a permanent right of residence in less than five years. You have a permanent right to reside if you:[377]

- were a worker (see p142) or self-employed person (see p159) and at the time you cease working you:
  - have reached retirement age, or (workers only) have taken early retirement, and you either:
    - have a spouse or civil partner who is a British citizen (or who lost that nationality by marrying you); *or*
    - have worked in the UK for the preceding year and resided in the UK continuously (see p199) for more than three years; *or*
  - stopped your activity as a worker or self-employed person in the UK because of a permanent incapacity (see p198) and:
    - you have a spouse or civil partner who is a British citizen (or who lost that nationality by marrying you); *or*

- you have resided in the UK continuously (see p199) for more than two years; *or*
- the incapacity was as a result of an accident at work or occupational disease that resulted in benefit entitlement – eg, industrial injuries disablement benefit; *or*
- have worked and resided in the UK continuously (see p199) for three years and you then work in another member state and return to the UK at least once a week; *or*
- are the family member (see p199) of a worker or self-employed person in any of the above groups and satisfy other conditions (see p199); *or*
- are the family member of a worker or self-employed person who died while still working and who did not acquire a permanent right of residence under one of the above groups and:
    - s/he had resided (see p199) in the UK for two years; *or*
    - the death resulted from an accident at work or an occupational disease; *or*
    - (EU Directive only) you lost your UK nationality as a result of marrying her/him.

Permanent incapacity
'**Permanent incapacity**' is the opposite of temporary incapacity.[378]
If your incapacity is not permanent, you may be able to retain your worker or self-employed status on the basis that you are temporarily unable to work due to illness or accident (see p156).

What can be treated as a period of work

If the basis on which you acquire a permanent right to reside in less than five years requires you to have worked for a period of time, in addition to the periods when you are actually working, the following are treated as periods of activity as a worker or self-employed person:[379]
- periods when you were not working for reasons not of your making;
- periods when you were not working because of an illness or accident;
- (workers only) periods of involuntary unemployment (see p150) recorded by the relevant employment office – ie, Jobcentre Plus.

Under the EEA Regulations, you must meet the requirements for retaining worker status during these periods (see p149). If you are a Croatian, A2 or A8 national, the additional restrictions that apply or applied to your residence rights can also affect whether you can count these periods as periods of work (see p129).[380]
Note: if you retire or become permanently incapable of work while you are in one of the above situations, since you are treated as being in a period of activity as a worker or self-employed person, provided you satisfy the other requirements,

you should be able to acquire permanent residence on that basis. This approach was followed by the Court of Appeal when determining the date a Portuguese national who had been off work sick became permanently incapable of work. The court upheld the decision that he had become permanently incapable as soon as he stopped work. Because this was before he had resided in the UK for two years, this meant he failed to acquire permanent residence. However, had he become permanently incapable of work after residing in the UK for two years, it was accepted that he would then have had a permanent right to reside, even though the permanent incapacity would have been preceded by temporary incapacity rather than actual employment.[381]

Residing in the UK

Some of the ways in which you can acquire permanent residence in less than five years require you to have resided in the UK continuously for specified periods. Whether or not you satisfy this may be affected by the way the phrase 'resided in the UK continuously' is interpreted. This can be affected by the fact that acquiring permanent residency in less than five years is the exception to the general rule. Of particular relevance are:

- how the period of continuous residence is calculated. It is arguable that certain absences should not affect your continuity of residence in the same way as for acquiring permanent residence after five years (see p195); *and*
- the quality of residence required. The Upper Tribunal has held that actual residence is sufficient,[382] and that earlier caselaw that interpreted 'reside' as 'legally reside' should not be followed.[383] However, the DWP's appeal against this decision is due to be heard in the Court of Appeal.[384] Guidance to decision makers advises that they 'stay' (do not decide) any claims in which the quality of residence is relevant, pending the appeal, and that they invite the First-tier Tribunal to do the same.[385]

Family members

You acquire permanent residence in less than five years if you are living in the UK and are the family member (see p171) of someone who has acquired a permanent right to reside under the first bullet point on p197. The requirements of the EU Directive and the EEA Regulations differ on the circumstances in which you have this right to reside.

- **The EU Directive** requires that you 'reside with' the family member in the UK. You do not have to live with the person; it is sufficient that you are living in the UK now.[386] You do not have to have lived in the UK for the same period as the person of whom you are a family member, and you do not need to have been her/his family member throughout this time.[387]
- **The EEA Regulations** require that you had a right to reside on the basis of being her/his family member at the point s/he ceased activity as a worker or self-employed person.[388] This more restrictive requirement has been in force

since 1 February 2017, with no protection for those who had a right to reside under the previous provision.

If you are refused benefit on the grounds you do not satisfy the EEA Regulations but you do satisfy the EU Directive, you should challenge the decision on the basis that you have a right to reside under the EU Directive.

Loss of permanent right to reside

Once you have a permanent right to reside (either because you have resided legally in the UK for five years or under the rules that enable you to acquire permanent residence in less than five years), you only lose this right if you are absent from the UK for more than two consecutive years.[389]

However, note in exceptional circumstances, your residence rights can be revoked or cancelled on grounds of public policy, public security or public health (see p41).[390] If you are told this has happened or will happen to you, get specialist immigration advice immediately.

Benefit entitlement

If you have a permanent right to reside, this satisfies the right to reside requirement for all the benefits that have this requirement (see p117).

If you acquired a permanent right to reside in less than five years, you are exempt from the habitual residence test for means-tested benefits (see p108). You therefore do not need to be 'habitually resident in fact' nor, for income-based JSA, to have lived in the common travel area for the three months prior to your claim.

Note: to claim benefit on the basis of your permanent residence, you must provide evidence of this. It may help you to refer to decision makers' guidance, including sections on evidence, if this supports your situation.[391] You should always provide as much documentary evidence that you satisfy the conditions for permanent residence as you can. However, if you are unable, for example, to prove you worked for a relevant period, the decision maker should use additional records available to her/him – eg, national insurance contribution records.[392] This is covered in more detail on p371. For more information on evidence, see Chapter 20.

Notes

2. **Non-European Economic Area nationals**
1 *Yesiloz v LB Camden and Another* [2009] EWCA Civ 415

4. **European Economic Area nationals**
2 Art 18 TFEU
3 Art 20 TFEU
4 Arts 20 and 21 TFEU
5 EEA Joint Committee Decision No.158/2007
6 *Agreement between the European Community and its Member States, of the one part, and the Swiss Confederation, of the other, on the free movement of persons*, Cmd 5639, 21 June 1999 (in force on 1 June 2002)
7 Reg 2(1) I(EEA) Regs
8 Reg 1(2) I(EEA) Regs – except reg 9, which was replaced from 25 November 2016
9 This approach is taken in the I(EEA) Regs – see reg 2(1), definition of 'EEA national', I(EEA) Regs
10 Art 3(1) EU Dir 2004/38
11 Regs 6 and 14(1) I(EEA) Regs
12 Arts 7 and 14 EU Dir 2004/38
13 *SSWP v JB (JSA)* [2011] UKUT 96 (AAC)

5. **Croatian, A2 and A8 nationals**
14 *TG v SSWP (PC)* [2015] UKUT 50 (AAC)
15 *SSWP v Gubeladze*, Court of Appeal hearing due in autumn 2017
16 DMG Memo 2/16, ADM Memo 4/16
17 Reg 8 AC(IWA) Regs
18 Regs 4 and 5 AC(IWA) Regs
19 Reg 9 A(IWA) Regs
20 Reg 6 A(IWA) Regs; reg 7B I(EEA) Regs 2006, as saved by reg 45 and Sch 4 para 2 I(EEA) Regs
21 Reg 7 A(IWR) Regs
22 Reg 5 A(IWR) Regs; reg 7A I(EEA) Regs 2006, as saved by reg 45 and Sch 4 para 2 I(EEA) Regs
23 *RP v SSWP (ESA) (Interim decision)* [2016] UKUT 422 (AAC) (case ref: *Prefeta* C-618/16)
24 CIS/1042/2008; *SSWP v JB* [2011] UKUT 96 (AAC)
25 Reg 2 AC(IWA) Regs; reg 2 A(IWA) Regs; *OB v SSWP (ESA)* [2017] UKUT 255 (AAC)

26 s33(2A) IA 1971
27 Reg 3 AC(IWA) Regs; reg 4 A(IWA) Regs
28 Reg 2 A(IWR) Regs
29 *JK v SSWP (SPC)* [2017] UKUT 179 (AAC)
30 Reg 2(5) AC(IWA) Regs; reg 2(12) A(IWA) Regs
31 *Miskovic and Another v SSWP* [2011] EWCA Civ 16
32 Reg 2(7) A(IWR) Regs
33 *Miskovic and Another v SSWP* [2011] EWCA Civ 16
34 Reg 7 A(IWR) Regs
35 *SSWP v ZA* [2009] UKUT 294 (AAC); *Szpak v SSWP* [2013] EWCA Civ 46
36 *BS v SSWP* [2009] UKUT 16 (AAC)

6. **Initial right of residence**
37 Reg 11 I(EEA) Regs
38 Reg 13(1) I(EEA) Regs; Art 6(1) EU Dir 2004/38
39 Reg 13(3) I(EEA) Regs; Art 14(1) EU Dir 2004/38
40 Reg 13(2) I(EEA) Regs; Art 6(2) EU Dir 2004/38

7. **Jobseekers**
41 Art 45 TFEU; Art 14 EU Dir 2004/38; *The Queen v Immigration Appeal Tribunal, ex parte Antonissen*, C-292/89 [1991] ECR I-00745; reg 6 I(EEA) Regs
42 Reg 6(1), (6) and (7) I(EEA) Regs
43 Reg 6(8)-(10) I(EEA) Regs
44 Art 45 TFEU; *The Queen v Immigration Appeal Tribunal, ex parte Antonissen*, C-292/89 [1991] ECR I-00745
45 Reg 5 AC(IWA) Regs
46 **A2** Reg 6 A(IWA) Regs
    A8 Regs 4(2) and (4) and 5(2) A(IWR) Regs
47 *The Queen v Immigration Appeal Tribunal, ex parte Antonissen*, C-292/89 [1991] ECR I-00745, para 21; confirmed in *SSWP v MB (JSA) (and linked cases)* [2016] UKUT 372 (AAC), para 49
48 Reg 6 I(EEA) Regs
49 Reg 6(8) I(EEA) Regs
50 Reg 6(1), (8) and (9) I(EEA) Regs
51 Confirmed in para 073080 DMG
52 para 073120 DMG
53 Reg 6(1) and (5)-(8) I(EEA) Regs

54 para 073107 DMG
55 para 073108 DMG
56 *KS v SSWP* [2016] UKUT 269 (AAC) and
    caselaw cited; paras 073096-073100
    DMG
57 *The Queen v Immigration Appeal
    Tribunal, ex parte Antonissen,* C-292/89
    [1991] ECR I-00745, para 21
58 *SSWP v MB (JSA)(and linked cases)* [2016]
    UKUT 372 (AAC), paras 49-60,
    especially paras 49 and 57
59 www.cpag.org.uk/genuine-prospects-
    of-work
60 *SSWP v MB (JSA) (and linked cases)*
    [2016] UKUT 372 (AAC), para 47
61 *OS v SSWP (JSA)* [2017] UKUT 107
    (AAC), para 5-7 and caselaw cited
62 *SSWP v RR (IS)* [2013] UKUT 21 (AAC)
63 *SSWP v MB (JSA) (and linked cases)*
    [2016] UKUT 372 (AAC)
64 paras 073099-073100 DMG
65 Rewritten October 2016; *KS v SSWP*
    [2016] UKUT 269 (AAC); *SSWP v MB
    (JSA) (and linked cases)* [2016] UKUT 372
    (AAC)
66 *SSWP v MB (JSA) (and linked cases)*
    [2016] UKUT 372 (AAC), paras 91 and
    127
67 *SSWP v MB (JSA) (and linked cases)*
    [2016] UKUT 372 (AAC), para 61
68 Confirmed in Vol 2, para 073122 DMG
69 CJSA/1080/2002, para 15; *GM v SSWP
    (JSA)* [2014] UKUT 57 (AAC)
70 CH/3314/2005
71 R(IS) 8/08, para 6; *SSWP v MB (JSA) (and
    linked cases)* [2016] UKUT 372 (AAC), in
    particular paras 32-33; CIS 1951/2008,
    para 21; see also *Shabani v SSHD (EEA –
    jobseekers; nursery education)* [2013]
    UKUT 315 (IAC)
72 s7 JSA 1995; reg 8 JSA Regs; *SSWP v MB
    (JSA) (and linked cases)* [2016] UKUT 372
    (AAC), paras 63-79
73 *The Queen v Immigration Appeal
    Tribunal, ex parte Antonissen,* C-292/89
    [1991] ECR I-00745, para 21; R(IS) 8/08,
    para 5; *GE v SSWP (ESA)* [2017] UKUT
    145 (AAC), para 46
74 Art 24(2) EU Dir 2004/38; see also
    Jobcentre Berlin Neukölln v Alimanovic, C-
    67/14 [2015]; *Vestische Arbeit Jobcenter
    Kreis Recklinghausen v García-Nieto,* C-
    299/14 [2016]
75 *Vatsouras and Koupatantze v
    Arbeitsgemeinschaft Nürnberg,* C-23/08
    [2009] ECR I-04585, paras 40 and 45
76 Reg 3 HB(HR)A Regs
77 Reg 70(3)(b) and (d) ESA Regs

78 *Vatsouras and Koupatantze v
    Arbeitsgemeinschaft Nürnberg,* C-23/08
    [2009] ECR I-04585, para 40
79 *Alhashem v SSWP* [2016] EWCA Civ 395

8. Workers
80 Regs 6(1) and 14(1) I(EEA) Regs; Arts
    7(1)(a) and 14(2) EU Dir 2004/38; Art
    45 TFEU
81 Reg 4(1)(a) I(EEA) Regs
82 *Levin v Staatssecretaris van Justitie,* C-53/
    81 [1982] ECR I-1035
83 *LN v Styrelsen for Videregående
    Uddannelser og Uddannelsesstötte,* C-46/
    12 [2013]
84 *MDB (Italy) v SSHD* [2012] EWCA Civ
    1015, paras 61-65
85 Reg 5 AC(IWA) Regs
86 Reg 6 A(IWA) Regs
87 Reg 5(2) A(IWR) Regs
88 *SSWP v Gubedladze,* Court of Appeal
    hearing due in autumn 2017
89 DMG Memo 2/16, ADM Memo 4/16
90 paras 073031-58 DMG; paras C1480-
    C1506 ADM; HB A3/2014; HMRC, *Child
    Benefit and Child Tax Credit: right to reside
    establishing whether an EEA national is/
    was a worker or a self-employed person
    under EU law,* February 2014
91 para 073040 DMG; para C1489 ADM;
    HB A3/2014 para 15; HMRC, *Child
    Benefit and Child Tax Credit: right to reside
    establishing whether an EEA national is/
    was a worker or a self-employed person
    under EU law,* February 2014, para 7
92 *Raulin v Minister van Onderwijs en
    Wetenschappen,* C-357/89 [1992] ECR I-
    01027, para 10
93 *SSWP v RR (IS)* [2013] UKUT 21 (AAC)
94 CIS/868/2008; CIS/1837/2006; see also
    VW v SSWP (PC) [2014] UKUT 573 (AAC)
95 *Steymann v Staatssecretaris van Justitie,*
    C-196/87 [1988] ECR I-06159; R(IS) 12/
    98
96 *Jany v Staatssecretaris van Justitie,* C-268/
    99 [2001] ECR I-08615, para 34
97 *SSWP v KP (JSA)* [2011] UKUT 241 (AAC);
    SSWP v MM (IS) [2015] UKUT 128
    (AAC), paras 31 and 36
98 *Bettray v Staatssecretaris van Justitie,* C-
    344/87 [1989] ECR I-01621, para 16; *JA
    v SSWP (ESA)* [2012] UKUT 122 (AAC);
    EP v SSWP (JSA) [2016] UKUT 445 (AAC),
    para 21
99 *EP v SSWP (JSA)* [2016] UKUT 445 (AAC)
    para 22

100 *Barry v London Borough of Southwark*
[2008] EWCA Civ 1440, para 45; *NE v
SSWP* [2009] UKUT 38 (AAC), para 4
101 *Bettray v Staatssecretaris van Justitie*, C-
344/87 [1989] ECR I-01621; *SSWP v KP
(JSA)* [2011] UKUT 241 (AAC)
102 *NE v SSWP* [2009] UKUT 38 (AAC), para
9; *SSWP v MM (IS)* [2015] UKUT 128
(AAC), paras 31 and 36
103 *EP v SSWP (JSA)* [2016] UKUT 445 (AAC),
para 21
104 *Levin v Staatssecretaris van Justitie*, C-53/
81 [1982] ECR I-01035, para 17
105 *Ninni-Orasche v Bundesminister für
Wissenschaft, Verkehr und Kunst*, C-413/
01 [2003] ECR I-13187, para 27
106 *Genc v Land Berlin*, C-14/09 [2010] ECR
I-00931
107 R(IS) 12/98
108 *Ninni-Orasche v Bundesminister für
Wissenschaft, Verkehr und Kunst*, C-413/
01 [2003] ECR I-13187, para 25
109 *Barry v London Borough of Southwark*
[2008] EWCA Civ 1440
110 *Ninni-Orasche v Bundesminister für
Wissenschaft, Verkehr und Kunst*, C-413/
01 [2003] ECR I-13187, para 19
111 In *NE v SSWP* [2009] UKUT 38 (AAC),
para 9; R(IS) 12/98
112 *Vatsouras and Koupantze v
Arbeitsgemeinschaft (ARGE) Nürnberg
900* [2009] C-22/08 and C-23/08
[2009] ECR I-04585, paras 27-28 and
caselaw cited
113 *Raulin v Minister van Onderwijs en
Wetenschappen*, C-357/89 [1992] ECR I-
01027
114 *NE v SSWP* [2009] UKUT 38 (AAC); CIS/
1793/2007; *SSWP v MM (IS)* [2015]
UKUT 128 (AAC)
115 *Genc v Land Berlin*, C-14/09 [2010] ECR
I-00931
116 *Barry v London Borough of Southwark*
[2008] EWCA Civ 1440, para 20
117 *SSWP v SY (IS)* [2012] UKUT 233 (AAC);
JR v SSWP (IS) [2014] UKUT 154 (AAC);
JR v Leeds City Council (HB) [2014] UKUT
154 (AAC)
118 *BS v SSWP* [2009] UKUT 16 (AAC); CIS/
4237/2007

9. Retaining worker status
119 Art 7(3) EU Dir 2004/38; reg 6(1)-(3)
and (5)-(7) I(EEA) Regs
120 *Saint Prix v SSWP*, C-507/12 [2014]
121 *Saint Prix v SSWP*, C-507/12 [2014], para
38

122 Reg 5(4) A(IWR) Regs; reg 7A(4) I(EEA)
Regs 2006, as saved by reg 45 and Sch 4
para 2 I(EEA) Regs
123 *SSWP v Gubedladze*, Court of Appeal
hearing due in autumn 2017
124 DMG Memo 2/16; ADM Memo 4/16
125 Art 7(3)(b) and (c) EU Dir 2004/38
126 Reg 6(2)(b) and (c) and (5)-(7) I(EEA)
Regs
127 CH/3314/2005, para 11; confirmed in
SSWP v EM (IS) [2009] UKUT 146 (AAC),
para 10; *SSWP v MK* [2013] UKUT 163
(AAC), paras 44-47
128 *SSWP v Elmi* [2011] EWCA Civ 1403;
paras 072826-27 DMG
129 Art 7(3)(b) EU Dir 2004/38; *SSWP v MM
(IS)* [2015] UKUT 128 (AAC), paras 53-
54
130 *SSWP v MM (IS)* [2015] UKUT 128
(AAC), paras 53-58
131 *SSWP v MM (IS)* [2015] UKUT 128
(AAC), paras 45-46
132 Reg 6(2)(b) and (5)-(8) I(EEA) Regs
133 Reg 6(1) and (2)(c), (3) and (5)-(7)
I(EEA) Regs
134 Art 7(3)(c) EU Dir 2004/38
135 Reg 6(1) and (7)-(10) I(EEA) Regs
136 Reg 6(2)(b) and (5)-(8) I(EEA) Regs
137 Confirmed in para 073080 DMG and
C1403 ADM
138 para 073120 DMG; para C1431 ADM
139 Reg 6(1), (2) and (5)-(8) I(EEA) Regs
140 para 073107 DMG and para C1421
ADM
141 para 073108 DMG and para C1422
ADM
142 *KS v SSWP* [2016] UKUT 269 (AAC) and
ECJ caselaw cited; paras 073096-
073100 DMG; paras C1412-16 ADM
143 *SSWP v MB (JSA) (and linked cases)*
[2016] UKUT 372 (AAC), paras 49-60,
especially paras 49 and 57
144 www.cpag.org.uk/genuine-prospects-
of-work
145 *SSWP v MB (JSA) (and linked cases)*
[2016] UKUT 372 (AAC), para 47
146 *OS v SSWP (JSA)* [2017] UKUT 107
(AAC), paras 5-7 and caselaw cited
147 *SSWP v RR (IS)* [2013] UKUT 21 (AAC)
148 *SSWP v MB (JSA) (and linked cases)*
[2016] UKUT 372 (AAC)
149 paras 073099-073100 DMG; paras
C1415-C1416 ADM
150 Rewritten October 2016; *KS v S SWP*
[2016] UKUT 269 (AAC); *SSWP v MB
(JSA) (and linked cases)* [2016] UKUT 372
(AAC)

151 *SSWP v MB (JSA) (and linked cases)*
[2016] UKUT 372 (AAC), paras 91 and
127
152 *SSWP v MB (JSA) (and linked cases)*
[2016] UKUT 372 (AAC), para 61
153 Confirmed in Vol 2, para 073122 DMG
154 CJSA/1080/2002, para 15; *GM v SSWP
(JSA)* [2014] UKUT 57 (AAC)
155 Art 7(3)(d) EU Dir 2004/38; reg 6(1) and
(2)(d) and (e) I(EEA)Regs
156 *SSWP v EM (IS)* [2009] UKUT 146 (AAC),
para 10; see also *OB v SSWP (ESA)* [2017]
UKUT 255 (AAC), para 32
157 *Brown v Secretary of State for Scotland*, C-
197/86 [1988] ECR I-03205
158 *Lair v Universität Hannover*, C-39/86
[1988] ECR I-03161, para 37
159 *Raulin v Minister van Onderwijs en
Wetenschappen*, C-357/89 [1992] ECR I-
01027, paras 18 and 19
160 Art 7(3)(a) EU Dir 2004/38; reg 6(2)(a)
I(EEA) Regs
161 CIS/4304/2007, para 35
162 CIS/3182/2005
163 *SSHD v FB* [2010] UKUT 447 (IAC), para
23; *LM v HMRC (CHB)* [2016] UKUT 389
(AAC)
164 CIS/3890/2005
165 *De Brito v SSHD* [2012] EWCA Civ 709;
*Konodyba v Royal Borough of Kensington
and Chelsea* [2012] EWCA Civ 982;
Samin v Westminster CC [2012] EWCA
Civ 1468 (this part of the decision was
not in dispute in the further appeal to
the Supreme Court); *LM v HMRC (CHB)*
[2016] UKUT 389 (AAC)
166 CIS/4237/2007
167 CIS/731/2007
168 CIS/4010/2006
169 *Saint Prix v SSWP*, C-507/12 [2014];
SSWP v SFF and Others [2015] UKUT 502
(AAC)
170 *SSWP v SFF and Others* [2015] UKUT 502
(AAC), para 35; confirmed in Vol 2 paras
073224 and 073230 (note) DMG and
para C1521 ADM
171 *SSWP v SFF and Others* [2015] UKUT 502
(AAC), para 26; *Weldemichael and
Another v SSHD* [2015] UKUT 540 (IAC),
paras 22-23
172 *SSWP v SFF and Others* [2015] UKUT 502
(AAC), paras 24 and 25
173 CIS/4304/2007, para 34; *SSWP v IR*
[2009] UKUT 11 (AAC); *SSWP v SFF and
Others* [2015] UKUT 502 (AAC), para 40;
GE v SSWP (ESA) [2017] UKUT 145
(AAC), para 41

174 CIS/1934/2006; *SSWP v IR (IS)* [2009]
UKUT 11 (AAC)
175 *SSWP v MK* [2013] UKUT 163 (AAC); *VP v
SSWP (JSA)* [2014] UKUT 32 (AAC), paras
56-61; *SSWP v MM (IS)* [2015] UKUT
128 (AAC), paras 47-52

10. Self-employed people
176 Reg 6(1)(c) J(EEA) Regs; Art 7(1)(a) EU
Dir 2004/38; Art 49 TFEU
177 Reg 4(1)(b) I(EEA) Regs refers to Art 49
TFEU
178 *Aldona Malgorzata Jany and Others v
Staatssecretaris van Justitie*, C-268/99
[2001] ECR I-08615
179 *Bristol City Council v FV (HB)* [2011] UKUT
494 (AAC)
180 *HMRC v IT (CTC)* [2016] UKUT 252
(AAC), paras 25-28
181 *DV v SSWP* [2017] UKUT 155 (AAC)
182 *SSWP v SY (IS)* [2012] UKUT 233 (AAC);
JR v SSWP (IS) [2014] UKUT 154 (AAC);
JR v Leeds City Council (HB) [2014] UKUT
154 (AAC)
183 paras 073031-58 DMG; HB A3/2014;
HMRC, *Child Benefit and Child Tax Credit:
right to reside establishing whether an EEA
national is/was a worker or a self-
employed person under EU law*, February
2014
184 Reg 4(1)(b) I(EEA) Regs
185 Art 49 TFEU; R(IS) 6/00
186 R(IS) 6/00, para 31
187 *TG v SSWP* [2009] UKUT 58 (AAC), para
5
188 *SSWP v JS (IS)* [2010] UKUT 240 (AAC),
paras 5 and 8; *RJ v SSWP (JSA)* [2011]
UKUT 477 (AAC), paras 9 and 17; *HMRC
v HD (interim decision) and HMRC v GP*
[2017] UKUT 11 (AAC)
189 *SSWP v JS (IS)* [2010] UKUT 240 (AAC),
para 5; para 072842 DMG; para C1452
ADM
190 CIS/1042/2008
191 *HMRC v HD (interim decision) and HMRC
v GP* [2017] UKUT 11 (AAC)
192 *Saint Prix v SSWP*, C-507/12 [2014]
193 *Gusa v Minister for Social Protection*
[2016] IECA 237 (case ref: *Gusa* C-442/
16, heard June 2017, awaiting
judgment)
194 *SSWP v JB (JSA)* [2011] UKUT 96 (AAC)

11. Retaining self-employed status
195 Art 7(3)(a) EU Dir 2004/38; reg 6(4)
I(EEA) Regs
196 *R (Tilianu) v SSWP* [2010] EWCA Civ
1397

197 *Gusa v Minister for Social Protection*
[2016] IECA 237 (case ref: *Gusa* C-442/
16, heard June 2017, awaiting
judgment)
198 Art 7(3)(a) EU Dir 2004/38; reg 6(4)
I(EEA) Regs
199 CIS/1042/2008
200 *HMRC v HD (interim decision) and HMRC
v GP* [2017] UKUT 11 (AAC)
201 CIS/4010/2006

12. Self-sufficient people and students

202 Art 7(1) EU Dir 2004/38; regs 4(1)(c)
and (2)-(4), 6(1) and 14(1) I(EEA) Regs
203 Art 7(1) EU Dir 2004/38; regs 4(1)(d)
and (2)-(4), 6(1) and 14(1) I(EEA) Regs
204 *VP v SSWP (JSA)* [2014] UKUT 32 (AAC),
paras 88-97
205 Reg 4 I(EEA)Regs
206 Art 8(4) EU Dir 2004/38
207 Reg 4 I(EEA) Regs
208 *SG v Tameside MBC (HB)* [2010] UKUT
243 (AAC)
209 *Zhu and Chen v SSHD*, C-200/02 [2004]
ECR I-09925; *AMS v SSWP (PC)* [2017]
UKUT 48 (AAC), para 62
210 *Commission of the European Communities
v Kingdom Belgium*, C-408/03 [2006]
ECR I-02647; *Zhu and Chen v SSHD*, C-
200/02 [2004] ECR I-09925
211 *VP v SSWP (JSA)* [2014] UKUT 32 (AAC),
paras 88-97
212 *Singh and Others v Minister of Justice and
Equality*, C-218/14 [2015]
213 *Pensionsversicherungsanstalt v Brey*, C-
140/12 [2013], paras 54-57
214 CH/1400/2006; *SG v Tameside MBC
(HB)* [2010] UKUT 243 (AAC);
Pensionsversicherungsanstalt v Brey, C-
140/12 [2013]
215 para 073244 DMG; para C1729 ADM
216 *Pensionsversicherungsanstalt v Brey*, C-
140/12 [2013], paras 64 and 75-78;
AMS v SSWP (PC) [2017] UKUT 48 (AAC)
217 *VP v SSWP (JSA)* [2014] UKUT 32 (AAC),
paras 77, 84 and 94
218 *W (China) and Another v SSHD* [2006]
EWCA Civ 1494
219 *SG v Tameside MBC (HB)* [2010] UKUT
243 (AAC); *VP v SSWP (JSA)* [2014] UKUT
32 (AAC); *SSWP v HH (SPC)* [2015] UKUT
583 (AAC); para 073246 DMG; para
C1730 ADM
220 *SSWP v HH (SPC)* [2015] UKUT 583
(AAC); *AMS v SSWP (PC)* [2017] UKUT
48 (AAC), para 7; para 073246 DMG;
para C1730 ADM

221 Arts 1(j) and (k) and 19 EU Reg 883/
2004; *I v Health Services Executive*, C-
255/13 [2014], para 59
222 *SSWP v GS (PC)* [2016] UKUT 394 (AAC);
[2017] AACR 7, paras 13-40; para
073246 DMG; para C1730 ADM; see
also Decision S1 of 12 June 2009 of the
Administrative Commission for the Co-
ordination of Social Security Systems, C-
106/08 [2010]
223 *FK (Kenya) v SSHD* [2010] EWCA Civ
1302; *VP v SSWP (JSA)* [2014] UKUT 32
(AAC); *SSWP v LL (SPC)* [2014] UKUT
136 (AAC); *Ahmad v SSHD* [2014] EWCA
Civ 988
224 *Baumbast and R v SSHD*, C-413/99
[2002] ECR I-07091
225 *KS v SSWP* [2016] UKUT 269 (AAC), para
6; *SSWP v GS (PC)* [2016] UKUT 394
(AAC), reported as [2017] AACR 7, paras
42-46R
226 Art 7(1) EU Dir 2004/38; regs 4(1)(d)
and (2)-(5), 6(1) and 14(1) I(EEA) Regs
227 Reg 4(1)(d)(i) I(EEA) Regs
228 Reg 4(1)(d)(iii) I(EEA) Regs
229 *Grzelczyk v Centre Public d'aide Sociale
d'Ottignies-Louvain-la-Neuve*, C-184/09
[2001] ECR I-06193
230 Art 7(4) EU Dir 2004/38; reg 7(2) I(EEA)
Regs
231 Art 7(4) EU Dir 2004/38

13. Family members of European Economic Area nationals

232 Arts 6(2) and 7(1)(d) and (2) EU Dir
2004/38; *Clauder*, C-E-4/11 [2011]
EFTACR 216, para 43; regs 13(2) and
14(2) I(EEA) Regs
233 Regs 6 and 14(1) I(EEA) Regs. The same
groups are covered in Arts 7 and 14 EU
Dir 2004/38, although the term
'qualified person' is not used.
234 Art 2(2) EU Dir 2004/38; reg 7(1) I(EEA)
Regs
235 Reg 7(3) I(EEA) Regs; CPC/3588/2006;
SS v SSWP (ESA) [2011] UKUT 8 (AAC);
SSWP v LZ (SPC) [2014] UKUT 147 (AAC)
236 *Aissatou Diatta v Land Berlin*, C-267/83
[1985] ECR I-00567
237 CF/1863/2007

238 CIS/2100/2007, which considers the findings of *Centre Public d'Aide Sociale de Courcelles v Lebon*, 316/85 [1987] ECR I-02811, *Zhu and Chen v SSHD*, C-200/02 [2004] ECR I-09925 and *Jia v Migrationsverket*, C-1/05 [2007] ECR I-00001; *SSWP v MB (JSA) (and linked cases)* [2016] UKUT 372 (AAC), paras 132-39

239 *Reyes v Migrationsverket* C-423/12 [2014]; *Centre Publique d'Aide Social de Courcelles v Lebon* C-316/85 [1987] ECR I-02811; *ECO v Lim (EEA dependency)* [2013] UKUT 437 (IAC)

240 *Pedro v SSWP* [2009] EWCA Civ 1358. Arguably, this remains good law despite the assumptions made in *Reyes v Migrationsverket*, C-423/12 [2014].

241 *SSHD v Rahman and Others*, C-83/11 [2012] ECR; *Oboh and Others v SSHD* [2013] EWCA Civ 1525; *AA (Algeria) v SSHD* [2014] EWCA Civ 1741

242 *Centre Publique d'Aide Social de Courcelles v Lebon*, C-316/85 [1987] ECR I-02811, para 20; *SSWP v MB (JSA) (and linked cases)* [2016] UKUT 372 (AAC), paras 132-39

243 Reg 7(3) I(EEA) Regs; CPC/3588/2006; *SS v SSWP (ESA)* [2011] UKUT 8 (AAC); *SSWP v LZ (SPC)* [2014] UKUT 147 (AAC)

244 Reg 7(3) and 8 I(EEA) Regs; the same groups are covered in Art 3 EU Dir 2004/38, but the term is not used.

245 *Dauhoo (EEA Regs – Reg 8(2)) v SSHD* [2012] UKUT 79 (IAC)

246 *SSHD v Rahman and Others*, C-83/11 [2012]; *Oboh and Others v SSHD* [2013] EWCA Civ 1525; *Soares v SSHD* [2013] EWCA Civ 575; *AA (Algeria) v SSHD* [2014] EWCA Civ 1741

247 Reg 8(7) I(EEA) Regs

248 *SSHD v Rahman and Others*, C-83/11 [2012]; Recital 6 and Art 3(2) EU Dir 2004/38

249 Art 3(1) EU Dir 2004/38 applies to people who 'move to or reside in' an EEA country 'other than that of which they are a national'. Reg 2(1) I(EEA) Regs achieves a similar effect by setting out the residence rights of EEA nationals and their family members, but defining an EEA national 'as a national of an EEA state who is not also a British citizen'.

250 Art 7(2) EU Dir 2004/38; *R v IAT and Singh ex parte SSHD*, C-370/90 [1992] ECR I-04265; *Minister voor Vreemdelingenzaken en Integratie v Eind*, C-291/05 [2007] ECR I-10719; *O and B v Minister voor Immigratie, Intergratie en Asiel*, C-456/12 [2014]

251 Regs 1, 7(4) and 9 I(EEA) Regs since 1 February 2017 and reg 4 and Sch 5 I(EEA) Regs for prior period from 25 November 2016

252 *O and B v Minister voor Immigratie, Integratie en Asiel*, C-456/12 [2014]; *VW v SSWP (PC)* [2014] UKUT 573 (AAC)

253 *O and B v Minister voor Immigratie, Intergratie en Asiel*, C-456/12 [2014]

254 *Minister voor Vreemdelingenzaken en Integratie v Eind*, C-291/05 [2007] ECR I-10719, para 45. The case relates to an earlier EU regulation, but the same reasoning applies to Art 7(2) EU Dir 2004/38.

255 Reg 9(7) I(EEA) Regs

256 Reg 9(4) I(EEA) Regs

257 Regs 1, 7(4) and 9 I(EEA) Regs since 9 February 2017 and reg 4 and Sch 5 I(EEA) Regs for the earlier period.

258 *Mary Carpenter v SSHD*, C-60/00 [2002] ECR I-06279, para 46

259 *S and G v Minister voor Immigratie, Integratie en Asiel*, C-457/12 [2014]

260 *McCarthy v SSHD*, C-434-09 [2011] ECR I-03375

261 Reg 2(1) I(EEA) Regs

262 *AA v SSWP* [2009] UKUT 249 (AAC); *HG v SSWP (SPC)* [2011] UKUT 382 (AAC)

263 Sch 3 I(EEA)A Regs 2012 up to, and Sch 6 para 9 I(EEA) Regs since, 1 February 2017

264 Reg 9 I(EEA) Regs

265 *Lounes v SSHD* [2016] EWHC 436 (Admin); AG Opinion in *Lounes v SSHD* C-165/16 (30 May 2017)

266 Regs 10 and 14(3) I(EEA) Regs

267 Reg 14(3) I(EEA) Regs

268 Reg 10(8) and (9) I(EEA) Regs

269 Art 12 EU Dir 2004/38

270 Art 12 EU Dir 2004/38

271 Art 13 EU Dir 2004/38

272 *Singh and Others v Minister of Justice and Equality*, C-218-14 [2015]

273 *SSHD v NA*, C-115/15 [2016]

274 Arts 12, 13 and 18 EU Dir 2004/38; *Ziolkowski and Szeja*, joined cases C-424/10 and C-425/10 [2011] ECR I-14035, para 44

14. Derivative residence rights

275 Reg 16 I(EEA) Regs

276 See also *London Borough of Harrow v Ibrahim and SSHD*, C-310/08 [2010] ECR I-01065; *Teixeira v London Borough of Lambeth and SSHD*, C-480/08 [2010] ECR I-01107; *GBC Echternach and A Moritz v Minister van Onderwijs en Wetenschappen*, joined cases 389/87 and 390/87 [1989] ECR I-00723; *Baumbast and R v SSHD*, C-413/99 [2002] ECR I-07091

277 See also *London Borough of Harrow v Ibrahim and SSHD*, C-310/08 [2010] ECR I-01065; *Teixeira v London Borough of Lambeth and SSHD*, C-480/08 [2010] ECR I-01107; *GBC Echternach and A Moritz v Minister van Onderwijs en Wetenschappen*, joined cases 389/87 and 390/87 [1989] ECR 00723; *Baumbast and R v SSHD*, C-413/99 [2002] ECR I-07091

278 See also *Zhu and Chen v SSHD*, C-200/02 [2004] ECR I-09925; *SSHD v NA*, C-115/15 [2016]

279 See also *Zambrano v ONEm*, C-34/09 [2011] ECR I-01177; *Dereci and Others v Bundesministerium für Inneres*, C-256/11 [2011] ECR I-11315

280 Reg 16(1) I(EEA) Regs

281 Reg 16(7)(c) I(EEA) Regs

282 *HMRC v IT (CTC)* [2016] UKUT 252 (AAC)

283 *SSWP v JS (IS)* [2010] UKUT 347

284 *DJ v SSWP* [2013] UKUT 113 (AAC)

285 Art 10 EU Reg 492/2011 (before 1 June 2012, Art 12 EC Reg 1612/68 was in identical terms)

286 *Baumbast and R v SSHD*, C-413/99 [2002] ECR I-07091

287 *Baumbast and R v SSHD*, C-413/99 [2002] ECR I-07091, para 57; *Alarape and Tijani (Article 12, EC Reg 1612/68) Nigeria* [2011] UKUT 413 (IAC), paras 28-29

288 *JS v SSWP (ESA)* [2016] UKUT 314 (AAC)

289 *MS v SSWP (IS)* [2016] UKUT 348 (AAC)

290 *IP v SSWP (IS)* [2015] UKUT 691 (AAC)

291 CIS/3960/2007

292 *SSWP v IM* [2011] UKUT 231 (AAC), paras 17 and 28

293 *Shabani v SSHD* [2013] UKUT 315 (IAC)

294 Reg 16(7)(a) I(EEA) Regs

295 Art 10 EU Reg 492/2011; *Landesamt für Ausbildungsförderung Nordrhein-Westfalen v Lubor Gaal*, C-7/94 [1995] ECR I-1031, paras 24 and 25; *Teixeira v LB Lambeth and SSHD*, C-480/08 [2010] ECR I-01107, paras 76-87; *Alarape and Tijani v SSHD*, C-529/11 [2013], paras 24, 25 and 31

296 *Teixeira v LB Lambeth and SSHD*, C-480/08 [2010] ECR I-01107, para 74; *Baumbast and R v SSHD*, C-413/99 [2002] ECR I-07091, para 63; *SSHD v NA*, C-115/15 [2016]

297 Reg 16(7)(b) I(EEA)Regs

298 Reg 10 EU Reg 492/2011 (before 1 June 2012, Art 12 EC Reg 1612/68 was in identical terms)

299 *London Borough of Harrow v Ibrahim and SSHD*, C-310/08 [2010] ECR I-01065; *Teixeira v London Borough of Lambeth and SSHD*, C-480/08 [2010] ECR I-01107; *Baumbast and R v SSHD*, C-413/99 [2002] ECR I-07091; *SSWP v Czop and SSWP v Punakova* joined cases, C-147/11 and C-148/11 [2012]; *Landesamt für Ausbildungsförderung Nordrhein-Westfalen v Lubor Gaal*, C-7/94 [1995] ECR I-01031

300 para 073401 DMG

301 *Echternach and Moritz v Netherlands Minister for Education and Science*, joined cases 389/87 and 390/87 [1989] ECR I-00723, paras 18-23

302 Reg 16(1) and (4) I(EEA) Regs

303 Art 10 EU Reg 492/2011 (before 1 June 2012, Art 12 EC Reg 1612/68 was in identical terms)

304 *Baumbast and R v SSHD*, C-413/99 [2002] ECR I-07091

305 *Teixeira v LB Lambeth and SSHD*, C-480/08 [2010] ECR I-01107, paras 84-86; *Alarape and Tijani v SSHD*, C-529/11 [2013]

306 *Teixeira v LB Lambeth and SSHD*, C-480/08 [2010] ECR I-01107, para 3

307 *Baumbast and R v SSHD*, C-413/99 [2002] ECR I-07091, para 75; see also *SSWP v RR (IS)* [2013] UKUT 21 (AAC)

308 Reg 16(8) I(EEA) Regs

309 *SSWP v MH (IS)* [2016] UKUT 526 (AAC)

310 Reg 16(8)-(10) I(EEA) Regs

311 Reg 16(11) I(EEA) Regs

312 Reg 16(1) and (2) I(EEA) Regs

313 *Zhu and Chen v SSHD*, C-200/02 [2004]
ECR I-09925; see also *Alokpa and
Moudoulou v Ministre du Travail, de
l'Emploi et de l'Immigration*, C-86/12
[2013], paras 27-29; *SSHD v NA*, C-115/
15 [2016]

314 Reg 4(5) I(EEA) Regs; DMG Memo 24/
16, para 13

315 Reg 16(1) and (5) I(EEA) Regs

316 *Zambrano v ONEm*, C-34/09 [2011] ECR
I-01177; *Dereci and Others v
Bundesministerium für Inneres*, C-256/11
[2011] ECR I-11315

317 *Harrison and AB v SSHD* [2012] EWCA
Civ 1736; *O and S v
Maahanmuuttovirasto and
Maahanmuuttovirasto v L*, joined cases
C-356/11 and C-357/11 [2012]

318 *Sanneh and Others v SSWP* [2015] EWCA
Civ 49. The appeal to the Supreme
Court in the joined case of *HC* was heard
in June 2017, judgment pending – file
reference: *R (on the application of HC) v
SSWP* UKSC 2015/0215

319 Reg 16(1) and (6) I(EEA) Regs

320 *SSWP v Czop and Punakova*, joined cases
C-147/11 and C-148/11 [2012]

321 Art 12 EC Reg 1612/68 replaced, in
identical terms, by Art 10 EU Reg 492/
2011 since 1 June 2012

322 *SSWP v Czop and Punakova*, joined cases
C-147/11 and C-148/11 [2012], para
33

323 *SSWP v Punakova* [2012] UKUT 352
(AAC) and *SSWP v Czop* [2012] UKUT
351 (AAC)

324 *RM v SSWP (IS)* [2014] UKUT 401 (AAC);
Hrabkova v SSWP [2017] EWCA Civ 794

325 *Hrabkova v SSWP* [2017] EWCA Civ 794

326 Reg 16(6) I(EEA) Regs

327 *Sanneh and Others v SSWP* [2015] EWCA
Civ 49. The appeal to the Supreme
Court in the joined case of *HC* was heard
in June 2017, judgment pending – file
reference: *R(on the application of HC) v
SSWP* UKSC 2015/0215

15. Permanent right to reside

328 Art 16(1) EU Dir 2004/38

329 Art 16(4) EU Dir 2004/38; reg 15(2)
I(EEA) Regs

330 Art 16(1) EU Dir 2004/38; reg 15(1)
I(EEA) Regs

331 Art 16(1) and (2) EU Dir 2004/38; reg
15(1)(a) and (b) and Sch 6 para 8 I(EEA)
Regs; Sch 4 para 6 (IEEA) Regs 2006

332 Arts 7 and 16(1) and (2) EU Dir 2004/
38; regs 6, 7, 14 and 15 I(EEA) Regs;
Ziolkowski and Szeja v Land Berlin, joined
cases C-424/10 and C-425/10 [2011]
ECR I-14035

333 *SSWP v Lassal*, C-162/09 [2010] ECR I-
09217; *Alarape and Tijani v SSHD*, C-
529/11 [2013]; *Ogieriakhi v Minister for
Justice and Equality*, C-244/13 [2014]

334 Sch 6 para 8 I(EEA) Regs; Sch 4 para 6
I(EEA) Regs 2006

335 *SSWP v Lassal*, C-162/09 [2010] ECR I-
09217; *SSWP v Dias*, C-325/09 [2011]
ECR I-06387; Sch 6 para 8(4) I(EEA) Regs

336 Regs 6(1)(a), 7, 14(1) and (2) and 15(1)
and Sch 6 para 8 I(EEA) Regs; *GE v SSWP
(ESA)* [2017] UKUT 145 (AAC)

337 Vol 2, para 073428 DMG; para C1807
ADM; HB Circular A8/15 para 19

338 Vol 2, para 073443 DMG; HB Circular
A8/15 para 27

339 *GE v SSWP (ESA)* [2017] UKUT 145
(AAC), para 46

340 Vol 2, para 073442 DMG; HB Circular
A8/15 para 26

341 *Ziolkowski and Szeja*, joined cases C-
424/10 and C-425/10 [2011] ECR, I-
14035

342 Regs 13 and 15(1) I(EEA) Regs; *GE v
SSWP (ESA)* [2017] UKUT 145 (AAC)

343 *Ziolkowski and Szeja*, joined cases C-
424/10 and C-425/10 [2011] ECR I-
14035; *GE v SSWP (ESA)* [2017] UKUT
145 (AAC), paras 59-66

344 Reg 14(2) I(EEA) Regs; *Clauder*, C-E-4/11
[2011] EFTACR 216, para 43

345 Regs 14(2) and 15(1)(a) and (b) I(EEA)
Regs

346 Reg 15(1)(f) I(EEA) Regs

347 Arts 12, 13 and 18 EU Dir 2004/38;
Ziolkowski and Szeja, joined cases C-
424/10 and C-425/10 [2011] ECR I-
14035

348 *Ziolkowski and Szeja*, joined cases C-
424/10 and C-425/10 [2011] ECR I-
14035

349 Art 18 EU Dir 2004/38

350 *SSWP v Gubedladze*, Court of Appeal
hearing due in autumn 2017

351 DMG Memo 2/16; ADM Memo 4/16

352 *JK v SSWP (SPC)* [2017] UKUT 179 (AAC)

353 *Ziolkowski and Szeja*, joined cases C-
424/10 and C-425/10 [2011] ECR I-
14035; Sch 6, para 8(1) and (3) I(EEA)
Regs; *SSWP v LS (IS)* [2012] UKUT 207
(AAC)

354 *Oakfor and Others v SSHD* [2011] EWCA Civ 499; *Alarape and Tijani v SSHD*, C-529/11 [2013]; *Bee and Another v SSHD* [2013] UKUT 83 (IAC); reg 15(2) I(EEA) Regs

355 Art 16(1) EU Dir 2004/38; reg 15(1) I(EEA) Regs

356 Art 16(3) EU Dir 2004/38; reg 3 I(EEA) Regs

357 *Babajanov v SSHD* [2013] UKUT 513 (IAC)

358 *Idezuna v SSHD* [2011] UKUT 474 (IAC); *Babajanov v SSHD* [2013] UKUT 513 (IAC)

359 Vol 2, paras 073360 and 073417 DMG; para C1796 ADM; HB Circular A8/2015, para 7; CIS/2258/08

360 *OB v SSWP (ESA)* [2017] UKUT 255 (ACC), para 28

361 Reg 3(3) I(EEA) Regs

362 *OB v SSWP (ESA)* [2017] UKUT 255 (ACC), paras 29-30 and 34

363 Following *SSWP v Dias*, C-325/09 [2011] ECR I-06387; see also *Saint Prix v SSWP*, C-507/12 [2014], paras 45 and 46

364 *SSHD v Ojo* [2015] EWCA Civ 1301

365 For example there is no discussion of *Saint Prix v SSWP*, C-507/12 [2014], paras 45 and 46

366 Vol 2, paras 073433-35 DMG; paras C1812-14 ADM; HB Circular A8/2015, paras 20-22

367 Vol 2, para 073439 DMG; para C1820 ADM; HB Circular A8/15, para 26

368 Vol 2, para 073440 DMG; para C1821 ADM; HB Circular A8/15, para 27

369 *GE v SSWP (ESA)* [2017] UKUT 145 (AAC), para 46

370 *Saint Prix v SSWP*, C-507/12 [2014], para 38

371 *Onuekwere v SSHD*, C-378/12 [2014]; reg 3(1) and (3) I(EEA) Regs

372 *Onuekwere v SSHD*, C-378/12 [2014] ECR, paras 24-26

373 Reg 3(1), (3) and (4) I(EEA) Regs; see also *SSHD v MG*, C-400/12 [2014]; Art 28(3) EU Dir 2004/38

374 Sch 6 para 8(4) I(EEA) Regs

375 Art 16(4) EU Dir 2004/38

376 *SSWP v Dias*, C-325/09 [2011] ECR I-06387; see also *SSWP v Lassal*, C-162/09 [2010] ECR I-09217

377 Regs 5 and 15 I(EEA) Regs; Art 17 EU Dir 2004/38

378 *SSHD v FB* [2010] UKUT 447 (IAC), para 23; *LM v HMRC (CHB)* [2016] UKUT 389 (AAC)

379 Reg 5(7) I(EEA) Regs; Art 17(1) EU Dir 2004/38

380 Regs 5(7) and 6(2) I(EEA) Regs; regs 7A(3) and 7B(3) I(EEA) Regs 2006, as saved by reg 45 and Sch 4 para 2 I(EEA) Regs

381 *De Brito v SSHD* [2012] EWCA Civ 709

382 *TG v SSWP (PC)* [2015] UKUT 50 (AAC)

383 *ID v SSWP (IS)* [2011] UKUT 401 (AAC), paras 17 and 18

384 *SSWP v Gubeladze*, Court of Appeal hearing due in autumn 2017

385 DMG Memo 2/16; ADM Memo 4/16

386 *PM (EEA – spouse – 'residing with') Turkey* [2011] UKUT 89 (IAC)

387 Art 17(3) EU Dir 2004/38; see also *RM (Zimbabwe) v SSHD* [2013] EWCA Civ 775, para 56 – cited in *TG v SSWP (PC)* [2015] UKUT 50 (AAC), para 33; paras 62-64 of the AG's opinion in *Givane*, C-257/00 [2003] ECR I-00345, although the ECJ did not address the issue itself.

388 Reg 15(1)(d) I(EEA) Regs

389 Art 16(4) EU Dir 2004/38; reg 15(2) I(EEA) Regs – note that the words 'only' and 'consecutive' were removed from these regulations from 1 February 2017, but EU law has not changed and should be followed.

390 Part 4 I(EEA) Regs

391 Vol 2, paras 073350-68 and 073414-43 DMG; paras C1750-77 and C1793-824 ADM; HB Circular A8/2015

392 Vol 2, paras 073429-32 DMG; C1810 ADM

Chapter 13

• •

Residence and presence: rules for individual benefits

This chapter covers:
1. Means-tested benefits (below)
2. Bereavement benefits (p215)
3. Child benefit and guardian's allowance (p216)
4. Disability and carers' benefits (p218)
5. Industrial injuries benefits (p221)
6. Contribution-based jobseeker's allowance and contributory employment and support allowance (p223)
7. Maternity allowance (p225)
8. Retirement pensions (p225)
9. Social fund funeral and winter fuel payments (p226)
10. Tax credits (p227)

This chapter explains the residence and presence rules for each benefit. It also covers how you may be assisted by the European Union (EU) co-ordination rules. Further information on the different residence and presence tests is in Chapter 10, further information on the habitual residence and right to reside tests is in Chapter 11, and further information on the EU co-ordination rules is in Chapter 16. This chapter does not explain the rules on being paid while you are abroad. These are covered in Part 5.

1. Means-tested benefits

To be entitled to income support (IS), income-based jobseeker's allowance (JSA), income-related employment and support allowance (ESA), housing benefit (HB), pension credit (PC) and universal credit (UC), you (and your partner for joint-claim JSA or UC) must:
- (except for HB – see p211) be present in Great Britain (see p94);[1] *and*
- satisfy the habitual residence test (see p106), unless you are exempt (see p108).[2]

To satisfy the habitual residence test for these benefits, in addition to being 'habitually resident in fact' (see p112), unless you have transitional protection (see p120), you must have a right to reside (see p117) in the common travel area – ie, the UK, Ireland, Channel Islands and the Isle of Man. For income-based JSA only, you must also have been living in the common travel area for the past three months (see p95 for details including exceptions).

Although there is no requirement to be present in Great Britain to be entitled to HB, the HB rules that require you to occupy your home, except during certain temporary absences, can mean that you cease to be entitled if you go abroad.[3] If you are temporarily absent from your home and outside Great Britain, your entitlement generally only continues during an absence of up to four weeks, unless you are covered by an exception (see p242).

For the means-tested benefits other than HB, the rules treat you as present in Great Britain during a temporary absence in certain circumstances, so you can continue to receive these benefits while you are abroad for limited periods (see p246).

For all means-tested benefits, the habitual residence test applies to the claimant.

If you live with a partner and claim UC or joint-claim JSA, the habitual residence test applies to both of you, as you are both claimants. If you satisfy the habitual residence test but your partner does not, the rules are different for each benefit. For UC, you claim and are paid as a single person, but your partner's income and capital are taken into account (see p110). For joint-claim JSA, you do not need to make a joint claim and are still paid as a couple (see p109).

If you come under the UC system, unless you are in a 'full service area', you must meet certain 'gateway' conditions, including having a national insurance number (see p354). In addition, you (and, if you are in an area where couples can claim, your partner) must:[4]

- be a British citizen; *and*
- have resided in the UK throughout the two years before the date of your claim; *and*
- not have left the UK for a continuous period of more than four weeks during the above period.

If you do not satisfy the 'gateway' conditions for UC, you may be able to claim existing means-tested benefits. For further details, see CPAG's *Welfare Benefits and Tax Credits Handbook*.

Note: looking for work abroad does not count towards satisfying the requirement that you be 'actively seeking work' for income-based JSA.[5]

If your partner is abroad

If you have a partner who is abroad, the effect this has on your benefit depends on whether the separation is permanent or, if temporary, whether you still count as members of the same household.

If you are still regarded as a couple, your partner's absence abroad can affect your benefit in two ways.

• At some point, you will cease to be paid an amount of benefit for your partner.

• Your partner's capital and income can continue to affect your entitlement.

If you separate permanently (ie, you do not intend to resume living with your partner), you no longer count as a couple and must claim as a single person.[6] Your partner's income and capital no longer affect your benefit.

If you and your partner are living apart temporarily, you continue to count as a couple because you are still treated as members of the same household, unless:[7]

• **for IS, income-based JSA, income-related ESA, PC and HB**, you are likely to be separated for more than 52 weeks. However, you still count as a couple if you are unlikely to be separated for 'substantially' longer than 52 weeks and there are exceptional circumstances, such as a stay in hospital, or if you have no control over the length of the absence;

• **for IS, income-based JSA, income-related ESA and PC**, you or your partner are detained in custody or in a high-security psychiatric hospital, or are on temporary release, or are living permanently in a care home;

• **for UC**, you have been separated (or expect to be separated) for more than six months.

Your partner's absence is from *you*, not from the family home, so these rules can apply even if your partner has never lived in your current home, and your former household need not have been in this country.[8] However, you must have been living with your partner in the same household before you can be treated as continuing to be members of that household.[9] The length of the absence is calculated from when it started to when it is likely to finish.

Where questions of 'intention' are involved (eg, when deciding whether you or your partner intend to resume living with your family), the intention must be 'unqualified'. This means that it must not depend on a factor over which you have no control – eg, the right of entry to the UK being granted by the Home Office[10] or the offer of a suitable job.[11]

If you still count as a couple, there are rules that allow you to continue to receive an amount of benefit for your partner while s/he is abroad for a limited period, depending on the circumstances. These rules vary between the different means-tested benefits (see Chapter 15).

If you cease to be paid for your partner because these rules do not apply, or at the end of the limited period:

- **for IS, income-based JSA, income-related ESA and HB,** your applicable amount no longer includes an amount for your partner. However, your partner's capital, income and work are still taken into account as s/he is still treated as part of your household;[12]
- **for PC,** you are paid as a single person. Your partner's income and capital are ignored because s/he is no longer treated as part of your household;[13]
- **for UC,** you cease to be entitled as joint claimants and must claim as a single person. Your award is based on the maximum amount for a single person, but your partner's income and capital are taken into account until you have been, or you expect to be, apart for six months (as then you cease to be treated as a couple).[14] **Note:** if your partner's absence abroad means s/he ceases to be habitually resident (including if s/he ceases to have a right to reside) in the common travel area, s/he is treated as no longer present. You can claim as a single person, but your partner's income and capital are taken into account.[15]

If your child is abroad

If you have a child who is abroad, the effect this has on your benefit depends on whether s/he is still treated as being part of your household, despite temporarily living away from you.

S/he ceases to be treated as part of your household if:[16]

- **for IS, JSA, ESA and HB,** s/he is not living with you and:
  - has no intention of resuming living with you; *or*
  - is likely to be absent for more than 52 weeks, unless there are exceptional circumstances, such as being in hospital, or if you have no control over the length of absence and the absence is unlikely to be substantially longer than 52 weeks;
- **for IS, JSA and ESA,** s/he is not living with you and has been abroad for more than:
  - four weeks; *or*
  - eight weeks (26 weeks for ESA) to get medical treatment;
- there are other reasons that are not related to residence or presence, such as being fostered. See CPAG's *Welfare Benefits and Tax Credits Handbook* for more information.

For IS or income-based JSA, once your child stops being treated as part of your household, s/he is no longer included in your applicable amount. If s/he returns to your household, you must claim child tax credit (CTC) (or if you are in a UC 'full service area', UC) for her/him instead.[17] See p248 for IS and p251 for income-based JSA.

For UC, you cease to be responsible for a child if s/he is absent from your household and the absence exceeds, or is expected to exceed, one month, or, in limited circumstances, two or six months (see p256).[18]

From 6 April 2017, you can only be paid means-tested benefits (and CTC) for your third and subsequent child in limited circumstances (known as the 'two-child limit'). These include for UC and HB, transitional rules (which may cease to apply if your child returns from abroad after payments for her/him, or your claim, ended because s/he ceased to be part of your household). **Note:** HB is always paid for a child for whom you receive CTC.

For HB, UC, IS and income-based JSA, if you have adopted a child or s/he has been placed with you for adoption, this is generally an exception that means you can be paid for the child even if s/he is your third or subsequent child (provided, for HB, that exception applies to a CTC claim). However, this does not apply if, prior to the adoption under UK law, you had adopted the child under the law of another country.[19]

Note: until 1 November 2018, if you are responsible for more than two children you cannot make a new claim for UC (unless it is linked by less than six months to a previous UC claim). You must claim CTC and other means-tested benefits instead.

The rules on the 'two-child limit' and the exceptions vary between the benefits. Check the details of the benefit you are claiming in CPAG's *Welfare Benefits and Tax Credits Handbook*.

European Union co-ordination rules

If you are covered by the European Union (EU) co-ordination rules, these can assist you to satisfy the habitual residence test for some of the means-tested benefits sooner than might otherwise be the case.

If you are covered by the EU co-ordination rules (see p281) and you are claiming:

- **income-based JSA, income-related ESA or PC**, you cannot be denied benefit solely on the basis that your length of actual residence is too short, because the period of your residence is only one relevant factor in determining whether you are 'habitually resident in fact' and can be outweighed by others (see p116);[20]
- **income-based JSA**, you may be able to argue that if you have come to the UK from another European Economic Area (EEA) country, you must be allowed to demonstrate your link with the UK labour market in ways other than living in the common travel area for three months (see p95).

Reciprocal agreements

Most means-tested benefits are not covered by reciprocal agreements. One exception is the agreement between Great Britain and Northern Ireland which, since 6 April 2016, has covered income-related ESA (as well as contributory ESA), and since 27 November 2016, has covered income-based JSA (as well as contribution-based JSA).[21]

If you moved to Great Britain from Northern Ireland (or vice versa) while claiming ESA before 6 April 2016, the DWP policy was to make an extra-statutory payment to cover any loss of income-related ESA (or contributory ESA) that resulted from having to make a new claim. See p310 for further details.

2. Bereavement benefits

If your spouse or civil partner died on or after 6 April 2017, you may be entitled to the new bereavement support payment if you were ordinarily resident (see p99) in Great Britain (or a specified territory) on the date s/he died.[22] The only 'specified territory' is Sark (see p315).

If your spouse or civil partner died before 6 April 2017, you may be entitled to one of the 'old' bereavement benefits. These do not have any residence or presence rules, except bereavement payment, which requires (unless one of the bullets below applies) you to be present in Great Britain when you make your claim.[23]

If you are absent from Great Britain when you claim bereavement payment, you can only be entitled if:[24]

- your late spouse or civil partner was present in Great Britain when s/he died; *or*
- you were present in Great Britain on the date of the death of your spouse or civil partner; *or*
- neither of the above two bullets apply, but you returned to Great Britain within four weeks of the death of your late spouse or civil partner; *or*
- your late spouse's/civil partner's national insurance (NI) contribution record is sufficient for you to satisfy the contribution conditions for widowed parent's allowance and bereavement allowance; *or*
- your spouse or civil partner died while abroad in another European Economic Area (EEA) state and the European Union (EU) co-ordination rules apply to you (see p281); *or*
- your spouse or civil partner died while abroad in a state which has a reciprocal agreement with the UK that covers your entitlement to bereavement payment.

DWP guidance states that if you and your late spouse or civil partner were outside Great Britain when s/he died and you do not return to Great Britain within four weeks of the death (and none of the last three bullets above apply), you are disqualified from bereavement payment, even if you claim within the necessary time limit when you are back in Great Britain.[25] It is arguable that this approach is incorrect and you should only be disqualified if you are absent from Great Britain when you make your claim (and none of the above bullets apply).

European Union co-ordination rules

If you are covered by the EU co-ordination rules (see p281) and the UK is your 'competent state' (see p288):[26]

- you can, if necessary, rely on NI contributions paid by your late spouse or civil partner in other EEA states to calculate your entitlement to bereavement benefits under the aggregation principle (see p298);
- you can be entitled to a bereavement support payment if you were residing in another EEA state at the date your spouse or civil partner died;
- you can be entitled to a bereavement payment if your late spouse/civil partner died in another EEA state, or you were in another EEA state at the date of her/his death.

Reciprocal and other international agreements

If you have lived and worked in a country with which the UK has a reciprocal agreement (see p309), you may be able to count periods of insurance paid in that country towards your bereavement benefit entitlement. Similarly, if you are covered by an international agreement between the EU and another state, you may be able to do the same (see p319). **Note:** the reciprocal agreements have been amended to include, from 6 April 2017, bereavement support payment.[27]

---

3. Child benefit and guardian's allowance

Child benefit

To be entitled to child benefit, you and your child(ren) must be present in Great Britain (see p94).[28]

You are treated as not present and, therefore, not eligible for child benefit if:[29]

- you are not ordinarily resident in the UK (see p99); *or*
- you do not have a right to reside in the UK (see p117); *or*
- you have not been living in the UK for the three months prior to your claim, unless you are exempt (see p95).

Note: you do not need to have a right to reside if you claimed child benefit before 1 May 2004 and you have been receiving it continuously since that date.

You are treated as present if you are:[30]

- a Crown servant posted overseas and:
  - you are, or immediately before your posting abroad you were, ordinarily resident in the UK; *or*
  - immediately before your posting you were in the UK in connection with that posting; *or*
- the partner of a Crown servant posted overseas and in the same country as her/ him, or temporarily absent from that country under the same exceptions that

enable child benefit to continue during a temporary absence from Great Britain (see p257); *or*
- a person who is in the UK as a result of your being deported or legally removed from another country.

You and/or your child can be treated as present for limited periods during a temporary absence (see p257).

While you are treated as present, you continue to satisfy that condition of entitlement. This means that you can continue to receive child benefit if it is already being paid and you can also make a fresh claim during your, or your child's, absence. If you, or your child, spend longer abroad than the permitted periods (see p257), you (or s/he) cease to satisfy the presence condition and your entitlement to child benefit ends.

Note: if you or your child are treated as present, you must satisfy all the other conditions of entitlement including, if your child is not living with you, contributing to the costs of her/him at least the amount of child benefit that would be payable for her/him.[31]

Guardian's allowance

Entitlement to guardian's allowance depends on entitlement to child benefit, so you must meet the conditions for child benefit set out above. In addition, at least one of the child's parents must have:[32]
- been born in the UK; *or*
- spent a total of 52 weeks in any two-year period in Great Britain at some time after reaching the age of 16.

In order to satisfy the second condition above, you are treated as being present in Great Britain during any absence abroad which is due to your employment as a serving member of the forces, an airman or airwoman, mariner or continental shelf worker.

European Union co-ordination rules

If you are covered by the European Union (EU) co-ordination rules (see p281), you may be able to:
- use certain periods of residence in another European Economic Area (EEA) country to satisfy the child benefit requirement to have been 'living in' the UK for the past three months under the aggregation principle. For further information, including on HM Revenue and Customs guidance that suggests this only applies to residence in four EEA countries, see p95;
- use time spent in another EEA state to satisfy the guardian's allowance requirement to have spent 52 weeks in any two-year period in Great Britain (see above). It may also be arguable that this condition should not apply to you

if you are covered by the co-ordination rules and have a 'genuine and sufficient link to the UK' (see p220);[33]

- be paid child benefit and, if applicable, guardian's allowance, for a child resident in another EEA country without her/his needing to satisfy the UK rules on temporary absences. However, you must still satisfy all the other conditions of entitlement, including contributing to the costs of the child an amount at least equal to the amount of child benefit payable for that child.[34] Child benefit and guardian's allowance are classified as 'family benefits' under the EU co-ordination rules. For more details on the payment of these, see p301.

4. Disability and carers' benefits

For attendance allowance (AA), disability living allowance (DLA), personal independence payment (PIP) and carer's allowance (CA), you must:[35]

- be present in Great Britain at the time of your claim;
- have been present in Great Britain for at least 104 weeks in the last 156 weeks (the 'past presence test'). See p94, but see also the exceptions below;
- be habitually resident in the common travel area (see p106) unless your award of AA, DLA or CA began before 8 April 2013, in which case you must be ordinarily resident, rather than habitually resident, until your award is revised or superseded.[36]

If the DLA claimant is a child under 16, her/his residence is generally determined by the residence of the person responsible for her/him (see p98).

For AA, DLA, PIP and CA, you are treated as being habitually resident (as well as treated as present) if you:[37]

- are abroad as a serving member of the armed forces; or
- are living with someone who is abroad as a serving member of the armed forces and s/he is your spouse, civil partner, son, stepson, daughter, stepdaughter, father, stepfather, father-in-law, mother, stepmother or mother-in-law.

For employment and support allowance (ESA) in youth, incapacity benefit (IB) in youth and severe disablement allowance (SDA), you must:[38]

- be present in Great Britain at the time of your claim (see p94);
- have been present in Great Britain for not less than 26 weeks in the last 52 weeks (the 'past presence' test – see p94);
- be ordinarily resident in Great Britain (see p99).

For ESA in youth, IB in youth and SDA, once you satisfy these tests, you do not need to do so again while you are in the same period of limited capability for work or incapacity for work.[39]

Note: in the future, the rules on AA, DLA, PIP and CA may be different in Scotland. See CPAG's online service and *Welfare Rights Bulletin* for updates.

When you can be treated as present

You are treated as being present during certain absences (see p259). Any period when you are treated as present can be counted to satisfy both the presence and the past presence tests.

Exceptions to the past presence test

If you are claiming the DLA care component for a baby under six months old, there is a shorter 13-week past presence test. If covered by this, it continues to apply until your child's first birthday. If your child becomes entitled to DLA aged between six months and 36 months, the past presence test is 26 weeks in the last 156 weeks.

For AA, DLA and PIP, the 104-week (or 26-week or 13-week) past presence test does not apply if you are terminally ill.[40]

The definition of 'terminal illness' is the same as applies for other purposes for these benefits – ie, that you have a progressive disease and your death as a result of that disease can reasonably be expected within six months.[41]

If you, or the family member who you have joined under the family reunion provisions (see p33), have been granted refugee leave or humanitarian protection, you are exempt from the past presence test.[42]

It may also be possible to argue that you should be exempt from the past presence test if you have discretionary leave and one of the documents in the *Autumn Statement 2016* suggests that the DWP accepts this.[43]

European Union co-ordination rules

If you are covered by the European Union (EU) co-ordination rules (see p281):
- you are not entitled to AA, DLA care component, the daily living component of PIP or CA unless the UK is your 'competent state' (see p288).[44] This might not be the case if you (or your family member who brings you within the co-ordination rules) receive a pension from another European Economic Area (EEA) state, or your family member is working in another EEA state (see p290);
- you may be able to claim AA, DLA, PIP and CA in the UK more quickly. Check below to see whether the past presence test does not apply to you (see p220) or whether periods of residence in another EEA state can be used to satisfy the test (see p220);
- you may be able to make a new claim for AA, DLA care component, the daily living component of PIP or CA if you live in another EEA state (see p221);
- you may be entitled to the mobility component of PIP or DLA sooner than you would otherwise be (see p221).

When the past presence test does not apply

The past presence test does not apply to AA, DLA, PIP and CA if:[45]
- you are habitually resident in Great Britain; *and*
- you are covered by the EU co-ordination rules (see p281); *and*
- you can demonstrate 'a genuine and sufficient link to the UK' (see below).

Note: the DWP interprets 'habitual residence' in this context in the same way as 'residence' is interpreted under the EU co-ordination rules (see p289).[46]

Genuine and sufficient link to the UK

The phrase **'genuine and sufficient link to the UK'** is not defined in regulations, but comes from a case decided by the Court of Justice of the European Union (CJEU).[47] The way this phrase is interpreted must therefore be consistent with this judgment.

Although the regulations require you to demonstrate a 'genuine and sufficient link to the UK *social security system*', the Upper Tribunal has held that the last three words must be disregarded as they are not authorised by the CJEU's judgment.[48]

The circumstances which applied in the CJEU case and which were held to have amounted to a 'genuine and sufficient link to the UK' are relevant, but they are not exhaustive. Other factors may be equally or more relevant in your case and may also be affected by the benefit you are claiming.[49] Relevant factors accepted by the CJEU include whether you:[50]
– have worked in the UK;
– have spent a significant part of your life in the UK;
– are receiving a UK contributory benefit;
– are dependent on a family member who has worked in the UK and/or receives a UK contributory benefit. 'Family member' in this context is not limited to the definition of 'member of the family' in the co-ordination rules (see p282). The Upper Tribunal held that a child claiming DLA had a 'genuine and sufficient link to the UK ' on the basis that he was dependent on his sister who had worked in the UK for at least five years.[51] This principle that your link can be established through someone else's link to the UK was also accepted in a subsequent case.[52]

Your presence in the Great Britain is also a factor, and the closer your period of presence comes to satisfying the two-year past presence requirement, the more significance should be attached to this when demonstrating your 'genuine and sufficient link to the UK'.[53]

Note: the interpretation of this phrase is still evolving and is affected by developments in caselaw. See CPAG's online service and *Welfare Rights Bulletin* for updates.

When the co-ordination rules can help you satisfy the past presence test

If you are covered by the EU co-ordination rules (see p281), but are not exempt from the past presence test because you are not accepted as having 'a genuine and sufficient link to the UK', you may be able to satisfy the test by adding certain periods of residence in another EEA state to periods of presence in Great Britain (the 'aggregation principle'[54]). **Note:** the Upper Tribunal has held that 'mere residence' in another EEA state cannot be aggregated in order to satisfy the past presence test.[55] For further details on this and the aggregation principle, see p298.

Making a new claim while living in another European Economic Area state

If you are living in another EEA member state, you can make a new claim for AA, DLA care component, the daily living component of PIP or CA without needing to satisfy the habitual residence, presence and past presence requirements if the UK is your 'competent state' (see p288)[56] and:[57]

- you are habitually resident in another EEA state or Switzerland; *and*
- you are covered by the EU co-ordination rules (see p281); *and*
- you can demonstrate a genuine and sufficient link to the UK (see p220).

Mobility component

You can only be entitled to the mobility component of DLA or PIP if you are habitually resident in the UK. This is because DLA mobility component is listed as, and PIP mobility component is treated by the DWP as, a special non-contributory benefit and therefore not 'exportable'.[58] You can only be paid these in the state where you are resident.[59] Under the EU co-ordination rules, this means where you 'habitually reside'.[60]

If you are covered by the EU co-ordination rules (see p281), these can still assist you to be entitled to the DLA or PIP mobility component sooner than you would otherwise be because:

- the past presence test does not apply to you if you are covered by the rules on p220; *and*
- you cannot be found to be not habitually resident and denied benefit solely on the basis that you have not been actually resident for an 'appreciable period' of time. Your length of actual residence is only one relevant factor in determining whether you are 'habitually resident in fact' and can be outweighed by other factors (see p116).

---

5. Industrial injuries benefits

Industrial injuries benefits are:

- industrial injuries disablement benefit;
- reduced earnings allowance;
- retirement allowance;
- constant attendance allowance;
- exceptionally severe disablement allowance.

To be entitled to any of these benefits, you must have been:

- in Great Britain when the accident at work happened;[61] *or*
- engaged in Great Britain in the employment that caused the disease (even if you have also been engaged outside Great Britain in that employment);[62] *or*

- paying UK national insurance (NI) contributions, either at class 1 rate or at class 2 rate as a volunteer development worker when the accident at work happened or you contracted the disease. Benefit is not payable until you return to Great Britain.[63]

There are exceptions to these rules, which mean you can qualify for benefit in respect of an accident which happens, or a disease which is contracted, outside Great Britain while you are:[64]
- employed as a mariner or airman or airwoman;
- employed as an apprentice pilot on board a ship or vessel;
- on board an aircraft on a test flight starting in Great Britain in the course of your employment.

In these cases, there are also more generous rules for defining when accidents arise 'out of and in the course of' your employment, and for complying with time limits under benefit rules.[65]

Note: in the future, the rules on industrial injuries disablement benefit may be different in Scotland. See CPAG's online service and *Welfare Rights Bulletin* for updates.

European Union co-ordination rules

If you are covered by the European Union (EU) co-ordination rules (see p281), you can, if necessary, rely on periods of employment and NI paid in other European Economic Area (EEA) states in order to qualify for industrial injuries benefits in the UK (under the aggregation principle – see p298).

Industrial injuries benefits, except retirement allowance, are classed as 'benefits for accidents at work and occupational diseases' under the EU co-ordination rules (see p284).

If you have an accident while travelling abroad in another member state, this can be deemed to have occurred in the state liable to pay benefits for accidents at work and occupational diseases. If one state determines that you have had an accident or contracted a disease, this should be accepted by the state liable to pay benefit in respect of that accident or disease. These outcomes are achieved under the principle of equal treatment of facts of events (see p298).[66]

If you have worked in two or more EEA states in jobs that gave you a prescribed industrial disease, you get benefit from the member state in which you last did work that, by its nature, is likely to cause that disease and which recognises that disease under its industrial injuries scheme.[67] If you make your claim to the state that does not have responsibility under this rule, your claim and all supporting evidence must be forwarded to the relevant institution in the correct state without delay.[68]

13

Reciprocal agreements

The UK has reciprocal agreements with several countries that cover industrial injuries benefits. The agreements determine which country is responsible for determining and paying your entitlement, and if and how you can combine injuries or take account of new accidents or diseases. For more information on reciprocal agreements covering industrial injuries benefits, see p315.

6. Contribution-based jobseeker's allowance and contributory employment and support allowance

To be entitled to contribution-based jobseeker's allowance (JSA) or contributory employment and support allowance (ESA), you must be in Great Britain.[69] The rules about when you can be paid during a temporary absence abroad are covered on p248 and p251. There are no residence conditions, unless you are claiming contributory ESA in youth (see p218).

Note: looking for work abroad does not count towards satisfying the JSA requirement that you be 'actively seeking employment'.[70]

See p210 for the residence and presence conditions for income-based JSA and income-related ESA.

European Union co-ordination rules

Contribution-based jobseeker's allowance

If you are covered by the European Union (EU) co-ordination rules (see p281) you can, if necessary, rely on the equivalent of national insurance (NI) contributions paid in another European Economic Area (EEA) state to entitle you to contribution-based JSA in the UK. This is achieved under the principle of aggregation (see p298). However, an additional condition applies for unemployment benefits that means that, in most cases, you can only aggregate your contributions if your most recent period of paying or being credited with those contributions was in the UK.[71] See p298 for more details.

If you are coming to, or returning to, the UK to look for work and have been insured in another EEA member state, you may be able to continue to receive that other member state's unemployment benefit for up to three months if:[72]

- you were getting that unemployment benefit immediately before coming to the UK;
- you have been registered as available for work for four weeks (or less if the member state's rules allow) in the other member state;

13

Chapter 13: Residence and presence: rules for individual benefits
6. Contribution-based JSA and contributory ESA

- you claim JSA within seven days after you were last registered in the other member state; *and*
- you meet the relevant jobseeking requirements for JSA.

The three months can be extended to a maximum of six months if the state from which you are claiming the unemployment benefit agrees.[73]

Contributory employment and support allowance

If you are covered by the EU co-ordination rules (see p281) you can, if necessary, rely on the equivalent of NI contributions paid in another EEA state to entitle you to contributory ESA in the UK. This is achieved under the principle of aggregation (see p298).

If you are covered by the EU co-ordination rules (see p281) and have moved to the UK from another EEA state, you may be able to continue to receive a sickness or invalidity benefit from that other EEA state if it continues to be your competent state for the payment of that benefit (see p288).

Reciprocal and other international agreements

If you have lived and worked in a country with which the UK has a reciprocal agreement (see p309), you may be able to count periods of insurance paid in that country towards your entitlement to contribution-based JSA or contributory ESA in the UK if the agreement covers you and that benefit. Similarly, if you are covered by another type of international agreement between the EU and another state, you may be able to do the same (see p319).

Although most reciprocal agreements do not cover income-based JSA, the reciprocal agreement between Northern Ireland and Great Britain was extended to cover income-based JSA (as well as contribution-based JSA) from 27 November 2016 (see p310).

Although most reciprocal agreements do not cover ESA (see p314), the reciprocal agreement between Northern Ireland and Great Britain was extended to cover contributory ESA (as well as income-related ESA) from 6 April 2016.[74] If you moved from Northern Ireland to Great Britain or vice versa while claiming ESA before this date, the DWP policy was to make extra-statutory payments to cover any loss arising from having to make a new claim. If you were receiving extra-statutory payments on this basis up to 27 November 2016, and do not satisfy the contributory conditions for entitlement to contributory ESA, you are treated as satisfying those conditions and as having made a claim for ESA from 27 November 2016 and your period of limited capability for work is treated as continuous (see p310).[75]

7. **Maternity allowance**

Entitlement to maternity allowance (MA) is based on past employment. There are no residence requirements, but you are disqualified if you are absent from Great Britain.[76] See p263 for the rules allowing you to be paid during a temporary absence.

European Union co-ordination rules

If you are covered by the European Union co-ordination rules (see p281) you can, if necessary, rely on periods of employment in other European Economic Area states in order to qualify for MA in the UK. This is achieved under the principle of aggregation (see p298).

8. **Retirement pensions**

Retirement pensions, other than a category D retirement pension, do not have any residence or presence entitlement conditions. They can be paid without time limit, whether or not you are present in Great Britain. However, going abroad can mean you are not paid the annual uprating, can be relevant to decisions on deferring your retirement and can prevent you from 'de-retiring' while you are abroad (see p267).[77]

To be entitled to a category D retirement pension, you must have been:[78]
- resident in Great Britain for at least 10 years in any continuous period of 20 years ending on or after your 80th birthday; *and*
- ordinarily resident (see p99) in Great Britain on either:
  – your 80th birthday; *or*
  – the date on which you claimed the category D pension, if later.

European Union co-ordination rules

If you are covered by the European Union (EU) co-ordination rules (see p281), you can, if necessary, rely on the equivalent of national insurance contributions paid in other European Economic Area (EEA) states to calculate your entitlement to retirement pensions in the UK. Similarly, you can count certain periods of residence in other EEA states to meet the residence requirement for a category D pension. Both these are achieved under the aggregation principle (see p298).

Note: your award may be reduced to reflect the proportion of years of contributions paid, or periods of residence completed, in the UK out of the total years of contributions paid or periods of residence completed in all states.[79]

The requirement to be ordinarily resident for a category D retirement pension may not apply to you if you are covered by the EU co-ordination rules and you can show that you have a 'genuine and sufficient link to the UK' (see p220).[80]

13

Chapter 13: Residence and presence: rules for individual benefits
9. Social fund funeral and winter fuel payments

Reciprocal and other international agreements

If you have lived and worked in a country with which the UK has a reciprocal agreement (see p309), you may be able to count periods of residence or insurance paid in that country towards your UK retirement pension entitlement. For further information on reciprocal agreements and retirement pensions, see p315.

Similarly, if you are covered by another international agreement between the EU and another state, you may be able to do the same (see p319).

9. Social fund funeral and winter fuel payments

The only two social fund payments that have residence conditions are funeral expenses payments and winter fuel payments.

Note: in the future, the rules on funeral expenses payments and winter fuel payments, as well as cold weather payments and Sure Start maternity grants, may be different in Scotland. See CPAG's online service and *Welfare Rights Bulletin* for updates.

Funeral expenses payment

To qualify for a funeral expenses payment:
- the deceased must have been ordinarily resident (see p99) in the UK;[81]
- the funeral must usually take place in the UK. However, it can take place in any European Economic Area (EEA) country if you or your partner are:[82]
  - an EEA national and a 'worker' (see p142), including if you have retained this status (see p149);
  - an EEA national and a self-employed person (see p159), including if you have retained this status (see p163);
  - a family member of one of the above (see p170);
  - an EEA national with a permanent right of residence acquired in less than five years, or you are the family member of such a person (see p197);
  - arguably, a person with any other right of residence in the UK under European Union (EU) law (see below).

It is arguable that you can also qualify for a funeral expenses payment for a funeral in another EEA state if you have *any* right to reside in the UK under EU law. This is because the EU law on residence rights has developed since the above rules were introduced and now covers additional groups of EEA nationals and their family members. The above rules were introduced following a case in which the Court of Justice of the European Union (CJEU) held that requiring a funeral to be in the UK was unlawfully discriminatory against EU migrant workers.[83] Arguably, the same applies to other groups who now have residence rights under EU law, but who are not listed in the funeral payment regulations – eg, people who have a permanent right of residence following five years of legal residence in the UK. Furthermore, EU Directive 2004/38 contains a general rule that (subject to certain limitations) prohibits discrimination against anyone with a right of residence.[84]

Winter fuel payment

To qualify for a winter fuel payment, you must be ordinarily resident (see p99) in Great Britain on any day in the qualifying week.[85]

The qualifying week
The '**qualifying week**' is the week beginning on the third Monday in September before the winter you want to be paid for.

European Union co-ordination rules

You are not required to be ordinarily resident in Great Britain in order to be entitled to a winter fuel payment if, on any day in the qualifying week, you are:[86]
- covered by the EU co-ordination rules (see p281);
- habitually resident in Switzerland or an EEA country (other than Cyprus, France, Gibraltar, Greece, Malta, Portugal, Spain or the UK); *and*
- can demonstrate a 'genuine and sufficient link to the UK' (see p220).

Was your application for a winter fuel payment refused before September 2013?
The EU rules were only included within the UK regulations from 16 September 2013. However, they are based on a judgment of the CJEU, dated 21 July 2011.[87] If you had your winter fuel payment refused because, at the relevant time, you were not ordinarily resident in Great Britain, but you satisfied the above rules, you can request that the decision be revised. The DWP will revise its decision on the grounds of official error if it was made on or after 21 July 2011.[88] If the decision was made before this date, the DWP's position is that it can only be revised if another ground for revision is available.[89] For a discussion of similar issues in relation to previous refusals of disability benefits, see p262.

10. **Tax credits**

To be entitled to **child tax credit** (CTC), you (and your partner if you are making a joint claim) must:[90]
- be present in the UK (see p94); *and*
- be ordinarily resident in the UK (see p99); *and*
- have a right to reside in the UK (see p117); *and*

● have been living in the UK for the three months prior to your claim (unless you are exempt – see p95).

To be entitled to **working tax credit** (WTC), you (and your partner if you are making a joint claim) must be:[91]
● present in the UK (see p94); *and*
● ordinarily resident in the UK (see p99).

There are, however, some exceptions.[92]
● There are several groups of people who are exempt from the requirement to have been living in the UK for three months prior to the date of your CTC claim (see p97).
● You do not need to have a right to reside for CTC if you claimed CTC before 1 May 2004 and you have been receiving it since then.
● You are treated as ordinarily resident in the UK for CTC and WTC and, for CTC, you are not required to have been living in the UK for the past three months, if you have been deported or otherwise legally removed from another country to the UK.
● You are treated as ordinarily resident in the UK for WTC if you have a right to reside under European Union (EU) Directive 2004/38 (see p126). However, in practice, being accepted as ordinarily resident is rarely a problem.
● You can be treated as present for either eight or 12 weeks during a temporary absence, or while you or your partner are a Crown servant posted overseas (see p269). While you are treated as present, you continue to satisfy the conditions of entitlement to tax credits. This means that you can continue to receive tax credits that are already in payment and can make a fresh or renewal claim during your absence. If you spend longer abroad than the permitted periods, you cease to satisfy the presence condition and your tax credit entitlement ends.

Note:
● If you are a self-employed European Economic Area (EEA) national, the definition of 'self-employed' for WTC purposes (ie, that you are carrying out a trade, profession or vocation that is organised and regular, on a commercial basis and with a view to making a profit[93]) is different from and does not affect the meaning of 'self-employed' for the purpose of having a right to reside that satisfies that requirement for CTC (see p159).
● If you are responsible for a child but do not have a right to reside and so cannot claim CTC, the number of hours you need to work to be entitled to WTC is still determined on the basis that you are responsible for a child.[94] If HM Revenue and Customs (HMRC) tells you that you cannot claim WTC unless you work 30 hours because you do not receive CTC, this is wrong.

Being absent (other than while you are treated as present), ceasing to be ordinarily resident or losing your right to reside are all changes that you must notify to HMRC within one month. Failure to notify may result in your being overpaid and/or being subject to a penalty.

Couples and children

If you are a member of a couple and make a joint tax credit claim, you must both satisfy the residence requirements. Your entitlement to tax credits as a couple ends if either you or your partner:
- are abroad for longer than a permitted temporary absence of eight or 12 weeks (see p269);
- (for CTC only) lose the right to reside;
- cease to be ordinarily resident.

The person who continues to satisfy the residence rules can make a fresh claim for CTC and/or WTC as a single person if s/he is entitled on that basis.

If your partner returns to the UK, or becomes ordinarily resident or acquires a right to reside, you must terminate your single person claim and claim again as a couple.

If you or your partner are abroad (even for a permitted temporary absence of less than eight or 12 weeks) and you (or s/he) were the only partner in full-time work, you may lose entitlement to WTC if the requirement to be in full-time work is no longer satisfied.

If at any point HMRC considers that you and your partner have separated and this is likely to be permanent, you stop being entitled to make a joint claim as a couple and each of you may be entitled to make single claim.[95]

You have a duty to notify HMRC of any of the above changes within one month of their taking place. Failure to do so may result in your being overpaid or being given a penalty, as well as missing out on any potential alternative entitlements that you may have as a single person or as a couple.

There are no presence or residence requirements for any child in your claim, but you must be responsible for her/him. You count as being responsible if the child normally lives with you or, if there are competing claims, you have main responsibility for her/him.[96]

If your partner or child is a non-EEA national, also check the rules in Part 3. In particular, see p77 if:
- your child is a non-EEA national with leave that is subject to a 'no recourse to public funds' condition; and/or
- your partner is a non-EEA national who does not have immigration leave to enter or remain in the UK and does not have a right to reside.

From 6 April 2017, you can only be paid CTC (and means-tested benefits) for your third and subsequent child in limited circumstances (the 'two-child limit'). These include if the child was born before 6 April 2017 or if an exception applies. One exception is if you have adopted the child or s/he has been placed with you for adoption. However, this exception does not apply if, prior to the adoption under UK law, you had adopted the child under the law of another country.[97] For details of the 'two-child limit' rule, including the exceptions, see CPAG's *Welfare Benefits and Tax Credits Handbook*.

European Union co-ordination rules

CTC is classed as a 'family benefit' under the EU co-ordination rules. If you are covered by the EU co-ordination rules (see p281), you may be able to:

- be paid CTC for a partner or child resident in another EEA country;
- use periods of residence in another EEA country to satisfy the requirement for CTC to have been living in the UK for the past three months under the 'aggregation principle'. For further information, including HMRC guidance that suggests this principle only applies to residence in four EEA countries, see p95.

For more details on the payment of family benefits, see p301.

WTC is not covered by the EU co-ordination rules. Therefore, if your partner is in another EEA country, although you may be able to make a joint claim for CTC as a couple, your WTC claim is treated as a single person's claim.[98] In this case, or if you are a single claimant with a child living in another EEA country, your CTC claim is decided in accordance with the EU co-ordination rules, but your WTC claim is decided solely under UK legislation. If you or your partner are working in another EEA country but live in the UK, and therefore remain present and ordinarily resident in the UK, this work can count for the purposes of your WTC claim.[99]

In any of the circumstances above, your claim(s) is likely to be deemed 'complex' and processed by the 'international team' at HMRC. Detailed guidance for decision makers on how these claims should be administered can be referred to if you experience difficulties.[100]

Although the co-ordination rules do not apply to WTC, other provisions of EU law mean that you cannot be refused the childcare element of WTC in respect of childcare costs solely because the childcare provider is located outside the UK in another EEA state.[101] This was the judgment of the Northern Ireland commissioners in a decision which is not binding in Great Britain. However it is strongly persuasive as it concerns UK legislation and has has been highlighted by the Upper Tribunal in Great Britain. At the time of writing, this decision had not been reflected in guidance, which continues to state that childcare costs can only be paid for approved childcare providers in the UK.[102]

Notes

1. Means-tested benefits
1   **IS** s124(1) SSCBA 1992
    JSA s1(2)(i) JSA 1995
    ESA s1(3)(d) WRA 2007
    PC s1(2)(a) SPCA 2002
    UC s4(1)(c) WRA 2012
2   **IS** Regs 21-21AA IS Regs
    JSA Regs 85-85A JSA Regs
    ESA Regs 69-70 ESA Regs
    HB Reg 10 HB Regs; reg 10 HB(SPC) Regs
    PC Reg 2 SPC Regs
    UC Reg 9 UC Regs
3   s130(1)(a) SSCBA 1992; reg 7 HB Regs; reg 7 HB(SPC) Regs
4   Sch 5 WRA(No.9)O, as applied in UC areas by subsequent commencement orders
5   *GP v SSWP (JSA)* [2015] UKUT 746 (AAC)
6   **IS** Reg 16(2)(a) IS Regs
    JSA Reg 78(2)(a) JSA Regs
    ESA Reg 156(3)(a) ESA Regs
    PC Reg 5(1)(a)(i) SPC Regs
    HB Reg 21(2)(a) HB Regs; reg 21(2)(a) HB(SPC) Regs
    UC Reg 3(6) UC Regs
7   **IS** Reg 16(1)-(3) IS Regs
    JSA Reg 78(1)-(3) JSA Regs
    ESA Reg 156(1)-(4) ESA Regs
    PC Reg 5 SPC Regs
    HB Reg 21(1) and (2) HB Regs; reg 21(1) and (2) HB(SPC) Regs
    UC Reg 3(6) UC Regs
8   CIS/508/1992
9   *Broxtowe Borough Council v CS (HB)* [2014] UKUT 186 (AAC)
10 CIS/508/1992; CIS/13805/1996
11 CIS/484/1993
12 **IS** Regs 4, 16 and 21 and Sch 7 paras 11 and 11A IS Regs
    JSA Regs 78 and 85 and Sch 5 paras 10 and 11 JSA Regs
    ESA Reg 156 and Sch 5 paras 6 and 7 ESA Regs
    HB Reg 21 HB Regs; reg 21 HB(SPC) Regs
13 Regs 3-5 SPC Regs
14 Regs 3(3) and (6), 18(2), 22(3) and 36(3) UC Regs
15 Regs 3(3), 9, 18(2), 22(3) and 36(3) UC Regs
16 **IS** Reg 16 IS Regs
    JSA Reg 78 JSA Regs
    ESA Reg 156 ESA Regs
    HB Reg 21 HB Regs; reg 21 HB(SPC) Regs
17 Reg 1(4B) and (8B) SS(WTCCTC)(CA) Regs
18 Reg 4(7) UC Regs
19 **IS** and **JSA** Regs 5 and 6 The Social Security (Restrictions on Amounts for Children and Qualifying Young Persons) Amendment Regulations 2017, No.376; Sch 12 para 3 UC Regs; DMG Memo 10/17, paras 13, 14 and 26
    UC Sch 12 para 3 UC Regs; ADM Memo 10/17, paras 15 and 29
    HB Reg 22 HB Regs; reg 22 HB(SPC) Regs
20 *Swaddling v Chief Adjudication Officer*, C-90/97 [1999] ECR I-01075
21 SS(NIRA) Regs; SS(GBRA)(NI) Regs; SS(NIRA)(A) Regs; SS(GBRA)(A) Regs

2. Bereavement benefits
22 s30(1) PA 2014
23 s113 SSCBA 1992
24 s113 SSCBA 1992; reg 4(1) and (2B) SSB(PA) Regs
25 para 077081 DMG, Example 2
26 Arts 5, 6, 7, 42 and 43 EU Reg 883/04
27 The Social Security (Reciprocal Agreements) Order 2017, No.159; SS(NIRA)(A) Regs; SS(GBRA)(A) Regs; DMG Memo 15/17

3. Child benefit and guardian's allowance
28 s146 SSCBA 1992
29 Reg 23 CB Regs
30 Regs 23, 30 and 31 CB Regs
31 s143(1)(b) SSCBA 1992
32 Reg 9 GA(Gen) Regs
33 *Stewart v SSWP*, C-503/09 [2011] ECR I-06497; *SSWP v JG (IS)* [2013] UKUT 298 (AAC); *SSWP v Garland* [2014] EWCA Civ 1550
34 s143(1)(b) SSCBA 1992; *RK v HMRC (CHB)* [2015] UKUT 357 (AAC); *JL v HMRC (CHB)* [2017] UKUT 193 (AAC)

4. Disability and carers' benefits
35 **AA** Reg 2 SS(AA) Regs
  DLA Reg 2 SS(DLA) Regs
  PIP Reg 16 SS(PIP) Regs
  CA Reg 9 SS(ICA) Regs
36 Reg 1 SS(DLA,AA&CA)(A) Regs
37 **AA** Reg 2(2) and (3A) SS(AA) Regs
  DLA Reg 2(2) and (3A) SS(DLA) Regs
  PIP Regs 19 and 20 SS(PIP) Regs
  CA Reg 9(3) SS(ICA) Regs
38 **ESA** Reg 11 ESA Regs; reg 12 ESA Regs
  2013
  IB Reg 16 SS(IB) Regs
  SDA Reg 3 SS(SDA) Regs
39 **ESA** Reg 11(4) ESA Regs; reg 12(4) ESA
  Regs 2013
  IB Reg 16(6) SS(IB) Regs
  SDA Reg 3(3) SS(SDA) Regs
40 **AA** Reg 2(3) SS(AA) Regs
  DLA Reg 2(4) SS(DLA) Regs
  PIP Reg 21 SS(PIP) Regs
41 **AA** s35(2C) SSA 1975
  DLA s66(2) SSCBA 1992
  PIP s82(4) WRA 2012
42 *MM and IS v SSWP (DLA)* [2016] UKUT
  149 (AAC), confirmed in DMG Memo
  20/16, ADM Memo 21/16, para
  071716 DMG and para C2027 ADM
43 HM Government, *Autumn Statement
  2016: policy costings*, November 2016,
  p9
44 ss65(7), 70(4A) and 72(7B) SSCBA
  1992; s84 WRA 2012
45 **AA** Reg 2A SS(AA) Regs
  DLA Reg 2A SS(DLA) Regs
  PIP Reg 22 SS(PIP) Regs
  CA Reg 9A SS(ICA) Regs
46 *SSWP v MM & BK v SSWP* [2016] UKUT
  547 (AAC), para 33. This case is being
  appealed to the Court of Appeal; Art 1(j)
  EU Reg 883/04; Art 11 EU Reg 987/09
47 *Stewart v SSWP*, C-503/09 [2011] ECR I-
  06497
48 *SSWP v MM & BK v SSWP* [2016] UKUT
  547 (AAC), paras 28-31. This case is
  being appealed to the Court of Appeal.
  See also DMG Memo 16/17 and ADM
  Memo 20/17
49 *SSWP v JG (IS)* [2013] UKUT 298 (AAC);
  SSWP v Garland [2014] EWCA Civ 1550
50 *Stewart v SSWP*, C-503/09 [2011] ECR I-
  06497
51 *PB v SSWP (DLA)* [2016] UKUT 280 (AAC)
52 *SSWP v MM & BK v SSWP* [2016] UKUT
  547 (AAC), para 38. This case is being
  appealed to the Court of Appeal.

53 *SSWP v MM & BK v SSWP* [2016] UKUT
  547 (AAC), para 32. This case is being
  appealed to the Court of Appeal.
54 Art 6 and Annex XI UK entry para 2 EU
  Reg 883/04
55 *SSWP v MM & BK v SSWP* [2016] UKUT
  547 (AAC), paras 18-27 and 35. This
  case is being appealed to the Court of
  Appeal. See also DMG Memo 16/17 and
  ADM Memo 20/17
56 ss65(7), 70(4A) and 72(7B) SSCBA
  1992; s84 WRA 2012
57 **AA** Reg 2B SS(AA) Regs
  DLA Reg 2B SS(DLA) Regs
  PIP Reg 23 SS(PIP) Regs
  CA Reg 9B SS(ICA) Regs
58 *Bartlett and Others v SSWP*, C-537/09
  [2011] ECR I-03417; para C2097 ADM
59 Art 70 EU Reg 883/04; *Swaddling v
  Adjudication Officer*, C-90/97 [1999] ECR
  I-01075
60 Art 1(j) EU Reg 883/04

5. Industrial injuries benefits
61 s94(5) SSCBA 1992
62 Reg 14 SS(IIPD) Regs
63 Reg 10C(5) and (6) SSB(PA) Regs
64 Reg 2 SS(II)(AB) Regs; reg 2 SS(II)(MB)
  Regs
65 Regs 3, 4, 6 and 8 SS(II)(MB) Regs; regs
  3 and 6 SS(II)(AB) Regs
66 Art 5 EU Reg 883/04
67 Art 38 EU Reg 883/04; Art 36 EU Reg
  987/09; *SSWP v OF (by MF) (II)* [2011]
  UKUT 448 (AAC)
68 Art 36(2) EU Reg 987/09

6. Contribution-based jobseeker's allowance and contributory employment and support allowance
69 **JSA** s1(2)(i) JSA 1995
  ESA ss1(3)(d) and 18(4)(a) WRA 2007
70 *GP v SSWP (JSA)* [2015] UKUT 476 (AAC)
71 Art 61(2) EU Reg 883/04
72 Art 64 EU Reg 883/04
73 Art 64(3) EU Reg 883/04
74 SS(NIRA) Regs; SS(GBRA)(NI) Regs
75 Sch Art 2A-2B SS(NIRA) Regs; Sch Art
  2A-2B SS(GBRA)(NI) Regs; see also DMG
  Memo 1/17 paras 4-7

7. Maternity allowance
76 s113(1) SSCBA 1992

8. Retirement pensions
77 s113 SSCBA 1992; reg 4(1) SSB(PA)
  Regs
78 Reg 10 SS(WB&RP) Regs

79 Art 52 EU Reg 883/04; for example, see
Vol 2, para 075771 DMG
80 *Stewart v SSWP*, C-503/09 [2011] ECR, I-
06497; *SSWP v Garland* [2014] EWCA
Civ 1550, paras 14 and 28; *SSWP v MM
and BK v SSWP* [2016] UKUT 547 (AAC).
This case is being appealed to the Court
of Appeal.

9. Social fund funeral and winter fuel payments

81 Reg 7(5) SFM&FE Regs
82 Reg 7(9) and (10) SFM&FE Regs
83 *O'Flynn v Adjudication Officer*, C-237/94
[1996] ECR I-02617; R(IS) 4/98
84 Art 24 EU Dir 2004/38
85 Reg 2 SFWFP Regs
86 Reg 2 SFWFP Regs
87 *Stewart v SSWP*, C-503/09 [2011] ECR I-
06497
88 Reg 3(5)(a) SS&CS(DA) Regs; para
73245 and Vol 2 Part 6 Appendix 1, para
10 DMG
89 Vol 2 Part 6 Appendix 1, para 11 DMG

10. Tax credits

90 s3(3) TCA 2002; reg 3(1) and (5) TC(R)
Regs
91 s3(3) TCA 2002; reg 3(1) TC(R) Regs
92 Reg 3 TC(R) Regs
93 Reg 2(1) WTC(EMR) Regs
94 Regs 2(2) and 4 (2nd condition)
WTC(EMR) Regs
95 s3(5A) TCA 2002
96 s8(2) TCA 2002; reg 3(1) CTC Regs
97 Reg 11(2) CTC Regs
98 CCM 20090, 20160, 20170 and 20260
99 TCM 0288580; see also *GC v CHMRC
(TC)* [2014] UKUT 251 (AAC)
100 CCM 20000
101 *NB v HMRC (TC)* [2016] NICom 47; Art
56 TFEU
102 CCM 20290

Part 5

Benefits while abroad

Chapter 14

Going abroad

This chapter covers:
1. Introduction (below)
2. How your benefits and tax credits are affected (p239)

This chapter provides an overview of the way your entitlement to benefits and tax credits is affected if you, or a member of your family for whom you claim, go abroad. The specific information about individual benefits and tax credits is in Chapter 15.

1. Introduction

Most benefits and tax credits are affected if you, or your partner or child, go abroad. The rules vary between different benefits and tax credits. Some can always be paid abroad, some can only be paid in certain circumstances and for limited periods, and some benefits have rules affecting the amount that can be paid if you are abroad.

Your entitlement while you, or your partner or child, are abroad depends on any or all of the following factors:
- the benefit or tax credit you are claiming (see Chapter 15);
- the reason for going abroad;
- whether the absence is temporary or permanent;
- the length of time the absence will last;
- the country to which you are, or s/he is, going;
- whether you are covered by the European Union (EU) co-ordination rules;
- whether you are covered by a reciprocal agreement the UK has with the country you, or your partner or child, are going to.

In addition to the above factors, other changes that occur indirectly as a consequence of your being abroad can also affect your entitlement – eg, if your income changes, or you cease to count as being in full-time work for the benefit or tax credit you are claiming. Further details on the way these other changes affect your entitlement are covered in CPAG's *Welfare Benefits and Tax Credits Handbook*.

Before you go abroad

If you are thinking about going abroad, check how your entitlement will be affected well in advance of your departure, as this could affect the decisions you make. It also ensures you have sufficient time to take any necessary action before you leave the UK. Notify the Jobcentre Plus/local authority/HM Revenue and Customs (HMRC) office that pays your benefit before you leave, providing details of your destination, purpose and expected duration of your absence abroad. If it is possible for you get your UK benefit paid abroad, you should give the relevant benefit authorities as much notice as possible, as they can be very slow in making these arrangements.

To see how going abroad affects your entitlement, check which rules apply (see below) and then check the rules for the specific benefit or tax credit you are claiming (see Chapter 15).

If you might want to claim a benefit from the country you are going to, it is worth checking what the conditions of entitlement are, as you might want to take relevant documents with you – eg, a statement of the national insurance contributions you have paid, which you can obtain from HMRC, or proof of your past employment. **Note:** check whether claiming a benefit in another country could affect your entitlement to benefits paid abroad by the UK – eg, if you claim a benefit in another European Economic Area (EEA) country, this can mean that the UK is no longer your 'competent state' for the purposes of paying a different benefit under the EU co-ordination rules (see p288).

Which rules apply

Your entitlement to UK benefits or tax credits while you, or a family member, are abroad can be affected by three different sets of rules.

- **The UK benefit and tax credit legislation** contains rules about how your absence, or the absence of your family member, affects your entitlement (see p239). You should check these rules first. If your circumstances mean that, under these rules, you can obtain the benefits you want when you or your family member are outside the UK, you do not generally need to check the other rules. However, if you want to be paid a disability or carer's benefit when you go to another EEA country and you are covered by the EU co-ordination rules, you should check whether they affect your entitlement.
- If you or your family member are going to another EEA country (see p40), even if you are not entitled under UK legislation, you may be able to receive UK benefits if the **EU co-ordination rules** override any specific UK rules that prevent you getting your benefit outside the UK (see p244).
- **Reciprocal agreements** exist between the UK and some other countries and can assist in similar ways to the EU co-ordination rules (see p244). In general, these only apply if the EU co-ordination rules do not assist you. Great Britain and Northern Ireland also have reciprocal agreements.

2. How your benefits and tax credits are affected

UK law

There are different ways in which the UK benefits and tax credits rules affect your entitlement when you (or your family member) go abroad. The main ways in which they result in your not receiving benefit (or not being paid for your family member) are as follows.

- During your (or her/his) absence you do not (or s/he does not) meet the requirement to:
  - be present in Great Britain (see below);
  - be ordinarily resident in the UK (see p241);
  - be habitually resident in the common travel area (ie, the UK, Ireland, Channel Isles and the Isle of Man) (see p241); *or*
  - have a right to reside (see p241).
- Your partner's absence abroad can mean you no longer count as a couple (see p242).
- Your child's absence abroad can mean s/he is no longer included in your claim (see p242).
- You stop being covered by the rules that allow you to receive housing costs for a certain period while you are absent from your home (see p242).

All of the above rules have exceptions. In particular, you can be treated as present in certain circumstances, provided (in most cases) your absence is temporary.

The way these different rules affect your entitlement when you go abroad is explained below. For details on how to satisfy the presence and residence rules when you are in the UK, see Part 4.

Presence and absence

Most benefits require you to be present in Great Britain (the UK for tax credits). You can be treated as present and, therefore, continue to be entitled to the benefit or tax credit, during a temporary absence in specified circumstances (see below). You are disqualified from entitlement to some benefits if you are absent from Great Britain, although there are exemptions for each benefit.

Presence and absence

'**Presence**' means being physically present in Great Britain (the UK for tax credits) and '**absence**' means 'not physically present' in Great Britain. If the DWP, HM Revenue and Customs or a local authority wants to disqualify you from benefit because you were absent from Great Britain, it must show that you were absent throughout that day. This means that, on the day you leave Great Britain and the day you arrive in Great Britain, you count as present.

Temporary absence

Many benefits or tax credits allow you to be treated as present, and therefore entitled to that benefit or tax credit, during a temporary absence in specified circumstances. Your entitlement depends on:

- whether your absence counts as 'temporary' for the benefit or tax credit you are claiming (see below); *and*
- how long (if at all) during your temporary absence the rules for that benefit or tax credit allow you to be treated as present (see Chapter 15).

Temporary absence

For attendance allowance (AA), disability living allowance (DLA), personal independence payment (PIP), tax credits and (for the claimant's, but not the child's, absence) child benefit, you are '**temporarily absent**' from the UK if, at the beginning of the period of absence, it is unlikely to exceed 52 weeks.[1]

For all other benefits, temporary absence is not defined. It is your responsibility to demonstrate that your absence will be temporary, and you should therefore provide full details of why you are going abroad, how long you intend to be away and what you intend to do while you are abroad.[2] However, although your intentions are relevant, they are not decisive.[3] The nature of an absence can also change over time. If your absence is found to be temporary at the beginning of the period, it does not mean that it will always remain temporary. If your circumstances change while you are abroad (eg, you go abroad for one reason and decide to stay for a different purpose), your absence may no longer be regarded as temporary.[4] Although there is no set period for a temporary absence (except for tax credits, child benefit, AA, DLA, and PIP), as a general rule, absences of more than 12 months are not considered to be temporary unless there are exceptional circumstances.[5]

If the purpose of your trip abroad is obviously temporary (eg, for a holiday, to visit friends or relatives or for a particular course of medical treatment) and you buy a return ticket, your absence should be viewed as temporary.

If your absence counts as temporary for the benefit or tax credit you are claiming, you are entitled to receive the benefit or tax credit for a specified period. This period varies for each benefit or tax credit and according to your circumstances. Many of the rules that entitle you to benefit during a specified period only do so if certain circumstances apply, but some simply state a maximum period. See Chapter 15 for information on the specific benefit you are claiming.

Note: for many benefits and tax credits, your intended absence still counts as temporary even if it is longer than the maximum period for which the benefit or tax credit is payable.

Example

Mohsen receives PIP. He goes to visit family in Iran and buys a return ticket to come back after seven months. Mohsen is entitled to PIP for the first 13 weeks of his absence (the maximum period in these circumstances – see p259). Although his intended period of absence is longer than this maximum period, it is still a temporary absence.

Ordinary residence

In order to be entitled to some benefits and tax credits, you must be ordinarily resident in Great Britain (the UK for tax credits). See p99 for a list of benefits and tax credits that require you to be ordinarily resident and an explanation of what 'ordinary residence' means. If, by going abroad, you cease to be ordinarily resident, your entitlement to any benefit or tax credit that requires you to be ordinarily resident ends. However, if your absence abroad is temporary and you intend to return to the UK, your ordinary residence is not usually affected.[6] Ceasing to be ordinarily resident will rarely be the reason why your entitlement ends when you go abroad. It is more likely that your entitlement ends simply because you are absent (see p239). If you receive a decision that your entitlement to a benefit or tax credit has ended because you have ceased to be ordinarily resident, ask for the decision to be looked at again and obtain specialist advice.

Habitual residence

In order to be entitled to some benefits, you must be habitually resident in the common travel area (the UK, Ireland, Channel Isles and the Isle of Man) or be exempt from this requirement. See p106 for a list of benefits that require habitual residence, an explanation of what it means to be 'habitually resident' and a list of who is exempt. If, by going abroad, you cease to be habitually resident, your entitlement to any benefit that requires you to be habitually resident ends. However, if your absence abroad is temporary and you intend to return to the UK, your habitual residence is not usually affected.[7] Ceasing to be habitually resident will rarely be the reason why your entitlement ends when you go abroad. It is more likely that your entitlement ends simply because you are absent (see p239) or, for housing benefit (HB), absent from your home (see p242).

Right to reside

In order to be entitled to some benefits and tax credits, you must have a right to reside in either the UK or the common travel area (the UK, Ireland, Channel Isles and the Isle of Man). See p117 for a list of benefits and tax credits that require a right to reside and an explanation of how this requirement operates. If, by going abroad, you lose your right to reside, your entitlement to any benefit or tax credit that requires you to have a right to reside ends. However, an absence does not necessarily mean you lose your right to reside – it depends on your circumstances.

Couples and children living apart

There are UK benefit and tax credit rules on when members of a couple who are living apart continue to count as a couple and when a child living elsewhere is still included in your claim. Although these rules are not only about situations where one member of a couple or a child is living abroad, when this is the case, these rules can affect your benefit.

If your partner goes abroad, this can affect your benefit or tax credit in one or more of the following ways.

- For tax credits and universal credit (UC), you may cease to be entitled to make a joint claim as a couple and may need to make a single claim.
- Depending on the circumstances, including the permanence or duration of your partner's absence, at some point you will stop being paid for your partner.
- Even if you are not paid for your partner, in some circumstances her/his income and capital can still affect your claim.

If your child goes abroad, depending on the circumstances, including the duration, s/he can cease to be part of your claim. This can affect your entitlement – either you stop being paid for her/him or your entitlement ends altogether.

From 6 April 2017, you can only be paid means-tested benefits and child tax credit for your third and subsequent child in limited circumstances (known as the 'two-child limit'). These include, for UC and HB, transitional rules. These may cease to apply when your child returns from abroad after payments for her/him, or your claim, ended because s/he was abroad. The rules and exceptions vary between the benefits, so check the details of the benefit you are claiming in CPAG's *Welfare Benefits and Tax Credits Handbook*.

For further details of the rules about couples and children for means-tested benefits, see p212, and for tax credits, see p229.

Absence from your home

If you are temporarily absent from the accommodation you normally occupy as your home, you can be treated as occupying it for a period. These rules apply to HB and to housing costs in income support (IS), income-based jobseeker's allowance (JSA), income-related employment and support allowance (ESA), pension credit and UC. They mean you can continue to receive payments during your temporary absence.

The absence rules are not (except for HB) specific to your being outside Great Britain, but can still affect you if you are absent from your home when abroad. They are only briefly summarised here – for further details, see CPAG's *Welfare Benefits and Tax Credits Handbook*.

A new period of absence starts if you return home, even for a short stay. A stay of at least 24 hours before you leave again may be enough.[8]

If you are temporarily absent from home, have not rented out your home and intend to return to it, you can continue to be paid housing costs in your **IS,**

income-based JSA, income-related ESA or PC (provided you remain entitled to these benefits). You can be paid for up to:

- **13 weeks** while you are absent, whatever the reason. You must be unlikely to be away for longer than this;[9]
- **52 weeks** in specific circumstances.[10] These include if you, your partner or child are in hospital, if you are undergoing or recovering from medical treatment, or if you are absent from home because of domestic violence. See CPAG's *Welfare Benefits and Tax Credits Handbook* for more details.

For **HB**, the above 13- or 52-week rule applies if your absence is within Great Britain.[11] However, from 28 July 2016, if you are temporarily absent from home and you are outside Great Britain, the period when you can be treated as occupying your home is different and, in most cases, shorter (see below). If you were already outside Great Britain on this date, the previous rules continue to apply to you until you return to Great Britain (unless you were abroad as a member of HM forces, a mariner or as a continental shelf worker, in which case the new rules apply).[12]

If you are temporarily absent from home while abroad, have not rented out your home and intend to return to it, you can continue to be paid HB for up to:[13]

- **four weeks**, if you are absent outside Great Britain and the absence is unlikely to be more than four weeks;
- **eight weeks**, if the absence abroad is in connection with the death of your partner, your (or your partner's) close relative, or a child for whom you (or your partner) are responsible: the above four weeks are extended by up to four weeks if the decision maker considers it unreasonable for you to return within the first four weeks;
- **26 weeks in specific circumstances.** These include if you, your partner or child are in hospital, if you are undergoing or recovering from medical treatment, or if you are absent from home because of domestic violence. See CPAG's *Welfare Benefits and Tax Credits Handbook* for more details. Your absence abroad must be unlikely to exceed (or in exceptional circumstances, substantially exceed) 26 weeks;
- **26 weeks**, if you are a member of HM forces posted overseas, a mariner or a continental shelf worker. Your absence abroad must be unlikely to exceed 26 weeks.

Note:

- The periods for which you can be paid HB while in Great Britain continue to run during any absence abroad. You may, therefore, be able to return to Britain and continue to be paid HB while absent from your home for the remainder of the 13- or 52- week period. However, if your entitlement has ended as a result of your absence abroad, you cannot qualify for HB again until you return home.[14]

- HB guidance contains a useful table summarising when you can receive HB during different periods of absence, both in Great Britain and abroad.[15]
- If you have a European Economic Area (EEA) right to reside in the UK (see p126) and you go abroad to another EEA country, it is arguable that the shorter period during which you can be entitled while abroad should not apply as it is indirect discrimination and potentially unlawful under European Union (EU) law (see p297). The Court of Justice of the European Union accepted a similar argument in relation to funeral payments, ruling that requiring the funeral to take place in the UK unlawfully discriminated against EU migrant workers (see p226).[16]

If you are temporarily absent from your home, you can continue to be paid UC housing costs for up to six months while you are absent for any reason. You are no longer treated as occupying your home once your absence has lasted, or is expected to last, longer than six months.[17] The main exception to this is if you are absent because of a fear of domestic violence, in which case you can be treated as occupying your home for up to 12 months.[18]

European Union co-ordination rules

If you are an EEA national (including a UK national) or a family member of an EEA national, and you are going to another EEA country, you may be able to benefit from the EU co-ordination rules. These can help you to be paid your benefits or tax credits when you go abroad for longer than would be the case under UK law. The EU co-ordination rules can also enable you to be paid benefit for a family member living in another EEA country. See Chapter 15 for information on the individual benefits and tax credits and Chapter 16 for further information on the co-ordination rules.

Reciprocal agreements

The UK has reciprocal agreements with several EEA and non-EEA countries. For a list of these and further information, see p309. In general, a reciprocal agreement only applies if the EU co-ordination rules do not assist you (see p311). They are therefore of most relevance for non-EEA countries, but they can also assist if you are moving between Great Britain and Northern Ireland, the Channel Islands or the Isle of Man. In addition, the EU and the Council of Europe have other agreements with some countries that can also affect your entitlement. See Chapter 17 for further information on all the agreements.

Notes

2. How your benefits and tax credits are affected

1 **AA** Reg 2(3C) SS(AA) Regs
   DLA Reg 2(3C) SS(DLA) Regs
   PIP Reg 17(2) SS(PIP) Regs
   CB Reg 24(2) CB Regs
   TC Reg 4(2) TC(R) Regs
2 *Chief Adjudication Officer v Ahmed and Others*, 16 March 1994, CA, reported as R(S) 1/96
3 *Chief Adjudication Officer v Ahmed and Others*, 16 March 1994, CA, reported as R(S) 1/96
4 R(S) 1/85
5 R(U) 16/62
6 *R v Barnet London Borough Council ex parte Shah* [1983] 2 AC 309, Lord Scarman at p342D
7 *KS v SSWP (SPC)* [2010] UKUT 156 (AAC)
8 *R v Penwith District Council ex parte Burt* [1988] 22 HLR 292 (QBD); para A3/3.460 GM
9 **IS** Sch 3 para 3(10) IS Regs
   JSA Sch 2 para 3(10) JSA Regs
   ESA Sch 6 para 5(10) ESA Regs
   PC Sch 2 para 4(10) SPC Regs
10 **IS** Sch 3 para 3(11)-(13) IS Regs
   JSA Sch 2 para 3(11)-(13) JSA Regs
   ESA Sch 6 para 5(11)-(13) ESA Regs
   PC Sch 2 para 4(11)-(13) SPC Regs
11 Reg 7(13), (16), (17) and (18) HB Regs; reg 7(13), (16), (17) and (18) HB(SPC) Regs
12 Reg 5 The Housing Benefit and State Pension Credit (Temporary Absence) (Amendment) Regulations 2016, No.624
13 Reg 7(13A)-(13G), (16), (17A)-(17D) and (18) HB Regs; reg 7(13A)-(13G), (16), (17A)-(17D) and (18) HB(SPC) Regs
14 Reg 7(13B) and (17B) HB Regs; reg 7(13B) and (17B) HB(SPC) Regs
15 HB Circular A7/2016
16 Art 18 TFEU; Art 24 EU Dir 2004/38; *O'Flynn v Adjudication Officer*, C-237/94 [1996] ECR I-02617; R(IS) 4/98
17 Sch 3 para 9(1) UC Regs
18 Sch 3 paras 6 and 9(3) UC Regs

Chapter 15

. . . .

Going abroad: rules for individual benefits

This chapter covers:

1. Means-tested benefits (below)
2. Bereavement benefits (p256)
3. Child benefit and guardian's allowance (p257)
4. Disability and carers' benefits (p259)
5. Incapacity benefit, severe disablement allowance and maternity allowance (p263)
6. Industrial injuries benefits (p265)
7. Contribution-based jobseeker's allowance and contributory employment and support allowance (p266)
8. Retirement pensions (p267)
9. Statutory payments (p269)
10. Tax credits (p269)

This chapter explains the UK benefit and tax credit rules on being paid when either you or your family members are abroad. It also covers the ways in which the European Union (EU) co-ordination rules may affect whether you can be paid benefit. See Chapter 14 for an overview of how the UK benefit rules and the EU co-ordination rules operate, and see Chapters 16 and 17 for more details on the EU co-ordination rules and international agreements.

1. Means-tested benefits

You cannot usually receive means-tested benefits when you are abroad, because the rules for each benefit require you to be present in Great Britain (although the rules are different for housing benefit (HB), as your absence from Great Britain affects whether you can be treated as occupying your home – see p254). However, you can be treated as present (or as occupying your home for HB) in certain circumstances. The rules differ between the different benefits.

. . . .

Income support

You cannot usually get income support (IS) if you are not in Great Britain.[1] However, IS can be paid while you are temporarily absent from Great Britain in the circumstances listed below, provided you meet the other conditions of entitlement.

If you were entitled to IS immediately before leaving Great Britain and are temporarily absent, your entitlement can continue:[2]

- **indefinitely** if your absence is for NHS treatment at a hospital or other institution outside Great Britain;
- during the first **four weeks** of your absence, if it is unlikely to exceed 52 weeks and:
  - you are in Northern Ireland; *or*
  - you and your partner are both abroad and s/he satisfies the conditions for one of the pensioner premiums, a disability premium or a severe disability premium; *or*
  - you are claiming IS on the grounds of being incapable of work and are abroad for the sole purpose of receiving treatment for that incapacity. The treatment must be carried out by, or under the supervision of, a person qualified to provide medical treatment, physiotherapy or similar treatment; *or*
  - you are incapable of work and:
    - you have been continuously incapable of work for the previous 28 weeks and you are terminally ill or receiving the highest rate of disability living allowance care component, the enhanced rate of the daily living component of personal independence payment or armed forces independence payment; *or*
    - you have been continuously incapable of work for 364 days; *or*
  - you come within one of the groups of people who can claim IS (see CPAG's *Welfare Benefits and Tax Credits Handbook* for these), other than if you are:
    - in 'relevant education'; *or*
    - involved in a trade dispute, or have returned to work for 15 days or less following the dispute; *or*
    - entitled to statutory sick pay; *or*
    - appealing a decision that you are not incapable of work;
- during the first **eight weeks** of your absence, if it is unlikely to exceed 52 weeks and is solely in connection with arrangements made for the treatment of a disease or disablement of a child or qualifying young person. The treatment must be carried out by, or under the supervision of, a person qualified to provide medical treatment, physiotherapy or similar treatment, and the child or young person must be someone for whom you count as responsible under the IS rules. See CPAG's *Welfare Benefits and Tax Credits Handbook* for who counts as a child or young person and when you count as responsible for her/him.

If you are entitled to housing costs in your IS, your temporary absence from your home can mean that you cease to be entitled to receive these (see p242).

If your partner is abroad

If you are the IS claimant and you stay in Great Britain, your IS applicable amount includes an amount for your partner who is abroad for:[3]

- the first **four weeks**; *or*
- the first **eight weeks**, if s/he meets the conditions of the eight-week rule on p247.

If you are the IS claimant and both you and your partner are abroad, your IS includes an amount for your partner for the first eight weeks if both of you meet the conditions of the eight-week rule on p247.[4]

After this four- or eight-week period, your benefit is reduced because your applicable amount is calculated as if you have no partner. However, your partner is still treated as being part of your household and, therefore, her/his work, income and capital affect your IS entitlement, unless you are no longer treated as a couple (see p242).[5]

If your child is abroad

If you were getting an amount in your IS for your child before s/he went abroad, you continue to be paid for her/him for:[6]

- the first **four weeks**; *or*
- the first **eight weeks**, if your child meets the conditions of the eight-week rule on p247.

After this four- or eight-week period, you cease to be paid IS in respect of your child. When s/he returns to Great Britain, unless you have continued to be paid IS for another child, you will not be able to receive IS for her/him and will need to claim child tax credit (CTC) for her/him instead.[7]

Note: if your child was born after 6 April 2017, you may not be able to receive IS for her/him when s/he returns to Britain if you are already receiving IS for two or more other children due to the 'two-child limit' (see p213).

European Union co-ordination rules

IS is not classified as a 'social security benefit' under the European Union (EU) co-ordination rules (see p285). This means that the co-ordination rules cannot assist you. If you go to another European Economic Area (EEA) state, you can only be paid under the UK rules above.

Income-based jobseeker's allowance

You cannot usually get jobseeker's allowance (JSA) if you are not in Great Britain.[8] However, both income-based JSA and contribution-based JSA can be paid when you are temporarily absent from Great Britain in the circumstances below, provided you meet the other conditions of entitlement.

You can be treated as available for, and actively seeking, work during certain temporary absences abroad. These are similar to, but more limited than, those listed below. See CPAG's *Welfare Benefits and Tax Credits Handbook* for details.[9] Similarly, if you are getting contribution-based JSA and you come under the universal credit (UC) system, you are exempt from the work search requirement and are treated as 'able and willing immediately to take up work' during these absences.[10]

If you are temporarily absent from Great Britain, you are treated as being in Great Britain and can therefore be paid JSA:[11]

- **indefinitely** if you are entitled to JSA immediately before leaving Great Britain and your absence is for NHS treatment at a hospital or other institution outside Great Britain;
- for up to **four weeks** if you are entitled to JSA immediately before leaving Great Britain and:
  - your absence is unlikely to exceed 52 weeks, you continue to satisfy the conditions of entitlement and you are in Northern Ireland. (Note also that the reciprocal agreements between Great Britain and Northern Ireland have been extended to cover income-based JSA – see p310); *or*
  - (except if you come under the UC system) your absence is unlikely to exceed 52 weeks, you continue to satisfy the conditions of entitlement and your partner is also abroad with you and satisfies the conditions for one of the pensioner premiums, a disability premium or a severe disability premium; *or*
  - (except if you come under the UC system) you get a specified type of training allowance that means you do not have to satisfy the JSA jobseeking conditions;[12]
- for up to **eight weeks** if you are entitled to JSA immediately before leaving Great Britain and your absence is unlikely to exceed 52 weeks and is solely in connection with arrangements made for the treatment of a disease or disablement of a child or qualifying young person. The treatment must be carried out by, or under the supervision of, a person qualified to provide medical treatment, physiotherapy or similar treatment and you must count as responsible for the child or young person in the same way as for the similar rule on temporary absence for IS (see p247);
- for an absence of up to **seven days** if you are attending a job interview and you notified the employment officer before you left (in writing if required). On your return, you must satisfy the employment officer that you attended the interview as stated;
- for an absence of up to **15 days** for the purpose of training as a member of the reserve forces.

If you are entitled to housing costs in your income-based JSA, your temporary absence from your home can mean that you cease to be entitled to receive these (see p242).

Joint-claim jobseeker's allowance if your partner is abroad

If you are a member of a 'joint-claim couple' (see CPAG's *Welfare Benefits and Tax Credits Handbook* for what this means) and your partner is temporarily absent from Great Britain on the date you make your claim, you are paid as a couple for:[13]
- an absence of up to **seven days** if your partner is attending a job interview;
- up to **four weeks** if your partner is:
  - in Northern Ireland and her/his absence is unlikely to exceed 52 weeks; *or*
  - getting a specified type of training allowance that means s/he does not have to satisfy the JSA jobseeking conditions.

If you are a joint-claim couple and your partner goes abroad after you claimed JSA, and her/his absence is for NHS treatment at a hospital or other institution outside Great Britain, you are paid as a couple for up to four weeks.[14]

After this seven-day/four-week period, your JSA is reduced because your applicable amount is calculated as if you have no partner.[15] However, your partner is still treated as part of your household if s/he is abroad for treatment in the circumstances above. Therefore, her/his work, income and capital affects your joint-claim JSA entitlement, unless s/he ceases to be treated as part of your household for another reason (see p212).[16]

If your partner has ceased to be treated as part of your household, you can claim income-based JSA as a single person.

Income-based jobseeker's allowance if your partner is abroad

If you are the income-based JSA claimant and you stay in Great Britain, your applicable amount includes an amount for your partner while s/he is abroad for:[17]
- the first **four weeks** of a temporary absence; *or*
- the first **eight weeks** if your partner meets the conditions of the eight-week rule on p249.

If you are the income-based JSA claimant and both you and your partner are abroad, your applicable amount includes an amount for your partner for the first eight weeks if both of you meet the conditions of the eight-week rule on p249.[18]

After this four- or eight-week period, your benefit is reduced because your applicable amount is calculated as if you have no partner. However, your partner is still treated as part of your household and, therefore, her/his work, income and capital affect your income-based JSA entitlement, unless you are no longer treated as a couple (see p212).[19]

Income-based jobseeker's allowance if your child is abroad

If you were getting JSA for your child before s/he went abroad, you can continue to be paid for her/him for:[20]
- the first **four weeks**; or
- the first **eight weeks** if your child meets the conditions of the eight-week rule on p249.

After this four- or eight-week period, you cease to be paid income-based JSA in respect of your child. When s/he returns to Great Britain, unless you have continued to be paid income-based JSA for another child, you cannot receive it for her/him and need to claim CTC for her/him instead.[21] **Note:** if your child was born after 6 April 2017, you may not be able to receive income-based JSA for her/him when s/he returns to Britain if you are already receiving income-based JSA for two or more other children due to the 'two-child limit' (see p213).

European Union co-ordination rules

Income-based JSA is classed as a 'special non-contributory benefit' under the EU co-ordination rules (see p287) and therefore cannot be exported. This means that if you go to another EEA country, the co-ordination rules cannot assist you and you can only be paid income-based JSA abroad under the UK rules explained above.

However, the EU co-ordination rules may enable you to be paid contribution-based JSA for up to three months if you go to another EEA country (see p266).

Income-related employment and support allowance

You cannot usually get employment and support allowance (ESA) if you are not in Great Britain.[22] However, both income-related ESA and contributory ESA can be paid when you are temporarily absent from Great Britain in the circumstances below, provided you meet the other conditions of entitlement.

If you were entitled to ESA immediately before leaving Great Britain and are temporarily absent, you can continue to be entitled:[23]
- **indefinitely** if:
  - your absence is for NHS treatment at a hospital or other institution outside Great Britain; or
  - you are living with your spouse, civil partner, son, daughter, stepson, stepdaughter, father, father-in-law, stepfather, mother, mother-in-law or stepmother who is a serving member of the armed forces;
- for the first **four weeks**, if your absence is unlikely to exceed 52 weeks;
- for the first **26 weeks**, if your absence is unlikely to exceed 52 weeks and is solely in connection with arrangements made for the treatment of:
  - your disease or disablement that is directly related to your limited capability for work which began before you left Great Britain; or
  - the disease or disablement of a dependent child who you are accompanying.

The treatment must be carried out by, or under the supervision of, a person qualified to provide medical treatment, physiotherapy or similar treatment.

If you are due to have a medical examination to assess your limited capability for work when you go abroad, you can ask for this to be carried out in the country you are going to, or to be postponed until you return. If your request is refused and you go abroad and miss your medical, your ESA will be stopped because you failed to attend your medical, unless it is accepted that you had a good cause for not attending. In deciding whether you had good cause, the decision maker must take all your circumstances into account, including the fact that you were outside Great Britain.[24] See CPAG's *Welfare Benefits and Tax Credits Handbook* for further details.

If you are entitled to housing costs in your income-related ESA, your temporary absence from your home can mean that you cease to be entitled to receive these (see p242).

Note: the work-related activity component was abolished for new claimants of ESA from 3 April 2017. If your entitlement to ESA ends because you are abroad, you will not be entitled to this component in a future claim, unless linking rules apply because your new claim for ESA:[25]

- follows a break in your period of limited capability for work of less than 12 weeks since a previous period of limited capability for work that began before 3 April 2017; *or*
- is within 12 weeks of your entitlement to maternity allowance (MA) ending, and immediately before your MA entitlement began you were entitled to ESA before 3 April 2017.

For details of all the groups that can be paid the work-related activity component, see CPAG's *Welfare Benefits and Tax Credits Handbook*.

If your partner is abroad

If you are the claimant and you stay in Great Britain, your income-related ESA includes an amount for your partner for:[26]

- the first **four weeks**; *or*
- the first **26 weeks** if s/he is accompanying a child abroad for treatment in line with the 26-week rule above.

If you are the claimant and both you and your partner are abroad, your income-related ESA includes an amount for your partner for the first 26 weeks if both of you are accompanying a child abroad for treatment in line with the 26-week rule above.[27]

After this four- or 26-week period, your benefit is reduced because your applicable amount is calculated as if you have no partner. However, your partner is still treated as part of your household and, therefore, her/his work, income and capital affect your income-related ESA entitlement, unless you are no longer treated as a couple (see p242).[28]

European Union co-ordination rules

Income-related ESA is listed under the co-ordination rules as a 'special non-contributory benefit' (see p287) and is therefore not exportable. This means that if you go to another EEA country, the EU co-ordination rules cannot assist you and you can only be paid income-related ESA abroad under the UK rules explained on pp251–52.

However, the co-ordination rules may enable you to continue to be paid contributory ESA if you go to live in another EEA country (see p266).

Reciprocal agreements

Reciprocal agreements have not been updated to include ESA (see p309), with the following exceptions.

- The reciprocal agreements between Northern Ireland and Great Britain have included ESA (both income-related and contributory) since 6 April 2016.[29] The purpose of these agreements is to ensure you do not lose out if you move from one territory to the other while claiming ESA. For more information on arrangements between Great Britain and Northern Ireland, including if you moved before 6 April 2016, see p310.
- If your award of contributory ESA was converted from an award of incapacity benefit (IB), it is covered by each of the agreements (with the exception of the Isle of Man, Israel and Switzerland) that cover IB (see Appendix 5).[30]

Pension credit

You cannot usually get pension credit (PC) if you are not in Great Britain.[31] However, PC can be paid when you are temporarily absent from Great Britain in the circumstances below, provided you meet the other conditions of entitlement.

From 28 July 2016, if you were entitled to PC immediately before leaving Great Britain and are temporarily absent, your entitlement can continue:[32]

- for up to **26 weeks**, provided your absence is not expected to exceed that and is solely in connection with medical treatment or medically approved convalescence or care as a result of medical treatment, for you, or your partner or a child who you are accompanying who normally lives with you; *or*
- for up to **eight weeks**, provided your absence is not expected to exceed that and is in connection with the death of your partner, your child who normally lived with you or a close relative of you, your partner or child who normally lives with you, and the decision maker considers it unreasonable for you to return to Great Britain within four weeks; *or*
- up to **four weeks**, provided your absence is not expected to exceed that.

If you were already outside Great Britain on 28 July 2016, the previous, more generous, rules continue to apply until you return.[33]

If you are entitled to housing costs in your PC, your temporary absence from home can mean that you cease to be entitled to receive these (see p242).

If your partner is abroad

If your partner is abroad and you are entitled to PC, either while in Great Britain or abroad because you are covered by the rules on p253, your PC only includes an amount for her/him if s/he is also covered by the above rules. After this, s/he is not treated as part of your household, you are paid as a single person and her/his income and capital do not affect your claim.[34]

Note: the above rules came into force on 28 July 2016. If your partner was already outside Great Britain on this date, the previous, more generous, rules continue to apply until s/he returns.[35]

For further information about your partner going abroad, see p242.

European Union co-ordination rules

PC is classed as a 'special non-contributory benefit' under the EU co-ordination rules (see p287) and therefore cannot be exported. This means that if you go abroad, the co-ordination rules cannot assist you. You can only be paid PC abroad under the UK rules.

Housing benefit

Although there is no requirement to be present in Great Britain to be entitled to HB, the rules that require you to occupy your home, except during certain temporary absences, can mean that you cease to be entitled if you go abroad.[36] If you are temporarily absent from your home and outside Great Britain, your entitlement generally only continues during an absence of up to four weeks, unless you are covered by an exception.

Note:
- The rules on absences abroad were introduced on 28 July 2016. If you were already temporarily absent abroad on this date, the previous, more generous, rules apply to you until you return to Great Britain.
- If you have an EEA right to reside in the UK and go abroad to another EEA state, it is arguable that the shorter period for which you can be entitled while outside Great Britain is discriminatory under EU law and should not apply.

For further details on all the above, see p242.

If your partner or child is abroad

Whether or not you have amounts included in your HB for your partner or child who is abroad depends on whether s/he is treated as part of your household (see p212 and p213). The amount of HB you are entitled to may also depend on whether s/he is treated as occupying the home (see p242).

From 6 April 2017, you can only be paid HB for your third or subsequent child in limited circumstances (known as the 'two-child limit'). These include transitional rules which may cease to apply when your child returns from abroad after payments for her/him, or your claim, ended because s/he was abroad. For further details, see p213.

Universal credit

You cannot usually be paid UC if you (and your partner if it is a joint claim) are not in Great Britain.[37] However, UC can be paid while you are temporarily absent from Great Britain in the circumstances outlined below, provided you meet the other conditions of entitlement.

If you were entitled to UC immediately before leaving Great Britain and are temporarily absent, you can continue to be entitled for:[38]

- **one month** if your absence is not expected to exceed, and does not exceed, one month; *or*
- **two months** if your absence is in connection with the death of your partner or child, or a close relative of yours (or of your partner or child), and it would be unreasonable for you to return to Great Britain within the first month; *or*
- **six months** if your absence is not expected to exceed, and does not exceed, six months and you are a mariner or continental shelf worker; *or*
- **six months** if your absence is not expected to exceed, and does not exceed, six months and is solely in connection with the medically approved care, convalescence or treatment of you, your partner or child. You are automatically exempt from the work search requirement and are also treated as 'able and willing immediately to take up work' during this period.[39]

If you are entitled to housing costs in your UC, your temporary absence from your home can mean that you cease to be entitled to receive these (see p242).

Note: the work-related activity component was abolished for new claimants of UC from 3 April 2017. If your entitlement to UC ends because you are abroad, you cannot be entitled to this component in a future claim unless limited linking rules apply.

For details of the rules on payment of the work-related activity component, see CPAG's *Welfare Benefits and Tax Credits Handbook*.

If your partner is abroad

If you have a joint claim for UC and both you and your partner go abroad, this does not affect your entitlement during the period when one of the situations listed above applies to both of you. After this time, if you both remain abroad, your entitlement ends.

If you stay in Great Britain while your partner is abroad, her/his absence does not affect your entitlement during the one-, two- or six-month period if the circumstances described above apply to her/him. After this time, you cease to be entitled as joint claimants and must claim as a single person. However, if you and your partner have been, and expect to be, apart for less than six months, you are still treated as a couple and although your award is based on the maximum amount for a single person, your partner's income and capital are taken into account.[40] Once you have been, or expect to be, apart for six months, you cease to be treated as a couple[41] and your entitlement is then unaffected by your absent partner.

In addition, if your partner's absence abroad means that s/he stops being habitually resident (including if s/he no longer has a right to reside) in the common travel area, s/he is treated as no longer present (see p94). You can claim as a single person, but your partner's income and capital are taken into account (unless you have ceased to be treated as a couple as described above).[42]

If your child is abroad

If your child is abroad, you cease to be entitled for her/him if her/his absence abroad is, or is expected to be, longer than the one-, two- or six-month periods allowed in the circumstances set out above. The circumstances must apply to your child.[43]

Note: from 6 April 2017, you can only be paid UC for your third or subsequent child in limited circumstances (known as the 'two-child limit'). For further details, see p213.

European Union co-ordination rules

The DWP considers that UC is not a 'social security benefit' under the EU co-ordination rules (see p287), and therefore these rules cannot assist you. If you go to another EEA state, you can only be paid under the UK rules on p255.

2. **Bereavement benefits**

In general, bereavement benefits are payable while you are abroad. However, if you are receiving one of the old bereavement benefits (because your spouse or civil partner died before 6 April 2017), your benefit is not uprated each year if, on the day before the annual uprating takes place, you have ceased to be 'ordinarily resident' (see p99) in Great Britain – unless you have gone to another European Economic Area (EEA) state and you are covered by the European Union (EU) co-ordination rules (see p281) or you can rely on a reciprocal agreement (see Chapter 17).[44]

If your spouse or civil partner died on or after 6 April 2017, you may be entitled to a bereavement support payment if you were ordinarily resident in Great Britain on the date s/he died. If you were abroad on that date, see p101 for whether your absence meant that you had ceased to be ordinarily resident in Great Britain.

If your spouse or civil partner died before 6 April 2017, you may be entitled to a bereavement payment if you were present in Great Britain when you claim or if other specific circumstances apply. See p215 for further details.

European Union co-ordination rules

Bereavement benefits are classed as 'survivors' benefits' under the EU co-ordination rules (see p285) and are therefore fully exportable. If you are covered by these rules (see p281) and you go to stay or live in another EEA state, you can be paid your bereavement support payment, bereavement allowance or widowed parent's allowance for as long as you would receive them if you remained in Great Britain, including any annual uprating.

If you are covered by the EU co-ordination rules (see p281) and the UK is your 'competent state' (see p288):[45]
- for **bereavement support payment**, the requirement to be ordinarily resident in Great Britain on the date your spouse or civil partner died does not apply if you were resident in another EEA state on that date;
- for **bereavement payment**, if your spouse or civil partner died in another EEA state, s/he can be treated as having died in the UK.

Reciprocal agreements

If you are covered by a reciprocal agreement this can assist in a similar way to the EU co-ordination rules (see above) in respect of the relevant country. The reciprocal agreements have been amended to include, from 6 April 2017, bereavement support payment.[46]

3. **Child benefit and guardian's allowance**

Child benefit

You and your child can be treated as present in Great Britain and, therefore, you can continue to be entitled to child benefit for a limited period during a 'temporary absence' (see p240).

Provided you are 'ordinarily resident' (see p99), you are treated as present during a temporary absence for:[47]
- the first **eight weeks**; or
- the first **12 weeks** of any period of absence, or any extension to that period, which is in connection with:
  - the treatment of an illness or disability of you, your partner, a child for whom you are responsible, or another relative of yours or your partner's; or

- the death of your partner, a child or qualifying young person for whom you or your partner are responsible, or another relative of yours or your partner's.

'**Relative**' means brother, sister, parent, grandparent, great-grandparent or child, grandchild or great-grandchild.[48]

Your child is treated as present during a temporary absence for:[49]

- the first **12 weeks** of any period of absence; *or*
- **any period** during which s/he is absent for the specific purpose of being treated for an illness or disability which began before her/his absence began; *or*
- **any period** when s/he is in Northern Ireland; *or*
- **any period** during which s/he is absent only because s/he is:
  - receiving full-time education at a school or college in another European Economic Area (EEA) state or in Switzerland; *or*
  - engaged in an educational exchange or visit made with the written approval of the school or college s/he normally attends; *or*
  - a child who normally lives with a Crown servant posted overseas who is either in the same country as her/him or is absent from that country for one of the reasons in the two bullet points immediately above.[50]

If a child is born outside Great Britain during the eight- or 12-week period in which you were treated as present in Great Britain, s/he is treated as being in Great Britain for up to 12 weeks from the start of your absence.[51]

While you and your child are present, or treated as present, you satisfy that condition of entitlement. This means that you can continue to receive any child benefit already being paid and can also make a fresh claim during your or her/his absence. **Note:** if you or your child are treated as present, you must satisfy all the other conditions of entitlement including, if your child is not living with you, contributing at least the amount of child benefit that would be payable to the costs of that child.[52] For information on all the conditions of entitlement for child benefit, see CPAG's *Welfare Benefits and Tax Credits Handbook*.

Guardian's allowance

Entitlement to guardian's allowance depends on entitlement to child benefit, so you can be paid guardian's allowance abroad for the same period as child benefit (see p257).

However, your guardian's allowance is not uprated each year if you have ceased to be ordinarily resident (see p99) in Great Britain on the day before the annual uprating takes place,[53] unless you have gone to another EEA state and you are covered by the European Union (EU) co-ordination rules (see p259) or you can rely on a reciprocal agreement.

European Union co-ordination rules

Child benefit and guardian's allowance are classed as 'family benefits' under the EU co-ordination rules (see p285). If these rules apply to you (see p281) and the UK is your 'competent state' (see p288):

- you can be paid child benefit and guardian's allowance for a child resident in another EEA country. The child does not have to be in education. However, you must still satisfy all the other conditions of entitlement, including contributing to the costs of the child an amount at least equal to the amount of child benefit payable for her/him;[54] *and/or*
- you can be paid child benefit and guardian's allowance if you are an EEA national and you go to stay or live in another EEA country, and your benefit is uprated in the normal way.

These rules can be complicated in certain circumstances – eg, if there is entitlement to family benefits in more than one state. See p301 for more information on the payment of family benefits under the EU co-ordination rules.

4. Disability and carers' benefits

If you go abroad, you can be treated as being present in Great Britain and therefore continue to be entitled to attendance allowance (AA), disability living allowance (DLA), personal independence payment (PIP) or carer's allowance (CA) for a limited period.

Provided you satisfy the residence condition (see p260), you are treated as present and can continue to receive AA, DLA, PIP or CA during an absence from Great Britain:[55]

- (for AA, DLA and PIP only) for the first **13 weeks** of a 'temporary absence' (see p240);
- (for AA, DLA and PIP only) for the first **26 weeks** of a 'temporary absence' (see p240), if the absence is solely in connection with medical treatment for your illness or disability that began before you left Great Britain;
- (for CA only) for up to **four weeks** if your absence is, and was when it began, for a temporary purpose and does not exceed four weeks. If you are not accompanied by the disabled person for whom you are caring, you must satisfy the rules that entitle you to CA during a break from caring. See CPAG's *Welfare Benefits and Tax Credits Handbook* for information;
- (for CA only) if your absence is temporary and for the specific purpose of caring for a disabled person who is also absent from Great Britain and who continues to receive AA, DLA care component paid at the highest or middle rate, the daily living component of PIP, armed forces independence payment or constant attendance allowance;

- if you were already abroad on 8 April 2013 but continued to be entitled to AA or DLA because your absence was temporary and for the specific purpose of being treated for an illness or disability that began before you left Great Britain, and the DWP has agreed you should be treated as present. You continue to be treated as being present in Great Britain until either you return or your award is revised or superseded;[56]
- while you are abroad as an airwoman/man or mariner or continental shelf worker;
- while you are a serving member of the armed forces, or you are living with your spouse, civil partner, son, daughter, stepson, stepdaughter, father, father-in-law, stepfather, mother, mother-in-law or stepmother who is a serving member of the armed forces.

The residence condition

You must be habitually resident (see p103), unless your current award of AA, DLA or CA began before 8 April 2013, in which case, you must be ordinarily resident (see p99) until that award is terminated, revised or superseeded.[57] You are treated as habitually resident if you are covered by the last bullet point above.

Note: at the time of writing, the DWP was due to introduce a rapid reclaim process if your entitlement to PIP stops because you are absent from Britain for more than 13 weeks but less than a year, you have not reached your award review date (generally, one year before the end of your award) and you can confirm your needs have not changed since you left.[58] It is not known if this will also apply to DLA and AA. See CPAG's online service and *Welfare Rights bulletin* for updates.

If you lose your entitlement to CA, you should still be eligible for a carer premium paid with your income support, income-based jobseeker's allowance, income-related employment and support allowance and housing benefit for a further period of eight weeks, provided you remain entitled to these benefits while you are away.[59] If you lose your entitlement to CA while you are abroad and the disabled person for whom you care is staying in the UK, s/he may be entitled to a severe disability premium during your absence instead. For further information on premiums, see CPAG's *Welfare Benefits and Tax Credits Handbook*.

You can continue to be paid an increase in your CA for your spouse/civil partner or dependent adult while s/he is abroad if:[60]

- you are entitled to CA; *and*
- you are residing with her/him. **Note:** you can be treated as residing together during a temporary absence from each other.[61]

European Union co-ordination rules

Since April 2013, if you move to another European Economic Area (EEA) state, you can continue to be paid (or make a new claim for) AA, DLA care component, PIP daily living component and CA without needing to satisfy the usual presence and residence requirements (see p218) if:[62]
- you are habitually resident in another EEA state or Switzerland; *and*
- you are covered by the European Union (EU) co-ordination rules (see p281); *and*
- you can demonstrate a 'genuine and sufficient link to the UK' (see p219).

Note: if you are covered by the EU co-ordination rules, you can continue to be paid for as long as the UK is your 'competent state' (see p288).[63]

Whether or not you could be paid in another EEA state before April 2013 depends on the date your entitlement began, as AA, DLA and CA have been categorised in different ways under the co-ordination rules at different times.

Before 1 June 1992, AA, DLA and CA were classed as 'invalidity benefits' (see p285). If your entitlement began before this date, you can export your benefit without any time limit to any EEA state.

From 1 June 1992, the UK government categorised AA, DLA and CA as 'special non-contributory benefits' (see p287). These are not exportable. However, the Court of Justice of the European Union (CJEU) declared that this was wrong and that these benefits (except DLA mobility component) were 'sickness benefits'.[64] This means they are exportable and you should continue to receive the benefit for as long as the UK remains your competent state (see p290).[65] The CJEU has recently reconfirmed that DLA care component is a sickness, and not an invalidity, benefit.[66]

DLA mobility component is listed as (and PIP mobility component is treated by the DWP as) a 'special non-contributory benefit' and is not exportable.[67] You can only be paid the mobility component in the state where you are resident under the co-ordination rules.[68] See p289 for details on where you are considered 'resident'.

The age cut-off for new claims for DLA mobility component or PIP mobility component at age 65 can mean that if you lose entitlement because you go abroad, you cannot re-establish entitlement when you return to the UK if, by then, you are aged 65 or over. The Upper Tribunal has held that this rule is *not* contrary to EU law in a case concerning a man who returned to the UK aged over 65 after living in France for several years.[69] **Note:** if you lose your entitlement to DLA or PIP because you went abroad and you reached the age of 65 before your entitlement ended, you can become entitled again (including, if you were previously entitled, to the mobility component, despite being aged 65 or over), provided you make a renewal claim within 12 months of the previous award ending.[70] For further details on DLA and PIP entitlement criteria and the rules on renewal claims, see CPAG's *Welfare Benefits and Tax Credits Handbook*.

If you receive CA while in the UK and the EU co-ordination rules apply to you (see p281), you may be able to continue to be paid an addition for an adult or child if s/he goes to stay or live in another EEA state. These additions count as 'family benefits' under the co-ordination rules (see p301).

Was your benefit stopped because you moved to another European Economic Area state on or after 8 March 2001?

If your AA, DLA care component or CA was stopped solely because you moved to another EEA state on or after 8 March 2001, this decision was wrong.[71]

The DWP can restore your entitlement and pay arrears from 18 October 2007 (or the date your payment was stopped, if this is later).[72] The DWP pays arrears from this date because it was when the CJEU decided these benefits had been wrongly categorised.

To get your entitlement restored and arrears paid for any period between 8 March 2001 and 18 October 2007, you should do the following.

1. If you appealed within the time limit against the decision that stopped your benefit, the First-tier Tribunal should be able to reinstate it from the date it was stopped. If your appeal is waiting to be determined, the DWP can revise the decision and pay your arrears of benefit in full.

2. If you did not appeal, the DWP can only correct its decision and pay arrears from the date your benefit was stopped if that decision was made because of an 'official error'. However, if a mistake in a decision was not known to be a mistake at the time, but is only shown to have been a mistake by a later court decision, it does not count as an official error.[73] It has been decided that it only became clear that AA, DLA care component and CA were exportable benefits under the EU co-ordination rules when the CJEU decided that they had been wrongly categorised (on 18 October 2007).[74] Therefore, if the decision stopping your benefit (solely because it was mistakenly categorised as a special non-contributory benefit and therefore not exportable) was made before 18 October 2007, this decision does not count as an official error. If the decision is revised, your benefit can only be restored from the date of the revision (although the DWP pays arrears outside these rules back to 18 October 2007).

3. You may be able to get around the above difficulty if you can identify another error in the decision to stop your benefit when you moved to another EEA state which can count as an official error, thus enabling the decision to be revised and your entitlement reinstated from the date it was stopped.[75] One fairly common mistake that may count as another error, if made before 10 April 2006, was a decision to stop your AA or DLA care component from the date you went abroad, rather than from the date of the decision.[76]

Chapter 15: Going abroad: rules for individual benefits
5. Incapacity benefit, severe disablement allowance and maternity allowance

15

Reciprocal agreements

Most reciprocal agreements do not cover disability and carers' benefits. However, the agreements with Guernsey, Jersey, the Isle of Man and Northern Ireland have relevant provisions. From 6 April 2016, new reciprocal arrangements between Great Britain and Northern Ireland that also cover PIP came into force (see p310).

5. Incapacity benefit, severe disablement allowance and maternity allowance

If you are temporarily absent from Great Britain, you can continue to be paid incapacity benefit (IB), severe disablement allowance (SDA) and maternity allowance (MA) if:[77]

- you are receiving attendance allowance (AA), disability living allowance (DLA), personal independence payment (PIP) or armed forces independence payment. For when AA, DLA or PIP can be paid abroad, see p259; *or*
- the DWP certifies that you should continue to be paid. You can then receive the benefit for the first 26 weeks of your temporary absence; *or*
- you are the spouse, civil partner, son, stepson, daughter, stepdaughter, father, stepfather, father-in-law, mother, stepmother or mother-in-law of a serving member of the armed forces and you are abroad only because you are living with her/him.

In addition:

- when you left Great Britain, you must have been continuously incapable of work for six months and have been continuously incapable since your departure; *or*
- your absence from Great Britain must be for the specific purpose of being treated for an incapacity which began before you left Great Britain; *or*
- for IB only, your incapacity for work is the result of a personal injury caused by an accident at work and your absence from Great Britain is for the specific purpose of receiving treatment for that injury. See CPAG's *Welfare Benefits and Tax Credits Handbook* for more information on industrial injuries.

If you are due to have a medical examination, this can be arranged abroad.
Note: most IB and SDA claims have been reassessed for transfer to employment and support allowance (ESA). If you are still receiving IB or SDA, at some future point you will be reassessed for ESA. If your award of IB or SDA is converted to an award of contributory ESA, you do not need to resatisfy the national insurance (NI) contribution conditions. However, if you are getting IB or SDA and lose entitlement because you go abroad for more than 26 weeks, you do not requalify for IB or SDA on your return to Great Britain, and you can only get contributory

15

Chapter 15: Going abroad: rules for individual benefits
5. Incapacity benefit, severe disablement allowance and maternity allowance

ESA if you satisfy all the conditions of entitlement, including the NI contribution conditions. Losing entitlement now could therefore result in a loss of potential future benefit.

You can continue to be paid an increase in your IB or SDA for your spouse/civil partner or dependent adult while s/he is abroad if you are residing with her/him.[78] **Note:** you can be treated as residing together during a temporary absence from each other.[79]

European Union co-ordination rules

Long-term IB and SDA are classed as 'invalidity benefits' under the European Union (EU) co-ordination rules (see p285). If these rules apply to you (see p281) and the UK continues to be your 'competent state' for the payment of this benefit (see p288), you can export your IB and SDA if you go to live in another European Economic Area (EEA) state. Provided you continue to satisfy the rules of entitlement, benefit is paid without any time limit and at the same rate as if you were still in the UK, including your annual uprating.

The state from which you claim benefit is the one that determines your degree of invalidity, but any checks and medicals take place in the state in which you live and the reports are then sent to the paying state.[80]

If the co-ordination rules apply to you and you remain in the UK, you may be able to continue to be paid an increase for an adult or child if s/he goes to stay or live in another EEA state. Such increases are classified as 'family benefits'. See p301 for details about when you can receive these for a family member living abroad.

MA is classed as a 'maternity benefit' under the EU co-ordination rules (see p285). If these rules apply to you (see p281) and the UK is your competent state for the payment of this benefit (see p288), you can be paid MA if you go to live or stay in another EEA country.[81] See p300 for more details.

Reciprocal agreements

The UK has reciprocal agreements with several countries that cover incapacity, sickness and maternity benefits. If you are going to one of these countries, the agreement may enable you to continue to be paid benefit, make a new claim for MA or use NI contributions paid, or periods of employment completed, in the UK to qualify for benefit in the country you are going to. For more information on reciprocal agreements covering sickness and invalidity benefits, see p314, and for maternity benefits, see p315.

6. **Industrial injuries benefits**

Industrial injuries benefits are:
- disablement benefit;
- reduced earnings allowance (REA);
- retirement allowance;
- constant attendance allowance;
- exceptionally severe disablement allowance.

Disablement benefit and retirement allowance are not affected if you go abroad.[82]

Constant attendance allowance and exceptionally severe disablement allowance are payable for the first six months of a temporary absence, or a longer period that the DWP may allow.[83]

REA can be paid while you are temporarily absent abroad for the first three months (or longer if the DWP allows) if:[84]
- your absence from Great Britain is not in connection with employment, trade or business; *and*
- your claim was made before you left Great Britain; *and*
- you were entitled to REA before going abroad.

Note: REA has now been abolished. If you break your claim, you may no longer be eligible for benefit.

European Union co-ordination rules

Industrial injuries benefits, with the exception of retirement allowance, are classed as 'benefits for accidents at work and occupational diseases' under the European Union co-ordination rules (see p285) and are therefore fully exportable. If these rules apply to you (see p281) and you go to stay or live in another European Economic Area state, you can be paid without any time limit and they will be fully uprated each year. See p300 for more details.

Reciprocal agreements

The UK has reciprocal agreements with several countries that cover industrial injuries benefits. These can enable you to continue to be paid benefit indefinitely when you go to a relevant country, and contain provisions for determining entitlement when more than one country is involved. For more information on reciprocal agreements covering industrial injuries benefits, see p315.

---

7. Contribution-based jobseeker's allowance and contributory employment and support allowance

You cannot usually get jobseeker's allowance (JSA) or employment and support allowance (ESA) if you are not in Great Britain.[85] However, contribution-based JSA can be paid when you are temporarily absent from Great Britain in the same circumstances as income-based JSA (see p248), and contributory ESA can be paid when you are temporarily absent from Great Britain in the same circumstances as income-related ESA (see p251).

European Union co-ordination rules

Contribution-based jobseeker's allowance

Contribution-based JSA is classed as an unemployment benefit under the European Union (EU) co-ordination rules (see p285). If these rules apply to you (see p281) and the UK is your 'competent state' (see p288), you can continue to be paid contribution-based JSA for up to three months if:[86]

- you satisfied the conditions for contribution-based JSA before you left the UK for at least four weeks, unless the DWP authorised you to go abroad before then; *and*
- you register as unemployed in the European Economic Area (EEA) state you go to within seven days and comply with its procedures.

Contributory employment and support allowance

If the EU co-ordination rules apply to you (see p281) and the UK is your competent state (see p288), you can generally continue to be paid contributory ESA if you go to live in another EEA state.

After the assessment phase, contributory ESA is classed as an 'invalidity benefit' under the co-ordination rules and is therefore fully exportable if you move to another EEA state. During the assessment phase, it is classed as a 'sickness benefit', which can be subject to limitations on exportability under the co-ordination rules. **Note:**

- If you have a long-term or permanent disability, it is arguable that contributory ESA during the assessment phase should be regarded as an 'invalidity benefit' (see p285).[87]
- In most cases, this distinction does not matter, as sickness benefits are exportable in similar circumstances to invalidity benefits (see p300).

If the UK continues to pay your contributory ESA while you are resident in another EEA state, the DWP continues to assess your limited capability for work and your limited capability for work-related activity. However, any checks and medicals take place in the state in which you are living, with reports then sent to the DWP.[88]

If you appeal against a decision on your limited capability for work-related activity while abroad, the tribunal should consider the hypothetical work-related activity that applies in the area of the UK where the tribunal hearing is held, unless you object. This area is usually Newcastle if you opt for a paper hearing.[89]

Reciprocal agreements

If the country you are going to has a reciprocal agreement that covers contribution-based JSA (see Appendix 5), check whether you are covered by it. Such agreements can, for example, enable you to be paid a contribution-based benefit for a limited period and/or to use periods of employment completed, or national insurance contributions paid, in Great Britain to entitle you to unemployment benefits in the country you are going to. See p314 for further information.

Most reciprocal agreements do not cover contributory ESA (see p314). The exceptions are:
- the agreement with Northern Ireland, which, since 6 April 2016, covers contributory ESA (as well as income-related ESA);[90] *and*
- if your award of contributory ESA was converted from incapacity benefit (IB), it is covered by each of the agreements (except the Isle of Man, Israel and Switzerland) that cover IB (see Appendix 5).[91]

If you moved from Great Britain to Northern Ireland (or vice versa) while claiming ESA before 6 April 2016, the DWP policy was to make an extra-statutory payment to cover any loss of ESA that resulted from your having to make a new claim. If you were receiving extra-statutory payments on this basis up to 27 November 2016, and do not satisfy the contributory conditions for entitlement to contributory ESA, you are treated as satisfying those conditions and as having made a claim for ESA from 27 November 2016 and your period of limited capability for work is treated as continuous.[92] For further information on the arrangements between Northern Ireland and Great Britain, see p310.

---

8. Retirement pensions

All retirement pensions are payable without time limit while you are abroad.[93] However, if you are not ordinarily resident (see p99) in Great Britain:[94]
- on the day before the annual uprating takes place, your benefit is not uprated each year;
- when you claim state pension (ie, if you reach pension age on or after 6 April 2016) that you have deferred, the upratings that occurred while you were

abroad are ignored when calculating both the deferral increase and rate payable;

- you cannot stop claiming ('de-retire') your 'old' retirement pension (ie, if you reached pension age before 6 April 2016) in order to accrue a deferral payment,[95] unless you have gone to another European Economic Area (EEA) state and you are covered by the European Union (EU) co-ordination rules, or you can rely on a reciprocal agreement (see below).

Although category D retirement pension is payable if you are abroad, you must meet the residence requirements at the date you make your claim (see p225).

If you live abroad, your retirement pension can be paid either into a bank in the country where you live or a bank or building society in the UK.

You can continue to be paid an increase in your category A retirement pension for your spouse/civil partner or dependent adult while s/he is abroad if:[96]

- you are entitled to the pension; *and*
- you are residing with her/him. You can be treated as residing together during a temporary absence from each other.[97]

European Union co-ordination rules

Retirement pensions are classed as 'old age benefits' under the EU co-ordination rules (see p285). If these rules apply to you (see p281), the UK is your 'competent state' (see p288) and you go to live in another EEA state:

- you can 'export' your retirement pension without time limit;
- your retirement pension is paid at the same rate as if you were still in the UK, including your annual uprating; *and*
- you can opt to stop claiming your pension ('de-retire') in order to accrue a deferral payment while living in another EEA state.

If the EU co-ordination rules apply and you remain in the UK, you may be able to continue to be paid an increase for an adult or child if s/he goes to stay or live in another EEA state. These increases count as 'family benefits' under the co-ordination rules. See p301 for more details.

Reciprocal agreements

If you are covered by a reciprocal agreement (see p309) that provides for uprating, you can continue to be paid your pension at the same rate as if you were still in the UK. **Note:** the agreements with Canada and New Zealand, and the former agreement with Australia, do not provide for uprating. For further information on reciprocal agreements and retirement pensions, see p315.

9. Statutory payments

There are no presence or residence rules for statutory sick pay (SSP), statutory maternity pay (SMP), statutory adoption pay (SAP), statutory paternity pay (SPP) and statutory shared parental pay (SSPP). You remain entitled to these benefits if you go abroad, provided you meet the usual rules of entitlement, including those relating to being an employee.[98]

Although you are generally required to be employed in Great Britain to count as an 'employee', you count as an employee for the purpose of these benefits, even while employed abroad, in certain circumstances, including if:[99]

- your employer is required to pay secondary class 1 national insurance (NI) contributions for you; *or*
- you are a continental shelf worker or, in certain circumstances, an airwoman/ man or mariner; *or*
- you are employed in another European Economic Area (EEA) state and, had you been employed in Great Britain you would be considered an employee, and the UK is the competent state under the European Union (EU) co- ordination rules (see p288).

Your employer is not required to pay you SSP, SMP, SAP, SPP or SSPP if:[100]

- your employer is not legally required to pay employer's class 1 NI contributions (even if these contributions are, in fact, made) because, at the time they become payable, your employer:
  – is not resident or present in Great Britain; *and*
  – does not have (or is treated as not having) a place of business in Great Britain; *or*
- because of an international treaty or convention, your employer is exempt from the Social Security Acts, or they are not enforceable against your employer.

European Union co-ordination rules

It is arguable that SSP is a 'sickness benefit' and SMP, SAP, SPP and SSPP are 'maternity/paternity benefits' or family benefits under the EU co-ordination rules (see p285).[101] However, given the generosity of the above UK rules, it is unlikely that you will need to rely on the EU co-ordination rules directly.

10. Tax credits

You can be treated as being present and, therefore, entitled to child tax credit (CTC) and working tax credit (WTC) for limited periods during a 'temporary absence' (see p240).

You are treated as present for both CTC and WTC during a temporary absence, provided you are ordinarily resident (see p99), for:[102]

- the first **eight weeks**; *or*
- the first **12 weeks** of any period of absence, or any extension to that period, which is in connection with:
  - the treatment of an illness or disability of you, your partner, a child for whom you are responsible, or another relative (see below) of either you or your partner; *or*
  - the death of your partner, a child or qualifying young person for whom you or your partner are responsible, or another relative (see below) of you or your partner.

'**Relative**' means brother, sister, parent, grandparent, grandchild or great-grandparent or child.[103]

You are also treated as present if you are:[104]

- a Crown servant posted overseas and:
  - you are, or immediately before your posting abroad you were, ordinarily resident in the UK; *or*
  - immediately before your posting you were in the UK in connection with that posting; *or*
- the partner of a Crown servant posted overseas and in the same country as her/him or temporarily absent from that country under the same exceptions that enable tax credits to continue during a temporary absence from Great Britain.

While you are treated as present in any of the ways above, you continue to satisfy that condition of entitlement. This means that you can continue to receive any tax credits that are already in payment and can make a fresh or renewal claim during your absence.

Your tax credit entitlement ends if:

- you (or your partner, if you are making a joint claim) spend longer abroad than the permitted temporary absence periods, as you cease to satisfy the presence condition; *or*
- you (or your partner, if you are making a joint claim) cease to be ordinarily resident; *or*
- you are making a joint claim and separate from your partner in circumstances in which the separation is likely to be permanent, as you cease to count as a couple.[105]

If your entitlement to a joint claim as a couple ends, you may be able to make a single claim. See p229 for considerations if you are making a joint claim as a couple.

From 6 April 2017, you can only be paid CTC for your third and subsequent child in limited circumstances (known as the 'two-child limit'). For further details, see p213.

European Union co-ordination rules

CTC is classed as a 'family benefit' under the European Union (EU) co-ordination rules (see p285). If these rules apply to you (see p281) and the UK is your 'competent state' (see p288), you can be paid CTC:

* for a child resident in another European Economic Area (EEA) state; *and/or*
* if you are an EEA national and you go to stay or live in another EEA state.

See p301 for more details on the payment of family benefits under the EU co-ordination rules.

WTC is not covered by the EU co-ordination rules. Therefore, if your partner is in another EEA country, although you may be able to make a joint claim for CTC as a couple, your WTC claim is treated as a single claim.[106]

If you or your partner are working in another EEA country but live in the UK and therefore remain present and ordinarily resident in the UK, this work can count for the purposes of your WTC claim.[107]

If your childcare provider is located outside the UK in another EEA state, you may still be entitled to the childcare element of WTC (see p230).

Notes

1. **Means-tested benefits**
1 s124(1) SSCBA 1992
2 Reg 4 IS Regs
3 Reg 21 and Sch 7 paras 11 and 11A IS Regs
4 Reg 21 and Sch 7 para 11A IS Regs
5 Reg 16 IS Regs
6 Reg 16(5) IS Regs
7 Reg 1(4B) and (4C) SS(WTCCTC)(CA) Regs
8 s1(2)(i) JSA 1995
9 Regs 14 and 19 JSA Regs
10 Reg 16 JSA Regs 2013
11 s21 and Sch 1 para 11 JSA 1995; reg 50 JSA Regs; reg 41 JSA Regs 2013
12 Regs 50(4) and 170 JSA Regs

13 Regs 3E(1) and (2)(c), 50(6B), 86C and 170 and Sch 5A para 7 JSA Regs; Vol 4, paras 24146-49 DMG
14 Regs 3E(1) and (2)(c), 50(6B) and 86(C) JSA Regs
15 Regs 50(6B) and 78(1A) and (3)(c) and Sch 5A para 7 JSA Regs
16 Reg 78 JSA Regs
17 Reg 85 and Sch 5 paras 10 and 11 JSA Regs
18 Reg 85 and Sch 5 para 11 JSA Regs
19 Reg 78 JSA Regs
20 Reg 78(5) JSA Regs
21 Reg 1(8B) and (8C) SS(WTCCTC)(CA) Regs
22 ss1(3)(d) and 18(4)(a) WRA 2007

23 Regs 151-55 ESA Regs; regs 88-92 ESA
   Regs 2013
24 Reg 24 ESA Regs; reg 20 ESA Regs 2013
25 Sch 2 paras 3 and 7 The Employment
   and Support Allowance and Universal
   Credit (Miscellaneous Amendments and
   Transitional and Savings Provisions)
   Regulations 2017, No.204; reg 145 ESA
   Regs
26 Regs 69 and 156 and Sch 5 paras 6 and
   7 ESA Regs
27 Regs 69 and 156 and Sch 5 para 7 ESA
   Regs
28 Reg 156 ESA Regs
29 SS(NIRA) Regs; SS(GBRA)(NI) Regs
30 SS(RA)O
31 s1(2)(a) SPCA 2002
32 Regs 3 and 4 SPC Regs
33 Reg 5 The Housing Benefit and State
   Pension Credit (Temporary Absence)
   (Amendment) Regulations 2016,
   No.624
34 Reg 5 SPC Regs
35 Reg 5 The Housing Benefit and State
   Pension Credit (Temporary Absence)
   (Amendment) Regulations 2016,
   No.624
36 s130(1)(a) SSCBA 1992; reg 7 HB Regs;
   reg 7 HB(SPC) Regs
37 ss3 and 4(1)(c) WRA 2012
38 Reg 11 UC Regs
39 Reg 99(1)-(3) UC Regs
40 Regs 3, 18, 22 and 36 UC Regs
41 Reg 3(6) UC Regs
42 Regs 3(3), 9, 18(2), 22(3) and 36(3) UC
   Regs
43 Reg 4(7) UC Regs

2. Bereavement benefits
44 Reg 5 SSB(PA) Regs
45 Arts 5, 7, 42 and 43 EU Reg 883/04
46 The Social Security (Reciprocal
   Agreements) Order 2017, No.159;
   SS(NIRA)(A) Regs; SS(GBRA)(A) Regs;
   DMG Memo 15/17

3. Child benefit and guardian's allowance
47 Reg 24 CB Regs
48 Reg 24(1) CB Regs
49 Reg 21 CB Regs
50 Reg 32 CB Regs
51 Reg 21(2) CB Regs
52 s143(1)(b) SSCBA 1992
53 Reg 5 SSB(PA) Regs
54 s143(1)(b) SSCBA 1992; *RK v HMRC
   (CHB)* [2015] UKUT 357 (AAC), reported
   as [2016] AACR 4; *JL v HMRC (CHB)*
   [2017] UKUT 193 (AAC)

4. Disability and carers' benefits
55 **AA** Reg 2(2), (3B) and (3C) SS(AA) Regs
   DLA Reg 2(2), (3B) and (3C) SS(DLA)
   Regs
   PIP Regs 17-20 SS(PIP) Regs
   CA Reg 9(2) and (3) SS(ICA) Regs
56 Reg 5 SS(DLA,AA&CA)(A) Regs
57 Reg 1(2), (3) and (4) SS(DLA,AA&CA)(A)
   Regs
58 House of Commons, *Hansard,* 20 April
   2017, HCWS603
59 **IS** Sch 2 para 14ZA IS Regs
   JSA Sch 1 para 17 JSA Regs
   ESA Sch 4 para 8 ESA Regs
   HB Sch 3 para 17 HB Regs
60 Reg 13 SSB(PA) Regs; Sch 2 para 7
   SSB(Dep) Regs
61 Reg 2(4) SSB(PRT) Regs
62 **AA** Reg 2B SS(AA) Regs
   DLA Reg 2B SS(DLA) Regs
   PIP Reg 23 SS(PIP) Regs
   CA Reg 9B SS(ICA) Regs
63 **AA** s65(7) SSCBA 1992
   DLA s72(7B) SSCBA 1992
   PIP s84 WRA 2012
   CA s70(4A) SSCBA 1992
64 *Commission of the European Communities
   v European Parliament and Council of the
   European Union,* C-299/05 [2007] ECR I-
   08695, 18 October 2007
65 ss65(7), 70(4A) and 72(7B) SSCBA
   1992; s84 WRA 2012
66 *SSWP v Tolley,* C-430/15 [2017]. This
   case relates to the old co-ordination
   rules.
67 *Bartlett and Others v SSWP,* C-537/09
   [2011] ECR I-03417; see also *NG v SSWP
   (DLA)* [2012] UKUT 26 (AAC), reported
   as [2012] AACR 2012
68 Art 70 EU Reg 883/04; *Swaddling v AO,*
   C-90/97 [1999] ECR I-01075
69 *GS v SSWP (DLA)* [2015] UKUT 687
   (AAC)
70 **DLA** Sch 1 paras 3 and 5 SS(DLA) Regs;
   Vol 10, para 61558 DMG
   PIP Regs 15 and 26 SS(PIP) Regs; para
   P4082 ADM
71 *Commission of the European Communities
   v European Parliament and Council of the
   European Union,* C-299/05 [2007] ECR I-
   08695, 18 October 2007
72 Reg 6(35)-(37) SS(C&P) Regs; reg 7(9A)
   SS&CS(DA) Regs
73 Reg 1(3) SS&CS(DA) Regs
74 *CK and JK v SSWP (CA, DLA)* [2013] UKUT
   218 (AAC)

75 *BD v SSWP (DLA)* [2013] UKUT 216
    (AAC), para 15, but note that this part of
    the decision is not binding; see also R(P)
    2/09
76 CIB/736/2004; *BD v SSWP (DLA)* [2013]
    UKUT 216 (AAC), para 14, but note that
    this part of the decision is not binding.

5. Incapacity benefit, severe disablement allowance and maternity allowance
77 Reg 2 SSB(PA) Regs
78 Reg 13 SSB(PA) Regs; reg 14 SS(IB-ID)
    Regs
79 Reg 2(4) SSB(PRT) Regs
80 Arts 5, 46 and 82 EU Reg 883/04; Arts
    27, 46, 49 and 87 EU Reg 987/2009
81 Arts 7 and 21 EU Reg 883/04

6. Industrial injuries benefits
82 Reg 9(3) SSB(PA) Regs
83 Reg 9(4) SSB(PA) Regs
84 Reg 9(5) SSB(PA) Regs

7. Contribution-based jobseeker's allowance and contributory employment and support allowance
85 s1(2)(i) JSA 1995; ss1(3)(d) and 18(4)(a)
    WRA 2007
86 Art 64 EU Reg 883/04
87 *Stewart v SSWP*, C-503/09 [2011]
88 Arts 5, 46 and 82 EU Reg 883/04; Arts
    27, 46, 49 and 87 EU Reg 987/2009
89 *BB v SSWP (ESA)* [2015] UKUT 545
    (AAC); see also *KC and MC v SSWP (ESA)*
    [2017] UKUT 94 (AAC)
90 SS(NIRA) Regs; SS(GBRA)(NI) Regs
91 s179(3), (4) and (5) SSAA 1992;
    SS(RA)O
92 Sch Art 2A-2B SS(NIRA) Regs; Sch Art
    2A-2B SS(GBRA)(NI) Regs

8. Retirement pensions
93 s113 SSCBA 1992; reg 4(1) SSB(PA)
    Regs
94 Regs 4(3) and 5 SSB(PA) Regs; ss18 and
    20 PA 2014; regs 21-23 The State
    Pension Regulations 2015, No.173; for
    state pension, see DMG Memo 6/16
95 Reg 6 SSB(PA) Regs
96 Reg 13 SSB(PA) Regs; reg 10 SSB(Dep)
    Regs
97 Reg 2(4) SSB(PRT) Regs

9. Statutory payments
98 **SSP** Reg 10 SSP(MAPA) Regs
    SMP Reg 2A SMP(PAM) Regs
    SAP/SPP Reg 4 SPPSAP(PAM) Regs
    SSPP Reg 6 SSPP(PAM) Regs
99 Art 6 EU Reg 883/04
    SSP s163(1) SSCBA 1992; reg 16 SSP
    Regs; regs 5-10 SSP(MAPA) Regs
    SMP s171(1) SSCBA 1992; regs 2, 2A, 5,
    7 and 8 SMP(PAM) Regs
    SAP/SPP ss171ZJ(2)-(3) and 171ZS(2)-
    (3) SSCBA 1992; regs 3, 4, 8 and 9
    SPPSAP(PAM) Regs
    SSPP s171ZZ4(2) SSCBA 1992; regs 5,
    6, 7, 9, 10 SSPP(PAM) Regs
100 **SSP** Reg 16(2) SSP Regs
    SMP Reg 3 SMP(PAM) Regs; reg 17(3)
    SMP Regs
    SAP/SPP Reg 2 SPPSAP(PAM) Regs; reg
    32(3) SPPSAP(G) Regs; reg 24(4)
    ASPP(G) Regs
    SSPP Reg 33(5) SSPP Regs; reg 4
    SSPP(PAM) Regs
101 *Caisse nationale des prestations familiales
    v Hiddal and Bernard*, C-216/12 and C-
    217/12 held that a parental leave
    allowance was a family benefit under EU
    Reg 1408/71.

10. Tax credits
102 Reg 4 TC(R) Regs
103 Reg 2(1) TC(R) Regs
104 Regs 3, 5 and 6 TC(R) Regs
105 s3(5A) TCA 2002
106 CCM 20090, 20160 and 20170; TCTM
    09374 and 09376
107 TCM 0288580; see also *GC v CHMRC
    (TC)* [2014] UKUT 251 (AAC)

Part 6

European co-ordination rules and international agreements

Chapter 16

....

European Union co-ordination rules

This chapter covers:
1. Introduction (below)
2. Who is covered (p281)
3. Which benefits are covered (p284)
4. Principles of co-ordination (p288)

This chapter describes the way in which the European Union social security co-ordination rules operate, both when you need to satisfy the entitlement conditions for UK benefits and tax credits if you have moved from another European Economic Area (EEA) state to the UK, and when you want to continue being paid benefits and tax credits after you or a family member go to live in another EEA state.

The residence and presence conditions for the individual benefits that affect your entitlement while you are in Great Britain are covered in Part 4, and the rules that affect your entitlement to benefits and tax credits if you go abroad are covered in Part 5.

If you are not an EEA national, check Part 3 first as your immigration status may exclude you from the benefit or tax credit you want to claim.

---

1. Introduction

If you are a European Economic Area (EEA) national (see p40), a family member (see p282) of an EEA national or, in some cases, a non-EEA national, your entitlement may be affected by the European Union (EU) social security co-ordination rules. These rules and the European caselaw that has interpreted their meaning apply in the UK and throughout the EEA.

Note: there are two main parts of EU law that are covered in this *Handbook*: the residence rights that enable you to satisfy the right to reside requirement, covered in Part 4, and the social security co-ordination rules, which are summarised in this chapter. In general, you do not need to know whether you have a right to reside in order to understand how the co-ordination rules affect you.

The co-ordination rules can affect whether you qualify for benefits in the UK.

In most cases, they make it easier to satisfy the UK rules – eg, by enabling you to count periods of residence, insurance and employment in any EEA state towards meeting the conditions of entitlement. However, in limited circumstances the co-ordination rules can prevent you from claiming a UK benefit. For the ways the co-ordination rules affect whether you qualify for individual UK benefits, see Chapter 13. The co-ordination rules can also help you to be paid a UK benefit in another EEA state for longer than you would be able to do under UK law alone. See Chapter 15 for the ways the co-ordination rules can help you claim, or continue to receive, individual UK benefits if you or your family member are in another EEA state.

The co-ordination rules

In order to secure and promote freedom of movement, EU law co-ordinates all the social security systems within the EEA. The intention is that people should not lose out on social security protection because they move to another member state. The rules do not seek to harmonise the social security systems of individual states; their sole objective is to co-ordinate the different schemes.

The co-ordination rules contain the following principles.

- **The single state principle.** You can generally only claim a particular category of benefit from one member state at any one time. The state responsible for paying your benefit is referred to as the 'competent state' (see p288).
- **Equal treatment of people.** Discrimination on the grounds of nationality in terms of access to, or the rate of payment of, the benefits that are covered is prohibited (see p297).
- **Equal treatment of benefits, income, facts and events.** If receipt of a benefit, or a fact or an event, has a legal consequence in one member state, this must be recognised in the same way by other member states (see p298).
- **Aggregation.** Periods of residence, insurance and employment in any EEA state can be used towards entitlement to benefit in another (see p298).
- **Exportability of certain benefits.** The co-ordination rules allow you to continue to be paid certain benefits abroad if you go to another member state. These rules generally mean that you can take benefit abroad for longer than under the UK rules (see p300).
- **Administrative co-operation.** Member states undertake to co-operate in the administration of the co-ordination rules.

The co-ordination rules set out the above general principles. There are exceptions for specific categories of benefits and, in some cases, there are more detailed provisions on how the principles should apply in certain circumstances. It is therefore helpful to understand the sources of the rules and the structure of the main regulation that sets these out (see below).

The current co-ordination rules succeed and build on, but do not repeal, the previous set of rules. The latter are referred to in this *Handbook* as 'the old co-ordination rules' (see p280).

Note: the co-ordination rules and their effect have not changed as a result of the UK's vote to leave the EU. They continue to apply until the UK formally leaves the EU.

Sources of the co-ordination rules

Article 48 of the Treaty on the Functioning of the European Union (TFEU) requires the European Parliament and the Council of Ministers to make such rules in the field of social security:

'as are necessary to provide freedom of movement for workers; to this end, they shall make arrangements to secure for employed and self-employed migrant workers and their dependants:

(a) aggregation, for the purpose of acquiring and retaining the right to benefit and of calculating the amount of benefit, of all periods taken into account under the laws of the several countries;

(b) payment of benefits to persons resident in the territories of Member States.';

Under this Article, the following further legislation has been made.

- **EU Regulation 883/2004** sets out the rules for co-ordinating the different social security systems of the various EU states. The structure of this regulation is as follows.
  - Preamble. This contains numbered 'recitals' that explain the purpose of the regulation and the principles it contains. These recitals can be used as an aid to interpret the subsequent substantive Articles.
  - General Provisions. Article 1 contains important definitions. Article 2 explains the 'personal scope' of the Regulation (the people to whom it applies – see p281). Article 3 sets out the 'material scope' (the categories of benefits to which the regulation applies – see p284). Articles 4 to 10 contain the general principles of the Regulation.
  - Determination of the Legislation Applicable. Articles 11 to 16 contain the general rules for working out which is the competent state (see p288).
  - Special Provisions Concerning the Various Categories of Benefits. Articles 17 to 70 contain more specific rules for different categories of benefits and are divided into chapters – one for each category of benefits.
  - Administrative Commission and Advisory Committee. Articles 71 to 75 establish organisations to oversee and implement the working of the regulation.
  - Miscellaneous Provisions. Articles 76 to 86 contain various miscellaneous rules on practical issues of administration.

- Transitional and Final Provisions. Articles 87 to 91 provide for the implementation of the regulation and transitional measures.
- Annexes. These contain further rules, most of which concern specific rules for individual member states.
- EU **Regulation 987/2009** contains procedures for implementing EU Regulation 883/2004.

Note: EU Regulation 883/2004 is the successor to **Regulation 1408/71**, which (together with its implementing regulation, EU Regulation 574/72) came into force on 1 April 1973 and is referred to in this chapter as the '**old co-ordination rules**'. The current co-ordination rules build on their predecessor, taking account of developments in European caselaw and national legislation to modernise and simplify the rules. However, the old co-ordination rules have not been repealed and continue to apply to limited groups of people (see p283). Since the majority of claims are now determined under the current co-ordination rules, this *Handbook* only covers these. For further information on the old co-ordination rules, see the 2012/13 edition of CPAG's *Welfare Benefits and Tax Credits Handbook*.

The other relevant law in the field of EU co-ordination comprises:
- the provisions in the TFEU on freedom of movement for workers and self-employed people, and citizenship. Even if the EU co-ordination rules do not provide for entitlement to benefits, these provisions may;
- the Charter of Fundamental Rights of the European Union;
- judgments of the Court of Justice of the European Union.

Using the co-ordination rules

In order to establish whether you can rely on the co-ordination rules, you must do the following.
- **Step one:** check whether you are covered by the current or the old co-ordination rules (see p283).
- **Step two:** check whether you are within the 'personal scope' of the co-ordination rules (see p281).
- **Step three:** check whether the particular benefit you want to claim is covered by the co-ordination rules, and into which category it falls (see p284).
- **Step four:** check which state is the 'competent state' for the benefit you are claiming (see p288).
- **Step five:** check the principle you want to apply – eg, exporting benefit or aggregating periods of insurance (see pp297–300).
- **Step six:** check the individual benefit and tax credit rules in Chapter 13 if you want to check entitlement in the UK, and in Chapter 15 if you want to be paid when you or your family are in another EEA state.

---

2. **Who is covered**

In order to be covered by the co-ordination rules, you must come within the range of people to whom the rules apply. This is known as the **'personal scope'** of the co-ordination rules. In addition, for the co-ordination rules to apply, your situation must involve more than one member state. This generally means that you must have moved between European Economic Area (EEA) states, or you live in one and work in another, or you live in one and are the national of another.[1]

You are within the 'personal scope' of the co-ordination rules if:[2]

- you have been 'subject to the legislation of one or more member states' (see below) and you are:
  - an EEA national; *or*
  - a refugee; *or*
  - a stateless person; *or*
- you are a family member (see p282) or a survivor of someone covered in the above bullet point. **Note:** the old co-ordination rules defined 'survivor' in terms of national legislation, so in the UK it meant a widow, widower or surviving civil partner.[3] However, there is no definition in the current rules, so it might be possible to argue a wider meaning could apply.

Subject to the legislation of a member state

You have been '**subject to the legislation of a member state**' if you have worked in and paid (or should have paid) the equivalent of national insurance (NI) contributions to that state, or you have paid contributions to that state on interest from assets,[4] or you have received any social security (see p285) or special non-contributory benefit (see p287) from that state. You may also be subject to the legislation if you are potentially eligible for any social security benefit or special non-contributory benefit.

'Legislation' is defined as 'in respect of each member state, laws, regulations and other statutory provisions and all other implementing measures relating to the social security branches covered by Article 3(1) of the Regulation.'[5]

The 'social security branches' referred to in this definition include UK benefits which are intended to assist you in the event of one of the risks covered by the co-ordination rules (see p285).[6] Examples include attendance allowance (AA), disability living allowance (DLA), personal independence payment (PIP), carer's allowance (CA), child benefit and child tax credit.

None of these depend on your being an employee or self-employed at any time. Potentially, therefore, even if you have never worked, including in some circumstances if you are a child, you can be covered by the co-ordination rules.

If you are covered by the co-ordination rules, check whether the benefit you are claiming or want to claim is covered by the co-ordination rules (see p284) and then check which state is the 'competent state' for that benefit (see p288).

Member of the family

A member of the family of someone covered by the co-ordination rules can also rely on, and be affected by, the rules that cover that person (which can vary depending on the type of benefit claimed).[7] The definition of a 'member of the family' under the co-ordination rules is different to the definition of a 'family member' in European Union (EU) residence law (see p170). It is also affected by national social security legislation and can therefore vary between member states.

Note: as economically inactive people, including in some circumstances children, are covered under the current co-ordination rules, you may be covered directly and not need to rely on being a member of someone else's family. If you are both a member of the family of a person covered by the rules and also covered by the rules yourself, you can usually rely on either coverage. However, the consequences of being a member of someone's family are not always favourable – eg, if it changes which state is competent to pay your benefits (see p288).

Member of the family
You are a '**member of the family**' of a person covered by the co-ordination rules if you are:[8]
– defined or recognised as a member of the family, or designated as a member of the household, by the legislation under which benefits are provided; *or*
– if the legislation under which benefits are provided does not make a distinction between the members of the family and other people to whom it applies, the covered person's spouse or child who is either under the age of majority (18 in England, Wales and Northern Ireland; 16 in Scotland) or older but dependent on the person covered.
If, under the legislation in either bullet above, you are only considered to be a member of the family or member of the household if you are living in the same household as the person, this condition is considered to be satisfied if you are mainly dependent on her/him.

The 'legislation under which benefits are provided' in the above definition should cover the legislation providing for the particular benefit you are claiming. However, it may be arguable that a broader category of social security legislation should apply. Obtain specialist advice if this affects you.

In a case concerning child benefit, the Upper Tribunal found that the relevant legislation was the child benefit legislation and held that the claimant's niece and nephew living in a different EU state did not count as members of the claimant's family.[9] **Note:** this case concerned the old co-ordination rules, and while the judge commented that the same would apply under the current co-ordination rules, it is arguable that insufficient consideration was given to the possibility of the children being designated as members of the household. Since they were not living in the same household as the claimant, this would have required the Upper Tribunal to have found that they were mainly dependent on the claimant.

In a case concerning DLA for a child, the Upper Tribunal, following the above case, found that the relevant legislation was the DLA legislation and held that the claimant's sister did not count as a member of his family under the current co-ordination rules. However, this did not affect his entitlement, as he was covered by the co-ordination rules himself.[10]

In a recent case concerning CA, the Upper Tribunal found that the relevant legislation was the CA legislation currently in force and since this no longer defined or recognised any particular persons as a member of the family or household, the second point above applied and the spouse was held to be the member of the family despite being separated and living in another EEA state.[11]

Note: if you are claiming 'sickness benefits' (eg, AA, CA, DLA care component and PIP daily living component), in limited circumstances a slightly different definition of member of the family member can be relevant and rules can apply to determine whether your rights as a member of the family or any independent rights you have take priority (see p290).

When the old co-ordination rules apply

The current co-ordination rules[12] apply to the vast majority of current benefit claims. However, the old co-ordination rules[13] (see p279) apply to you if:

- you are receiving a benefit because you claimed it before the current rules came into force.[14] This depends on your nationality (see the dates on p284). However, if you claimed your benefit before the current rules came into force but did not need to rely on co-ordination rules until after that date (eg, when moving between states), the current rules apply.[15] If the old rules apply to you, they continue to do so during a transitional period of up to 10 years, provided your circumstances do not change. This transitional period is intended to protect anyone who might otherwise have lost benefit under the new rules. However, you can ask to be transferred and considered under the new rules if this would be better for you. If so, the new rules take effect from the start of the following month.[16] **Note:** it is possible that the old co-ordination rules applied to you and then, subsequently, the current rules applied, so a decision maker or First-tier Tribunal may need to consider both sets of rules;[17] *or*
- you are a national of a non-EEA state (other than a refugee), you are legally resident in the UK or another member state,[18] and you have been employed or self-employed and subject to the legislation of a member state because you have paid (or should have paid) NI contributions, or you have been a student and subject to the legislation of an EEA state. You continue to be covered by

the old co-ordination rules if the UK is one of the member states where you have legally resided. This is because the UK obtained an opt-out, allowing it not to extend the current rules to 'third-country nationals' – ie, nationals of non-EEA states.[19]

Note: for the co-ordination rules to apply, your situation must involve more than one member state. This generally means that you must have moved between EEA states, or you live in one and work in another, or you live in one and are the national of another.[20]

Relevant dates
The current co-ordination rules apply to nationals (and their family members) of:[21]
– the EU member states (and refugees and stateless people) from 1 May 2010;
– Switzerland from 1 April 2012;
– Iceland, Liechtenstein and Norway from 1 June 2012.

As most claims are now determined under the current co-ordination rules, this *Handbook* only covers these. For further information on the old co-ordination rules, see the 2012/13 edition of CPAG's *Welfare Benefits and Tax Credits Handbook*.

3. **Which benefits are covered**

The benefits to which the co-ordination rules apply are referred to as being within the **'material scope'** of the rules.

Individual social security benefits are not directly referred to. Instead, the rules have broad categories of benefits such as for 'old age' or 'maternity'. The rules refer to these categories as benefits designed to cover certain 'risks'. Any social security benefit in a member state designed to provide assistance in the event of a particular risk comes into that particular category of benefit. Each state must then list the benefits it considers to be designed to assist with that risk.[22] However, the categorisation of a benefit can be challenged, as ultimately it depends on its characteristics rather than on how an individual state lists it.

Benefits are also divided into the following types, depending on the conditions of eligibility:
• social security benefits (see p285);
• special non-contributory benefits (see p287);
• social and medical assistance (see p287).

Those benefits deemed to be social security benefits have the most rights, and special non-contributory benefits provide fewer rights. Social and medical assistance is not covered by the co-ordination rules.

Social security benefits

Social security benefits are categorised according to the risk against which they are designed to provide financial protection.[23]

Risk	UK benefit
Sickness	Attendance allowance (AA)
	Disability living allowance (DLA) care component
	Personal independence payment (PIP) daily living component
	Carer's allowance (CA)
	Statutory sick pay
	Contributory employment and support allowance (ESA) in the assessment phase (but see p286)
Maternity and paternity	Maternity allowance
	Statutory maternity, adoption, paternity and shared parental pay (but see p286)
Invalidity	AA, DLA care and mobility components and CA if you were in receipt of benefit before 1 June 1992. If you claimed after this date, see the note on p286
	Long-term incapacity benefit
	Severe disablement allowance
	Contributory ESA after the assessment phase
	Arguably, contributory ESA during the assessment phase (see p286)
Old age	State pension
	Category A, B and D retirement pensions
	Additional pension
	Graduated retirement benefit
	Winter fuel payments
	Increments – eg, to pensions
	Increases of retirement pension for an adult
	Age addition in pensions
Pre-retirement	None
Survivors	Bereavement benefits
Death grants	Bereavement support payment (lump-sum payment)
	Bereavement payment

Accidents at work and occupational diseases	Industrial injuries disablement benefit
	Constant attendance allowance
	Exceptionally severe disablement allowance
	Reduced earnings allowance
	Retirement allowance
Unemployment	Contribution-based jobseeker's allowance (JSA)
Family benefits (see p301)	Child benefit
	Guardian's allowance
	Child tax credit
	Increases in other benefits for an adult or a child

Note: AA, DLA care component and CA have been categorised as assisting with different risks at different times. Until 1 June 1992, they were categorised as invalidity benefits. They were then categorised as special non-contributory benefits until this was held to be wrong and they were then re-categorised as sickness benefits.[24] The Court of Justice of the European Union has recently reconfirmed that DLA care component should be categorised as a sickness, and not an invalidity, benefit.[25] For the relevance of the changing categorisations when you want to be paid one of these benefits in another European Economic Area state, see p261.

The mobility component of DLA continues to be listed as a special non-contributory benefit and this has been held to be lawful.[26] The mobility component of PIP is treated by the DWP as a special non-contributory benefit. Therefore, you cannot export either mobility component (see p261).

Note:

- If you have a long-term or permanent disability, it is arguable that contributory ESA during the assessment phase, as well as after, should be regarded as an invalidity benefit.[27] However, in most cases, whether it is classed as an invalidity benefit or a sickness benefit makes no difference to whether you can export contributory ESA (see p300).
- For rules on exporting family benefits, see p301.
- The DWP considers that statutory maternity, adoption, paternity and shared parental pay are treated as pay rather than social security or special non-contributory benefits.[28] However, it is strongly arguable that these benefits should be classed as maternity and paternity benefits or family benefits.[29] In practice, the scope of the UK rules means that it will be rare for you to need to rely on the co-ordination rules directly.
- The DWP considers that universal credit (UC) is neither a social security nor a special non-contributory benefit and so the co-ordination rules do not apply to it.[30]

Special non-contributory benefits

Special non-contributory benefits are:[31]
* intended to provide supplementary or ancillary cover against the risks on pp285–86 or specific protection for disabled people closely linked to a person's social environment in the state concerned; *and*
* funded solely from general taxation and do not depend on having made contributions as a condition of entitlement; *and*
* listed as such in European Union (EU) Regulation 833/2004 (see below).

The last criterion above requires each member state to list in an annex to EU Regulation 833/2004 the benefits it considers to be 'special non-contributory benefits'. The UK government has only listed the four benefits below.[32] However, it is expected that the mobility component of PIP will also be listed as a special non-contributory benefit and, until then, the DWP is treating it as such.[33] Income-related ESA replaced income support (IS) in the list from 28 June 2012.

Special non-contributory benefits
DLA mobility component
Income-related ESA
Income-based JSA
Pension credit

Special non-contributory benefits can only be paid in the state in which you are 'resident'.[34] See p289 for details of when you count as resident.

Although you cannot 'export' special non-contributory benefits, all the other co-ordination principles apply.[35]

Social and medical assistance

Benefits which are neither 'social security' nor 'special non-contributory' benefits are considered to be social assistance and consequently excluded from the co-ordination rules.

The UK does not specify which benefits it considers to be social assistance, but it has made it clear that it does not consider UC to be either a social security or a special non-contributory benefit.[36]

It has also been decided that housing benefit[37] and working tax credit[38] are not social security or special non-contributory benefits. It is likely that the government might argue that IS is now also outside the scope of the EU co-ordination rules, since its removal from the list of special non-contributory benefits on 28 June 2012.

4. Principles of co-ordination

The co-ordination rules set out several general principles. There are exceptions to these principles for specific categories of benefits and, in some cases, there are more detailed provisions on how the principles should apply in certain circumstances. The following information provides an overview of the principles, as it is beyond the scope of this *Handbook* to cover all the exceptions and additional provisions in detail. You should therefore get specialist advice about the way the co-ordination rules apply to your particular circumstances.

The single competent state

In general, under the co-ordination rules you can only claim a particular category of benefit from one member state and are only liable to pay national insurance (NI) contributions (or their equivalent) to one member state at any one time. This is expressed as the general principle that you can be subject to the legislation of a single member state only.[39]

> ### The competent state and competent institution
> The '**competent state**' is the state that is responsible for paying your benefit and to which you must pay NI contributions. It is the state in which the 'competent institution' is situated.[40]
> The '**competent institution**' is broadly the institution that is responsible for paying your benefit and to which you are laible to pay NI contributions.[41] In the UK, this is the DWP and HM Revenue and Customs (HMRC).

The general rule is that the competent state is the one in which you are:[42]
- employed or self-employed;
- resident and from which you receive an unemployment benefit;
- a conscripted member of the armed forces or someone doing compulsory civilian service; *or*
- a civil servant.

If none of the above bullet points apply, the competent state is the state in which you are 'resident' (see p289 for how this is determined). However, sometimes other co-ordination rules may mean that a different state is deemed competent. The caselaw on when this applies is currently developing, but see p290 for when a state other than the one in which you are resident has been held to be competent.[43]

Note: there are exceptions for 'sickness benefits' if you (or your family member who brings you within the co-ordination rules) receive a pension from a state other than the one in which you reside (see p290). There are also exceptions for family benefits if you receive a pension (see p302).

You are treated as still employed or self-employed if, as a result of that activity, you are receiving cash benefits (other than for the risks of invalidity, sickness, old age, being a survivor or accidents at work).[44]

If you work simultaneously in two or more member states, you are subject to the legislation of the state of residence if you pursue a substantial part (generally, at least 25 per cent) of your activities there.[45]

If your employer's business is normally in one state but you are sent to another to work and it is anticipated that the posting will last for no more than 24 months, you remain subject to the legislation of the first state. Similarly, if you are self-employed in one state and go to another state to pursue a similar activity as a self-employed person, you remain subject to the legislation of the first state, provided the anticipated duration of your activity in the other state does not exceed 24 months.[46]

Note: you may continue to be subject to the legislation of the member state where you previously lived and were self-employed if, although you move to live in another state, you continue to be self-employed in the previous state.[47]

If you make a claim, declaration or appeal to the competent institution in a state that is not your competent state, it must be forwarded to the competent state without delay andtreated as if it had been submitted to the competent state on the date it was originally submitted.[48] For further information, including if there is a dispute between states over which is your competent state, see p296.

How residence is determined

'Residence' is defined in the co-ordination rules as 'the place where a person habitually resides'.[49] The following information outlines the factors that should be considered when determining where you habitually reside. Although this list of factors is in a rule which explains what should be done if there is a difference of views between two states or institutions about where you are resident, it should also be used where there is no such dispute. Firstly, it should be established by common agreement where your centre of interests lies. This is based on an overall assessment of the relevant facts, including:[50]

- the duration and continuity of presence in the state(s) concerned;
- your personal situation, including:
  - the nature and specific characteristics of any activity pursued, in particular the place where such activity is habitually pursued, the stability of the activity, and the duration of any work contract;
  - your family status and family ties;
  - any unpaid activity, such as voluntary work;
  - if you are a student, the source of your income;
  - your housing situation, in particular how permanent it is;
  - the member state in which you are deemed to reside for tax purposes.

If there is still a dispute about your place of residence, your intentions should be considered, especially the reasons why you moved. This is decisive in establishing your actual place of residence.[51]

If there is a dispute between states over which is your competent state, see p296.

When the UK remains the competent state

If you are subject to the legislation of the UK, either because you last worked in the UK or you are resident in the UK, the UK remains your competent state until:[52]
- you start to work in another European Economic Area (EEA) member state;
- (unless you last worked in the UK) you receive a pension from another EEA member state and request that the UK ceases to be your competent state;[53]
- in some circumstances, you move to another EEA member state and become resident there (see below).

These general rules can be supplemented by other rules which are specific to the category of benefit being paid.[54] For example, if you are receiving a 'sickness benefit' from the UK because the UK is the competent state on the basis of your residence in the UK and you then begin receiving a 'pension' from another EEA state, this can mean that your competent state ceases to be the UK (see below).[55]

The point at which the UK stops being responsible for paying your benefit if you move to another state is not always clear and most of the caselaw has considered the old co-ordination rules, which differ in significant respects from the current ones (see p279).[56] However, in general, if you continue to be entitled to a UK benefit when you move to another EEA state, the UK remains the competent state for paying that benefit until either you become employed/self-employed in the other state or, in certain circumstances, you start to receive a benefit from that state.[57] If you were self-employed in the UK and move to live in another EEA state, you may, depending on your circumstances, continue to be self-employed in the UK, in which case the UK remains your competent state.[58]

Sickness benefits

If you are covered by the co-ordination rules, you are only entitled to attendance allowance (AA), disability living allowance (DLA) care component, the daily living component of personal independence payment (PIP) and carer's allowance (CA) (which are all classed as sickness benefits) if the UK is the competent state for paying 'cash' sickness benefits.[59] The UK must be the competent state to pay *your* sickness benefits. So, for example, for you to receive CA, the UK must be the competent state to pay you that benefit, even if there is a different competent state for paying sickness benefit to the person you care for.[60]

In most cases, the competent state is determined under the general rule explained on p288. However:

- If the only basis for the UK being the competent state to pay your cash sickness benefits is that you are resident in the UK, other provisions of the co-ordination rules may mean that another state is deemed competent.[61] One such provision states that an insured person and members of her/his family residing or staying in a state other than the competent state shall be entitled to cash benefits provided by the competent state.[62] The Upper Tribunal recently held that, as a result of this provision, the UK was not the competent state to pay CA to a woman resident in the UK because her husband (from whom she was separated but not divorced) was working and insured in the Netherlands. Since the Netherlands was his competent state, and she was a member of his family residing in another state, the Netherlands was held to be the competent state for her CA claim.[63] **Note:** the Upper Tribunal is due to hear two linked cases on whether the claimants' competent state is affected by their family member being employed in another state.[64] See CPAG's online service and *Welfare Rights Bulletin* for updates and get specialist advice if you think this could affect your entitlement.

- The way of determining the competent state for paying your cash sickness benefits is different if you, or the member of your family who brings you within the co-ordination rules, receive a 'pension' from an EEA state other than the one where you reside (see below).

If you or a member of your family receive a pension from another European Economic Area state

If you, or the member of your family (see p282) who brings you within the co-ordination rules, receive a 'pension' (see below) from an EEA state other than the one you are residing in, the competent state for paying your cash sickness benefits is the one responsible for meeting the cost of your sickness benefits in kind – eg, in the UK, NHS treatment.[65] **Note:** although you receive sickness benefits in kind in the state where you are resident, the *cost* of these can be borne by another state. This means that to work out which state is competent for paying a cash sickness benefit, you must establish which state must bear the cost of sickness benefits in kind. Various scenarios are set out on pp292–95. It may also be helpful to refer decision makers to the DWP guidance, *Deciding the Competent State to Pay Cash Sickness Benefits.*[66]

Pension and pensioner

'Pension', for the purpose of the co-ordination rules, includes more than old age pensions. It includes lump-sum benefits that can be substituted for pensions and reimbursement of contributions, and can include revaluation increases and supplementary allowances.[67] It has been accepted that, under the old co-ordination rules, a pension can include incapacity benefit, employment and support allowance (ESA), DLA and severe disablement allowance.[68] However, a more recent case has held that DLA is not a pension under the current co-ordination rules. It also held that the term 'pension' must have the same meaning throughout the European Union (EU) regulations and that a Dutch survivors' benefit is a pension.[69] It may be arguable that the term 'pension' includes pension credit (PC) since this is a supplementary allowance.[70] Although the Upper Tribunal recently commented that PC is not a 'pension', as it is a special non-contributory benefit (see p287),[71] the argument was not considered in depth, and the Court of Justice of the European Union (CJEU) has held that a benefit can be both a special non-contributory benefit and a supplementary allowance.[72]

'Pensioner' is not defined, but refers to someone receiving a 'pension'.

Who is a member of the family for sickness benefits in kind

The definition of 'member of the family ' for sickness benefits in kind is slightly different to the general definition (see p282). The difference is highlighted below in italics.

You are a member of the family of a person covered by the co-ordination rules for the purpose of sickness benefits in kind if you are:[73]

- a person defined or recognised as a member of the family, or designated as a member of the household, by the legislation *of the member state in which you reside; or*
- if the legislation under which benefits are provided does not make a distinction between the members of the family and other people to whom it applies, the covered person's spouse or child who is either under the age of majority (18 in England, Wales and Northern Ireland; 16 in Scotland) or older but dependent on the person covered.

If, under the legislation in either bullet above, you are only considered to be a member of the family or member of the household if you are living in the same household as the person, this condition is considered to be satisfied if you are mainly dependent on her/him.

If you have a right to benefits in kind as a member of the family, as well as an independent right to benefits in kind, your independent right takes priority unless this is only based on residence.[74] Examples are given below.

Scenarios if a pension is paid by another European Economic Area state

If you, or the member of your family (see p282) who brings you within the co-ordination rules, receive a 'pension' (see p291) from an EEA state other than the one you are living in, check the possible scenarios, and exceptions, to determine which state is competent for paying your cash sickness benefits.

If you reside in the UK (or another state in which entitlement to sickness benefits in kind is on the basis of residence, rather than insurance or employment) and you (or your family member who brings you within the co-ordination rules) receive a 'pension' from another state, *but not* from the UK (or the other state of residence), the cost of sickness benefits in kind received in the UK (or other state) is borne by the state that pays the pension, to the extent that you would be entitled to receive sickness benefits in kind from that state if you lived there. Therefore, the state that pays your pension, rather than the UK, is responsible for paying your cash sickness benefit.[75]

Example
Emil is a Swedish national and receives a small Swedish old age state pension. Emil moves to the UK and claims AA. As he receives a pension from another state (Sweden), that state is responsible to the UK for reimbursing the cost of any NHS treatment he has. Consequently, provided Emil would be entitled to sickness benefits in kind (eg, healthcare) if he were resident in Sweden, he is not entitled to AA (but may be able to claim a Swedish cash sickness benefit).

If you receive a pension from two or more states and one of them is the state in which you reside, that state is responsible for the cost of your sickness benefits in kind (and is therefore the competent state for paying cash sickness benefits).[76]

Example
Emil becomes eligible for and claims a category D retirement pension. He now receives a pension from two or more states, including the one in which he resides (the UK). That state (the UK) is responsible for the cost of his NHS treatment, so Emil can be entitled to AA.

If you reside in the UK (or another state in which entitlement to sickness benefits in kind is on the basis of residence) and you receive a pension from two or more states other than the UK (or other state of residence), the cost of your healthcare in kind is met by the state in which you were subject to pensions legislation for the longest period (or if that is more than one state, the state in which you were last subject to its pensions legislation).[77] That state is therefore the competent state for paying your cash sickness benefits.

Example
Jonas worked 10 years in Germany and 18 years in France and now resides in the UK. He receives pensions from both Germany and France. France is the state responsible for the cost of any NHS treatment he has while he lives in the UK and so France is the competent state for paying cash sickness benefits.

If you are the member of the family of a person receiving a pension and reside in a different state to her/him, whichever state must meet the cost of the sickness benefits in kind for her/him must also meet the cost of sickness benefits in kind for you (and is therefore the competent state for paying cash sickness benefits).[78]

However, check whether you also have an independent right to benefits in kind and, if so, whether these take priority. See the second bullet point below.

Example
Reka is a Hungarian national living in the UK. Her husband Roland is a Dutch national. He lives in Ireland and his only income is his Dutch pension. The Netherlands is the state that must meet the cost of the sickness benefits in kind for Roland and, therefore, is also the state that must meet these costs for Reka.

The above rules do not apply in the following cases.
* You (or your family member who is a pensioner) are entitled to benefits under the legislation of a state because that state is the competent one on the basis of an activity as an employed or self-employed person.[79] **Note:** the DWP guidance suggests that undertaking activity as an employed or self-employed person in the UK is sufficient to mean that the UK becomes the competent state for paying cash sickness benefits.[80]

Example
Sophia is Portuguese and lives in the UK. She receives a small pension from Portugal. Sophia works part time as a self-employed cleaner and claims child benefit and child tax credit (CTC) for her disabled granddaughter who lives with her and receives DLA middle rate care component. Sophia can claim CA, as the UK is the competent state for paying benefits to her on the basis of her self-employment here.

* You are the family member of a pensioner, but you have an independent right to benefits in kind, either under the legislation of a state or under the co-ordination rules. Your independent right takes priority, unless it exists solely because of your residence in that state.[81]

Examples
Krista is Latvian and resides in the UK with her Latvian husband Andris. Krista and Andris both receive a pension from Latvia, but Krista also receives contributory ESA. Krista wants to claim the daily living component of PIP. She can do so because her independent rights take priority over her rights as the member of Andris' family. Because Krista receives a 'pension' from the UK as well as one from Latvia, the UK is the state responsible for the cost of her sickness benefits in kind, and is therefore the competent state for paying cash sickness benefits.

Ryan is a 13-year-old Irish national living in the UK with his Irish mother Megan who receives an invalidity pension from Ireland. Ryan wants to claim the care component of

DLA. However, because his independent rights are only based on his residence in the UK, the rights he has as the member of his mother's family take priority. Therefore, Ireland is the state responsible for the cost of his sickness benefits in kind, and is therefore the competent state for paying cash sickness benefits.

To check the sickness benefits payable by other EEA states, see the European Commission's website: 'Your rights country by country'.

If the rules exclude you

If you are residing in the UK and you receive a decision that the rules determining the competent state for sickness benefits exclude you from entitlement to AA, DLA care component, the daily living component of PIP or CA, or you think these rules might exclude you, check the following.

Are you excluded from 'sickness benefits'?

1. If it is suggested that you (or your family member who brings you within the co-ordination rules) are receiving a 'pension' from another state, check whether it is a pension received under the legislation of a member state. Private and occupational pensions should not bring you within the above rules. See p290 for the meaning of 'pension'.

2. Do, or could, you (or your family member who brings you within the co-ordination rules) receive a pension from the UK as well as from another state? If so, the UK is responsible for the cost of your NHS treatment and so is the competent state for paying sickness benefits (see the example of Emil on p293).

3. Although withdrawing your (or your family member's) claim for a pension from the other state could mean the above rules no longer apply to you (or her/him), get advice before doing so as it could affect your (or her/his) future pension entitlement.

4. If the DWP has decided that the UK is not the competent state, see p296.

5. It may be possible to argue that your particular circumstances mean that the exclusion from AA, DLA care component or the daily living component of PIP on the basis that the UK is not your competent state does not apply due to one of the following arguments.

– If you are the dependent family member of an EEA worker, the exclusion is prohibited by the principle of equal treatment (see p297) if the refusal of a disability benefit reduces or impedes her/his ability to work or disadvantages her/him in relation to a British worker.[82]

 Note: a recent Upper Tribunal decision rejected an argument that refusal of AA was disproportionate and discriminatory, but arguably did not fully consider this discrimination argument.[83] However, the argument was considered in a subsequent case when it was put in broad terms.[84] Although the judge dismissed the argument as presented, he left open the possibility that the principle of equal treatment could prohibit exclusion from sickness benefits for a family member of a worker in particular circumstances. Such an argument may be accepted if there is no equivalent sickness benefit payable by the competent state and exclusion would result in your being deprived of any entitlement at all.[85]

– If you have previously worked and paid taxes in the UK, the co-ordination rules should not deprive you of entitlement to a benefit paid for by taxation. If this would be the result of the co-ordination rules, a state is not prevented from awarding the benefit, even when it is not the competent state for paying it.[86] However, the Upper Tribunal has considered this line of argument developed through recent European caselaw, but did not find that it applied in that particular case as the person had not contributed through general taxation.[87]

If the decision maker decides the UK is not the competent state

If, when you claim a UK benefit, the decision maker decides the UK is not the competent state to pay that benefit, s/he must forward the claim to the relevant institution in the state that is considered competent without delay, unless there is evidence that state takes a different view (see below). The date of claim is the date the claim was made in the UK.[88]

If there is a difference of views between the institutions of two or more states on which state is the competent state for paying a cash benefit or meeting the cost of a benefit in kind, while the issue is being resolved you can get **provisional payments** from, and under the legislation of:[89]

- your state of residence, if you are resident in one of the states concerned; *or*
- the state to which you first applied, if you are not resident in any of the states concerned.

These rules on provisional payments apply if forwarding the claim triggers a different view and also if there is evidence of a different view when the claim is received, in which case it should not be forwarded.[90] The legislation only requires there to be a 'difference of views' between the relevant institutions. It says nothing about the form in which the view must be expressed nor the evidence required to prove it. The Upper Tribunal has considered this issue and noted that although documentary evidence will 'put the matter beyond doubt', it may not be available and oral evidence could, particularly at tribunals, be accepted.[91] A subsequent case accepted the claimant's oral evidence as sufficient to show the difference of view and therefore held that the DWP had to determine the claim and, if the claimant met the other conditions of entitlement, make provisional payments.[92] However, the DWP has been granted permission to appeal this decision to the Court of Appeal.[93]

Even if there is clear evidence of a 'difference of views', the benefit authorities do not always comply with their duty to pay provisional payments, so you may need to request these in wiriting, and include in your request references to the relevant legislation and caselaw.

If no agreement is reached between the states after one month, the matter can be brought before the Administrative Commission for the Co-ordination of Social

Security Systems by the competent authorities, which will seek to reconcile the dispute within six months.[94]

If it is established that the state that made provisional payments is not the competent state, it is reimbursed.[95]

The DWP has issued guidance on action to be taken once competency has been decided.[96] **Note:** this states that if there is a difference of view on which state is competent to pay benefit with a state that does not have a similar benefit to the one claimed in the UK, provisional payments need not be made.[97] No reference is given for this assertion and it is arguable that provisional payments should still be made.[98]

Although in most cases the issue is which state is competent to make the payment, if there is a difference of views between states concerning the determination of the applicable legislation, you are provisionally subject to the legislation of one state in the following order of priority:[99]

• if you only work in one state, the state where you work;
• if you either work in two or more states and live in one of them, or do not work, the state where you reside;
• in all other cases, of the states in which you work, the state to which you first applied.

Equal treatment of people

If you are covered by the co-ordination rules, you are entitled to the same benefits under the legislation of the 'competent state' (see p288) as a national of that state.[100] Equal treatment is one of the fundamental rights of EU law,[101] and the principle of non-discrimination prohibits discrimination based on your nationality. Both direct discrimination and, if it cannot be justified as proportionate and in pursuit of a legitimate aim, indirect discrimination are prohibited.

Direct discrimination arises when one person is treated less favourably than another. Indirect discrimination arises when rules which, although apparently neutral and non-discriminatory, have, in practice, a greater adverse impact on some people than others – eg, non-nationals of the competent state over nationals of the competent state. For example, the right to reside test in UK law appears to apply equally to all EEA nationals. However, British and Irish citizens always have a right to reside in the common travel area and therefore satisfy the test for means-tested benefits, whereas other EEA nationals only satisfy it in certain circumstances. Therefore, the test is indirectly discriminatory. However, the Supreme Court decided in a case concerning PC that this discrimination is justified and, therefore, legal.[102] Similarly, the CJEU has held that the right to reside test for child benefit and CTC was not directly discriminatory and, although indirectly discriminatory, this was justified.[103] Although a different view was taken by the Northern Ireland Chief Commissioner who found that, for the purposes of child benefit, the right to reside test was either directly or indirectly discriminatory, this was overturned by the Court of Appeal in Northern Ireland.[104]

Equal treatment of facts and events

The co-ordination rules provide for the 'equal treatment of benefits, income, facts or events'.[105] This is sometimes referred to as the 'principle of the assimilation of facts'. This principle is designed to ensure that if the competent state regards the receipt of a particular benefit or income, or the occurrence of certain facts or events, as producing certain legal effects, it should regard the receipt of an equivalent benefit or income from another state, or the occurrence of particular facts or events in another state, as producing the same effect. For example, a person receiving AA is entitled to a disability premium in her/his housing benefit (HB). Therefore, someone receiving a benefit equivalent to AA from another state who claims HB can argue that s/he should get the disability premium in her/his applicable amount. Similarly, if one member state has determined that a person has had an industrial accident, that fact must be accepted, for the purpose of awarding benefit, in another member state.

There are exceptions to the general principle of the assimilation of facts, some of which are set out in the co-ordination rules, and others arise as a result of a conflict between this principle and other principles of the co-ordination rules. An example of the latter is that the assimilation of facts cannot render another member state competent.[106] The competent state should first be determined (see p288) and then that state should assimilate the facts for the purposes of its own legislation. Another example of the assimilation principle not being absolute is that it should not interfere with the principle of aggregation (see below).[107] So, the competent state should count periods of insurance in another member state (under the aggregation principle) without needing to address the question of whether they count as periods of insurance for the assimilation principle to apply. If it counts as a period of insurance under the legislation of the state in which it took place, that period can be aggregated.

Aggregation

The principle of aggregation for the purpose of acquiring and calculating entitlement to benefits is a key co-ordinating principle.[108] To ensure and promote freedom of movement, the aim of this principle is to remove disadvantages that arise when claiming benefit after moving from one state to another.

'**Aggregation**' means adding together periods of insurance (such as NI contributions in the UK), residence or employment/self-employment completed under the legislation of other member states to satisfy the conditions of entitlement for a benefit. For example, if you want to claim a UK contribution-based benefit such as contributory ESA, but you have not paid sufficient NI contributions in the UK, you can rely on contributions you have paid in other EEA states in order to satisfy the UK contribution rules.

The competent institution must contact the competent institutions in the other relevant states to determine the periods completed under their legislation.[109]

What constitutes a period of residence, employment or insurance is determined by the legislation of the state in which it took place.[110]

Note: the EU co-ordination rules allow 'residence' in another EEA state to be aggregated together with presence in Great Britain to satisfy the past presence test for AA, DLA, PIP and CA (see p218).[111] However, the Upper Tribunal has held that 'mere residence' in another EEA state does not count for this purpose. Although, in the cases being decided, it was not necessary to decide what qualities the residence must have in order to count, it was suggested that insurance-based, or contribution-based, residence would count.[112] **Note:** this case has been appealed to the Court of Appeal.[113] See CPAG's online service and *Welfare Rights Bulletin* for updates.

Example
Sancha is a Portuguese national who has worked for many years in Portugal. She leaves her job in Portugal and moves to the UK. She works for three weeks before being made redundant. Sancha is expecting a baby in two months' time and claims maternity allowance (MA). She is entitled to MA because she can add her periods of employment in Portugal to her period of employment in the UK to satisfy the condition of having worked for 26 out of the last 66 weeks.

Unemployment benefits

When determining entitlement to unemployment benefits, your periods of insurance (if entitlement depends on insurance) or employment/self-employment (if entitlement depends on employment/self-employment) completed in all member states are only aggregated if you were last insured or you last worked (whichever is required) under the legislation of the state from which you are claiming benefit.[114]

Example
Tomasz is Polish and after working and being insured in Poland for four years became unemployed, and so moved to the UK to look for work. If he claims contribution-based jobseeker's allowance (JSA), he cannot use his periods of insurance from Poland to satisfy the NI contribution conditions. However, if he takes two weeks' full-time temporary work in the UK and then claims contribution-based JSA, he can then aggregate his periods of insurance in Poland and the NI contributions paid in the UK to be able to qualify for contribution-based JSA.

However, this additional condition does not apply if, during your last period of employment or self-employment, you resided in a state other than your competent state. In this case, if you claim an unemployment benefit in the state in which you reside, you *can* aggregate periods of insurance or employment or self-employment in order to be entitled to that benefit.[115]

Example
Monique was employed and insured in Belgium where she resided for a year. She then got a job in France for 18 months. As this involved mainly working from home, she did this work while residing in the UK with her boyfriend. She has been made redundant and wants to claim contribution-based JSA. She can aggregate the contributions paid in both Belgium and France to qualify for contribution-based JSA.

Exporting benefits

The co-ordination rules allow you to 'export' certain social security benefits to another state if you cease to be resident in the member state in which your entitlement arose.

This means that certain benefits may not be reduced, modified, suspended, withdrawn or confiscated just because you go to live in a different member state.[116] The rules for exporting vary according to the benefit concerned: some are fully exportable, some may be exportable on a temporary basis, and some are not exportable at all.

Check the individual benefit rules in Chapter 15 to see whether that benefit can be exported. If it can, you should contact the office that pays your benefit well in advance so that arrangements can be made to pay you in the other EEA state. The rules covering periodic reassessments still apply so, for example, if you export contributory ESA, the DWP continues to assess your limited capability for work and your limited capability for work-related activity. However, any checks and medicals take place in the state in which you are living, with reports then sent to the DWP.[117]

Under the co-ordination rules, all benefits categorised as social security benefits are exportable. See p285 for a list of the UK benefits covered.

The following benefits can be exported indefinitely:
• invalidity benefits;
• old age benefits;
• survivors' benefits;
• pensions for accidents at work or occupational diseases;
• death grants.

The following benefits can be exported for a limited period or subject to certain restrictions:
• unemployment benefits;

• sickness, maternity and paternity benefits. However, in most cases, these benefits are exportable in a similar way to the fully exportable benefits.

Special non-contributory benefits (see p287) cannot be exported. They are paid only in the state in which you are 'resident'.[118] See p289 for details of when you count as resident.

Overlapping benefit rules

A general principle of the EU rules on co-ordination is that you should not use one period of compulsory insurance to obtain more than one benefit derived from that period of insurance.[119] In general, you are only insured in one EEA member state for any one period, so you cannot use insurance from that one period to obtain entitlement to benefits of the same kind from more than one member state. Usually, benefits are adjusted to ensure that either only one state (the 'competent state' – see p288) pays the benefit, taking into account periods of insurance in other EEA member states, or the benefit is paid pro rata according to the lengths of the periods of insurance in different member states.

In certain cases, however, you may be paid both the full level of a UK benefit and a proportion of a benefit from another member state, accrued as a result of having paid NI contributions there. EEA states are not allowed to apply provisions preventing the overlapping of their own benefits with those of other member states if it would reduce what you would have received from your years of contributions in the first member state alone.[120]

There are particular overlapping rules on specific categories of benefits – eg, family benefits (see p302),[121] old age and survivors' benefits.[122]

Family benefits

Under the co-ordination rules, family benefits in the UK include child benefit, CTC, guardian's allowance and child dependants' additions in other benefits.

If you are covered by the co-ordination rules, you can export family benefits without any time limit provided there is no change in your competent state.[123] If you export family benefits, they are uprated in the normal way. You can also be paid for family members living in another member state (see p302).[124] For the definition of member family member, see p282.

If you are entitled to family benefits from more than one member state in respect of the same person and for the same period, there are rules that determine which state has priority if your entitlements overlap (see p302).

Note: working tax credit (WTC) has been held not to be a social security benefit or a special non-contributory benefit under the EU co-ordination rules and therefore these rules do not apply to WTC (see p284).[125] However, other provisions of EU law mean that you cannot be refused the childcare element of WTC in respect of childcare costs solely because the childcare provider is located outside the UK in another EEA state (see p230).[126]

Family members resident in another state

Generally, you are entitled to receive family benefits from your competent state, determined in the usual way (see p288), even when the family member for whom you are claiming is resident in another state.[127] In this case, your family member is treated as if s/he were resident in the competent state.

Example
Carla is Italian. She is working in the UK and sending money to her two children who live in Italy with their grandmother. Carla is entitled to child benefit and CTC in respect of her children.

However, if you are receiving a 'pension', the member state that is competent for paying this is the one from which you claim family benefits.[128] See p290 for definition of 'pension'.[129]

Example
Julien is a French national. He receives a small state pension from France and has moved to the UK. Julien's 15-year-old twin daughters remain living in France. Julien also runs a small business in the UK. Normally, because Julien is working in the UK, the UK would be the competent state for paying family benefits. However, because Julien is in receipt of a pension from France, he is only entitled to claim French family benefits.

Note: if you can claim benefit for your child who is resident in another member state, you must still satisfy all the other conditions of entitlement including, for child benefit, contributing to the costs of the child an amount at least equal to the amount of child benefit payable for her/him.[130]

HMRC guidance for decision makers covers how the co-ordination rules enable you to be paid for a family member living in another member state.[131] It lists workers and self-employed people paying NI contributions in the UK as examples of those eligible to use these rules, and can therefore easily be misunderstood as meaning that the rules only apply to these groups of people. This mistaken suggestion that the current co-ordination rules are limited in a similar way to the old co-ordination rules (see p279) has appeared in several HMRC appeal submissions and has been confirmed as wrong by the Upper Tribunal.[132]

Priority when family benefits overlap

It is not uncommon for there to be entitlement to family benefits provided for under the legislation of more than one EEA state in respect of the same family member and for the same period. This can arise when two people are entitled to benefit for the same child (eg, if a mother resides in one state and the father in another and both can claim family benefits for their child), or if the same person has an entitlement from more than one state – eg, if a parent lives in one state with her/his children, but works in another.

To ensure that equivalent family benefits are not payable by more than one state in respect of the same family member for the same period, the co-ordination rules set out which member state has 'priority' – ie, must pay the family benefits.

Note: these priority rules only need to be considered if there is an actual overlap of entitlement because a claim has been made for a family benefit in another member state (unless entitlement does not require a claim to have been made.[133]

The way the priority rules operate depends on the basis on which each family benefit is paid and, in some cases, the state in which the child lives.[134]

Different member states have different criteria for entitlement. In some states, you must reside in that state (family benefits payable on the basis of 'residence'); in others, you must work in that state (family benefits payable on the basis of 'employment or self-employment'); and some states require you to receive a pension (family benefits payable on the basis of 'receipt of a pension'). It can be difficult to work out the basis on which a family benefit is paid, but the European Commission has online information on the conditions for each state.[135] In the majority of states, including the UK, family benefits are mostly payable on the basis of residence – eg, there are no employment conditions or a requirement to receive a pension in order to obtain child benefit or CTC.

If the family benefits from each state are payable on a *different* basis, the state which has priority (ie, must pay) is the one whose family benefits are payable on the first of the following bases:[136]

- activity as an employed or self-employed person. This can include temporary periods not working for reasons such as sickness, maternity or unemployment, provided you receive either wages or benefits other than a 'pension' (see p290);[137]
- receipt of a pension (see p290);
- residence.

If the family benefits from each state are payable on the *same* basis, the state which has priority (ie, must pay) is as follows.[138]

- If family benefits are based on employment/self-employment in both states, the state with priority is the one where the child resides, if you (or if there is another potential claimant, s/he) work there, otherwise it is the state that pays the highest amount.[139]
- If family benefits are based on receipt of a pension in both states, the state with priority is the one where the child resides if that state also pays the pension;

otherwise it is the state where you (or the other potential claimant) have been insured or resided for the longest period.

- If family benefits are based on residence, the state with priority is the one where the child resides.

If there is an entitlement to family benefits from the state that has priority, the entitlement to family benefits from the other state(s) with lower priority is suspended up to the amount provided under the legislation of the former state. If this suspension does not wipe out all entitlement, a supplement is paid to 'top up' the family benefits paid by the priority state.[140] However, this top-up need not be paid for children residing in another state when entitlement to family benefits in both states is based on residence only.[141]

Examples

Marie and her two children moved to the UK from Belgium four months ago when she separated from their father, Arnaud. Marie is looking for work, but has not found a job yet. She claims child benefit and CTC. However, Arnaud, who is working in Belgium, is still receiving the Belgian family benefit and sending this money to Marie for the children. The Belgian family benefit is payable on the basis of employment and, therefore, has priority over the UK family benefits, since the latter are based on residence. If the UK family benefits are more than the Belgian family benefits, Marie should be paid the difference to top up the Belgian family benefits.

Alicia moved to the UK from Slovakia to take up a job, but was made redundant after four months. Her husband and their two children stayed in Slovakia. Alicia's husband receives Slovakian family benefits, which are payable on the basis of residence. Alicia claims child benefit and CTC. Since these are also payable on the basis of residence, Slovakia has priority since the children live there. The UK does not need to pay a top-up, even though its family benefits are more generous than the Slovakian ones.

Note: if entitlement to a family benefit in one state depends on a claim having been made and no claim has been made, entitlement to the family benefit that has been claimed in another state cannot be suspended.[142] It is therefore not necessary to consider whether family benefits in another member state have priority or are payable at a higher rate if a claim is required for entitlement but no claim has been made.[143]

If family benefits are paid to someone who is not using them to maintain her/his family member, the EEA state paying the benefit can make payments to the person who is, in fact, maintaining the family member. This is done at the request of, and through, the relevant institution in the state where the person who is maintaining the family member lives.[144]

Administration of family benefits

There are rules that cover the administration of claims for family benefits where more than one state could potentially be involved.[145]

If a claim is submitted to the relevant institution in a state whose legislation is applicable but which does not have priority under the rules above, that institution should make a provisional decision on the priority rules and then forward the claim to the relevant institution in the state with priority without delay. The date of claim is the date it was made to the first state. The relevant institution in the other state should then make a decison within two months. If it fails to do so, benefit should be awarded on the basis of the provisional decision, including any 'top-up' from the state where the benefit was claimed.[146] However, if there is a difference of view between the states about which has priority, provisional payments must be made by the state in which the child resides (or where the benefit was first claimed if the child does not reside in any of the relevant states). If agreement is not reached between the states within a month, the matter may be referred to the Administrative Commission for the Co-ordination of Social Security to resolve within six months.[147]

If you are claiming in the UK and HMRC advises you that another state has priority, you might need to remind HMRC of its duty to forward the claim to the relevant institution in the other state. If this has been done and there is evidence of a difference of view between HMRC and the relevant institution in the other state, remind HMRC of its duty to make provisional payments. Although the Upper Tribunal caselaw on provisional payments under the EU co-ordination rules has concerned sickness benefits, it can still be helpful to refer to because it sets out how these rules work (see p296).[148]

It can also be useful to check, and refer to when helpful, HMRC guidance for decision makers, which covers the priority rules, when family benefits can be 'topped up', administrative procedures and provisional payments.[149]

Notes

2. Who is covered
1 *Petit v Office National de Pensions*, C-153/91 [1992] ECR I-04973
2 Art 2 EU Reg 883/04
3 Art 1(g) EU Reg 1408/71
4 *Ministre de l'Économie et des Finances v Ruyter*, C-623/13 [2015]
5 Art 1(l) EU Reg 883/04
6 Art 3 EU Reg 883/04
7 Art 2 EU Reg 883/04
8 Arts 1(i) and 2 EU Reg 883/04
9 *KT v HMRC (CB)* [2013] UKUT 151 (AAC)
10 *PB v SSWP (DLA)* [2016] UKUT 280 (AAC), paras 8-10
11 *AM v SSWP* [2017] UKUT 26 (AAC), para 15

12 EU Reg 883/04
13 EU Reg 1408/71
14 Art 87(8) EU Reg 883/04; Recital (2),
Decision H1 of 12 June 2009 of the
Administrative Commission for the Co-
ordination of Social Security Systems
[2010] OJ C-106/13; SSWP v PW (CA)
[2013] UKUT 296 (AAC)
15 KG v SSWP (DLA) [2015] UKUT 146
(AAC)
16 Art 87(8) EU Reg 883/04
17 For example, SL v SSWP (DLA) [2014]
UKUT 108 (AAC)
18 Art 1 EU Reg 859/2003
19 Recital 18 EU Reg 1231/2010
20 Petit v Office National de Pensions, C-
153/91 [1992] ECR I-04973
21 The UK's attempt to challenge this
extension of the current co-ordination
rules failed in relation to:
Switzerland: UK v Council of the European
Union, C-656/11 [2014];
Iceland, Liechtenstein and Norway: UK v
Council of the European Union, C-431/11
[2013]

3. Which benefits are covered
22 Art 9 EU Reg 883/04
23 Art 3 EU Reg 883/04
24 Commission of the European Communities
v European Parliament and Council of the
European Union, C-299/05 [2007] ECR I-
08695
25 SSWP v Tolley C-430/15 [2017]. This
case relates to the old co-ordination
rules.
26 Bartlett and Others v SSWP, C-537/09
[2011] ECR I-03417
27 Stewart v SSWP, C-503/09 [2011] ECR I-
06497
28 para 070153 DMG
29 Caisse nationale des prestations familiales
v Hiddal and Bernard, C-216/12 and C-
217/12 held that a parental leave
allowance was a family benefit under EU
Reg 1408/71.
30 SSAC, Universal Credit and Related
Regulations Report and Government
Response, December 2012
31 Art 70(1) and (2) and Annex X EU Reg
883/04
32 Annex X EU Reg 883/04
33 Ch C2, para C2097 ADM
34 Art 70 EU Reg 883/04
35 Art 3(3) EU Reg 883/04; Dano v
Jobcenter Leipzig, C-333/13 [2014],
paras 46-55

36 SSAC, Universal Credit and Related
Regulations Report and Government
Response, December 2012
37 CH/1400/2006, paras 37-40
38 MR v HMRC (TC) [2011] UKUT 40 (AAC),
para 17

4. Principles of co-ordination
39 Art 11 EU Reg 883/04
40 Art 1(s) EU Reg 883/04
41 Art 1(q) EU Reg 883/04
42 Art 11 EU Reg 883/04
43 Art 11(3)(e) EU Reg 883/04
44 Art 11(2) EU Reg 883/04
45 Art 13 EU Reg 883/04
46 Art 12 EU Reg 883/04
47 AR v HMRC (CHB) [2014] UKUT 553
(AAC); HB v HMRC (CHB) [2014] UKUT
554 (AAC), paras 37-39
48 Arts 67, 68 and 81 EU Reg 883/04; Arts
2 and 60 EU Reg 987/2009; SSWP v AK
(AA) [2015] UKUT 110 (AAC)
49 Art 1(j) EU Reg 883/04
50 Art 11 EU Reg 987/2009
51 Art 11(2) EU Reg 987/09
52 Arts 11-16 EU Reg 883/04
53 Art 16(2) EU Reg 883/04
54 Title III EU Reg 883/04
55 LD v SSWP [2017] UKUT 65 (AAC). Note
that permission to appeal to the Court of
Appeal is being sought.
56 See for example, Kuusijärvi v
Riksförsäkringsverket, C-275/96 [1998]
ECR I-03419; AR v HMRC (CHB) [2014]
UKUT 553 (AAC); HB v HMRC (CHB)
[2014] UKUT 554 (AAC)
57 See for example, Kuusijärvi v
Riksförsäkringsverket, C-275/96 [1998]
ECR I-03419; AR v HMRC (CHB) [2014]
UKUT 553 (AAC); HB v HMRC (CHB)
[2014] UKUT 554 (AAC); SSWP v Tolley,
C-430/15 [2017]
58 AR v HMRC (CHB) [2014] UKUT 553
(AAC); HB v HMRC (CHB) [2014] UKUT
554 (AAC), paras 37-39
59 **AA** s65(7) SSCBA 1992
DLA s72(7B) SSCBA 1992
PIP s84 WRA 2012
CA s70(4A) SSCBA 1992
60 SSWP v AH [2016] UKUT 148 (AAC)
61 Art 11(3)(e) EU Reg 883/04
62 Art 21(1) EU Reg 883/04
63 AM v SSWP [2017] UKUT 26 (AAC)
64 File refs: CSDLA/136/2017 and CSG/95/
2017
65 Art 29 EU Reg 883/04
66 DMG Memo 26/15; ADM Memo 20/15
67 Art 1(w) EU Reg 883/04

68 *JS v SSWP (DLA)* [2012] AACR 7, para 14; *KS v SSWP (DLA)* [2014] UKUT 19 (AAC), para 81; both in relation to EU Reg 1408/71
69 *LD v SSWP* [2017] UKUT 65 (AAC). Permission to appeal to the Court of Appeal is being sought.
70 *Perry v Chief Adjudication Officer* [1998]; *EC v SSWP (SPC)* [2010] UKUT 95 (AAC), para 40
71 *IG v SSWP* [2016] UKUT 176 (AAC), para 25
72 *Skalka v Sozialversicherungsanstalt der Gewerblichen Wirtschaft,* C-160/02 [2004] ECR I-05613; *Naranjo v CRAM Nord-Picardie,* C-265/05 [2007] ECR I-00347
73 Art 1(i)(1) and (ii), (2) and (3) EU Reg 883/04
74 Art 32(1) EU Reg 883/04
75 Art 25 EU Reg 883/04; *SSWP v AK (AA)* [2015] UKUT 110 (AAC), reported as [2015] AACR 27
76 Art 23 EU Reg 883/04; *SSWP v HR (AA)* [2013] UKUT 66 (AAC); *SL v SSWP (DLA)* [2014] UKUT 108 (AAC)
77 Arts 24(2)(b) and 25 EU Reg 883/04; *Helder and Farrington v College voor Zorgverzekeringen,* C-321/12 [2013]
78 Art 26 EU Reg 883/04
79 Art 31 EU Reg 883/04
80 DMG Memo 26/15, note to para 22; ADM Memo 20/15, note to para 22
81 Art 32(1) EU Reg 883/04
82 *INASTI v Hervein and Others,* C-393/99 and C-394/99 [2002] ECR I-02829, para 51; *Leyman v INAMI,* C-3/08 [2009] ECR I-09085, para 45
83 *SSWP v AK (AA)* [2015] UKUT 110 (AAC), paras 11-12
84 *IG v SSWP* [2016] UKUT 176 (AAC), paras 11-12
85 *IG v SSWP* [2016] UKUT 176 (AAC), paras 32 and 40-42 and caselaw cited
86 *Hudzinski and Wawrzyniak v Agentur für Arbeit Wesel – Familienkasse,* joined cases C-611/10 and C-612/10 [2012]
87 *IG v SSWP* [2016] UKUT 176 (AAC), para 32 and caselaw cited
88 Art 81 EU Reg 883/2004; Art 2 EU Reg 987/2009; *SSWP v AK (AA)* [2015] UKUT 110 (AAC), reported as [2015] AACR 27
89 Art 6(2) EU Reg 987/2009; *SSWP v HR (AA)* [2014] UKUT 571 (AAC), reported as [2015] AACR 26
90 *SSWP v AK (AA)* [2015] UKUT 110 (AAC), reported as [2015] AACR 27, paras 29-30

91 *SSWP v HR (AA)* [2014] UKUT 571 (AAC), reported as [2015] AACR 26, paras 16-19
92 *SSWP v FF* [2015] UKUT 488 (AAC)
93 *Fileccia v SSWP,* C3/2016/0358, due to be heard in the Court of Appeal in November 2017
94 Art 6(3) EU Reg 987/2009
95 Arts 6(4)-(5) and 73 EU Reg 987/2009
96 DMG Memo 27/15; ADM Memo 21/15
97 DMG Memo 27/15, note to para 4; ADM Memo 21/15, note to para 4
98 *SSWP v HR (AA)* [2014] UKUT 571 (AAC), reported as [2015] AACR 26, para 18
99 Art 6(1) EU Reg 987/2009
100 Art 4 EU Reg 883/04
101 Art 18 TFEU; Art 24 EU Dir 2004/38; Art 7 EU Reg 492/2011
102 *Patmalniece v SSWP* [2011] UKSC 11
103 *European Commission v UK,* C-308/14 [2016]
104 *Commissioners for HMRC v Aiga Spiridonova,* 13/115948
105 Art 5 EU Reg 883/04
106 Recital 11 EU Reg 883/04
107 Recital 10 EU Reg 883/04
108 Art 6 EU Reg 883/04; see also Annex XI UK entry, para 2, and Art 48 TFEU
109 Art 12 EU Reg 987/09; see *PB v SSWP (DLA)* [2016] UKUT 280 (AAC), para 10, second ground of appeal
110 Art 6 EU Reg 883/04; *Decision H6 of 16 December 2010 of the Administrative Commission for the Co-ordination of Social Security Systems* [2011] OJ C-45/04
111 Art 6 and Annex XI UK entry para 2 EU Reg 883/04; *SSWP v MM & BK v SSWP* [2016] UKUT 547 (AAC), para 25
112 *SSWP v MM & BK v SSWP* [2016] UKUT 547 (AAC), paras 18-27 and 35. See also DMG Memo 16/17 and ADM Memo 20/17
113 *Kavanagh v SSWP* CDLA/373/2016
114 Art 61 EU Reg 883/04
115 Arts 61(2) and 65(2) and (5)(a) EU Reg 883/04
116 Art 7 EU Reg 883/04
117 Arts 5, 46 and 82 EU Reg 883/04; Arts 27, 46, 49 and 87 EU Reg 987/2009
118 Art 70 EU Reg 883/04
119 Art 10 EU Reg 883/04
120 *Teresa and Silvana Petroni v Office National des Pensions Pour Travailleurs Salariés (ONPTS), Bruxelles* 24-75 [1975] ECR I-01149
121 Art 68 EU Reg 883/04
122 Arts 53-55 EU Reg 883/04

123 Art 67 EU Reg 883/04; *HB v HMRC (CHB)*
 [2014] UKUT 554 (AAC)
124 Art 67 EU Reg 883/04; *HMRC v Ruas*
 [2010] EWCA Civ 291
125 *MR v HMRC (TC)* [2011] UKUT 40 (AAC),
 para 17
126 *NB v HMRC (TC)* [2016] NICom 47; Art
 56 TFEU
127 Art 67 EU Reg 883/04; *HMRC v Ruas*
 [2010] EWCA Civ 291
128 Art 67 EU Reg 883/04, second sentence;
 Würker v Familienkasse Nurnberg, C-32/
 13 [2014] ECR
129 Art 1(w) EU Reg 883/04
130 s143(1)(b) SSCBA 1992; *RK v HMRC
 (CHB)* [2015] UKUT 357 (AAC), reported
 as [2016] AACR 4; *JL v HMRC (CHB)*
 [2017] UKUT 193 (AAC)
131 TCTM 2810; para 10203 CBTM
132 *BM v HMRC* [2015] UKUT 526 (AAC)
133 *Gudrun Schwemmer v Agentur für Arbeit
 Villingen-Schwenningen – Familienkasse*,
 C-16/09 [2010] ECR I-09717;
 *Bundesagentur für Arbeit – Familienkasse
 Sachsen v Trapkowski*, C-378/14 [2015];
 JL v HMRC (CHB) [2017] UKUT 193
 (AAC)
134 Art 68 EU Reg 883/04; Art 60 EU Reg
 987/09
135 http://ec.europa.eu/social
136 Art 68(1)(a) EU Reg 883/04; Art 60 EU
 Reg 987/09
137 *Decision F1 of 12 June 2009 of the
 Administrative Commission for the Co-
 ordination of Social Security Systems*
 [2010] OJ C-106/04
138 Art 68(1)(b) EU Reg 883/04; Art 60 EU
 Reg 987/09
139 See also Art 58 EU Reg 987/2009
140 Art 68(2) EU Reg 883/04; see, for
 example, *Slanina v Unabhängiger
 Finanzsenat, Außenstelle Wien*, C-363/08
 [2009] ECR I-11111
141 Art 68(2) EU Reg 883/04; Art 60 EU Reg
 987/09
142 *Gudrun Schwemmer v Agentur für Arbeit
 Villingen-Schwenningen – Familienkasse*,
 C-16/09 [2010] ECR I-09717;
 *Bundesagentur für Arbeit – Familienkasse
 Sachsen v Trapkowski*, C-378/14 [2015]
143 *JL v HMRC (CHB)* [2017] UKUT 193
 (AAC)
144 Art 68a EU Reg 883/04
145 Art 68(3) EU Reg 883/04; Arts 6 and 58-
 61 EU Reg 987/2009
146 Art 68(3) EU Reg 883/04; Art 60(2) and
 (3) EU Reg 987/2009

147 Arts 6(2)-(3) and 60(4) EU Reg 987/
 2009; TCTM 2835; para 10208 CBTM
148 Art 6(2) EU Reg 987/09
149 TCTM 2815-75; paras 10204-13 CBTM

Chapter 17

. . . .

International agreements

This chapter covers:
1. Reciprocal agreements (below)
2. Council of Europe conventions and agreements (p317)
3. European Union co-operation and association agreements (p319)

The rules in this chapter may help you to obtain benefits in the UK, or to export benefits to certain countries. However, if you are moving within the European Economic Area, the European Union co-ordination rules may be more generous. See Chapter 16 for whether these apply to you.

---

1. Reciprocal agreements

A reciprocal agreement is a bilateral agreement made between the UK and another country. Reciprocal agreements are part of UK law and their purpose is to protect your entitlement to benefits if you move from one country that is a party to an agreement to the other.[1] A reciprocal agreement can help you qualify for certain benefits by allowing periods of residence and contributions paid in each of the two countries to be added together (this is similar to the aggregation principle in the European Union (EU) co-ordination rules – see p298). It can also mean that you are paid more generously when you go abroad than you would be under the UK rules. In addition, they often specify that you must receive equal treatment with nationals of the country to which you have moved.

In general, a reciprocal agreement only applies if the EU co-ordination rules do not assist you (see p311). They are therefore of most relevance for non-European Economic Area (EEA) countries, but they can also assist if you are moving to or from Northern Ireland, the Channel Islands or the Isle of Man.

The scope of the reciprocal agreements differs greatly, not only in terms of the benefits covered and the provisions made, but also in respect of the people covered. It is therefore crucial to check the individual agreement. You can find the agreements in the *Law Related to Social Security* at http://lawvolumes. dwp.gov.uk – go to the 'List of Statutory Instruments' and search under the relevant country to find the number and year of the statutory instrument.

However, although this site is more helpful as it is specific to social security, it has not been updated since October 2015, so for amendments since then you also need to check www.legislation.gov.uk.

This section provides an outline of the benefits covered and the general principles relating to the agreements. A list of all the countries and the benefits covered is in Appendix 5.

Note: the following benefits are *not* covered by any of the agreements:

- housing benefit;
- income support;
- income-based jobseeker's allowance (JSA) – but see below;
- employment and support allowance (ESA) – but see below;
- pension credit;
- personal independence payment (PIP) – but see below;
- social fund payments;
- universal credit;
- child tax credit;
- working tax credit.

Note:
- Income-based JSA (in addition to contribution-based JSA) is now covered by the agreement with Northern Ireland (see below).
- Although amendments have been made enabling reciprocal agreements to be extended to ESA and PIP,[2] in general the necessary amendments to the individual agreements have not been made. However, the agreements with Northern Ireland do cover both ESA and PIP (see below). Most agreements cover your award of contributory ESA if it was converted from incapacity benefit (see p314). It may be arguable that the agreement with the states of former Yugoslavia (Bosnia-Herzegovina, Kosovo, Macedonia, Montenegro and Serbia) does not need to be amended to cover ESA and PIP. This is because it contains provision for cover to be extended to amendments, supplements and consolidations of listed legislation, provided the contracting parties agree.[3]

Agreements with non-European Economic Area countries

The UK has reciprocal agreements with some countries outside the EEA.

Each reciprocal agreement is different in terms of who is covered, which benefits are included and what arrangements are provided.

For a full list of the countries and the benefits covered, see Appendix 5.

Agreements with Northern Ireland, the Channel Islands, the Isle of Man and Gibraltar

The rules relating to most social security and tax credits apply only to Great Britain – ie, England, Wales and Scotland. This does not include Northern Ireland, the Channel Islands, the Isle of Man or Gibraltar, which have their own social security legislation. There are reciprocal agreements between all of these to ensure you do not lose out if you move between them. However, not all benefits and circumstances are covered, so it is essential that you check the provisions of the relevant agreement. **Note:** the reciprocal agreement between the UK and the Channel Islands does not cover Sark. However, regulations provide that you are not disadvantaged by being there.[4]

See p315 for information on retirement pensions and bereavement support payment and Sark and the Isle of Man.

Replacement reciprocal arrangements between Northern Ireland and Great Britain came into force on 6 April 2016.[5] These mirror, but also update and extend, the previous arrangements, and continue to co-ordinate the social security systems with the aim of creating a coherent system of social security throughout the UK. The purpose of the arrangements is to ensure that when moving between the two territories, you are entitled to the same rights and benefits paid at the same rates, and that you do not need to return to the previous territory if you appeal a decision made there.[6] Although some benefits are still not covered (most means-tested benefits, tax credits and all statutory payments), the new arrangements have been extended to include ESA (both contributory and income-related), PIP, state pension and, from 27 November 2016, income-based JSA (contribution-based JSA was already covered) and, from 6 April 2017, bereavement support payment.[7]

Note: before the agreements were extended to ESA, the DWP policy on ESA was to make extra-statutory payments to make up any loss of ESA that resulted from having to make a new claim when moving from Northern Ireland to Great Britain or vice versa.[8] If you were receiving extra-statutory payments on this basis before 27 November 2016 and do not satisfy the contributory conditions for entitlement to contributory ESA, you are treated as satisfying these conditions and as having made a claim for ESA from 27 November 2016, and your period of limited capability for work is treated as continuous.[9]

Gibraltar is a British overseas territory and the only one which is part of the EU. For social security purposes, it is treated as part of the UK in relation to other EU members under the EU co-ordination rules. However, the reciprocal agreement between Gibraltar and Great Britain provides that, except for family benefits, you are treated as having the same rights under the EU co-ordination rules as you would have if the UK and Gibraltar were separate member states.[10]

Agreements with European Economic Area states

The UK has reciprocal agreements with most, but not all, of the EEA member states. For a list of the states with which the UK has social security agreements and the benefits covered by each, see Appendix 5.

In general, reciprocal agreements can be relied on by EEA nationals if the EU co-ordination rules (see Chapter 16) do not apply.[11] This means, in most cases, you cannot qualify for benefits using a reciprocal agreement if you:

- come within the 'personal scope' of the co-ordination rules (see p281);[12] *and*
- acquired your right to benefit on, or after, the date the EU co-ordination provisions applied.[13]

However, reciprocal agreements between EEA states can continue to apply if either:

- you are not covered by the co-ordination rules;[14] *or*
- you are covered by the co-ordination rules, but:
  - the provisions of an agreement are more beneficial to you than the EU co-ordination provisions; *and*
  - your right to benefit from the reciprocal agreement was acquired (eg, because you moved between the relevant member states) before the EU co-ordination provisions applied.[15]

Note: the UK's agreement with Denmark applies in both the Faroes and Greenland, as they are not part of the EU/EEA. Greenland left what was then the European Economic Community on 1 February 1985.

People covered by the agreements

Some of the reciprocal agreements cover nationals of the contracting countries, while others apply to 'people going from one member state to another'. This may be particularly significant if you are a non-EEA national who has worked in two or more EEA states but you cannot benefit under the co-ordination rules (see p281). Of the member states that now comprise the EEA (see p40), the agreements with Belgium, Denmark, France, Italy and Luxembourg are confined to nationals only.[16] The convention with the Netherlands covers those who have been subject to the legislation of one or both member states and their family members and survivors.[17]

The reciprocal agreements define who is counted as a national for the purpose of the agreement, where nationality is an issue. In all of these, a UK national is defined as a 'citizen of the United Kingdom and Colonies'.[18]

This category of people disappeared on 1 January 1983 when the British Nationality Act 1981 came into force. On this date, if you previously had citizenship of the UK and Colonies, you might have become:

- a British citizen;
- a British overseas territories citizen (subsequently renamed British dependent territories citizen); *or*
- a British overseas citizen.

You might also have become one of the above after 1 January 1983, including if you were born after this date. The rules on this are beyond the scope of this *Handbook*.

For the purpose of the UK social security 'nationals only' conventions with Belgium, Denmark, France, Italy and Luxembourg, a UK national now includes anyone in one of the categories above.

See p15 for further details of British nationality.

The definition of nationality contained in the agreements with Denmark, Italy and Luxembourg is simply that of a 'Danish' or 'Italian' or 'Luxemburger' national.[19] These agreements confer no rights if you are not a national of one of these states. The agreement with Belgium, however, covers a 'person having Belgian nationality or a native of the Belgian Congo or Ruanda-Urundi'. The agreement with France refers to 'a person having French nationality' and 'any French-protected person belonging to French Togoland or the French Cameroons'.

When these agreements came into force in 1958, the Belgian Congo and Ruanda-Urundi and French Togoland and the French Cameroons were Belgian and French territories respectively. Which Belgian and French nationals are covered by the agreements is a matter for the Belgian and French authorities. If you come from one of these countries (present-day Democratic Republic of Congo, Rwanda, Burundi, Togolese Republic and the Republic of Cameroon), check with the Belgian or French authorities whether you are covered by these agreements.

The agreements give equal treatment to nationals of the contracting countries, stating that a 'national of one contracting party shall be entitled to receive the benefits of the legislation of the other contracting party under the same conditions as if he were a national of the latter contracting party'.[20]

The agreements with Finland, Iceland, Ireland, Portugal, Spain and Sweden are not confined to nationals but give rights to:

- 'people who go from one country to another' (Ireland);
- 'a person subject to the legislation of one contracting party who becomes resident in the territory of the other party' (Portugal);
- 'a national of one contracting party, or a person subject to the legislation of that party, who becomes resident in the territory of the other contracting party' (Spain);
- 'a national of the state and person deriving their rights from such nationals and other people who are, or have been, covered by the legislation of either of the states and people deriving their rights from such a person' (Sweden).

The agreements with Austria and Norway have nationality restrictions that apply to the protocol on benefits in kind (eg, medical treatment), but not to social security contributions and benefits. A national of the UK is defined as anyone who is recognised by the UK government as a UK national, provided s/he is 'ordinarily resident' in the UK.

The agreement with Germany is not restricted to nationals of either agreement member state insofar as social security benefits are concerned. However, a nationality provision applies to the Articles relating to contribution liability.

Even if you are not a national of one of the contracting parties to these agreements, you may still be able to benefit from their provisions.

Benefits covered by the agreements

The following benefits are covered by some of the reciprocal agreements. See Appendix 5 for a full list of which benefits apply to which countries.

Unemployment benefits

The relevant benefit in the UK is contribution-based JSA. Since 27 November 2016, the agreements between Great Britain and Northern Ireland also cover income-based JSA (see p310).

None of the agreements allow you to receive unemployment benefits outside the country in which you have paid your national insurance (NI) contributions. However, some allow NI paid in one country to count towards satisfying the conditions of entitlement in another. This is the case with the UK agreements with Austria, Canada, Cyprus, Finland, Iceland, Isle of Man, Jersey, Guernsey, Malta, New Zealand and Norway, as well as the agreements between Great Britain and Northern Ireland.

Sickness and invalidity benefits

In the UK, the relevant sickness benefit was short-term incapacity benefit (IB) and the relevant invalidity benefit was long-term IB. In 2008, IB was abolished for new claims and replaced by ESA, with existing IB claimants being reassessed for possible conversion to ESA. There are now very few remaining claimants of long-term IB, but if you still receive this the agreements continue to apply.

Although amendments have been made to enable reciprocal agreements to be extended to ESA,[21] in general, the necessary amendments to the individual agreements have not been made.[22] There are two exceptions. The reciprocal agreements cover:

- contributory ESA if your award was converted from IB. Your ESA is covered by each of the agreements (except the Isle of Man, Israel and Switzerland) that cover invalidity benefits (see Appendix 5);[23]
- both contributory and income-related ESA under the agreement between Great Britain and Northern Ireland (see p310).

It may be arguable that the agreement with the states of former Yugoslavia (Bosnia-Herzegovina, Kosovo, Macedonia, Montenegro and Serbia) does not need to be amended in order to cover ESA. This is because it contains provision for the agreement to be extended to amendments, supplements and consolidations of listed legislation, provided the contracting parties agree.[24]

The agreements in relation to 'sickness' or 'invalidity' benefits vary. For example, some enable you to be paid in another country, and some enable contributions paid under one country's scheme to be taken into account to help you satisfy the conditions of entitlement in another. The agreements with Austria, Cyprus, Iceland, Norway and Sweden allow you to continue to receive your invalidity benefit in these countries, subject to medical checks being undertaken in the agreement country. Similarly, you can receive the other country's invalidity benefits in the UK. The agreement with Barbados allows a certificate of permanent incapacity to be issued, permitting you to receive your 'invalidity benefit' without medical checks.

Maternity benefits

In the UK, the relevant maternity benefit is maternity allowance (MA).

If you are entitled to maternity benefits, some of the agreements allow you to receive your benefit in another country. You may be entitled to MA, or continue to be paid MA, when absent from the UK, under the reciprocal agreements with: Barbados, Cyprus, the Isle of Man, Jersey and Guernsey, Switzerland, Turkey and the countries of the former Republic of Yugoslavia (Bosnia-Herzegovina, Croatia, Kosovo, Macedonia, Montenegro, Serbia and Slovenia), and when you have moved from Great Britain to Northern Ireland or vice versa. The circumstances under which you may be able to claim or retain MA differ from agreement to agreement.

Benefits for industrial injuries

The relevant benefits in the UK are industrial injuries disablement benefit (including constant attendance allowance or exceptionally severe disablement allowance), reduced earnings allowance and retirement allowance.

Most of the agreements include industrial injuries benefits. The arrangements determine which country's legislation applies to new accidents or diseases, depending on where you are insured at the time. Many of the agreements allow you to combine industrial injuries incurred in each country when assessing the degree of your latest injury. Furthermore, if you work in one country and remain insured under the other country's scheme and you have an industrial injury, you can be treated as though the injury arose in the country in which you are insured. Most agreements include arrangements to allow you to receive all three of the UK benefits for industrial injuries indefinitely in the other country.

Retirement pensions and bereavement benefits

All the agreements include retirement pensions and bereavement benefits. In the UK, the relevant benefits are retirement pensions, bereavement allowance and widowed parent's allowance. All the agreements have been amended to include the new state pension from 6 April 2016[25] and bereavement support payment from 6 April 2017.[26]

There is a new reciprocal agreement between the Isle of Man and the UK covering arrangements for all retirement pensions.[27] The new state pension does not apply in the Isle of Man, so if you reach retirement age on or after 6 April 2016 and have worked in both the UK and the Isle of Man, you must make two claims under the two different systems. If you receive a UK pension while resident in the Isle of Man, it is uprated as if you were in the UK. For further details on receiving either or both pensions while resident in the Isle of Man, see the government of the Isle of Man website.[28]

Note: the reciprocal agreement between the UK and the Channel Isles does not cover Sark, but regulations provide for entitlement to state pension and bereavement support payment if you are ordinarily resident on Sark.[29]

The provisions of the reciprocal agreements vary. In most cases, the agreements can enable you to receive a retirement pension or bereavement benefit in the agreement country at the same rate as you would be paid in the country where you are insured. This is, however, not the case under the agreements with Canada, New Zealand and (for those still covered by the agreement revoked on 1 March 2001, subject to limited savings provisions[30]) Australia, as they do not permit these benefits to be uprated. If you go to live in one of these countries, your retirement pension (and any other long-term benefit) is 'frozen' at the rate payable either when you left the UK or when you became entitled to your pension abroad.

The agreements with Canada, New Zealand and (for those still covered by the agreement revoked on 1 March 2001, subject to limited savings provisions[31]) Australia, allow you to be treated as having paid NI contributions in the UK during periods when you were resident in that country. From 1 April 2015, periods of habitual residence in another EEA member state or Switzerland count as period of residence in the UK if you:[32]

• are an EEA national (see p40);
• are covered by the EU co-ordination rules (see p281); *and*
• have a 'genuine and sufficient link to the UK' (see p219).

The agreement with Chile is limited and relates to the continuing liability to pay NI contributions to your home country if you go to work in the other country for a period of up to five years.[33]

If you do not qualify for a retirement pension or bereavement benefit from either the UK or the other country, or you qualify for a pension or bereavement benefit from one country but not the other, the agreements with the following countries allow you to be paid basic old age and bereavement benefits on a pro rata basis, with your insurance under both schemes taken into account: Austria, Barbados, Bermuda, Cyprus, Finland, Iceland, Israel, Jamaica, Malta, Mauritius, Norway, the Philippines, Sweden, Switzerland, Turkey, the USA and the countries of the former Republic of Yugoslavia (Bosnia-Herzegovina, Croatia, Kosovo,[34] Macedonia, Montenegro, Serbia and Slovenia).[35]

Family benefits

In the UK, the relevant family benefits are child benefit and guardian's allowance. The provisions concerning these two benefits enable periods of residence and/or presence in the other country to be treated as residence and/or presence in Great Britain. Arguably, these provisions could enable you to to use periods of residence in the other country to satisfy the requirement for child benefit to have been living in the UK for the past three months (see p95). The extent to which reciprocity exists varies, however, according to the particular agreement. For example, residence or contributions paid in Cyprus, Jamaica, Jersey/Guernsey, Isle of Man, Israel, Mauritius and Turkey count towards your satisfying UK residence conditions for guardian's allowance.

If you are a 'person subject to immigration control' (see p57) and you are covered by a reciprocal agreement for child benefit, your immigration status does not exclude you from entitlement to child benefit (see p71). In practice, this is most helpful if you are covered by the agreement with former Yugoslavia which applies to Bosnia-Herzegovina, Kosovo, Macedonia, Montenegro, and Serbia.[36] You must still meet the other conditions of entitlement, including the residence and presence requirements (see p216).

Dependants' benefits

In the UK, a dependant's benefit is an increase to the benefit covered by the agreement. Dependants' increases can be paid if the dependant is in either country to the agreement.

2. Council of Europe conventions and agreements

There are numerous European conventions and agreements. These are prepared and negotiated within the Council of Europe. The most well known is perhaps the European Convention on Human Rights. The purpose of these conventions is to address issues of common concern in economic, social, cultural, scientific, legal and administrative matters and in human rights. However, such agreements and conventions are not legally binding in the UK unless or until they are incorporated into UK law, or legislation is enacted to give specific effect to the treaty obligations in question – eg, the UK Human Rights Act in respect of the European Convention on Human Rights. They are statements of intent of the individual countries that are signatories. The UK is a signatory to a number of these agreements, including two that are significant for social security.

The European Convention on Social and Medical Assistance

The European Convention on Social and Medical Assistance has been in force since 1954. It requires that ratifying states provide assistance in cash and in kind to nationals of other ratifying states, who are lawfully present in their territories and who are without sufficient resources on the same conditions as their own nationals. It also prevents ratifying states repatriating a lawfully present national of other ratifying states simply because s/he is in need of assistance.

All the European Economic Area (EEA) countries (see p40) plus Turkey have signed and ratified this agreement. The rights given are recognised in UK law. However, the European Union (EU) co-ordination rules are more generous than the Convention, so EEA nationals would not usually need to rely on it. It mainly assists you if you are a Turkish national and a 'person subject to immigration control' (see p57), as the Convention exempts those covered from being excluded from means-tested benefits (see p67) and working tax credit (WTC) (see p72).

You can only benefit from the Convention if you are 'lawfully present' in the UK. If you are a Turkish national, this means, in practice, you must be within a period in which you have leave to enter or remain in the UK.

Note: you still must satisfy the other conditions of entitlement including, for means-tested benefits, having a right to reside (see p117).[37] Consequently, although the House of Lords held that an asylum seeker with temporary admission is 'lawfully present' and so potentially can benefit from the Convention,[38] this will rarely assist you, as temporary admission does not give you a right to reside.[39] However, if you are within a period of leave, you do have a right to reside (see p125).

The 1961 European Social Charter

This agreement is similar to the European Convention on Social and Medical Assistance. The ratifying states are all EEA countries (see p40), plus Macedonia and Turkey. The main relevance of this agreement for entitlement to benefits and tax credits is that if you are a national of Macedonia or Turkey and you are lawfully present, as with the Convention (see above), you are not excluded from means-tested benefits or WTC if you are a 'person subject to immigration control'.

It is only this 1961 Charter that gives access to UK social security benefits. If you are a national of a country that has signed a later charter only and are a 'person subject to immigration control', you are not exempt from being excluded from means-tested benefits and WTC.

3. European Union co-operation and association agreements

The Treaty on the Functioning of the European Union provides for agreements to be made with countries outside the European Union (EU).[40]

The EU co-operation and association agreements can be divided into those that include a rule on equal treatment and have quite a wide scope and those that do not include an equal treatment rule and whose scope is much narrower (see p320).

Agreements with equal treatment provisions

The agreements that most directly affect benefits in the UK are those with Algeria,[41] Morocco, San Marino, Tunisia and Turkey.[42]

All these agreements contain provisions specifying that there must be equal treatment for those covered by the agreement in matters of 'social security'.

UK regulations specify that if you are defined as a 'person subject to immigration control' (see p57) but you are covered by one of these agreements (see below), you are exempt from the exclusion from certain non-contributory benefits (see p69) and tax credits (see p72) that would otherwise apply.

However, the EU agreements offer equal treatment to a wider range of benefits. The Court of Justice of the European Union (CJEU) found, in one case, the Turkish agreement and, in another, the Algerian agreement, to be inspired by the old EU co-ordination rules and that these rules should be looked to for guidance in interpreting the agreements. The CJEU held that the benefits covered by these agreements were those classed as 'social security benefits' under the co-ordination rules.[43] See p285 for a full list of these benefits.

Who is covered

To benefit from the agreements, you must be within their 'personal scope' – ie, you must be a national of Algeria, Morocco, Tunisia, San Marino or Turkey and you must be lawfully working in the UK.

Lawfully working

'**Lawfully working**' has been equated with being an 'insured person' under the EU co-ordination rules. In broad terms, this means that you must have been insured by paying, or being credited with, national insurance (NI) contributions.[44] It is likely that you will only be accepted as 'lawfully working' if your work does not breach any work restrictions attached to your leave or, if you are an asylum seeker, you have permission to work from the Home Office.

Other agreements: Israel

The EU also has various agreements with other countries. In general, these do not contain any provisions on the co-ordination of social security schemes, with the exception of the agreement with Israel.[45] This agreement is narrower in scope than those containing an agreement on equal treatment in matters of social security.

The agreement with Israel covers nationals of the European Economic Area (EEA) and Israel who are legally working in the EEA (for Israelis) or Israel (for EEA nationals) and members of their family who are legally resident.

The agreement covers benefits designed to protect against the risks of old age, invalidity and accidents at work, benefits for survivors and family benefits. The EU co-ordination rules, which should be used as an aid to interpret this agreement, also cover these, and other, risks (see p285).

However, the agreement does not go as far as either the EU co-ordination rules or the agreements that contain an equal treatment provision (see p297), but it provides that:

- for Israelis, all periods of residence, insurance and employment fulfilled by a person covered by the agreement in different EEA states are totalled for the purpose of working out entitlement to the benefits covered;
- the benefits covered (except non-contributory benefits) can be exported to (for Israelis) Israel or (for EEA nationals) from Israel to the EEA.

Note: Israel also has a reciprocal agreement with the UK.[46] See Appendix 5 for the benefits covered.

Notes

1. **Reciprocal agreements**
1 s179 SSAA1992
2 s179(3), (4) and (5) SSAA 1992
3 Art 2 FANIII(Y)O
4 In particular, reg 12, SS(PA) Regs
5 SS(NIRA) Regs; SS(GBRA)(NI) Regs
6 Explanatory memorandum to SS(NIRA) Regs, para 4.2
7 SS(NIRA)(A) Regs; SS(GBRA)(A) Regs; see also DMG Memo 1/17

8 DWP guidance, *Extra-statutory Payments for Claimants Moving from Northern Ireland to Great Britain*, available at www.cpag.org.uk/content/dwp-guidance-extra-statutory-payments-esa
9 Sch Art 2A-2B SS(NIRA) Regs; Sch Art 2A-2B SS(GBRA)(NI) Regs; see also DMG Memo 1/17 paras 4-7
10 Sch para 2 The Family Allowances, National Insurance and Industrial Injuries (Gibraltar) Order 1974, No.555; see also *SSWP v Garland* [2014] EWCA Civ 1550, para 33

11 Art 8 EU Reg 883/04
12 Art 2 EU Reg 883/04
13 *Walder v Bestuur der Sociale Verzekeringsbank*, C-82/72 [1973] 599; *Jean-Louis Thévenon and Stadt Speyer-Sozialamt v Landesversicherungsanstalt Rheinland-Pfalz*, C-475/93 [1995] ECR I-03813; *Balazs v Casa Judeteana de Pensii Cluj*, C-401/13 [2015]
14 Art 2 EU Reg 1408/71; Art 2 EU Reg 883/04; *Galinsky v Insurance Officer*, C-99/80 [1981] 503; R(P) 1/81
15 *Rönfeldt v Bundesversicherungsanstalt für Angestellte*, C-227/89 [1991] ECR I-323; *Jean-Louis Thévenon and Stadt Speyer-Sozialamt v Landesversicherungsanstalt Rheinland-Pfalz*, C-475/93 [1995]; *Edmund Thelen v Bundesansalt für Arbeit*, C-75/99 [2000] ECR I-09399
16 Art 3 to each of the relevant reciprocal agreements
17 Art 2 The Social Security (Netherlands) Order 2007, No.631
18 Art 1 to each of the relevant reciprocal agreements
19 Art 1 to each of the relevant reciprocal agreements
20 Art 1 to each of the relevant reciprocal agreements
21 s179(3), (4) and (5) SSAA 1992
22 para 070312 DMG
23 SS(RA)O
24 Art 2 FANIII(Y)O
25 SS(NIRA) Regs
26 The Social Security (Reciprocal Agreements) Order 2017, No.159; DMG Memo 15/17
27 The Social Security (Reciprocal Agreement) (Isle of Man) Order 2016, No.157
28 www.gov.im. See, for example, *An Introduction to Pensions for People Reaching Retirement Age On or After 6 April 2016*
29 Reg 8, The Bereavement Support Payment Regulations 2017, No.410
30 s299 Pensions Act 2004
31 s299 Pensions Act 2004
32 The Social Security (Application of Reciprocal Agreements with Australia, Canada and New Zealand) (EEA States and Switzerland) Regulations 2015, No.349

33 Convention on Social Security between the Government of the United Kingdom of Great Britain and Northern Ireland and the Government of the Republic of Chile, reproduced as Schedule to The Social Security (Contributions) (Republic of Chile) Order 2015, No.828
34 *AP v SSWP (RP)* [2011] UKUT 64 (AAC)
35 FANIII(Y)O
36 FANIII(Y)O

2. Council of Europe conventions and agreements
37 *Yesiloz v London Borough of Camden and DWP* [2009] EWCA Civ 415
38 *Szoma v SSWP* [2005] UKHL 64; [2006] 1 All ER 1, reported as R(IS) 2/06
39 R(IS) 3/08

3. European Union co-operation and association agreements
40 Art 217 TFEU
41 Euro-Mediterranean Agreement establishing an Association between the European Community and its Member States, of the one part, and the People's Democratic Republic of Algeria, of the other part, 2005/690/EC, 18 July 2005
42 Decision No.3/80 of the Council of Association, set up under the EEC-Turkey Association Agreement (sometimes referred to as the 'Ankara Agreement')
43 *Sema Sürül v Bundesanstalt für Arbeit*, C-262/96 [1999] ECR I-02685; *Babahenini v Belgian State*, C-113/97 [1998] ECR I-00183; see also CFC/2613/1997
44 *Sema Sürül v Bundesanstalt für Arbeit*, C-262/96 [1999] ECR I-02685, in particular paras 85-86 and 93
45 Euro-Mediterranean Agreement establishing an Association between the European Communities and their Member States, of the one part, and the State of Israel, of the other part, 2000/384/EC, 20 November 1995. In force on 1 June 2000.
46 The National Insurance and Industrial Injuries (Israel) Order 1957, No.1879

Part 7

Claims and getting paid

Chapter 18

. . . .

Delays

This chapter covers:
1. Dealing with delays (below)
2. Waiting for a decision on a claim (p326)
3. Delays when challenging a decision (p341)
4. Delays getting paid (p347)

1. Dealing with delays

All benefit authorities should act promptly to process your claim, to process any challenge you make to a decision and to issue payments due to you.

Although all benefit claimants can experience delays in the administration of their benefits and tax credits, you are more likely to experience delays if you are, or someone included in your claim is, a migrant.

If you experience a delay, in order to resolve the matter it can be helpful if you:
- can establish the reasons for the delay (see below);
- are clear at which stage the delay occurs (see p326).

The reasons for the delay

There can be many reasons for delays in benefit and tax credit administration. These are broadly due to the need for decision makers to have sufficient information, which can take time to collect, and the volume of work that decision makers have. This chapter focuses on the rules that are most relevant to migrants, but the cause of the delay in your case can also be due to reasons that apply to all benefit claimants.

If you or your family member have moved to or from the UK or are not British, a delay in the administration of your benefit or tax credit can be because of the following.
- The complexity of the rules on immigration status, residence and presence, and the effect of the European Union (EU) co-ordination rules. This complexity often means that all these decisions are made by specialist decision makers, and these individuals or teams often have a backlog.

- The initial benefit or tax credit claim form may not ask for all the information that the decision maker needs to be clear about the effect of the rules on immigration status, residence, presence and EU co-ordination. The decision maker must therefore write to you or to other agencies requesting further information, and this takes extra time.
- You may have difficulties obtaining and providing evidence which the decision maker has requested – eg, evidence about your immigration status or residence rights. See Chapter 20 for more details on this and what you can do in this situation.
- If you are covered by the EU co-ordination rules, the benefit authorities may need to get information from benefit authorities in other European states and this can take a long time. See Chapter 16 for more information on the EU co-ordination rules.
- There may be a query about whether you need or have, or have applied for, a national insurance (NI) number. See Chapter 19 for more information on NI numbers.

When the delay occurs

What you can do to resolve a delay depends on the benefit you have claimed and also the stage at which the delay occurs. Delays can occur when you have:
- made a claim for benefit and are waiting for a decision on it (see below);
- had a decision on your entitlement and you have challenged that decision (see p341);
- had a decision on your entitlement and you are awaiting payment (see p347).

Note: although the information in this chapter focuses on delays in decisions on claims, challenges to refusals of claims and payment once an award has been decided, similar issues arise if there is a delay in superseding a decision on your claim – eg, to award you increased benefit after you have reported your partner or child moving into your household. For information about supersessions, including the date they take effect, see CPAG's *Welfare Benefits and Tax Credits Handbook*.

2. **Waiting for a decision on a claim**

If you have been waiting for a decision on your claim, what you can do depends on which benefit or tax credit you have claimed.

Are you waiting for a decision on your claim?

1. Check that your claim has been received. If it has not, if possible provide the benefit authority with a copy of the claim and/or any evidence that was previously submitted. If the benefit authority says that it has not received your claim and you have no copy, you must submit a new claim and may be able to ask for it to be backdated. See CPAG's *Welfare Benefits and Tax Credits Handbook* for details on the backdating rules for the different benefits and tax credits.

2. If your claim has been received, but not dealt with, you should ask why. See below for your options.

3. If the decision maker is not making a decision on your claim because there is a test case pending, see p341.

4. When trying to resolve delays, it is helpful to show the history of your previous contact. Therefore, keep a copy of any letters you send or receive. If you make your claim, or submit supporting information online, take screenshots as evidence. Take the name and job title of anyone you speak to on the phone and note the date.

5. In all communication, give your national insurance (NI) number (if you have one).

Note: administrative policy guidance is sometimes issued to decision makers on the processes to be followed when determining claims from particular groups of migrants – eg, to fast track certain claims or accept certain standard pieces of evidence. It can be helpful to refer to this guidance to ensure that it is appropriately applied. For an example of such a policy on the habitual residence test, see p107. Although this guidance is often internal, if you contact organisations that work a lot with particular groups (such as recently arrived refugees), they may be able to give you details of current decision-making policies and practices.

Benefits administered by the DWP and HM Revenue and Customs

The rules about making decisions on claims for benefits and tax credits administered by the DWP or HM Revenue and Customs (HMRC) (ie, all benefits except housing benefit (HB) – see p338) do not state explicitly how long it should take to determine a claim and issue a decision.

However, the decision maker must decide claims for benefit[1] within 'a reasonable time'.[2]

Whether or not the decision maker has taken longer than 'a reasonable time' to make a decision on your claim depends on:

- the volume of other claims waiting for consideration and the number of decision makers available to deal with them;[3]
- the facts of your individual case, including how long you have waited for a decision and the effect on you of your having to wait. For example, if you have no income while you wait for your claim to be decided, this is more serious for

you than if the benefit, once awarded, would top up your existing income. Similarly, if you or a dependent family member has a health condition which is exacerbated by the lack of income, this may be relevant.

If there are specific reasons, such as the examples given above, which mean that the delay is making things particularly difficult for you or your family, you can suggest that it is not appropriate for your claim to be dealt with as part of a normal queuing system (whereby claims are determined in the order they are received). Tell the decision maker of any specific reasons why the delay is causing hardship for you.

If a delay continues, you could:
- request a short-term advance (certain benefits only) (see p329);
- request an interim payment of child benefit and guardian's allowance (see p333);
- apply for help from your local welfare assistance scheme (see p462);
- make a complaint in writing and follow the complaints procedure and consider requesting help from your MP (see p334, and for HB, see p339);
- escalate a complaint to the Parliamentary and Health Service Ombudsman (see p336);
- obtain legal advice about sending a 'letter before action' for judicial review (see p337);
- check whether you can get provisional payments if the delay is due to a dispute about which is the competent state to pay your benefit or tax credit under the European Union (EU) co-ordination rules (see p296).

You can pursue more than one of these options – eg, you can make a complaint and if this does not resolve the delay, obtain legal advice about sending a letter before action for judicial review.

Note: you cannot get an advance or interim payment of tax credits.

While waiting for your claim to be decided, you may be able to get help from your local welfare assistance scheme (see p462).

Is the delay due to the DWP determining whether you have a right to reside?
If the delay is due to the DWP determining whether you have a right to reside for your claim for income support (IS), income-related employment and support allowance (ESA) or (for men aged between pension credit (PC) age and men's retirement age) PC and you have a right to reside as a jobseeker, you may want to claim income-based jobseeker's allowance (JSA). Your income-based JSA claim is likely to be determined more quickly, as it is easier to establish your right to reside as a jobseeker than other residence rights that satisfy the right to reside requirement for the other benefits (see p117). However, as the DWP computer system cannot have two claims open at once, in practice, you must request that you still want your IS (or the other benefit) claim determined but that it should be done clerically and taken off the computer system to enable the JSA claim to be

determined and put into payment. If the IS (or other benefit) is then awarded, it should be paid from the date you first claimed it. The decision to award JSA should then be revised, either because it was based on a mistake about your entitlement to IS (or other benefit) and the decision was more advantageous to you[4] or because you were awarded benefit (JSA) and then awarded another benefit (IS) for a period including the date the first benefit award (JSA) was made.[5] The IS (or other benefit) should then continue. Get advice if you experience difficulty with this.

Official targets

If there are published targets for the time in which a claim should be processed, it can be helpful to refer to these, and they should be taken into account when determining whether or not your claim has been dealt with as soon as is reasonably practicable. HMRC states that it will handle all new child benefit and tax credit claims and changes of circumstances for UK claimants within an average of 22 days, and for international claimants within an average of 92 days.[6]

The DWP's claim processing times are five days for IS, 10 days for JSA and 16 days for ESA.[7]

If you are a non-UK claimant and are either covered by the co-ordination rules (see p281) or you are a European Economic Area (EEA) national exercising your rights as a 'worker' (see p142) in the UK, you may be able to argue (in any judicial review – see p337) that it is unlawful for HMRC to have a policy that takes substantially longer to deal with your claim than a UK claimant's claim. The argument is that you should receive equal treatment and/or should not be deterred from exercising your right of free movement between EEA states as a worker.[8] For more information on equal treatment, see p297.

Short-term advances

If you are waiting for a decision on your claim, or you are waiting to be paid (either your first or increased payments) and you are in 'financial need' (see p330), you may be able to get an advance payment of your future benefit award. This is called a 'short-term advance' or, for universal credit (UC), a 'universal credit advance'. In this *Handbook* both are referred to as 'short-term advances'.

Short-term advances are discretionary – ie, the decision maker does not have to give you a short-term benefit advance, but must take all the circumstances of your case into account when making her/his decision. Given their discretionary nature, it is helpful to be aware of the DWP's guidance on short-term advances. This guidance, together with further information, is available on 'Ask CPAG online'.[9]

Note: the decision maker should always determine your benefit claim and pay any benefit due, if this is possible, before considering a short-term advance.[10] Consequently, requesting a short-term advance can be a way of getting your claim processed and your benefit paid.

The decision maker can only make a short-term advance if:[11]

- you have made a claim for a benefit in respect of which you can be paid a short-term advance (see below). The only exception to this requirement is if you are not required to make a claim for benefit in order to be entitled, which only applies in very limited circumstances; *and*
- you are in 'financial need' (see below); *and*
- either:
  - your claim has not been determined, but it appears likely to the decision maker that you are entitled to the benefit. **Note:** if there is no reason preventing the DWP from determining your claim, the decision maker should just do so, rather than consider a short-term advance;[12] *or*
  - your claim has been determined and you have been awarded benefit but:
    - you are waiting for your first payment; *or*
    - you have received your first payment, but it was for a shorter period than subsequent payments will be paid for and you are waiting for your next payment; *or*
    - you have had a change of circumstances that increases your entitlement, but your benefit has not yet been increased and paid to you; *or*
    - you are entitled to a payment, but it is impracticable to pay some or all of it on the date on which it is due.

You cannot get short-term advance if there is an appeal pending on the benefit in respect of which the advance would otherwise be paid.[13]

You can get a short-term advance of any benefit *except*: [14]

- HB, although if your HB is delayed and you are a private or housing association tenant, you might be able to get a 'payment on account' (see p338);
- attendance allowance;
- disability living allowance;
- personal independence payment;
- child benefit or guardian's allowance, although you might be able to get an interim payment (see p333);
- statutory sick pay, statutory maternity pay, statutory adoption pay, statutory paternity pay or statutory shared parental pay;
- tax credits.

Financial need

'**Financial need**' means that because you have not received your benefit, there is a serious risk of damage to the health or safety of you or a member of your family.[15] Guidance notes that situations that are considered 'serious risk' are not easily defined, but that examples include fleeing domestic violence and being without money for food or for gas/electricity meters.[16]

'**Family**' means your partner and any child in your household for whom you or your partner are responsible.[17]

Applications and decisions

You can request a short-term advance in person at, or by writing (by post, fax or email) to, your local jobcentre, or by telephoning the number for the specific benefit at www.gov.uk/short-term-benefit-advance.

To apply for a UC advance, the DWP encourages you to phone the UC helpline on 0345 600 0723 (textphone: 0345 600 0743), but you can also ask at your intial UC interview. The phone calls are not free, but you can ask the DWP to call you back or use the telephone in your local job centre.

Your application should set out why you meet the criteria. You should give the relevant history of your benefit claim and explain how you satisfy all the conditions of entitlement, including the immigration status, residence and presence requirements. Provide evidence for any areas where there may be a doubt – eg, provide the basis of your right to reside (see Chapter 12 and also p332) or the reason why you are not a 'person subject to immigration control' (see Chapter 7). You must also give the reasons why you are in 'financial need' (see above). See 'Ask CPAG online' for sample application statements.[18]

The DWP guidance sets out the procedure that should be folllowed in determining your application.[19] This confirms that, before considering your application, the DWP should always check whether it can simply determine your claim and issue you a payment. If so, it should telephone you to let you know.[20] If your benefit cannot be paid, the DWP should determine your application and contact you by telephone (or text if it cannot reach you) to either give you the decision or to request more information.[21] If you do not have a phone, provide the DWP with the number of a friend or relative. If you cannot do that, the DWP will tell you to ring the benefit enquiry line after a certain period of time for an update on your request.[22]

There are no rules on how much a short-term advance should be. The DWP considers how much you have asked for, how much you can afford to repay within the time period (see below) and what your benefit entitlement will be. For a UC advance, the DWP usually offers a maximum of 50 per cent of your estimated award (or estimated increase in your award due a change of circumstances).[23] For other benefits, the potential maximum is based on 60 per cent of your daily personal allowance multiplied by the number of days until your benefit is due to be paid.[24]

Recovering the advance

A short-term advance is recovered by making deductions from subsequent payments of your benefit, either in one lump sum from your next benefit payment or weekly. You (and your partner if it is an advance of UC) must be notified of your liability to have the advance recovered by deductions, and to repay any amount not recovered in this way.[25]

A UC advance is usually recovered within six months (or 12 if you are transferring to UC from another benefit), at up to 40 per cent of your monthly UC standard allowance. In exceptional circumstances, after you have been awarded the advance, you can request that recovery be deferred for up to three months.[26]

A short-term advice of other benefits is usually recovered within 12 weeks at no more than 25 per cent of your benefit.[27] Recovery can be deferred, by up to 12 weeks, if you are fleeing domestic violence.[28] In exceptional circumstances, you can request that recovery be rescheduled, over a maximum of 24 weeks. The DWP guidance gives a list of examples, including if your benefit has been reduced as a result of a sanction or a drop in your household income, and an unforseen and unavoidable event.[29]

You can appeal against the decision about the repayment from subsequent payments of your benefit, including the rate of the deductions.[30]

If you are refused a short-term advance

You cannot appeal against a refusal to award you a short-term advance.[31] The only legal remedy is judicial review (see p337). However, you can ask for the decision to be reconsidered during the phone call in which you are told your request has been refused. If possible, provide any additional information to support your application. If you are aware that the decision was based on incorrect information, correct this during the call. The decision maker should then reconsider your application based on the revised information. If you wait until after this phone call, you will be asked to make a new request.[32]

You can also make a complaint to the DWP, including if you were prevented from requesting a short-term advance, and this can be effective in either obtaining an advance or in getting your claim processed.

You can contact your MP to see if s/he can help with either a complaint or to get the decision reconsidered.

Note: you may be able to get help from your local welfare assistance scheme (see p462) as well as, or instead of, a short-term advance. However, you should not be prevented from requesting a short-term advance just because local welfare assistance is available.

Are you having problems getting a short-term advance?

1. Be aware of the DWP's guidance on short-term advances and UC advances and refer to it when helpful.[33]

2. Do not be deterred from requesting an advance by recorded messages on DWP helplines that tell you not to contact it until you have waited for a certain period of time. There is no minimum period of time you must wait before applying.

3. You may be told to seek help from your local welfare assistance scheme (see p462) or be referred to a food bank (see p472) instead. If you consider that you meet the criteria for a short-term advance, insist on your request being passed to the decision maker to consider. Decisions on advances must be made by a decision maker, not frontline staff.

4. The decision maker who considers your application may not be an expert on the benefit rules for migrants. This can be a problem because s/he can only make a short-term

advance if it appears to her/him that you are likely to be entitled to benefit. It may therefore assist your application if you set out clearly how you satisfy the relevant immigration, residence and presence conditions.

5. If you are told you cannot receive an advance because the habitual residence test has not yet been applied to you, you should explain how you satisfy, or are exempt from, this and ask the decision maker to reconsider her/his decision. The DWP guidance lists an outstanding habitual residence test as an example of when it is likely someone would not be entitled to benefit and therefore when an advance should be refused.[34] However, decision makers should not refuse your request without considering all your circumstances, and taking such a 'blanket' approach is contrary to earlier paragraphs in the guidance and is arguably unlawful.[35]

6. If the reason your claim cannot be processed is because you are waiting to obtain evidence showing that you satisfy all the conditions of entitlement, it may help to explain the cause of the delay, summarise any other evidence that you have already submitted and explain how it is consistent with the evidence you are waiting for to show that you are entitled to benefit. For more information on the evidence required for the immigration and residence tests, see Chapter 20.

7. The decision maker may suggest that you are not entitled to a short-term advance because you do not have an NI number. If this happens, point out that the DWP guidance states that a short-term advance should still be considered, provided you can prove your identity and are complying with other requests for evidence. The guidance also states that the DWP must ensure that all necessary action to allocate an NI number is taken promptly to ensure the claim can be finalised and paid.[36] See Chapter 19 for further information on the NI requirement.

8. If you are, or think you might be, refused a a short-term advance on the grounds that you cannot repay it within the usual timescale, note the following:

– the short-term advance regulations do not require you to be able repay the advance within any particular period;
– DWP guidance covers circumstances in which the standard repayment rates can be exceeded if you agree to higher repayment rates and (other than for UC advances) in exceptional circumstances recovery can be rescheduled over a longer period or deferred (see p331).[37]
– if your circumstances are likely to change in the future and improve your ability to repay a short-term advance, make sure the decision maker is aware of this.

Interim payments of child benefit and guardian's allowance

An interim payment of child benefit or guardian's allowance can be made if it appears to HMRC that you may be entitled to benefit and:[38]

- you have not claimed correctly and it is impracticable for such a claim to be made immediately; *or*
- you have claimed correctly and all the conditions of entitlement are satisfied *except* the NI number requirement (see p354) and it is impracticable for that to be satisfied immediately; *or*

- you have claimed correctly, but it is impracticable for the claim to be dealt with immediately; *or*
- you have been awarded benefit, but it is impracticable to pay you immediately, other than by an interim payment.

Note:
- You cannot appeal against a refusal to award you an interim payment. The only legal remedy is judicial review (see p337). You can ask HMRC to reconsider its refusal and you can complain. You can also contact your MP to see whether s/he can help to get the decision reconsidered.
- An interim payment can be deducted from any later payment of the benefit and, if it is more than your actual entitlement, the overpayment can be recovered. You should be notified of this in advance.[39]
- An interim payment cannot be paid if you have an appeal pending.[40]

Making a complaint

Making a complaint when there is an ongoing problem (such as a claim that has not been decided) is different from making a complaint about a situation that you think should not have happened but which is no longer producing a problem – eg, if your claim has been decided, but you are unhappy it took so long. The information in this section is aimed at enabling you to use the complaints process in order to get the situation resolved (ie, to get a decision on your claim), rather than at seeking compensation or highlighting to the DWP/HMRC the hardship it has caused after a delay has been resolved.

When you make a complaint to try to resolve an ongoing delay, it is important to highlight that the problem persists, that this is therefore an urgent matter and be clear what you want to be done about it – eg, ask for your claim to be determined within X number of days.

The DWP and HMRC have different procedures for complaining.

Complaints about the DWP

If you want to complain about how a particular DWP agency has dealt with your case, you should first contact the office that is dealing with your claim. If you are unsure which office this is, contact numbers and information about the complaints procedure are provided on the DWP website.[41] You can also make a complaint about JSA or UC online via the DWP website.

You should receive a response to your complaint within 15 working days.

If you are still dissatisfied, you can ask that your complaint be passed to a complaints resolution manager. This is referred to as a 'tier one' complaint. S/he should contact you, usually by phone, to discuss your complaint. It should be dealt with, or you should be told when it will be dealt with, within 15 working days.

If you remain dissatisfied, you can ask for your complaint to be passed to a more senior DWP officer. The DWP refers to this as a 'tier two' complaint. All 'tier two' complaints should receive a written response, or you should be be told when you can expect a response, within 15 days. If you are still not satisfied, you can complain to the Independent Case Examiner (ICE), and you may also have grounds to make a complaint to the Ombudsman (see p336).

The ICE deals with complaints about DWP agencies and its contracted providers.

A complaint can only be made to the ICE if you have already completed the complaints procedure of the particular agency concerned. This usually means that you have had a response to a tier two complaint. A complaint should be made to the ICE no later than six months after the final response from the agency you are complaining about.

The ICE first considers whether it can accept the complaint. If so, it attempts to settle it by suggesting ways in which you and the agency concerned can come to an agreement. If this fails, the ICE prepares a formal report, setting out how the complaint arose and how it believes it should be settled. The ICE considers whether there has been maladministration. It cannot deal with legal matters or cases that are being appealed, or subject to judicial review or other legal procedures.

If you remain unhappy, ask your MP to consider referring your concerns to the Parliamentary and Health Service Ombudsman (see p336).

If you are unhappy with the way the ICE dealt with your case, use the ICE internal complaints process.

Complaints about HM Revenue and Customs

If you want to complain about how HMRC has dealt with your claim for tax credits, child benefit or guardian's allowance, first raise the complaint with the office dealing with your case, or the named contact person on the letters you have received, setting out the nature of your complaint – eg, the delay in processing information you have submitted, requesting supplementary information or evidence or in actually determining your claim. Set out the history of your claim and any telephone contact or written correspondence and say what you think HMRC has done wrong. Also include in the complaint any loss that you have incurred, or difficulty you or your family members have had as a result.

If you are not happy with the response to your complaint, you can ask for it to be passed to an HMRC complaints handler. If you are dissatisfied with her/his response, you can ask that your complaint be reviewed by another complaints handler.

HMRC's complaints procedure is set out in its factsheet *Complaints* (C/FS), available on its website.[42]

If you are not happy with HMRC's reply, you can ask the Adjudicator's Office to look into it.

The Adjudicator only investigates a complaint if you have first exhausted the HMRC internal complaints procedure. A complaint should be made within six months of the final correspondence with HMRC.

Complaints can be made about delays, inappropriate staff behaviour, misleading advice or any other form of maladministration. The Adjudicator cannot, however, investigate disputes about matters of law. The Adjudicator can recommend that compensation be paid. HMRC has undertaken to follow the Adjudicator's recommendations in all but exceptional circumstances.

If you are still unhappy, you can ask your MP to consider referring your concerns to the Parliamentary and Health Service Ombudsman (see below).

For further details on complaints about tax credits, see CPAG's *Tax Credits and Complaints Factsheet.*[43]

Complaining to the Parliamentary Ombudsman

If you have an ongoing delay in getting a decision made on your claim for benefit, a complaint, or the threat of a complaint, to the Parliamentary and Health Service Ombudsman may result in the DWP or HMRC taking action to determine your claim. You can also make a complaint to the Ombudsman after the issue is resolved.

The role of the Ombudsman is to investigate complaints from members of the public who believe they have experienced an injustice because of maladministration by a government department.[44] 'Maladministration' means poor administration and can include avoidable delays, failure to advise about appeal rights, refusal to answer reasonable questions or respond to correspondence, and discourteous, racist or sexist behaviour.

The Ombudsman does not usually investigate a complaint unless you have first exhausted the internal complaints procedure. However, if the DWP or HMRC is not acting on your complaint, or there are unreasonable delays, this delay may also form part of your complaint. The time limit for lodging a complaint with the Ombudsman is 12 months from the date you were notified of the matter complained about. However, a delay in bringing a complaint does not necessarily prevent a complaint being heard if there are good reasons for the delay.

A public body, such as the DWP or HMRC, is required to follow the recommendations of a complaints panel unless there are good reasons not to. If a public body has failed to do so, you may have grounds to complain to the Ombudsman and, in some circumstances, may have grounds for a judicial review.

The Parliamentary and Health Service Ombudsman deals with complaints about all central government departments. This includes the DWP, HMRC, HM Courts and Tribunals Service and any agencies carrying out functions on their behalf. In order to make a complaint, you must write to your MP, who then refers the complaint to the Ombudsman. To find out who your MP is, contact the House of Commons Information Office on 020 7219 4272 or see www.parliament.uk/ mps-lords-and offices/. The Ombudsman can only investigate complaints of maladministration and not complaints about entitlement, which should be dealt with by challenging the decision on this. The Ombudsman has powers to look at documents on your claim held by the benefit authority. You may be interviewed to check any facts. The Ombudsman can recommend financial compensation if you have been unfairly treated or have experienced a loss as a result of the maladministration.

Judicial review

Judicial review is a process by which you can ask a court to look at an action (or, in the case of delay, inaction) of any public authority that affects you, on the grounds that such (in)action is unlawful. If the High Court (Court of Session in Scotland) accepts that the (in)action is unlawful, it can order the decision maker to determine your benefit claim (or otherwise resolve the issue).

There are many steps that must be taken before the High Court (or Court of Session) gives such a decision, and if you want to apply for judicial review about a benefit delay, it is strongly advisable only to do so with the help of legal advice. In particular, you risk having to pay the legal costs of the decision maker (which could be thousands of pounds) if your challenge is unsuccessful. In order to protect against this risk, it is necessary to obtain a legal aid certificate before proceedings are issued (and this is another reason to obtain legal advice).

However, in cases of benefit delay, often a 'letter before action', in which your adviser states that judicial review action will start unless your claim is determined by a certain date, can lead to its being decided promptly. If the adviser works for an organisation that does not have a solicitor able to get legal aid in a public law matter, the letter should state that if your claim is not determined by a certain date, the matter will be referred to such a solicitor with a view to starting judicial review action. The letter should be sent to the solicitor for the DWP or HMRC, together with a copy to the manager of the section responsible for dealing with your claim. Although a 'letter before action' is currently only a requirement in England and Wales, it can still be used in Scotland to help resolve delays.

A template for a pre-action letter (for use in England and Wales) is available online.[45] The letter should include all the details required in that template.

Completing a pre-action letter

Under the section entitled 'the issue', you should include the following.

1. Set out the history of your claim for benefit – ie, which benefit you claimed and when, plus the details of all further correspondence and any complaints you have made. It is useful to do this in chronological date order.

2. Explain why you believe you are entitled to the benefit claimed. Address how you meet the conditions of entitlement, including how you meet the rules about immigration status, residence or the EU co-ordination of social security, and the evidence of this that you have submitted.

3. Explain that there is a legal duty to determine claims within a reasonable time (see p327).

4. Explain why you believe the claim has not been determined within a reasonable time in your particular case and/or why a short-term advance should have been made. It is important to explain in as much detail as possible why you believe the DWP or HMRC has all the information needed to determine your claim, or why it should be able to obtain it. Also explain any specific reasons why the delay is causing you difficulties.

Housing benefit

Your HB claim must be determined within 14 days (or as soon as reasonably practicable after that) of your submitting a valid claim and providing all the information and evidence requested and reasonably required by the local authority.[46]

What counts as 'as soon as reasonably practicable' is the same as for benefits administered by the DWP and HMRC (see p327). In addition, the fact that your home may be at risk of repossession if the rent is not paid can often be a relevant factor in determining how long it should take to make a decision.

If you experience a delay in deciding your claim for HB, you can:
- request a 'payment on account' if you are a private or housing association tenant – ie, not a council tenant (see below);
- make a complaint in writing (see p339);
- escalate a complaint to the Local Government and Social Care Ombudsman (see p340);
- obtain legal advice about sending a 'letter before action' for judicial review (see p340).

You can pursue more than one of these options – eg, you can make a complaint and if this does not resolve the delay, get legal advice about sending a 'letter before action' for judicial review.

Payments on account

The local authority must make a 'payment on account' if:[47]
- you have claimed HB as a private or housing association tenant; *and*
- it is impracticable for it to make a decision on your claim within 14 days of its being made; *and*
- this is not due to your failure (without good cause) to provide the information it has requested.

A payment on account is sometimes called an 'interim payment'.

A payment on account is not discretionary. The local authority *must* pay the amount it considers 'reasonable', based on the information it has about your circumstances. If your actual entitlement is less, the local authority recovers the overpayment, or pays your arrears if your entitlement is greater.[48] The local authority must notify you of the amount of a payment on account and that it can recover any overpayment resulting from your actual HB entitlement being lower.[49]

You do not need to ask the local authority to make a payment on account and you do not need to make a separate claim.[50] However, in practice, it is often necessary to write and request a payment on account, and/or make a complaint (see below), and/or write to the solicitor for the local authority and threaten judicial review (see p340) in order to get a payment.

Making a complaint

Making a complaint when there is an ongoing problem (such as an HB claim that has not been decided) is different from making a complaint about a situation that you think should not have happened but which is no longer producing a problem – eg, if your claim has been decided, but you are unhappy it took so long. The information in this section is aimed at enabling you to use the complaints process in order to get the situation resolved (ie, get a decision on your HB claim), rather than at seeking compensation or highlighting to the local authority the hardship it has caused after a delay has been resolved.

When you make a complaint to resolve an ongoing delay, it is important to say clearly that the problem persists, that this is therefore an urgent matter and what you want to be done about it – eg, ask for your claim to be determined within X number of days. In particular, you should include any relevant details of steps your landlord is taking to obtain possession of the property as a consequence of the rent arrears arising from the HB delay.

Local authorities must have an effective complaints procedure, which should be made available to the public. If you are unhappy about the actions of your local authority and wish to make a complaint, ask for a copy of its complaints policy. If you are unable to obtain the policy or there is no formal complaints procedure, begin by writing to the supervisor of the person dealing with your claim, making it clear why you are dissatisfied. If you do not receive a satisfactory reply, take up the matter with someone more senior in the department and, ultimately, the principal officer. Send a copy of the letter to your ward councillor and to the councillor who chairs the relevant committee responsible for HB (local authority officers are always accountable to the councillors). If this does not produce results, or if the delay is causing you severe hardship, consider a complaint to the Ombudsman (see p340) or obtain legal advice about a judicial review (see p340).

Government departments also monitor local authorities, so you could contact your MP or write to the relevant minister.

If you want to make a complaint about an elected member of a council, you must write to the local authority. In England, the Localism Act requires all local authorities to promote and maintain high standards of conduct by elected members. However, they can choose whether or not to set up standards committees to consider complaints about the conduct of councillors. The practice may therefore vary and you should ask your local authority for its procedure for complaints against members. In Wales and Scotland, elected members of a council are subject to a code of conduct. Complaints about Scottish councillors can be made to the Commissioner for Ethical Standards in Public Life in Scotland who can refer cases to the Standards Commission for Scotland. Complaints about Welsh councillors can be made to the Public Services Ombudsman for Wales.

Complaining to the Ombudsman

If you have tried to sort out your complaint with the local authority but you are not satisfied with the outcome, you can apply to the Local Government and Social Care Ombudsman (in England), the Scottish Public Services Ombudsman (in Scotland) or the Public Services Ombudsman for Wales (in Wales). The Ombudsman can investigate any cases of maladministration by local authorities, but not matters of entitlement, which are dealt with by the First-tier Tribunal.

You can complain to the Ombudsman either by completing an online form or by telephone. The Ombudsman has powers to look at documents on your claim held by the local authority. You may be interviewed to check any facts. Straightforward cases can be dealt with in about three months. The Ombudsman can recommend financial compensation if you have been unfairly treated or experienced a loss as a result of the maladministration. A complaint may also make the authority review its procedures, which could benefit other claimants.

One outcome of your complaint may be a 'local settlement'. This is where the local authority agrees to take some action that the Ombudsman considers is a satisfactory response to your complaint and the investigation is then discontinued. If you are unhappy with the way in which the Ombudsman has dealt with your complaint, you can use its complaints process and, if you are still unhappy, obtain legal advice as quickly as possible.

Judicial review

Judicial review when there is a delay in making a decision on an HB claim is similar to when there is a delay in deciding a claim for a benefit administered by the DWP or HMRC (see p337). However, as there are different rules for how quickly a HB claim must be decided, any 'letter before action' for judicial review must refer to these. In particular, if you are a private tenant, your letter should note the rules about payments on account (see p338).

The letter should be sent to the solicitor for the local authority, together with a copy to the manager of the HB section responsible for dealing with your claim.

Note: because of the potential consequences, including costs, it is strongly advised that you obtain legal advice, and a legal aid certificate, before initiating judicial review proceedings.

Pending test cases

The general requirement to decide your claim does not apply if there is a appeal pending against a decision of the Upper Tribunal or a court in a 'test case' that deals with issues relevant to your claim. If this applies, the decision maker must consider whether it is possible that the outcome of the test case would mean you would have no entitlement. If so, the decision maker can postpone ('stay') making a decision on your claim (or revision or supersession request) until the test case is decided.[51] This prevents you appealing until a decision is made in the test case.

If the decision on your claim (or request for a revision or supersession) is postponed, once a decision has been made in the test case, the decision maker makes the decision in your case.[52]

If you would be entitled to benefit even if the test case were decided against you, the decision maker can make a decision.[53] This is done on the assumption that the test case has been decided in the way that is most unfavourable to you. However, this does mean that you are at least paid something while you wait for the result of the test case. Then, if the decision in the test case is in your favour, the decision maker revises her/his decision.

If you already have a decision in your favour, the decision maker can suspend payment of your benefit (see p349).

If you have already appealed to the First-tier Tribunal, see p343.

---

3. **Delays when challenging a decision**

If you have challenged a decision on your entitlement to a benefit or tax credit, there can be a delay while the:

- decision maker considers whether or not to revise (or review) the decision (see p342);
- decision maker prepares the appeal to send to the First-tier Tribunal (see p343);
- appeal is with the First-tier Tribunal waiting for a hearing date.

Note: for benefits other than housing benefit (HB), if you want to appeal to the First-tier Tribunal, you must have first applied for a revision (or, for tax credits, a review) of the decision. The DWP and HM Revenue and Customs (HMRC) call this 'mandatory reconsideration'. In addition, the following must apply.

- For child benefit and guardian's allowance, HMRC must have decided not to revise the decision. If HMRC revises the decision, but not to award you all you wanted, you can appeal against the original decision as revised without having to apply for another revision.[54]
- For tax credits, HMRC must have reviewed the decision and given you notice of its conclusion.[55]

• For other benefits, the DWP must have considered whether or not to revise the decision. You must have been notified in writing that you must apply for a revision of the decision before you can appeal (see below).[56]

The DWP or HMRC gives or sends you a mandatory reconsideration notice, telling you the result of your application for a revision or review. The notice is proof that it has accepted and considered your application. You must send a copy of this to the tribunal when you appeal. If the DWP or HMRC only provides a mandatory reconsideration notice after a long delay, this may put you at a disadvantage – eg, if it makes it difficult to obtain evidence to support your appeal. This is something the tribunal should take into account if you subsequently appeal, so you should explain how you think the delay has affected your chances of winning your appeal.[57]

For DWP decisions only, you do not need to request a revision before you appeal if you were not sent a written notice of the decision that included a statement that you were required to do this.[58]

For further information on challenging decisions, see CPAG's *Welfare Benefits and Tax Credits Handbook*.

Delay in carrying out a revision

When you submit your request for a revision to the DWP, make it clear that you are asking for a revision, include the fact that this is also referred to as a 'mandatory reconsideration', and ask for your request to be sent immediately to the Dispute Resolution Team. The Dispute Resolution Team should then decide whether the decision will be revised and send you the mandatory reconsideration notice. If the DWP responds to your revision request with a letter telling you that the decision has been looked at again, but not changed, and either inviting you to request a mandatory reconsideration or informing you that your request is being forwarded to the Dispute Resolution Team, you may be able to argue that your right of appeal has arisen. However, to safeguard your appeal rights, you should also continue with the mandatory reconsideration process and resubmit your revision request, explaining what has happened and clearly asking that it be sent immediately to the Dispute Resolution Team. You should also submit a complaint, as you should not need to request a mandatory reconsideration twice.

There is no specified time limit in the legislation for how long it should take the decision maker to carry out a revision (or, for tax credits, a review). However, revision requests should be dealt with within a reasonable time. Tax credit reviews should be carried out as soon as is 'reasonably practicable', and HMRC's stated target is 42 days.[59] See p327 for the factors that are relevant when determining what is reasonable. You should ensure that you highlight any specific circumstances of your case that mean it is urgent for you, and therefore not appropriate for your request to be dealt with in the order in which it was received.

If a delay in carrying out a revision or review continues, the options for resolving it are the same as those for resolving a delay in determining a claim and include:

- making a written complaint (see p334 for benefits administered by the DWP or HMRC and p339 for HB);
- escalating a complaint to the relevant Ombudsman (see p336 for benefits administered by the DWP or HMRC and p340 for HB);
- obtaining legal advice about sending a 'letter before action' for judicial review (see p337).

Note:
- The decision maker can postpone making a decision on your revision request if there is a 'test case' pending (see p341).
- The DWP has recently stated that its internal target is to clear 90 per cent of mandatory reconsiderations in 10–20 days.[60] It publishes quarterly statistics online, which show average clearance times for work capability assessment mandatory reconsiderations.[61]

Delay while an appeal is prepared

The rules on the time in which the decision maker must send her/his response to the First-tier Tribunal and the possible solutions if there are delays depend on whether or not you were required to request a mandatory reconsideration before appealing.

If your appeal concerns your rights under European Union (EU) law (eg, your right to reside under EU law or the effect of the EU co-ordination rules), see also p350 for a possible argument that some payments should be paid to you while you wait for your appeal to be heard.

Delay preparing your appeal following a mandatory reconsideration

Once you have sent your appeal to HM Courts and Tribunals Service (HMCTS), you may experience a delay in its being progressed. You should first establish what stage the appeal is at. Contact HMCTS and check whether:

- your appeal has been received. You may wish to obtain proof of receipt – eg, by sending the appeal by a type of postal service that requires a signature or using the Royal Mail tracking service. Once it has been received by the tribunal, it is responsible for ensuring that the case is dealt with 'fairly and justly', which includes 'avoiding delay so far as compatible with proper consideration of the issues';[62]
- your appeal has been sent onto the DWP or HMRC and, if so, on what date;
- the DWP/HMRC has responded (see p344). A copy of this response should be sent to you and/or your representative;
- you have been sent an enquiry form or, if you have returned this, whether it has been received;
- your appeal is ready to be listed for a hearing date.

The decision maker must send her/his response to the appeal to the First-tier Tribunal within 28 days of having received it.[63] If the DWP/HMRC has not done so, you can ask the tribunal to make a direction that it does so within a further short period, after which time the appeal is listed and the DWP/HMRC is barred from taking any further part in proceedings.[64]

If your situation is particularly urgent, you can ask the tribunal to shorten the 28-day time limit.[65]

If the DWP/HMRC applies for a direction to extend the 28-day time limit, you should be notified of this in writing and you can then apply for a direction setting this direction aside.[66]

If you apply for a direction, you should clearly explain the consequences for you of a continuing delay and explain why it would be fair and just to determine the case more quickly than would otherwise happen.

If you request that your appeal be dealt with quickly in this way, you must also be as flexible as possible in terms of preparing your case quickly and making yourself, and any representative, available for hearings at short notice.

If the tribunal refuses to expedite your appeal, and it is arguable that this means your case is not being dealt with fairly and justly, you should get advice on whether there are grounds for a judicial review (see p337).

If your appeal is delayed because of a pending 'test case', see p346.

Delay preparing your appeal without a mandatory reconsideration

The information in this section applies if your appeal is about an HB decision or, in very rare cases, a decision that did not correctly notify you that you were required to request a revision before appealing. For more information on when this applies, see CPAG's *Welfare Benefits and Tax Credits Handbook*. In these cases, you send your appeal to the decision maker in the local authority (or DWP or HMRC). If there is a delay in your appeal being processed, first establish what stage the appeal is at. Contact the relevant benefit authority and check whether:

- your appeal has been received;
- the decision maker has written her/his response and sent it to HMCTS. A copy should also be sent to you and/or your representative;
- you have been sent an enquiry form or, if you have returned this, whether it has been received; *and*
- your appeal is ready to be listed for a hearing date.

The decision maker must send her/his response to your appeal to HMCTS as soon as reasonably practicable.[67] You are entitled to have your appeal heard within a reasonable period of time, so the decision maker should prepare the response and send it to the First-tier Tribunal without delay.[68] Following a complaint about an HB appeal, the Ombudsman said that the local authority should forward an appeal within 28 days.[69]

If your appeal has been received but has not been sent to HMCTS, you should request that this be done. You can complain about the delay using the complaints procedure (see p339 for local authorities, and p334 for the DWP and HMRC).

If there are special reasons why your appeal should be dealt with urgently or there has already been significant delay, you can write to the First-tier Tribunal asking it to direct the decision maker to produce the response and/or list the appeal for a hearing.[70] Set out the history of the appeal, what you have done to try to get the matter resolved and the effect of the delay on you and your family as clearly as possible and include all documents that you have about the decision. Bear in mind that the tribunal expects normal procedures to be followed in the vast majority of cases, but, if necessary, can deal with your appeal differently. This includes admitting the appeal directly if it has not yet been received from the decision maker or by prioritising the hearing date, so it is not listed in the order in which the appeal was received.

How should you ask the First-tier Tribunal to deal with your appeal if it has not been sent by the decision maker?

If you write to the First-tier Tribunal, there is a risk of a misunderstanding. The tribunal clerk (an administrative officer who processes appeals) may be confused if s/he receives documents concerning an appeal which the decision maker has not told the tribunal about. In order to minimise the chances of confusion, you should do the following.

1. Clearly head your letter 'Application for a Direction under Rule 6 of the Tribunal Procedure Rules' and mark it 'urgent'.

2. Explain at the start of the letter that the papers have not been sent by the decision maker and you would like the case to be referred to a tribunal judge to give a direction to resolve this problem.

3. Set out the history of when your appeal was submitted and the contact you have made with the benefit authority since then. If possible, enclose a copy of your appeal request and any accompanying documents.

4. Refer to the caselaw that confirms that HMCTS has the power to issue directions in relation to an unnotified appeal.[71]

5. Clearly explain the consequences for you of a continuing delay and explain why it would be fair and just to determine the case more quickly than would otherwise happen.

6. Follow up your letter or fax with a phone call to the tribunal to establish that it has been received and passed to a judge.

7. See CPAG's website for a sample letter, which you may want to adapt.[72] This does not specify timescales, because what is reasonable depends on the facts of your case and the consequences of the continued delay. For example, if you are at imminent risk of losing your home as a consequence of HB not being awarded, the timescale should reflect this.

If you request that your appeal be dealt with quickly in this way, you must then be as flexible as possible in terms of preparing your case quickly and making yourself, and any representative, available for hearings at short notice.

If a tribunal judge refuses to direct the decision maker to submit her/his response to the tribunal and to expedite the appeal, you should consider whether there are grounds for judicial review against this refusal (see p337). Depending on the particular facts, it may be arguable that a failure to give such directions has resulted in procedural impropriety because the tribunal has failed to deal with your case fairly and justly as required.[73] You should obtain legal advice before doing this (there is a risk of costs in applying for judicial review) and you should act promptly. As with delays in processing benefit claims, a 'letter before action' for judicial review in such circumstances can often lead to the issue being resolved (in this case, the requested direction being given). In England and Wales, judicial review proceedings against action (or inaction) of the First-tier Tribunal must be started in the Upper Tribunal.[74] In Scotland, you must begin judicial review proceedings against action (or inaction) of the First-tier Tribunal by applying to the Court of Session. If certain conditions are satisfied, your case can then be transferred to the Upper Tribunal.[75]

Appeal delayed because of a pending test case

If you have appealed to the First-tier or Upper Tribunal and there is a 'test case' pending against a decision of the Upper Tribunal or a court that deals with issues raised in your case, the decision maker can serve a notice requiring the tribunal in your appeal:[76]

- not to make a decision and to refer your case back to her/him; *or*
- to deal with your appeal by either:
  - postponing making a decision (known as 'stay' or, in Scotland, 'sist') until the test case is decided; *or*
  - deciding your appeal as if the test case had been decided in the way most unfavourable to you, but only if this is in your interests. If this happens and the test case is eventually decided in your favour, the decision maker must make a new decision superseding the decision of the First-tier Tribunal or Upper Tribunal in the light of the decision in the test case.

If the decision on your appeal has been postponed, once a decision has been made in the test case, the decision is made on your appeal.

If your appeal concerns European law, see p350.

4. Delays getting paid

Once you have a positive decision stating that you are entitled to benefit, there may be delays in the DWP, HM Revenue and Customs (HMRC) or local authority implementing it and making any payments due.

It is important to check first that there is a decision in place awarding you a specified amount of benefit (see below). If there is, unless payments can be suspended (see p348), payment should be made to you as soon as reasonably practicable.[77]

If you do not have a bank account, you should be paid through the 'simple payment' service, which enables you to collect your payment from a PayPoint outlet.[78]

If benefit is not paid promptly, you have a right to start action in the county court (England and Wales) or sheriff court (Scotland) for payment of the money owed.[79] However, it is extremely rare that this action is required to obtain benefit that has been awarded but not paid.

The decision awarding you benefit

In most cases, it is clear that there has been a decision awarding you a specified amount of benefit. However, in some cases, you may get a decision which does not award benefit but only decides one or more conditions of entitlement. For example, if you appeal to the First-tier Tribunal against the DWP's decision that it cannot pay you income support (IS) because you do not have a right to reside, the tribunal can allow your appeal if it decides that the DWP was wrong because you do have a right to reside. However, the tribunal's decision is not a decision awarding you benefit, because it only relates to one condition of entitlement and does not decide whether you meet all the other conditions of entitlement for IS. The question of your entitlement to IS is therefore passed back to the DWP decision maker to make a decision on whether you meet all the conditions of entitlement to award you a specified amount of benefit.

If your appeal about one condition of your entitlement is allowed and there is then a delay in a decision being made to award you benefit:
- check whether the decision maker has received notification of the tribunal's decision;
- if the decision maker has received notification, establish what is the cause of the delay. A long time may have elapsed since your initial claim was made, and so to ensure that you have met the other conditions of entitlement since your date of claim, the decision maker may write asking you to confirm this, often by completing a claim or review form. Any further delays can be reduced if you provide the information or complete and return any forms as soon as you can;
- if you are advised that the decision maker has all the information s/he requires, but there is still a delay in deciding your claim, your options are the same as for

someone who experiences a delay in getting a decision on an initial claim (see p326). You should include in any correspondence the fact that you have already had a significant wait while your appeal was determined.

Note: you only have the right to sue for benefit awarded but not paid once there is a decision actually awarding you a specified amount of benefit.

Suspension of benefit

In certain circumstances, a decision maker can suspend payment of part or all of your benefit or tax credits. In this case, you have no right to the payment (and so cannot take court action). See CPAG's *Welfare Benefits and Tax Credits Handbook* for all the circumstances in which benefit can be suspended. **Note:** the tax credit regulations use the term 'postponement' rather than 'suspension' of payment, but as HMRC uses the term 'suspension', this is used for both benefits and tax credits in this section.

There are two situations when payment of benefit or tax credits can be suspended that are most relevant to the way the immigration, residence, presence and European Union (EU) co-ordination rules operate. These are:

- because the decision maker wants more information to decide whether you continue to be entitled to benefit (see below); *and*
- while an appeal against a positive decision is pending (see p349).

Has your benefit been suspended?

1. The decision maker may be willing to continue to pay your benefit, or at least some of it, if you can show that you will experience hardship otherwise. Guidance to decision makers is clear that, in almost all decisions to suspend benefit, consideration must be given to whether hardship would result and whether this would make the suspension unacceptable. In addition, the decision to suspend your benefit can be reconsidered if the decision maker receives additional information.[80]

2. If you receive a letter telling you that your benefit has been suspended, write explaining how the suspension affects you and ask for the suspension decision to be reconsidered. In addition to hardship, there may be other arguments why your benefit should not be suspended, based on the information below.

3. You cannot appeal to the First-tier Tribunal against the decision to suspend your benefit. The only way to change the decision is to negotiate to get your benefit reinstated or to challenge the decision in the courts by judicial review (see p337).

The decision maker requires further information

You can be required to supply information or evidence if the decision maker needs this to determine whether your award of benefit should be revised or superseded.[81]

If you do not provide the information and evidence, payment of all or part of your benefit can be suspended if:[82]
- a question has arisen about your entitlement or whether a decision should be revised or superseded;[83] *or*
- you apply for a revision or supersession; *or*
- you do not provide certificates, documents, evidence or other information about the facts of your case as required.[84]

If the decision maker wants you to provide information or evidence, s/he must notify you in writing. Within 14 days (one month for child benefit, guardian's allowance and housing benefit (HB); seven days for contribution-based jobseeker's allowance if you come under the universal credit system; or by the date specified, which must not be less than 30 days after the date of the notice, for tax credits) of being sent the request, you must:
- supply the information or evidence.[85] You can be given more time if the decision maker is satisfied that this is necessary; *or*
- satisfy the decision maker that the information does not exist or you cannot obtain it.[86]

If the decision maker has not already done so, your benefit can be suspended if you do not provide the information or evidence within the relevant time limit.[87] Similarly, your tax credits can be suspended if you do not provide information or evidence by the date requested.[88]

The complexity of the immigration, residence, presence and EU co-ordination rules, together with the additional information and evidence requirements these rules generate, means that the likelihood of your benefit being suspended on the above grounds is increased. For information on some of the practical issues involved in satisfying the information and evidence requirements, see Chapter 20.

If an appeal is pending

Your benefit or tax credit can be suspended if the DWP, HMRC or local authority is appealing (or considering an appeal) against:[89]
- a decision of the First-tier Tribunal, Upper Tribunal or court to award you benefit (or to reinstate benefit); *or*
- a decision of the Upper Tribunal or court about someone else's appeal if the issue could affect your claim. For HB only, the other case must also be about a HB issue.

The DWP, HMRC or local authority must (although for tax credits this is only guidance[90]) give you written notice as soon as reasonably practicable if it intends to:[91]
- request the statement of reasons for the First-tier Tribunal's decision;

- apply for leave to appeal; *or*
- appeal,

whichever is the first that is yet to be done.

The decision maker must then take that action within the usual time limits for doing so (generally within one month in each case). If s/he does not, the suspended benefit must be paid to you.[92] The suspended benefit must also be paid to you if the decision maker withdraws an application for leave to appeal, withdraws the appeal or is refused leave to appeal and it is not possible for her/him to renew the application.

The decision maker still has discretion not to suspend if s/he considers it would result in hardship and s/he should keep her/his decision under review so that the suspension can be lifted if your circumstances, including level of hardship experienced, change.[93] You should therefore write to the relevant benefit authority if the suspension will cause, or is causing, you hardship.

Suspension on this ground is particularly common following appeals about the right to reside requirement. This is due to decision makers seeking to appeal to the Upper Tribunal against the First-tier Tribunal's decision, and the large number of ongoing cases about right to reside that are in the higher courts.

If your appeal concerns your rights under EU law (eg, your right to reside or the effect of the EU co-ordination rules), see below.

If your appeal concerns European law

If the issue in your appeal concerns EU law, you may be able to argue that your benefit or tax credit should not be suspended, or that you should receive some form of interim payment. It has been established in European caselaw that national governments cannot automatically refuse requests for interim relief to individuals seeking to exercise their rights under European law, and that national courts must be able to grant interim relief to ensure EU rights are respected.[94]

This argument could be used, for example, if the issue in your appeal is whether you have a right to reside in EU law (see Chapter 12) or whether you are entitled to benefit because of the EU co-ordination rules (see Chapter 16).

It may be possible to make this argument:

- if you are waiting for your appeal to be heard by the First-tier Tribunal. You may be able to argue that you should be paid a short-term advance or that you should receive some form of interim payment while waiting for your appeal. You must request a payment outside the benefit rules from the benefit authority, because its decision is that you are not entitled under these rules;
- if action on your appeal has been deferred (known as your appeal having been 'stayed', or, in Scotland, 'sisted') because there is a test case pending (see p346). You may be able to argue either that these rules deferring action should not be applied or that you should receive some form of interim payment until your appeal can be determined; *or*

- if you have won your First-tier Tribunal appeal and the decision maker suspends payment of your benefit or tax credit because s/he has appealed, or intends to appeal, to the Upper Tribunal. You may be able to argue that your benefit should not be suspended, or that you should receive some form of interim payment pending the further appeal.

If there is a difference of views between the relevant institutions in the UK and another EEA state over which state is the competent state under the EU co-ordination rules for paying your benefit or tax credit, you may be entitled to receive provisional payments (see p296).

Note: if your appeal concerns EU law, the benefit authorities can still lift the suspension on grounds of hardship.

Notes

2. Waiting for a decision on a claim

1 **WTC/CTC** s3 TCA 2002
   Other benefits s8(1)(a) SSA 1998
2 *SSHD v R (S)* [2007] EWCA Civ 546, para 51
3 *R v Secretary of State for Social Services and Chief Adjudication Officer ex parte Child Poverty Action Group* [1990] 2 QB 540
4 Reg 3(5)(b) SS&CS(DA) Regs
5 Reg 3(7) SS&CS(DA) Regs
6 HMRC, *Single Departmental Plan 2015-2020*
7 DWP, *Single Departmental Plan: 2015 to 2020 headline indicators technical detail*
8 Art 4 EU Reg 883/04; Arts 18 and 45 TFEU; Art 24 EU Dir 2004/38; Art 7 EU Reg 492/2011
9 www.cpag.org.uk/content/welcome-ask-cpag-online
10 DWP guidance, *Short Term Benefit Advances: benefit centres*, paras 3, 5, 55 and 80
11 Regs 5 and 6 SS(PAB) Regs
12 DWP guidance, *Short Term Benefit Advances: benefit centres*, paras 3, 5, 55 and 80
13 Reg 4(2) SS(PAB) Regs
14 Reg 3 SS(PAB) Regs
15 Reg 7 SS(PAB) Regs
16 DWP guidance, *Short Term Benefit Advances: benefit centres*, paras 22-23
17 Reg 7 SS(PAB) Regs; s137 SSCBA 1992
18 www.cpag.org.uk/content/welcome-ask-cpag-online
19 DWP guidance, *Short Term Benefit Advances: benefit centres*
20 DWP guidance, *Short Term Benefit Advances: benefit centres*, paras 3, 5, 55, 80 and 90
21 DWP guidance, *Short Term Benefit Advances: benefit centres*, paras 89-94
22 DWP guidance, *Short Term Benefit Advances: benefit centres*, para 93
23 DWP guidance, *Universal Credit Advances*, November 2015, p3
24 DWP guidance, *Short Term Benefit Advances: benefit centres*, para 35
25 Reg 8 SS(PAB) Regs
26 DWP guidance, *Universal Credit Advances*, November 2015, p3 (see also p13)
27 DWP guidance, *Short Term Benefit Advances: benefit centres*, para 29
28 DWP guidance, *Short Term Benefit Advances: benefit centres*, paras 16 and 29-32

29 DWP guidance, *Short Term Benefit Advances: benefit centres*, paras 175-181
30 Sch 2 para 20A SS&CS(DA) Regs allows a right of appeal against decisions on deductions under reg 10 SS(PAB) Regs.
31 Sch 2 para 20A SS&CS(DA) Regs
32 www.gov.uk/short-term-benefit-advance; DWP guidance, *Short Term Benefit Advances: benefit centres*, paras 193-95
33 Both available at www.cpag.org.uk/content/welcome-ask-cpag-online
34 DWP guidance, *Short Term Benefit Advances: benefit centres*, paras 17 and 72
35 DWP guidance, *Short Term Benefit Advances: benefit centres*, paras 7-11
36 DWP guidance, *Short Term Benefit Advances: benefit centres*, paras 66-67
37 DWP guidance, *Universal Credit Advances*, November 2015, p13 and *Short Term Benefit Advances: benefit centres*, paras 16, 29-32 and 175-181
38 Reg 22 CB&GA(Admin) Regs
39 Regs 22(3), 41 and 42 CB&GA(Admin) Regs
40 Reg 22(2) CB&GA(Admin) Regs
41 www.gov.uk/government/organisations/department-for-work-pensions/about/complaints-procedure
42 www.gov.uk/guidance/complain-to-hm-revenue-and-customs
43 www.cpag.org.uk/content/tax-credits-and-complaints
44 s5(1)(a) Parliamentary Commissioner Act 1967
45 www.justice.gov.uk/courts/procedure-rules/civil/protocol/prot_jrv
46 Reg 89 HB Regs; reg 70 HB(SPC) Regs
47 Reg 93(1) HB Regs; reg 74(1) HB(SPC) Regs
48 Reg 93(2) and (3) HB Regs; reg 74(2) and (3) HB(SPC) Regs
49 Reg 93(2) HB Regs; reg 74(2) HB(SPC) Regs
50 *R v Haringey London Borough Council ex parte Azad Ayub* [1992] 25 HLR 566 (QBD)
51 **HB** Sch 7 para 16 CSPSSA 2000
   Other benefits s25 SSA 1998
52 **HB** Sch 7 para 18(2) CSPSSA 2000
   Other benefits s27(2) SSA 1998

53 **HB** Sch 7 para 16(3) and (4) CSPSSA 2000; reg 15 HB&CTB(DA) Regs
   CB/GA s25(3) and (4) SSA 1998; reg 22 CB&GA(DA) Regs
   UC/PIP/JSA&ESA under UC s25(3) and (4) SSA 1998; reg 53 UC,PIP,JSA&ESA(DA) Regs
   Other benefits s25(3) and (4) SSA 1998; reg 21 SS&CS(DA) Regs

3. Delays when challenging a decision
54 s12(1), (2) and (3D) SSA 1998; r22(9)(b) TP(FT) Rules; HMRC Form CH24A, *What To Do If You Think Your Child Benefit or Guardian's Allowance Decision is Wrong*
55 s38(1A) TCA 2002
56 s12(2)(b) and (3A)-(3C) SSA 1998; reg 3ZA SS&CS(DA) Regs; reg 7 UC,PIP,JSA&ESA(DA) Regs; r22(9)(a) TP(FT) Rules
57 *MM v SSWP (PIP)* [2016] UKUT 36 (AAC)
58 Reg 3ZA SS&CS(DA) Regs; reg 7 UC,PIP,JSA&ESA(DA) Regs; r22(9)(a) TP(FT) Rules
59 s21A(2) TCA 2002; David Gauke MP, Exchequer Secretary to the Treasury, Eighth Delegated Legislation Committee, 26 March 2014
60 DWP response to Public Law Project's Freedom of Information request, 29 June 2017
61 DWP, *Employment and Support Allowance: outcomes of work capability assessments*, available on www.gov.uk
62 r2(2)(e) TP(FT) Rules
63 r24(1)(c) TP(FT) Rules
64 rr2, 5, 6 and 8 TP(FT) Rules
65 rr5(3)(a) and 6 TP(FT) Rules
66 r6(5) TP(FT) Rules
67 r24(1A) TP(FT) Rules
68 Art 6 European Convention on Human Rights; s6 HRA 1998; CH/3497/2005; *MB v Wychavon DC* [2013] UKUT 67 (AAC)
69 Complaint 01/C/13400 against Scarborough Borough Council
70 R(H) 1/07; *FH v Manchester City Council(HB)* [2010] UKUT 43 (AAC)
71 R(H) 1/07; *FH v Manchester City Council (HB)* [2010] UKUT 43 (AAC)
72 www.cpag.org.uk/sites/default/files/CPAG-How-to-expedite-social-security-appeal-Aug-13.pdf
73 r2(3)(a) TP(FT) Rules
74 ss15-21 TCEA 2007 and the Direction of the Lord Chief Justice on classes of cases specified under s18(6) TCEA 2007

75 ss20 and 21 TCEA 2007; Act of Sederunt (Transfer of Judicial Review Applications from the Court of Session) 2008, No.357; *Currie, Petitioner* [2009] CSOH 145, [2010] AACR 8; R(IB) 3/09
76 **HB** Sch 7 para 17 CSPSSA 2000
Other benefits s26 SSA 1998

4. Delays getting paid
77 **HB** Reg 91 HB Regs; reg 72 HB(SPC) Regs
UC/PIP/ESA&JSA under UC Reg 45 UC,PIP,JSA&ESA(C&P) Regs
WTC/CTC Regs 8 and 9 TC(PC) Regs
Other benefits Reg 20 SS(C&P) Regs
78 Vol 3, paras 08011-12 DMG; paras B1006-07 ADM; see also www.gov.uk/simple-payment
79 *Murdoch v DWP* [2010] EWHC 1988 (QB), paras 75-79; and for HB see *Jones v Waveney DC* [1999] 33 HLR 3
80 DWP, *Suspension and Termination Guide*, paras 1350, 2050-52 and 2301-02, www.gov.uk/government/uploads/system/uploads/attachment_data/file/424064/suspension-termination-guide.pdf
81 **HB** Reg 86(1) HB Regs; reg 67(1) HB(SPC) Regs
CB/GA Reg 23 CB&GA(Admin) Regs
UC/PIP/JSA&ESA under UC Reg 38(2) UC,PIP,JSA&ESA(C&P) Regs; reg 45 UC,PIP,JSA&ESA(DA) Regs
WTC/CTC s16(3) TCA 2002
Other benefits Reg 32(1) SS(C&P) Regs; reg 17 SS&CS(DA) Regs
82 **HB** Reg 13 HB&CTB(DA) Regs
CB/GA Reg 19 CB&GA(DA) Regs
UC/PIP/JSA&ESA under UC Reg 45(6) UC,PIP,JSA&ESA(DA) Regs
WTC/CTC Reg 11 TC(PC) Regs
Other benefits Reg 17(2) SS&CS(DA) Regs
83 **HB** Reg 11(2)(a)(i) HB&CTB(DA) Regs
CB/GA Reg 18(2)(a) CB&GA(DA) Regs
UC/PIP/JSA&ESA under UC Reg 44(2)(a)(i) UC,PIP,JSA&ESA(DA) Regs
WTC/CTC Reg 11(3A) TC(PC) Regs
Other benefits Reg 16(3)(a) SS&CS(DA) Regs
84 **HB** Reg 86(1) HB Regs; reg 67(1) HB(SPC) Regs
CB/GA Reg 23 CB&GA(Admin) Regs
UC/PIP/JSA&ESA under UC Reg 38(2) UC,PIP,JSA&ESA(C&P) Regs
WTC/CTC Reg 11(3A) TC(PC) Regs
Other benefits Reg 32(1) SS(C&P) Regs

85 **HB** Reg 13(4)(a) HB&CTB(DA) Regs
CB/GA Reg 19(2) CB&GA(DA) Regs
UC/PIP/JSA&ESA under UC Reg 45(4)(a) UC,PIP,JSA&ESA(DA) Regs
WTC/CTC Reg 32 TC(CN) Regs
Other benefits Reg 17(4)(a) SS&CS(DA) Regs
86 **HB** Reg 13(4)(b) HB&CTB(DA) Regs
CB/GA Reg 19(2)(b) CB&GA(DA) Regs
UC/PIP/JSA&ESA under UC Reg 45(4)(b) UC,PIP,JSA&ESA(DA) Regs
WTC/CTC HMRC leaflet, *Tax Credits: suspension of payments*, WTC/FS9, April 2017
Other benefits Reg 17(4)(b) SS&CS(DA) Regs
87 **HB** Reg 13(4) HB&CTB(DA) Regs
CB/GA Reg 19(5) CB&GA(DA) Regs
UC/PIP/JSA&ESA under UC Reg 45(6) UC,PIP,JSA&ESA(DA) Regs
Other benefits Reg 17(5) SS&CS(DA) Regs
88 Reg 11 TC(PC) Regs
89 **HB** Sch 7 para 13(2) CSPSSA 2000; reg 11(2)(b) HB&CTB(DA) Regs
CB/GA Reg 18(3) CB&GA(DA) Regs
WTC/CTC Reg 11 TC(PC) Regs
Other benefits s21(2)(c) and (d) SSA 1998; reg 16(3)(b) SS&CS(DA) Regs; reg 44(2)(b) and (c) UC,PIP,JSA&ESA(DA) Regs
90 TCM 0014360 Step 1
91 **HB** Reg 11(3) HB&CTB(DA) Regs
CB/GA Reg 18(4) and (5) CB&GA(DA) Regs
Other benefits Reg 16(4) SS&CS(DA) Regs; reg 44(5) UC,PIP,JSA&ESA(DA) Regs
92 **HB** Reg 12(1)(b) HB&CTB(DA) Regs
CB/GA Reg 21 CB&GA(DA) Regs
Other benefits Reg 20(2) and (3) SS&CS(DA) Regs; reg 46(b) and (c) UC,PIP,JSA&ESA(DA) Regs
93 DWP, *Suspension and Termination Guide*, paras 2050-52 and 2354
94 *The Queen v Secretary of State for Transport ex parte Factortame and Others*, C-213/89 [1990] ECR I-02433, para 23; *Unibet (London) Ltd and Unibet (International) Ltd v Justitiekanslern*, C-432/05 [2007] ECR I-02271, especially para 77; see also *obiter* (not binding) comments in *R (Sanneh) v SSWP and HMRC* [2013] EWHC 793 (Admin), paras 104-14

Chapter 19

· ·

National insurance numbers

This chapter covers:
1. The national insurance number requirement (below)
2. Obtaining a national insurance number (p357)
3. Common problems (p360)

This chapter covers the rules on the national insurance number requirement for benefits and tax credits and the issues that arise in satisfying this, particularly if you or a member of your family are not British.

1. The national insurance number requirement

In general, in order to be entitled to any social security benefit or tax credit, or, in England and Wales, council tax reduction (see p457), you must satisfy the national insurance (NI) number requirement.[1] This means that you and any partner included in your claim must:

- provide an NI number, together with evidence to show that it is the one allocated to you; *or*
- provide evidence or information to enable your NI number to be traced; *or*
- make an application for an NI number, accompanied with sufficient information or evidence for one to be allocated. There is no requirement for an NI number to have been allocated to you.

Certain groups of people are exempt from the requirement (see p355).

If you live in a universal credit (UC) 'gateway area', in order to come under the UC system you (and your partner) must meet certain gateway conditions, including that you (and s/he) have an NI number and also that you (and s/he) are British. This is the only benefit that requires you to actually have a NI number as a condition of entitlement (see p360).

Note:
- The NI number requirement is only one requirement that must be satisfied as part of making a valid claim. For general information on the main

requirements, see p365. For detailed information on the requirements for each benefit and tax credit, see CPAG's *Welfare Benefits and Tax Credits Handbook*.
* You, and any person included in your application, must satisfy the NI number requirement to be entitled to council tax reduction (except in Scotland) (see p460).[2]

When the requirement applies

The NI requirement applies when you make a claim for benefit. It also applies when someone who will be included in an existing award of benefit joins your family – eg, if your partner joins you from abroad.[3]

The requirement applies to you, and also to your partner if you are claiming means-tested benefits or tax credits as a couple.[4]

This is the case even if, for income support (IS), income-based jobseeker's allowance (JSA), or income-related employment and support allowance (ESA), you are not going to receive any extra benefit for her/him because s/he is a 'person subject to immigration control' for benefit purposes.[5]

The situation is different, however, if your partner is not included in your claim, which can be the case for universal credit (UC) and pension credit (PC). For UC, if your partner is defined as a person subject to immigration control (and not in an exempt group), you must claim UC as a single person and, consequently, your partner does not need to satisfy the NI requirement. (**Note:** your partner's income and capital still affect your UC entitlement). If you are claiming PC and your partner is a person subject to immigration control, s/he is treated as not being part of your household and so does not need to satisfy the NI requirement.

For the definition of 'person subject to immigration control', see p57, and for more information about your entitlement if your partner is a person subject to immigration control, see p74 for means-tested benefits and p77 for tax credits.

See p356 for when your partner does not have to satisfy the NI number requirement.

Who is exempt

You do not need to satisfy the NI number requirement:
* if you are under 16 and you are claiming disability living allowance;[6]
* for statutory sick pay, statutory maternity pay, statutory paternity pay, statutory shared parental pay, statutory adoption pay or a social fund payment;[7]
* for housing benefit (HB) if you live in a hostel;[8]
* for tax credits if you have a 'reasonable excuse' for failing to satisfy the requirement (see p356).[9]

If a child or qualifying young person is included in your claim for HB or UC, or still included in your award of IS or income-based JSA, s/he does not need to satisfy the NI number requirement.[10]

If you are the benefit claimant and your partner is included in your claim, your partner does not have to satisfy the NI number requirement if:[11]

- s/he is a 'person subject to immigration control' because s/he requires leave to enter or remain in the UK, but does not have it (see p58); *and*
- s/he has not previously been given an NI number; *and*
- you are claiming IS, income-based JSA, income-related ESA or PC and your partner is not entitled to that benefit her/himself, or you are claiming HB and your partner fails the 'habitual residence test' (see p106). However, in practice, it is difficult to see who could satisfy the first bullet point and not satisfy this.

You may still be asked for information about an NI number application for your partner, even though s/he is exempt. An NI number will then be refused, but this does not prevent you from being entitled to benefits or tax credits or council tax reduction.[12]

Note:

- The above exemption for partners does not apply to UC. This is because if your partner is defined as a 'person subject to immigration control' because s/he requires leave, you must claim UC as a single person and your partner is not required to have an NI number.[13]
- The above exemption for partners, and the exemption for a child or qualifying young person included in your claim, also applies to your application for council tax reduction in England or Wales (see p460).[14]
- Any of the above exemptions that apply to someone in respect of whom benefit is claimed, do not apply to the claimant. For example if you are a child claiming HB you are not exempt from the NI number requirement even though a child included in the claim is exempt.[15]

Tax credits

The NI number requirement for tax credits is as described above, including the exemption for partners who require leave but do not have it. If you live with your partner, you must make a joint claim for tax credits and both of you must satisfy the NI number requirement unless one of you is exempt.

However, the NI number requirement does not apply if the Tax Credit Office is satisfied that you (and/or your partner if it is a joint claim) have a 'reasonable excuse' for not complying with it.[16] A 'reasonable excuse' is not defined: whether or not the Tax Credit Office is satisfied that you have one is a matter of discretion. Guidance to decision makers stresses that their discretionary decision must be reasonable, which includes being fair and taking into account all relevant considerations, including available evidence.[17] A 'reasonable excuse' could include if you are unable to prove your identity because the Home Office has all your documents and you can show this – eg, with a letter from your solicitor.

If the decision maker decides that you have not made a valid claim because you have not satisfied the NI number requirement and you believe you had a reasonable excuse for not doing so, you can appeal against that decision.[18] You must request a 'mandatory reconsideration' of the decision first.

2. Obtaining a national insurance number

The DWP allocates all national insurance (NI) numbers.

NI numbers are allocated automatically to children shortly before their 16th birthday, provided child benefit is being claimed for them. If child benefit was being claimed for you when you were that age, you should have an NI number. If you are under 20, you were in the UK when you turned 16 and you did not receive an NI number, you can phone HM Revenue and Customs (HMRC) (tel: 0300 200 3500).

If you have been allocated an NI number but do not know what it is, or if you want written confirmation of your NI number, you should complete Form CA5403 (available online[19]) and send it to HMRC. If you attend your Jobcentre Plus office with evidence of your identity, a member of staff may be able to tell you what your NI number is.

If you do not have an NI number, see p358.

DWP guidance on tracing or allocating an NI number is available online. As the procedures are often misunderstood and/or not followed, it can be helpful to refer to this. The guidance is split into documents covering specific groups or circumstances, and stages of the procedures. All these are available on one website and all the DWP guidance referred to in this chapter can be found there.[20]

NI number applications may be completed as part of the process of applying for immigration leave and/or a biometric immigration document. Guidance for immigration officers covers the procedures for completing an NI number application during an asylum interview, forwarding the application to the DWP if leave is granted, and notifying you of the NI number if one is allocated.[21] DWP guidance covers the procedures for tracing or allocating an NI number at the request of the Home Office to enable it to be included in the biometric immigration document.[22] These procedures are not always followed and do not always result in an NI number being allocated.

If an NI number has been allocated before a biometric immigration document is issued, it may be included on this document.[23] If you have not been allocated an NI number as part of the process of your immigration application, you should apply for an NI number in the usual way (see p358).

Guidance to claimants who have been granted leave following an asylum application confirms you should receive written notification of your NI number, but also that if you have not you should make your benefit claim as you do not need an NI number to claim benefits.[24]

Applying for a national insurance number

If you have not been allocated an NI number, you can apply for one by telephoning the NI number application line on 0345 600 0643 or by contacting your local Jobcentre Plus office.

There are a number of reasons why you may need an NI number, including for employment purposes, for a student loan, to open an Individual Savings Account (ISA), or to claim benefits or tax credits.[25]

If you do not have an NI number, you do not need to obtain one before you make your benefit or tax credit claim, unless you are claiming UC in a 'gateway' area (see p360).[26]

If you claim a benefit or tax credit, or you apply for a supersession of an award of benefit (eg, to include your partner), when you (or s/he) do not have an NI number, the DWP, HMRC or local authority should complete Form DCI1 and send it to the NI number centre.[27] This counts as your having made an application for an NI number. It is advisable to state clearly on the form or letter that you do not have an NI number and you wish to apply for one when you make your claim for benefit or when you notify the benefit authority that your family member has joined you.

Note: if your partner is a 'person subject to immigration control' because s/he has leave which is subject to a 'no recourse to public funds' condition and s/he is included in your claim, s/he can be allocated an NI number even if you do not receive an increased personal allowance for her/him.[28] (For details of when you are paid for your partner who is a 'person subject to immigration control', see p74).

When the NI number centre receives Form DCI1, it carries out a number of checks to ensure that you do not already have an NI number. It should then contact you to arrange an interview at your local DWP office if this is required (usually the case for European Economic Area (EEA) nationals), otherwise the application can be done by post (often the case for non-EEA nationals who have leave to enter or remain in the UK, or if the claimant or partner included in the claim is living outside the UK). The interview is generally referred to as an 'evidence of identity interview'. DWP guidance states that whether or not you have a right to work in the UK is 'not a consideration' when this interview is carried out.[29]

You should be told what documents to take to your interview. It is important to take as many as possible that establish your identity. The www.gov.uk website on applying for a NI number gives the following non-exhaustive list of examples of documents that prove your identity:[30]

- passport;
- identity card;
- residence permit;
- birth or adoption certificate;

- marriage or civil partnership certificate;
- driving licence.

If you have any of these documents, take them to your interview. If not, take any documents you do have that could help prove your identity. These could include:
- an immigration status document;
- a biometric immigration document;
- Form NASS35 or another document confirming the end of your asylum support;
- a current travel document issued by any national government, including the UK;
- a residence document issued to EEA nationals (see p375);
- a certificate of registration or naturalisation as a British citizen;
- a standard acknowledgement letter issued by the Home Office;
- an application registration card issued by the Home Office to an asylum seeker;
- an expired passport, travel document or EEA identity card;
- a local authority rent book or card;
- a tenancy agreement;
- council tax documents;
- life assurance/insurance policies;
- mortgage repayment documents;
- recent fuel or telephone bills in your name;
- divorce or annulment papers;
- civil partnership dissolution or annulment papers;
- a wage slip from a recent employer;
- a trade union membership card;
- a travel pass with photograph affixed;
- vehicle registration or insurance documents;
- a work permit.

These are only some of the documents that you can use to prove your identity. If you have other documents that are not in the above list, these may also help. Photocopies of documents can be relied on to establish your identity, but you should take the originals if you have them. If not, explain why you do not have the original documents. For example, if some of your documents are with the Home Office, explain this and, if possible, provide proof in the form of a solicitor's letter or some other evidence. The DWP should not ask you to provide documents which you obviously do not possess.

If you are unable to provide any documentary evidence of your identity (eg, because you are homeless or fleeing domestic violence), a holistic approach should be taken and a decision made on the information which you are able to provide.

At the interview, you are asked to complete Form CA5400. The DWP may also ask you to complete a form allowing it to contact third parties to establish your identity.

An NI number might be refused for various reasons – eg, if you:

- have been unable to prove your identity;
- have failed to provide sufficient information;
- provided identity documents that are considered not genuine;
- failed to attend an evidence of identity interview (you should be given two opportunities to attend[31]); *or*
- failed to respond to correspondence.

If your application for an NI number is refused, the reason should be recorded and notified to you.

You cannot appeal directly against a decision not to allocate you an NI number.[32] However, you can appeal against any decision refusing benefit because the NI number requirement is not met (see p362).

3. **Common problems**

Migrants often have problems with the national insurance (NI) number requirement because, unlike most British citizens, they are not issued with an NI number when they turn 16. The three most common problems are:

- being told you cannot apply for benefit unless you have an NI number (see below);
- delays in benefit because of the NI number requirement (see p361);
- being refused benefit on the grounds that the NI number requirement is not met (see p362).

Making a claim

If you (or your partner if s/he is included in your claim) do not have an NI number, you may be told by Jobcentre Plus, HM Revenue and Customs or the local authority that you cannot claim a benefit or tax credit. This is only correct if you are claiming universal credit (UC) in a 'gateway' area (see below). Similarly, you may find it impossible to claim online if you cannot provide an NI number.

If you live in a UC 'gateway' area, in order to come under the UC system you (and your partner) must meet certain gateway conditions. These include having an NI number and being British.[33] If you (and your partner) do not satisfy the gateway conditions, you do not come under the UC system, you cannot claim UC but you can instead claim one of the benefits that UC replaces.

For more details on the roll-out of UC, including all the gateway conditions, see CPAG's *Welfare Benefits and Tax Credits Handbook*.

For all other claims, including for UC in a 'full service' area, you do not need an NI number in order to claim a benefit or tax credit. You can satisfy the NI number requirement by applying for an NI number and accompanying your application with sufficient information or evidence for one to be allocated (see p354). You should not be prevented from making a claim for benefit and it should be treated as the first stage in your application for an NI number (see p354).[34]

For all benefits except UC, if you are unable to make your claim online because you do not have an NI number, you should be able to claim by telephone or on a paper claim form.

There are no paper claim forms for UC, as it is intended that all UC claims will be made online. Although the regulations allow for a telephone claim to be accepted if the DWP is willing to do so,[35] in practice the DWP tends to advise you to use a computer at your local job centre or local support service.

At the time of writing, an NI number was not required to make a claim in a 'full service area'. On receiving your claim, the DWP usually arranges for you to provide further information in support of it by attending a meeting with a work coach. You are likely to be asked to take proof of your identity and other information relevant to your entitlement to this meeting.

Have you been told you cannot apply for benefit because you do not have a national insurance number?

If you have lost benefit entitlement because you were prevented from making a claim because you did not have an NI number, you may be able to get a new claim backdated. If the rules for the benefit or tax credit you are claiming do not allow backdating at all, or for the full period, or if the arrears do not cover the full amount lost, consider requesting compensation. For the rules on backdating and further information on obtaining compensation, see CPAG's *Welfare Benefits and Tax Credits Handbook*.

Delays

Payment of benefit or tax credits can often be delayed because you (or your partner) need to satisfy the NI number requirement or you are waiting for an NI number to be allocated.

Is your benefit delayed?

1. Check whether you or your partner are exempt from the requirement to have an NI number (see p355).

2. If you or your partner have applied for an NI number, but there is a delay in one being allocated, ask that your claim be determined, as there is no requirement for a number to be allocated (see p354). It is likely that your claim will have to be processed clerically before the NI number has been allocated, but this should not prevent payment.

3. If it is a new claim for benefit, or you are adding a partner to your claim that will result in your award increasing, you may be able to obtain a short-term advance (see p329). This can be paid if you do not have an NI number, provided you meet the usual conditions, including that the decision maker considers it likely you will be entitled to the benefit.[36] The guidance on short-term advances states they should be considered if you do not have an NI number, provided you can prove your identity and are complying with other requests for evidence. This guidance also states that the DWP should ensure that all action needed to allocate an NI number is taken promptly.[37] Applying for a short-term advance may therefore be a way of getting your NI number allocated more quickly.

4. If you have made a new claim for child benefit and/or guardian's allowance, you may be able to obtain an interim payment (see p333).

5. If you have made a new claim for housing benefit (HB), you may be able to obtain a 'payment on account' (see p338).

6. If you are adding your partner to your existing claim and s/he does not have an NI number, your benefit may be suspended (see p348). You may be able to argue that payment should not be suspended if it is clear that the NI number requirement is likely to be met and the only factor is a question of time.

For further information on your options if your benefit or tax credit payments are delayed, see Chapter 18.

Benefit is refused

You cannot appeal against a decision not to allocate you an NI number.[38] However, if you are refused benefit or tax credits (or are refused an increase when your partner joins your household) because you (or s/he) do not satisfy the NI number requirement, you can ask for a mandatory reconsideration of the decision and then appeal if the decision is not changed. For HB, you can appeal directly or ask for a revision and then appeal if the decision is not changed. In your mandatory reconsideration, revision and appeal, you can argue that the NI number requirement was met.[39]

Usually, if benefit is refused because the benefit authority says the NI number requirement is not met, the issue in dispute is whether your application was accompanied by sufficient information or evidence to enable a number to be allocated, even if the benefit authority has not considered this point.[40]

Even if you have been refused an NI number, it is possible to argue successfully that you still satisfy the NI number requirement if your application was accompanied by sufficient information or evidence to enable a number to be allocated. However, the law is unclear about whether you can satisfy the NI number requirement if you have not attended an interview,[41] or if you must have attended an interview and completed and signed Form CA5400.[42] If you have been refused an NI number after failing to attend an interview, the reasons why you failed to attend are relevant.[43]

Have you been refused tax credits?
If the decision maker decides you have not made a valid claim for tax credits because you or your partner do not satisfy the NI number requirement, you can challenge this decision. The Upper Tribunal has held that you have a right of appeal if the basis of your appeal is that your partner is exempt from the NI number requirement because s/he requires leave to enter or remain in the UK but does not have it (see p355).[44] In a subsequent case, the Upper Tribunal went further and held that there is also a right of appeal if you or your partner had a reasonable excuse for not satisfying the NI number requirement (see p356).[45] You must request a mandatory reconsideration before you can appeal.

Other remedies

If you are refused an NI number, you can write to your MP and ask her/him to help. Your MP can also complain to the Parliamentary and Health Service Ombudsman on your behalf. See CPAG's *Welfare Benefits and Tax Credits Handbook* for more information.

Problems with NI numbers also raise issues about race discrimination since, in practice, the NI number requirement often prejudices black and minority ethnic communities. You may therefore want to refer to the DWP's Equality and Diversity statement when you contact it.[46] The Equality Advisory and Support Service may be able to advise or, in certain cases, take up the issue (see Appendix 2).

Notes

1. **The national insurance number requirement**
   1 **TC** Reg 5(4) TC(CN) Regs
     CB/GA s13(1A) and (1B) SSAA 1992
     Other benefits s1(1A) and (1B) SSAA 1992
   2 **E** Sch 8 para 7 CTRS(PR)E Regs
     W Sch para 111 CTRS(DS)W Regs; Sch 13 para 5 CTRSPR(W) Regs
   3 s1(1A) and (1B) SSAA 1992; reg 5(4) TC(CN) Regs; *Leicester City Council v OA* [2009] UKUT 74 (AAC), paras 27 and 28
   4 s1(1A) SSAA 1992; reg 5(4) TC(CN) Regs
   5 *SSWP v Wilson* [2006] EWCA Civ 882, reported as R(H) 7/06

   6 Reg 1A SS(DLA) Regs
   7 s1(4) SSAA 1992 and s122 SSCBA 1992
   8 Reg 4(a) HB Regs; reg 4(a) HB(SPC) Regs
   9 Reg 5(6) TC(CN) Regs
   10 **IS** Reg 2A(a) IS Regs has continued effect in these cases due to the transitional protection in reg 1(3) SS(WTCCTC)(CA) Regs
     JSA Reg 2A(a) JSA Regs has continued effect in these cases due to the transitional protection in reg 1(7) SS(WTCCTC)(CA) Regs
     HB Reg 4(b) HB Regs; reg 4(b) HB(SPC) Regs
     UC Reg 5 UC,PIP,JSA&ESA(C&P) Regs

11 **IS** Reg 2A IS Regs
JSA Reg 2A JSA Regs
ESA Reg 2A ESA Regs
PC Reg 1A SPC Regs
HB Reg 4(c) HB Regs; reg 4(c) HB(SPC)
Regs
TC Reg 5(8) TC(CN) Regs
**Bereavement benefits and
retirement pensions** Reg 1A(c)
SS(WB&RP) Regs
12 Vol 1, paras 02184-86 DMG; Ch A2,
para A2153 ADM; TCTM 06110
13 Ch A2, para A2154 ADM
14 **E** Sch 8 para 7(3) CTRS(PR)E Regs
W Sch para 111(3) CTRS(DS)W Regs;
Sch 13 para 5(3) CTRSPR(W) Regs
15 *Westminster City Council v AT & SSWP
(HB)* [2013] UKUT 321 (AAC)
16 Reg 5(6) TC(CN) Regs
17 TCTM 06110
18 *CI v HMRC (TC)* [2014] UKUT 158 (AAC)

2. Obtaining a national insurance number
19 On www.gov.uk/lost-national-
insurance-number
20 www.gov.uk/government/publications/
national-insurance-number-allocations-
staff-guide
21 Home Office guidance, *Procedures for
Issuing a NINO to Asylum Claimants
Granted Leave to Enter or Remain in the
UK*, available on www.gov.uk
22 DWP guidance, *Home Office Biometric
Residence Permit Verification Allocation:
in-country allocation process; Home Office
Biometric Residence Permit Verification
Allocation: in-country trace process; Home
Office Biometric Residence Permit
Verification Allocation: out of country
allocation process,* available on
www.gov.uk
23 Reg 15 The Immigration (Biometric
Registration) Regulations 2008,
No.3048, as amended by reg 13
Immigration (Biometric Registration)
(Amendment) Regulations 2015,
No.433
24 www.gov.uk/government/publications/
refugees-guidance-about-benefits-and-
pensions/help-available-from-the-
department-for-work-and-pensions-
for-people-who-have-been-granted-
leave-to-remain-in-the-uk para 8
25 www.gov.uk/national-insurance/your-
national-insurance-number; DWP
guidance, *Introduction to National
Insurance Number Allocation,* para 13
26 Sch 5 WRA(No.9)O

27 CH/4085/2007; HB/CTB Circular A13/
2010, paras 14 and 15; TCM 0066140
and 0316020; DWP guidance, *Benefit
Inspired Evidence of Identity (DCI1
Process)* and *Contact Centre Appointment
Booking Process,* para 92, and *Completing
the DCI1 Form,* all available on
www.gov.uk.
28 DWP guidance, *Completing the EDCI1
Form,* para 43, scenario 1
29 DWP guidance, *Benefit Inspired Evidence
of Identity (DCI1 Process),* para 23
30 www.gov.uk/apply-national-insurance-
number
31 DWP guidance, *Benefit Inspired Evidence
of Identity (DCI1 Process),* para 19
32 CH/4085/2007, paras 19-22; *Leicester
City Council v OA* [2009] UKUT 74 (AAC),
para 33

3. Common problems
33 All 'gateway' conditions are listed in Sch
5 WRA(No.9)O, as applied in UC areas
by subsequent commencement orders
34 CH/4085/2007; HB/CTB Circular A13/
2010, paras 14 and 15; TCM 0066140
and 0316020; DWP guidance, *Benefit
Inspired Evidence of Identity (DCI1
process)* and *Contact Centre Appointment
Booking Process,* para 92 and *Completing
the EDCI1 Form;* www.gov.uk/
government/publications/refugees-
guidance-about-benefits-and-pensions/
help-available-from-the-department-
for-work-and-pensions-for-people-who-
have-been-granted-leave-to-remain-
in-the-uk, para 8
35 Reg 8 UC,PIP,JSA&ESA(C&P) Regs; para
A2030 ADM
36 Reg 5 SS(PAB) Regs
37 DWP guidance, *Short Term Benefit
Advances: benefit centres,* paras 66-67
38 CH/4085/2007, paras 19-22; *Leicester
City Council v OA* [2009] UKUT 74 (AAC),
para 33
39 CH/1231/2004; CH/4085/2007;
Leicester City Council v OA [2009] UKUT
74 (AAC)
40 CH/1231/2004
41 CH/4085/2007, para 30
42 *Leicester City Council v OA* [2009] UKUT
74 (AAC), para 35
43 CH/4085/2007, para 32
44 *ZM and AB v HMRC (TC)* [2013] UKUT
547 (AAC)
45 *CI v HMRC (TC)* [2014] UKUT 158 (AAC)
46 www.gov.uk/government/
organisations/department-for-work-
pensions/about/equality-and-diversity

Chapter 20

Providing evidence

This chapter covers:
1. General points about evidence (below)
2. Evidence of immigration status (p373)
3. Evidence of residence rights (p374)
4. Types of evidence (p376)

This chapter covers some of the issues that arise when you are required to provide evidence to show that you satisfy the immigration conditions (see Part 3), the residence conditions (see Part 4) or that you are covered by the European Union co-ordination rules (see Chapter 16).

1. General points about evidence

There are some issues and principles that apply to the evidence you may be asked to provide, or that you should provide, when you make a claim for a benefit or tax credit, or when you challenge a decision about your entitlement.

Evidence required when you make your claim

When you claim a benefit or tax credit, you must normally:
- satisfy the national insurance (NI) number requirement (see Chapter 19); *and*
- provide proof of your identity, if required (see below); *and*
- ensure your claim is valid (see p366).

To determine your claim, the decision maker needs evidence that you satisfy all the conditions of entitlement (see p367) and that you are not covered by any of the exceptions that mean you are not entitled (see p367). You can be asked for evidence to show that you satisfy all the conditions of entitlement, including the immigration, residence or presence conditions, or that the European Union (EU) co-ordination rules apply to you.

Proving your identity

You may be asked to produce further documents or evidence that prove your identity. If your partner is included in your claim, even if you do not receive an amount for her/him (eg, because s/he is a 'person subject to immigration control' – see p74), you may also be asked to prove her/his identity. In addition, if your claim includes an amount for your child, you may be asked to prove her/his identity.

There are various documents that you can provide to the benefit authorities as proof of your identity. You should not be required to supply any document which is unreasonable for you to have or obtain, and you should not be refused a benefit or tax credit simply because you can not provide a particular document.

The www.gov.uk website on applying for an NI number has a list of examples of documents that prove your identity, and you should provide one or more of these if possible. For these and other documents that could be used to prove your identity, see p358. It can be helpful to provide details of anyone who can confirm what you have stated – eg, your solicitor or other legal representative or official organisation.

Note: if you are claiming universal credit, you may be required to prove your identity online using the gov.uk/verify system. This uses various private companies to check your identity. You should not be prevented from making your claim just because you do not have the preferred form of proof.[1] If you cannot prove your identity online, the DWP requires you to do so in person at the job centre.

Making a valid claim

To be entitled to a benefit or tax credit, you must make a valid claim. This means you must claim in the correct way and your claim must not be 'defective'. The DWP, HM Revenue and Customs (HMRC) or the local authority should inform you if your claim is defective and must then give you the opportunity to correct the defect.

What counts as a valid claim varies between the individual benefits and tax credits. What you are required to do to make your claim in the correct way is also affected by the method by which you can make your claim – ie, in writing, only on a certain form, online and/or also by telephone. You may also have to attend an interview to complete your claim, or be sent a written statement to sign and return. The rules for each benefit and tax credit are covered in CPAG's *Welfare Benefits and Tax Credits Handbook*.

If your claim is refused because it is not valid, you can challenge that decision.

Note: your right to challenge a decision that your claim for tax credits is not valid is based on caselaw, rather than legislation.[2] The relevant case concerned a claim that was not accepted as valid because it did not satisfy the NI number requirement (see p362), but the principle that there is a right of appeal (after a mandatory reconsideration) also applies when a claim is not accepted as valid for a different reason.

In all cases, if you challenge a decision that your claim is not valid, you should also make a fresh claim.

If your claim is accepted as valid, the decision maker must make a decision on your entitlement. However, even if your claim has been accepted as valid, you may still be required to provide additional documentation and evidence. If you fail to do so within the time allowed (this can be extended if it is reasonable), adverse conclusions can be drawn (but see below).

Evidence that you are entitled

When you claim a benefit or tax credit you must generally show, on the balance of probabilities, that you meet the conditions of entitlement.[3] If you do not meet these under the UK rules, but the EU co-ordination rules (see Chapter 16) enable you to be entitled, you must provide evidence of this.

The inquisitorial nature of benefit adjudication means that decision makers, who know what information and evidence is needed to decide whether you satisfy the conditions of entitlement, must ask you for that information. If you have been asked for information or evidence and fail, to the best of your abilities, to provide it, the decision maker can assume that you do not meet that particular condition of entitlement. However, the decision maker cannot do this if s/he fails to ask the relevant questions and does not give you a reasonable opportunity to provide the necessary information and evidence.[4]

If you have documentary evidence showing that you meet the entitlement conditions, you should always submit it because it corroborates and reinforces your evidence. However, if you cannot do so, your own evidence, given in the process of making your claim or subsequently, can be accepted without its being corroborated.

Corroborative evidence is not necessary unless there are reasons to doubt your evidence – eg, if it is self-contradictory or inherently improbable.[5]

If you are asked for a particular document that you do not have, ask why this is needed so that you have the opportunity to provide alternatives. If you cannot provide any documentary proof of a particular fact, explain why not (eg, because all your documents are with the Home Office) and, if possible, provide proof of this – eg, a letter from your legal representative. If you consider any requests for information are unreasonable, you can complain. Get advice if you think you have experienced discrimination – eg, from the Equality Advisory and Support Service (see Appendix 2).

Evidence that you are not excluded

If there is an exception to entitlement that excludes you from a benefit or a tax credit to which you would otherwise be entitled (eg, because you are not habitually resident or because you are defined as a 'person subject to immigration control'), the burden of proving that this exception applies to you lies with the relevant benefit authority.[6]

If you have evidence that an exception does not apply to you, you should always submit this.

If you do not provide evidence that you are not excluded from entitlement when you make your claim, the decision maker must ask you for the information and evidence required for her/him to make a decision. Because the process of benefit adjudication is inquisitorial, rather than adversarial, the decision maker knows what information is required to determine whether you are entitled to benefit or whether you are excluded from entitlement, and the decision maker must therefore ask for that information.[7]

If some relevant facts are still unknown after all the enquiries have been made, the question of whether an exception applies that excludes you from entitlement should be decided in your favour.[8]

If the decision maker failed to ask all the relevant questions, the First-tier Tribunal must ask you those questions (it also has an inquistorial role).[9] However, if you have evidence that an exception to entitlement does not apply to you, submit this in advance of the hearing if possible.

If you cannot provide the evidence required to determine whether or not you are excluded, but that evidence is available to the benefit authorities, see p371.

Decisions to end your entitlement

If you are receiving benefits or tax credits and the benefit authority terminates your award on the basis that you no longer satisfy the immigration, residence or presence rules, the burden of proof is on the benefit authority to show the evidence on which this decision is based. If the decision maker has not shown this and based her/his decision on the fact that you failed to provide evidence that nothing has changed, you should challenge the decision, pointing out that the burden of proof lies with the benefit authority. However, you should still set out clearly the reasons why you are not excluded from entitlement by the rules.

The same burden of proof also applies to the First-tier Tribunal.

There are a number of Upper Tribunal decisions concerning tax credits that confirm that the burden of proof is on HMRC to establish that there are grounds for revising a decision that you are entitled to tax credits, and that the same burden of proof applies to the First-tier Tribunal. This applies if HMRC wants to revise an entitlement decision:

- for the current year. HMRC must show the evidence for its 'reasonable grounds for believing' that the decision is wrong;[10] *and*
- for a previous year for which the award has already been finalised.[11]

However, if HMRC decides that you have ceased to be entitled during the tax credit renewal period, the onus of proof is on you to show your continued entitlement.[12]

Example

Nardos is an Eritrean national with discretionary leave to remain in the UK, with no restriction on receiving public funds, for two and a half years. She claimed child tax credit (CTC), provided proof of her leave and was awarded CTC. Her leave was due to expire two months ago, but before it did Nardos applied for a further period of discretionary leave. She received an acknowledgement letter from the Home Office, and forwarded a copy of this to the Tax Credit Office, but has not yet had a decision from the Home Office. Her discretionary leave to remain is extended while she waits for the Home Office to decide her application for further leave (see p374).

The Tax Credit Office wrote to Nardos asking her to provide evidence that she was entitled to receive public funds – both now and since the start of her claim. Nardos did not know how she could show this and so did not reply. She then received a decision letter, informing her that, as she has not shown she can receive public funds, HMRC has decided she is a 'person subject to immigration control' (see p57) and not entitled to CTC. Her award was terminated and HMRC decided to recover the overpaid CTC since the start of her claim.

Nardos can challenge this decision, by requesting a mandatory reconsideration. HMRC has not provided any evidence to show that her entitlement has ended, nor that the original decision awarding her CTC was incorrect. The evidence that Nardos had already given HMRC shows that she has leave to remain in the UK with no restriction on receiving public funds. She does not need to provide any further evidence that she is not excluded by her immigration status because it has not changed. She should explain this in her mandatory reconsideration request and remind HMRC that the Upper Tribunal has confirmed that the onus of proof is on HMRC to show the evidence relied upon in its decision that she is not entitled to CTC and has not been since the start of her claim.

For information on when a decision to award you benefits or tax credits can be revised or superseded, see CPAG's *Welfare Benefits and Tax Credits Handbook*.

If you make another benefit claim

A decision that you do or do not satisfy the immigration status, residence or presence requirements, or that the EU co-ordination rules do, or do not, apply to you for one benefit claim is not conclusive if you make another claim, either for a different benefit or for the same benefit but at a later date.[13] However, it is a factor that should be taken into account.

There are limited exceptions to this, including if you claim housing benefit (HB) and the DWP has made a decision to award you income support (IS), income-related employment and support allowance or pension credit. In this case, you are exempt from the habitual residence test for the purpose of HB (see p108).

In practice, if you have had a successful benefit claim, mandatory reconsideration or appeal, it is helpful to tell this to the decision maker or First-tier Tribunal that is considering a separate claim. If you have a written notice of a decision, provide a copy to support your case, even if you think the decision maker already has access to this. If some time has passed since the earlier decision, explain why it is still relevant to your current situation.

Example

Carmen is a Spanish national and in 2015 she claimed IS. Her claim was initially refused on the grounds that she did not satisfy the habitual residence test, but was subsequently awarded IS after she requested a mandatory reconsideration. The decision maker decided that Carmen satisfied the right to reside part of the habitual residence test because she had acquired a permanent right to reside as a result of having worker status in the UK from 2009 to 2015. When her daughter turns five, Carmen is no longer entitled to IS and so she makes a new claim for universal credit (UC). She submits a copy of the IS mandatory reconsideration decision to the UC decision maker, together with evidence that she has not been out of the UK for a continuous period of two years to show that she has not lost her right of permanent residence (see p108).

If a decision on a previous claim was not favourable to you and you make a separate claim, or challenge a refusal of a separate claim, it may be helpful to remind the decision maker (or tribunal) that the earlier decision does not prevent her/him from making a different decision. Explain why the earlier decision was wrong or incomplete and note any challenge that you have submitted or intend to submit.

If you are a European Economic Area (EEA) national and you claim HB and have been awarded income-based jobseeker's allowance (JSA), the DWP may have recorded that you have a right to reside as an EEA jobseeker.

Although the local authority can take the DWP's findings into account, they are not conclusive and it must make its own decision on whether you have another right to reside (as the right to reside as a jobseeker is an excluded residence right for HB – see p118), including, for example, whether you have retained worker status.[14]

Note: if the DWP has supplied information, including evidence, which was used in connection with a DWP benefit claim to a local authority, it should be accepted without its accuracy being verified for the purpose of the HB claim. This does not apply if the information was supplied more than 12 months after being used or if there are reasonable grounds for believing it has changed. This also applies in reverse – ie, if the local authority supplied information to the DWP.[15] However, this does not prevent the decision maker from requesting additional information – eg, if the information supplied is insufficient to determine your entitlement.

If evidence is not available to you

If your potential exclusion from benefit entitlement depends on evidence that is not available to you, but which is available to the benefit authority, the benefit authority must take the necessary steps to obtain it. If it fails to do so and consequently it is not known whether or not you are excluded from benefit, the matter must be decided in your favour – ie, that you are not excluded.[16]

This principle was established by the House of Lords in the case of *Kerr*[17] and is significant for migrants. For example, if the decision maker needs evidence of your immigration status which the Home Office has but you do not, s/he must use her/his channels of communication with the Home Office to obtain it.[18]

The principle is also significant if your entitlement depends on someone else's circumstances and the relevant information about these is not available to you, but it could be available to the benefit authority if the decision maker made enquiries or checked records. For example, the decision maker may need evidence of your right to reside which depends on the current or past economic activity of a family member (see p171), but you cannot contact her/him or s/he will not provide you with the information you need. Examples include if your right to reside depends on your being:

- the spouse or civil partner of an EEA national from whom you are now separated or the child under 21 of an EEA national, and in either case the EEA national is in the UK with a right to reside:
  - as a worker (see p142);
  - with retained worker status (see p149);
  - as a self-employed person (see p159);
  - with retained self-employed status (see p163);
  - with a permanent right to reside (see p190);
- previously a family member of an EEA national legally resident in the UK for five years and you are trying to prove that you now have a permanent right to reside (see p190);
- the primary carer of a child in education and you need to prove that one of the child's parents had worker status in the UK while child was also in the UK (see p185).

If this applies to you, you should provide as much information as possible to the benefit authority to enable it to trace the evidence you cannot provide, but which could be available to the decision maker if s/he made enquiries or checked records.

Example

Kristina is a 19-year-old Slovakian national who came to the UK last week. She came to the UK because she is due to give birth next week and wanted the support of her father, Pavol, who has been in the UK for two years. However, Pavol disapproves of Kristina's pregnancy and has said that he never wants to hear from her again. Kristina is sleeping on a friend's sofa and has claimed IS. If Pavol has 'worker' status, Kristina, as his family member, is exempt from the habitual residence test for IS.

Kristina has her own birth certificate which names Pavol as her father and confirms his nationality. However, she cannot get evidence of Pavol's worker status from him as he will not speak to her. Kristina has heard that Pavol was made redundant two months ago and is now claiming JSA. Therefore, if she can provide sufficient information to the DWP for it to be able to trace Pavol's JSA claim, the DWP will be able to obtain details of his previous work from it and assess whether that work gave him worker status and whether he has retained that status while claiming JSA. The DWP holds this information and therefore must take the necessary steps to enable it to be traced. If it fails to do so, Kristina can argue that she cannot be excluded from IS on the basis of not being habitually resident, as this has not been proved by the DWP.

How do you get the benefit authority to check someone's residence rights?

If your right to reside depends on someone else's residence rights, but you cannot obtain proof of these, you should ask the benefit authority to carry out the necessary investigations.

1. Although there is a duty on the benefit authority to take the necessary steps to trace information which is available to it and not you,[19] it is unlikely it will do so unless you clearly ask it to. Explain why you are unable to obtain the necessary information and remind it of its duty to trace the information, citing the principles established in the *Kerr* case.[20]

2. Explain your right to reside in your letter, how this results from your relationship with the other person (eg, as her/his family member or primary carer of her/his child) and what information needs to be obtained – eg, evidence of current or past employment.

3. Provide as much information as possible on the relevant person's:
– name;
– date of birth;
– NI number;
– last known address;
– last known place of work;
– nationality;
– previous benefit claims – eg, which benefit and when claimed.

4. The benefit authority must then take the necessary steps to trace the information, by checking records of any benefit claims or NI contributions.

Note: guidance confirms that decision makers should use additional records available to them (eg, NI contribution records) to confirm whether a claimant has permanent residence.[21]

5. If the benefit authority fails to make the necessary investigations, you cannot be excluded from benefit on the basis of not having a right to reside, as the burden of proof is on the benefit authority to show that you do not have a right to reside (see p367).

6. If the benefit authority refuses to carry out the investigations, including if it tells you it is prohibited from doing so under data protection legislation, you should appeal. Ask the

First-tier Tribunal for a direction requiring the decision maker to carry out the necessary investigations. It can make such a direction once you have appealed.[22] If you request a direction before your appeal hearing, this avoids the need for the hearing to be adjourned. It can also mean that, once the necessary information has been traced, the decision refusing your claim is revised, you are awarded benefit and your appeal lapses.

2. Evidence of immigration status

If you are not a European Economic Area (EEA) national and you are claiming any of the benefits or tax credits listed on p66, the decision maker needs evidence of your immigration status to determine whether you are a 'person subject to immigration control' (see p57).

If you are claiming means-tested benefits or tax credits and your partner lives with you and is not an EEA national, the decision maker also needs evidence of her/his immigration status to determine whether s/he is a 'person subject to immigration control' (see p74).

It is rare for a decision maker to need evidence of your child's immigration status, as this does not affect whether or not you can be paid for her/him. However, if your child is the claimant (eg, for disability living allowance), the decision maker requires evidence of her/his immigration status to determine whether s/he is a 'person subject to immigration control'.

Note: if your partner or child has leave which is subject to a 'no recourse to public funds' condition, this condition may be breached if s/he is included in your (or someone else's) claim and this could jeopardise her/his immigration status (see p59).

Further information on checking your immigration status is in Chapter 6. If you are unclear about your, or your partner's or child's, immigration status, you should get immigration advice (see Appendix 2) before making any claim for benefits or tax credits.

Problems with evidence

Problems can arise if you do not have documentary evidence or if the documents you have are unclear. The general points about evidence all apply (see p365). You should not be refused benefit because you cannot provide a particular document, and you should ask why a document is being requested so you can provide the evidence through another means. If you cannot provide a document (eg, because it is with the Home Office), it can help if you provide a letter confirming this from your legal representative. S/he may also be able to confirm your current immigration status and the significance of any applications you have pending.

If evidence of immigration status is not available to you, but is available to the decision maker (eg, by emailing the Home Office), s/he must take the necessary steps to obtain this (see p371).

Changes in immigration status

If you have time-limited leave to enter or remain, you can apply to extend your leave or apply for further leave to remain on a different basis. Provided you apply before your existing leave expires, this leave is extended until your application is decided by the Home Office.[23] If your original leave was not subject to a 'no recourse to public funds' condition, you were not a 'person subject to immigration control' and were therefore entitled to all benefits and tax credits, subject to the usual rules of entitlement. When your leave is extended, you continue not to be a person subject to immigration control and your benefit entitlement remains the same. It is important to notify the benefit authorities, as otherwise, they may assume your leave has expired and that you are no longer entitled to benefit (because you are a person subject to immigration control on the basis of being someone who requires leave but does not have it – see p57).

The benefit authorities need evidence that you applied to vary your leave before your existing leave ended. If possible, you should submit documents showing when your leave was due to expire (which the benefit authorities may already have on your file), together with confirmation of the date when your application to vary that leave was submitted – eg, a letter from a legal representative who helped you with the application, proof of date of posting and any letter confirming the date your application was received. Although it should not be necessary, in practice it also helps if you submit a covering letter. In this, explain that your previous leave is extended because you applied to vary your leave before your previous leave expired,[24] you therefore continue not to be a person subject to immigration control, and so your benefit or tax credit entitlement also continues. Include the relevant legal references in your letter.

Note: if your application to vary your leave is refused and your leave is extended while your appeal against that refusal is pending, you *may* count as a person subject to immigration control (see p63).

3. **Evidence of residence rights**

Establishing your residence rights under European Union (EU) law can be complex and involve many steps, each requiring certain conditions to be met. It is advisable to set out your residence rights to the decision maker as clearly as possible and, wherever possible, provide evidence of every requirement. If you do not have documentary evidence of one requirement, but you have provided evidence of others, it is more likely that the decision maker will accept your uncorroborated evidence on the remaining requirement (unless it is self-contradictory or inherently improbable – see p367).

The actual requirements vary depending on the residence right you are asserting (see Chapter 12). See p376 for some of the most commonly required types of evidence.

Residence documents

The only circumstance when you need a residence document in order to have a right to reside is if you are an 'extended family member' (see p173). In this case, you need a relevant residence document in order to be *treated as* a 'family member' of someone who can confer a right of residence on you (see p173).

For any other right to reside, you do not need a residence document because your right to reside depends on the facts of your situation.

Documentation only confirms your residence rights; it cannot give you a right to reside if either the document was issued in error or it correctly confirmed your right to reside when it was issued but your circumstances have now changed so that you cease to have that right to reside.[25]

However, obtaining a residence document can make it easier for you to demonstrate your residence rights and may avoid your having to to provide all your evidence every time you make a benefit claim. For example, once you have acquired a permanent right of residence, it is easier to provide a permanent residence document, together with evidence that you have not lost this right by leaving the UK for more than two years (see p200) than it is, for example, to provide weekly payslips spanning a five-year period. In addition, although it is not yet known what rights European Economic Area (EEA) nationals and their family members will have once the UK leaves the EU, getting a document confirming your current residence *may* assist you in the future. You should obtain specialist immigration advice if you are concerned about your future residence rights.

You can be issued with the following residence documents.
- A **registration certificate** if you are an EEA national with a right of residence under the EEA Regulations.[26]
- A **residence card** if you are a non-EEA national and you have a right to reside as the family member of an EEA 'qualified person' (see p128) or an EEA national with a permanent right of residence.[27]
- A **derivative residence card** if you have a derivative right to reside (see p181).[28]
- A **document certifying a permanent right of residence** if you are an EEA national with a permanent right of residence, or a **permanent residence card** if you are a non-EEA national with permanent residency.[29]
- A **residence document**, issued, or treated as issued, under previous EEA Regulations. These are treated as issued under the current EEA Regulations.[30]
- A **family permit** issued for entry to the UK if you are a non-EEA family member of an EEA national and do not have any of the other residence documentation.[31]

Forms and further information, including about application fees, are available on the UK Visas and Immigration website (see Appendix 3).

4. **Types of evidence**

Certain types of evidence are of particular significance for migrants and are discussed below. Depending on your circumstances and the benefit or tax credit being claimed, this evidence may be required by all claimants to satisfy the entitlement conditions, or because it affects the amount to which you are entitled. If the evidence is required by all claimants, you should not be required to submit more evidence because you are a migrant than would be required of a British person in the same circumstances. If you are asked for more evidence because you are not British, you may want to get advice from the Equality Advisory and Support Service (see Appendix 2).

It can be helpful to check the guidance issued to decision makers on acceptable evidence and refer to this where it supports your situation. Check both the general guidance applicable to all benefits on evidence in general[32] or specific types (eg, of age, marriage and death[33]), and guidance specific to migrants,[34] including on the right to reside and habitual residence tests.[35] For example, part of the DWP guidance covers evidence for establishing permanent residence.[36]

Evidence from other countries

If your documentary evidence is from another country and is not in English, it can be helpful to submit an authorised translation. If obtaining a translation will cause any delay, you should make sure you do not miss any deadlines for submitting evidence. For example, you could take the original document to a local benefit office to take an authorised copy and accompany this with a letter explaining that you are obtaining a translation.

The authenticity of a document issued outside the UK should not automatically be questioned just because it was not issued in the UK. Decision makers are reminded in guidance that certificates of birth, marriage, civil partnerships and deaths issued abroad can all be accepted as evidence of that event, unless there is a reason to doubt their authenticity.[37]

Even if a document originates in a country in which it is relatively easy to obtain fraudulent documents, a decision maker (or First-tier Tribunal) cannot presume that your document is not genuine. The decision maker (or tribunal) can conclude that a document is not genuine on the balance of probabilities, but it is rarely necessary to decide whether or not a document is forged because the decision maker (or tribunal) should determine the 'weight' given to any single piece of evidence. This weighting is affected by factors such as whether there is any information or evidence of the accuracy of record keeping by the issuing body, whether other evidence corroborates the document issued abroad, and the overall view taken of your credibility.[38]

Evidence of your nationality

The most common acceptable evidence of your nationality is a current passport, a current European Economic Area (EEA) identity card or, if you are a non-EEA national, a current travel document or biometric residence permit. However, if you cannot provide one of these, other official documents should be accepted (see p358). As with all evidence requirements, it helps if you can provide more than one form of evidence of your nationality.

If you are relying on someone else's nationality for your own rights (eg, to argue you have a right to reside as the family member of an EEA worker), you must provide evidence of her/his nationality – eg, to show s/he is an EEA national.

Evidence of your relationship to someone

If your rights are based on being someone's family member or primary carer, you must provide evidence of this relationship. This can enable you to show that you:

- are covered by the European Union (EU) co-ordination rules (see p282);
- are a family member of an EEA national exercising EU Treaty rights and are therefore not a 'person subject to immigration control' (see p58);
- can claim a benefit despite being a person subject to immigration control because you are in an exempt group (see p67);
- have a right to reside as a family member of an EEA national (see p170) or as the primary carer of someone who can confer residence rights on you (see p181); or
- are exempt from the habitual residence test as the family member of an EEA worker or self-employed person (see p108).

You must also provide evidence of the other factors that are relevant. For example, if you need to show you are the family member of an EEA worker, in addition to evidence that you are her/his family member, you must also provide evidence of her/his EEA nationality and her/his employment.

Non-European Economic Area nationals

If you are a non-EEA national and are the family member of an EEA national who confers residence rights on you, you are not a 'person subject to immigration control' (see p58).

If you entered the UK as the family member of an EEA national who is in the UK exercising her/his treaty rights (eg, as a worker), you usually have an entry clearance document that states this. You should provide this to the benefit authority, as it is the most significant documentary evidence required. However, depending on your circumstances, the benefit authority may also want evidence that you are still a family member of an EEA national in the UK exercising her/his treaty rights, or that you come within limited circumstances that enable you to retain residence rights as a former family member (see p177).

If you are a non-EEA national and are the primary carer of someone who confers a derivative right to reside on you (see p181), the benefit authorities require evidence of each requirement that must be satisfied for you to have this right to reside. For example, if you are asserting that you are the primary carer of a worker's child in education, you must show:

- you are the primary carer of the child (see p186);
- s/he is currently in education (see p184);
- one of her/his parents (or step-parents) is an EEA national (see p377);
- that parent (or step-parent) had worker status in the UK (see p184) while the child was in the UK.

Evidence of marriage or civil partnership

If you have been given leave to enter or remain on the basis of being a spouse or civil partner of someone, evidence of that leave is generally accepted as sufficient evidence of your relationship for the purposes of proving your entitlement to a benefit or tax credit.

Spouses and civil partners have far greater rights under EU law than partners who are not married or who are not civil partners. Consequently, it can be important to show that someone is your spouse or civil partner – eg, when s/he can confer residence rights on you. If you need to prove that you are someone's spouse or civil partner, you must show that you are still married or in a civil partnership. If you have separated and are no longer living together or in a relationship, you are still her/his spouse or civil partner until you are finally divorced or the civil partnership is finally dissolved.[39]

A marriage or civil partnership certificate is the best evidence. If the certificate was issued outside the UK by the appropriate registration authority, it should be accepted as valid evidence (see p376).[40]

If you do not have a marriage or civil partnership certificate, other evidence confirming your marriage or civil partnership can be accepted. Official documents that refer to your marriage or civil partnership, as well as official correspondence confirming you live together, can be be taken into account.

There is extensive guidance for decision makers on evidence of marriage and civil partnerships, including religious and national variations.[41]

If you are refused benefits or tax credits because your marriage or civil partnership is not recognised or is deemed to have been a marriage or civil partnership 'of convenience', get specialist immigration advice.

Evidence of parentage

If you have been given leave to enter or remain on the basis of being a parent or child of someone, evidence of that leave is generally accepted as sufficient evidence of your relationship for the purposes of proving your entitlement to a benefit or tax credit.

If you are showing that you are the parent or child of someone who can confer residence rights on you, it is important to show that you meet all the conditions for being defined as a 'family member'.

To be a 'family member' as a child, you must show:

- s/he is your parent; *and*
- either you are aged under 21 *or* you are dependent on her/him.

To be a 'family member' as a parent, you must show:

- you are her/his parent; *and*
- you are dependent on her/him.

A birth certificate, or official DNA test results, that name both child and parent should be sufficient evidence. If the document is from outside the UK, see p376.

If you do not have a birth certificate or official DNA test results, other documents can also be accepted. If you do not have anything decisive, submit the evidence you have to back up your own evidence and ask for the decision maker to decide on the balance of probabilities (see p367).

Example

Nadifa is 18 and a Dutch national. She has health problems and wants to claim income-related employment and support allowance and housing benefit (HB). She came to the UK four years ago with her mother, who is also a Dutch national, having acquired Dutch citizenship after fleeing to the Netherlands as a refugee 15 years ago. Nadifa's mother is a self-employed translator and has extensive evidence of this. However, Nadifa does not have any evidence that she is her mother's daughter. Her mother fled to the Netherlands without any documents. Nadifa therefore submits evidence of her mother's Dutch nationality and self-employment, together with a letter setting out the relevant details of her life history and documents showing that she was given leave to remain in the Netherlands as a dependant on her mother's asylum claim, evidence that she travelled with her mother to the UK four years ago and letters from her GP and dermatologist discussing Nadifa's eczema and the likelihood of its being linked to her mother's eczema.

Note: if you are trying to show that you are someone's father or that someone is your father, until officially declared otherwise, a man is deemed to be a child's father if he was married to the child's mother at the time of the child's birth or his name was registered on the birth certificate.[42]

Evidence of your age

Your age (or someone else's age) can affect whether or not you meet the basic conditions of entitlement to a benefit, and the amount to which you are entitled. Your age (or someone else's age) can also affect your residence rights, whether your immigration status excludes you from benefits and tax credits and/or whether you are covered by the EU co-ordination rules. In addition, age can affect whether you (or someone else) are defined as a 'family member' or as 'dependent'.

A birth certificate, passport or identity card is usually accepted as proof of your date of birth. Other evidence that can show your date of birth includes school, medical or army records. Guidance to decision makers states that the 'primary' or best evidence of age is a certified copy of an entry which must be made in a register by law, such as a birth certificate or adoption certificate.[43] If you were born abroad and have a certificate issued by the appropriate registration authority, this should be accepted unless there is reason to doubt its validity (see p376).[44] See also the other evidence that can be accepted as proof of your identity on p358, and guidance to decision makers on 'secondary' evidence of age.[45]

You may be able to show your date of birth by referring to the accepted birth dates of other relatives, such as siblings.[46] For example, if you are recorded as the eldest child and your sister has been accepted as born in 1995, you must have been born before then.

If you have no record of your date of birth, or there is conflicting evidence, it is possible for an age assessment to be carried out. However, there is no accurate scientific test that can establish a person's age, and such an assessment can be disputed. See p412 for age assessments for unaccompanied asylum-seeking children. Guidance to decision makers covers the possibility of arranging a physical examination of an adult by medical services, but notes that this is generally only reliable five years either way.[47] However, getting your GP to state her/his opinion of your age, together with her/his reasons, can be helpful supporting evidence, particularly if it is clear that the GP has known you for some time and is familiar with your medical conditions.[48]

A common problem is conflicting evidence due to past errors. Your date of birth may have been wrongly recorded in your passport when it was issued – eg, because you gave the wrong date or because of an administrative error. The date in the passport may then have been used in many other official documents and it may be difficult to persuade the benefit authorities that all these dates are wrong. You should explain that all these dates come from one document and give a detailed account about how the wrong date came to be recorded. This explanation counts as evidence, but if you have (or can obtain) other evidence showing that date is not correct, you should submit it.[49]

While each piece of evidence must be considered, the oldest documents may be more reliable, since they were made nearer to the time of the events to which they refer.

Passports and other immigration documents are commonly recorded as '1 January' when your exact date of birth is unclear. However, if you obtain evidence of your exact date of birth later, this can be accepted.

The decision maker, or First-tier Tribunal, should weigh up all the available evidence and determine your age on the balance of probabilities, not by any higher standard.[50]

If there is no documentary evidence, the benefit authorities should accept your own statements, unless they are contradictory or improbable (see p367).

Evidence of work

Evidence of your (or someone else's) current or past employment or self-employment can be required in order to prove that you satisfy, or are exempt from, immigration or residence conditions, or that you are covered by the EU co-ordination rules. The exact evidence required depends on what you need to prove, so it is essential that you check the rules for the specific condition you are trying to satisfy or be exempt from.

Examples

Samir is a national of Algeria and is in the UK to study. He has a student visa, which gives him leave to be in the UK for the next two years, subject to the condition that he does not have recourse to public funds. Samir is therefore a 'person subject to immigration control' (see p57). He works 15 hours a week, which is permitted under his student visa. Samir wants to claim child benefit and child tax credit (CTC) because his girlfriend's 14-year-old French son has come to live with him while she goes to Canada for a year. Samir can claim both child benefit and CTC if he can show that he is 'lawfully working', as this shows he is in a group of people who can claim despite being a 'person subject to immigration control' (see p71 for child benefit and p73 for CTC). Samir must provide HM Revenue and Customs (HMRC) with evidence of his employment (eg, a payslip or letter from his employer), together with confirmation that his work is allowed under the conditions of his immigration leave, proof of his Algerian nationality and his student visa.

Dimitra is a Greek national who wants to claim income support (IS) and HB as she is due to have a baby in three weeks. She came to the UK six years ago and got a job after being here a month. She stayed in this job until she was made redundant last month. If Dimitra can show that she had a right to reside as a 'worker' for a continuous period of five years, she will have a permanent right to reside (see p190), which satisfies the right to reside requirement for IS and HB. Dimitra must provide evidence confirming that she was in an employment relationship (see p144) doing 'genuine and effective' work (see p146) for a continuous period of five years.

There is no definitive list of what counts as acceptable evidence. The evidence of work is considered stronger if it has several ways of showing it relates to you – eg, if it shows your full name, your date of birth, your address and your national insurance (NI) number, rather than just one or two of these.

Evidence of employment includes:

- a contract of employment;
- payslips;
- correspondence from your employer to you – eg, offering you the job or confirming a change in hours;
- a letter from an employer confirming your employment;
- documents relating to your total pay and tax over a period, such as P60 and P45 forms;
- bank statements showing wages being paid in from the employer or, if you are paid 'cash in hand', showing you have deposited your wages on a regular basis.

If you are not actually working (eg, because you are on sick leave or maternity leave), you may not have ceased to have a right to reside as a 'worker' (see p148). You need to provide evidence that you are still under a contract of employment, such as a letter from your employer stating this. Alternatively, if you have ceased to be a worker, you may be able to retain your worker status and must provide evidence of the basis of this (see p149) in addition to the evidence of the worker status you had.

Evidence of self-employment includes:

- documents from HMRC confirming your registration as a self-employed person;
- evidence of paying class 2 NI contributions;
- business accounts;
- samples of marketing;
- documents showing you have purchased the equipment needed to carry out your trade.

If you want to demonstrate that you have a right to reside as a self-employed person, it should be enough to show that you have established yourself in order to undertake activity as a self-employed person (see p160).

If you are not actually working, you may not have ceased to have a right to reside as a self-employed person. You must provide evidence of all the factors that are relevant in your circumstances (see p161).

You may be able to retain your self-employed status (see p163) and need to provide evidence of this in addition to the evidence of your self-employment.

If your right to reside depends on someone else being, or having been, a worker or self-employed, all the above points apply to evidence of their work. However, if you do not have any documentary evidence of this because you cannot contact the person or s/he will not provide you with the evidence, you may be able to argue that the benefit authorities should obtain this evidence (see p371).

Croatian, A2 and A8 nationals

There are additional restrictions which can affect your residence rights based on employment that currently apply to Croatian nationals and which previously applied to A2 nationals and A8 nationals (see p129). If these apply, or applied, to you, you must supply additional evidence. If you need to show that you have (or had) a right to reside as a 'worker', or that you have (or had) retained 'worker' status, you must show that, at the time of working, you:

- were exempt from restrictions (see p131 for Croatian and A2 nationals, and p132 for A8 nationals); or
- (for Croatian and A2 nationals) worked in accordance with a valid authorisation document (see p130); or
- (for A8 nationals) worked for an 'authorised employer' (see p133). **Note:** a registration certificate that was applied for after the first month of work is not retrospective, and so is only evidence that you were working for an authorised employer from the date it was issued.[51] Also, because you were classed as working for an authorised employer for the first month of any employment, you do not need to provide a registration certificate for this first month.

If you are unable to provide your authorisation document or registration certificate because it has been lost or stolen, you should provide the benefit authority with as much information as you can about your employment and when it was authorised or registered, and ask the decision maker to confirm this through her/his contacts with the Home Office. You can also contact the Home Office yourself and ask for a letter confirming the details of your authorisation or registration(s), but do not delay making your claim while you do this. Your employer at the relevant time may also be able to assist you with evidence confirming your authorisation or registration.

There are no additional restrictions, and therefore no additional evidence requirements, if you (or the person whose right to reside you are relying on) was self-employed.

Evidence of jobseeking

You must provide evidence that you are seeking employment and have a 'genuine chance of being engaged' to have a right to reside as a jobseeker (see p135) or, under the EEA regulations, to retain your worker status while involuntarily unemployed (see p150).[52]

These requirements are similar to the requirements to be 'actively seeking' and 'available for' work for the purposes of being entitled to jobseeker's allowance (JSA) or NI credits, and to the work search and work availability requirements if you come under the universal credit (UC) system. This means that, in most cases, if the decision maker accepts that you have provided evidence that satisfies these requirements for JSA, UC or NI credits on the basis of unemployment, this evidence should also be accepted as satisfying the requirements for you to have a right to reside as a jobseeker. For the circumstances when this might not apply and for more information on the type of work you must be seeking, see p140.

However you do not need to receive, or claim, benefit to have a right to reside as a jobseeker, as long as you provide evidence that you are seeking employment and have a 'genuine chance of being engaged' (see p140).[53]

Under European law, there is no time limit on how long you can have a right to reside as a jobseeker – it continues for as long as you provide evidence that you are looking for work and have a genuine chance of being engaged.[54] There is also no time limit on how long you can retain your worker status while involuntarily unemployed, provided you were employed for at least a year (see p151).[55]

However, under the EEA Regulations, in order to continue to have a right to reside as a jobseeker for longer than 91 days, or to continue to retain your worker status while involuntarily unemployed for longer than six months, the evidence that you are seeking employment and have a genuine chance of being engaged must be 'compelling'.[56] This requirement is referred to as the 'genuine prospects of work test' (see p137 for jobseekers and p152 if you are retaining your worker status while involuntarily unemployed).

Examples of evidence

Evidence that you are seeking employment could include details of all your:

- work search activities;
- enquiries made to potential employers;
- applications for employment, together with responses;
- requests to attend interviews, together with responses.

Evidence that you have a genuine chance of being engaged could include evidence of:

- your work history in the UK;
- your work history in other countries;
- your qualifications;
- training you have undertaken;
- voluntary work (in the UK and abroad);
- your language skills;
- security checks you have satisfied;
- your proximity to potential employers;
- completion of a course on obtaining work as part of the Work Programme;
- the broad range of types of work you are looking for and/or the hours of work you are able to do;
- your arrangements for adequate childcare to enable you to attend interviews and take up employment.

Whether you have a genuine chance of being engaged also depends on future events,[57] so you should provide evidence of any qualifications you hope to obtain and experience you will gain in the near future.

Although it is arguable that you should not be required to change the quality of your evidence after a particular length of time, in practice, the longer you have been a jobseeker without obtaining work, the more likely it is that the decision maker will argue that this shows that you do not have a genuine chance of getting work. The Upper Tribunal has held that if you have been seeking employment without success for at least six months, this is relevant, but is only one factor that must be considered and can be outweighed by others.[58] You should therefore provide as much evidence as possible to demonstrate that, on the balance of probabilities, you have a genuine chance of being engaged, despite the long period of unemployment.

If you are asked to provide 'compelling' evidence under the 'genuine prospects of work test', see p137 for jobseekers and p152 if you are retaining your worker status while involuntarily unemployed.

Notes

1. General points about evidence

1 www.whatdotheyknow.com/request/254608/response/638477/attach/2/FOI%20IR172%20reply.pdf
2 *CI v HMRC (TC)* [2014] UKUT 158 (AAC)
3 *LS v SSWP (SPC)* [2014] UKUT 249 (AAC)
4 *Kerr v Department for Social Development (Northern Ireland)* [2004] UKHL 23, paras 15-17 and 61-63; *SS v HMRC (TC)* [2014] UKUT 383 (AAC), paras 28-30
5 R(I) 2/51, paras 6 and 7; R(SB) 33/85, para 14; *EP v SSWP (JSA)* [2016] UKUT 445 (AAC), para 21
6 R(IS) 6/96, para 15; see also *Kerr v Department for Social Development (Northern Ireland)* [2004] UKHL 23, paras 16-17 and 61-69; CIS/1697/2004, paras 18-20; R(PC) 1/09, paras 16-18
7 *R v Medical Appeal Tribunal (North Midland Region) ex parte Hubble* [1958] 2 QB 228; *Kerr v Department for Social Development (Northern Ireland)* [2004] UKHL 23, paras 15-17 and 61-63; R(PC) 1/09, paras 16-20

8 *Kerr v Department for Social Development (Northern Ireland)* [2004] UKHL 23, paras 61-69; R(PC) 1/09, para 19
9 R(IS) 11/99
10 s16(1) TCA 2002; *NI v HMRC (TC)* [2015] UKUT 490 (AAC) – see also caselaw listed in para 4; *JR v HMRC (TC)* [2015] UKUT 192 (AAC)
11 s19 TCA 2002; *TS v HMRC (TC)* [2015] UKUT 507 (AAC); *CS v HMRC (TC)* [2015] UKUT 407 (AAC)
12 s14 TCA 2002; *SB v HMRC (TC)* [2014] UKUT 543 (AAC), para 12
13 See for example, s17 SSA 1998; Sch 7, para 11 CSPSSA 2000
14 *EP v SSWP (JSA)* [2016] UKUT 445 (AAC), paras 24-27
15 Social Security (Claims and Information) Regulations 2007, No.2911
16 *Kerr v Department for Social Development (Northern Ireland)* [2004] UKHL 23, paras 61-69; R(PC) 1/09, paras 16-19
17 *Kerr v Department for Social Development (Northern Ireland)* [2004] UKHL 23
18 R(PC) 1/09, paras 16-19

19 *Kerr v Department for Social Development
(Northern Ireland)* [2004] UKHL 23,
especially para 62
20 *Kerr v Department for Social Development
(Northern Ireland)* [2004] UKHL 23,
paras 61-69
21 Vol 2, para 073431 DMG
22 rr5, 6 and 15 TP(FT) Rules; *PM v SSWP
(IS)* [2014] UKUT 474 (AAC)

2. Evidence of immigration status
23 s3C(2)(a) IA 1971
24 s3C IA 1971

3. Evidence of residence rights
25 *SSWP v Dias*, C-325/09 [2011] ECR I-
06387; *EM and KN v SSWP* [2009] UKUT
44 (AAC); *MD v SSWP (SPC)* [2016]
UKUT 319 (AAC); regs 17(8), 18(7),
19(4) and 20(5) I(EEA) Regs
26 Reg 17 I(EEA) Regs
27 Reg 18 I(EEA) Regs
28 Reg 20 I(EEA) Regs
29 Reg 19 I(EEA) Regs
30 Reg 45 and Sch 6 para 2 I(EEA) Regs
31 Reg 12 I(EEA) Regs

4. Types of evidence
32 For example, Vol 1 Ch 1 DMG or Ch A1
ADM
33 For example, Vol 3 Ch 10 DMG or Ch B3
ADM
34 For example, Vol 2 DMG or Ch 20 CCM
35 For example, Vol 2 Ch 7 DMG
36 Vol 2, paras 073429-32 DMG
37 See for example, Vol 3 Ch 10 DMG
38 *SW v SSWP (SPC)* [2016] UKUT 163
(AAC), in particular paras 28 and 41
39 *Diatta v Land Berlin*, C-267/83 [1985]
ECR I-00567
40 Vol 3, para 10155 DMG
41 For example, paras 10120-43 DMG
42 **EW** ss2 and 4 CA 1989
S s3 C(S)A 1995
43 paras 10030 and 10064-65 DMG; para
B3016 ADM
44 para 10035 DMG; para B3021 ADM; *SW
v SSWP (SPC)* [2016] UKUT 163 (AAC), in
particular paras 28 and 41
45 paras 10036 and 10070-73 DMG; paras
B3022 and B3051-58 ADM
46 para 10071, example 10 DMG; para
B3051 example ADM
47 paras 10098-102 DMG; paras B3073-74
and B3086-89 ADM
48 For example, *SW v SSWP (SPC)* [2016]
UKUT 163 (AAC)

49 For example, *SW v SSWP (SPC)* [2016]
UKUT 163 (AAC)
50 *LS v SSWP (SPC)* [2014] UKUT 249
(AAC), para 5
51 *SSWP v ZA* [2009] UKUT 294 (AAC);
Szpak v SSWP [2013] EWCA Civ 46
52 Reg 6(1), (2), (5) and (6) I(EEA) Regs
53 *The Queen v Immigration Appeal
Tribunal, ex parte Antonissen*, C-292/89
[1991] ECR I-00745, para 21; *R(IS)* 8/08,
para 5; *GE v SSWP (ESA)* [2017] UKUT
145 (AAC), para 46
54 *The Queen v Immigration Appeal Tribunal
ex parte Antonissen*, C-292/89 [1991]
ECR I-00745, para 21
55 Art 7(3)(b) EU Dir 2004/38
56 Reg 6(1), (2), (5), (6) and (7) I(EEA) Regs
57 *SSWP v MB (JSA) (and linked cases)*
[2016] UKUT 372 (AAC), para 47
58 *SSWP v MB (JSA) (and linked cases)*
[2016] UKUT 372 (AAC), paras 49-60

Part 8

Support for asylum seekers

Part 8

Support for asylum seekers

Chapter 21

· ·

Asylum support

This chapter covers:
1. Introduction (below)
2. Support for asylum seekers (p391)
3. Temporary support (p397)
4. Support for failed asylum seekers (p398)
5. Support for people on temporary admission, temporary release or immigration bail (p407)
6. Support from your local authority (p408)

1. **Introduction**

Types of support for asylum seekers

There are three main types of government support for people who have made an application for asylum in the UK:

- support for the period until a final decision on an asylum application is made. This is known as **section 95 support** (see p391);[1]
- **temporary support** (often called emergency support), available to asylum seekers waiting for a decision on their application for section 95 support. This is known as **section 98 support** (see p397);[2]
- support available to failed asylum seekers and other migrants who meet certain criteria. This is known as **section 4 support** (see p398).[3]

Section 95 support consists of accommodation and cash, or the option of cash only. Temporary support is full-board accommodation, and section 4 support is accommodation and a payment card (known as an ASPEN card) that can be used in participating shops.

Background to the current system of support

Before 5 February 1996, asylum seekers without funds received income support, at the urgent cases rate of 90 per cent, and housing benefit. Those without accommodation and in 'priority need' were entitled to local authority housing under the homelessness legislation. In February 1996, the government decided that providing benefits was a factor that attracted asylum seekers to the UK. Access to state benefits was removed from many asylum seekers, who therefore sought assistance from local authorities under safety-net legislation.

From 6 December 1999, the Immigration and Asylum Act 1999 restricted the ability of asylum seekers and other migrants to access support from local authorities. These restrictions have been extended, so they now apply to the following local authority support:[4]

- s2 of the Chronically Sick and Disabled Persons Act 1970;
- s21 and Schedule 8 of the National Health Service Act 1977;
- ss17, 23C, 24A and 24B of the Children Act 1989;
- s2 of the Local Government Act 2000;
- s1 of the Localism Act 2011;
- Part 1 of the Care Act 2014.

Note: the exclusions do not prevent a local authority from providing support under the above provisions to a child,[5] or if failing to do so would result in a breach of a person's human rights (see p408).[6]

The Immigration and Asylum Act 1999 also retained the general exclusion of asylum seekers and others from most state benefits and other welfare provisions on the basis that they are 'persons subject to immigration control' (see p57).[7] Instead, the current system of support for asylum seekers was introduced.

Until early 2005, failed asylum seekers could only receive 'hard cases support' under section 4 of the Immigration and Asylum Act 1999, provided entirely at the Home Office's discretion. On 31 March 2005, regulations were introduced specifying entitlement to support under section 4(2) (known as section 4 support) for certain failed asylum seekers and their dependants (see p398).[8] If your asylum application has been refused, accommodation and support may be provided under section 4 of the Act, but with strict eligibility criteria.

Note: the Immigration Act 2016 abolishes section 4 support and replaces it with much more restrictive support for failed asylum seekers. At the time of writing, the part of the Act dealing with asylum support is not yet in force, but may be brought into force during 2018.

Home Office agencies

Since the Immigration and Asylum Act 1999 came into force, the role of providing accommodation and support to asylum seekers has passed between several different Home Office agencies. Until April 2006, the support scheme for asylum seekers and failed asylum seekers was administered by the National Asylum Support Service (NASS). In April 2006, NASS ceased to exist and its role was taken over by the Border and Immigration Agency (BIA). On 7 April 2008, the UK Border Agency (UKBA) was formed, taking over the support role of the BIA, as well as the immigration and asylum functions of the Immigration and Nationality Department. The UKBA was abolished on 26 March 2013 and all its functions were returned to the Home Office. Asylum support applications are now dealt with by the UK Visas and Immigration (UKVI) Department in the Home Office. For simplicity, we refer to the 'Home Office' in this *Handbook*.

You may find that advisers and even officials still refer to asylum support as 'NASS' or 'UKBA' support, even though these agencies no longer exist.

Home Office guidance

The Home Office publishes internal guidance for its decision makers on deciding and processing applications for asylum support. This is published on the government's website at www.gov.uk/government/collections/asylum-support-asylum-instructions. The guidance is in the form of policy bulletins and process instructions. It is important to be familiar with the guidance in addition to the law. It is regularly amended, so always check the website for the latest versions.

There are currently two main policy documents: one dealing with section 95 support (*Asylum Support Instructions: policy bulletins*) and the other with section 4 support (*Asylum Support, Section 4 Policy and Process*). There are also several other shorter supplemental policies. The guidance is not legally binding, but is a useful indication as to how applications are likely to be processed by the Home Office – although it is not the law, the Home Office should follow its own written policies. However, if it is not an accurate representation of the law and less favourable than the law if applied to your particular case, you can argue that it should not be followed.

Asylum Help

Asylum Help is a national confidential and impartial advice service for asylum seekers, funded by the Home Office and provided by the charity Migrant Help. It can help you make your application for support and give general advice about the asylum process. For contact details and a list of other organisations that provide advice services to asylum seekers, see Appendix 2.

---

2. **Support for asylum seekers**

You are entitled to asylum support under section 95 of the Immigration and Asylum Act 1999 (known as **section 95 support**) if:[9]
- you are an asylum seeker or a dependant of an asylum seeker; *and*
- you are destitute or likely to become destitute; *and*
- unless you made your application before 8 January 2003, you have made your application for asylum 'as soon as reasonably practicable' after you entered the UK.[10]

See p397 for who is entitled to temporary support. The criteria are similar, but you must be destitute, not simply likely to become destitute.

Who is an asylum seeker for support purposes

For the purposes of asylum support, you are an asylum seeker if:[11]
• you are over 18 years; *and*
• you have made an application for asylum; *and*
• your application has been recorded by the Secretary of State (see below); *and*
• the application has not yet been determined (see below).

Your asylum application may be made either under the 1951 Refugee Convention (see p12) or under Article 3 of the European Convention on Human Rights. If you have made a different type of application, such as under Article 8 of the European Convention on Human Rights or an application for indefinite leave to remain (see p23), and you have not also made an asylum or Article 3 application, you cannot claim section 95 support, but may be eligible for section 4 support (see p398) or support from your local authority (see p407). For further details on asylum applications, see p31.

When an asylum application is recorded

Asylum applications made 'at port' (ie, on entry to the UK) are recorded immediately. If you are already in the UK and making an 'in-country' asylum application for the first time, it is processed at the Home Office's Asylum Screening Unit (ASU) in Croydon. You must make an appointment to attend the ASU by telephone in advance, unless you have nowhere to live, in which case you can turn up at the ASU and apply on the same day. Your application is normally 'recorded' at your screening interview on the same day.

If your asylum application has been refused, your appeal rights are exhausted and you make a fresh asylum application (ie, a subsequent claim), this is not recorded until the Home Office accepts that it constitutes a fresh application – ie, it is significantly different to the material considered in your first asylum application.[12] While you are waiting for your further representations to be considered, you may be eligible for section 4 support (see p398).

When an asylum application is determined

An asylum application remains undetermined during the time allowed for any appeal to be made and during any appeal lodged within that time (or any appeal accepted out of time) to the First-tier Tribunal (Immigration and Asylum Chamber), or a further appeal. However, an asylum application is not considered undetermined while a judicial review is outstanding.

For support purposes, you continue to be treated as an asylum seeker for 28 days after:[13]
• your application for asylum is granted; *or*

- you are granted leave to remain; *or*
- your asylum appeal is allowed.

Alternatively, you continue to be an asylum seeker for 21 days after your asylum application has been refused by the Home Office or, if there is an appeal, for 21 days after that appeal is finally dismissed.

Families with children

If you have a dependent child when your application for asylum is determined, you continue to be treated as an asylum seeker for support purposes until her/his 18th birthday, provided s/he remains in the UK.[14] Therefore, families with children aged under 18 continue to receive section 95 support, even after their asylum application has been refused.

The asylum support adjudicators (as the appeal tribunal was called at that time) dismissed an appeal by an asylum seeker who had a dependent child with her in the UK, but was not claiming asylum support at the relevant time.[15] This decision relied on the word 'continuing' in section 94(5) of the Immigration and Asylum Act 1999 which says, 'he is to be treated (for the purposes of this Part) as continuing to be an asylum-seeker'. This interpretation, however, is challengeable as it can be argued that the word 'continuing' means that someone continues to be an asylum seeker for support purposes, not that there must be some pre-existing support that will be continued. If you are refused support on this basis, you should appeal.

This provision does not apply if your children were born after your asylum application was refused and you had exhausted all your rights of appeal. In this case, you cease to be an asylum seeker for support purposes and are no longer eligible for section 95 support. However, you and your children may be eligible for section 4 support as a failed asylum seeker (see p398) or for support under the Children Act 1989 (see p408).

The Home Office can withdraw section 95 support from failed asylum-seeker families who, in its opinion, have not taken steps to leave the UK voluntarily.[16] This means that you are expected to demonstrate that you are taking steps to arrange your departure from the UK to return home. However, this power was piloted across the UK in 2005, but has not been adopted as general practice. If the Home Office decides to withdraw your support because it says that you are not taking steps to leave the UK with your family, you can appeal against this decision to the First-tier Tribunal (Asylum Support). For more information, see Chapter 24.

Note: once the relevant section of the Immigration Act 2016 is in force (which may be in 2018), refused asylum-seeker families will no longer be able to continue to receive section 95 support.

Who is a dependant for support purposes

Support is provided to asylum seekers and their dependants, provided they are destitute. You are a 'dependant' of an asylum seeker if you are:[17]

- her/his spouse or civil partner;
- a child aged under 18 years of the asylum seeker or her/his spouse/civil partner and you are dependent on her/him;
- a child aged under 18 years of the close family of the asylum seeker/spouse/ civil partner (you do not have to be dependent on her/him);
- a child aged under 18 years and you have lived in the asylum seeker's household for six out of the last 12 months, or since birth;
- now over 18 years old, but you were under 18 and came within one of the above categories when the asylum support application was made or when you entered the UK;
- a close family member, or someone who has lived with the asylum seeker for six out of the last 12 months (or since birth), and you are disabled and in need of care and attention from a member of the household;
- her/his partner and you were living with her/him as an unmarried couple for at least two of the three years before the application for support or before entering the UK.[18] If you are in an unmarried couple and want to be included as a dependant in your partner's existing asylum support, it can be difficult to comply with this condition. You may be caught in a 'catch-22' situation – eg, your relationship may have started at a time when either you or your partner were already on asylum support and you will not have been allowed to join their household. Therefore, you will have never been able to build up two years of having lived together before the application for support;[19]
- someone who has applied to the Home Office to remain in the UK as a dependant on your relative's asylum claim.

Note: being a dependant for support purposes is not always the same as being a dependant on another person's asylum claim. Whether the Home Office allows you to be a dependant on someone else's asylum claim (and whether this would be in your interests) and, therefore, whether you can be a dependant on her/his asylum support claim, is not always simple. The issue of who can be a dependant overall is a complex one and you should obtain specialist advice if this affects you. Further information is in the Asylum Support Appeals Project Factsheet 11, *Asylum Support for Dependants*.[20]

The definition of destitute

You are considered destitute if:[21]

- you do not have adequate accommodation or any means of obtaining it (whether or not you can meet your other essential living needs); *or*

- you have adequate accommodation or the means of obtaining it, but cannot meet your other essential living needs.

When you make an application for support, you are regarded as destitute if there is a likelihood of destitution within 14 days.[22] If you already receive support, you continue to be regarded as destitute if there is a likelihood of destitution within 56 days.[23]

See p416 for what income and assets are taken into account when deciding whether or not you are destitute.

Who is excluded from support

Even if you are eligible for section 95 support, you can be excluded from getting support if:[24]
- you are not excluded from getting social security benefits because of your immigration status (see p67);
- you are not being treated as an asylum seeker or the dependant of an asylum seeker for immigration purposes;
- you apply for support as part of a group and every person is excluded under either of the above.

If you do not have dependent children and you apply for cash-only support and not accommodation (see p427),[25] you can also be excluded if you did not claim asylum 'as soon as reasonably practicable' on entering the UK.[26]

There is no statutory definition of the term 'as soon as reasonably practicable'. When the rule was first introduced, this led to substantial numbers of in-country asylum seekers (ie, people who did not claim asylum at the port of entry, but only after they had entered UK) being refused support, and subsequent judicial review cases in the High Court. The Home Office has since issued a policy stating that any claim made within three days of arrival is treated as having been made 'as soon as reasonably practicable'.[27]

Support should not be withheld if a refusal of support would be in breach of a person's human rights.[28]

Other exclusions
The following people are excluded from section 95 support:[29]
- people with refugee status granted by a European Economic Area (EEA) state and their dependants;[30]
- EEA nationals and their dependants.[31]

Note: a child cannot be excluded from support, nor can someone if the provision of support is necessary to avoid a breach of human rights.[32]

When support can be suspended or discontinued

If you have been granted section 95 support, the Home Office can discontinue or suspend it in certain circumstances.[33] This is a discretionary power, which the Home Office must exercise lawfully. Support can be suspended or discontinued if:

- the Home Office has reason to believe that you or your dependant have committed a serious breach of the rules of the accommodation, if accommodated in 'collective accommodation' – eg, a hostel or shared house.[34] Each accommodation provider is likely to have a set of 'house rules', which everyone must follow – eg, to be respectful of other residents and not to make any noise late at night;
- the Home Office has reason to believe that you or your dependant have committed an act of seriously violent behaviour;[35]
- you or your dependant have committed a criminal offence under Part VI of the Immigration and Asylum Act 1999.[36] This includes making a false claim to get support and failing to report a change of circumstances to the Home Office – eg, a change in your financial resources;
- you fail within five working days to provide the Home Office with information about an application for, or receipt of, support;[37]
- you fail to attend an interview relating to your or your dependant's support and do not have a reasonable excuse;[38]
- you fail within 10 working days to provide information about your dependant's asylum application;[39]
- the Home Office has reason to believe that you or your dependant have concealed financial resources and unduly benefited from asylum support;[40]
- you or your dependant fail to comply with reporting requirements;[41]
- the Home Office has reason to believe that you or your dependant have made, or you attempted to make, a second application for asylum before the first application is determined;[42]
- there are 'reasonable grounds' to suspect that you have abandoned your 'authorised address' (see p430) without first informing the Home Office or without its permission.[43]

Your support may be suspended (ie, for a temporary period) if the Home Office requires time or more information to decide whether to discontinue your support – ie, to terminate it entirely. If it is satisfied that there has been a breach of conditions, it must take into account the extent of the breach when deciding whether or not to continue to provide support. **Note:** even if the grounds for suspension or discontinuation are established, you can still retain your entitlement to support if you can show that you are destitute and require support to avoid a breach of your human rights.

If you apply for support again after it has been discontinued, unless there are exceptional circumstances that justify considering it, the Home Office may refuse to consider your application if there has been no 'material change in circumstances' since the original decision to suspend or discontinue the support.[44] This means a change of any of the circumstances that you must notify to the Home Office (see p422).[45]

If the Home Office decides to consider your application for support in these circumstances, it may still refuse support.[46]

A decision to refuse or discontinue support can be appealed to the First-tier Tribunal (Asylum Support). See Chapter 24 for more details.

3. Temporary support

While the Home Office considers your application for section 95 support, it can provide a temporary form of support to you or your dependant(s) under section 98 of the Immigration and Asylum Act 1999.[47] This is known as **section 98 support** and is also commonly called 'emergency support' or (if accommodation is also requested) 'initial accommodation'.

Temporary asylum support can be provided if it appears that you *may* be destitute at the time of the application – ie, even if there is some uncertainty.[48] The definition of 'destitution' is the same as for section 95 support (see p416),[49] except that temporary support cannot be provided solely on the basis that you are likely to become destitute within 14 days.[50]

Temporary support may be provided subject to conditions, which must be given in writing. It can only be provided until the Home Office decides whether or not section 95 support is to be provided. If the Home Office refuses section 95 support, temporary support ends at the same time.

There is no right of appeal to the First-tier Tribunal (see p440) against a refusal or withdrawal of temporary support.[51] The only method of challenging such a decision is by judicial review proceedings.

Who is excluded from temporary support

You are excluded from temporary support if:[52]
- you are not excluded from getting social security benefits because of your immigration status (see p67);
- you apply as a dependant, but you are not being treated as a dependant of an asylum seeker for immigration purposes;
- you apply as part of a group and every person in the group is excluded under either of the above provisions.

---

4. Support for failed asylum seekers

If you are a failed asylum seeker who has reached the end of the appeal process and exhausted all your appeal rights, you are generally not entitled to support from the Home Office; it expects you to return to your country of origin. If you are unable to leave the UK, you may be able to claim support under section 4(2) of the Immigration and Asylum Act 1999. This is known as **section 4 support**.

To get section 4 support you must:

- be destitute (see below); *and*
- meet one of the five criteria for support (see p399).[53]

The Home Office can also provide support under section 4(1) of the Immigration and Asylum Act 1999 to people who have been temporarily admitted to the UK or who are on bail from immigration detention, regardless of whether they have claimed asylum (see p407).[54]

The definition of destitute

The definition of 'destitute' is the same as for section 95 support (see p394).[55] If you apply for section 4 support within 21 days of your section 95 support ending, the Home Office automatically accepts that you are destitute. However, if you have not recently had support, the Home Office usually insists that the onus is on you to prove that you are now destitute, and requires detailed information on how you have survived and how your situation has now changed to leave you destitute. In these circumstances, the Home Office asks you to provide evidence, such as letters from friends, family and charities, explaining what support they have given you in the past and why that cannot continue. You may have survived from working (legally or illegally) in the past and so may need to explain this to the Home Office, so that it can fully understand your new situation. If this evidence cannot be obtained, tell the Home Office (and the First-tier Tribunal in any appeal) why this is the case – eg, the friendship may have now deteriorated because you have overstayed your welcome.

Note: the test of destitution is as set out in the regulations (see p394). If you have relied on friends and relatives, you may still have been destitute within the meaning of the regulations, even while receiving that help – eg, you may have spent nights sleeping on various friends' floors without a key to gain access, and walking the streets during the day, or have had no money and/or little food. In this situation, you have been destitute under the regulations throughout this period, as you have not had adequate accommodation and/or have been unable to meet your essential living needs. When applying for section 4 support in these circumstances, it is important to give full details about what support has been made available in the past.

Criteria for support

As well as being destitute, to qualify for section 4 support, you must also prove that you are in one of the following situations.

- You are taking all reasonable steps to leave the UK (see below).
- You are unable to leave the UK because a medical condition prevents you from travelling (see p400).
- You are unable to leave the UK because there is no viable route of return (see p401).
- You have applied for judicial review (see p401).
- Section 4 support is necessary to avoid a breach of human rights (see p401).

You are taking all reasonable steps to leave the UK

To qualify for section 4 support, you must be taking all reasonable steps to leave the UK or place yourself in a position in which you are able to leave the UK, including, if relevant, applying for a travel document.[56]

The Home Office runs a 'voluntary returns service', through which failed asylum seekers and others without leave to remain in the UK can receive assistance and, in some cases, cash, to return home. If you apply to the Home Office for assisted or voluntary return, this should be sufficient to satisfy the requirement for section 4 support. An application to the Home Office for assisted or voluntary return is not the sole means to demonstrate that you are taking all reasonable steps to leave the UK. However, the emphasis is on expecting you to be proactive in attempting to get travel documents – eg, by visiting your embassy.

After granting support, the Home Office reviews your case every six weeks or so and asks you for documentary proof of what you have done. It is advisable to keep a diary of the steps you take. It is also important to keep copies of all letters and emails, and notes of telephone calls, emails and visits to, for example, the voluntary returns service and your embassy.

If you get support on these grounds, it is likely to be terminated after three months: it is the Home Office's view that a three-month period of support is sufficient for most people to be able to arrange their departure from the UK.[57] Support only continues in exceptional circumstances or if the initial voluntary return application is not successful within three months of its being made (six months for Palestinians). This policy may not be lawful as it does not reflect the test in the regulations, which refers to whether a failed asylum seeker 'is' taking all reasonable steps to leave the UK. So, the question is what steps you are currently taking and not solely what have you done in the past. If you are refused support on this basis, you should appeal to the First-tier Tribunal (Asylum Support). See Chapter 24 for details.

Support is often withdrawn on the grounds that someone has not taken *all* reasonable steps. It could be argued that the Home Office's view on this is often unrealistic, bearing in mind that applicants are destitute, desperate and may speak little English. However, on appeal, the First-tier Tribunal may take the view that, if any reasonable step can be identified that you have not taken, even if you did not previously think of it, you have not satisfied the requirement and will be refused support. Each case should be considered on its own merits.

You are unable to leave the UK because a medical condition prevents you from travelling

To get section 4 support, you must be unable to travel (ie, to make a single journey from the UK to your country of origin) because of 'a physical impediment' or other medical reason.[58] 'Unable' has been interpreted to mean more than 'unreasonable' or 'undesirable', but not 'impossible'.[59]

If you apply for support on this ground, you must submit a completed medical declaration. The form is available from Appendix B of the *Asylum Support, Section 4 Policy and Process*.[60] Arguably, a letter containing the same information on headed paper should be sufficient, but it is advisable to use the form if possible.

The medical declaration must be completed by your GP, consultant or psychiatrist and must state that you are unable to leave the UK because of your medical condition. The Home Office reimburses doctors their fees for completing this form.[61]

When asking the medical professional to complete the declaration, point out the method of travel (eg, by plane) and how many hours it will take to travel to, and wait at, the UK international airport, as well as the number of hours to travel by air to your country of origin and home area. When deciding whether to grant support, the Home Office does not consider your doctor's opinion that you should be allowed to stay in the UK – eg, on compassionate grounds or to finish a course of treatment or to get medical treatment that may be unavailable in your own country. Indeed, if your doctor says this, the Home Office might discount the report, believing that s/he has applied the wrong test.

The Home Office accepts that a woman cannot travel during the period of 'around' six weeks before the expected date of giving birth and six weeks after the birth.[62] You must provide medical documentation (usually Form MATB1 issued by your GP or midwife) to confirm the pregnancy and expected date of birth, or the birth certificate with your application form. The Home Office recognises that a woman may be unable to travel for a longer period if there are particular medical problems with the pregnancy, so you may be eligible for section 4 support earlier in your pregnancy. You can also argue that, according to the NHS, 'the length of a normal pregnancy varies between about 37 and 42 weeks', although the expected delivery date is 'calculated at 40 weeks from the first day of your last period'.[63] However, only 5 per cent of babies are born on their due date. This means that, in practice, a substantial number of babies are born up to three weeks before the expected due date. The First-tier Tribunal has accepted this argument, in combination with evidence of complications in pregnancy, as evidence of the need to provide support earlier than six weeks before the expected date of delivery.

You should also consider providing evidence of how your social circumstances are impacting on your pregnancy. So, for example, if you are experiencing any form of abuse or if you are unable to sleep and eat properly, include this information on the application form.

You are unable to leave the UK because there is no viable route of return

To qualify for section 4 support under this ground, the Secretary of State must have made a declaration that, in her/his opinion, there is no viable route to a particular country.[64]

At the time of writing, there is no country to which this applies. Irrespective of your personal circumstances, therefore, you will not succeed in claiming support under this criterion unless, by the time of your application, the Secretary of State has made a declaration that there is no safe route. The only time the Secretary of State has made such a declaration was in 2005 for a six-month period with regard to Iraq.[65] If your application under this ground is refused, you might be able to argue that this is a breach of your human rights (see p405).

You have applied for judicial review

To get section 4 support under this ground, you must have lodged with the court an application for judicial review to challenge a decision refusing your application for asylum and, in England and Wales, you must have been granted permission to proceed (or leave to proceed in Northern Ireland).[66] Simply lodging a judicial review application at court in Scotland is sufficient.

If you have lodged an application and are waiting for the court to consider whether to grant permission, you are likely to be able to receive support to avoid a breach of your human rights (see p404).

Section 4 support is necessary to avoid a breach of human rights

You qualify for section 4 support if you can show that the provision of accommodation is necessary to avoid a breach of human rights.[67] The courts have said that denying support to asylum seekers whose claims are outstanding, in the context in which they are not allowed to work and would be faced with street homelessness, constitutes 'inhuman and degrading treatment'.[68] This is prohibited under Article 3 of the European Convention on Human Rights.

If you are a failed asylum seeker, you must also show that it is not reasonable for you to leave the UK. You may be able to rely on the fact that:

- you have lodged fresh representations with the Home Office (see p402);
- you have made an 'out-of-time' appeal to the First-tier Tribunal (Immigration and Asylum Chamber) (see p403);

- you have applied for a judicial review challenging a refusal of your fresh representations, or you have sent a letter threatening proceedings (see p404);
- you have an outstanding application to the European Court of Human Rights (see p404);
- you have no safe route of return (see p405);
- there are other human rights arguments (see p405).

You have lodged fresh representations with the Home Office

This is the most usual situation in which a failed asylum seeker is given support to avoid a breach of her/his human rights. You must show that:

- you have made a further application to the Home Office to remain in the UK (see p38). This is usually in the form of 'further submissions' that you want the Home Office to accept as a fresh asylum claim. It can, however, include an application to remain in the UK under Article 8 of the European Convention on Human Rights (see p34); *and*
- this application is still outstanding – eg, the Home Office has not yet decided whether it amounts to a fresh asylum application; *and*
- it would not be reasonable for you to leave the UK at this stage and to be left destitute (while you remain) would be a breach of your human rights (under Article 3).

The High Court has stated that section 4 support should be provided in the above circumstances.[69]

Since 30 March 2015, if you want to make further submissions, you must book an appointment and travel in person to the Further Submissions Unit (FSU) in Liverpool. If you have exceptional reasons why you cannot travel to Liverpool, such as illness, disability or childcare difficulties, you can apply to submit them by post. Previously, only people whose initial claim was made before 5 March 2007 had to travel to Liverpool, as all others could make further submissions at their local reporting centre.

The First-tier Tribunal has granted support on human rights grounds if someone has prepared fresh representations and has an appointment to attend the FSU and submit them on a future date and, in exceptional cases, if further submissions are still being prepared.[70] This is because the applicant has done all that s/he reasonably can to submit the fresh representations. However, the approach of judges varies and some may refuse support unless the representations have been submitted in person.

Even if the representations have been submitted, the Home Office can refuse support if:[71]

- the fresh claim or representations contain no detail whatsoever – eg, if you are still fearful of returning to your country of origin, but do not give any further information or simply state that you will send new information later; *or*

- the evidence or arguments that you have submitted as part of your fresh claim have already been seen and rejected by the Home Office, or rejected on appeal and they do not rely on any change in the law since the previous refusal.

Once the Home Office has looked at any fresh representations, you are informed in writing whether they have been accepted as a new asylum application. If so, a fresh asylum application is recorded. At this point, you become an asylum seeker again and should reapply for section 95 support (see p391). If your representations are not accepted as an asylum application, your section 4 support is discontinued unless you can prove that you meet one of the other criteria for support.

Note: the Home Office used to have a policy of delaying making a decision on a section 4 support application for at least 15 working days to allow time to consider the further submissions. In 2012, the High Court ruled that this policy was unlawful, because it led to a 'significant risk' that Article 3 of the European Convention on Human Rights would be breached if applicants were left destitute while waiting for a decision.[72] The Home Office amended its policy to comply with the ruling. According to the current instructions:[73]

- the caseworker must make every effort to consider the further submissions at the same time as considering the section 4 application;
- the decision about support should not be delayed because of administrative or other problems in assessing the merits of the further submissions;
- 'as a general rule', caseworkers must make a decision on support applications made on the basis of further submissions within five working days;
- if the application is a higher priority, the caseworker must make 'every reasonable effort' to decide the application within two working days;
- there is a non-exhaustive list of cases requiring extra prioritisation, including people who are street homeless, families with children, people who are disabled, elderly or pregnant, and potential victims of torture and trafficking;
- caseworkers must 'check that the further submissions are not clearly abusive, manifestly unfounded or repetitious'.

You have made an application for leave under Article 8 of the European Convention on Human Rights

You may qualify for section 4 support if you have an outstanding application for leave under Article 8 of the European Convention on Human Rights (see p34), provided it has some merit and is not obviously hopeless or abusive.[74]

You have made an 'out-of-time' appeal to the First-tier Tribunal

If you want to appeal against the refusal of your asylum application but the time for appealing has expired, you must ask the First-tier Tribunal (Immigration and Asylum Chamber) for permission for an 'out-of-time' appeal to proceed. If you have made such an application, the Home Office and the First-tier Tribunal (Asylum Support) usually grant section 4 support, considering that it would be unreasonable to expect you to leave the UK in the meantime.

If the First-tier Tribunal (Immigration and Asylum Chamber) gives you permission to appeal out of time, you become an asylum seeker again and are eligible for section 95 support (and, at that stage, no longer eligible for section 4 support).

If you appeal within the prescribed time limits, you are still considered to be an asylum seeker and so you may still be eligible for section 95 support (see p391).

You have issued or threatened judicial review proceedings on an asylum matter

If your further submissions are rejected, you can challenge this by judicial review. You are not eligible for support unless you have been granted permission by the High Court.[75] This can take some time. In the meantime, and while you are preparing to take a judicial review, you may be eligible for support to avoid a breach of your human rights.

A judicial review in the High Court on this issue in 2009 held that the criteria may be satisfied 'in a variety of factual circumstances'. The judge declined to define exactly what these would be, but the implication of the judgment is that they would include if your solicitor has sent the required 'pre-action' letter to the Home Office threatening judicial review proceedings or if you have already issued proceedings and are waiting for a decision on whether you can proceed.[76] You must show that your case is not 'entirely without merit'.

You have applied to the European Court of Human Rights

Failed asylum seekers who have exhausted their appeal rights in the UK, but who claim that their removal would lead to a breach of their human rights, can apply to the European Court of Human Rights in Strasbourg for an order preventing their imminent removal (called a Rule 39 order).

If this applies to you and you are waiting for a decision from the European Court and you are destitute, you may be eligible for section 4 support. In a decision in 2011, a judge in the First-tier Tribunal (Asylum Support) gave criteria for deciding when support should be granted.[77] You must show that:

- your application to the European Court 'has some merit'. This includes showing that it contains details and these are specific to your case. The level of detail required depends on the case;
- you exhausted all remedies in the UK before applying to the European Court, including making a fresh application for asylum and challenging any refusal by judicial review. However, there is no need to have applied for a remedy if it was 'bound to fail'. So, for example, if you have been refused legal aid for a judicial review because of existing UK caselaw, you may still satisfy this ground;
- you have 'raised the prospect of imminent risk on return'. This is usually satisfied if you have applied for a Rule 39 order.

Note: this decision is not binding on other judges in the First-tier Tribunal, but is persuasive.

You have no safe route of return

In the case *M Ahmed v Asylum Support Adjudicator and the Secretary of State,* Mr Ahmed argued that there was no safe route for him to return to his home in Iraq and, therefore, he could not leave the UK and so should be given section 4 support to avoid a breach of his human rights.[78] The High Court ruled that he did not have sufficient evidence to establish that the route back to his home was so dangerous that it would be a breach of his human rights to require him to leave the UK. The Secretary of State, however, agreed that there may be cases in which this argument could succeed and the judge agreed that such an argument might succeed if there were sufficient evidence to support it. However, the Home Office (or the First-tier Tribunal) may conclude that the risks of a return journey would have been considered when your asylum application was refused, and so you would have to show that circumstances had since changed. The issue may need to be tested again in the light of the deteriorating situation in Iraq and Syria.

Other human rights arguments

Many cases depend on their own particular facts. The First-tier Tribunal has granted support on human rights grounds when a medical condition would make travel risky or harmful, but which was not so bad as to mean someone was 'unable to travel'. It has also granted support to a mentally ill person on the basis that he should remain on support while still in the UK.[79]

In one case, the First-tier Tribunal decided that a failed asylum seeker could not be expected to leave the UK while on probation and subjected to reporting requirements and medical tests because of drug offences. Leaving the UK would have meant that he could not comply with the probation order made by the court and support was required to prevent his destitution.

Who is excluded from support

Certain people are excluded from section 4 support. They are the same people who are excluded from section 95 support (see p395).

When support can be suspended or discontinued

The Home Office has no power to suspend section 4 support. This may have been an oversight in drafting the regulations or it may have been thought that, as the nature of the support is in theory temporary, it can simply be terminated.

The Home Office may discontinue your support if it believes that you are no longer eligible – eg, because you are not taking all reasonable steps to leave the UK, your further representations for asylum have been refused or an application for judicial review has failed.

The Home Office's policy is to review section 4 support:[80]

* six weeks after it is granted on the basis that you are taking all reasonable steps to leave the UK, and every six weeks thereafter;

- six weeks after the birth of a baby if you have received support on the basis of late pregnancy or birth of a baby (the Home Office accepts that a woman cannot travel six weeks before or six weeks after giving birth); or
- at the end of the period estimated by the Home Office medical adviser or your doctor as the period within which you should recover sufficiently from an illness or disability that has prevented you from travelling earlier.

Before discontinuing support on the basis that you are not taking all reasonable steps to leave the UK or you no longer have a medical impediment to travel, the Home Office should send you a review letter, asking you to provide evidence that you are still eligible. If you do not provide a satisfactory response justifying why it should continue, the Home Office then sends a further letter terminating support. In all other cases where you no longer qualify (eg, because your further submissions have been rejected), Home Office policy is simply to terminate support without first sending a review letter. You can appeal against the decision. See Chapter 24 for details.

If you have breached the conditions of support

Section 4 support can be granted subject to certain conditions. The conditions must be given to you in writing and must involve:[81]

- specified standards of behaviour; or
- a reporting requirement; or
- a requirement:
  - to reside at an authorised address; or
  - if absent from an authorised address without the Home Office's permission, to ensure that the absence is for no more than seven consecutive days and nights or for no more than a total of 14 days and nights in any six-month period; or
- specified steps to facilitate your departure from the UK.

The Home Office usually writes to you about an alleged breach of conditions before terminating your support. If support is terminated, either with or without prior warning, you should appeal immediately to the First-tier Tribunal, as the time limit for doing so is very short (see p444). Once you have lodged the appeal, your support should continue until the date of your appeal.

The best interests of children

The Home Office has a duty to ensure that all its decisions take into account the need to safeguard and promote the welfare of children.[82] It has a policy of not discontinuing section 4 support to families, which attempts to reflect this.[83]

If the breach of conditions is a minor one, it may not be appropriate to discontinue support. In any event, the Home Office should liaise with the local authority so that social services can carry out a child in need assessment, with a view to taking over the support. The policy is unclear on what should happen if the local authority refuses to provide support because it has emerged that you and your family are not, in fact, destitute – eg, if you have been concealing funds. In this situation, if funds are still available to you, the local authority may also not have a duty to support you under the Children Act as the children in the family would not be 'in need' (see p408).

5. **Support for people on temporary admission, temporary release or immigration bail**

If you are on temporary admission or temporary release, or you have been released from immigration detention on bail, or you are currently in detention and intend to seek bail, you can apply for accommodation and support from the Home Office under section 4(1) of the Immigration and Asylum Act 1999 (see p424).[84] You do not need to be an asylum seeker or a failed asylum seeker to apply for this type of **section 4 support**.[85]

Unlike support for failed asylum seekers under section 4(2), there are no regulations setting out the criteria for support.

If you have been given temporary admission or are on temporary release, you will have been given Form IS96, and will probably be required to report to an immigration officer. It is a different status from being on immigration bail. See p14 for more details. Whether or not you can receive support is at the Home Office's discretion. In April 2013, it issued its policy on how applications are decided.[86]

- This type of support is not provided to asylum seekers or to failed asylum seekers.
- Support may be provided to unaccompanied asylum-seeking children who have reached the age of 18, but whose asylum application was determined before their 18th birthday. This is because they do not come within the definition of an asylum seeker or failed asylum seeker. You must show that you are destitute, that you meet the conditions for section 4 support and that you are not eligible for support from your local authority.
- Applications are only considered from people in other immigration categories (eg, overstayers who have never made a claim for asylum) 'in truly exceptional circumstances'. You must show that you are destitute and that support is required to avoid a breach of human rights. This generally means that it is not reasonable for you to leave the country – eg, because you are waiting for travel documents, you are too ill to travel or you have an outstanding application for leave to remain. The guidance states that support should not be provided

solely because you have an outstanding application for leave to remain under Article 8 of the European Convention on Human Rights or based on long residence. However, as it is now accepted that section 4(2) support can be granted on the basis of an outstanding Article 8 application (see p403), it is also possible to obtain section 4(1) support on this basis, depending on the facts.

The First-tier Tribunal has granted support to the following destitute people on temporary admission who had never claimed asylum:[87]

- a 21-year-old man who arrived in the UK aged 15 claiming he was a British citizen. He had been waiting for seven years for the Home Office to decide his case;[88]
- a man with severe mental health problems who had been certified by his doctor as unable to travel and who had applied for leave to remain outside the Immigration Rules;[89]
- a 43-year-old homeless man who had applied for voluntary return and was waiting for a travel document so that he could return to India;[90]
- a separated father, who was involved in bringing up his British citizen child;
- a homeless man who had been in the UK for 23 years, and was waiting for his human rights immigration appeal.

You can also apply for section 4 support if you are currently detained and need to be able to demonstrate to the judge who will hear your bail application that you will have accommodation if you were to be released.[91] Alternatively, you may already have been released on bail to a particular address and your host can no longer let you stay.

Whether you are on temporary admission or bail, there is nothing in the law to say that you should be destitute. However, the Home Office policy refers to the destitution test (see p398).[92] You may wish to argue that there is no requirement to be destitute (eg, if you have received compensation for having been unlawfully detained), but as providing support under section 4(1) is discretionary, you may not be successful. If you are refused support, you can appeal to the First-tier Tribunal. You can appeal even if you are still in detention at the time. See Chapter 24 for details.

6. **Support from your local authority**

You may be eligible for support from your local authority if you have care needs or if there is a child in your family. Failed asylum seekers with children generally do not need to apply for local authority support as they remain on asylum support.

Note: this is a complex area of law and beyond the scope of this *Handbook*. What follows is a brief description of the support available for asylum seekers and failed asylum seekers under the Care Act 2014 and the Children Act 1989. If you believe that you may be entitled to support from your local authority, get expert advice from a community care adviser.

Local authority support is not listed as a 'public fund' in the Immigration Rules. Therefore, if you have been granted leave to enter or remain subject to the condition that you do not have 'recourse to public funds' (see p25), receiving community care support does not breach this condition.

Who is excluded from support

You are not eligible for local authority support if you come into an excluded group, unless to exclude you would be a breach of human rights (see below). You are excluded if:[93]

- you have, or you are the dependant of someone who has, been granted refugee status by another European Economic Area (EEA) state;
- you are, or you are the dependant of someone who is, an EEA national;
- you are, or you are the dependant of someone who is, a failed asylum seeker who has not complied with removal directions;
- you are not an asylum seeker and you are in the UK unlawfully – ie, in breach of immigration laws;
- you are a failed asylum seeker with children, you are treated as an asylum seeker for support purposes, and the Secretary of State has stated that you have failed, without reasonable excuse, to take reasonable steps to leave, or place yourself in a position to leave, the UK. **Note:** this exclusion is rarely used.

The above exclusions do not apply to children, or where support is necessary to avoid a breach of human rights.[94] There are various situations in which support may be necessary to avoid a breach. In particular, failed asylum seekers and other migrants who are unlawfully in the UK, but who have made a fresh application for asylum or for permission to remain in the UK on human rights grounds, may be able to argue that a local authority should provide support in order to avoid a breach of their human rights while their further submissions are outstanding. However, the submissions must not be 'manifestly unfounded', or merely repeat grounds you have previously made.[95]

Adults with care needs

If you do not have children but have care needs (eg, because of an illness or disability), you may qualify for support, including accommodation, from your local authority social services department (in Scotland, social work department).[96] This is called 'community care' or 'social care' support.

The fact that you are receiving, or may be eligible for, section 95 support from the Home Office must be ignored by the local authority when deciding whether or not to provide community care support and at what level.[97] So, if you qualify for community care support, this takes precedence over section 95 support and therefore you are supported by the local authority, not the Home Office.

The courts have considered where the dividing line is between the two types of support (and therefore which you receive) several times. The authoritative case on this issue is *SL v Westminster City Council*.[98] In this case, it was decided that the applicant should have an accommodation-related need in order to be eligible for local authority support. So, someone with a physical disability who needs help with tasks in the home would be more likely to qualify for local authority support than a person who is mentally ill, whose care could take place outside the home.

The legislation covering community care support changed in 2015.[99] Recently, the courts have established that caselaw before this date continues to apply.[100] Different rules apply depending on where you are in the UK.

- In England, from April 2015, support is provided under the Care Act 2014, which replaces most of the previous legislation covering community care. Local authorities can provide support, including accommodation in a care home or other premises, to adults whom they assess as having a need for care and support.[101] There are national eligibility criteria setting out the minimum thresholds for support to be provided. Your care needs must arise from, or be related to, a physical or mental impairment or illness, and as a result you must be unable to achieve at least two specified 'outcomes', as a consequence of which there is likely to be a significant impact on your wellbeing.[102] The outcomes are:
  - managing and maintaining nutrition;
  - maintaining personal hygiene;
  - managing toilet needs;
  - being appropriately clothed;
  - being able to make use of your home safely;
  - maintaining a habitable home environment;
  - developing and maintaining family or other personal relationships;
  - accessing and engaging in work, training, education or volunteering;
  - making use of necessary facilities or services in the local community, including public transport and recreational facilities or services;
  - carrying out any caring responsibilities you have for a child.
- In Wales, in April 2016, similar provisions to those in England came into force under the Social Services and Well-being (Wales) Act 2014.
- In Scotland, local authorities have a general duty to promote social welfare by making available advice, guidance and assistance to 'persons in need'.[103]

Note: if you are a 'person subject to immigration control' (see p57), which includes asylum seekers and failed asylum seekers on temporary admission, your care needs must not arise solely from being destitute or from the anticipated effects of being destitute.[104] In other words, you cannot get community care support if the only reason you need looking after is because you are destitute. There must be some additional reason why you need to be looked after. This test has become known as the 'destitution plus' test.

Support for children

Local authorities have a duty to safeguard and promote the welfare of children who are 'in need' in the area.[105] If you are destitute and have children, you may therefore be eligible for accommodation or support from your local authority under the Children Act 1989 (in Scotland, the Children (Scotland) Act 1995). A child who is destitute is generally considered to be 'in need', but a child can also be in need if s/he is disabled, or if s/he is unlikely to achieve or maintain a reasonable standard of health or development without the provision of services by a local authority.[106]

Although the duty is to support the child, it extends to supporting parents or other family members if this is in the child's best interests.[107]

If you request accommodation under the Children Act for yourself and your children, some local authorities may suggest that a breach of human rights can be avoided by providing accommodation for the child only and not you, the parent. This is often unlawful. If this happens, you should obtain expert advice from a community care adviser or lawyer, as it may be possible to challenge the local authority's decision by judicial review.

Asylum seekers

If you are eligible for section 95 support (see p391), you and your dependants are excluded from help under the Children Act 1989 or Children (Scotland) Act 1995.[108] However, if you or your children cannot claim section 95 support (eg, because you have breached the conditions of support), you may be eligible for local authority support. **Note:** you cannot be entitled to section 95 support if you are aged under 18. Therefore, if you are an unaccompanied asylum seeker under 18, you are not excluded from Children Act support (see p412). When you turn 18, the local authority may have a duty to continue to provide you with support.[109]

Failed asylum seekers

The parents of a child (although not the child her/himself) who are failed asylum seekers unlawfully in the UK are excluded from local authority support, unless support is necessary to avoid a breach of human rights. Support may be necessary to avoid a breach if you are destitute and you have an arguable application for leave to remain on human rights grounds which is outstanding.[110]

The fact that you may be eligible for section 4 support (see p398) does not exclude you from claiming Children Act support (unlike section 95 support – see above).[111] This is because section 4 is a 'residual power' and any duty to support under the Children Act should come first.[112] Despite this, some local authorities still refuse support on this basis. If this happens, you should get expert advice, as it may be possible to challenge the local authority's refusal by judicial review.

Unaccompanied asylum-seeking children

Local authorities are responsible for supporting children under the age of 18 years who arrive in the UK alone and claim asylum (often referred to as 'unaccompanied minors').

Unaccompanied asylum-seeker children are dispersed around the country, rather than assisted in the areas in which the UK ports and airports are situated.[113] The local authority in the new area should then make arrangements for suitable accommodation, which can include foster care.

If you have already been supported by a local authority as an unaccompanied minor, it may continue to have a duty to provide you with support when you turn 18 under the Children (Leaving Care) Act 2000.[114] This allows for a needs assessment and potential support up to the age of 21, or 24 if you continue in education.

There may be a dispute about your age. If you claim asylum as an unaccompanied minor, the Home Office should refer you to social services for support unless it strongly believes that you are over 18 years old. If the social services department (in Scotland, social work department) has any doubt about your age, it can carry out an age assessment.[115] Get specialist advice if your age has been disputed: refugee organisations, such as the Refugee Council, can assist you (see Appendix 2).

Notes

1. Introduction
1 s95 IAA 1999
2 s98 IAA 1999
3 s4 IAA 1999
4 Sch 3 para 1 NIAA 2002
5 Sch 3 para 2 NIAA 2002
6 Sch 3 para 3 NIAA 2002
7 s115(9) IAA 1999
8 IA(PAFAS) Regs; see also www.gov.uk/
  immigration-operational-guidance/
  asylum-policy

2. Support for asylum seekers
9 ss94(1) and 95(1) and Sch 9 paras 1-3
  IAA 1999; regs 2(1) and 3 AS Regs
10 s55 NIAA 2002
11 ss94(1) and 95(1) and Sch 9 para
  1(1)(2) IAA 1999; reg 3(1) AS Regs
12 para 353 IR
13 s94(3) IAA 1999; regs 2 and 2A AS Regs
14 s95(4) IAA 1999
15 ASA/02/02/1877
16 s9 AI(TC)A 2004

17 s94(1) IAA 1999; reg 2 (4) AS Regs;
Home Office guidance, Asylum Support
(Asylum Instructions), *Dependants on an*
Asylum Support Application, available at
www.gov.uk/government/collections/
asylum-support-asylum-instructions
18 Reg 2(4)(f) and (6)(a) and (b) AS Regs
19 *R (Chen) v SSHD* [2012] EWHC 2531
20 http://www.asaproject.org/uploads/
Factsheet_11_Asylum_support_for_
dependants.2_.pdf
21 s95(3) IAA 1999
22 Reg 7 AS Regs
23 Reg 7(b) AS Regs
24 s95(2) IAA 1999; reg 4 AS Regs
25 *R (Limbuela and Others (Shelter*
intervener)) v SSHD [2005] UKHL 66
26 s55 NIAA 2002
27 Home Office guidance, Asylum Support
(Asylum Instructions), *Asylum Support:*
policy bulletins, Ch 5, available at
www.gov.uk/government/collections/
asylum-support-asylum-instructions
28 s55 IAA 1999
29 Sch 3 NIAA 2002
30 Sch 3 para 4 NIAA 2002
31 Sch 3 para 5 NIAA 2002
32 Sch 3 paras 2 and 3 NIAA 2002
33 Reg 20(1) AS Regs provides that support
'may' be suspended or discontinued.
34 Reg 20(1)(a) AS Regs
35 Reg 20(1)(b) AS Regs
36 Reg 20(1)(c) AS Regs
37 Reg 20(1)(e) AS Regs
38 Reg 20(1)(f) AS Regs
39 Reg 20(1)(g) AS Regs
40 Reg 20(1)(h) AS Regs
41 Reg 20(1)(i) AS Regs
42 Reg 20(1)(j) AS Regs
43 Reg 20(1)(d) AS Regs
44 Reg 21(1) AS Regs; Home Office
guidance, Asylum Support (Asylum
Instructions), *Asylum Support*
Instructions: policy bulletins, 84, available
at www.gov.uk/government/
collections/asylum-support-asylum-
instructions
45 Reg 21(1)(c) and (2) AS Regs, with
reference to reg 15 AS Regs
46 Reg 21(3) AS Regs

3. Temporary support
47 s98 IAA 1999
48 s98(1) IAA 1999; Home Office
guidance, Asylum Support (Asylum
Instructions), *Asylum Support*
Instructions: policy bulletins, para 1.1,
available at www.gov.uk/government/
collections/asylum-support-asylum-
instructions
49 s98(3) IAA 1999, applying s95(11)

50 As compared with the position relating
to asylum support under s95(1) IAA
1999.
51 This is because s103 IAA 1999, which
deals with appeals, does not refer to s98
support.
52 Reg 4(8)(9) AS Regs

4. Support for failed asylum seekers
53 Reg 3(1)(a) IA(PAFAS) Regs
54 s4(1)(a) IAA 1999
55 These are listed in reg 3(2)(a-e)
IA(PAFAS) Regs
56 Reg 3(1)(b) and (2)(a) IA(PAFAS) Regs;
ASA/06/03/12859
57 Home Office guidance, Asylum Support
(Asylum Instructions), *Asylum Support,*
Section 4 Policy and Process, para 4.2.1,
available at www.gov.uk/government/
collections/asylum-support-asylum-
instructions
58 Reg 3(1)(b) and (2)(b) IA(PAFAS) Regs
59 *R (SSHD) v ASA and Osman, Yillah,*
Ahmad and Musemwa (interested parties)
[2006] EWHC 1248
60 Home Office guidance, Asylum Support
(Asylum Instructions), *Asylum Support,*
Section 4 Policy and Process, Appendix B,
available at www.gov.uk/government/
collections/asylum-support-asylum-
instructions
61 Home Office guidance, Asylum Support
(Asylum Instructions), *Asylum Support,*
Section 4 Policy and Process, para 1.11.2,
available at www.gov.uk/government/
collections/asylum-support-asylum-
instructions
62 Home Office guidance, Asylum Support
(Asylum Instructions), *Asylum Support,*
Section 4 Policy and Process, para 1.11.3,
available at www.gov.uk/government/
collections/asylum-support-asylum-
instructions
63 See www.nhs.uk, 'Your pregnancy and
baby guide'
64 Reg 3(1)(b) and (2)(c) IA(PAFAS) Regs
65 *R (Rasul) v ASA* [2006] EWHC 435; ASA/
06/03/12859
66 Reg 3(1)(b) and (2)(d) IA(PAFAS) Regs
67 Regs 3(1)(b) and (2)(e) IA(PAFAS) Regs
68 *R (Limbuela and Others (Shelter*
intervener)) v SSHD [2005] UKHL 66
69 *R (Nigatu) v SSHD* [2004] EWHC 1806
(Admin), para 20
70 See, for example, AS/14/06/31490, 11
June 2014
71 Reg 3(2)(e) IA(PAFAS) Regs
72 *R (MK and AH) v SSHD* [2012] EWHC
1896

73 Home Office guidance, Asylum Support (Asylum Instructions), *Asylum Support Section 4 Policy and Process*, para 1.11.2, available at www.gov.uk/government/collections/asylum-support-asylum-instructions

74 *R (Malumba) v First-tier Tribunal (Asylum Support)*, unreported. The Home Office conceded in the 2015 judicial review that 'provision of s4 may in any particular case be necessary to avoid a breach of a person's Article 8 rights'; AS/14/11/32141, 10 August 2015

75 Reg 3(2)(d) IA(PAFAS) Regs

76 *R (NS) v First-tier Tribunal* [2009] EWHC 3819 (Admin)

77 AS/11/06/26857, 18 August 2011

78 *M Ahmed v Asylum Support Adjudicator and the Secretary of State* [2008] EWHC 2282 (Admin), judgment given 2 October 2008

79 *Khan*: AS/15/09/34157, 8 October 2015

80 Home Office guidance, Asylum Support (Asylum Instructions), *Asylum Support, Section 4 Policy and Process* and *Section 4 Review: instruction*, available at www.gov.uk/government/collections/asylum-support-asylum-instructions

81 Reg 6 IA(PAFAS) Regs

82 s55 Borders, Citizenship and Immigration Act 2009

83 Home Office guidance, Asylum Support (Asylum Instructions), *Section 4 Review: instruction* para 10.2, available at www.gov.uk/government/collections/asylum-support-asylum-instructions

5. Support for people on temporary admission, temporary release or immigration bail

84 Support provided under section 4(1)(a) and (b) is essentially the same: section 4(1)(a) refers to those on temporary admission and section 4(1)(b) to those who have been in detention and are on temporary release.

85 Home Office guidance, Asylum Support (Asylum Instructions), *Asylum Support, Section 4 Policy and Process*, para 5.7.3, available at www.gov.uk/government/collections/asylum-support-asylum-instructions

86 Home Office guidance, Asylum Support (Asylum Instructions), *Asylum Support, Section 4 Policy and Process*, para 1.1.3, available at www.gov.uk/government/collections/asylum-support-asylum-instructions

87 s4(1)(a) IAA 1999

88 AS/11/09/27448, 30 September 2011

89 AS/11/11/76787, 22 November 2011

90 AS/11/12/27777, 12 January 2012

91 s4(1)(c) IAA 1999

92 Home Office guidance, Asylum Support (Asylum Instructions), *Asylum Support, Section 4 Policy and Process*, para 5.7.3, available at www.gov.uk/government/collections/asylum-support-asylum-instructions

6. Support from your local authority

93 Sch 3 NIAA 2002

94 Sch 3 para 2 NIAA 2002

95 *R (AW) v Croydon London Borough Council* [2005] EWHC 2950; *Birmingham City Council v Clue* [2010] EWCA Civ 460

96 CA 2014

97 *R (Westminster) v NASS* [2002] UKHL 38; *R (AW) v Croydon London Borough Council* [2005] EWHC 2950

98 *SL v Westminster* [2013] UKSC 27

99 CA 2014

100 *R (SG) v Haringey LBC* [2017] EWCA Civ 322, 3 May 2017

101 ss8,18 and 19 CA 2014

102 Reg 2 The Care and Support (Eligibility Criteria) Regulations 2015, No.313

103 Support is provided under s12 of the Social Work (Scotland) Act 1968.

104 **E** s21 CA 2014
W s21(1A) NAA 1948
S s12(2A) Social Work (Scotland) Act 1968

105 s17 CA 1989; s22 C(S)A 1995

106 s17(10) CA 1989

107 s17(3) CA 1989; s22(3) C(S)A 1995

108 s122(5) IAA 1999

109 Home Office guidance, Asylum Support (Asylum Instructions), *Transition at Age 18: instruction*, available at www.gov.uk/government/collections/asylum-support-asylum-instructions; s20 CA 1989; Children (Leaving Care) Act 2000

110 *Birmingham City Council v Clue* [2010] EWCA Civ 460

111 *Birmingham City Council v Clue* [2010] EWCA Civ 460

112 *R (VC and K) v Newcastle CC* [2011] EWHC 2673 (Admin)

113 s69 IA 2016

114 *R (SO) v London Borough of Barking and Dagenham* [2010] EWCA Civ 1101; Home Office guidance, Asylum Support (Asylum Instructions), *Transition at Age 18: instruction*, available at www.gov.uk/government/collections/asylum-support-asylum-instructions

115 *R (C) v London Borough of Merton* [2005] EWHC 1753 (Admin)

Chapter 22

Applying for asylum support

This chapter covers:
1. Applying for section 95 support (below)
2. Making a decision on your application (p416)
3. Applying for section 4 support (p423)

---

1. Applying for section 95 support

If you are either an asylum seeker or a dependant of an asylum seeker for support purposes, you can apply for section 95 support from the Home Office.[1] The application can be for you alone, or for yourself and your dependants.[2] See p423 for how to apply for section 4 support if you are a failed asylum seeker who has reached the end of the appeal process, or if you have been temporarily admitted to the UK or are on immigration bail.

You can apply for accommodation and cash support or, if you have somewhere to live, just for the cash support to meet your 'essential needs' (known as 'subsistence-only support'). Most people apply for both.

You must apply for support on Form ASF1, available from the Asylum Help service at Migrant Help (see p391) and from www.gov.uk/asylum-support/how-to-claim.[3] Even if the application is for both yourself and your dependants, you only need to complete one form. If you wish to obtain support as a dependant of a person who is already being supported by the Home Office, you do not need to complete the application form again – the Home Office will consider providing additional support for you if notified of your existence in writing.[4] However, it is advisable to complete a separate application form, as this should ensure that any subsequent refusal is issued in writing, thereby giving you a right of appeal. This may not happen if an asylum seeker simply notifies the Home Office that s/he has been joined by a dependant.[5]

Migrant Help can help you complete Form ASF1 and submit it to the Home Office. It is strongly advisable to get assistance from Migrant Help or a local advice agency if you can. You must complete the form in full and in English.[6] There are detailed notes accompanying it, which give further information about the application procedure and guidance on how to complete the form.

The form asks for details of the stage your asylum application has reached, the kind of support you need, your current accommodation, any other kind of support you receive (including support from friends or relatives, details of cash, savings, investments or other property you own, any employment you have and state benefits you receive, both for yourself and your dependants), and details of any disabilities or special needs you have. You must send documents to confirm the information you give. It is a criminal offence to make false representations in order to obtain asylum support (it is believed that the Home Office has not carried out any prosecutions).[7]

Form ASF1 can be downloaded, printed and filled in by hand, or completed and saved to a computer. With either method, it then must be emailed, faxed or posted to the Home Office. At the time of writing, all applications, whether by email, fax or post, must be sent via Migrant Help. The address for this purpose is Asylum Support Casework Team, PO Box 471, Dover CT16 9FN.

The methods of, and addresses for, communicating with the Home Office frequently change, and if it is unclear from the website how to submit the form, contact a specialist agency for advice.

The Home Office may ask you for further information on any of the details contained in the application form.[8]

2. Making a decision on your application

Deciding whether you are destitute

If you apply for section 95 support for yourself, the Home Office must be satisfied that you are 'destitute'. If you apply for support for yourself and your dependants, it decides whether the group as a whole is destitute.[9]

'Destitute' includes if you are 'likely to become destitute within 14 days'.[10] You are destitute if either:[11]

- you do not have 'adequate accommodation' (see p418), or any means of getting adequate accommodation; *or*
- you cannot meet your essential living needs (see p420), even if you have adequate accommodation.

It is an either/or test, so you are 'destitute' and therefore eligible for both accommodation and cash support, if you are without adequate accommodation *or* without the means to feed yourself.

The Home Office must follow rules that set out what is and what is not relevant in deciding these questions. These apply when you make an application for support and at any stage if there is a question of whether support should continue.

When considering whether you are destitute, the Home Office must take into account any of the following that are available to you or to any of your dependants:[12]
- any income you have, or which you may reasonably be expected to have;
- any other support that is available, or which may reasonably be expected to be available, to you;
- any of the following assets that are available to you, or which might reasonably be expected to be available to you:
  - cash;
  - savings;
  - investments;
  - land;
  - vehicles;
  - goods for trade or business.

This might include support from friends and relatives in the UK (or abroad, depending on the facts) or from voluntary sector organisations. Any income your partner receives (eg, from wages or social security benefits) may be taken into account when assessing whether you are destitute, but only if her/his income is actually available, or might reasonably be expected to be available, to meet your essential living needs.[13]

Land may include property, such as a house and other outbuildings. Investments include business investments, income bonds, life assurance policies, pension schemes, stocks and shares, and unit trusts (but not jewellery[14]). Your land, assets and investments could be in the UK or abroad and must all be disclosed on Form ASF1.

Although jewellery is excluded, you should disclose any items of jewellery or watches belonging to you or your dependants that are worth over £1,000 at the current market value in your application for support, and inform the Home Office immediately if any of these items are subsequently sold and for how much.[15] The money you receive as a result of the sale may be taken into account.

The Home Office examines any visa application you may have made to come to the UK and compares it with the information on Form ASF1. For example, you may have come to the UK on a student or visitor's visa and then claimed asylum. Therefore, it is important to explain how your situation has changed and why you are now destitute.

The Home Office may provide you with support on a limited basis to allow you time to sell items of property – eg, six months if it is a house. The Home Office treats the money received from the sale as cash or savings and takes it into account when deciding whether or not to provide support. If you do not consider it reasonable that you should have to sell your property, give your reasons for this when you send in your application form.[16]

When deciding whether you are destitute, the Home Office must ignore any:
- assets you or your dependants have that are not listed on p417;[17]
- Home Office support which you are already being provided with.[18]

Note: since 2015 the Home Office has been refusing many more applications for section 95 support, finding applicants 'not destitute'. In the Home Office's view, these people have assets or access to assets. You are therefore strongly advised to obtain specialist help with completing Form ASF1. You may need to appeal against the Home Office's decision and your chances of winning the appeal depend on the information you initially submitted.

Adequate accommodation

If you are applying for support but you have some form of accommodation, the Home Office must decide whether or not this is 'adequate'. The Home Office must take into account whether:[19]
- it is 'reasonable' for you to continue to occupy the accommodation;
- you can afford to pay for the accommodation;
- you can gain entry to the accommodation;
- if the accommodation is a houseboat, a caravan or some other moveable structure that can be lived in, whether there is somewhere you can place it and have permission to live in it;
- you can live in the accommodation with your dependants;
- you or your dependants are likely to experience harassment, threats or violence if you continue to live in the accommodation.

Accommodation may be considered inadequate, for example, if you are staying with a friend and sleeping on her/his floor, or if you cannot gain entry to it during the day, or if it is unsuitable for you because of your health needs or a physical disability.

Note: even if the accommodation is adequate, you are still destitute if you cannot meet your essential living needs.

If you have told the Home Office that you want to stay in your current accommodation and only want financial assistance, the factors listed above are not taken into account when deciding whether you are destitute, except for the question of whether you can afford the accommodation.[20]

Note: if you have sufficient savings to be able to rent accommodation for yourself, since 1 February 2016 in England you must obtain permission from the Home Office for the 'right to rent'.[21] Landlords can only grant tenancies or rent rooms to those with a right to rent. At the request of the landlord, the Home Office checks that you are still a current asylum seeker and is likely to grant permission within 48 hours.

Is it reasonable for you to continue to occupy the accommodation?

The Home Office must consider whether it is 'reasonable' for you to continue to occupy the accommodation.[22] In considering this, it may take into account the general housing circumstances in the district[23] of the local government housing authority in which the accommodation is situated.[24] So if your accommodation is worse or more overcrowded than other accommodation generally found in the area in which you live, it may not be reasonable for you to continue to live there.

Can you afford to pay for the accommodation?

The Home Office must consider whether you can afford to pay for your existing accommodation.[25] It must take into account:[26]

- any income or assets (see p416), other than from Home Office support or temporary support, available to you or any of your dependants, or which might be expected to be available;
- the costs of living in the accommodation;
- your other reasonable living expenses.

Do you have access to the accommodation?

Circumstances in which you would be considered not to have access to your accommodation include if you have been illegally evicted from the accommodation, or squatters have unlawfully moved in.

Is there harassment, threats or violence?

The Home Office must consider whether it is 'probable' that your continued occupation of the accommodation will lead to domestic violence against you or any of your dependants.[27] The domestic violence must be:[28]

- from a person who is, or who has been, a 'close family member'; *and*
- in the form of either actual violence, or threats of violence that are likely to be carried out.

There is no definition of 'close family member'. Depending on the circumstances, it may cover a married or unmarried partner and ex-partner, those to whom you have a blood relationship, in-laws, relatives of your partner and others who live (or have lived) in your household. **Note:** the family member does not have to live with you.[29] You may fear that because your address is known to her/him, your continued occupation of that accommodation is likely to lead to domestic violence.

Although the asylum support rules only specifically refer to *domestic* violence, it is arguable that other forms of violence or threats which you have received from anyone not normally associated with you are also relevant when deciding whether your current accommodation is adequate. This may be in the form of racial harassment or attacks,[30] sexual abuse or harassment, and harassment because of your religion or for other reasons.

Your essential living needs

When deciding whether you can meet your essential living needs, certain items are not treated as essential.[31] When deciding whether you are destitute, your inability to provide any of the following items for yourself is not relevant:[32]

- the cost of sending or receiving faxes, photocopying or buying or using computer facilities;
- travelling expenses;
- toys and entertainment expenses.

If you are granted support, the cost of travelling to your new accommodation is paid for by the Home Office.

If you have another need that is not referred to in these rules, it does not necessarily mean that it is an 'essential living need'.[33] The Home Office must decide whether the need is essential, taking into account your individual circumstances. Once you are in receipt of support, it is possible to apply for additional support if your needs are 'exceptional' (see p432).

Clothing

When deciding whether you can meet your essential living needs in terms of clothing, the Home Office cannot take into account your personal preferences.[34] However, it can take into account your individual circumstances when deciding whether you can meet your clothing requirements, including:[35]

- whether you can afford to provide clothes for yourself that are suitable for the different weather conditions in the UK;
- whether you have sufficient changes of clothes required for cleanliness; *and*
- whether you have clothes that are suitable for any particular health or other individual needs that you have.

Decisions and temporary support

The Home Office may decide not to consider your application if you have not completed the form properly or accurately, or if you have not co-operated with enquiries.[36] This is known as a 'section 57 decision'. There is no right of appeal against this, so it is therefore important to answer all further questions from the Home Office (known as 'further inquiry requests') as best you can and within the time limit given to you. The only remedy against a section 57 decision is judicial review.

While you are waiting for a decision on your application, if you appear destitute, you should be provided with temporary (section 98) support (see p397).[37] You can also apply for temporary support before you have completed Form ASF1.

In practice, obtaining temporary support can be difficult, with the Home Office adopting an overly restrictive test of destitution.[38] In late 2016, the Home office sought to improve the section 98 decision-making process and to keep it line with Home Office guidance. If you apply for asylum on arrival or shortly afterwards at the Asylum Screening Unit in Croydon and are street homeless, you should be given initial accommodation (usually, a full-board hostel). If you need to apply for support at a later stage and also need to apply for temporary support, it is probably quickest to apply via Migrant Help, although it is also possible to apply via other voluntary sector organisations.

There is no application form for temporary support, but there is an initial accommodation referral form, which Migrant Help will complete on your behalf, if it is helping you.

If the Home Office refuses you temporary support, it emails its reasons to Migrant Help. There is no right of appeal; the only method of challenging a decision is by judicial review proceedings.

If the Home Office decides to provide you with support, it informs you in writing that your application has been accepted and about the package of support you will receive. If your application is refused, you receive a letter explaining why, and informing you of your right of appeal, together with an appeal form.[39]

Conditions attached to the support

The Home Office may provide you with support, subject to certain conditions – eg that the accommodation is not sublet, that noise is kept to a reasonable level in the interests of neighbours or that you must live at the address the Home Office has provided and inform it of any changes in your circumstances.[40] The conditions must be in writing[41] and given to the person who is being supported.[42]

Even if you have only asked the Home Office for financial support and not accommodation (eg, because a friend has offered to let you stay with her/him), you must inform it of your address for support purposes, and this becomes your authorised address. You must tell the Home Office if you need to leave this address, and you are not allowed to leave the address for more than 14 days.

The Home Office may take into account any previous breach of conditions when deciding whether or not to provide you with support, whether to continue to provide support, and in deciding the level or kind of support to be provided.[43]

Dispersal

The Home Office's general policy is to provide support and accommodation outside London.[44] Under this 'dispersal' policy, most people who are entitled to support are provided with accommodation outside London and the south east of England, unless they can show a strong reason for staying where they currently live. For example, if you are receiving treatment from Freedom from Torture, which is based in London, Birmingham, Manchester, Newcastle and Glasgow, the Home Office takes this into account. It also delays dispersal if your child is about to take her/his GCSEs or A levels. There is detailed guidance on how someone who is pregnant or who has a serious medical condition should be dispersed.[45] It is generally very difficult to succeed in arguing against being dispersed away from London and the South East or against being moved away from the area in which you already live (see p430).

Health benefits

If your application for support is accepted, the Home Office should also issue you with a certificate (HC2), enabling you to get free NHS prescriptions, dental treatment, sight tests and wigs. You may also be able to get vouchers towards the cost of glasses and contact lenses. The HC2 certificate itself tells you how to use it and what you can use it for. If you have already paid for any of the above items or for travel to and from hospital for NHS treatment, you may be able to claim the money back.

Change of circumstances

If you are provided with support, you must notify the Home Office of certain relevant changes in your circumstances.[46] These are if you (or any of your dependants):[47]

- are joined in the UK by a dependant;
- receive or obtain access to any money or savings, investments, land, cars or other vehicles, or goods for the purposes of trade or other business, which you have not previously declared;
- become employed or unemployed;
- change your name;
- get married or divorced;
- begin living with another person as if you were married to her/him, or if you separate from a spouse or from a person with whom you have been living as if you were married;
- become pregnant or have a child;
- leave school;
- begin to share your accommodation with another person;
- move to a different address or otherwise leave your accommodation;
- go into hospital;
- go into to prison or some other form of custody;
- leave the UK;
- die.

If there is a relevant change of circumstances, a decision may be made to change the nature or level of the existing support, or to provide or withdraw support for different individuals.

Note: unless you have a reasonable excuse, it is a criminal offence not to notify the Home Office of a change in circumstances.[48]

Eviction from accommodation

The usual law on security of tenure does not apply to Home Office accommodation.[49] Tenancies or licences created when Home Office support is provided can come to an end when asylum support is terminated – ie, if:[50]
- your support is suspended or discontinued (see p396) because:
  - there has been a breach of the conditions or a criminal offence;
  - you have concealed financial resources;
  - you have been absent from the address without permission;
  - you have ceased to reside at the address;
- your application for asylum has been determined;
- you are no longer destitute;
- you move to be supported in other accommodation.

In any of the above circumstances, any tenancy or licence is terminated at the end of the period (minimum of seven days) specified in a 'notice to quit' given to you.[51]

Further applications for support

If you are refused support, in most cases you can make a further application at any time and this must be considered by the Home Office. The exception to this is if your support is suspended or terminated because you breach its conditions.[52] In this case, the Home Office has the discretion not to accept a new application from you unless there has been a 'material change of circumstances' (see p397)[53] or if there are 'exceptional circumstances'. **Note:** the Home Office has discretion and so a change of circumstances is not always necessary.

---

3. Applying for section 4 support

The procedure for applying for section 4 support is very similar to applying for section 95 support (see p415). There is the same requirement to be destitute and the definition of destitution is the same.[54] You use the same Form ASF1, which can be obtained from Migrant Help or online from the government website (www.gov.uk/asylum-support/how-to-claim). There are additional sections at the end of Form ASF1 that you should complete to show the grounds on which you are eligible for section 4 support.

It is crucial to submit all the necessary information and documentation with your application form. If you supply insufficient or ambiguous information, your application will be rejected or the Home Office will write to you requesting more information, which delays support being provided. There is no interim or emergency support available.

The Home Office previously had a target of making a decision on a section 4 application within two days. In October 2009, this target was removed for people applying for support on the basis that they had submitted a fresh asylum claim. Home Office caseworkers were instructed to delay considering an application for section 4 support for 15 working days in order to first make a decision on the fresh asylum claim/further submissions. In 2012, the High Court found this blanket instruction to be unlawful because it involved a significant risk of human rights being breached.[55] The Home Office then revised its policy instruction to comply with this judgment. The policy is now to make all decisions on applications for section 4 support based on further submissions within five working days and, for priority applicants, within two working days.[56]

However, you may still experience significant administrative delays in decision making. Although the Home Office should provide support as soon as your eligibility is established, there are routine delays. Home Office policy is to give accommodation providers up to nine days in which to provide accommodation, but this often takes longer.

Section 4 support if you have temporary admission or are on temporary release

There is no particular form for applying for section 4 support if you have temporary admission or are on temporary release, so you should use Form ASF1. Make it clear on the form that you are applying for support under section 4(1)(a) or (b) and the basis of your application, taking into account the Home Office's policy.[57] **Note:** the policy does not accurately reflect the law in stating that section 4(1)(a) and (b) support cannot be granted to someone who has an outstanding 'Article 8 application'.

Section 4 support if you are applying for bail from immigration detention

If you are detained under the Immigration Acts (or were detained and still on immigration bail) and want to apply for support (under section 4(1)(c)) and an address for bail (see p407), the application form is a very simple four-page form. This is because the destitution test and other detailed section 4 criteria do not apply. Although there is no statutory basis for the destitution test, the Home Office still considers whether you are destitute.[58] You should therefore be ready to provide information on your assets and income, even though you are not required to complete Form ASF1.

How your application is dealt with

Most section 4 applications are dealt with by a centralised team in Leeds, including if your original asylum application was before March 2007. Applications for section 4(1)(c) support from immigration detainees and those on immigration bail are made to a different part of the Home Office in Liverpool (known as the Complex Casework Directorate, Case Assurance and Audit Unit, or Older Live Cases Unit), and some more complex cases are also sent there. Applications to Leeds can be made by email, fax or post.

When the Home Office has decided that you should receive support and has made the necessary arrangements with an accommodation provider, you are notified of the travel arrangements to the dispersal area (see p430).

Notes

1. Applying for section 95 support
1 Reg 3(1) AS Regs
2 Reg 3(2) AS Regs
3 Reg 3(3) AS Regs
4 Reg 3(6) AS Regs
5 See wording of s103 IAA 1999
6 Reg 3(3) AS Regs. See also Form ASF1 on www.gov.uk/asylum-support/how-to-claim
7 ss105-07 IAA 1999
8 Reg 3(5) AS Regs

2. Making a decision on your application
9 s95(4) IAA 1999; reg 5(1) AS Regs
10 Reg 7 AS Regs
11 s95(3) IAA 1999
12 s95(5) and (7) IAA 1999; reg 6(4)-(5) AS Regs
13 R (SSHD) v Asylum Support Adjudicator and (1) Berkadle (2) Perera [2001] EWHC 811
14 Reg 6(6) AS Regs; Form ASF1 guidance notes, 'Cash, savings and assets'
15 Form ASF1 guidance notes, 'Jewellery'
16 Form ASF1 guidance notes, section 10
17 Reg 6(6) AS Regs
18 Reg 6(3) AS Regs
19 s95(5)(a) IAA 1999; reg 8(1)(a)-(b) and (3) AS Regs
20 Reg 8 (2) AS Regs
21 IA 2014
22 Reg 8(3)(a) AS Regs
23 Reg 8(6)(b) AS Regs. 'District' for these purposes has the same meaning as in s217(3) Housing Act 1996.
24 Reg 8(4) AS Regs

25 Reg 8(3)(b) AS Regs
26 Reg 8(5)(a)-(c) AS Regs
27 Reg 8(3)(g) AS Regs
28 Reg 8(3)(g) and (6)(a) AS Regs; Home Office guidance, Asylum Support (Asylum Instructions), *Asylum Support Instructions: policy bulletins*, Ch 23, available at www.gov.uk/government/collections/asylum-support-asylum-instructions
29 Although Form ASF1 guidance notes ask for information about people who 'normally stay with you as members of your family'.
30 See Home Office guidance, Asylum Support (Asylum Instructions), *Asylum Support Instructions: policy bulletins*, 81, available at www.gov.uk/government/collections/asylum-support-asylum-instructions
31 s95(7)-(8) IAA 1999
32 Reg 9(3)(4) AS Regs
33 Reg 9(6) AS Regs
34 s95(7)(b) IAA 1999; reg 9(1)(2) AS Regs
35 Reg 9(2) AS Regs
36 s57 NIAA 2002; reg 3(5A-5B) AS Regs; see also Home Office guidance, Asylum Support (Asylum Instructions), *Asylum Support Instructions: policy bulletins*, Ch 10, available at www.gov.uk/government/collections/asylum-support-asylum-instructions
37 s98 IAA 1999
38 See www.refugee-action.org.uk/wp-content/uploads/2017/06/Slipping-through-the-cracks-final4-A4-1.pdf

39 Form ASF1 guidance notes, 'What Happens Next?'
40 s95(9) IAA 1999; regs 19 and 20 AS Regs
41 s95(10) IAA 1999
42 s95(11) IAA 1999
43 Reg 19 AS Regs
44 Home Office guidance, Asylum Support (Asylum Instructions), *Allocation of Accommodation Policy*, available at www.gov.uk/government/collections/asylum-support-asylum-instructions
45 Home Office guidance, Asylum Support (Asylum Instructions), *Healthcare Needs and Pregnancy Dispersal Policy*, available at www.gov.uk/government/collections/asylum-support-asylum-instructions
46 Reg 15(1) AS Regs
47 Reg 15(2) AS Regs
48 s105(1)(c) IAA 1999
49 They are 'excluded tenancies' under s3A (7A) Protection from Eviction Act 1977.
50 Reg 22(2) AS Regs
51 Reg 22(1) AS Regs
52 Reg 21(1) AS Regs
53 Regs 15 and 21(2) AS Regs

3. Applying for section 4 support
54 Regs 2 and 3(1)(a) IA(PAFAS) Regs
55 *MK and AH (Refugee Action Intervening) v SSHD* [2012] EWHC 1896 (Admin)
56 Home Office guidance, Asylum Support (Asylum Instructions), *Asylum Support, Section 4 Policy and Process*, Ch 1.15, available at www.gov.uk/government/collections/asylum-support-asylum-instructions
57 Home Office guidance, Asylum Support (Asylum Instructions), *Asylum Support, Section 4 Policy and Process*, para 1.1.3, available at www.gov.uk/government/collections/asylum-support-asylum-instructions
58 Home Office guidance, Asylum Support (Asylum Instructions), *Asylum Support, Section 4 Policy and Process*, para 5.7.3, available at www.gov.uk/government/collections/asylum-support-asylum-instructions

Chapter 23

. . . .

Payment and accommodation

This chapter covers:
1. Section 95 support (below)
2. Section 4 support (p433)
3. Recovery of support (p435)

1. Section 95 support

Section 95 asylum support includes:[1]
- accommodation and 'subsistance' (cash) to cover your and your dependants' essential living needs;
- subsistence-only support for your essential living needs if you already have accommodation;
- expenses, other than legal expenses, in connection with your asylum application;
- if your circumstances are exceptional, any other form of support that the Home Office thinks is necessary.[2]

Note: the Home Office can disregard any preference you or your dependants have as to how the support is provided or arranged.[3]

When deciding what support to give you, the Home Office takes into account any income, support or assets (see p416) that you or your dependants have, or which might reasonably be available to you.[4]

Support for your essential living needs

If the Home Office decides you need support for your essential living needs, the general rule is that you are provided with cash on a weekly basis.[5]

Amount of support

Since 10 August 2015, the amount of support, regardless of age, is £36.95.[6]

There are additional payments of:[7]
- £3 a week for pregnant women;
- £5 a week for babies under one;
- £3 a week for children between the ages of one and three.

In 2017, the Home Office rolled out a new method of issuing financial support via an 'ASPEN' card. This replaces the system whereby asylum seekers collected their support on a weekly basis from a designated post office. The ASPEN card is a pre-paid visa chip and pin and can be used in the same way as a debit card to pay for items in shops or to withdraw cash from most ATMs. The support is uploaded onto the card weekly. There is no limit on the amount that can be carried over from one week to the next, but the Home Office monitors spending. At the time of writing, some issues have been reported with the new system, including the Home Office claiming that it cannot provide emergency support payments in the event of the card being lost, stolen or failing to work.

Legal challenge to the rates of asylum support

Before August 2015, different amounts were paid to adults and children, and to couples and single people. In the past, the rates were based on the equivalent of 70 per cent of the applicable amount of income support (IS), without any premiums, to which an adult would otherwise be entitled if s/he qualified for IS and had no other income (see CPAG'S *Welfare Benefits and Tax Credits Handbook* for more details). Initially, the rates were increased in April every year, but from April 2011 the rates were frozen, meaning a cut in real terms over several years.

In 2013, the charity Refugee Action brought a judicial review challenge against the Home Secretary's decision to freeze the rate of asylum support. This was upheld by the High Court in April 2014,[8] which ruled that the Home Secretary had acted irrationally and failed to take all relevant factors into account, in accordance with her duties under the European Union Reception Directive and the Immigration and Asylum Act 1999 to provide for asylum seekers' essential living needs.[9] Following the judgment, the Home Secretary reconsidered the level of support, but decided it should remain unchanged. In April 2015, the rate for single asylum seekers over 18 was increased by by 33 pence and then, from August 2015, the rates were cut to the above amounts. This is a significant reduction in the rate previously paid for children in families (£52.96 per week).

Exceptional payments

The Home Office can provide additional support if the normal rate of support is not enough to meet your essential living needs and you can show that your particular circumstances are 'exceptional'.[10] The Home Office's ability to provide exceptional payments was a key part of its case in the Refugee Action judicial review (see above), and so you should apply for exceptional payments if you need to. For instance, the High Court found that it was unreasonable to refuse a separated father help with the travel costs he incurred in visiting his young child because the Home Office was unable to provide him with accommodation closer than 130 miles.[11] The court suggested that reasonable travel costs should enable him to visit his son at least fortnightly. In March 2017, the Home Office produced an application form (Form ASF2)[12] and guidance that allows asylum seekers to apply for exceptional payments for any 'exceptional needs'.[13] You must give details on the form of your needs and circumstances, the support required and its likely duration, together with documentary evidence to support your application.

If your application is refused, the Home Office should provide the reasons in writing. However, if an application is refused, the only remedy is judicial review proceedings.

Maternity payments

You may be eligible for a one-off maternity payment of £300.[14] You must apply in writing between one month before the expected birth and two weeks after, enclosing evidence – eg, a birth certificate, Form MAT B1 from your GP or some other original formal evidence. A payment can also be made if you are a supported parent or a parent applying for support and you have a child under three months old who was born outside the UK. It is important to make this application in time. If it is made late, it is likely to be refused. The Home Office policy bulletin that allows maternity payments does not say whether or not it is possible to make a late claim, but it may be worth trying if you can give good reasons for the delay.[15]

Backdating support

There is often a delay between applying for support and getting paid. This can be serious if you are without support in the meantime. With social security benefits, regulations normally stipulate the start date of the particular benefit. This is not the case with asylum support as there are no rules in the legislation identifying the date from when support must be provided. It is, therefore, unclear whether you are entitled to support from, for example, the date the Home Office receives your application or the date it makes a decision.

In the absence of legislation stating otherwise, it is arguable that support should be payable from the date the Home Office receives a full and valid claim – ie, an application that shows that you are destitute and eligible for support. This should be the case, no matter what delays are caused by the Home Office or the appeal procedure.

However, in practice, the Home Office usually only awards support from the date it makes its decision.

In its policy, the Home Office recognises that awards of asylum support can be backdated if payments have been missed and the applicant has not caused it.[16] This relates to missed payments of support after a favourable decision on eligibility has already been made, not to Home Office delays in processing an initial application for support and before a favourable decision has been made.

Contributions to support

When deciding what level of support to give you as a destitute asylum seeker, the Home Office must take into account any income, support and assets that are available (or might reasonably be expected to be available) to you (see p416).[17] However, if you have income and/or assets, it can decide that you should make a contribution to the cost of your support rather than reducing the level of support provided.[18] If this is the case, you are notified of the amount and you must make payments directly to the Home Office.[19] If you are required to make a contribution, the Home Office may also make it a condition of your support that you pay your contributions promptly.[20] In practice, the Home Office tends to delay the start of the financial support or deduct the relevant amount from the initial support payment.

Accommodation

The majority of applications for asylum and asylum support are made in the south-east of England. However, the Home Office has a strict policy of **'dispersal'**.[21] This means that, apart from a few exceptions, the accommodation and support it provides are outside London and south-east England.

The Home Office does not own and provide accommodation itself. It makes arrangements with private contractors, which provide the accommodation throughout the UK.[22] These arrangements, which include transport, are a crucial part of the dispersal scheme.

When deciding the location and nature of the accommodation you are given, the Home Office must consider:[23]

- the fact that you are only being provided with accommodation on a temporary basis until your application for asylum has been dealt with (including any period during which you are appealing);
- the fact that it is desirable to provide accommodation for asylum seekers in areas where there is a good supply of accommodation – eg, outside London, given that there is an acute shortage of accommodation in the London area.[24]

The Home Office does not take into account your preferences on:

- the area in which you would like the accommodation to be located;[25]
- the nature of the accommodation to be provided;[26]
- the nature and standard of the fixtures and fittings in the accommodation.[27]

However, the Home Office may still take into account your individual circumstances if they relate to your accommodation needs.[28] These include:[29]

- your ethnic group and/or religion. Ethnicity is taken into account, although it does not usually prevent dispersal since the Home Office considers asylum dispersal accommodation to be located in areas where there is either an already established ethnic minority community or where one can be sustained.[30] Your freedom to practice your religion is also taken into account and, if you can demonstrate that you should be allocated accommodation in an area because it is the only place you can worship, this may be accepted. However, if others

of the same religion have been dispersed, the Home Office is likely to consider it possible that you can practise your religion with others in the dispersal area;
- any special dietary needs you or your dependants may have;
- your or your dependants' medical or psychological condition, any disabilities you have and any treatment you are receiving for these.

The Home Office should delay dispersal on medical grounds, pending further medical advice if:[31]
- you are HIV positive or have tuberculosis, and you are having specialist treatment;
- you have severe mental health problems and you are engaged with psychological and psychiatric services and/or dispersal would adversely affect your mental health;
- you are pregnant and four weeks from your expected due date, or you have experienced complications, or you have medical advice against travel, or you are a new mother whose baby is less than four weeks old. You are not expected to travel for longer than four hours to your dispersal accommodation at any point during your pregnancy;
- you are receiving ongoing treatment which is only available in the area where you currently live or which would be hard to replicate elsewhere;
- you are booked to receive invasive surgery within a month, or you are recovering from an operation, or surgery has been booked to take place in more than a month's time but any delay would have an adverse impact on your health;
- delaying dispersal is necessary to arrange continuity of care – eg, if you are undergoing kidney dialysis;
- an infectious and notifiable disease is present or suspected;
- you have been referred to or admitted to secondary care services due to acute need.

The list is not exhaustive, so the Home Office may consider delaying dispersal in other circumstances.

If you are receiving treatment from Freedom from Torture or the Helen Bamber Foundation, the Home Office should provide you with accommodation in London travel zones 1–6 or within one hour travelling distance from a regional office, so you can continue to receive treatment.[32]

Note: the Home Office must apply the above criteria when deciding how and where support should be provided, even though a private contractor makes the actual arrangements.

Expenses in connection with your asylum application

The Home Office may meet some of the expenses connected to your asylum application.[33] These do not include 'legal' expenses – eg, the costs of paying your lawyer to prepare your case and represent you.

Eligible expenses include the cost of preparing and copying documents and travelling to Home Office interviews,[34] and may include the cost of:

- sending letters and faxes in order to obtain further evidence;
- medical reports and expert reports on your country of origin;
- your travel expenses (or those of your witnesses) to attend your appeal;
- medical or other examinations in connection with your application.

Note: you may also be able to apply for exceptional payments (see p428).

In practice, the difficulties and bureaucratic nature of dealing with the Home Office often make the process of claiming overwhelming and uneconomic. In addition, the Home Office is aware that funding from the Legal Aid Agency is available to pay for assessments and reports to support your asylum application.

Although not paid as asylum support, the cost of your fares incurred in travelling to comply with any immigration reporting requirements can be reclaimed from the Home Office if you live more than three miles from the reporting centre.[35] You must claim these at the reporting centre. It is only possible to claim the travel costs for attending your next reporting date (ie, in advance), not the costs already incurred. Some reporting centres are very strict in applying the wording of the guidance. This says that the test is a three-mile 'radius', interpreted as the straight-line distance between the reporting centre and your accommodation, not whether the distance that you must travel is over three miles. The Home Office has, however, been pressed to interpret the guidance more sensibly.

Services

If you are receiving asylum support, the Home Office may provide the following services:[36]

- education, including English language lessons;
- sporting or other developmental activities.

The Home Office has the power to provide these services, but it is not under a duty to do so. In addition, the services may only be provided in order to 'maintain good order' among supported asylum seekers.[37] This does not mean that 'good order' must have broken down before these services are provided. However, the Home Office must, at least, be able to anticipate that 'good order' is less likely to be maintained without the stimulation of education, language lessons and developmental activities, and general access to, and integration into, the wider community.

Note: at the time of writing, the Home Office is not providing these services.

2. Section 4 support

Section 4 support is provided as a package of accommodation and financial support. There is no subsistence-only support. In 2017, the Home Office began issuing section 4 support recipients with ASPEN cards (see p427). These replace the 'Azure card', which was a pre-paid payment card which could only be used in designated shops. However, unlike section 95 support, section 4 recipients cannot use their ASPEN card to withdraw cash from ATMs and are only able to use the card to make payments in participating shops.

Unlike section 95 support, there are no specific provisions to reduce the value of any support provided under section 4, to require you to make contributions, or to recover the value of support if it has been provided to someone who is not entitled to it.

The value of the payment card

The financial element of section 4 support is not fixed in the legislation, but is decided by the Secretary of State for the Home Department. When the regulations were made in 2005, the value of the vouchers was set at £35 per individual – ie, for each adult and child. This amount has only been increased once since 2005 – in early 2010, it was raised to £35.39 for each member of the household.

It is possible to carry your balance over from one week to the next – eg, in order to save for more expensive items. However, if too much balance is accrued, the Home Office may query whether you are destitute.

Additional support

There has been criticism of the low level of financial support provided under section 4 and, in order to comply with a European Directive, the government introduced additional section 4 support in 2007.[38] This additional support can be claimed by failed asylum seekers (and/or their dependants) in certain prescribed circumstances. **Note:** this additional support is not provided automatically. You must make an application to the Home Office, using the form *Application for Provision of Services or Facilities for Section 4 Service Users*. The application form includes useful guidance.[39]

You can claim additional support:[40]
- for the costs of travel to receive healthcare treatment where a 'qualifying journey' is necessary. A **'qualifying journey'** is a single journey of at least three miles, or of any distance if:
  - you or your child are unable, or virtually unable, to walk up to three miles because of a physical impediment or for some other reason; *or*
  - you have at least one dependant aged under five years;
- for the costs of travel to register a birth;
- to obtain a child's full birth certificate;

- for telephone calls and letters (ie, stationery and postage) about medical treatment or care and to communicate with:
  - the Home Office;
  - a 'qualified person' – ie, a solicitor, barrister or authorised immigration adviser;
  - a court or tribunal;
  - a voluntary sector partner;
  - a Citizens Advice Bureau;
  - a local authority;
  - an immigration officer;
  - the Secretary of State;
- if you are pregnant (up to £3 a week);
- if have a child under one year (up to £5 a week);
- if have a child between one and five years (up to £3 a week);
- for clothing for a child under 16 years old (up to £5 a week);
- for exceptional specific needs. The Home Office must be satisfied that there is an exceptional need (which may not be met by the above) for travel, telephone calls, stationery and postage, or essential living needs. This could include travel to your embassy.

There is also a one-off additional payment for pregnant women and new mothers similar to the maternity payment that can be made with section 95 support – see p429). The amount is £250 (£500 if twins) and it is provided as a credit on your payment card. You should apply on the application form, with a MAT B1 certificate or birth certificate. You must apply between eight weeks before the expected due date and six weeks after the birth.

Many failed asylum seekers and others in receipt of section 4 support are required to sign in at an immigration reporting centre at regular intervals and may be able to reclaim their travel costs (see p14).

Accommodation

If you have friends or family who can provide you with accommodation, but who cannot support you, the Home Office cannot provide you with the financial element of section 4 support unless you occupy Home Office accommodation.[41] You must therefore take up the offer of Home Office accommodation in order to receive payment card credits.

This situation can cause severe hardship and can seem absurd. You may have friends who can provide you with accommodation, companionship and social, psychological and moral support which may be crucial to you and, in this case, it would be substantially less expensive for the government simply to provide you with the payment card without accommodation. You may therefore be left with the stark choice of living with your friends but remaining destitute (with the risk that your friends may then refuse to accommodate you), or being dispersed – possibly far from your friends to a place where you know no one and, if you are a single person, where you may have to share a room with strangers.

The Home Office has split adults (ie, over 18 years old) from their families in this way when they have had separate asylum applications. It is therefore important that you obtain advice from your immigration lawyer on the inclusion of a family member in the asylum claim of another as a dependant.

In one case, the High Court found that a refusal to provide support to a refused asylum seeker in a way that allowed him to continue to live with his British partner and child did not breach their right to family life under Article 8 of the European Convention on Human Rights, but the Home Office stated that it would make 'every effort' to house the applicant within a 'reasonable walking distance' of close family members.[42] If you are dispersed to accommodation that is a long distance from your family, you may still be able to challenge the dispersal by judicial review.

3. **Recovery of support**

There are four circumstances in which you may be required to repay your asylum support. These only apply to section 95 support. You do not have to repay any section 4 support you have received.

The Home Office may require you to repay your support if:
- you had assets at the time of your application for support that you can now convert into money (see below);[43]
- you have been overpaid support as a result of an error (see p436);[44]
- you have misrepresented or failed to disclose a 'material fact' (see p436);
- it transpires that you were not destitute.[45]

In addition, the Home Office may try to recover any support provided to you from a person who has sponsored your stay in the UK (see p436).[46]

The Home Office can recover the support through deductions from your existing asylum support[47] or through the civil courts as though it were a debt.[48]

You have convertible assets

Apart from any overpayments, the Home Office can require you to repay the value of any section 95 support if, at the time of your application for support, you had assets (eg, savings, investments, property or shares) either in the UK or elsewhere that you could not convert into money that is available to you, but you now can (even if you have not done so).[49]

The Home Office cannot require you to repay more than either:[50]
- the total monetary value of all the support provided to you up to the date that it asks you to make a repayment; *or, if it is a lesser amount,*
- the total monetary value of the assets which you had at the time of the application for support and which you have since been able to convert into money.

You were overpaid support

The Home Office may require you to repay any section 95 support that has been provided to you as a result of an 'error' by the Home Office.[51] Unlike recovery of overpayments of most social security benefits, you do not need to have been responsible for the overpayment in any way.

The Home Office may recover the support from you whether or not you are still being supported.[52] It cannot recover more than the total monetary value of the support provided to you as a result of its mistake.[53]

You have misrepresented or failed to disclose a material fact

If the Home Office believes that you have received support as a result of misrepresenting or failing to disclose a material fact, it may apply to a county court (or, in Scotland, the sheriff court) for an order to require you (or the person who made the misrepresentation, or who was responsible for the failure to disclose) to repay the section 95 support.[54] This means that recovery is possible from people other than you and your dependants. The total amount that the court can order to be repaid is the monetary value of the support paid as a result of the misrepresentation or failure to disclose, which would not have been provided had there not been that misrepresentation or failure to disclose.[55]

Recovery from a sponsor

Support may be recovered from a sponsor of someone who receives asylum support.[56] A **'sponsor'** is a person who has given a written undertaking under the Immigration Rules to be responsible for the maintenance and accommodation of someone seeking to enter or remain in the UK (see p26).[57] This form of recovery is intended to deal with the situation in which someone obtains admission to the UK under a sponsorship agreement in a non-asylum capacity and then applies for asylum and becomes entitled to asylum support during the process. The sponsor is only liable to make payments for the period during which the undertaking was in effect.[58] S/he should not, therefore, be liable for payments for any period of leave given subsequent to the original leave for which the undertaking was given, unless a further undertaking was also given. The sponsor is not liable for payments during any period of residence without leave.

In order to recover asylum support, the Home Office must apply to a magistrates' court (the sheriff court in Scotland) for an order. The court may order the sponsor to make weekly payments to the Home Office of an amount which the court thinks is appropriate, taking into account all the circumstances of the case and, in particular, the sponsor's own income.[59] The weekly sum must not be more than the weekly value of the support being provided to the asylum seeker.[60] The court can order that payments be made to cover any period before the time the Home Office applied to the court. If it does so, it must take into account the sponsor's income during the period concerned, rather than her/his current income.[61] The order can be enforced in the same way as a maintenance order.[62]

Notes

1. **Section 95 support**
   1 s96(1) IAA 1999
   2 s96(2) IAA 1999
   3 s97(7) IAA 1999
   4 Reg 12(3) AS Regs
   5 Reg 10(1)(2) AS Regs
   6 Reg 2(2) Asylum Support (Amendment No.3) Regulations 2015, No.1501
   7 Reg 10A AS Regs, introduced by The Asylum Support (Amendment) Regulations 2003, No.241; see also Home Office guidance, Asylum Support (Asylum Instructions), *Asylum Support Instructions: policy bulletins*, para 25.5, available at www.gov.uk/government/collections/asylum-support-asylum-instructions
   8 R (Refugee Action) v SSHD [2014] EWHC 1033 (Admin)
   9 R (Refugee Action) v SSHD [2014] EWHC 1033 (Admin)
   10 s96(2) IAA 1999
   11 R (MG) v SSHD [2015] EWHC 3142 (Admin)
   12 Available at www.gov.uk/government/publications/application-for-additional-asylum-support-form-asf2
   13 See Home Office guidance, Asylum Support (Asylum Instructions), *Applications for Additional Support*, available at www.gov.uk/government/collections/asylum-support-asylum-instructions

   14 Home Office guidance, Asylum Support (Asylum Instructions), *Asylum Support Instructions: policy bulletins*, para 25.2, available at www.gov.uk/government/collections/asylum-support-asylum-instructions
   15 Home Office guidance, Asylum Support (Asylum Instructions), *Asylum Support Instructions: policy bulletins*, para 25.2, available at www.gov.uk/government/collections/asylum-support-asylum-instructions
   16 Home Office guidance, Asylum Support (Asylum Instructions), *Asylum Support Instructions: policy bulletins*, para 15.2, available at www.gov.uk/government/collections/asylum-support-asylum-instructions
   17 Reg 12(3) AS Regs
   18 Reg 16(2) AS Regs
   19 Reg 16(3) AS Regs
   20 Reg 16(4) AS Regs. Conditions may generally be imposed under s95(9)-(12) IAA 1999.
   21 Home Office guidance, Asylum Support (Asylum Instructions), *Allocation of Accommodation Policy*, available at www.gov.uk/government/collections/asylum-support-asylum-instructions
   22 ss94(2) and 99-100 IAA 1999
   23 s97(1)(a) IAA 1999
   24 IAA 1999, Explanatory Notes, para 303
   25 s97(2)(a) IAA 1999
   26 Reg 13(2)(a) AS Regs
   27 Reg 13(2)(b) AS Regs

28 Reg 13(2) AS Regs
29 Home Office guidance, Asylum Support (Asylum Instructions), *Allocation of Accommodation Policy*, available at www.gov.uk/government/collections/asylum-support-asylum-instructions
30 Home Office guidance, Asylum Support (Asylum Instructions), *Allocation of Accommodation Policy*, available at www.gov.uk/government/collections/asylum-support-asylum-instructions
31 Home Office guidance, Asylum Support (Asylum Instructions), *Allocation of Accommodation Policy*, available at www.gov.uk/government/collections/asylum-support-asylum-instructions
32 Home Office guidance, Asylum Support (Asylum Instructions), *Allocation of Accommodation Policy*, Ch 3, available at www.gov.uk/government/collections/asylum-support-asylum-instructions
33 s96(1)(c) IAA 1999
34 Expressly included in IAA 1999, Explanatory Notes, para 300
35 Home Office, *Enforcement Instructions and Guidance*, Ch 22, para 22a.3.3, available at www.gov.uk/government/collections/enforcement-instructions-and-guidance
36 Sch 8 para 4 IAA 1999; reg 14 AS Regs
37 Reg 14(1) AS Regs

2. Section 4 support
38 The Immigration and Asylum (Provision of Services or Facilities) Regulations 2007, No.3627; Home Office guidance, Asylum Support (Asylum Instructions), *Asylum Support, Section 4 Policy and Process*, Ch 10, available at www.gov.uk/government/collections/asylum-support-asylum-instructions
39 www.gov.uk/government/uploads/system/uploads/attachment_data/file/309984/section_4_service_users_2014.pdf
40 Home Office guidance, Asylum Support (Asylum Instructions), *Asylum Support, Section 4 Policy and Process*, Ch 10, available at www.gov.uk/government/collections/asylum-support-asylum-instructions
41 *R (Kiana and Musgrove) v SSHD* [2010] EWHC 1002 (Admin); *MK v SSHD* [2011] All ER(D) 158 (CA); s4(1) and (2) IAA 1999
42 *R (Kiana and Musgrove) v Secretary of State for the Home Department* [2010] EWHC 1002 (Admin)

3. Recovery of support
43 Reg 17 AS Regs
44 s114 IAA 1999
45 Reg 17A AS Regs
46 s113 IAA 1999
47 Regs 17(4) and 18 AS Regs
48 s114(3) and Sch 8 para 11(2)(a) IAA 1999
49 Sch 8 para 11 IAA 1999; reg 17(1) AS Regs. Note that it is unclear whether the Home Office can require a person who is no longer being supported to repay the value of the support. There is no equivalent wording in para 11 or reg 17 to that effect in s114(2) IAA 1999, which expressly refers to both those who are, and those who have ceased to be, supported persons for the purposes of recovery as result of Home Office errors.
50 Reg 17(2)(3)(5) AS Regs
51 s114(1) IAA 1999; Home Office guidance, Asylum Support (Asylum Instructions), *Asylum Support Instructions: policy bulletins*, Ch 15, available at www.gov.uk/government/collections/asylum-support-asylum-instructions
52 s114(2) IAA 1999
53 s114(2) IAA 1999
54 s112 IAA 1999
55 s112(2)(3) IAA 1999
56 s113 IAA 1999
57 s113(1)(a) IAA 1999
58 s113(1)(b) IAA 1999
59 s113(3) IAA 1999
60 s113(4) IAA 1999
61 s113(5) IAA 1999
62 s113(6) IAA 1999

Chapter 24

Appeals

This chapter covers:
1. Introduction (below)
2. The right to appeal (p440)
3. How to appeal (p440)
4. Decisions the First-tier Tribunal can make (p450)

1. Introduction

If your application for either section 95 support or section 4 support is refused by the Home Office or, in some circumstances, if your support is discontinued, you can appeal to the First-tier Tribunal (Asylum Support), which is based in east London.

A decision of the First-tier Tribunal (Asylum Support) cannot be appealed to the Upper Tribunal and can only be legally challenged by judicial review, except in limited circumstances when the First-tier Tribunal can 'set aside' some of its own decisions (see p452).

The Tribunal Procedure (First-tier Tribunal) (Social Entitlement Chamber) Rules 2008 (referred to as the 'tribunal rules' in this chapter) contain the rules for appeals in the Social Entitlement Chamber.[1] Most of these are common to all tribunals in the Social Entitlement Chamber, but a few refer solely to the First-tier Tribunal (Asylum Support).

In all asylum support appeals, a single judge considers the appeal and makes the decisions. Tribunal judges have no power to make an order relating to the parties' costs, so even if you lose your appeal you cannot be ordered to pay any legal costs to the Home Office or to the First-tier Tribunal.

2. **The right to appeal**

The circumstances in which you have the right to appeal to the First-tier Tribunal
are limited. You can only appeal if you have been refused support by the Home
Office or your support has been stopped – ie:[2]

- you have applied for section 95 or section 4 support and it has been refused; *or*
- your section 95 support has been stopped for a reason other than because you
  have ceased to be an asylum seeker (unless the Home Office has made a mistake
  and you are still an asylum seeker);[3] *or*
- your section 4 support is stopped for any reason.

Further information is in the Asylum Support Appeals Project Factsheet 3,
Appealing to the Support Tribunal.

Any other Home Office decision about your support (such as the level of
support or the place of dispersal) or *any* decision about temporary support can
only be challenged by judicial review. In addition, it is not possible to appeal a
decision refusing you support if the reason for the refusal is that:

- you failed to provide complete or accurate information in connection with
  your application;[4] *or*
- you failed to co-operate with enquiries made in respect of the support
  application;[5] *or*
- you did not make your application for asylum as soon as reasonably possible.[6]

These decisions must be challenged by judicial review, although the Home Office
reconsiders an application if missing information is later provided.

Note: if you are appealing a discontinuation of your section 4 support and you
appeal within the time limits (or a late appeal is accepted) while you are still living
in the section 4 accommodation, your support should continue until the day of
the appeal.[7]

3. **How to appeal**

Notice of appeal

If the Home Office refuses your application for support or terminates your
support, it gives you a written decision with its reasons. It also informs you in the
decision letter whether you have a right of appeal and, if so, provides an appeal
form. You can also get an appeal form from the First-tier Tribunal website at http:
//hmctsformfinder.justice.gov.uk.

The Home Office does not always get this right. So if you want to appeal, but
the Home Office says you do not have the right to appeal, you should get legal
advice immediately.

You must use the prescibed form if you want to appeal.[8] It must be completed in English (or in Welsh).[9] This is known as the **'notice of appeal'**. See Asylum Support Appeals Project Factsheet 4, *Filling in the Notice of Appeal*, for more information.

You must state the grounds for your appeal on the form (ie, why you disagree with the Home Office's decision) and include a copy of the decision you are appealing against. If your notice of appeal does not include all the necessary information and/or is not accompanied by the written Home Office decision, the tribunal sends it back to you and any later attempt to appeal may not be within the time limit.

If you have any further information or evidence which relates to your application for support or your appeal, you should (if possible) send copies of the relevant documents to the First-Tier Tribunal with the notice of appeal.[10] However, do not delay submitting your appeal in order to obtain any further evidence – this can be faxed or emailed to the tribunal later. It is very important that you provide the First-tier Tribunal with any evidence that proves you are entitled to support. For example, if the Home Office does not accept that you are destitute, you may want to provide letters from someone who has been providing you with support, but who cannot continue to do so, or from a voluntary agency who knows your situation.

There is a database of the most significant First-tier Tribunal decisions at www.gov.uk/asylum-support-tribunal-decisions, which you may want to use to see how the tribunal has dealt with similar issues in the past. Although the legal positions expressed in the decisions are not legally binding, they may be persuasive and help support your appeal.

Once you have completed the appeal form, you[11] (or your representative – see p442[12]) must sign it.

Deciding whether to have a hearing

The notice of appeal form asks whether you want to attend, or be represented at, an oral hearing or whether you are content for the appeal to be decided on the papers submitted to the First-Tier Tribunal. An appeal can be decided on the papers without a hearing if both sides agree and the tribunal believes it can make a decision without a hearing.[13] Even if you ask for a paper appeal without an oral hearing, the tribunal may still hold an oral hearing if there are issues to be explored that are raised, but not explained, in the papers (see p446). It is usually advisable to attend the hearing in person. The tribunal judge is likely to understand your appeal much better if you are present to explain your situation.

If you choose to have an oral hearing, the Home Office sends you tickets to travel to the hearing.

If your partner is a British national or has leave to remain and is in receipt of state benefits, it is usually important for her/him to attend the appeal in order to be able to give full details of her/his benefits (with documentary evidence) and to explain why s/he cannot support you. However, unless you specifically request it and the tribunal directs the Home Office to comply with your request, you are only sent travel tickets for yourself.

If you might find it difficult to travel to the hearing (eg, because of medical problems, pregnancy or lack of childcare), you can request on the appeal form for it to be heard by video link. If the tribunal approves, you attend the hearing from a court in your local area, with a video line linking you to the tribunal in London, where the interpreter, Home Office representative and judge attend.

In the notice of appeal you must also state whether you will need an interpreter at the hearing and, if so, in what language and dialect. If you have any difficulties with the English language, you should ask for an interpreter. If required, an interpreter is supplied by HM Courts and Tribunals Service.

Time limits

Your notice of appeal must be received by the First-Tier Tribunal within three working days of the day on which you received the notice of the decision on your asylum support application.[14] If you receive the Home Office's decision letter more than two days after the date it was written, it is advisable to state in your appeal the date on which you received it to show that you are not (or not fully) responsible for any delay. You can submit it to the tribunal by email or fax – the details are on the appeal form.

If you do not appeal in time, ask the tribunal in the notice of appeal to extend the time limit.[15] You should explain why you could not appeal earlier – eg, if you were ill and incapable of dealing with your affairs at the time you received the notice, or if you needed advice. The First-tier Tribunal usually treats applications for an extension of time favourably, provided a sufficient explanation is given for the delay. Judges recognise that the time limit to appeal is very short, and an extension of a two or three days (or longer) is often granted, especially for destitute people who may not speak English and may be relying for advice on an advice agency that is only open during certain hours. The judge must consider your application fairly and justly,[16] including why you (or your representative) could not comply with the time limit.

If the tribunal refuses to extend the time limit, your only alternative is to seek a judicial review of the decision on your asylum application and/or of the decision of the First-tier Tribunal to refuse to give you more time.[17] Alternatively, it may be possible to reapply for support.

Representatives

You may be represented throughout the appeal procedure by a representative of your choice. S/he does not have to be legally qualified.[18] If you are represented, the name and address of your representative must be given in writing to the First-tier Tribunal.[19] This can be done by including the details in the appeal notice. If your representative is unable to attend the hearing with you, you should tick 'no' when asked this question on the form. An adviser should *not* state that s/he is your representative if s/he is simply helping you to complete and submit the appeal form and perhaps acting as a mail box for you. In these circumstances, s/he should write on the form that this is the limit of her/his involvement.

It is generally understood that 'representation' implies an ongoing responsibility for the prompt conduct of all stages of the appeal including:

- securing and preparing all available relevant evidence and submitting it to the First-tier Tribunal;
- dealing with all correspondence with the First-tier Tribunal and the Home Office;
- responding in writing to the directions given by the First-tier Tribunal;
- advising you on each of these steps and at every stage;
- representing you or arranging for a legal adviser to represent you at the First-tier Tribunal;
- advising you on the outcome of the appeal and on any steps to be taken – eg, to secure support if the appeal has been successful or any further challenge (eg, by judicial review) if the appeal was unsuccessful.

If you state that you have a representative, the First-tier Tribunal must give her/his details to the Home Office. Any documents that the Home Office is required to serve must be served on the representative (and need not be served on you).[20] Anyone else who accompanies you to the appeal hearing cannot assist in presenting your case without the First-tier Tribunal's approval.[21]

Advice through legal aid may be available in asylum support cases if you are at risk of homelessness, but only to prepare your case, not to represent you in a First-tier Tribunal hearing.[22]

The Asylum Support Appeals Project (ASAP) attends the First-tier Tribunal, Monday to Friday, to provide free representation and advice to as many people as possible (see Appendix 2). This service is provided by ASAP staff and volunteer solicitors and barristers. You can ask ASAP to represent you when you arrive at the tribunal on the day. Alternatively, and preferably, you can ask your representative (if you have one) to refer your case to ASAP in advance. If you do not have a representative, you can make the referral yourself. If your named representative on the notice of appeal form is a firm of solicitors (and not an advice agency), the First-tier Tribunal may not allow ASAP to represent you, unless you or your solicitor refer the case to ASAP in advance of the hearing.

Response from the Home Office

On the same day as the First-tier Tribunal receives your notice of appeal or, if not reasonably practicable, as soon as possible on the next day, it must fax a copy to the Home Office, together with any supporting documents that you sent with it.[23]

By the third day after your notice of appeal is received by the First-tier Tribunal, the Home Office must send to the tribunal:[24]
- a statement saying whether or not the Home Office opposes the appeal;
- a copy of the decision letter refusing or withdrawing support;
- any other evidence that the Home Office took into account when refusing you support;
- any other grounds and reasons for the decision that have not been included in the decision letter;
- copies of all documents the Home Office has that are relevant to the case.

At the same time, the Home Office must provide you (or your representative) with a copy of all the above information and documents.[25]

This is commonly referred to as the tribunal 'bundle'. It is important that you receive a copy of the bundle before the hearing so that you are aware of all the evidence in the appeal. If you or your representative have not received the bundle on time, you should alert the tribunal and/or contact the Home Office.

The appeal timetable

The tribunal rules set out a timetable for appeals to the First-tier Tribunal, a summary of which is set out below.[26]

Day	Event
Day one	Notice of decision is received by you.
Day four (latest)	Notice of appeal must be received by the First-tier Tribunal. Delivery of a notice of appeal at any time up to midnight on the relevant day is sufficient. If not lodged in time, you must apply for an extension of time (see p442).
Day four or day five	First-tier Tribunal faxes notice of appeal to the Home Office.
Day seven (latest)	Home Office sends its response and documentation to the First-tier Tribunal by fax/hand, and to you by first-class post or by hand.
Day seven or thereafter 'with the minimum of delay'	First-tier Tribunal judge decides whether to hold an oral hearing and: – if no oral hearing is to be held, determines the appeal and sends a notice of the decision and a statement of reasons for the decision to you and the Home Office; *or* – fixes the hearing date for the oral hearing, giving both parties one to five days' notice. It is likely that, at the same time, directions are given (see p446).

	If the judge believes the appeal should be 'struck out' (eg, if the First-tier Tribunal does not have jurisdiction – see p449), s/he must give you an opportunity to make representations. It is likely that a hearing date is arranged to consider striking out, and the full hearing follows immediately if the appeal is not struck out.
Day nine or thereafter 'with the minimum of delay'	Oral hearing held. The First-tier Tribunal judge notifies the decision to you and the Home Office at the end of the hearing or, if not present, sends a decision notice.
Within three days after an oral hearing	First-tier Tribunal judge sends a statement of reasons for the decision to you and the Home Office.

Appeals to the First-tier Tribunal should be processed with the minimum of delay.[27] Taking into account the above time limits, the tribunal usually holds an oral hearing within two weeks of receiving your notice of appeal.

Notices or documents can be sent to the tribunal by post, fax or email or given by hand. If you choose to send documents by fax or email, do not also send them by post.[28]

If a time limit expires on a non-working day (Saturday, Sunday and bank holidays), it is treated as expiring on the next working day.[29]

The hearing

Paper hearings

After it receives the Home Office's response, the tribunal judge must consider all the documents and decide whether it is necessary to hold an oral hearing, or whether the appeal can be determined simply by considering the papers. The tribunal can only decide the appeal without a hearing if both parties agree, but it can decide that an oral hearing is necessary even if you ask for a paper appeal.

You may have stated on the notice of appeal form that you did not want an oral hearing, but may not have been aware of all of the information or evidence relied on by the Home Office until afterwards – eg, new papers might subsequently be disclosed to you by the Home Office or the tribunal. If, having seen any new material, you change your mind and decide that you want an oral hearing in order to make direct representations to the tribunal, you should notify the tribunal as soon as possible by fax, email or telephone. The judge must then take this into account when deciding whether to grant an oral hearing. If you want to make written representations to the tribunal about this further evidence, you should do so as soon as possible.

The decision

In all cases, the First-tier Tribunal must make a decision with minimum delay.[30] If no oral hearing is required, the tribunal judge proceeds to decide the appeal. S/he must send a copy of the decision notice, together with the written statement of reasons for the decision, to both parties on the same day as the appeal is decided.[31]

Oral hearings

Hearing date

If an oral hearing is necessary, the First-tier Tribunal must promptly inform the parties of the time and date. It is likely that the hearing will take place within two weeks or so of the tribunal receiving your notice of appeal.

Tribunal directions

When sending out the notice of a hearing date, the First-tier Tribunal usually also sends 'directions' (a 'directions notice') to both you and the Home Office – eg, to produce further evidence.[32] This is information and evidence which a judge at the tribunal (not necessarily the same judge who will hear your appeal) has considered on looking through the papers will be useful for both sides to produce in order to make a fair decision on the appeal. It may include evidence of your destitution, medical evidence or copies of a previous asylum determination. If possible, these documents should be sent to the tribunal and the Home Office before the hearing. The directions notice tells you to send the information by midday on the day before the hearing. Even if you cannot meet this deadline, you should still send the documents and take them to the appeal hearing. It is important to comply with any directions, because if you do not, the tribunal may not have all the evidence needed to make a decision on your appeal. However, if you cannot provide the documents, you should still go to your appeal.

If an agency or solicitor has helped you to complete the appeal form, the directions may be sent to her/him, so it is important to keep in close and regular contact to check that they have been received and whether your adviser/solicitor can help you respond.

You should also note what further information the Home Office has been directed to provide and make sure you see its response. The Home Office does not always respond in time to the directions notice and may only produce the information at the hearing, if at all.

Further evidence

If you decide that you want to submit more evidence in support of your appeal which you did not send with your notice of appeal, you may still send it to the First-tier Tribunal to be considered. In particular, you may wish to rely on evidence which shows a change in your circumstances after the date of the Home Office decision or which has only now come into your possession. You should send this evidence to the tribunal judge before the date s/he will determine the appeal. Do this immediately and by fax or email if possible, especially if no oral hearing is to be held, as the tribunal will determine the appeal very quickly. This further evidence may overlap with what the tribunal has asked you to provide in the directions notice.

You should also send a copy of this further evidence to the Home Office.[33] Although the tribunal rules no longer require you to do so, the First-tier Tribunal judge will want to ensure that the Home Office has seen the further evidence. There is even the (very unlikely) risk that the judge will refuse to allow evidence that is provided late and which has not been seen by the Home Office.[34]

In any event, you should take copies of all the appeal papers, including your evidence and the Home Office's documents and any new evidence, to the appeal hearing as you may need to refer to them. At the start of the hearing, you should also ensure that none of the papers have gone astray and that the judge has all your evidence.

The Home Office can also send further evidence to the tribunal before the appeal is determined. It is likely that the Home Office and/or the tribunal will send copies to you (or your representative) or, if there is not sufficient time, provide you with copies at the hearing. In any event, you must be provided with copies of any documents on which the Home Office intends to rely at the hearing and you must have time to consider them.

Travel to the hearing

You are sent tickets for your travel to and from the First-tier Tribunal. If you live too far away to travel on the day and arrive on time for your hearing, overnight accommodation is arranged and paid for by the Home Office. If tickets are not sent, a travel warrant can be requested from the Home Office travel bureau.[35] If your tickets have not arrived in time for you to travel, inform the tribunal urgently and your appeal will be relisted. If you decide to travel anyway and purchase your own ticket, it is unlikely that the Home Office will agree to refund it. If there are good reasons why the Home Office should also provide tickets for dependants or witnesses, ask the tribunal to direct the Home Office to do this.

The hearing

In principle, oral hearings before the First-tier Tribunal take place in public, but it is extremely rare for members of the public to attend.[36] The tribunal judge can decide that a hearing, or part of it, should be in private and can exclude anyone who is likely to cause a disruption or defeat the purpose of the hearing. In practice, judges politely check who is in the hearing room in order to ensure that there is no one present who may intimidate you or otherwise hinder a fair hearing. If, for any reason, you think that someone should be excluded, tell the tribunal either before or at the start of the hearing.

As there are no rules setting out the procedure which must be adopted at the oral hearing, this is decided by the tribunal judge.[37] S/he should explain the procedure to you at the outset. There are no strict rules on evidence, and so hearsay and letters from third parties can be considered. You can provide oral evidence and call any witnesses to give oral evidence in support of your case. The Home Office is usually represented by a 'presenting officer', who sets out its case and asks you questions. Sometimes the Home Office is unrepresented at the hearing. You or your representative must also have the opportunity of directly addressing the tribunal about the decision it should make and commenting on all of the evidence, documentary or oral. If witnesses are called, they may be required to give their evidence under oath or affirmation.[38]

If either you or the Home Office attend the hearing with further evidence which has not previously been provided, the other party must be given the opportunity to photocopy and look at it in order to comment on it before the hearing proceeds. The judge often checks at the beginning of the hearing whether anything further needs to be photocopied.

If possible, take notes of what is said at the hearing. It is usual for the judge to make her/his own written record. If you later want to challenge the decision by judicial review, you can request a copy of this.

If you do not arrive at the hearing in time, it may go ahead without you (or in the absence of a Home Office representative) if the judge:[39]

- is satisfied that you/the Home Office have been notified of the hearing or that reasonable steps have been taken to notify you/the Home Office of the hearing; *and*
- considers that it is in the interests of justice to proceed.

The judge waiting usually waits 30 minutes from the listed start time before starting the appeal without you.

The decision

At the end of the hearing, the judge must tell you and the Home Office representative the decision that has been reached.[40] The judge may retire for a period in order to consider the decision before telling you the outcome.

The judge must provide both parties with a 'decision notice' (ie, without reasons) at the end of the hearing.[41] This simply states whether the appeal has been allowed, dismissed or remitted (see p450). The notice is also sent on the same day to any party (ie, you or the Home Office) who was not present at the hearing of the appeal. In addition, whether or not you were at the hearing, the judge must send a 'statement of reasons' for her/his decision to both parties within three working days of the hearing.[42]

Withdrawing an appeal

If, at any stage before the hearing, you decide you do not wish to carry on with your appeal, you can give written notice of withdrawal.[43] If the withdrawal is made on the day of the hearing, the judge's consent is required. The tribunal rules imply that if either party withdraws from the case in writing before the day of the appeal, the consent of a judge is not required and therefore no reasons need be given.

If the Home Office withdraws, this can be unfair on you because, unless it immediately substitutes its negative decision with a positive one awarding you support, you still need your appeal to go ahead.

If the Home Office withdraws from an appeal when you are not yet receiving support, you should refer it to its policy on withdrawals.[44] Under this, if the Home Office serves a notice of withdrawal before 12 noon on the day before the hearing, it should immediately make a fresh decision, which must be posted or faxed to you or your representative. If this decision is again negative (but for a different reason than the first), you need to appeal immediately again. This will have caused a delay in your getting support (assuming you win your eventual appeal). Make sure you compare the two decisions and if there is no substantial difference, draw this to the judge's attention.

Under the withdrawal policy, if the Home Office withdraws after 12 noon on the day before the hearing, it must apply to do so at the hearing itself. The judge only consents to the withdrawal if:

- the Home Office confirms in writing that the decision under appeal is being withdrawn and you are to be granted support immediately; *or*
- the Home Office serves you with a copy of a fresh refusal or discontinuation decision letter, and you or your representative agree that the hearing can proceed on the basis of this new decision; *or*
- both parties agree to adjourn the proceedings (for no longer than 14 days) and the Home Office confirms in writing that you will be provided with support in the meantime.

In practice, the First-tier Tribunal allows the Home Office to withdraw from appeals at any time before the day of the hearing (as opposed to only up to midday) without providing reasons and it is very difficult to prevent this. If you are not immediately provided with a new decision letter, whether positive or negative, refer the Home Office to its policy and consider judicial review if there continues to be a delay.

Striking out an appeal

The First-tier Tribunal can decide that your appeal cannot continue, even before a hearing takes place. This is called 'striking out' your appeal. The tribunal must strike out your appeal if it does not have jurisdiction to decide the matter – eg, it cannot consider an appeal about how much money the Home Office should pay you each week in asylum support.[45] The tribunal may also strike out your appeal without a hearing if it considers your case has no reasonable prospect of success.[46]

In either case, before striking out your appeal, the tribunal must give you the opportunity to make representations. It may direct you to make these in writing by a certain deadline, following which a decision is made by the judge 'on the papers'. Alternatively, the tribunal may fix a date for you and the Home Office to attend to make any representations and, if the appeal is not struck out, the appeal then proceeds to a full hearing on the same day.

4. Decisions the First-tier Tribunal can make

When deciding the appeal, the First-tier Tribunal judge can:[47]
* substitute her/his own decision for the decision made by the Home Office and thus allow the appeal, meaning you are entitled to support; *or*
* dismiss the appeal, so that the decision of the Home Office stands; *or*
* require the Home Office to reconsider the matter. The First-tier Tribunal calls this 'remitting' the appeal (see below).

The effect of remitting a decision is to set aside the decision of the Home Office. This requires the Home Office to reconsider and come to a new decision on whether you should be provided with support. This puts you back into the position you were in before the decision was made. So if you had been receiving support and the Home Office's decision to withdraw your support is remitted by the tribunal, the Home Office must immediately reinstate the support until it comes to a new decision. If you were previously without support and are appealing the Home Office's decision to refuse your application, a tribunal decision to remit that refusal decision leaves you in your previous position of being without support, at least until the Home Office comes to a new decision.[48]

Cases come before the First-tier Tribunal in which people are not sure of their immigration status or it has changed since an appeal has been lodged. It may become apparent at the hearing that you have applied for the wrong form of support – eg, the tribunal may find that you are eligible for section 95 support as an asylum seeker, although you have applied for section 4 support as a failed asylum seeker or vice versa. Previously, the practice would have been for the tribunal to dismiss your appeal, suggesting that you reapply on the correct form. However, in 2011, the Home Office introduced a combined application form for both kinds of support (Form ASF1 – see p415). Since then, most judges have been willing to grant section 95 support if eligibility is established, even if the wrong type was applied for. This fits with the First-tier Tribunal's power to substitute its decision for the decision appealed against.[49]

First-tier Tribunal judges decide issues of fact on a balance of probabilities. This simply means deciding which facts in your case are more likely than not to be true. In appeals against a *refusal* of an application for support, it is up to you to prove, on a balance of probabilities, that you are entitled to support and meet the relevant criteria. If you are appealing a decision to *withdraw* support, it is up to the

Home Office to establish, on the balance of probabilities, that the support should be terminated.

The tribunal can take into account any change of circumstances that took place between the date on which the decision of the Home Office was made and the date of the appeal.[50]

A decision on an appeal by the First-tier Tribunal is legally binding and, if the appeal is allowed, the Home Office is obliged to provide support on that day.

If your appeal is successful, you may be left with a difficult choice. The Home Office offers 'emergency' accommodation situated in a hostel in south-east London while you wait to be allocated 'dispersal' accommodation elsewhere in the UK.[51] This emergency accommodation can be requested from the Home Office representative at the hearing or, if the Home Office did not attend your hearing, you can ask the tribunal clerk to put you in contact with the representative on duty that day. The accommodation is offered on condition that you stay there on the night of your appeal. If you are then allocated accommodation in a different part of the UK to where you were previously living, the Home Office does not provide travel costs to allow you to go back and collect any belongings.

Alternatively, after the hearing, you can return to the town in which you were living, using the return ticket provided by the Home Office. The Home Office should then contact you directly, or through your advice agency, to arrange your accommodation. This usually takes several days to arrange, in some cases even longer, during which time you may be left homeless. You are given travel tickets to get to your new accommodation. This option is therefore more appropriate if you need to collect belongings and you have somewhere to stay and the ability to feed yourself in the short term.

This arrangement is clearly particularly unsatisfactory if you are street homeless but have left belongings (eg, medication) in the town where you were sleeping. If there is any delay by the Home Office in providing support immediately after a successful appeal, it is acting unlawfully and should be challenged in judicial review proceedings.

If your appeal was heard by video link, the Home Office can provide emergency accommodation at your nearest initial accommodation centre. You should request this at the end of the hearing.

After the hearing

There is no right of appeal against the decision of the First-tier Tribunal. If you are dissatisfied with the decision, in limited circumstances you can ask the tribunal to set it aside (see p452).[52] Otherwise, the only way of challenging the decision is by judicial review.

Setting aside a decision

The First-tier Tribunal can only set aside its own decision and make a new decision (or set aside and remake part of a decision) if:[53]

- it was a decision 'disposing of the proceedings' – ie, a final decision or a decision to strike out the appeal and:
  - a document relating to the proceedings was not sent or was not received at an appropriate time by either party or her/his representative; *or*
  - a document relating to the proceedings was not sent to the First-tier Tribunal at an appropriate time; *or*
  - a party or representative was not present at a hearing; *or*
  - there has been some other procedural irregularity in the proceedings; *and*
- the First-tier Tribunal considers that it is in the interests of justice to do so.

You cannot, therefore, ask the First-tier Tribunal to set aside a decision simply because you do not agree with it. Remember that, even if one of these conditions does apply, the tribunal may still decide that it is not in the interests of justice to set aside the decision. For example, even if you did not receive a relevant document at the appropriate time, it may still consider that this did not make any difference to the decision that was eventually made, and so it is not in the interests of justice to set it aside.

If you wish to apply to set aside a decision, your application must be in writing and received by the First-tier Tribunal no later than one month after the date on which it sent the decision to you.[54]

Judicial review

A judicial review is when a judge in the High Court considers the lawfulness of a decision of a public body, including a decision of the First-tier Tribunal. There must be an error in law for an application for judicial review to succeed – it is not enough that you do not agree with the decision the judge made (unless you can clearly show that no reasonable tribunal could have come to that decision). To be successful in judicial review proceedings, you will need help from a solicitor.

An application for judicial review must be made promptly and, in any event, within three months of the decision complained of. It must be in writing, laying out the facts and legal arguments, and be accompanied by copies of all relevant documents.

You must get the permission of a High Court judge to take judicial review proceedings. A judge looks at the papers you send to establish whether there is an arguable point of law and, if not, refuses you permission to proceed. In any event, a judge has a discretion to refuse you permission (or to reject your case at the full hearing) if s/he does not think an order should be made. If you think judicial review might be appropriate in your case, you should immediately get legal advice. Legal aid is available for this.

Decision to remit

If the First-tier Tribunal decides to remit the matter (see p450) and the Home Office then makes a new decision refusing you support, you may appeal again to the First-tier Tribunal against the new decision.

Making a new application for support

Following an unsuccessful appeal, the Home Office cannot consider any further application for support from you, unless it is satisfied that there has been a 'material change of circumstances' between the time of the appeal and the new application.[55] However, if you are destitute and believe that your application or appeal may now be successful, you should reapply. The Home Office and tribunal will want to see evidence that your situation has changed since the last decision. If you decide to reapply for support after a dismissed appeal, make sure your application deals with the points raised in the 'statement of reasons', including by providing information or evidence that the judge considered to be lacking and, hence, why s/he dismissed your appeal.

Notes

1. Introduction
1 TP(FT) Rules

2. The right to appeal
2 s103(1)-(3) IAA 1999
3 s103(2) IAA 1999. Note that the legislation provides a right of appeal where a decision is made to stop providing support 'before that support would otherwise have come to an end'. The wording is ambiguous, but the intention is to allow a right of appeal in any case where support is terminated before the asylum seeker has ceased to be an asylum seeker for support purposes. See IAA 1999, Explanatory Notes, para 317.
4 s57 NIAA 2002
5 s57 NIAA 2002
6 s55 NIAA 2002

7 Home Office guidance, Asylum Support (Asylum Instructions), *Asylum Support Instructions: policy bulletins*, para 6.6, available at www.gov.uk/government/collections/asylum-support-asylum-instructions

3. How to appeal
8 Practice Direction, 'Social Entitlement Chamber, First-tier Tribunal Asylum Support Cases', 30 October 2008
9 r22(3) TP(FT) Rules
10 The standard appeal form itself indicates this.
11 r22(3) TP(FT) Rules
12 r11(5) TP(FT) Rules
13 r27(1) TP(FT) Rules
14 rr12 and 22(2)(a) TP(FT) Rules
15 rr5(3)(a) and 22(6) TP(FT) Rules
16 r2 TP(FT) Rules
17 Note that, in judicial review proceedings, the court may refuse to interfere with the decision you wish to challenge if you have failed to exercise a right of appeal.

18 r11(1) TP(FT) Rules. Note also that asylum support law is not immigration law, and so an adviser does not have to be registered with the Office of the Immigration Services Commissioner.
19 r11(2) TP(FT) Rules
20 r11(6a) TP(FT) Rules
21 r11(7) TP(FT) Rules
22 Sch 1 Part 1, para 31 Legal Aid, Sentencing and Punishment of Offenders Act 2012
23 r22(7)(a) TP(FT) Rules
24 r24(2) and (4) TP(FT) Rules
25 r24(5) TP(FT) Rules
26 rr22(2)(a) and (7)(a), 24(1)(a), 29, 33 and 34 TP(FT) Rules
27 s104(3) IAA 1999 requires the appeal regulations to provide for this.
28 r13(1) TP(FT) Rules
29 r12(2) and (3) TP(FT) Rules
30 s104(3) IAA 1999
31 s103(4) IAA 1999; r34(1)(b) TP(FT) Rules
32 r15 TP(FT) Rules
33 This used to be the case under r8(1)(2) ASA(P) Rules
34 r15(2)(b)(1) TP(FT) Rules
35 s103(9) IAA 1999
36 r30(1) TP(FT) Rules
37 TP(FT) Rules
38 r15(3) TP(FT) Rules
39 r31 TP(FT) Rules
40 r33 TP(FT) Rules
41 r33(2)(a) TP(FT) Rules
42 s103(4) IAA 1999; r34(1)(a) TP(FT) Rules
43 r17(1) TP(FT) Rules
44 Home Office guidance, Asylum Support (Asylum Instructions), *Asylum Support Instructions: policy bulletins*, para 6.5, available at www.gov.uk/government/collections/asylum-support-asylum-instructions
45 r8(2) TP(FT) Rules
46 r8(3) TP(FT) Rules

4. Decisions the First-tier Tribunal can make

47 s103(3) IAA 1999
48 In an application for section 95 support you could, in theory, receive temporary support under s98 IAA 1999 until a new decision is made.
49 s103(3)(b) IAA 1999
50 r10(2) ASA(P) Rules

51 Home Office guidance, Asylum Support (Asylum Instructions), *Asylum Support, Section 4 Policy and Process*, para 1.18.1, available at www.gov.uk/government/collections/asylum-support-asylum-instructions
52 Some other tribunals have the power to review their own decisions under r40 TP(FT) Rules, but the First-tier Tribunal is expressly excluded from doing so by r40(1). If an application is made to the First-tier Tribunal to review one of its own decisions, it can instead treat the application as a request for the decision to be set aside: r41 TP(FT) Rules
53 r37(1) TP(FT) Rules
54 r37(3) TP(FT) Rules
55 s103(6) IAA 1999

Part 9

Other sources of help

Chapter 25

Other sources of help

This chapter covers:
1. Council tax reduction (below)
2. Local welfare assistance schemes (p462)
3. Healthy Start food and vitamins (p463)
4. Education benefits (p466)
5. Free milk for children (p468)
6. Community care support from the local authority (p468)
7. Support under the Children Act 1989 (p470)
8. NHS healthcare (p470)
9. Other financial help (p472)

This *Handbook* is primarily concerned with migrants' entitlement to social security benefits, tax credits and asylum support. However, you may also be entitled to other financial help.

---

1. Council tax reduction

If you need help to pay council tax, you may be able to get a reduction under your local authority's council tax reduction scheme. **Note:** a council tax reduction is *not* a social security benefit or a tax credit, and how the scheme operates depends on where you live.[1]

- In England and Wales, local authorities can devise their own local schemes, which must meet minimum requirements. In Wales, if a local authority does not set up its own scheme, a default scheme applies. Check with your local authority whether it has its own local scheme or whether the default scheme applies.
- In Scotland, there is a national scheme, administered by local authorities.

The regulations for all the schemes are in CPAG's *Housing Benefit and Council Tax Reduction Legislation* and a short overview is also provided in CPAG's *Welfare Benefits and Tax Credits Handbook*.

All the schemes have immigration and residence rules. To be entitled to council tax reduction, you must:

- not be defined as a 'person subject to immigration control' (see below); *and*
- be habitually resident in, including having a right to reside in, the common travel area (see p459), unless you are exempt.

You are not entitled to council tax reduction if you are absent from the property, although certain temporary absences are disregarded. These rules can be affected by whether your absence is in or outside Great Britain (see p461).

To be entitled to council tax reduction in England and Wales you, and anyone included in your application, must satisfy the national insurance (NI) number requirement (see p460).

People subject to immigration control

Unless you are exempt, you are not entitled to council tax reduction if you are defined as a 'person subject to immigration control' (see p57).[2]

You are not excluded from council tax reduction on the basis of being a person subject to immigration control if you are: [3]

- a national of a country that has ratified either the European Convention on Social and Medical Assistance or the European Social Charter (1961). The only non-European Economic Area (EEA) countries to which this applies are Turkey and Macedonia; *and*
- lawfully present in the UK. You satisfy this if you currently have leave to enter or remain in the UK. However, see below if your leave is subject to a condition that you do not have recourse to public funds.

Note: you must satisfy all the other conditions of entitlement for council tax reduction, including the requirement to have a right to reside (see below). Therefore, if you are an asylum seeker with temporary admission in the UK, although you are 'lawfully present', you are likely to be excluded from council tax reduction, as having temporary admission does not give you a right to reside.[4]

Public funds

Council tax reduction is defined as a public fund in the Immigration Rules.[5]

If your leave to enter or remain in the UK is subject to a 'no recourse to public funds' condition, you are defined as a 'person subject to immigration control' (see p59) and (unless you come into the above exception) you are not entitled to council tax reduction.

However, if you are exempt, and are therefore entitled to council tax reduction, this is still regarded as having recourse to public funds. It breaches one of the conditions of your leave and could affect your right to remain in the UK (see p22).[6]

If your leave is subject to a 'no recourse to public funds' condition, you should also avoid being included in someone else's claim because if s/he receives a larger council tax reduction because of your presence, this also breaches your 'no recourse to public funds' condition and could affect your right to remain in the UK (see p22).[7]

Note: although council tax reduction is defined as a 'public fund', a discount in your council tax liability is not. If you get a discount (eg, because you live alone), this does not breach any condition not to have recourse to public funds.

Asylum support

In Wales and Scotland only, asylum support counts as income for council tax reduction purposes, except if you are defined as a 'pensioner'.[8] In England, some local authorities also treat asylum support as income, so you should check your local scheme.

Residence requirements

To be entitled to council tax reduction, you must satisfy both parts of the habitual residence test: you must be habitually resident, and have a right to reside (see p460), in the 'common travel area' (ie, the UK, Ireland, Channel Islands and the Isle of Man), *unless* you are exempt from the habitual residence test.[9]

You are exempt from the habitual residence test for council tax reduction if you:[10]

- are an EEA national and a 'worker' (see p142), including if you retain this status (see p149);
- are an EEA national and a 'self-employed person' (see p159), including if you retain this status (see p163);
- are the family member (see p170) (other than an 'extended family member', except in Scotland) of someone in either of the above two groups;
- are an EEA national with a permanent right of residence acquired in less than five years (the main people affected are certain former workers or self-employed people who have retired or are permanently incapacitated, and their family members – see p197);
- are a refugee;
- have humanitarian protection;
- have discretionary leave (see p36), leave granted under the 'destitution domestic violence concession' (see p35) or temporary protection granted under the displaced persons' provisions;
- have been deported, expelled or otherwise legally removed from another country to the UK and you are not a 'person subject to immigration control' (see p57);
- (England and Wales only) are a Crown servant or member of HM Forces posted overseas and immediately prior to your posting you were habitually resident in the UK;

- receive income support (IS) or income-related employment and support allowance (ESA);
- receive income-based jobseeker's allowance (JSA) and (except in Scotland) either:
  - you have a right to reside other than one that is excluded (see below); or
  - you were receiving both income-based JSA and council tax reduction on 31 March 2015. Your exemption on this basis ends when you cease to be entitled to income-based JSA or you make a new application for council tax reduction.[11]

Note: receipt of pension credit (PC) does not exempt you from the habitual residence test.

If you are *not* in one of the above exempt groups, to be entitled to council tax reduction you must be accepted as 'habitually resident in fact' (see p112) and have a right to reside (see below).

If you are not accepted as 'habitually resident in fact' and/or you do not have a non-excluded right to reside (see below), you are 'treated as not being in Great Britain' and consequently not entitled to council tax reduction.

Note: a local authority cannot require you to have resided in that local authority area for a set period of time before you can be entitled to council tax reduction.[12]

Right to reside

To satisfy the right to reside requirement for council tax reduction, you must have a right to reside in the common travel area, other than as:[13]

- an EEA national with an initial right of residence during your first three months in the UK (see p134);
- a family member of the above;
- (except Scotland) an EEA jobseeker (see p135);
- (except Scotland) a family member of an EEA jobseeker;
- (except Scotland) the 'primary carer' of a British citizen who is dependent on you and would have to leave the European Union if you were required to leave (see p187).

For information on who has a right to reside, see Chapter 12.

National insurance number requirement

If you apply for council tax reduction in England and Wales, you and anyone included in your application must satisfy an NI number requirement that is similar to that for benefits (see p354).[14] However, this does not apply to a child or young person, or if:[15]

- you are defined as a 'person subject to immigration control' because you require leave but do not have it (see p58); and

- you have not not previously had an NI number; *and*
- you do not satisfy the habitually residence test. **Note:** this is always likely to apply if you satisfy the first point, as you do not have a right to reside (see p459).

Absences abroad

Although you must be living in your property to qualify for council tax reduction, certain temporary absences are disregarded. An overview of the rules is provided below, but you should also check the details of your local or national scheme.

In England if you are a 'pensioner' (ie, you have reached the qualifying age for PC and you are not receiving universal credit, IS, income-related ESA or income-based JSA), you continue to receive council tax reduction during an absence for up to:[16]

- **four weeks** if you are absent outside Great Britain, provided the absence is unlikely to exceed four weeks. This can be extended by up to four weeks if the absence is in connection with the death of your partner, a child for whom you (or your partner) is responsible, or a close relative of you or your partner or child, and the decision maker considers it unreasonable for you to return within the first four weeks;
- **13 weeks** if you are absent in Great Britain and the absence is not intended to be longer or is due to your being in residential accommodation;
- **26 weeks** if you are absent outside Great Britain and you are a member of HM Forces posted overseas, a mariner or a continental shelf worker, and the absence is unlikely to exceed 26 weeks;
- **52 weeks** in limited circumstances. These include if you are a hospital inpatient (or your partner or dependent child is), undergoing or recovering from medical treatment, or you are absent from home because of domestic violence.

The above rules for absences abroad came into force on 1 April 2017. The previous rules were similar to those in Wales (see below). If you were already outside Great Britain on this date, these more generous rules continue to apply to you until you return to Great Britain, unless you are a member of HM Forces posted overseas, a mariner or a continental shelf worker.[17]

If you are not a 'pensioner', there are no prescribed rules on absences, so check the details of your local scheme.

In Wales, you can continue to receive council tax reduction during an absence for up to:[18]

- **13 weeks** if your absence is not intended to be longer or is due to your being in residential accommodation;
- **52 weeks** in limited circumstances. These include if you are a hospital inpatient (or your partner or dependent child is), undergoing or recovering

from medical treatment, or you are absent from home because of domestic violence.

In Scotland, you can continue to receive council tax reduction during an absence for up to:[19]

- **one month** if you are absent outside Great Britain, provided you have not been absent on more that two occasions in the previous 52 weeks. This may be extended by a further month if the absence abroad is in connection with the death of your partner or a child for whom you (or your partner) is responsible;
- **13 weeks** if you are absent within Great Britain, provided your absence is not intended to be longer or is due to your being in residential accommodation;
- **six months** if the absence is abroad solely in connection with your treatment, or recovery from treatment, for an illness or disability, or you are accompanying someone else for such treatment;
- **52 weeks** in limited circumstances. These include if you are a hospital inpatient (or your partner or dependent child is), undergoing or recovering from medical treatment, or you are absent from home because of domestic violence;
- **indefinitely** if you are abroad in your capacity as (or accompanying your partner in her/his capacity as) an aircraft worker, mariner, continental shelf worker, Crown servant or member of HM Forces and you satisfy, or are exempt from, the habitual residence test (see p459).

---

2. **Local welfare assistance schemes**

Help may be available under local welfare assistance schemes set up by your local authority (in England) or by the devolved governments (in Wales and Scotland). The DWP may refer to this as 'local welfare provision'.

Depending on your circumstances and where you live, you may qualify if you need help – eg:

- with immediate short-term needs in a crisis – eg, if you do not have sufficient resources, or you need help with expenses in an emergency or as a result of a disaster, such as a fire or flood in your home;
- to establish yourself in the community following a stay in institutional or residential accommodation, or to help you remain in the community;
- to set up a home in the community as part of a planned resettlement programme;
- to ease exceptional pressure on your family;
- to enable you to care for a prisoner or young offender on temporary release;
- with certain travel expenses – eg, to visit someone in hospital, to attend a funeral, to ease a domestic crisis, to visit a child living with her/his other parent or to move to suitable accommodation.

In Wales, the Discretionary Assistance Fund for Wales offers non-repayable emergency assistance payments and individual assistance payments.

In Scotland, the Scottish Welfare Fund is a national scheme administered in accordance with the Scottish government's national guidance, but local authorities have some discretion. You can apply for community care grants and crisis grants, and can be entitled if you are, or are about to be, resident in the local authority's area, if you are homeless or stranded in the area, or if there are other exceptional circumstances.[20] The guidance excludes you from the scheme if you are an asylum seeker, despite there being no such exclusion in legislation.[21]

In England, the local scheme is entirely at your local authority's discretion. Check with your local authority to find out what help is available, whether you qualify and how to apply. However, it is arguable that a local authority cannot require you to have resided in that local authority area for a set period of time before you can be entitled to local welfare assistance. This argument is based on a High Court case in which it was held to be unlawful for a local authority to require you to have resided in its area for a set period of time before you can be entitled to council tax reduction (see p459).

See www.cpag.org.uk/lwas for details of the different schemes.

Public funds

Local welfare assistance scheme payments, other than from the Discretionary Fund for Wales, have been defined as a 'public fund' under the Immigration Rules since 6 April 2016.[22] If you have leave to enter or remain in the UK which is subject to a condition that you do not have recourse to public funds (see p25), you will have breached this condition if you receive a payment from one of these schemes on or after this date. Get immigration advice before you make a claim. The guidance on the Scottish Welfare Fund excludes 'expenses to meet the needs of people who have no recourse to public funds'.[23]

3. Healthy Start food and vitamins

If you qualify for Healthy Start food and vitamins, you get free vitamins as well as vouchers that can be used to buy specified types of food.

Note in Scotland:
- in the future, the rules on Healthy Start food and vitamins may be different. See CPAG's online service and *Welfare Rights Bulletin* for updates;
- if you are pregnant, you are entitled to free vitamins regardless of your income;
- if you are pregnant, you can register with your midwife to receive a free 'baby box' of essential items for your baby.

Healthy Start food

If you qualify for Healthy Start food (see below), you:[24]

- get fixed-value vouchers (worth £3.10 each at the time of writing) that can be exchanged for 'Healthy Start food' at registered food outlets; *or*
- you are paid an amount equal to the value of the vouchers to which you are entitled, if there is no registered food outlet within a reasonable distance of your home.

Healthy Start food

'**Healthy Start food**' means liquid cow's milk and cow's milk-based infant formula, fresh or frozen fruit and vegetables including loose, pre-packed, whole, sliced, chopped or mixed fruit or vegetables (but not fruit or vegetables to which fat, salt, sugar, flavouring or any other ingredients have been added).[25]

Who can claim Healthy Start food

You qualify for Healthy Start food vouchers:[26]

- **if you are more than 10 weeks pregnant** and you are:
  - 18 or over and are entitled to (or are a member of the family of someone who is entitled to) a 'qualifying benefit' (see p465); *or*
  - under 18, unless you are defined as a 'person subject to immigration control' (see p57); *or*
- **if you are a mother** who has 'parental responsibility' for a child and:
  - you are 16 or over and entitled to (or you are a member of the family of someone who is entitled to) a qualifying benefit other than income-related employment and support allowance (ESA). If you are entitled to universal credit (UC), your child must be under one year old. For other qualifying benefits, your child must be under one or it must be less than a year since her/his expected date of birth. This means you can continue to qualify for vouchers for a period after your child is one – ie, if s/he was born prematurely; *or*
  - it is less than four months since your baby's expected date of birth and you have not yet notified Healthy Start that s/he was born. You must have been getting a qualifying benefit before your baby was born. This allows your entitlement to vouchers to continue until you notify the birth. Once you do, you can then qualify under the rule above (if you are 16 or over). **Note:** as long as you provided the notification within the four-month period, you can also get extra vouchers for your child from her/his date of birth.

  If you qualify for vouchers for more than one child under this rule (eg, you have twins), you get a voucher for each. If you do not have parental responsibility but would otherwise qualify for vouchers, your child qualifies instead of you;

- **for a child under four** who is a member of your family. You or a member of the family must be entitled to a qualifying benefit (see below) other than income-related ESA.

In practical terms, this means that each week you get one voucher for each of your children aged between one and four, two vouchers for each child under one (or within one year of her/his expected date of birth), plus one voucher if you are pregnant.

Definitions

The **'qualifying benefits'** are income support, income-based jobseeker's allowance and income-related ESA (in some cases). Child tax credit (CTC) is a qualifying benefit, provided gross income for CTC purposes is not more than £16,190 and there is no entitlement to working tax credit (WTC), other than during the four-week WTC 'run-on' period. Universal credit (UC) is a qualifying benefit if, during the last complete assessment period (or the previous one), you (and your partner if you have a joint claim) had earned income of £408 or less. If your earned income subsequently increases to more than £408, you continue to qualify for a further eight weeks after the last complete assessment period.[27]

'Parental responsibility' means parental responsibility as defined in section 3(1) of the Children Act 1989 (in England or Wales) or section 1(1) of the Children (Scotland) Act 1995 (in Scotland).[28]

'Family' means a person and her/his partner and any child or qualifying young person who is a member of her/his household and for whom s/he or her/his partner counts as responsible.[29] So for example, if you are not entitled to a qualifying benefit, but are included in your mother's or father's claim for one of these, you can qualify for Healthy Start food vouchers.

Claims

You must make an initial claim for Healthy Start food vouchers in writing, and must provide specified information and evidence.[30] You can:

- complete the form in the Healthy Start leaflet (HS01), available from midwives, health visitors, maternity clinics and some doctors' surgeries or from 0345 607 6823;
- download a form, or complete it online and print it off, or email yourself a form from www.healthystart.nhs.uk/healthy-start-vouchers/how-to-apply.

The form must be countersigned by a health professional (eg, a midwife or health visitor) who certifies when your baby is due (if you are pregnant) and that you have been given appropriate advice about healthy eating and breastfeeding. If you are under 16, your claim must also be signed by your parent or carer. Send the completed form to: Healthy Start Issuing Unit, Freepost RRTR-SYAE-JKCR, PO Box 1067, Warrington WA55 1EG.

If you are getting Healthy Start food vouchers while you are pregnant and then inform Healthy Start of your baby's birth by telephone while s/he is under four months old, you can get extra vouchers for her/him from her/his date of birth.[31] You may need to make a claim for CTC for her/him (or add her/him to your existing CTC or UC claim) to ensure that you continue to get the vouchers.

If you do not get vouchers to which you think you are entitled, or have any other problems with these, contact the Healthy Start helpline on 0345 607 6823.

Healthy Start vitamins

If you qualify for Healthy Start food vouchers, you also qualify for Healthy Start vitamins.[32]

In addition, in Scotland all pregnant women are entitled to free vitamins.

Mothers and pregnant women are entitled to 56 vitamin tablets, and children under four to 10 millilitres of vitamin drops, every eight weeks. Ask your local health professional what the local arrangements are for getting your free vitamins.

You do not have to make a separate claim for Healthy Start vitamins; you are sent Healthy Start vitamin coupons with your Healthy Start food vouchers. However, you must show evidence to the vitamin supplier that you are entitled (ie, the letter to which your most recent Healthy Start vouchers were attached) and, if requested, proof of your child's age.[33]

The ways that vitamins are made available varies through out the UK. For details see www.healthystart.nhs.uk.

4. **Education benefits**

Financial help is available from your local authority if you are in school or are a student, or if you have a child in school or college.

Free school lunches

School children are entitled to free school lunches if their families receive:[34]
- income support (IS), income-based jobseeker's allowance or income-related employment and support allowance (ESA);
- child tax credit (CTC) and have annual taxable income of £16,190 (in England) or £16,105 (in Scotland or Wales), or less. This does not apply if the family is entitled to working tax credit (WTC) unless:
  - this is during the four-week 'WTC run-on' period. See CPAG's *Welfare Benefits and Tax Credits Handbook* for when this applies; *or*
  - in Scotland only, the WTC award is based on annual taxable income of £6,420 or less – ie, the family gets maximum WTC;
- universal credit (UC). In Scotland from 1 August 2017, your (and your partner's if you have claimed jointly) earned income must not exceed £610 in the

assessment period immediately preceding your application for free school lunches. The government has indicated that an earnings threshold will also be introduced in England, but at the time of writing, it was not clear if it will also be introduced in Wales. See CPAG's online service and *Welfare Rights Bulletin* for updates;[35]

- in England and Wales only, guarantee credit of pension credit (PC). PC claimants in Scotland may qualify if they receive CTC, as on p466.

Also entitled are:

- 16–18-year-olds receiving the above benefits or tax credits in their own right;[36]
- asylum seekers in receipt of asylum support (see p391);[37]
- in Scotland, a child attending pre-school nursery (or similar) who is entitled under any of the six bullet points above, or if her/his family receives PC, incapacity benefit or severe disablement allowance, or if since the age of two the child is being, or has been, looked after by a local authority or is the subject of a kinship care or guardianship order.[38]

Note: in England and Scotland, free school lunches are provided to all children during the first three years of primary school. In Wales, free school breakfasts are provided to all children in primary schools maintained by the local authority.[39]

School transport and school clothes

Local authorities must provide **free transport to school** for pupils aged five to 16 if it is considered necessary to enable that pupil to get to the 'nearest suitable school'. This applies if s/he lives more than a set distance from that school. However, if there is no safe walking route, a pupil must be given free transport irrespective of how far away s/he lives from the nearest suitable school. Free school transport must also be be provided to pupils with special educational needs and to those whose parents are on a low income – ie, if they receive a benefit that would qualify them for free school lunches or the maximum rate of WTC.

Local authorities can give **grants for school uniforms and other school clothes.** Each authority determines its own eligibility rules. Some school governing bodies or parents' associations also provide help with school clothing.

Education maintenance allowance and 16 to 19 bursaries

Education maintenance allowance is a means-tested payment for young people who are aged 16 to 19, resident in Wales and Scotland, and who stay on in further education. Payments are made directly to the young person and are conditional on regular course attendance. The young person receives a weekly allowance during term time. The amount depends on the household income. Entitlement depends on your being 'ordinarily resident' in Wales / Scotland. Note: this is not just determined by where you live, but can also be affected by your nationality and immigration status. For further details of each scheme, see www.studentfinancewales.co.uk/fe/ema or www.mygov.scot/ema.

16 to 19 bursaries are payments for young people aged 16 to 19 who stay on in further education or training in England. These are available through the school, college or training provider. Certain vulnerable young people (eg, young people in care, care leavers, young people who get IS or UC, or who get ESA and either disability living allowance or personal independence payment) can get the maximum bursary. Discretionary bursaries are available to those in financial difficulty. You should apply as close to the start of the academic year as possible, or as soon as you become in financial need if this is later. See www.gov.uk/1619-bursary-fund for further information.

Neither payment counts as income for any benefits or tax credits the parent may be getting. They are also not affected by any income the young person has from part-time work.

Note: if you are a student, to find out what help is available to finance your studies contact your local authority or college or university, or see www.gov.uk/student-finance. Also see CPAG's *Student Support and Benefits Handbook* and *Benefits for Students in Scotland Handbook*.

5. **Free milk for children**

Children under five are entitled to 189–200 millilitres of free milk on each day they are looked after for two hours or more:[40]

- by a registered childminder or daycare provider; *or*
- in a school, playcentre or workplace nursery which is exempt from registration; *or*
- in local authority daycare.

Children under one are allowed fresh or dried milk.

In Wales, children in key stage one are entitled to free milk.

6. **Community care support from the local authority**

If you have care needs, you may be able to get support, including accommodation, from your local authority or NHS primary care trust under community care legislation.

This is a complex area of law and beyond the scope of this *Handbook*, but see p408 for a brief description of the support available for asylum seekers and failed asylum seekers under the Care Act 2014.

There are restrictions and exclusions that affect all groups of migrants, but there are also exceptions to these rules which mean you may still be able to get support.

Note: community care support is not listed as a 'public fund' in the Immigration Rules. Therefore, if you have leave to enter or remain in the UK which is subject to a 'no recourse to public funds' condition, receiving community care support does not breach this condition. For more information on public funds, see p25.

Community care law is complex, and community care support is often misunderstood and poorly administered by local authorities and other providers. You are strongly recommended to obtain specialist advice before applying to your local authority for support and, in all cases, if you want to challenge a refusal of support.

Adults with care and support needs

Local authorities can provide support, including accommodation, to adults who have a need for care and support. However, if you are defined as a 'person subject to immigration control' (see p57), you are excluded if your need for care and support is solely as a result of being destitute or the physical effects, or anticipated physical effects, of being destitute.[41] This means that, even if you are destitute, there must be another reason for your needing the care and support – eg, because of your age, disability, or physical or mental health problem. This test has become known as the **'destitution plus'** test.

There are other exclusions that may also mean you cannot access support. For a summary of the exclusions that affect migrants, see p409.

For a summary of local authority support available to adults, see p408.

Other types of support

There are a number of other types of community care support that may be available from local authority social services departments or from NHS primary care trusts. The type of support available depends on your individual circumstances. The support available may be just services, but could include accommodation – eg, if you have been detained, admitted or transferred to hospital under various sections of the Mental Health Act 1983, you are now no longer detained and you leave hospital, the clinical commissioning group, primary care trust or local health board and the local social services department have joint duties to provide you with aftercare services, which can include accommodation. A summary of the different community care provisions is in the *Disability Rights Handbook,* published annually by Disability Rights UK. The legislation under which these types of support can be provided is complex and frequently miunderstood. You are strongly advised to obtain expert advice from a community care adviser.

---

7. **Support under the Children Act 1989**

Local authorities have a duty to safeguard and promote the welfare of children who are 'in need' in their area.[42] If you are destitute and have children, you may be eligible for accommodation or support from your local authority under the Children Act 1989 (in Scotland, the Children (Scotland) Act 1995). A child who is destitute is generally considered to be 'in need', but a child can also be in need if s/he is disabled, or if s/he is unlikely to achieve or maintain a reasonable standard of health or development without the provision of services by a local authority.[43] Although the duty is to support the child, it extends to supporting parents or other family members if this is in the child's best interests.[44]

Some people are excluded from Children Act support, including some groups of adult migrants, but there are also exceptions. Children are always eligible for support under the Children Act regardless of immigration status.[45]

The provision of support can be complex, and is often misunderstood and poorly administered by local authorities. You are strongly recommended to obtain specialist advice before applying to your local authority for support and, in all cases, if you want to challenge a refusal of support or if the local authority tells you it can only accommodate your child, and not you as well.

This *Handbook* does not cover support available under the Children Act. However, for limited further information about the rules affecting this support for asylum seekers and failed asylum seekers, see p411.

---

8. **NHS healthcare**

The UK's NHS is a residence-based healthcare system. However, not all healthcare is provided free of charge to everyone, and the charges can be considerable.

The legislation setting out the rules for NHS charges is different in England, Wales and Scotland. The legislation and policies implementing it are currently changing rapidly, and are not always administered correctly. You are strongly recommended to obtain expert advice in advance of obtaining services or if you have been told that you will be charged for your healthcare, and always if you want to challenge charges you have been told to pay. The following information gives a broad overview.

At the time of writing, there is a charge for hospital healthcare service, unless:

- the specific service is exempt; *or*
- you are exempt; *or*
- you are accepted as 'ordinarily resident' in the UK (see p471).

NHS services are not listed in the definition of 'public funds' in the Immigration Rules (see p25). If you have leave to enter or remain in the UK which is subject to a 'no recourse to public funds' condition, you have not breached this condition if you receive NHS services. However, if you have an outstanding debt for NHS treatment with a total value of at least £500, you will normally be refused certain types of immigration leave.[46] The NHS should only contact the Home Office about debts of more than £500 in accordance with guidance that requires, for example, there to be no genuine outstanding challenges to the debt and no meaningful repayment plan that is being adhered to.[47]

Services exempt from charges

Health services that are currently exempt from charges, regardless of immigration or residence status, are broadly:[48]
- accident and emergency services, but not any provided after you have been admitted as an inpatient or at a follow-up outpatient appointment;
- services not provided in a hospital and not provided by staff employed to work in, or under the direction of, a hospital;
- services for diagnosing and treating specified conditions, including food poisoning, HIV, measles, malaria, tuberculosis, viral hepatitis and whooping cough;[49]
- services for diagnosing and treating sexually transmitted infections;
- services for treating conditions caused by torture, female genital mutilation, domestic violence or sexual violence, provided you have not travelled to the UK for the purpose of seeking that treatment;
- in England only, family planning services (this does not include maternity services or services providing terminations of pregnancies).

Note: there are currently no residence-related charges for primary healthcare, including services delivered through GP practices, NHS walk-in centres, dentists, pharmacists and optometrists. However, some of these services have other charges (eg, for dental care or prescriptions), and these have different exemption criteria. For details of who is exempt from these charges, see CPAG's *Welfare Benefits and Tax Credits Handbook*.

Who is exempt from charges

You are charged for NHS hospital services, unless you are exempt or you are accepted as 'ordinarily resident' in the UK.

The groups of people who are exempt from charges or who are accepted as ordinarily resident vary between England, Wales and Scotland. The rules are complex and can be affected by many factors, including your nationality and period of actual residence. If you are a European Economic Area (EEA) national, relevant factors can also include whether or not you are temporarily in the UK and whether you are exercising particular residence rights. If you are a non-EEA national, relevant factors can also include your immigration status and whether you have paid, or are exempt from, the health surcharge (see p18).

For details, check both regulations[50] and guidance[51] for the relevant country in which you intend to access the services. See also sources of further information below.

The meaning of 'ordinarily resident' for this purpose is currently evolving, and it is therefore useful to refer to current government guidance. **Note:** you may be of any nationality, including British, and not be accepted as 'ordinarily resident' in the UK.

Further information

The rules on health services charges are changing rapidly, so remember to check the current legislation and guidance.

Maternity Action has produced two factsheets on the NHS charging rules – in England, and in Wales, Scotland and Northern Ireland. These are available on its website, together with other resources, including details of its Maternity Care Access Advice line.[52]

Useful information on accessing healthcare in the UK, including if you are having difficulties in registering with a GP, is available online from Doctors of the World.[53]

9. Other financial help

Other financial help is available, to which you may be entitled, especially if you are on a low income, have children, are an older person, or have an illness, disability or other special needs.

See the *Disability Rights Handbook*, published by Disability Rights UK, for help if you have needs resulting from disability, health problems or caring responsibilities.

Food banks

If you are experiencing severe financial hardship (eg, caused by debt, or by having your benefits delayed or refused), you may be able to get vouchers for food which can be redeemed at a food bank. Vouchers are available from frontline care professionals, such as doctors, health visitors, social workers and advice workers. Jobcentre Plus staff may also provide vouchers. Further information and contact details for many food banks can be found at www.trusselltrust.org or by contacting your local authority.

You may be able to get help with food or meals through local community groups that are part of the FareShare network. Further information is available at www.fareshare.org.uk.

Repairs, home improvements and energy efficiency

Your local authority may be able to provide you with a grant to help with the cost of improving your home. The main types of grant available are:
* home improvement grants; *and*
* disabled facilities grants.

You may also be able to get:
* assistance from a home improvement agency (a local not-for-profit organisation) to repair, improve, maintain or adapt your home – sometimes called 'care and repair' or 'staying put' schemes – or with small repairs, safety checks and odd jobs from a handyperson service. or information see, in England, www.foundations.uk.com, in Wales, www.careandrepair.org.uk and in Scotland, www.careandrepairscotland.co.uk;
* a grant for help with insulation and other energy efficiency measures in your home. Help with fuel bills may also be available. Different schemes operate in England, Wales and Scotland. For further information, contact the Energy Saving Advice Service on 0300 123 1234 (calls charged at standard national rates) (in Scotland, Home Energy Scotland on 0808 808 2282) or at www.energysavingtrust.org.uk. For more details, see CPAG's *Fuel Rights Handbook*.

Special funds for sick or disabled people

A range of help is available for people with an illness or disability to assist with things like paying for care services in their own home, equipment, holidays, furniture and transport needs, and for people with haemophilia or HIV contracted via haemophilia treatment. Grants are also available for practical support to help people do their jobs – eg, to pay for specialist equipment and travel. For more information, see the *Disability Rights Handbook*, published by Disability Rights UK.

Payments for former members of the armed forces

If you are a former member of the UK armed forces, or your spouse or civil partner died while in service, you may be able to claim under the one of the various schemes administered by the Ministry of Defence. The benefits and lump-sum payments include pensions, disablement benefits and compensation payments. Your entitlement depends on your circumstances, including the dates of service and, where relevant, the degree and effect of any disablement or ill health and the final salary. Further details are available from Veterans UK (www.gov.uk/government/organisations/veterans-uk).

Charities

There are many charities that provide various types of help to people in need. Your local authority social services department or local advice centre may know of appropriate charities that could assist you, or you can consult publications, such as *A Guide to Grants for Individuals in Need* and the *Charities Digest*, in your local library. The organisation turn2us has a website (www.turn2us.org.uk) with an A–Z of charities that can provide financial help. In many cases, applications for support can be made directly from the website. Information on grants available for individuals can also be found on the website www.grantsforindividuals.org.uk.

Notes

1. Council tax reduction

1 **E** CTRS(PR)E Regs
   W CTRS(DS)W Regs; CTRSPR(W) Regs
   S CTR(S) Regs; CTR(SPC)S Regs
2 **E** Reg 13 CTRS(PR)E Regs
   W Reg 29 CTRSPR(W) Regs; Sch para 20 CTRS(DS)W Regs
   S Reg 19 CTR(SPC)S Regs; reg 19 CTR(S) Regs
3 **E** Reg 13(1A) CTRS(PR)E Regs
   W Reg 29(2) CTRSPR(W) Regs; Sch para 20(2) CTRS(DS)W Regs
   S Reg 19(2) CTR(SPC)S Regs; reg 19(2) CTR(S) Regs
4 *Szoma v SSWP* [2005] UKHL 64, reported as R(IS) 2/06 and see *Yesiloz v London Borough of Camden* [2009] EWCA Civ 415
5 para 6 IR
6 para 6A IR. Council tax reduction is not included in the regulations that are referred to in para 6B IR, which disregards claims made as a result of exemptions.
7 para 6A IR
8 **S** Reg 39(11) CTR(S) Regs
   W Sch 6 para 17(10) CTRSPR(W) Regs; Sch para 51(10) CTRS(DS)W Regs

9 **E** Reg 12 CTRS(PR)E Regs
   W Reg 28 CTRSPR(W) Regs; Sch para 19 CTRS(DS)W Regs
   S Reg 16 CTR(SPC)S Regs; reg 16 CTR(S) Regs
10 **E** Reg 12 CTRS(PR)E Regs
   W Reg 28 CTRSPR(W) Regs; Sch para 19 CTRS(DS)W Regs
   S Reg 16 CTR(SPC)S Regs; reg 16 CTR(S) Regs
11 **E** Reg 3 The Council Tax Reduction Schemes (Prescribed Requirements) (England) (Amendment) (No.2) Regulations 2014, No.3312
   W Reg 31 The Council Tax Reduction Schemes (Prescribed Requirements and Default Scheme) (Wales)(Amendment) Regulations 2015, No.44
12 *R (Winder and Others) v Sandwell MBC* [2014] EWHC 2617 (Admin)
13 **E** Reg 12 CTRS(PR)E Regs
   W Reg 28 CTRSPR(W) Regs; Sch para 19 CTRS(DS)W Regs
   S Reg 16 CTR(SPC)S Regs; reg 16 CTR(S) Regs
14 **E** Sch 8 para 7 CTRS(PR)E Regs
   W Sch 13 para 5 CTRSPR(W) Regs; Sch para 111 CTRS(DS)W Regs
15 **E** Sch 8 para 7(3) CTRS(PR)E Regs
   W Sch 13 para 5(3) CTRSPR(W) Regs; Sch para 111(3) CTRS(DS)W Regs
16 Sch 1 para 5 CTRS(PR)E Regs

17 Reg 3 The Council Tax Reduction Schemes (Prescribed Requirements) (England) (Amendment) Regulations 2016, No.1262
18 Reg 26 CTRSPR(W) Regs; Sch para 17 CTRS(DS)W Regs
19 Regs 15, 17 and 18 CTR(SPC)S Regs; regs 15, 17 and 18 CTR(S) Regs

2. Local welfare assistance schemes
20 Reg 4 The Welfare Funds (Scotland) Regulations 2016, No.107; *Scottish Welfare Fund: statutory guidance*, April 2017, paras 4.3-4.10
21 Scottish government, *Scottish Welfare Fund: statutory guidance*, April 2017, para 6.8
22 para 6 IR
23 Scottish government, *Scottish Welfare Fund: statutory guidance*, April 2017, Annex A para 19; see also para 6.7

3. Healthy Start food and vitamins
24 Regs 5(2) and 8 HSS&WF(A) Regs
25 Regs 2(1) and 5(1) and Sch 3 HSS&WF(A) Regs; HSS(DHSF)(W) Regs
26 Reg 3 HSS&WF(A) Regs
27 Reg 3 HSS&WFA(A) Regs
28 Reg 2(1) HSS&WF(A) Regs
29 Reg 2(1) HSS&WF(A) Regs
30 Reg 4 and Sch 2 HSS&WF(A) Regs
31 Reg 4(2) and (3A) HSS&WF(A) Regs
32 Reg 3 HSS&WF(A) Regs
33 Reg 8A HSS&WF(A) Regs

4. Education benefits
34 **E** s512ZB Education Act 1996; The Education (Free School Lunches) (Prescribed Tax Credits) (England) Order 2003, No.383
W s512ZB Education Act 1996; The Education (Free School Lunches) (Prescribed Tax Credits) (Wales) Order 2003, No.879 (W.110)
S s53(3) Education (Scotland) Act 1980; The Education (School Lunches) (Scotland) Regulations 2009, No.178
35 House of Commons, *Hansard*, 1 December 2014, written answer 216015
36 For CTC, the legislation only provides for this in Scotland.
37 Provided under Part VI of IAA 1999
38 The Education (School Lunches) (Scotland) Regulations 2015, No.269
39 s88 School Standards and Organisation (Wales) Act 2013

5. Free milk for children
40 Reg 18 WF Regs

6. Community care support from the local authority
41 **E** s21 CA 2014
W s21(1A) NAA 1948
S s12(2A) Social Work (Scotland) Act 1968

7. Support under the Children Act 1989
42 s17 CA 1989; s22 C(S)A 1995
43 s17(10) CA 1989
44 s17(3) CA 1989; s22(3) C(S)A 1995
45 Sch 3 para 2(1)(b) NIAA 2002

8. NHS healthcare
46 paras 320(22) and V3.14 Appendix V and Appendix FM IR
47 Department of Health guidance, *Overseas Chargeable Patients, NHS Debt and Immigration Rules: guidance on administration and data sharing*, available on www.gov.uk
48 **E** Reg 9 The National Health Service (Charges to Overseas Visitors) Regulations 2015, No.238
W Reg 3 The National Health Service (Charges to Overseas Visitors) Regulations 1989, No.306
S Reg 3 The National Health Service (Charges to Overseas Visitors) (Scotland) Regulations 1989, No.364
49 **E** Sch 1 The National Health Service (Charges to Overseas Visitors) Regulations 2015, No.238
W Sch 1 The National Health Service (Charges to Overseas Visitors) Regulations 1989, No.306
S Sch 1 The National Health Service (Charges to Overseas Visitors) (Scotland) Regulations 1989, No.364
50 **E** The National Health Service (Charges to Overseas Visitors) Regulations 2015, No.238
W The National Health Service (Charges to Overseas Visitors) Regulations 1989, No.306
S The National Health Service (Charges to Overseas Visitors) (Scotland) Regulations 1989, No.364
NI Provision of Health Services to Persons Not Ordinarily Resident Regulations (Northern Ireland) 2015, No. 27

51 **E** Department of Health guidance,
*Guidance on Implementing the Overseas
Visitor Hospital Charging Regulations
2015*, available on www.gov.uk
W www. gov.wales/topics/health/
publications/health/guidance/
implementing
S www.gov.scot/topics/health/services/
overseas-visitors
52 www.maternityaction.org.uk/advice-2/
maternitycareaccess
53 www.doctorsoftheworld.org.uk/useful-
resources

Appendices

Appendices

Appendix 1

Glossary of terms

A2 national. A national of the European Union member states Romania and Bulgaria.

A8 national. A national of the European Union member states Czech Republic, Estonia, Hungary, Latvia, Lithuania, Poland, Slovakia and Slovenia.

Absent. Not physically in an area such as Great Britain; the alternative to present.

Accession states. The newer members of the European Union: Croatia, the A2 states and the A8 states.

Administrative removal. A legal mechanism used to remove foreign nationals who have entered the UK illegally, including by deception, or to remove those who have breached the conditions of their leave, including overstaying.

Applicable amount. The maximum amount of benefit set by the government, taking account of certain factors such as age and whether someone is single or part of a couple.

Application registration card. The form of identification for those who have claimed asylum.

ASPEN card. A pre-paid visa chip and pin card, given to asylum seekers in receipt of asylum support. It is credited by the Home Office and can be used in a similar way to a debit card to pay for items in shops or (for those getting section 95 support) to withdraw cash from most ATMs.

Association agreement. A treaty signed between the European Union and a country outside the European Union, giving reciprocal rights and obligations.

Asylum. Leave to enter or remain in the UK as a refugee, given under the Refugee Convention or Article 3 of the European Convention on Human Rights (including protection under the Refugee Qualification Directive).

. . . .

Asylum seeker. A person who has applied for asylum and whose application has yet to be decided, or whose appeal against a refusal of an asylum application remains outstanding.

Asylum support. Support provided by the Home Office to various categories of asylum seekers and failed asylum seekers. In the past, this was provided by a section of the Home Office called the National Asylum Support Service (NASS). This was abolished in 2007, but the term 'NASS support' continues to be used.

Certificate of entitlement. A certificate of entitlement to the right of abode demonstrates that a person has the right of abode – ie, the right to travel freely to and from the UK. British citizens have the right of abode and can demonstrate this by producing their passports. A few Commonwealth nationals also have the right of abode and can obtain a certificate of entitlement, endorsed in their own national passport, to demonstrate this.

Common travel area. The UK, Ireland, Isle of Man and the Channel Islands.

Commonwealth countries. Antigua and Barbuda, Australia, Bahamas, Bangladesh, Barbados, Belize, Botswana, Brunei Darussalam, Cameroon, Canada, Cyprus, Dominica, Fiji Islands, Gambia, Ghana, Grenada, Guyana, India, Jamaica, Kenya, Kiribati, Lesotho, Malawi, Malaysia, Maldives, Malta, Mauritius, Mozambique, Namibia, Nauru, New Zealand, Nigeria, Pakistan, Papua New Guinea, Samoa, Seychelles, Sierra Leone, Singapore, Solomon Islands, South Africa, Sri Lanka, St Kitts and Nevis, St Lucia, St Vincent and the Grenadines, Swaziland, Tanzania, Tonga, Trinidad and Tobago, Tuvalu, Uganda, Vanuatu, Zambia.

Competent state. The European Economic Area country responsible under the European Union co-ordination rules for paying your benefit and to which you are liable to pay national insurance contributions.

Court of Justice of the European Union. The European Union institution that ensures that European Union law is observed by member states. It sits in Luxembourg. Previously known as the **European Court of Justice**.

Deportation. A legal mechanism used to remove a foreign national on the recommendation of a criminal court following her/his conviction for a criminal offence, or if the Home Secretary has decided that a person's presence in the UK is 'not conducive to the public good'. If an order has been signed to deport a foreign national, s/he may not return unless and until the order has been revoked.

Derivative right to reside. The term given to certain residence rights that are derived from someone else in specific ways.

Destitute. For asylum support purposes, someone who does not have access to adequate accommodation or who cannot meet her/his essential living needs.

Destitution domestic violence concession. A provision under which people who have immigration leave on the basis of a relationship, but which has broken down as a result of domestic violence, can be granted three months' leave in which to apply for indefinite leave to remain.

Discretionary leave. Permission to enter or remain in the UK given to a person outside the Immigration Rules or to someone who is refused asylum but who cannot be removed under another Article of the European Convention on Human Rights or for other humanitarian reasons.

Enforcement. A term used to refer to any of the different ways in which a person can be forced to leave the UK for immigration reasons – ie, having been refused entry at a port, having been declared an illegal entrant, or having been notified that s/he is someone who is liable for administrative removal, or who is being deported.

Entry clearance officer. An official at a British post overseas who deals with immigration applications made to that post.

European Community. The European Union was previously known as the European Community and, before that, the European Economic Community. In this *Handbook*, the legislation of all three is referred to as European Union law.

European Convention on Human Rights. An international instrument agreed by the Council of Europe. The rights guaranteed by it have now largely been incorporated into UK law by the Human Rights Act 1998.

European Convention on Social and Medical Assistance. An agreement signed by all the European Economic Area states, plus Turkey, requiring the ratifying states to provide assistance in cash and kind to nationals of other ratifying states who are lawfully present in their territory and who are without sufficient resources on the same conditions as their own nationals.

European Economic Area. Covers all European Union states plus Iceland, Liechtenstein and Norway. European Economic Area nationals have free movement within these and all European Union member states. From 1 June 2002, the right to free movement also applies to Switzerland.

European Social Charter. The 1961 Council of Europe Social Charter, signed by all the European Economic Area countries, plus Macedonia and Turkey.

European Union. Austria, Belgium, Bulgaria, Croatia, Cyprus, Czech Republic, Denmark, Estonia, Finland, France, Germany, Greece, Hungary, Ireland, Italy, Latvia, Lithuania, Luxembourg, Malta, Netherlands, Poland, Portugal, Romania, Slovakia, Slovenia, Spain, Sweden and the UK (including Gibraltar).

European Union/European Economic Area national. The term used in this *Handbook* to describe citizens of European Union member states/European Economic Area countries.

Exceptional leave. A form of leave to remain granted outside the Immigration Rules that has now been replaced with humanitarian protection and discretionary leave for those seeking asylum.

First-tier Tribunal (Asylum Support). The tribunal that decides appeals against the refusal or termination of asylum support. It sits in east London, but hears appeals nationwide (by video link if necessary).

First-tier Tribunal (Immigration and Asylum Chamber). The tribunal that hears and determines appeals against decisions made by the Secretary of State for the Home Department about asylum, immigration and nationality.

First-tier Tribunal (Social Entitlement Chamber). The tribunal that hears and determines appeals against decisions made by the Department for Work and Pensions and local authorities about benefit entitlement.

Habitual residence. The type of residence someone must usually have to get income support, income-based jobseeker's allowance, income-related employment and support allowance, housing benefit, pension credit, universal credit, attendance allowance, disability living allowance, carer's allowance and personal independence payment. The term 'habitually resident' is not defined in the benefit regulations and is determined by looking at all the person's circumstances.

Home Office. The government department responsible for asylum, immigration and nationality issues.

Humanitarian protection. Permission to enter or remain in the UK given to a person who needs to be protected from harm, but whose case does not fit the criteria for refugee status.

Illegal entrant. A person who immigration officials decide has entered the UK in breach of the immigration laws. This could be by deception or clandestinely.

Immigration judge. A person who determines appeals in the First-tier Tribunal (Immigration and Asylum Chamber) or Upper Tribunal (Immigration and Asylum Chamber).

Immigration officer. An official, usually stationed at a British port of entry, who decides whether to grant or refuse leave to enter. Immigration officers also have responsibility for enforcing immigration control.

Immigration Rules. Rules made by the Home Secretary, setting out the requirements for granting or refusing entry clearance, leave to enter and leave to remain to people applying in the different categories.

Indefinite leave. Permission to enter or remain that has no time limit.

Integration loan. An interest-free loan made to assist people who have recently been given refugee status or humanitarian protection to integrate into UK society.

Lawfully working. Depending on the context, either working with the permission of the Home Office or, for accession state nationals, working in accordance with any employment restrictions that apply.

Limited leave. Permission to enter or remain that is given for a certain period of time only. Also referred to as 'time-limited leave'.

Maintenance undertaking. A written undertaking given by someone under the Immigration Rules to be responsible for the maintenance and accommodation of another person who is applying to come to or stay in the UK.

Ordinarily resident. A residence requirement for several benefits and tax credits. A person is ordinarily resident where s/he has her/his home that s/he has adopted for a settled purpose and where s/he lives for the time being.

Past presence test. A requirement for some benefits to have been present in Great Britain for a period of time before the date of claim.

Person from abroad. A social security definition that refers to a person who has failed the habitual residence test for the purposes of income support, income-based jobseeker's allowance, income-related employment and support allowance or housing benefit.

Person subject to immigration control. A person in one of four specific groups of non-European Economic Area nationals who are excluded from entitlement to most social security benefits and whose entitlement to support under the Care Act 2014 is restricted.

Points-based system. The system of controlling migration to the UK from outside the European Union for economic purposes or studies.

Present. Physically in an area such as Great Britain; the alternative to absent.

Public funds. These are defined in the Immigration Rules as: housing provided by local authorities, either for homeless people or allocated from the local authority's housing register; attendance allowance; carer's allowance; child benefit; child tax credit; council tax benefit; council tax reduction; disability living allowance; income-related employment and support allowance; housing benefit; income support; income-based jobseeker's allowance; local welfare assistance (except the Discretionary Assistance Fund for Wales); pension credit; personal independence payment; severe disablement allowance; social fund payments; working tax credit; and universal credit.

Reciprocal agreement. A bilateral agreement made between the UK and another country, with the purpose of protecting benefit entitlement for people moving between the two.

Refugee. A person who satisfies the definition of someone who needs international protection under Article 1A(2) of the 1951 Convention Relating to the Status of Refugees.

Refugee Convention. The 1951 United Nations Convention Relating to the Status of Refugees, a multilateral treaty defining who is a refugee and setting out the rights of people who are granted asylum.

Removal. The final procedure for sending a person refused entry, or who is being treated as an illegal entrant, or who is subject to the administrative removal or deportation process, away from the UK.

Resident. A requirement of a category D retirement pension and a necessary part of ordinary residence and habitual residence. Residence is more than presence and is usually where you have your home for the time being.

Restricted leave. Leave to remain given outside the Immigration Rules to someone who is excluded from refugee or humanitarian protection leave but who cannot be removed from the UK for human rights reasons. Replaced discretionary leave.

Right of abode. The right to enter, remain, leave and return freely to the UK without needing to obtain leave from the immigration authorities. All British citizens, and some Commonwealth nationals, have the right of abode.

Right to reside. A residence requirement for entitlement to some benefits and tax credits. For child benefit and child tax credit, a person must have a right to reside in the UK, and, to satisfy the habitual residence test for means-tested benefits, s/he must have a right to reside in the common travel area. The right to reside depends on someone's nationality, immigration status and whether s/he has rights under European Union law.

Secretary of State for the Home Department (the Home Secretary). The government minister with primary responsibility for decisions made by the Home Office on immigration, asylum and nationality.

Section 4 support. A form of asylum support for destitute asylum seekers whose asylum application has been refused and who fit certain eligibility criteria. Also a discretionary form of support from the Home Office for those on immigration bail and with temporary admission.

Section 95 support. A form of support for people who have make an application for asylum in the UK.

Settlement/settled status. Defined in immigration law as being ordinarily resident in the UK without any restrictions on the time the person is able to remain here. Those with indefinite leave are generally accepted as being settled in the UK.

Sponsor. The person (usually a relative) with whom someone is applying to join, or remain with, in the UK, and/or a person who is to be responsible for the applicant's maintenance and accommodation in the UK.

Stateless person. Someone who is not considered a national by any country.

Subject to immigration control. Often used to refer to those who need leave to enter or remain in the UK – and this is the definition given in the Asylum and Immigration Act 1996. However, the Immigration and Asylum Act 1999 gives a different, narrower, definition, which is used to exclude people from most benefits and tax credits and certain services provided by local authorities' social services departments. This *Handbook* uses the term as it is defined in the 1999 Act.

Temporary admission. A temporary licence given to people to be in the UK while they are waiting for a decision to be made on their immigration status or while they are waiting to be removed from the UK. The alternative to temporary admission is detention.

Third country. Usually used to refer to a country to which the Home Office wishes to send an asylum seeker for her/his application for asylum to be considered, other than the country of which s/he is a national, rather than in the UK.

The United Kingdom. Comprises England, Wales, Scotland and Northern Ireland. The Channel Islands of Jersey and Guernsey, and the Isle of Man, are Crown dependencies and not part of the UK.

UK Visas and Immigration. The Home Office department that deals with immigration control.

Unmarried partners. A term used in the Immigration Rules to refer to couples (heterosexual or same-sex) who have been together for two or more years, who are in a relationship 'akin to marriage' and who cannot marry according to the law – eg, because they are of the same sex or one of them is already married. The Immigration Rules give unmarried partners some rights to enter and remain in the UK if one partner is settled in the UK or has limited leave to enter or remain here.

Upper Tribunal (Immigration and Asylum Chamber). The tribunal that hears and determines appeals against determinations made by the First-tier Tribunal (Immigration and Asylum Chamber) and most immigration-related applications for judicial review.

Upper Tribunal (Social Entitlement Chamber). The tribunal that hears and determines appeals against decisions made by the First-tier Tribunal (Social Entitlement Chamber) about benefit entitlement.

Visa national. A person who must obtain entry clearance before travelling to the UK for most purposes, unless s/he is a person with indefinite leave returning within two years or returning within a period of earlier leave granted for more than six months. For a list of countries covered, see Appendix 1 to the Immigration Rules.

Work permit. A document issued by UK Visas and Immigration to employers, allowing them to employ a named individual in a particular job.

Appendix 2

Information and advice

Immigration and asylum

If you need help with an immigration problem, you should obtain advice from your local law centre, a solicitor specialising in immigration work or one of the agencies listed below.

Note: anyone who gives immigration advice must be professionally regulated. For further details, see p7.

AIRE Centre (Advice on Individual Rights in Europe)
Room 505
Institute of Advanced Legal Studies
Charles Clore House
17 Russell Square
London WC1B 5DR
Tel: 020 7831 4276
info@airecentre.org
www.airecentre.org

Promotes awareness of European legal rights and assists people to assert these.

Asylum Aid
Migrants Resource Centre
Berol House
25 Ashley Road
London N17 9LJ
Tel: 020 7354 9631
info@migrants.org.uk
www.asylumaid.org.uk
Advice line: 020 7354 9264 (Tues 1–4pm)

Law Centres Network
Floor 1, Tavis House
1–6 Tavistock Square
London WC1H 9NA
Tel: 020 3637 1330
www.lawcentres.org.uk

Does not give advice, but can provide details of your nearest law centre.

Asylum Help

Language	For advice	Support applications
English (or any other language)	0808 800 0630	0808 800 0631
Albanian	0808 800 0620	0808 800 0621
Amharic	0808 800 0622	0808 800 0623
Arabic	0808 800 0624	0808 800 0625
Bengali	0808 800 0626	0808 800 0627
Chinese Mandarin	0808 800 0628	0808 800 0629
Farsi	0808 800 0632	0808 800 0633
French	0808 800 0634	0808 800 0635
Punjabi	0808 800 0636	0808 800 0637
Pushto	0808 800 0638	0808 800 0639
Somali	0808 800 0640	0808 800 0641
Tamil	0808 800 0642	0808 800 0643
Tigrinya	0808 800 0644	0808 800 0645
Urdu	0808 800 0646	0808 800 0647
Vietnamese	0808 800 0648	0808 800 0649

www.asylumhelpuk.org

Provides confidential advice and information for asylum seekers about the asylum process and applying for accommodation and support.

Asylum Support Appeals Project (ASAP)
Studios 11 and 12
Container City Building
48 Trinity Buoy Wharf
London E14 0FN
Tel: 020 3716 0284
Advice line (advisers only): 020 3716 0283 (Mon, Wed and Fri 2pm–4pm)
www.asaproject.org

British Red Cross
44 Moorfields
London EC2Y 9AL
Tel: 0344 871 1111
information@redcross.org.uk
www.redcross.org.uk

Provides support for refugees and vulnerable migrants in specific areas across the UK.

Civil Legal Advice

Tel: 0345 345 4345
www.gov.uk/civil-legal-advice
www.gov.uk/check-legal-aid

A legal aid eligibility checker.

http://find-legal-advice.justice.gov.uk

A directory of legal aid suppliers in England and Wales.

Greater Manchester Immigration Aid Unit

1 Delaunays Road
Crumpsall Green
Manchester M8 4QS
Tel: 0161 740 7722
info@gmiau.org
www.gmiau.org
Provides free, confidential immigration and asylum legal advice and representation to people in the local community.

Immigration Law Practitioners' Association

Lindsey House
40–42 Charterhouse Street
London EC1M 6JN
Tel: 020 7251 8383
info@ilpa.org.uk
www.ilpa.org.uk

A professional association aiming to promote and improve advice and representation in immigration, nationality and asylum law.

Joint Council for the Welfare of Immigrants

115 Old Street
London EC1V 9RT
Tel: 020 7251 8708
info@jcwi.org.uk
www.jcwi.org.uk

Migrant Help

Charlton House
Dour Street
Dover CT16 1AT
Tel: 01304 203 977
info@migranthelpuk.org
www.migranthelpuk.org

Delivers support and advice services to migrants in the UK.

• •

Migrant Legal Action (formerly Afro-Asian Advisory Service)
53 Addington Square
London SE5 7LB
Tel: 020 7701 0141
www.aaas.org.uk
Advice line: 0845 618 5385 (Mon – Fri 2–5pm).

Provides a specialist legal service, free of charge.

Refugee Action
Victoria Charity Centre
11 Belgrave Road
London SW1V 1RB
Tel: 020 7952 1511
info@refugee-action.org.uk
www.refugee-action.org.uk
Bradford: 01274 924 982
Greater Manchester: 0161 831 5420
Birmingham: 0121 201 3070

Refugee Council
PO Box 68614
London E15 9DQ
Tel: 020 7346 6700
www.refugeecouncil.org.uk

Scottish Refugee Council
6th Floor, Portland House
Glasgow G2 5AH
Tel: 0141 248 9799
info@scottishrefugeecouncil.org.uk
www.scottishrefugeecouncil.org.uk

Welsh Refugee Council
120–122 Broadway
Cardiff CF24 1NJ
Tel: 02920 489 800
www.wrc.wales

Social security
Independent advice and representation

It is often difficult for unsupported individuals to get a positive response from the Department for Work and Pensions, local authority or HM Revenue and Customs (HMRC). It can help if you obtain advice about your entitlement and how you can demonstrate this. If you can get good quality assistance from an adviser who will take on your case, this is even more helpful, particularly if you need to challenge a decision.

If you want advice or help with a benefit problem, the following agencies may be able to assist.

- Citizens Advice Bureaux (CABx) and other local advice centres provide information and advice about benefits and may be able to represent you. You can find out where your local CAB is from the Citizens Advice website at www.citizensadvice.org.uk (England and Wales) or www.citizensadvice.org.uk/Scotland (Scotland).
- Law centres can often help in a similar way to CABx and advice centres. You can find your nearest law centre at www.lawcentres.org.uk.
- Local authority welfare rights workers provide a service in many areas and some arrange advice sessions and take-up campaigns locally.
- Local organisations for particular groups of claimants may offer help – eg, unemployed centres, pensioners' groups and centres for disabled people.
- Claimants' unions give advice in some areas.
- Some social workers help with benefit problems, especially if they are already working with you on another problem.
- Solicitors can give some free legal advice. This does not cover the cost of representation at an appeal hearing, but can cover the cost of preparing written submissions and obtaining evidence, such as medical reports. However, solicitors do not always have a good working knowledge of the benefit rules and you may need to shop around until you find one who does.
- Civil Legal Advice (tel: 0345 345 4345 or www.gov.uk/civil-legal-advice). **Note:** help with welfare benefits is limited to appeals in the Upper Tribunal and the higher courts.

Advice from CPAG

Unfortunately, CPAG is unable to deal with enquiries directly from members of the public, but if you are an adviser you can phone or email for help with advising your client.

Advisers in England, Wales and Northern Ireland can call from 10am to 12pm and from 2pm to 4pm (Monday to Friday) on 020 7812 5231. Email advice is now limited to possible judicial review cases and enquiries that are specifically about universal credit, child benefit, tax credits or other HMRC-administered benefits. Our email address is advice@cpag.org.uk.

Organisations based in Scotland can contact CPAG in Scotland at Unit 9, Ladywell, 94 Duke Street, Glasgow G4 0UW or email advice@cpagscotland.org.uk. A phone line is open for advisers in Scotland from 10am to 4pm (Monday to Thursday) and from 10am to 12pm (Friday) on 0141 552 0552.

For more information, see www.cpag.org.uk/advisers.

CPAG takes on a small number of test cases each year. We focus on cases that have the potential to improve the lives of families with children in poverty. If you are an adviser and would like to refer a test case to us, please see www.cpag.org.uk/test-case-referrals.

Human rights

Information, advice and support on discrimination and human rights issues, and the relevant law.

Equality Advisory and Support Service

FREEPOST EASS HELPLINE FPN6521
Tel: 0808 800 0082
Textphone: 0808 800 0084
www.equalityadvisoryservice.com

Appendix 3

Useful addresses

Immigration and asylum

UK Visas and Immigration
Lunar House
40 Wellesley Road
Croydon CR9 2BY
www.gov.uk/government/organisations/uk-visas-and-immigration

UK Visas and Immigration Contact Centre
Tel: 0300 123 2241

Asylum Customer Contact Centre
Tel: 0300 123 2235

Voluntary returns service
18th floor
Lunar House
40 Wellesley Road
Croydon CR9 2BY
Tel: 0300 004 0202
voluntaryreturns@homeoffice.gsi.gov.uk
www.gov.uk/return-home-voluntarily

Note: contacting the Home Office directly to discuss your assisted voluntary return may have an impact on any outstanding protection or human rights-based claim that you may have made. You may therefore wish to obtain independent advice before doing so.

Enquiries from European citizens
Tel: 0300 123 2253

Sponsor, Employer and Education helpline
Tel: 0300 123 4699
businnesshelpdesk@homeoffice.gsi.gov.uk
educatorshelpdesk@homeoffice.gsi.gov.uk

• •

Citizenship and nationality
Tel: 0300 123 2253
nationalityenquiries@homeoffice.gsi.gov.uk

Passport Office
PO Box 767
Southport PR8 9PW
0300 222 0000
www.gov.uk/government/organisations/hm-passport-office

Independent Chief Inspector of Borders and Immigration
5th Floor
Globe House
89 Eccleston Square
London SW1V 1PN
chiefinspector@icinspector.gsi.gov.uk
http://icinspector.independent.gov.uk

First-tier Tribunal (Immigration and Asylum Chamber)
PO Box 6987
Leceister LE1 6ZX
Tel: 0300 123 1711
customer.service@hmcts.gsi.gov.uk
www.gov.uk/immigration-asylum-tribunal

Note: these are not the contact details you must use when appealing.

Upper Tribunal (Immigration and Asylum Chamber)
1A Field House
15–25 Breams Buildings
London EC4A 1DZ
Tel: 0300 123 1711
www.gov.uk/upper-tribunal-immigration-asylum

First-tier Tribunal (Asylum Support)
2nd Floor
Anchorage House
2 Clove Crescent
London E14 2BE
Freephone: 0800 681 6509 (to discuss your appeal or the appeal process)
www.gov.uk/appeal-first-tier-asylum-support-tribunal

Office of the Immigration Services Commissioner
5th Floor
21 Bloomsbury Street
London WC1B 3HF
Tel: 0345 000 0046
info@oisc.gov.uk
www.gov.uk/government/organisations/office-of-the-immigration-services-commissioner

Solicitors Regulation Authority
The Cube
199 Wharfside Street
Birmingham B1 1RN
Tel: 0370 606 2555
www.sra.org.uk

Legal Ombudsman
PO Box 6806
Wolverhampton WV1 9WJ
Tel: 0300 555 0333
enquiries@legalombudsman.org.uk
www.legalombudsman.org.uk

For complaints about lawyers.

European Commission Representation in the UK
Europe House
32 Smith Square
London SW1P 3EU
Tel: 020 7973 1992
comm-rep-london@ec.europa.eu
http://ec.europa.eu/unitedkingdom

Social security

HM Courts and Tribunals Service

Tribunal areas

Birmingham
Administrative Support Centre
PO Box 14620
Birmingham B16 6FR
Tel: 0300 123 1142
ASCBirmingham@hmcts.gsi.gov.uk

● ●

Cardiff
Eastgate House
35–43 Newport Road
Cardiff CF24 0AB
Tel: 0300 123 1142
SSCSA-Cardiff@hmcts.gsi.gov.uk

Glasgow
Wellington House
134–136 Wellington Street
Glasgow G2 2XL
Tel: 0141 354 8400
SSCSA-Glasgow@hmcts.gsi.gov.uk

Leeds
York House
31–36 York Place
Leeds LS1 2ED
Tel: 0300 123 1142
SSCSA-Leeds@hmcts.gsi.gov.uk

Liverpool
36 Dale Street
Liverpool L2 5UZ
Tel: 0300 123 1142
SSCSA-Liverpool@hmcts.gsi.gov.uk

Newcastle
Manorview House
Kings Manor
Newcastle upon Tyne NE1 6PA
Tel: 0300 123 1142
SSCSA-Newcastle@hmcts.gsi.gov.uk

Sutton
Copthall House
9 The Pavement
Grove Road
Sutton SM1 1DA
Tel: 0300 123 1142
SSCSA-Sutton@hmcts.gsi.gov.uk

Direct lodgement of appeals

England and Wales
HMCTS SSCS Appeals Centre
PO Box 1203
Bradford BD1 9WP

Scotland
HMCTS SSCS Appeals Centre
PO Box 27080
Glasgow G2 9HQ

First-Tier Tribunal (Tax)
PO Box 16972
Birmingham B16 6TZ
Tel: 0300 123 1024
taxappeals@hmcts.gsi.gov.uk
www.gov.uk/tax-tribunal

The Upper Tribunal (Administrative Appeals Chamber)

England and Wales
5th Floor
7 Rolls Buildings
Fetter Lane
London EC4A 1NL
Tel: 020 7071 5662
adminappeals@hmcts.gsi.gov.uk
www.gov.uk/administrative-appeals-tribunal

Scotland
George House
126 George Street
Edinburgh EH2 4HH
Tel: 0131 271 4310
utaacmailbox@Scotland.gsi.gov.uk

Northern Ireland
Tribunal Hearing Centre
2nd Floor
Royal Courts of Justice
Chichester Street
Belfast BT1 3JF
Tel: 028 9072 4848

The Upper Tribunal (Tax and Chancery Chamber)

England and Wales
5th floor
7 Rolls Buildings
Fetter Lane
London EC4A 1NL
Tel: 020 7612 9730
uttc@hmcts.gsi.gov.uk
www.gov.uk/tax-upper-tribunal

Scotland
Upper Tribunal for Scotland
4th Floor
1 Atlantic Quay
45 Robertson Street
Glasgow G2 8JB
Tel: 0141 302 5880
uppertribunalforscotland@scotcourtstribunals.gov.uk
www.scotcourts.gov.uk/the-courts/court-locations/the-upper-tribunal-for-scotland

Department for Work and Pensions
Caxton House
Tothill Street
London SW1H 9NA
www.gov.uk/dwp

Government Legal Department
One Kemble Street
London WC2B 4TS

Department for Work and Pensions (Overseas Healthcare)
Room M0401
Durham House
Washington N138 7SF
Tel: 0191 218 1999
overseas.healthcare@dwp.gsi.gov.uk

Disability and Carers Service

Attendance Allowance Service Centre
Mail Handling Site A
Wolverhampton WV98 2AD
Tel: 0345 605 6055
Textphone: 0345 604 5312
www.gov.uk/attendance-allowance

Disability Living Allowance Unit
  Claimants born on or before 8 April 1948:
  Disability Living Allowance DLA65+
  Mail Handling Site A
  Wolverhampton WV98 2AH
  Tel: 0345 605 6055
  Textphone: 0345 604 5312
  www.gov.uk/dla-disability-living-allowance-benefit

  Claimants born after 8 April 1948 who are over 16 years old:
  Disability Living Allowance
  Mail Handling Site A
  Wolverhampton WV98 2AH
  Tel: 0345 712 3456
  Textphone: 0345 722 4433
  www.gov.uk/dla-disability-living-allowance-benefit

  Claimants aged under 16 years:
  Disability Benefit Centre 4
  Post Handling Site B
  Wolverhampton WV99 1BY
  Tel: 0345 712 3456
  Textphone: 0345 722 4433
  www.gov.uk/disability-living-allowance-children

Personal Independence Payment Unit
  New claims
  Post Handling Site B
  Wolverhampton WV99 1AH
  Claims: 0800 917 2222 (textphone 0800 917 7777)
  Helpline: 0345 850 3322 (textphone 0345 601 6677)
  www.gov.uk/pip

Carer's Allowance Unit
  Mail Handling Site A
  Wolverhampton
  WV98 2AB
  Tel: 0345 608 4321
  Textphone: 0345 604 5312
  www.gov.uk/carers-allowance

• •

Exporting benefits overseas
   Exportability Co-ordinator
   Room B201
   Pension, Disability and Carers Service
   Warbreck House
   Warbreck Hill Road
   Blackpool FY2 0YE
   www.gov.uk/exportability-team

Jobcentre Plus (income support, jobseeker's allowance, employment and support allowance and incapacity benefit)

New benefit claims
   Tel: 0800 055 6688
   Tel: 0800 012 1888 (Welsh speakers)
   Textphone: 0800 023 4888
   www.gov.uk/contact-jobcentre-plus

Enquiries about ongoing claims
   Tel: 0345 608 8545
   Tel: 0345 600 3018 (Welsh speakers)
   Textphone: 0345 608 8551
   www.gov.uk/contact-jobcentre-plus

To change or cancel an appointment
   Universal credit appointments:
   Tel: 0345 600 0723
   Tel: 0345 600 3018 (Welsh speakers)
   Textphone: 0345 600 0743
   Other appointments:
   Tel: 0345 604 3719
   Tel: 0345 604 4248 (Welsh speakers)
   Textphone: 0345 608 8551
   www.gov.uk/contact-jobcentre-plus

Universal credit
   Tel: 0345 600 0723
   Tel: 0800 012 1888 (Welsh speakers: to make a claim)
   Tel: 0345 600 3018 (Welsh speakers: to report a change)
   Textphone: 0345 600 0743
   www.gov.uk/universal-credit

The Pension Service
Tel: 0800 731 7898 (new claims)
Textphone: 0800 731 7339
Tel: 0345 606 0265 (to report a change of circumstances)
Textphone: 0345 606 0285
www.gov.uk/contact-pension-service

Winter fuel payments
Winter Fuel Payment Centre
Mail Handling Site A
Wolverhampton WV98 1LR
Tel: 0345 915 1515
Textphone: 0345 606 0285
www.gov.uk/winter-fuel-payment

International Pension Centre
The Pension Service 11
Mail Handling Site A
Wolverhampton WV98 1LW
Tel: 0191 218 7777
Textphone: 0191 218 7280
www.gov.uk/international-pension-centre

HM Revenue and Customs (tax credits)

Tax Credit Office
Preston PR1 4AT
www.gov.uk/child-tax-credit
www.gov.uk/working-tax-credit

Tax Credit Helpline
Tel: 0345 300 3900
Textphone: 0345 300 3909
Intermediaries helpline: 0345 300 3946

HM Revenue and Customs (child benefit and guardian's allowance)

Child benefit
Child Benefit Office
PO Box 1
Newcastle upon Tyne NE88 1AA
Tel: 0300 200 3100
Textphone: 0300 200 3103
Advice line for advisers and intermediaries: 0300 200 3102
www.gov.uk/child-benefit

● ●

Guardian's allowance
PO Box 1
Newcastle upon Tyne NE88 1AA
Tel: 0300 200 3101
Textphone: 0300 200 3103
www.gov.uk/guardians-allowance

HM Revenue and Customs (Solicitor's Office)
South West Wing
Bush House
Strand
London WC2B 4RD

HM Revenue and Customs (national insurance)
National Insurance Contributions and Employer Office
HM Revenue and Customs
BX9 1AN
Tel: 0300 200 3500
www.gov.uk/personal-tax/national-insurance

HM Revenue and Customs (Statutory Payments Disputes Team)
Room BP2301
Benton Park View
Newcastle upon Tyne NE98 1YS
Tel: 0300 056 0630

NHS Business Services Authority (Help with NHS Costs)
Tel: 0300 330 1343 (low income scheme)
Tel: 0300 330 1341 (medical and maternity exemption certificates)
Tel: 0300 330 1347 (NHS tax credit exemption certificates)
www.nhsbsa.nhs.uk/healthcosts

Local Government and Social Care Ombudsman

England
PO Box 4771
Coventry CV4 0EH
Tel: 0300 061 0614
www.lgo.org.uk

Scottish Public Services Ombudsman
4 Melville Street
Edinburgh EH3 7NS
Tel: 0800 377 7330
www.spso.org.uk

● ● ● ●

Public Services Ombudsman for Wales
1 Ffordd yr Hen Gae
Pencoed CF35 5LJ
Tel: 0300 790 0203
www.ombudsman-wales.org.uk

The Parliamentary and Health Service Ombudsman
Millbank Tower
30 Millbank
London SW1P 4QP
Tel: 0345 015 4033
www.ombudsman.org.uk

The Adjudicator
Helen Megarry
The Adjudicator's Office
PO Box 10280
Nottingham NG2 9PF
Tel: 0300 057 1111
www.adjudicatorsoffice.gov.uk

Independent Case Examiner
The Independent Case Examiner
PO Box 209
Bootle L20 7WA
Tel: 0345 606 0777
ice@dwp.gsi.gov.uk
www.gov.uk/government/organisations/independent-case-examiner

Judicial Conduct Investigations Office
81–82 Queens Building
Royal Courts of Justice
Strand
London WC2A 2LL
Tel: 020 7073 4719
inbox@jcio.gsi.gov.uk
https://judicialconduct.judiciary.gov.uk

Standards Commission for Scotland
Room T2.21 Scottish Parliament
Edinburgh EH99 1SP
Tel: 0131 348 6666
enquiries@standardscommission.org.uk
www.standardscommissionscotland.org.uk

. . . .

Commissioner for Ethical Standards in Public Life in Scotland
Thistle House
91 Haymarket Terrace
Edinburgh EH12 5HE
Tel: 0300 011 0550
info@ethicalstandards.org.uk
To make a complaint: investigations@ethicalstandards.org.uk
www.ethicalstandards.org.uk

Appendix 4

Useful publications

Immigration, nationality and asylum

Macdonald's Immigration Law and Practice
(9th edition), I Macdonald and R Toal, LexisNexis Butterworths, 2015

Immigration Law Handbook
(9th edition), M Phelan and J Gillespie, Oxford University Press, 2015

Support for Asylum-seekers and Other Migrants
(3rd edition), S Willman and S Knafler, Legal Action Group, 2009

Best Practice Guide to Asylum and Human Rights Appeals,
M Henderson and A Pickup, ILPA, 2015 (available only from www.ein.org.uk)

Children

Working with Children and Young People Subject to Immigration Control: guidelines for best practice
(2nd edition), H Crawley, ILPA, 2012, www.ilpa.org.uk/pages/publications.html

Children in Need: local authority support for children and families
(2nd edition), I Wise QC and others, Legal Action Group, 2013

Resources Guide for Practitioners Working With Refugee Children
(4th edition), S Gillan, A Harvey and S Myerscough, ILPA, 2014,
www.ilpa.org.uk/pages/publications.html

Working With Migrant Children: community care law for immigration lawyers,
A Hundt and Z Yazdani, ILPA, 2012, www.ilpa.org.uk/pages/publications.html

Separated Children and Legal Aid Provision,
S Valdez, ILPA, 2012, www.ilpa.org.uk/pages/publications.html

Working With Refugee Children: current issues in best practice
(2nd edition), S Bolton and others, ILPA, 2012, www.ilpa.org.uk/pages/
publications.html

Social security legislation

The Law Relating to Social Security
All the legislation but without any commentary. Available at
http://lawvolumes.dwp.gov.uk

Social Security Legislation, Volume I: Non-Means-Tested Benefits and Employment and Support Allowance, N Wikely, I Hooker, R Poynter and R White (Sweet & Maxwell)
Legislation with commentary. 2017/18 edition (September 2017): £113 for the main volume.

Social Security Legislation, Volume II: Income Support, Jobseeker's Allowance, State Pension Credit and the Social Fund, N Wikeley, R Poynter and J Mesher (Sweet & Maxwell)
Legislation with commentary. 2017/18 edition (September 2017): £113 for the main volume.

Social Security Legislation, Volume III: Administration, Adjudication and the European Dimension, N Wikeley, M Rowland and R White (Sweet & Maxwell)
Legislation with commentary. 2017/18 edition (September 2017): £113 for the main volume.

Social Security Legislation, Volume IV: Tax Credits and HMRC-Administered Social Security Benefits, N Wikeley and I Hooker (Sweet & Maxwell)
Legislation with commentary. 2017/18 edition (September 2017): £113 for the main volume.

Social Security Legislation, Volume V: Universal Credit, J Mesher, R Poynter, N Wikeley and P Wood (Sweet & Maxwell)
Legislation with commentary. 2017/18 edition (November 2016): £90 for the main volume.

Social Security Legislation – updating supplement to Volumes I – IV (Sweet & Maxwell)
The spring 2017 update to the 2016/17 main volumes: £70.

CPAG's Housing Benefit and Council Tax Reduction Legislation, L Findlay, R Poynter, C George, S Wright, M Williams, S Mitchell and M Brough (CPAG)
Legislation with detailed commentary. 2017/18 (30th edition, winter 2017): £125 including Supplement.

Social security official guidance
Decision Makers' Guide
Available at www.gov.uk/government/collections/decision-makers-guide-staff-guide.

Advice for Decision Making: staff guide
Available at www.gov.uk/government/publications/advice-for-decision-making-staff-guide.

Housing Benefit Guidance Manual
Available at www.gov.uk/government/collections/housing-benefit-claims-processing-and-good-practice-for-local-authority-staff.

Tax credits manuals
Available at www.gov.uk/government/collections/tax-credits-hmrc-manuals

Budgeting Loan Guide
Available at www.gov.uk/government/publications/budgeting-loan-guide-for-decision-makers-reviewing-officers-and-further-reviewing-officers.

National insurance number allocation guidance
Available at www.gov.uk/government/publications/national-insurance-number-allocations-staff-guide

Child Benefit Technical Manual
Available at www.gov.uk/hmrc-internal-manuals/child-benefit-technical-manual

Leaflets
The DWP publishes many leaflets available free from your local DWP or Jobcentre Plus office. To order more than 50 leaflets, contact iON, 2nd floor, One City West, Gelderd Road, Leeds LS12 6NJ, email: ion-pass@xerox.com. To order up to 50 copies of a leaflet, fax order form to 0845 850 0479. www.gov.uk/government/collections/dwp-leaflets-and-how-to-order-them. Leaflets on housing benefit are available from your local council.

Periodicals
Welfare Rights Bulletin (CPAG, bi-monthly)
Covers developments in social security law, including Upper Tribunal decisions. The annual subscription is £40 but it is sent automatically to CPAG Rights members (more information at www.cpag.org.uk/membership).

Articles on social security and immigration can also be found in *Legal Action* (Legal Action Group), *Adviser* (Citizens Advice) and the *Journal of Social Security Law* (Sweet & Maxwell).

Other social security publications

Welfare Benefits and Tax Credits Handbook (CPAG)
£61/£15 for claimants (2017/18, April 2017)

Welfare Benefits and Tax Credits Handbook Online (CPAG)
Includes the full text of the *Welfare Benefits and Tax Credits Handbook* updated throughout the year. Annual subscription £70 per user (bulk discounts available). More information at www.shop.cpag.org.uk.

Universal Credit: what you need to know (CPAG)
£15 (4th edition, June 2017)

Winning Your Benefit Appeal: what you need to know (CPAG)
£15 (2nd edition, autumn 2016)

Help with Housing Costs: guide to housing benefit 2017/18 (Shelter/CIH)
£39.99 (June 2017)

Help with Housing Costs: guide to universal credit and council tax rebates 2017/18 (Shelter/CIH)
£39.99 (June 2017)

Disability Rights Handbook 2017/18 (Disability Rights UK)
£33.99 (May 2017)

Tribunal Practice and Procedure (Legal Action Group)
£65 (4th edition, autumn 2016)

For CPAG publications and most other publications, contact:

CPAG, 30 Micawber Street, London N1 7TB, tel: 020 7837 7979, email: bookorders@cpag.org.uk. Order via www.shop.cpag.org.uk. Postage and packing: free for online subscriptions and orders up to £10 in value; for order value £10.01–£100, add a flat rate charge of £3.99; for order value £100.01–£400, add £7.49; for order value £400+, add £11.49.

Appendix 5

Reciprocal agreements

Reciprocal agreements with European Economic Area states

State	Retirement pension	Bereavement benefits	Guardian's allowance	'Sickness benefit'	Incapacity benefit	Contribution-based jobseeker's allowance	Maternity allowance	Disablement benefit	Industrial injuries benefits	Child benefit	Attendance allowance and disability living allowance	Carer's allowance
Austria	✓	✓	✓	✓	✓	✓	✓	✓	✓	✓	–	–
Belgium	✓	✓	✓	✓	✓	✓	✓	✓	✓	✓	–	–
Croatia	✓	✓	–	✓	✓	✓	✓	✓	✓	✓	–	–
Cyprus	✓	✓	✓	✓	✓	✓	✓	✓	✓	–	–	–
Denmark	–	✓	✓	✓	✓	✓	✓	✓	✓	✓	✓	–
Finland	✓	✓	–	✓	✓	✓	✓	✓	✓	✓	–	–
France	✓	✓	✓	✓	✓	✓	✓	✓	✓	✓	–	–
Germany	–	✓	✓	✓	✓	✓	✓	✓	✓	✓	✓	–
Iceland	✓	✓	✓	✓	✓	✓	–	✓	✓	–	–	–
Ireland	✓	✓	✓	✓	✓*	✓	✓	✓	✓	–	–	–
Italy	✓	✓	✓	✓	✓	✓	✓	✓	✓	–	–	–
Luxembourg	✓	✓	✓	✓	✓	–	✓	✓	✓	–	–	–
Malta	✓	✓	✓	✓	✓	✓	–	✓	✓	–	–	–
Netherlands	✓	✓	✓	✓	✓	✓	✓	✓	–	–	–	–
Norway	✓	✓	✓	✓	✓	✓	✓	✓	✓	✓	✓	–
Portugal	✓	✓	✓	✓	✓	✓	✓	✓	✓	✓	–	–
Slovenia	✓	✓	–	✓	✓	✓	✓	✓	✓	✓	–	–
Spain	✓	✓	✓	✓	✓	✓	✓	✓	✓	✓	–	–
Sweden	✓	✓	✓	✓	✓	✓	✓	✓	✓	✓	–	–
Northern Ireland*	✓	✓	✓	✓	✓	✓	✓	✓	✓	✓	✓	✓

*Although Northern Ireland is part of the UK, there is an agreement between Great Britain and Northern Ireland. This is because benefits in Northern Ireland and Great Britain are separate and administered under different social security legislation. The reciprocal arrangements between Great Britain and Northern Ireland were replaced and extended to include employment and support allowance (ESA) and personal independence payment from 6 April 2016, income-based jobseeker's allowance from 27 November 2016 as well as the new state pension and bereavement support payment. For details of the previous policy if you were claiming ESA and moved between the two territories, and for details of the current reciprocal arrangements, see p310.

There is an agreement with Gibraltar, which provides that the UK and Gibraltar are treated as separate European Economic Area countries (except for child benefit).

For more information on reciprocal and other agreements, see Chapter 17.

Reciprocal agreements with non-European Economic Area states

State	Retirement pension	Bereavement benefits	Guardian's allowance	'Sickness benefit'	Incapacity benefit and 'converted' employment and support allowance	Contribution-based jobseeker's allowance	Maternity allowance	Disablement benefit	Industrial injuries benefits	Child benefit	Attendance allowance and disability living allowance	Carer's allowance
Barbados	✓	✓	✓	✓	✓	–	✓	✓	✓	✓	–	–
Bermuda	✓	✓	–	–	–	–	–	✓	✓	–	–	–
Bosnia-Herzegovina	✓	✓	–	✓	✓	✓	✓	✓	✓	✓	–	–
Canada	✓	–	–	–	–	✓	–	–	–	✓	–	–
Chile	✓	✓	–	–	–	–	–	–	–	–	–	–
Israel	✓	✓	✓	✓	✓*	–	✓	✓	✓	✓	–	–
Jamaica	✓	✓	✓	–	–	–	–	✓	✓	–	–	–
Kosova	✓	✓	–	✓	✓	✓	✓	✓	✓	✓	–	–
Macedonia	✓	✓	–	✓	✓	✓	✓	✓	✓	✓	–	–
Mauritius	✓	✓	✓	–	–	–	–	✓	✓	✓	–	–
Montenegro	✓	✓	–	✓	✓	✓	✓	✓	✓	✓	–	–
New Zealand	✓	✓	✓	✓	–	✓	–	–	–	✓	–	–
Philippines	✓	✓	–	–	–	–	–	✓	✓	–	–	–
Serbia	✓	✓	–	✓	✓	✓	✓	✓	✓	✓	–	–
Switzerland	✓	✓	✓	✓	✓*	–	✓	✓	✓	✓	–	–
Turkey	✓	✓	✓	✓	✓	–	✓	✓	✓	–	–	–
USA	✓	✓	✓	✓	✓	–	–	–	–	–	–	–
Guernsey	✓	✓	✓	✓	✓	✓	✓	✓	✓	✓	✓	–
Isle of Man	✓	✓	✓	✓	✓*	✓	✓	✓	✓	✓	✓	✓
Jersey	✓	✓	✓	✓	✓	–	✓	✓	✓	✓	✓	–

* Not employment and support allowance on conversion.

You can find the agreements in the *Law Related to Social Security* at http//lawvolumes.dwp.gov.uk by going to the 'List of Statutory Instruments' and searching under the relevant country.

The UK also has other types of agreements with other countries.

For more information on all agreements, see Chapter 17.

The agreement with Chile has only been in force since 1 June 2015.

The agreements with Bosnia-Herzegovina, Croatia, Kosovo, Macedonia, Montenegro and Serbia are in a single agreement with former Yugolsavia, but are treated as separate agreements.

Until 1 March 2001, there was an agreement with Australia. This was then revoked, subject to limited savings provisions in relation to retirement pensions and bereavement benefits.

There is an agreement with Japan, but it only covers liability for contributions.

Appendix 6

Passport stamps and other endorsements

Figure 1: UK passport

Figure 2: Certificates certifying naturalisation and registration as a British citizen

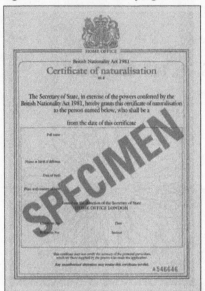

Figure 3: Certificate of entitlement to the right of above

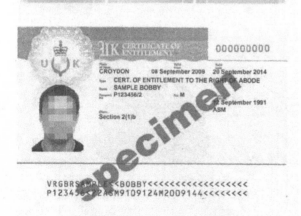

Figure 4: Immigration status document

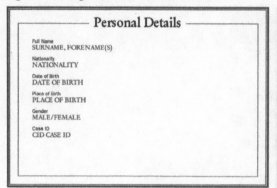

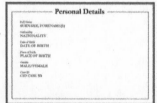

Figure 5: Biometric residence permit

The card's design is set by European Union (EU) regulation. It is a standard credit card size (86mm x 54mm) and will look similar to identity cards issued by other EU countries. The card is made from polycarbonate plastic and contains a chip to make it more secure against forgery and abuse.

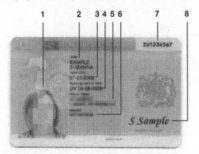
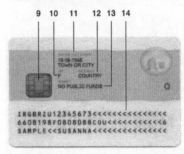

1. Holder's digital image
2. Holder's name
3. Valid until – the date the card expires. This date is at the end of the time the holder is allowed to stay; or five or 10 years if the holder has been given permission to settle in the United Kingdom (known as indefinite leave to remain)
4. Place and date of issue – this is the UK followed by the date the card was issued
5. Type of permit – this is the immigration category the holder is in (for example, STUDENT)
6. Remarks – these are the immigration entitlements for the length of the holder's stay, and may continue on the back of the card
7. ZU1234567 – unique card number
8. Holder's signature

9. Biometric chip
10. Holder's gender
11. Holder's date and place of birth
12. Holder's nationality
13. Remarks – this is a continuation of immigration entitlements for the length of time of the holder's stay (see 6 above)
14. Machine readable zone (MRZ) – this area allows information printed on the card to be read quickly by machine

Figure 6: Registration certificate or document certifying permanent residence

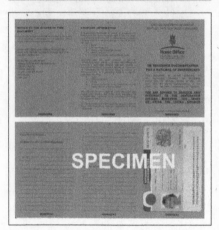
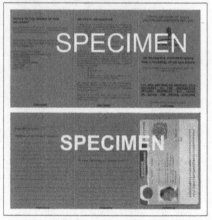

Figure 7: Residence card (including an accession residence card or a derivative residence card) issued by the Home Office to a non-European Economic Area national who is a family member of a national of a European Economic Area country or Switzerland or who has a derivative right of residence

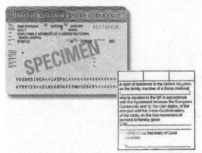
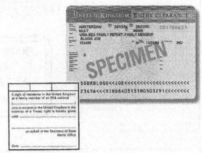

Figure 8: Historic ink stamp endorsements (top left, top middle and bottom left), application registration card (top right and bottom right), visa vignettes (bottom middle and bottom left), and residence permit vignette

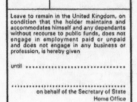

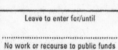

Figure 9: Entry clearance vignette

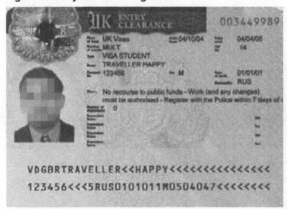

Figure 10: Date stamp on entry clearance vignette

Figure 11: Refugee Convention travel document

Figure 12: Notice of liability for removal

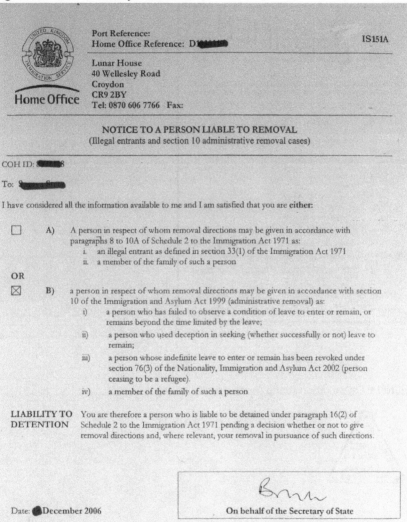

Port Reference:
Home Office Reference: D1████████

IS151A

Home Office

Lunar House
40 Wellesley Road
Croydon
CR9 2BY
Tel: 0870 606 7766 Fax:

NOTICE TO A PERSON LIABLE TO REMOVAL
(Illegal entrants and section 10 administrative removal cases)

COH ID: ████████

To: ████████

I have considered all the information available to me and I am satisfied that you are **either:**

☐ A) A person in respect of whom removal directions may be given in accordance with
paragraphs 8 to 10A of Schedule 2 to the Immigration Act 1971 as:
    i.   an illegal entrant as defined in section 33(1) of the Immigration Act 1971
    ii. a member of the family of such a person

OR

☒ B) a person in respect of whom removal directions may be given in accordance with section
10 of the Immigration and Asylum Act 1999 (administrative removal) as:
    i)   a person who has failed to observe a condition of leave to enter or remain, or
        remains beyond the time limited by the leave;
    ii)   a person who used deception in seeking (whether successfully or not) leave to
        remain;
    iii) a person whose indefinite leave to enter or remain has been revoked under
        section 76(3) of the Nationality, Immigration and Asylum Act 2002 (person
        ceasing to be a refugee).
    iv) a member of the family of such a person

LIABILITY TO You are therefore a person who is liable to be detained under paragraph 16(2) of
DETENTION Schedule 2 to the Immigration Act 1971 pending a decision whether or not to give
removal directions and, where relevant, your removal in pursuance of such directions.

Date: ██December 2006

On behalf of the Secretary of State

Important notice for persons detained under the Immigration Act 1971.

You may on request have one person known to you or who is likely to take an interest in your welfare informed at
public expense as soon as practicable of your whereabouts.

IS151A 04/06

Figure 13: Notice of temporary admission

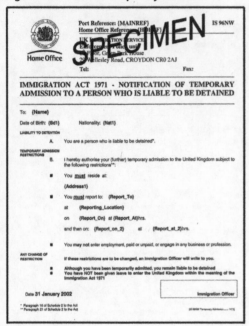

Figure 14: Embarkation stamp (not currently in use)

Appendix 7

Abbreviations used in the notes

AAC	Administrative Appeals Chamber
AACR	Administrative Appeals Chamber Reports
AC	Appeal Cases
Admin	Administrative Court
AG	Advocate General
All ER	All England Law Reports
All ER(D)	All England Law Reports (Digest)
Art(s)	Article(s)
CA	Court of Appeal
Ch	chapter
Civ	Civil Division
CJEU	Court of Justice of the European Union
Crim App R	Criminal Appeal Reports
CSIH	Court of Session, Inner House
CSOH	Court of Session, Outer House
Dir	Directive
EC	European Community
ECJ	European Court of Justice
ECR	European Court Reports
EEA	European Economic Area
EFTACR	European Free Trade Association Court Reports
EU	European Union
EWCA	England and Wales Court of Appeal
EWHC	England and Wales High Court
FLR	Family Law Reports
HC	High Court
HL	House of Lords
HLR	Housing Law Reports
IAC	Immigration and Asylum Chamber
IEAC	Ireland Court of Appeal

Imm AR	Immigration Appeal Reports
NICom	Northern Ireland Commissioner
OJ	Official Journal of the European Union
p(p)	page(s)
para(s)	paragraphs(s)
QB	Queen's Bench Reports
QBD	Queen's Bench Division
r(r)	rule(s)
Reg(s)	regulation(s)
s(s)	section(s)
Sch(s)	Schedule(s)
SLT	Scots Law Times
SSAC	Social Security Advisory Committee
SSH	Secretary of State for Health
SSHD	Secretary of State for the Home Department
SSWP	Secretary of State for Work and Pensions
TFEU	Treaty on the Functioning of the European Union
UKAIT	United Kingdom Asylum and Immigration Tribunal
UKHL	United Kingdom House of Lords
UKSC	United Kingdom Supreme Court
UKUT	United Kingdom Upper Tribunal
Vol	volume
WLR	Weekly Law Reports

Acts of Parliament

AI(TC)A 2004	Asylum and Immigration (Treatment of Claimants, etc.) Act 2004
BNA 1981	British Nationality Act 1981
CA 1989	Children Act 1989
CA 2014	Care Act 2014
C(S)A 1995	Children (Scotland) Act 1995
CSPSSA 2000	Child Support, Pensions and Social Security Act 2000
HRA 1998	Human Rights Act 1998
IA 1971	Immigration Act 1971
IA 1978	Interpretation Act 1978
IA 1988	Immigration Act 1988
IA 2014	Immigration Act 2014
IA 2016	Immigration Act 2016
IAA 1999	Immigration and Asylum Act 1999
JSA 1995	Jobseekers Act 1995
NAA 1948	National Assistance Act 1948

NIAA 2002	Nationality, Immigration and Asylum Act 2002
PA 2014	Pensions Act 2014
SPCA 2002	State Pension Credit Act 2002
SSA 1975	Social Security Act 1975
SSA 1998	Social Security Act 1998
SSAA 1992	Social Security Administration Act 1992
SSCBA 1992	Social Security Contributions and Benefits Act 1992
TCA 2002	Tax Credits Act 2002
TCEA 2007	Tribunals, Courts and Enforcement Act 2007
WRA 2007	Welfare Reform Act 2007
WRA 2012	Welfare Reform Act 2012

Regulations and other statutory instruments

Each set of regulations has a statutory instrument (SI) number and date. You ask for them by giving their date and number.

A(IWA) Regs	The Accession (Immigration and Worker Authorisation) Regulations 2006 No.3317
A(IWR) Regs	The Accession (Immigration and Worker Registration) Regulations 2004 No.1219
AC(IWA) Regs	The Accession of Croatia (Immigration and Worker Authorisation) Regulations 2013 No.1460
AS Regs	The Asylum Support Regulations 2000 No.704
ASA(P) Rules	The Asylum Support Appeals (Procedure) Rules 2000 No.541
ASPP(G) Regs	The Additional Statutory Paternity Pay (General) Regulations 2010 No.1056
CB Regs	The Child Benefit (General) Regulations 2006 No.223
CB&GA(Admin) Regs	The Child Benefit and Guardian's Allowance (Administration) Regulations 2003 No.492
CB&GA(DA) Regs	The Child Benefit and Guardian's Allowance (Decisions and Appeals) Regulations 2003 No.916
CTC Regs	The Child Tax Credit Regulations 2002 No.2007
CTR(S) Regs	The Council Tax Reduction (Scotland) Regulations 2012 No.303
CTR(SPC)S Regs	The Council Tax Reduction (State Pension Credit) (Scotland) Regulations 2012 No.319
CTRS(DS)E Regs	The Council Tax Reduction Schemes (Default Scheme) (England) Regulations 2012 No.2886

● ●

CTRS(DS)W Regs	The Council Tax Reduction Schemes (Default Scheme) (Wales) Regulations 2013 No.3035 (W.303)
CTRS(PR)E Regs	The Council Tax Reduction Schemes (Prescribed Requirements) (England) Regulations 2012 No.2885
CTRSPR(W) Regs	The Council Tax Reduction Schemes and Prescribed Requirements (Wales) Regulations 2013 No.3029 (W.301)
ESA Regs	The Employment and Support Allowance Regulations 2008 No.794
ESA Regs 2013	The Employment and Support Allowance Regulations 2013 No.379
ESA(TP)(EA) Regs	The Employment and Support Allowance (Transitional Provisions, Housing Benefit and Council Tax Benefit) (Existing Awards) (No.2) Regulations 2010 No.1907
FANIII(Y)O	The Family Allowances, National Insurance and Industrial Injuries (Yugoslavia) Order 1958 No.1263
GA(Gen) Regs	The Guardian's Allowance (General) Regulations 2003 No.495
HB Regs	The Housing Benefit Regulations 2006 No.213
HB(HR)A Regs	The Housing Benefit (Habitual Residence) Amendment Regulations 2014 No.539
HB(SPC) Regs	The Housing Benefit (Persons who have attained the qualifying age for state pension credit) Regulations 2006 No.214
HB&CTB(DA) Regs	The Housing Benefit and Council Tax Benefit (Decisions and Appeals) Regulations 2001 No.1002
HSS(DHSF)(W) Regs	The Healthy Start Scheme (Description of Healthy Start Food) (Wales) Regulations 2006 No.3108
HSS&WF(A) Regs	The Healthy Start Scheme and Welfare Food (Amendment) Regulations 2005 No.3262
I(EEA) Regs	The Immigration (European Economic Area) Regulations 2006 No.1003
I(EEA)A Regs 2012	The Immigration (European Economic Area) (Amendment) Regulations 2012 No.1547
I(EEA)A Regs 2013	The Immigration (European Economic Area)(Amendment) (No.2) Regulations 2013 No.3032
I(EEA)A Regs 2014	The Immigration (European Economic Area) (Amendment) Regulations 2014 No.1451

I(EEA)A(No.3) Regs	The Immigration (European Economic Area) (Amendment) (No.3) Regulations 2014 No.2761
IA(PAFAS) Regs	The Immigration and Asylum (Provision of Accommodation to Failed Asylum-Seekers) Regulations 2005 No.930
ILRFO Regs	The Integration Loans for Refugees and Others Regulations 2007 No.1598
IS Regs	The Income Support (General) Regulations 1987 No.1967
JSA Regs	The Jobseeker's Allowance Regulations 1996 No.207
JSA Regs 2013	The Job Seeker's Allowance Regulations 2013 No.378
JSA(HR)A Regs	The Jobseeker's Allowance (Habitual Residence) Amendment Regulations 2013 No.3196
SFM&FE Regs	The Social Fund Maternity and Funeral Expenses (General) Regulations 2005 No.3061
SFWFP Regs	The Social Fund Winter Fuel Payment Regulations 2000 No.729
SMP Regs	The Statutory Maternity Pay (General) Regulations 1986 No.1960
SMP(PAM) Regs	The Statutory Maternity Pay (Persons Abroad and Mariners) Regulations 1987 No.418
SPC Regs	The State Pension Credit Regulations 2002 No.1792
SPPSAP(G) Regs	The Statutory Paternity Pay and Statutory Adoption Pay (General) Regulations 2002 No.2822
SPPSAP(PAM) Regs	The Statutory Paternity Pay and Statutory Adoption Pay (Persons Abroad and Mariners) Regulations 2002 No.2821
SS(AA) Regs	The Social Security (Attendance Allowance) Regulations 1991 No.2740
SS(C&P) Regs	The Social Security (Claims and Payments) Regulations 1987 No.1968
SS(DLA) Regs	The Social Security (Disability Living Allowance) Regulations 1991 No.2890
SS(DLA,AA&CA)(A) Regs	The Social Security (Disability Living Allowance, Attendance Allowance and Carer's Allowance) (Amendment) Regulations 2013 No.389
SS(GBRA)(NI) Regs	The Social Security (Great Britain Reciprocal Arrangements) Regulations (Northern Ireland) 2016 No.149
SS(GBRA)(A)NI Regs	The Social Security (Great Britain Reciprocal Arrangements)(Amendment) Regulations (Northern Ireland) 2016 No.393

SS(HR)A Regs	The Social Security (Habitual Residence) Amendment Regulations 2004 No.1232
SS(IA)CA Regs	The Social Security (Immigration and Asylum) Consequential Amendments Regulations 2000 No.636
SS(IB) Regs	The Social Security (Incapacity Benefit) Regulations 1994 No.2946
SS(IB-ID) Regs	The Social Security (Incapacity Benefit – Increases for Dependants) Regulations 1994 No.2945
SS(ICA) Regs	The Social Security (Invalid Care Allowance) Regulations 1976 No.409
SS(II)(AB) Regs	The Social Security (Industrial Injuries) (Airmen's Benefits) Regulations 1975 No.469
SS(II)(MB) Regs	The Social Security (Industrial Injuries) (Mariners' Benefits) Regulations 1975 No.470
SS(IIPD) Regs	The Social Security (Industrial Injuries) (Prescribed Diseases) Regulations 1985 No.967
SS(NIRA) Regs	The Social Security (Northern Ireland Reciprocal Arrangements) Regulations 2016 No. 287
SS(NIRA)(A) Regs	The Social Security (Northern Ireland Reciprocal Arrangements) (Amendment) Regulations 2016 No.1050
SS(PA) Regs	The Social Security (Persons from Abroad) Regulations 1975 No.563
SS(PA)A Regs	The Social Security (Persons From Abroad) Amendment Regulations 2006 No.1026
SS(PAB) Regs	The Social Security (Payments on Account of Benefit) Regulations 2013 No.383
SS(PFA)MA Regs	The Social Security (Persons From Abroad) Miscellaneous Amendments Regulations 1996 No.30
SS(PIP) Regs	The Social Security (Personal Independence Payment) Regulations 2013 No. 377
SS(RA)O	The Social Security (Reciprocal Agreements) Order 2012 No.360
SS(SDA) Regs	The Social Security (Severe Disablement Allowance) Regulations 1984 No.1303
SS(WB&RP) Regs	The Social Security (Widow's Benefit and Retirement Pensions) Regulations 1979 No.642
SS(WTCCTC)(CA) Regs	The Social Security (Working Tax Credit and Child Tax Credit) (Consequential Amendments) Regulations 2003 No.455
SSB(Dep) Regs	The Social Security Benefit (Dependency) Regulations 1977 No.343

SSB(PA) Regs	The Social Security Benefit (Persons Abroad) Regulations 1975 No.563
SSB(PRT) Regs	The Social Security Benefit (Persons Residing Together) Regulations 1977 No.956
SS&CS(DA) Regs	The Social Security and Child Support (Decisions and Appeals) Regulations 1999 No.991
SSP Regs	The Statutory Sick Pay (General) Regulations 1982 No.894
SSP(MAPA) Regs	The Statutory Sick Pay (Mariners, Airmen and Persons Abroad) Regulations 1982 No.1349
SSPP Regs	The Statutory Shared Parental Pay (General) Regulations 2014 No.3051
SSPP(PAM) Regs	The Statutory Shared Parental Pay (Persons Abroad and Mariners) Regulations 2014 No.3134
TC(CN) Regs	The Tax Credits (Claims and Notifications) Regulations 2002 No.2014
TC(Imm) Regs	The Tax Credits (Immigration) Regulations 2003 No.653
TC(PC) Regs	The Tax Credits (Payments by the Board) Regulations 2002 No. 2173
TC(R) Regs	The Tax Credits (Residence) Regulations 2003 No.654
TP(FT) Rules	The Tribunal Procedure (First-tier Tribunal) (Social Entitlement Chamber) Rules 2008 No.2685
UC Regs	The Universal Credit Regulations 2013 No. 376
UC(TP) Regs	The Universal Credit (Transitional Provisions) Regulations 2013 No. 386
U-C,PIP,JSA&ESA(C&P) Regs	The Universal Credit, Personal Independence Payment, Jobseeker's Allowance and Employment and Support Allowance (Claims and Payments) Regulations 2013 No.380
UC,PIP,JSA&ESA(DA) Regs	The Universal Credit, Personal Independence Payment, Jobseeker's Allowance and Employment and Support Allowance (Decisions and Appeals) Regulations 2013 No. 381
WF Regs	The Welfare Food Regulations 1996 No.1434
WRA(No.9)O	The Welfare Reform Act 2012 (Commencement No.9 and Transitional and Transitory Provisions and Commencement No.8 and Savings and Transitional Provisions (Amendment)) Order 2013 No.983
WTC(EMR) Regs	The Working Tax Credit (Entitlement and Maximum Rate) Regulations 2002 No. 2005

● ●

Other information

ADM	*Advice for Decision Making*
CBTM	*Child Benefit Technical Manual*
CCM	*Claimant Compliance Manual* (HMRC guidance on investigation of tax credit claims)
DMG	*Decision Makers' Guide*
GM	*Housing Benefit/Council Tax Benefit Guidance Manual*
IDI	Immigration Directorate Instructions
IR	Immigration Rules
TCM	*Tax Credits Manual*
TCTM	*Tax Credits Technical Manual*

References like CIS/142/1990 and R(IS) 1/07 are to commissioners' decisions.

References like *TG v SSWP (PC)* [2015] UKUT 50 (AAC) are references to decisions of the Upper Tribunal.

References like ASA/02/02/1877 are references to decisions of the First-tier Tribunal (Asylum Support).

Index

....

How to use this Index

Entries against the bold headings direct you to the general information on the subject, or where the subject is covered most fully. Sub-entries are listed alphabetically and direct you to specific aspects of the subject. The following abbreviations are used in the index:

AA	Attendance allowance	I-ESA	Income-related employment and
CA	Carer's allowance		support allowance
C-ESA	Contributory employment and	I-JSA	Income-based jobseeker's
	support allowance		allowance
C-JSA	Contribution-based jobseeker's	JSA	Jobseeker's allowance
	allowance	MA	Maternity allowance
CTA	Common travel area	NI	National insurance
CTC	Child tax credit	PC	Pension credit
DLA	Disability living allowance	PIP	Personal independence payment
EC	European Community	SAP	Statutory adoption pay
EEA	European Economic Area	SMP	Statutory maternity pay
ESA	Employment and support allowance	SPP	Statutory paternity pay
EU	European Union	SSP	Statutory sick pay
HB	Housing benefit	SSPP	Statutory shared parental pay
IB	Incapacity benefit	UC	Universal credit
IS	Income support	WTC	Working tax credit

16-19 bursaries 467

A
A2 nationals
    derivative right to reside 183
    evidence of work 383
    family member of an EEA national 171
    jobseekers 136
    legally working 133
    not subject to worker authorisation 131
    permanent right to reside 194
    restrictions on employment 130
    restrictions on residence rights 130
    retaining self-employed status 163
    retaining worker status 149
    right to reside 129
    self-employed 160
    self-sufficient people 165
    workers 143
A2 states 129
A8 nationals
    authorised employer 133
    derivative right to reside 183

    evidence of work 383
    family member of an EEA national 171
    jobseekers 136
    legally working 133
    not required to register with authorised
        employer 132
    permanent right to reside 194
    restrictions on employment 130
    restrictions on residence rights 130
    retaining self-employed status 163
    retaining worker status 149
    right to reside 129
    self-employed 160
    self-sufficient people 165
    workers 143
A8 states 129
abroad
    benefit abroad 235, 246
        AA 259
        bereavement benefits 256
        C-ESA 266
        C-JSA 266

CA 259
child benefit 257
CTC 269
DLA 259
guardian's allowance 258
HB 254
I-ESA 251
I-JSA 248
IB 263
industrial injuries benefits 265
IS 247
MA 263
PC 253
PIP 259
retirement pensions 267
statutory employment benefits 269
UC 255
WTC 269
child abroad 185, 213, 242
effect of EU law on benefits and tax
    credits 244
effect of UK law on benefits and tax
    credits 239
indefinite leave 24
ordinary residence 101
partner abroad 212, 242
preparing to go abroad 238
temporary absence abroad 240
absence 239
absence from home 242
child abroad 185, 213, 242
indefinite leave 24
ordinary residence 101
partner abroad 212, 242
temporary absence 240
accession worker document 143
accident
retaining worker status 155, 164
accommodation
asylum seekers 418, 430
dispersal 421
eviction 423
failed asylum seekers 434
overcrowding 27
recourse to public funds 27
section 4 support 434

actively seeking work 140, 383
administrative removal 20
administrative review 19
advance benefit claims 114
advice 7
age
evidence 380
agency workers
EEA workers 145
aggregation
EU co-ordination rules 298
aircrew
leave to enter or remain 22
Algeria
CTC 73
EU agreements 319
non-means-tested benefits 71
appeals 18, 439
asylum support decisions 439
benefit decisions 343
EEA decisions 19
immigration decisions 18
leave to remain extended for an appeal 63
section 4 support 439
section 95 support 439
application registration card 49
armed services
financial help for former members 473
leave to enter or remain 22
single competent state 288
Article 8 leave to remain 34
ASPEN card 389, 428
association agreements 319
Turkish nationals 22
Asylum Help 391
asylum seekers 31, 49, 80
16/17-year-olds leaving care 412
accommodation 430, 434
adequate accommodation 418
appealing against refusal of application
    403
application expenses 432
application refused 38
application registration card 49
applying for asylum 31
bail 14
benefits 80
care needs due to sickness or disability
    409

children 412
Children Act support 411
claiming as soon as reasonably
    practicable 395
community care 409
definition 31, 392
definition of dependants 394
destitute 397, 398, 416
detention 32
determining an asylum application 392
discretionary leave 36
dispersal 421, 430
duty to report 432
entitlement to benefits and tax credits 390
essential living needs 427
eviction from accommodation 423
failed asylum seekers 398
further submissions to Home Office 402
health benefits 422
humanitarian protection 32
in-country applications 32
leaving the UK 399
means-tested benefits 69
permission to work 32
recording an asylum application 392
right to reside 125
standard acknowledgement letter 49
support 389
temporary admission 14
temporary protection 31
travel expenses 432
asylum support 387, 427
    accommodation 423, 430
    adequate accommodation 418
    amount of support 427
    appeals 439
    application expenses 432
    applications 415
    assets 435
    backdating 429
    background to current system 389
    change of circumstances 422
    children 409, 412
    Children Act support 411
    claiming asylum as soon as reasonably
        practicable 395
    clothing 420
    community care support 409
    conditions attached 421

contributing to own support costs 429
council tax reduction 459
decisions on asylum support 420
definition of asylum seeker 392
dependants 394
destitute 394, 397, 416
dispersal 421, 430
education costs 432
emergency support 397
essential living needs 420, 427
exceptional payments 428
exclusions 395
families with children 393
further applications 423, 453
health benefits 422
Home Office guidance 391
legal aid 443
local authority support 408
maternity payment 429
misrepresentation 436
organisations providing support 391
overpayments 436
payment 428
recovery from a sponsor 436
repaying support 435
section 4 support 398
section 95 support 389, 391
section 98 support 397
suspension 396
temporary support 397, 420
travel expenses 432
treated as income
    means-tested benefits 81
types of support 389
attendance allowance
    abroad 259
    EU co-ordination rules 219, 261
    habitual residence test 106
    person subject to immigration control 69
    residence rules 218
available for work 140, 383

B
backdating
    asylum support 429
bail 14
    applying for support 424
    section 4 support 407

benefit claims
claiming another benefit 369
claiming without an NI number 360
delays 325
ending an award 368
evidence is unavailable 371
exclusions from benefit 367
making a valid claim 366
providing evidence 365
proving entitlement 367
refusal of benefit 362
who may be entitled 67
bereavement
leave to remain following bereavement 35
recourse to public funds 35
bereavement allowance
abroad 256
EU co-ordination rules 216
residence rules 215
bereavement benefits
abroad 256
EU co-ordination rules 216, 257, 285
reciprocal agreements 216, 315
residence rules 215
bereavement payment
abroad 256
EU co-ordination rules 216
residence rules 215
bereavement support payment
abroad 256
EU co-ordination rules 216, 257
residence rules 215
biometric residence permits 47
Brexit 3
EU co-ordination rules 279
British citizens
dual British and other EEA state citizens 176
family members 174
primary carer of British citizen 187
proof of status 44
reciprocal agreements 312
right of abode 16
right to reside 125, 127
British citizenship 15
citizenship at birth 16
British dependent territories citizens
reciprocal agreements 312

British nationals 15
proof of status 43
right of abode 15
British overseas citizens
reciprocal agreements 312
British overseas territories citizens
reciprocal agreements 312

C
care and support needs 409, 468
carer's allowance
abroad 259
EU co-ordination rules 219, 261
habitual residence test 106
person subject to immigration control 69
residence rules 218
cash in hand
EEA workers 145
certificate of patriality 44
certificate of travel 48
challenging a decision
asylum support appeals 451
benefits 341
ending an award of benefit 368
immigration decisions 18
change of circumstances
sponsorship 27
Channel Islands
reciprocal agreements 310
charities 474
child benefit
abroad 257
child subject to immigration control 76
EEA jobseekers 141
EU co-ordination rules 217, 259
interim payments 333
living in UK for three months 97
person subject to immigration control 69
reciprocal agreements 317
refugees 83
residence rules 216
right to reside test 117, 119
child tax credit
abroad 269
EEA jobseekers 141
EU co-ordination rules 230, 271
living in UK for three months 97
NI numbers 356, 363
partner subject to immigration control 77

person subject to immigration control 72

refugees 83

residence rules 227

right to reside test 117, 119

transfers from IS or I-JSA 74

children

asylum support 412

child abroad 185, 213

Children Act support 411, 470

discretionary leave for unaccompanied children 37

education benefits 466

family members of EEA nationals 172

free milk 468

in education 183

leave to remain as parent of British child 35

primary carer of worker's child in education 185

proof of parentage 377, 378

residence requirements 98

civil partners

partner of EEA national 172

person subject to immigration control benefits 74

proof of relationship 377, 378

residence rights when partnership ends 178

sponsorship 26

civil servants

single competent state 288

clothing grants

school clothes 467

co-operation and association agreements 319

common travel area 95, 106

residence 112

Commonwealth citizens

freely landed 46

right of abode 16

right to reside 125

community care support 409, 468

competent state 288

determining competent state 289

disputes over competent state 296

how long the UK remains competent state 290

sickness benefits 290

complaints

benefit delays 327

HB 339

Council of Europe

conventions and agreements 317

Social Charter 318

council tax reduction 457

absences abroad 461

habitual residence test 107, 459

NI number requirement 460

partner subject to immigration control 76

person subject to immigration control 458

recourse to public funds 458

residence rules 459

right to reside 460

couples

partner abroad 212, 242

proof of relationship 377

criminal offence

breach of conditions of leave to remain 22

exclusion from refugee status 33

suspension of section 95 support 396

crisis loans

local welfare assistance 462

Croatia

derivative right to reside 183

evidence of work 383

family member of an EEA national 171

jobseekers 136

legally working 133

not subject to worker authorisation 131

permanent right to reside 194

restrictions on employment 130

restrictions on residence rights 130

retaining self-employed status 163

retaining worker status 149

right to reside 129

self-employed 160

self-sufficient people 165

workers 143

D

date of birth

providing evidence of age 380

death

leave to remain following bereavement 35

right to reside of family members 178

death grants
EU co-ordination rules 285
decisions
benefit decisions 326
delays with benefits 323
appeals 343
challenging a decision 341
HB 338
NI number delays 361
payment 347
reasons for delay 325
revisions 342
short-term advances 329
suspension of benefits 348
test case pending 341
dental treatment
asylum seekers 422
Department for Work and Pensions
benefit decisions 327
complaints 334
dependants
dependants' benefits, reciprocal
agreements 317
dependent on EEA national 172
deportation 20
derivative right to reside 181, 188
A2 nationals 183
A8 nationals 183
benefit entitlement 189
child of primary carer 188
Croatian nationals 183
permanent right to reside 194
primary carer of a worker's child in
education 185
primary carer of British citizen 187
primary carer of self-sufficient child 186
who has derivative right to reside 182
worker's child in education 183
destitute 472
community care support 468
definition 416
expenses of applying for asylum 432
section 4 support 398
section 95 support 394
temporary asylum support 397
destitution domestic violence concession 35
detention 14
asylum seekers 32
section 4 support 407, 424

diplomatic staff
leave to enter and remain 22
single state principle 288
disability
asylum seekers with care needs 409
failed asylum seekers unable to leave UK
400
financial support 473
disability living allowance
abroad 259
EU co-ordination rules 219, 261
habitual residence test 106
mobility component 221
person subject to immigration control 69
residence rules 218
special non-contributory benefit 287
Discretionary Assistance Fund for Wales 463
discretionary leave 36
benefits and tax credits 81
unaccompanied children 37
discrimination
EU co-ordination rules 297
dispersal
asylum seekers 421, 430
divorce
right to reside for EEA nationals 172, 178
domestic violence
asylum seekers accommodation 419
leave to remain 35, 61
recourse to public funds 35, 61
dual nationality 176

E
education
benefits 466
who is in education 184
education maintenance allowance 467
employment
asylum seekers 32
ceasing to be a worker 148
checks by employers 24
conditions 24
discretionary leave 36
employed in two or more EU member
states 289
evidence of employment record 381
genuine and effective work 146
genuine chance of obtaining 140
lawfully working 71

legally working 133
migrant workers 24
points-based system 29
remuneration 145
sponsorship 29
what counts as employed 144
employment and support allowance in youth
person subject to immigration control 69
residence rules 218
employment and support allowance, contributory
abroad 266
EU co-ordination rules 224, 266
reciprocal agreements 224, 267, 314
residence rules 223
employment and support allowance, income related
abroad 251
child abroad 213
EEA jobseekers 141
EU co-ordination rules 214, 253
habitual residence test 106
partner abroad 212, 252
partner subject to immigration control 74
person subject to immigration control 67
reciprocal agreements 253, 314
residence rules 210
right to reside test 117, 118
special non-contributory benefit 287
English language lessons
asylum seekers 432
entry clearance
applying from outside UK 16
proof of leave to enter or remain 44
proof of limited leave to enter 46
entry clearance officers 13
equal treatment 297, 298
agreements 319
European Convention on Social and Medical Assistance 318
discretionary leave 36
European Court of Human Rights
failed asylum seekers 404
European Economic Area
member states 40
reciprocal agreements 311
benefits covered 314
people covered 312

European Economic Area nationals 40
British nationals 177
checklist of residence rights 128
EU co-ordination rules 277
exclusion from UK 41
family members 171, 282
habitual residence test 108
initial right of residence 134
jobseeker 135
legal basis of residence rights 126
member of family 282
permanent right of residence 190
proof of status 41, 50
qualified person 128
registration certificate 41, 50
removal from UK 41
residence documents 41, 375
right of admission to UK 40
right to reside 117, 126
section 95 support 395
self-employed person 159
worker 142
European Free Trade Association 40
European Union
co-operation and association agreements 319
co-ordination of social security 244, 275
member states 40
reciprocal agreements
benefits covered 314
people covered 312
UK referendum 3
European Union co-ordination of benefits 244, 275
aggregation 298
benefits covered 284
bereavement benefits 216
competent state 288
death grants 285
discrimination 297
equal treatment 297, 298
exporting benefits 300
family benefits 286
habitual residence 116
how to use the rules 280
industrial injuries benefits 222, 286
insured person 71
invalidity benefits 285
legislative basis 279

maternity benefits 225, 285
member of family 282
old age benefits 225, 285
old co-ordination rules 280, 283
overlapping benefit rules 301
paternity benefits 285
personal scope of the rules 281
principles 278, 288
satisfying past presence rules 220
sickness benefits 285, 290
single state principle 288
social and medical assistance 287
social security benefits 285
special non-contributory benefits 287
subject to legislation of member state 281
survivors' benefits 257, 285
unemployment benefits 286
who is covered 281
evidence 365
age 380
benefit claims 365
challenging a decision to end a benefit
award 368
employment record 381
evidence is unavailable 371
from other countries 376
genuine prospect of work 137
immigration status 373
jobseeking 137, 383
relationships 377
exceptional leave to enter or remain 37
exporting benefits
EU co-ordination rules 300

F
failed asylum seekers
accommodation 434
additional section 4 support 433
appealing to European Court of Human
Rights 404
appeals 403
applying for section 4 support 423
Children Act support 411
community care support 409
criteria for section 4 support 399
destitution 398
detention 32
fresh applications 38, 402
human rights 401, 405

judicial review 401, 404
no viable route of return 401, 405
pregnancy 434
reasonable steps to leave UK 399
section 4 support 398, 433
sick or disabled 400
family benefits
EU co-ordination rules 286, 301
exporting benefits 301
overlapping benefits 302
reciprocal agreements 317
family life
enjoyment of private and family life 34
family members of EEA nationals 170
benefit entitlement 119, 180
British citizens 174
child abroad 213
Croatian, A2 and A8 nationals 171
EU co-ordination rules 282
evidence of family relationship 377
extended family 173
family benefits 301
family permits 41
former family members 177
habitual residence 108
initial right of residence 134
non-EEA nationals 193, 377
non-means-tested benefits 70
partner abroad 212
permanent right to reside 192
residence card 50, 375
residence rights 126, 127, 170
right of admission to UK 40
who is a family member 70, 171
family permit 375
family reunion 33
benefits and tax credits 82
fees
appeals 19
applications 17
health surcharge 18
fiancé(e)s
sponsorship 26
financial need
benefit delays 330
First-tier Tribunal (Asylum Support)
attending the hearing 441
challenging a decision 451
decision to remit 453

decisions 450
hearing procedure 447
Home Office response 443
how to appeal 440
notice of appeal 440
oral hearings 446
paper hearings 445
representation 442
right to appeal 440
setting aside a decision 452
striking out an appeal 449
time limits 442
timetable for appeals 444
withdrawing the appeal 448
First-tier Tribunal (Immigration and Asylum Chamber) 18
food banks 472
former workers 149
free school lunches 466
freedom of movement
EEA nationals 278
funeral payments
residence rules 226

G
genuine and sufficient link to the UK 220
genuine prospects of work test 137
Gibralter
reciprocal agreements 310
guardian's allowance
child abroad 258
EU co-ordination rules 217, 259
interim payments 333
reciprocal agreements 317
residence rules 217

H
habitual residence 103, 106
definition 112
EU co-ordination rules 116
habitual residence in fact 112
habitual residence test 106
benefits affected 103, 106
EEA nationals 108
establishing habitual residence 107, 112
evidence 112
exempt from habitual residence test 108
failing the test 110
length of residence period 114

refused benefit 110
residence 112
returning residents 115
satisfying the test 107
settled intention 113
voluntary residence 112
who is covered by the test 109
health benefits
asylum seekers 422
health surcharge 18
exceptions 18
Healthy Start food and vitamins 463
HM Passport Office 13
HM Revenue and Customs
benefit decisions 327
complaints 335
home improvement grants 473
Home Office
asylum support 390
hours of work
EEA workers 147
household
partner abroad 242
housing benefit
abroad 254
child abroad 213
complaints 339
delays 338
EEA jobseekers 142
habitual residence test 106
partner abroad 212, 254
partner subject to immigration control 75
payments on account 338
person subject to immigration control 67
residence rules 210
right to reside test 117, 118
housing repairs 473
human rights
asylum seekers 31
discretionary leave 36
failed asylum seekers 401, 403, 405
leave to remain for compassionate reasons 34
restricted leave 37
humanitarian protection 32
benefits and tax credits 81
exclusions 33
family reunion 33
integration loans 84

leave to remain 33
local welfare assistance 84

I

Iceland
residence rights 126
identity
proving identity 365
proving identity for NI number 358
illegal entry 49
administrative removal 20
temporary admission 14
immigration law 11
immigration officers 12
immigration status 13
benefit entitlement 56, 66
checking your status 43
evidence 373
immigration status document 48
in-country applications 32
incapable of work
permanent incapacity 198
temporary incapacity 155
incapacity benefit
abroad 263
EU co-ordination rules 264
reciprocal agreements 314
residence rules 218
income support
abroad 247
child abroad 213, 248
EEA jobseekers 141
EU co-ordination rules 214, 248
habitual residence test 106
partner abroad 212, 248
partner subject to immigration control 74
person subject to immigration control 67
refugees studying English 83
residence rules 210
right to reside test 117, 118
special non-contributory benefit 287
indefinite leave to enter or remain 23
absence abroad 24
entitlement to claim benefits 23
industrial injuries benefits
abroad 265
EU co-ordination rules 265, 286
reciprocal agreements 315
residence conditions 221

initial right of residence 134, 192
insured person 71
integration loans 84
how to apply 85
payment 86
repayments 86
who can apply 84
invalidity benefits
EU co-ordination rules 285
reciprocal agreements 314
Irish citizens
right to reside 126
Isle of Man
reciprocal agreements 310
Israel
EU co-ordination rules 320

J

jobseeker's allowance, contribution-based
abroad 266
EU co-ordination rules 223, 266
reciprocal agreements 224, 267, 314
residence rules 223
jobseeker's allowance, income-based
abroad 248
child abroad 213, 251
EEA jobseekers 141
EU co-ordination rules 214, 251
habitual residence test 106, 109
living in CTA for three months 95
moved from another EEA state 96
partner abroad 212, 250
partner subject to immigration control 74
person subject to immigration control 67
reciprocal agreements 314
residence and presence rules 210
right to reside test 117, 118
jobseekers 135
benefit entitlement 118, 141
Croatian, A2 and A8 nationals 136
entitlement of family members to benefits
119
evidence of jobseeking 137, 383
genuine chance of obtaining work 140
permanent right to reside 192
registering as a jobseeker 151
retaining worker status 150
right to reside 135
time limit on being a jobseeker 136

judicial review 19
  asylum support appeals 452
  benefit delays 337
  failed asylum seekers 401, 404
  HB 340

L
leave outside the rules 38
leave to enter or remain 21
  applications 17
  Article 8 leave to remain 34
  conditions of leave 22
  death of spouse or partner 35
  discretionary leave to remain 36
  domestic violence 35, 61
  employment conditions 24
  entry clearance 16, 44
  exceptional leave 37
  exemptions from usual conditions 22
  extended to allow appeal 63
  extending leave 23
  Immigration Rules 21
  indefinite leave 23
  leave outside the Immigration Rules 38
  port of entry applications 46
  proof of status 44, 373
  recourse to public funds 25, 59
  refugees 33
  restricted leave 37
  right to reside 125
  sponsorship 26
  stateless people 34
  time-limited leave 23
  travel documents 48
  who needs leave to enter or remain 21, 58
leaving the UK
  passport endorsements 50
legal aid
  asylum support appeals 443
  judicial reviews 452
Liechtenstein
  residence rights 126
limited leave to enter or remain 23
  bereavement 36
  domestic violence 36
  entry clearance 46
  overstayers 49
  proof of extension of stay 47
  recourse to public funds 25

living in UK or CTA for three months 95
local authorities
  asylum seekers 408
  community care support 468
  support under the Children Act 411
local welfare assistance schemes 462

M
Macedonia
  means-tested benefits 68
  WTC 73
maintenance undertakings 28, 61
  claiming benefits 62
  means-tested benefits 68
  non-means-tested benefits 70
  tax credits 72
**mandatory reconsiderations of benefit
  decisions** 341
maternity allowance
  abroad 263
  EU co-ordination rules 225, 264
  reciprocal agreements 315
  residence conditions 225
maternity benefits
  EU co-ordination rules 285
  Healthy Start food 464
  Healthy Start vitamins 466
  reciprocal agreements 315
maternity payment
  asylum seekers 429
  failed asylum seekers 434
means-tested benefits
  abroad 246
  person subject to immigration control 67
  reciprocal agreements 214
  residence and presence rules 210
medical treatment
  discretionary leave 36
Migrant Help 391
migrant workers
  checks by employer 24
  sponsorship under points-based system
    29
milk
  free milk 468
Morocco
  CTC 73
  EU agreements 319
  non-means-tested benefits 71

multiple nationalities 15

N
National Asylum Support Service 390
national insurance numbers 354
    applying for a number 358
    claiming benefits without a number 360
    delays 361
    obtaining a number 357
    refusal 362
    requirement 354
        who is exempt 355
    tax credits 356, 363
nationality
    British nationality 15
    evidence of nationality 377
    multiple nationalities 15
    nationality law 11
NHS healthcare charges 470
    asylum seekers 422
    services exempt from charges 471
    who is exempt from charges 471
non-contributory benefits
    EU co-ordination rules 287
non-means tested benefits
    partner subject to immigration control 76
    person subject to immigration control 69
    transitional protection 72
Northern Ireland
    reciprocal agreements 310
Norway
    residence rights 126

O
occupational diseases
    EU co-ordination rules 286
old age benefits
    EU co-ordination rules 285
Ombudsman
    benefit complaints 336
    HB 340
ordinary residence 99, 241
    absence from the UK 101
    access to healthcare 471
    benefits affected 99
    involuntary residence 100
    legal residence 102
    on arrival 100
    temporary purpose 100

overlapping benefits
    EU co-ordination rules 301
overpayments
    asylum support 436
overstayers 49

P
parents
    leave to remain as parent of British child 35
    proof of parentage 377, 378
part-time workers
    EEA workers 147
passports 50
    confirmation of status if passport expires 51
    illegible stamps 51
    proof of immigration status 43
past presence test 94
    exceptions 219
    when past presence test does not apply 220
paternity benefits
    EU co-ordination rules 285
payment of benefit
    delays 347
    suspension of payment 348
pension credit
    abroad 253
    child abroad 213
    EEA jobseekers 141
    EU co-ordination rules 214, 254
    habitual residence test 106
    partner abroad 212, 254
    partner subject to immigration control 75
    person subject to immigration control 67
    residence rules 210
    right to reside test 117, 118
    special non-contributory benefit 287
permanent residence card 375
permanent right to reside 190
    after five years 190
    benefit entitlement 200
    continuity of residence 194
    legally resided 191
    loss of permanent right to reside 200
    workers 197

person subject to immigration control 53
  asylum seekers 80
  benefits 66, 67
  children 74
  definition 57
  entry clearance 16
  evidence of status 373
  leave to remain extended for appeal 63
  maintenance undertaking 61
  means-tested benefits 67
  non-means-tested benefits 69
  partners 74
  recourse to public funds 59
  right to reside 125
  social fund payments 74
  sponsored people 62
  tax credits 72
  temporary admission 407
personal independence payment
  abroad 259
  EU co-ordination rules 219, 261
  habitual residence test 106
  mobility component 221
  person subject to immigration control 69
  residence rules 218
points-based system 29
police
  powers 13
pregnancy
  additional section 4 support 434
  asylum seekers 429
  Healthy Start food 464
  Healthy Start vitamins 466
  retaining worker status 156
  section 4 support 400
  self-employed EEA nationals 162, 164
prescription charges
  asylum seekers 422
presence rules 89, 210
  benefits affected 92
  definition 94, 239
  past presence 94
primary carer
  child of primary carer 188
  of British citizen 187
  of self-sufficient child 186
  of worker's child in education 185
prison
  continuity of residence 196

private health insurance 167
public funds
  definition 25

Q
qualified person
  EEA national 128
  family members 178

R
reciprocal agreements 244, 309
  benefits covered 314
  benefits not covered 310
  EEA member states 311
  means-tested benefits 214
  non-EEA countries 310
  non-means-tested benefits 71
  people covered 312
recourse to public funds 25
  accommodation 27
  adequate maintenance 26
  asylum seekers 80
  child with no recourse to public funds
    child benefit 77
  community care support 469
  council tax reduction 458
  death of spouse or partner 35
  definition 25
  discretionary leave 36
  domestic violence 35, 61
  leave outside the rules 38
  leave under Article 8 35
  local welfare assistance schemes 463
  NHS healthcare 470
  partner with no recourse to public funds
    council tax reduction 76
    HB 76
    IS/I-JSA 75
    WTC/CTC 78
  person subject to immigration control 59
refugees 32, 80
  backdated child benefit and tax credits 83
  benefits 81
  definition 32
  EU co-ordination rules 281
  exclusions 33
  family members 109
  family reunion 33, 82
  habitual residence 108

humanitarian protection 32
integration loans 84
leave to remain 33
local welfare assistance 84
past presence test 219
section 95 support 395
studying English 83
tax credits 81
travel documents 48
registration certificate
EEA nationals 41, 50, 375
removal 20
asylum seekers 32
EEA nationals 41
residence
checklist for EEA nationals, family
members or carers 128
continuity of residence 194
definition 98
derivative right to reside 181
EU co-ordination rules 289
evidence of residence rights 374
habitual residence 103
ordinary residence 99
right to reside 103, 124
residence cards 41, 50, 375
residence documents 375
residence permits
leave to remain granted in UK 46
residence rules for benefits 89, 210
AA 218
benefits affected 92
bereavement benefits 215
C-ESA 223
C-JSA 223
CA 218
child benefit 216
council tax reduction 459
CTC 227
DLA 218
guardian's allowance 217
habitual residence 103
HB 210
I-ESA 210
I-JSA 210
IB in youth 218
industrial injuries benefits 221
IS 210
living in UK or CTA for three months 95

MA 225
mobility component of PIP and DLA 221
ordinary residence 99
past presence 94
PC 210
PIP 218
presence 94
retirement pensions 225
right to reside 103
SAP 269
SMP 269
social fund 226
SPP 269
SSP 269
SSPP 269
UC 210
WTC 227
residence tests
habitual residence 103
living in UK or CTA for past three months
95
ordinary residence 99
past presence 94
presence 94
right to reside 103
restricted leave 37
retired people
right of residence 197
retirement pensions
abroad 267
EU co-ordination rules 225, 268, 291
reciprocal agreements 226, 315
residence rules 225
revisions of benefit decisions 341
delays 342
right of abode 15
evidence of right of abode 43
right of admission
EEA nationals 40
right of residence 124
initial right of residence 134
right to reside 117, 124
A2 nationals 129
A8 nationals 129
benefits with right to reside requirement
103, 117
British citizens 125
checklist for EEA nationals, family
members or carers 128

Croatian nationals 129
derivative right to reside 181
EEA nationals 126, 127
evidence of right to reside 374
family members of British citizens 174
family members of EEA nationals 170
initial right to reside 134
jobseekers 135
non-EEA nationals 125
permanent right to reside 190
registration certificate 50
self-employed EEA nationals 159
self-sufficient people 165
students 165
transitional protection 120
workers 143
right to reside test
benefits covered 117
who is covered by the test 120

S
San Marino
CTC 73
EU agreements 319
non-means-tested benefits 71
savings
asylum support 435
school transport 467
Scottish Welfare Fund 463
seamen
leave to enter or remain 22
section 4 support 398, 433
accommodation 434
additional section 4 support 433
amount of payments 433
appealing to European Court of Human
    Rights 404
appeals 439
applications 423
bail 407, 424
breach of conditions 406
children 406
criteria for support 399
decisions 424
destitution 398
disability 400
discontinued 405
exclusions 405
further submissions to Home Office 402

human rights 401, 403, 405
judicial review 401, 404
leaving the UK 399
no viable route of return 401, 405
out of time appeal 403
payment 433
pregnancy 400
review letter 406
sickness 400
suspension 405
temporary admission 407, 424
section 95 support 391, 427
accommodation 430
adequate accommodation 418
amount of support 427
appeals 439
application expenses 432
applications 415
assets 435
backdating support 429
change of circumstances 422
clothing 420
conditions attached 421
contributing to own support costs 429
decisions 420
destitute 394, 416
dispersal 421, 430
essential living needs 420, 427
exceptional payments 428
exclusions 395
further applications 423, 453
health benefits 422
legal aid 443
maternity payment 429
misrepresentation 436
overpayments 436
payment 428
recovery from a sponsor 436
suspension of support 396
temporary support 420
travel expenses 432
who is entitled 391
section 98 support 397, 420
exclusions from support 397
self-employed EEA nationals 159
benefit entitlement 162, 164
Croatian, A2 and A8 nationals 160, 163
deciding what is self-employment 160
evidence of work 381

jobseeker 140
permanent residence 197
pregnancy 164
retaining self-employed status 163
right to reside 159
temporarily unable to work 164
self-sufficient EEA nationals 165
benefit entitlement 170
comprehensive sickness insurance 167
Croatian, A2 and A8 nationals 165
primary carer of self-sufficient child 186
sufficient resources 166
separation
right to reside for EEA nationals 172, 178
settled status 23
severe disablement allowance
abroad 263
EU co-ordination rules 264
residence rules 218
short-term advances of benefit 329
applications 331
refusal of application 332
repaying the advance 331
sickness
comprehensive sickness insurance 167
discretionary leave 36
failed asylum seekers unable to leave UK 400
financial support 473
retaining worker status 155, 164
sickness benefits
competent state 290
EU co-ordination rules 285, 290
exclusion from benefits 295
reciprocal agreements 314
sight tests
asylum seekers 422
single state principle
EU co-ordination rules 288
social and medical assistance
EU co-ordination rules 287
social care support 468
asylum seekers with care needs 409
Social Charter 318
social fund
funeral expenses payments 226
person subject to immigration control 74
residence conditions 226
winter fuel payments 227

special non-contributory benefits 287
sponsorship 26, 62
accommodation 27
asylum seekers 436
change of circumstances 27
claiming benefits 26, 62
death of sponsor
means-tested benefits 68
tax credits 73
employment 29
financial requirements 26
person subject to immigration control 62
undertakings 28
spouses
ending a marriage 178
leave to remain following bereavement 35
person subject to immigration control benefits 74
proof of relationship 377, 378
sponsorship 26
spouse of EEA national 172
stamps
checking immigration status 43
standard acknowledgement letter 49
stateless people 34
co-ordination of social security 281
travel documents 48
statutory adoption pay
abroad 269
EU co-ordination rules 269, 286
residence conditions 269
statutory maternity pay
abroad 269
EU co-ordination rules 269, 286
residence conditions 269
statutory paternity pay
abroad 269
EU co-ordination rules 269, 286
residence conditions 269
statutory shared parental pay
abroad 269
EU co-ordination rules 269, 286
residence conditions 269
statutory sick pay
abroad 269
EU co-ordination rules 269
residence conditions 269

students
benefit entitlement 170
comprehensive sickness insurance 167
EEA nationals 165
family members of EEA students 169
no recourse to public funds 59
points-based system 29
right to reside 168
survivors' benefits
EU co-ordination rules 285
suspension of benefits 348
Switzerland
exclusion and removal from UK 41
registration certificate 41, 50
residence rights 127
right of admission to UK 40

T
temporary absence abroad 240
EEA nationals 195
indefinite leave 24
ordinary residence 101
temporary admission 14
applying for support 424
asylum seekers 32
section 4 support 407, 424
temporary protection 31
terminal illness
discretionary leave 36
past presence test 219
test case pending 341, 346
time limits
asylum support appeals 442
jobseeking 136
trafficking
discretionary leave for victims 36
EEA nationals, treatment as workers 145
travel expenses
asylum applications 432
asylum support appeals 447
exceptional payments for asylum seekers 428
school transport 467
tribunals 13
First-tier Tribunal 18
Tunisia
CTC 73
EU agreements 319
non-means-tested benefits 71

Turkey
CTC 73
EC association agreement 22
EU agreements 319
means-tested benefits 68
non-means-tested benefits 71
WTC 73
two-child limit
CTC 78
HB 75
UC 76

U
UK nationals
reciprocal agreements 312
UK Visas and Immigration 12
asylum support 391
unemployment
retaining worker status 149, 150
unemployment benefits
aggregation 299
EU co-ordination rules 286
reciprocal agreements 314
universal credit
abroad 255
child abroad 213, 256
EEA jobseekers 141
EU co-ordination rules 256
habitual residence test 106, 110
partner abroad 212, 255
partner subject to immigration control 76
person subject to immigration control 67
residence and presence rules 210
right to reside test 117, 118

V
vignettes 44
visas
entry clearance 16
visitors
employment 24
entry clearance 16
leave to enter or remain 21
vocational training
EEA workers 155
voluntary return
asylum seekers 399

W
widowers' benefits
    EU co-ordination rules 257
widows' benefits
    EU co-ordination rules 257
winter fuel payments
    EU co-ordination rules 227
    residence rules 227
work permits 24
worker authorisation 130
workers 142
    benefit entitlement 148, 158
    ceasing to be a worker 148
    changing basis of worker status 157
    child in education 183
    Croatian, A2 and A8 nationals 143
    deciding who is a worker 144
    employment relationship 144
    evidence of work 381
    gaps in worker status 157
    genuine and effective work 146
    habitual residence 108
    permanent residence 197
    pregnancy 156
    primary carer of worker's child in
        education 185
    remuneration 145
    retaining worker status 149
    right to reside 143
    temporary inability to work 155
    unemployed 150
    vocational training 155
working tax credit
    abroad 269
    EU co-ordination rules 230, 271
    NI numbers 356, 363
    partner subject to immigration control 77
    person subject to immigration control 72
    refugees 83
    residence rules 227
workseekers
    see: jobseekers

Y
young people
    family members of EEA nationals 172

Z
zero-hour contract
    EEA workers 147

• • • •